MLIWK

STRATEGIC
MARKETING
MANAGEMENT

STRATEGIC MARKETING MANAGEMENT

Jean-Jacques Lambin

Professor at Université Catholique de Louvain,
Louvain-la-Neuve, Belgium

The McGraw-Hill Companies

London · New York · St Louis · San Francisco · Auckland · Bogotá · Caracas · Lisbon
Madrid · Mexico · Milan · Montreal · New Delhi · Panama · Paris · San Juan · São Paulo
Singapore · Sydney · Tokyo · Toronto

Published by
McGraw-Hill Publishing Company
Shoppenhangers Road, Maidenhead, Berkshire, SL6 2QL, England
Telephone 01628 23432
Facsimile 01628 770224

British Library Cataloguing in Publication Data
Lambin, Jean-Jacques
  Strategic marketing management
  1. Marketing – Management   2. Strategic planning
  I. Title
  658.8

ISBN 0077092279

Library of Congress Cataloging-in-publication Data
Lambin, Jean-Jacques
   [Marketing stratégique.   English]
   Strategic marketing management / Jean-Jacques Lambin.
    p. cm.
   Includes bibliographical reference and index.
   ISBN 0-07-709227-9 (pbk. : ak. paper)
   1. Marketing—Europe—Management. I. Title.
  HF5415.13.L33213   1996
  658.8′02—dc20
                               96-27234
                                  CIP

First published in French as *Le Marketing Stratégique* be McGraw-Hill France. (French edition copyright © 1989 by McGraw-Hill France. All rights reserved.) First published in English as *Strategic Marketing* by McGraw-Hill Book Company, Maidenhead, England. (English edition copyright © 1993 by McGraw-Hill International (UK) Limited. All rights reserved.)

McGraw-Hill   

A Division of The McGraw·Hill Companies

12345 CUP 99987

Typeset by Paston Press Limited, Loddon, Norfolk
Printed and bound in Great Britain at the University Press, Cambridge

Printed on permanent papers in compliance with ISO Standard 9706

CONTENTS

PREFACE

Why yet another textbook in marketing? In other words, what distinctive qualities does this new product claim to offer? This question, central in strategic marketing, is just as relevant for an author as it is for an innovative firm.

WHY THIS NEW INTRODUCTORY TEXT?

A first objective is to close a cultural gap. In Europe, the marketing textbook market is largely dominated by American writers and I feel that there is a need for a text presenting the European perspective in English. In North America, the slogan: *What is good for Business is good for Society* is largely undisputed and, to my knowledge, there are few radicals among North-American marketing academicians or practitioners, questioning the premises underlying the marketing discipline. Elsewhere, and in particular in European societies exposed to other social and political currents, this is not as obvious and the role of marketing is always controversial and often seriously challenged by different social groups. A first objective of this book is, therefore, to clarify the ideological foundations of marketing and to explain its role as a key determinant in a democratic economic system. This objective is particularly important for Eastern European countries who have recently chosen the road to a market economy.

A second objective of this book is to introduce upfront the strategic dimension in marketing while the most popular marketing textbooks tend to treat marketing management as a stand-alone business function and to overlook the hidden part of the marketing iceberg, i.e. the strategic choices on which marketing management decisions must be based. Similarly, most strategic marketing texts examine strategic decisions that are made at the corporate level but devote only scant attention to how these decisions are implemented at the operational level for individual brands or products. Our objective in writing this book is to propose a broader treatment of marketing integrating both its dimensions—strategic and operational. Marketing is both a business philosophy and an action-oriented process. Too often, the tendency among practitioners and the general public is to reduce marketing to its active dimension and to overlook the underlying business philosophy without which marketing is simply a set of short-term selling tools.

Structure of the book

The overall structure of the book is summarized in Fig. 1.1 (p.2). It comprises five parts and sixteen chapters in total.

Part 1 is devoted to the analysis of *the changing role of marketing* in the European market. In Chapter 1, we introduce a distinction between operational marketing (the action dimension) and strategic marketing (the analytic and philosophy dimension). In the new European macro-marketing environment (Chapter 2), marketing is confronted with new challenging roles and priorities which require a reinforcement of strategic marketing and the adoption of a market orientation within the entire organization. The proactive firm must evolve from marketing management to market-driven management.

The objective of Part 2 is to analyse *the buyer's purchase and response behaviour*, be it an individual or an organization. Strategic marketing is, to begin with the analysis of the needs of individuals and organizations (Chapter 3). From the marketing viewpoint, the buyer's choice behaviour (Chapter 4) is not after a product as such, but after a product that may provide the solution to a problem. The role of marketing research (Chapter 5) is essential to gain certified knowledge to understand and predict the buyer's behaviour and response (Chapter 6).

Part 3 analyses the specific tasks to be performed by *strategic marketing*. The role of strategic marketing is to follow the evolution of the firm's *reference market* and to identify various potential product markets or segments on the basis of an analysis of the needs that must be met (Chapter 7). Once the potential product markets are identified, the *attractiveness* of the economic opportunities must be evaluated. The appeal of a product market is quantitatively measured by the notion of market potential and dynamically measured by its economic life or its life cycle (Chapter 8). For any given firm, the appeal of a product market depends on its *competitiveness*, in other words, on having a better capacity than its rivals to meet buyers' needs. This competitiveness will exist as long as the firm holds a competitive advantage, either because it can differentiate itself from its rivals due to sustainable distinctive qualities, or because of higher productivity putting it at a cost advantage (Chapter 9). On the basis of this strategic audit, the market-driven firm can formulate an appropriate *marketing strategy* for each business unit included in its product portfolio (Chapter 10). The strategic *marketing plan* describes objectives, positioning, tactics and budgets for each business unit of the company's portfolio in a given period and geographical zone (Chapter 11).

In Part 4, we examine the *implementation issues of strategic marketing* decisions. In order to be profitable, operational marketing must be founded upon a strategic design, which is itself based on the needs of the market and its expected evolution. The two roles of marketing are therefore closely complementary and cannot be dissociated. It is the classical commercial process of achieving a targeted market share through the use of tactical means related to the product (Chapter 12), distribution (Chapter 13), price (Chapter 14) and communication (Chapter 15) decisions—the four P's, or the marketing mix as it is called in professional jargon.

Distinctive features

This text offers full coverage of both strategic marketing principles and key marketing decisions. Chapter 11 concentrates on the strategic and operational marketing plan by providing a set of questionnaires and forms which review the key concepts and issues that must be addressed in a strategic plan. In addition, other features characterize this book:

■ It discusses the ideological foundations of marketing and its role in the turbulent environment of today's market economy.

■ It introduces the concept of market orientation as a substitute to the traditional marketing concept.

■ It analyses the structure of needs of both the individual consumer and the business or organizational buyer.

- It integrates important theoretical concepts such as utility theory, buyer behaviour theory, attitude models, information theory, and stresses the application of this conceptual material to the realities of marketing.

- It provides an integrated treatment of consumer and business marketing, underlining practical differences and conceptual similarities.

- It offers thorough coverage of macro- and micro-segmentation analyses illustrated by numerous examples taken from the European scene.

- It provides an overview of marketing research methods and particularly of survey research.

- It gives a general overview of the most popular market response measures provided by marketing research, void of all technical development.

- It integrates international and global marketing throughout the text rather than relegating it to a single chapter.

- It contains a section devoted to the distributor's strategic marketing, a topic often neglected in marketing textbooks.

- It is well illustrated with real-life examples and up-to-date European data and statistics.

WHY A EUROPEAN PERSPECTIVE?

Another claim of this book is to propose to the reader a 'European perspective' in strategic marketing. The question that comes readily to mind is: 'Is European marketing really different from, for example, American or Japanese ways of conducting marketing?' I strongly believe that significant differences do exist, not so much in terms of concepts or methods but rather in terms of priorities, complexity and business philosophy. Three factors explain these differences:

- The challenge of European market integration

- European cultural diversity and pluralism

- The social accountability of European society.

European countries are confronted with a formidable challenge, the idea of unifying the European market by removing all non-tariff barriers that have existed in some countries for centuries. At a business level, European companies are analysing the impact of this market transformation, redefining their reference market, reassessing their competitiveness and determining appropriate strategies and organizational structure. In this new European context, sound strategic thinking and analysis become priority preoccupations, not only for multinational firms, but also for small and medium-sized companies.

The European market is highly fragmented both in terms of culture and of consumer habits. The elimination of all barriers among European countries will create a borderless single market but not, however, a homogeneous single market. Cultural differences and variations in consumer attitudes across Europe will remain, even if European firms will have the possibility of executing a common marketing programme throughout Europe. Thus European firms will have to cope with this cultural complexity and find adequate solutions. A level of standardization of consumer behaviour similar to that observed in the US market will never be reached in Europe. The capacity to respect this diversity and to discover supranational segments will be a key factor to success.

European society is more concerned than American society by the integration of individual, family and social values in economic life and public policy. The European firm has to cope with more severe societal constraints than the American firm. The slogan '*the business of business is business*', largely accepted until recently by the business community, is no longer true and the European firm cannot remain immune from societal interference and accountability. These societal constraints are the expressions of new needs in society and come from public policy regulations, EU directives, green consumerists or environmentalists. They induce companies to widen the traditional marketing concept and to develop an increased consciousness of fallout generated by their marketing activity. In today's European socio-economic context, this greater societal sensitivity makes the concept of 'accountable marketing' particularly relevant.

Finally, in Part 5 (Chapter 16), the book offers a European perspective, with the vast majority of examples and case histories being drawn from the European scene. It is also well illustrated with up-to-date European data and statistics.

Acknowledgements

This book is the third edition of the French book *Le marketing stratégique* (Paris, Ediscience International, 1994). This new English edition is the result of several years of research, teaching and consulting in Europe. This experience, the exchange of ideas and discussions with business professionals within various executive seminars or consulting assignments have done much to further my knowledge of the marketing process.

Several persons have directly or indirectly contributed at various stages to the development of this new edition, and in particular my colleagues from the marketing unit at our school, the Institut d'Administration et de Gestion (IAG): Chantal de Moerloose, Paul Pellemans, Marie-Paule Kestemont, Dany Oda, Isabelle Schuiling and Claudine Laperche. A word of gratitude also to Boris Lifliandchik from the Leti-Lovanium International School of Management of Saint Petersburg, responsible for the Russian translation of the book and who reviewed the first three chapters of this edition. I also thank the teaching assistants of the Marketing Unit of IAG, and in particular to Jean-Philippe de Moreau who was very helpful in the design of the charts, Corine Leurquin for her editing work. Amélie Lauve provided her generous assistance in the translation. Last but not least, I am grateful to my students, captive customers, but nevertheless very attentive and demanding and who helped me to improve this text over the years. Personal thanks to each of them.

Jean-Jacques Lambin
Bousval.

The Changing Role of Marketing

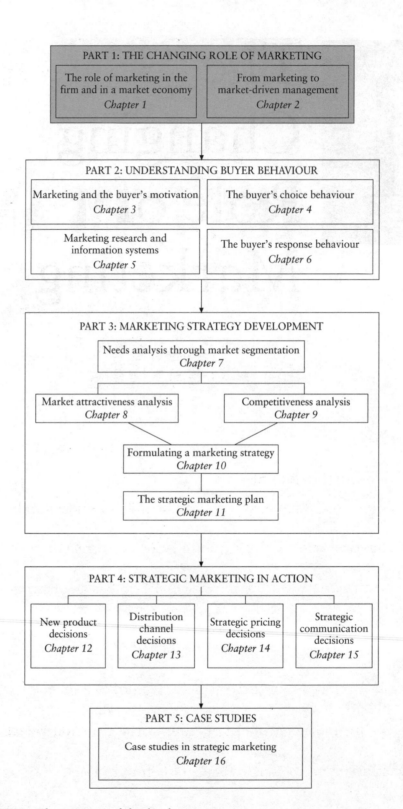

FIGURE PT1.1 *The structure of this book*

THE ROLE OF MARKETING IN THE FIRM AND IN A MARKET ECONOMY

LEARNING OBJECTIVES

After reading this chapter, you should be able to understand:

■ the theoretical and ideological foundations of marketing

■ the difference between 'operational' and 'strategic' marketing

■ the role of marketing in the firm in relation with the other functions

■ the tasks performed by marketing in a market economy

■ the steps in implementing marketing in the firm's organization

■ the limitations of the traditional marketing concept.

M arketing is both a business philosophy and an action-oriented process. This first chapter aims to describe the *system of thought*, to clarify the ideological foundations of marketing and their main implications regarding the firms operations and organization. As an *active process*, marketing fulfils a number of tasks necessary to the smooth functioning of a market economy. A second objective of this chapter is to describe these tasks, the importance and complexity of which have evolved with changes in technology, economics, competitiveness and the international environment. Within this framework, we shall examine the implications of these environmental changes for the management of the firm and, particularly, for the marketing function.

1.1 THE IDEOLOGICAL FOUNDATIONS OF MARKETING

The term *marketing*, which has even entered the non-English vocabulary, is a word heavily loaded, debased and often misunderstood, not only by its detractors, but also by its proponents. Three popular meanings recur regularly.

■ Marketing is advertising, promotion and hard selling; in other words, a set of particularly aggressive *selling instruments* used to penetrate existing markets. In this first, very mercantile sense of the word, marketing is viewed as mainly applicable to mass consumer markets and much less to more sophisticated sectors, such as high technology, financial services, public administration, social and cultural services.

■ Marketing is a set of *market analysis tools*, such as sales forecasting methods, simulation models and market research studies, used to develop a prospective and more scientific approach to needs and demand analysis. Such methods can be complex and costly, and are often considered to be available only to large enterprises and not to small and medium-sized ones. The image projected is often that of unnecessarily sophisticated tools which entail high costs and are of little practical value.

■ Marketing is the hype, *the architect of the consumer society*; that is, a market system where individuals are commercially exploited by sellers. It is necessary to create new needs continuously in order to sell more and more. Consumers become alienated from the seller, just as workers have become alienated from the employer.

Behind these somewhat oversimplified views there are three characteristic dimensions to the concept of marketing: an *active* aspect (the penetration of markets), an *analytic* aspect (the understanding of markets) and an *ideological* aspect (a market-oriented culture). More often than not, the tendency is to reduce marketing to its active dimension—that is, to a series of sales techniques (operational marketing)—and to underestimate its analytic dimension (strategic marketing).

Implicit in this vision of the role of marketing is the idea that marketing and advertising are omnipotent, that they are capable of making the market accept anything through powerful methods of communication. Such hard-selling methods are often devised independently of any desire to satisfy the real needs of buyers. The focus is on the needs of the seller, i.e. to achieve a sale.

The myth of the supremacy of marketing is a persistent theme despite the fact that there exists abundant proof to the contrary. For example, the high proportion of new products and brands that fail bears witness to the capacity of the market's resistance to the allegedly seductive powers of producers.

1.1.1 The principle of consumer sovereignty

Although this misunderstanding goes very deep, the theory or ideology that is the basis of marketing is totally different. The philosophy at the base of marketing—what may be called the marketing concept—rests in fact on a theory of individual choice through the *principle of consumer sovereignty*. In this framework, marketing is no more than the social expression of the principles advocated by classical economists, at the turn of the eighteenth century and translated into operational rules of management. These principles, which were set forth by Adam Smith (1776), form the basis of the market economy and can be summarized as follows:

> Society's well-being is the outcome, not so much of altruistic behaviour, but rather of the matching, through competitive exchange, of the buyer and seller's self-interest.

Starting from the principle that the pursuit of personal interest is an unfailing tendency in most human beings—which might be morally regrettable but remains a fact—Adam Smith suggested accepting people as they are, but developing a system that would make egocentric individuals contribute to the common good despite themselves. This is then the system of voluntary and competitive exchange, administered by the *invisible hand*, or the selfish pursuit of personal interests which in the end serves the interests of all.

Although in modern economics this basic principle has been amended with regard to social (solidarity) and societal (external effects, collective goods, government regulations) issues, it nevertheless remains the main principle driving the economic activity of a successful firm operating in a freely competitive market. Furthermore, it is now clearer than ever before that those countries that rejected Adam Smith's ideas are now discovering, to their cost, that they have regressed economically. The recent turmoil in Eastern Europe and in the republics of the former Soviet Union gives a clear illustration of this.

At the root of the market economy, we find four central ideas. These ideas seem simple, but have major implications regarding the philosophical approach to the market.

■ Individuals strive for *rewarding experiences*; it is the pursuit of one's self-interest that drives individuals to produce and to work. This search is the engine of growth, of individual development, and eventually determines the overall well-being.

- *Individual choice* determines what is rewarding. This varies according to tastes, culture, values, etc. Apart from respecting the ethical, moral and social rules imposed by society, no other judgement is implied as to the value or the triviality of this choice, or what might be regarded as 'true' or 'false' needs. The system is pluralistic and respects the diversity of tastes and preferences.

- It is through *free and competitive exchange* that individuals and the organizations they deal with will best realize their objectives. When exchange is free, it only takes place if its terms generate utility for both parties; when it is competitive, the risk of producers abusing their market power is limited (Friedman and Friedman, 1980).

- The mechanisms of the market economy are based on the principle of individual freedom and, more particularly, on the *principle of consumer sovereignty*. The moral foundation of the system rests on the recognition of the fact that individuals are responsible for their own actions and can decide what is or is not good for them.

1.1.2 The fields of marketing

Marketing is rooted in these four principles. This gives rise to a philosophy of action valid for any organization serving the needs of a group of buyers. The areas of marketing can be subdivided into three main fields:

- *Consumer marketing*, where transactions are between companies and end-consumers, individuals or households

- *Business marketing* (or business-to-business marketing), where the two parties in the exchange process are organizations

- *Social marketing*, which covers the field of activity of non-profit organizations such as museums, universities, etc.

This approach implies that all activity within the organization must have the satisfaction of its users' needs as its main objective. Given that this is the best way of achieving its own goals of growth and profitability, it is not altruism, but the organization's self-interest that dictates this course of action.

Such is the ideology on which marketing is based. One can imagine that there may be a large gap between what marketing claims to be and what it is in reality. Flaws come readily to mind. Nevertheless, the successful firm must pursue the ideal of marketing. It may be a myth, but it is a *driving myth*, which must continuously guide the activities of the firm.

1.1.3 The two faces of marketing

The application of this philosophy of action assumes a two-fold approach on the part of the firm, as shown in Fig. 1.1.

- The objectives of *strategic marketing* typically include: a systematic and continuous analysis of the needs and requirements of key customer groups and the design and production of a product or service package that will enable the company to serve selected groups or segments

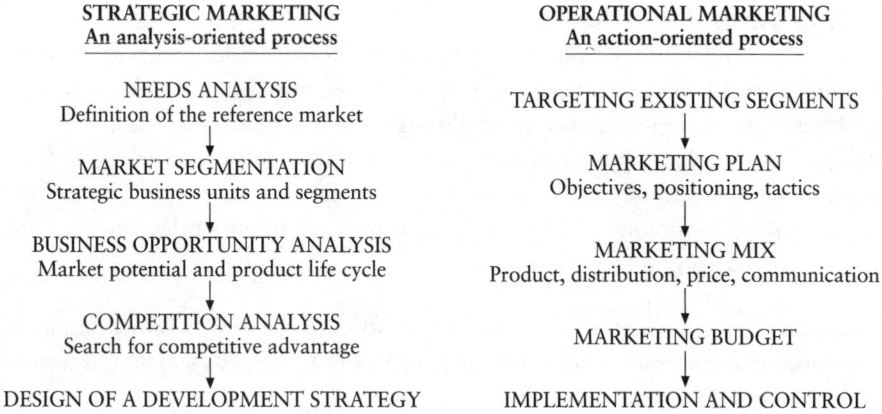

STRATEGIC MARKETING	OPERATIONAL MARKETING
An analysis-oriented process	An action-oriented process

STRATEGIC MARKETING
An analysis-oriented process

NEEDS ANALYSIS
Definition of the reference market
↓
MARKET SEGMENTATION
Strategic business units and segments
↓
BUSINESS OPPORTUNITY ANALYSIS
Market potential and product life cycle
↓
COMPETITION ANALYSIS
Search for competitive advantage
↓
DESIGN OF A DEVELOPMENT STRATEGY

OPERATIONAL MARKETING
An action-oriented process

TARGETING EXISTING SEGMENTS
↓
MARKETING PLAN
Objectives, positioning, tactics
↓
MARKETING MIX
Product, distribution, price, communication
↓
MARKETING BUDGET
↓
IMPLEMENTATION AND CONTROL

FIGURE 1.1 *The two faces of marketing*

more effectively than its competition. In serving these objectives, a firm is ensured a sustainable competitive advantage.

■ The role of *operational marketing* involves the organization of distribution, sales and communication policies in order to inform potential buyers and to promote the distinctive qualities of the product while reducing the information costs.

These objectives are implemented by the firm's branding policy—a key instrument for the application of the marketing concept. We therefore propose the following definition of marketing:

> Marketing is a social process, geared towards satisfying the needs and wants of individuals and organizations, through the creation of free competitive exchange of products and services that generate values to the buyer.

The three key concepts in this definition are need, product and exchange. The notion of *need* calls into question the motivations and behaviour of the buyer, the individual consumer or the organizational client; *product* or service refers to the producers' response to market expectations; and *exchange* directs attention to the market and the mechanisms that ensure the interplay of demand and supply.

1.2 THE ROLE OF MARKETING IN THE FIRM

The term *marketing*—literally the process of delivering to the market—does not express the inherent duality of the process very well and emphasizes the 'active' side of marketing more than the 'analytic' side. (As an aside, we may point out that to avoid the ambiguity—and the use of an English word in the common vocabulary—the French Academy (l'Académie Française) coined the terms *la mercatique* and *le marchéage* to illustrate these two facets of marketing. In practice, however, these terms are seldom used by the French business community.) The terms *strategic* and *operational* marketing are therefore used in practice.

1.2.1 Operational marketing

Operational marketing is an action-oriented process which is extended over a short- to medium-term planning horizon and targets existing markets or segments. It is the classical commercial process of achieving a target market share through the use of *tactical* means related to the product, distribution (place), price and communication (promotion) decisions (the four P's, or the 'marketing mix', as they are called in professional jargon). The operational marketing plan describes objectives, positioning, tactics and budgets for each brand of the company's portfolio in a given period and geographical zone.

The economic role that marketing plays in the operation of the firm is shown in Fig. 1.2. The main relationships between the four major managerial functions (Research and development, operations, marketing and finance) are illustrated.

The main task of operational marketing is to generate sales revenues, i.e. the target turnover. This means to 'sell' and to get purchase orders by using the most efficient sales methods while at the same time minimizing costs. The objective of realizing a particular sales volume translates into a manufacturing programme as far as the operations department is concerned, and a programme of storage and physical distribution for the sales department. Operational marketing is therefore a determining factor which directly influences the short-term profitability of the firm.

The vigour of operational marketing is a decisive factor in the performance of the firm, especially in those markets where competition is fierce. Every product, even those of superior quality, must have a price acceptable to the market, be available in the network of distribution adapted to the purchasing habits of the targeted customers, and be supported by some form of communication which promotes the product and enhances its distinctive qualities. It is rare to find market situations where demand exceeds supply or where the firm is well known by potential users or where competition is non-existent.

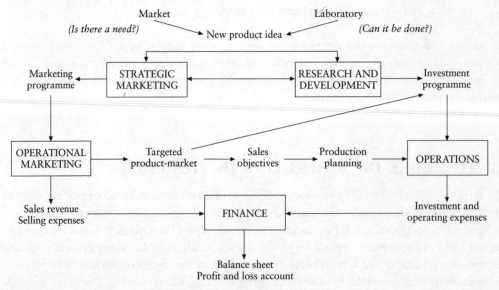

FIGURE 1.2 *The role of marketing in the firm*

There are many examples of promising products that have failed to prevail in the market due to insufficient commercial support. This is particularly the case in firms where the 'engineering' spirit predominates, whereby it is believed that a good quality product can gain recognition by itself and the firm lacks the humility to adapt to the needs of customers.

> Latin culture is especially susceptible to this attitude. Mercury was the god of merchants as well as of thieves and Christ expelled the tradesmen from the Temple; as a result, selling and advertising are still often viewed as shameful diseases.   (Pirot, 1987, p. 87)

Operational marketing is the most dramatic and the most visible aspect of the discipline of marketing, particularly because of the important role played by advertising and promotional activities. Some firms—banks, for example (Kotler, 1991, pp. 26–7)—have embarked on marketing through advertising. On the contrary, some other firms—like many producers of industrial goods—have for a long time tended to believe that marketing doesn't apply to their business, thus implicitly linking marketing to advertising.

Operational marketing is therefore the firm's commercial arm without which even the best strategic plan cannot lead to satisfactory results. However, it is also clear that without solid strategic options there can be no ultimately profitable operational marketing. Dynamism without thought is merely unnecessary risk. No matter how powerful an operational marketing plan, it cannot create demand where there is no need, just as it cannot keep alive activities that are doomed to disappear. Hence, in order to be profitable, operational marketing must be founded upon a strategic design, which is itself based on the needs of the market and its expected evolution.

1.2.2 Strategic marketing

Strategic marketing is, to begin with, the analysis of the *needs* of individuals and organizations. From the marketing viewpoint, the buyer is not seeking a product as such, but a product that might provide the *solution to a problem*. This solution may be obtained via different technologies which are themselves continually changing. The role of strategic marketing is to follow the evolution of the reference market and to identify various existing or potential product markets or segments on the basis of an analysis of the needs to be met.

Once the product markets are identified, they represent economic opportunities whose *attractiveness* needs to be evaluated. The appeal of a product market is quantitatively measured by the notion of the potential market, and dynamically measured by its economic life, or its *life cycle*. For a given firm, the appeal of a product market depends on its own competitiveness, in other words on a better capacity than its rivals to meet buyers' needs. This competitiveness will exist as long as the firm holds a competitive advantage, either because it can differentiate itself from its rivals due to sustainable distinctive qualities, or because of higher productivity, putting it at a cost advantage.

Figure 1.2. shows the various stages of strategic marketing in relation to the firm's other major functions. Irrespective of whether a product is *market-pull* or *technology-push*, it has to undergo the process of strategic marketing to evaluate its economic and financial viability. The interface

TABLE 1.1 *Contrasting operational and strategic marketing*

Operational marketing	Strategic marketing
Action-oriented	Analysis-oriented
Existing opportunities	New opportunities
Non-product variables	Product market variables
Stable environment	Dynamic environment
Reactive behaviour	Proactive behaviour
Day-to-day management	Longer range management
Marketing department	Cross-functional organization

between research and development, operations and strategic marketing plays a decisive role in this respect. The choice of the product market that results from this confrontation is of crucial importance in determining production capacity and investment decisions, and hence is vital to the equilibrium of the firm's overall financial structure.

The role of strategic marketing is therefore to lead the firm towards attractive economic opportunities; that is, opportunities that are adapted to its resources and know-how and offer a potential for growth and profitability. The process of strategic marketing has a medium- to long-term horizon; its task is to specify the firm's *mission*, define objectives, elaborate a development strategy and ensure a balanced structure of the product portfolio. By way of summary, the contrasting roles of operational and strategic marketing are presented in Table 1.1.

1.2.3 The integrated marketing process

This job of reflection and strategic planning is very different from operational marketing and requires different talents in the individuals who exercise it. Nevertheless, the two roles are closely complementary in the sense that the design of a strategic plan must be done in close relation to operational marketing. Operational marketing emphasizes non-product variables (distribution, pricing, advertising and promotion), while strategic marketing tends to emphasize the ability to provide a product with superior value at a competitive cost. Strategic marketing leads to the choice of product markets to be exploited in order of priority and the forecast of total demand in each of these product markets. Operational marketing, on the other hand, sets out market share objectives to reach in the target product market, as well as the marketing budgets necessary for their realization.

As shown in Fig. 1.3, the comparison of the market share objective and total demand forecast in each product market makes it possible to develop a sales objective first in volume and then in terms of turnover, given the chosen pricing policy. The expected gross profit is obtained after deducting direct manufacturing costs, possible fixed costs for specific structures, marketing expenditure attributed to the salesforce, and advertising and promotion, as allowed for in the marketing budget. This gross profit is the contribution of the product market to the firm; it must cover overhead costs and leave a net profit.

FIGURE 1.3 *The integrated marketing process*

1.2.4 The new role of strategic marketing

Some firms tend to confine strategic thinking to the managerial staff who support the managing director and who are based in headquarters, far from the field. But to be efficient, a strategy must be based on a deep knowledge of the market, and its implementation requires coherent plans of market penetration as well as distribution, price and advertising policies. Without these, even the best plan has little chance of success. The chosen marketing organization must reflect this necessity and ensure that the main goals of strategic marketing are adhered to at all levels of the firm through cross-functional co-ordination. In large firms, a product management organization has proved to be very successful; in small or medium-sized firms, the same results can be obtained by temporary and periodic structures such as a strategic planning task force of the key managers. Today, the trend is to consider that strategic marketing is the job of the entire organization and not simply of the marketing function.

Most successful firms adopt some form of strategic planning. This function is clearly becoming significantly more important with the technological, economic, competitive and sociocultural changes characterizing the 1980s and the 1990s and the advent of the single market in Europe.

These changes emphasize the need by the firm to consolidate its strategic marketing in order (1) to base its activities on *strategic options* which are solid and well defined, (2) to develop *systems of monitoring* the marketing environment and *analysing competitiveness*, (3) to reinforce the *capacity to adapt* to changes in the environment and (4) to regularly *re-evaluate the portfolio of businesses.*

Various empirical studies, both in Europe and in the United States, have shown the effectiveness of strategic marketing. Cooper, for example (1979, 1993), analyses the causes for the success of more than two hundred new industrial products. He finds that two out of the three key factors of success are direct results of the quality of strategic marketing: (1) superior quality from the buyer's point of view and the existence of distinctive qualities; (2) the understanding of the market and marketing know-how. It is worth noting that Booz *et al.* (1982) reached the same conclusions in their study of more than 13 000 new products. Narver and Slater (1990), using a sample of 140 strategic business units, have found that a market orientation has a substantial, positive effect on the profitability of the business units studied. More recently, Lambin (1996) reached the same conclusion in a study of the private insurance sector in Belgium.

There is nothing particularly sophisticated about the marketing concept as stated by Ames and Hlavacek (1989, p. 30). In today's competitive environment, no one really argues with the importance of marketing. In fact, it would probably be difficult to find anyone to argue against the idea that gearing all activities of a business to be responsive to customer or user needs is not only sensible, but the only way to run a business. Despite this general agreement, many companies are simply paying lip service to the concept or are not particularly happy with what marketing has done for them. Understanding the marketing concept is one thing; following through with the commitment to implementing this philosophy of action is quite another.

A company that adopts this philosophy of action will have to set up a *market-driven* organization whose behaviour and actions are consistent with the marketing concept. Creating superior value for the buyer at a profit is much more than a marketing function; it is the focus of the entire organization and not merely that of a single department.

Thus strategic marketing covers a field which is much broader than the traditional domain of marketing management, since it includes the organizational culture and climate that most effectively encourages the behaviours that are necessary for the successful implementation of the marketing concept. We therefore propose the following definition of strategic marketing:

> The process adopted by a firm, having a market-driven orientation, to achieve above-normal market performance by continuously creating products or services which provide the buyer with a higher quality product than the competition.

The key concepts here are value to the buyer, competitive superiority and above-normal profit performance.

1.3 THE ROLE OF MARKETING IN A MARKET ECONOMY

In a market economy, the role of marketing is to organize free and competitive exchange in order to ensure efficient matching of supply and demand of goods and services. This matching is not spontaneous, but requires liaison activities at two levels:

■ Organization of *exchange*—in other words, the physical flow of goods between the manufacturing and the consumption sites.

■ Organization of *communication*—in other words, the flow of information to precede, accompany and follow exchange in order to ensure that the supply is sufficient for the demand.

The role of marketing in society is therefore to *organize exchange and communication between sellers and buyers*. This definition emphasizes the tasks and functions of marketing, irrespective of the purpose of the process of exchange. As such, it applies to both commercial and non-profit-making activities, and in general to any situation where free exchange takes place between an organization and the users of the products and services it offers.

1.3.1 Organization of exchange transactions

The organization of the exchange of goods and services is the responsibility of the distribution process, whose task is to move goods from a state of production to a state of consumption. This flow of products to the consumption state creates three types of utility, thus giving distribution a higher value added.

■ *State utility*. The set of all material transformations putting goods in a consumable state: these are operations such as fragmenting, packaging, assortment, etc.

■ *Place utility*. Spatial transformations, such as transport, geographical allocation, etc., which contribute to putting goods at the disposal of users at places of utilization, transformation or consumption.

■ *Time utility*. Temporal transformations, such as storage, which make goods available at the time chosen by the user.

It is these various functions that make manufactured goods accessible and available to the targeted customers, and thus allow the actual matching of supply and demand.

Historically, these tasks of distribution have mainly been performed by autonomous intermediaries, such as sales agents, wholesalers, retailers and industrial distributors—in other words, by what is called the *distribution sector*. Some functions of the distribution process have been integrated, for instance on the manufacturing side (direct marketing), on the consumption side (consumers' co-operatives), and on the distribution side (supermarkets, chainstores, etc.). Furthermore, some vertical marketing systems have been developed which group together independent firms involved at various stages of the production and/or distribution process. This is done in order to co-ordinate their commercial activities, to realize economies in operating costs and thus to reinforce their impact on the market. Examples include voluntary chains, retailer co-operatives and franchise organizations. In many sectors, vertical marketing systems tend to supplant the very fragmented traditional distribution channels. They form one of the most significant developments in the tertiary sector, which has helped to intensify the competitive struggle between various forms of distribution and to improve the productivity of distribution significantly.

The value added of distribution is measured by the *distribution margin*, which is the difference between the price paid to the producer by the first buyer and the price paid by the ultimate user or consumer of the product. The distribution margin may therefore include the margins of one or many distributors; for example, those of the wholesalers and the retailers. Therefore, the distributive margin remunerates the functions performed by the intermediaries. In the consumer goods sector, it is estimated that the cost of exchange, covering the whole range of tasks performed by distribution, is about 40 per cent of the retail price. The cost of distribution represents a significant part of the price paid by the buyer in all sectors of activity.

1.3.2 Organization of communication flows

The merging of the various practical conditions for exchange is not sufficient to ensure efficient adjustment of demand and supply. For exchange of goods to take place, potential buyers must be equally aware and informed of the existence of goods or of the combination of alternative attributes likely to meet their needs. Communication activities are aimed at accumulating knowledge for manufacturers, distributors and buyers. As shown in Fig. 1.4, it is possible to distinguish seven different flows of communication in a typical market.

1. Before investing, the producer initiates the collection of information in order to identify the buyers' needs and wants, which constitute an attractive marketing opportunity. This is typically the role of *market research* prior to an investment decision.
2. Similarly, the potential buyer (mostly industrial) initiates a study of the possibilities offered by suppliers and invitations to tender (sourcing research.)
3. After production, the manufacturer's communication programme is oriented towards distribution—*a push strategy*—with the objective of obtaining product referencing and the co-operation of distributors with regards to selling space, promotion and price.
4. The manufacturer initiates the collection of information on all forms of brand advertising or direct selling activities aimed at making end-buyers aware of the existence of the brand's distinctive qualities: *a pull strategy*.
5. Activities of promotion and communication are prompted by distributors aimed at creating store loyalty, building traffic through promotional activities, supporting proprietary brands, informing about sales terms, etc.
6. After utilization or consumption of goods, the measurement of *satisfaction* or *dissatisfaction*, through surveys or consumer panels, is carried out by the marketer to enable the firm to adjust the supply to buyers' reactions.
7. After utilization or consumption of goods, *claims* and evaluations through comparative testing are transmitted spontaneously by buyers, acting alone or in organized groups (consumerism).

In small markets, communication takes place spontaneously between the various parties of the exchange process. In large markets, there is a significant physical and psychological gap between the parties, and communication needs to be specifically organized.

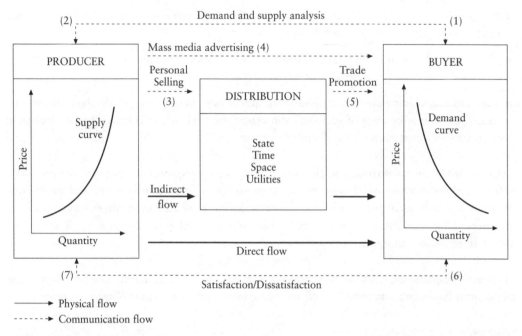

FIGURE 1.4 *The role of marketing in a market economy* (Source: *Lambin and Peeters, 1977*)

1.3.3 Marketing as a factor of economic democracy

Marketing, and specifically strategic marketing, has an important role to play in a market economy, not only because it contributes to an efficient matching between demand and supply but also because it triggers a virtuous circle of economic development, as illustrated in Fig. 1.5.

The steps of this development process are as follows:

■ Strategic marketing helps identifying poorly satisfied or unmet market needs and stimulates the development of new or improved products.

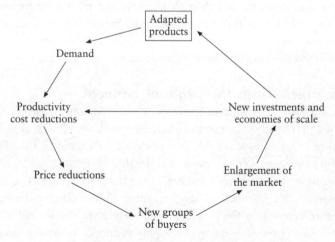

FIGURE 1.5 *Virtuous circle of development triggered by strategic marketing*

- Operational marketing designs a dynamic marketing programme to create and/or develop market demand for these new products.

- This increased demand generates cost decreases which make possible price reductions, thereby opening the market to new groups of buyers.

- The resulting enlargement of the market requires new investments in production capacity which generate economies of scale and stimulate further efforts in research and development to create new generations of products.

Strategic marketing contributes to the development of an economic democracy because (a) it starts with the analysis of consumers expectations, (b) it guides investment and production decisions on the basis of anticipated market needs, (c) it is respectful of the diversity of tastes and preferences by segmenting markets and developing adapted products and (d) it stimulates innovativeness and entrepreneurship.

As already emphasized, reality is not always in line with theory. The market orientation business philosophy has been progressively accepted and implemented by firms in Western economies.

1.4 THE CHANGING PRIORITY ROLE OF MARKETING

Viewed from the standpoint of the organization of communication and exchange in a market economy, it is clear that, despite its current prominence, marketing is not a new activity, given that it covers tasks that have always existed and have always been taken care of in some form in any system based on free exchange. Even in an autarky, founded on the most elementary form of exchange (i.e. barter), there are flows of exchange and communication, but their manifestation is spontaneous and requires neither the allocation of specific resources nor any form of organization to ensure their functioning.

It is the complexity of the technological, economic and competitive environment that has gradually led firms first to create and then to reinforce the marketing function. Hence, it is interesting to follow the history of this evolution in order to understand better the present role of marketing. One can distinguish three stages, each characterized by different priority marketing objectives: passive marketing, organizational marketing and active marketing.

1.4.1 Passive marketing: the product concept

Passive marketing is a form of organization prevalent in an economic environment characterized by the existence of a potentially important market, but where *supply is scarce*, with insufficient available production capacity to meet the market's needs. Demand is, therefore, higher than supply. A successful passive marketing strategy implies that needs are known and stable and that technological innovation in the reference market proceeds at a slow pace. This type of economic situation was observed, for instance, at the beginning of the century during the industrial revolution, and more recently in the period immediately after the Second World War. This environment continues to prevail in many developing countries at present, and particularly in Eastern Europe.

It is clear that in a situation characterized by scarce supply, marketing has a limited and passive role. Given that needs are known, strategic marketing is performed naturally, operational marketing is reduced to organizing the flow of manufactured goods, and promotional activity is rendered superfluous, given that the firm cannot supply the market as it would have liked. Contacts with the market are often limited to the first echelon—that is, the first buyer of the product—who is usually an intermediary, wholesaler or industrial distributor. There is therefore little contact with final demand and market research is infrequent. This state of affairs is also reflected in the organization of the firm, which is dominated by the operations function, with the development of production capacity and improvement of productivity as the main priorities. Marketing is there to sell what has already been produced.

When a firm adopts the 'product concept' it is, in general, structurally organized with the following characteristics:

■ A *functional disequilibrium* in the sense that, in the organizational chart, marketing does not occupy the same hierarchical level as the other functions, such as operations, finance or personnel.

■ The first level of marketing is *commercial service*, in charge of sales administration and in contact with the first buyer in the distributive chain, not necessarily with the end-user.

■ The product decisions are made by operations management; selling prices and sales forecasts are the responsibility of the financial department. There is typically a *dispersion of responsibilities* as far as the marketing instruments are concerned (the four P's).

This kind of organization fosters the development of the *product concept* based on the implicit assumption that the firm knows what is good for the buyer and the latter shares this conviction. Moreover, the managers of such firms are often convinced that they are producing a superior good and tend to take it for granted that buyers will continue to want their products. They tend to have an *inside-in perspective*, where the emphasis is placed on internal constraints and preoccupations and not on the customer's requirements or expectations. Such a viewpoint— typical of a bureaucratic organization—is therefore completely opposed to the idea of the buyer who views a product as a solution to a problem.

This state of mind is conceivable in an environment where demand exceeds supply, where buyers are prepared to buy any kind of product if they can find it. In reality, such market conditions are exceptional, and when they prevail they are temporary. The danger of the product concept is that it makes the firm myopic in its outlook and does not encourage a proactive behaviour, i.e. one that will anticipate a change in the environment and prepare itself accordingly.

Passive marketing is a form of marketing organization which is now no longer suitable for the environment facing the majority of firms in industrialized countries. The product concept nevertheless persists in some firms, mainly among industrial firms or financial services firms, such as insurance companies. The lack of market orientation is not only a major cause of many bankruptcies but is also the dominant state of mind observed among Eastern European firms, which have found themselves suddenly confronted with the formidable challenge of the market and of competition.

Until recently, the product concept also dominated in developing countries, mainly among experts of economic development. But even there marketing can play an active role and contribute towards economic development, to the extent however that such methods are now adapted to situations which are totally different from industrialized countries. (See the excellent article by de Maricourt (1987, pp. 5–17) on this subject).

1.4.2 Organizational marketing: the selling concept

Organizational marketing puts the emphasis on the *selling concept*. In Western European countries this approach to management was progressively adopted by firms in the consumer goods industry during the 1950s, when demand was expanding rapidly and production capacity was available. On the other hand, although these markets were in full growth, the distributive system was often deficient and unproductive.

The following changes in the economy are the cause of this new approach to marketing management:

■ The appearance of *new forms of distribution*, mainly self-service, have helped to modify the productivity of conventional distribution networks which were not adapted to the requirements of mass distribution.

■ The *geographical widening of markets* and the resulting physical and psychological gap between producers and consumers has made it increasingly necessary to resort to means of communication such as mass media advertising.

■ The development of *branding policies* has been seen as a requirement for self-service selling and a way for the firm to control its final demand.

The priority objective of marketing at this stage is to create an efficient commercial organization. The role of marketing becomes less passive. Now the task is to *find* and *organize* markets for the products that have been made. At this stage, most firms concentrate on the needs of the central core of the market, with products which satisfy the needs of the majority of buyers. Markets are therefore weakly segmented and strategic decisions regarding product policy remain the responsibility of the operations department. The main function of marketing is to organize the efficient distribution of products and to manage all tasks that fall under this process of commercialization.

As far as the organizational structure is concerned, these changes in priorities translate into the creation of a *sales* or a *commercial department*, and one can observe a readjustment of functions. These sales departments are given the task of setting up a sales network, organizing physical distribution, advertising and promotion. They also manage market research programmes, which are beginning to manifest their importance, for example, in analysing buying habits, the effectiveness of advertising and the impact of branding and packaging policies, etc.

The selling concept

The selling concept is a characteristic often present in organizational marketing. Its implicit assumptions are as follows:

- Consumers naturally tend to resist buying 'unsought products'.

- Consumers can be pushed to buy more by using different means of sales stimulation.

- The firm must create a powerful sales department and use substantial promotional means to attract and keep customers (Kotler, 1991, p. 15).

Thus, within the firm, marketing people tend to have an *inside-out perspective* and to give priority to the company's objectives over the customer's post-purchase satisfaction. The underlying assumption is that good selling is always 'salesperson driven'.

Some industries which make products that are not naturally sought by buyers, such as life insurance or control instruments, have developed hard-selling techniques which have become popularized through various writings on the 'Art of Selling'. Furthermore, when there is extra capacity in a sector, it is not unusual to see firms wanting to liquidate their stocks employing these methods by aggressively using television commercials, direct mail, newspaper advertisements, etc. It is not, therefore, surprising to see that the public at large, as well as some firms, tends to equate marketing with hard selling or even forced selling.

During the last few years, the notion of the role of the seller has changed greatly in firms with a market orientation (see, for example, Miller and Heiman, 1987). The marketing concept has replaced and reversed the logic of the selling concept. As stated by the General Electric Company shortly after the Second World War:

> Rather than making what you have always made, then trying to sell it, find out what will sell, then try to make it.

In this framework, the role of the seller becomes less one of 'trying to sell' as one of 'helping to buy'. The process of selling initially bases itself on the needs of the buyer. This kind of commercial attitude can only be practical in an organization where the marketing orientation dominates. To quote Drucker (1973, p. 86):

> There will always, one can assume, be need for some selling. But the aim of marketing is to make selling superfluous. The aim of marketing is to know and understand the customer so well that the product or service fits him and sells itself. Ideally, marketing should result in a customer who is ready to buy. All that should be needed then is to make the product or service available.

This ideal situation will only rarely be achieved, but it is important to remember that such is the objective of the marketing theory discussed earlier.

The risk of manipulative or wild marketing

Operational marketing has encouraged the development of the selling concept, which implies a degree of *commercial aggressiveness*, with the implicit assumption that the market can absorb everything, if enough pressure is applied. Judging by the high growth rate of private consumption and the level of household equipment purchased since 1945, this selling policy did prove to be efficient.

However, the efficiency of the selling concept must be evaluated by keeping in mind the situation at the time, i.e. a fundamentally expanding market, weakly differentiated products, and consumers who were less experienced as buyers. The risk run by the selling concept is to consider this commercial approach as being valid in any situation and to confuse it with the marketing concept. Levitt (1960, p. 48) compares the two concepts as follows:

> Selling focuses on the needs of the seller, marketing on the needs of the buyer. Selling is preoccupied with the seller's need to convert his product into cash; marketing with the idea of satisfying the needs of the customer by means of the product and the whole cluster of things associated with creating, delivering and finally consuming it.

An overenthusiastic use of advertising and selling can lead to *manipulative marketing* or *wild marketing*, which tries to mould demand to the requirements of supply rather than adapt supply to the expectations of demand. Here we have some examples of commercial practices that can be classified as wild marketing:

- Sales of defective or dangerous products.

- Exaggeration of the product's content through the use of flashy packaging design.

- Resorting to fraudulent practices with regard to price and delivery policies.

- Resorting to promotional techniques which exploit impulsive buyer behaviour.

- Advertisements which exaggerate the product's attributes and the promises that these attributes represent.

- Advertisements which exploit the agonies and anxieties of individuals.

- Enticing people to over-consume using hard-selling methods.
  . . .

(In the long run, wild marketing is self-destructive for a company or for a brand and goes against its best interests.)

The excesses of wild marketing have led to the birth of a countervailing power in the form of consumers' organizations, initiated by consumers, and in the form of legislation which increasingly reinforces the protection of consumers' legal rights prompted by public authorities.

1.4.3 Active marketing: the strategic marketing concept

The phase of active marketing is characterized by the development and/or reinforcement of the role of strategic marketing and by the adoption of a customer orientation within the firm. Three factors are at the root of this evolution:

■ Acceleration in the rate at which *technological progress* diffuses and penetrates.

■ Maturity of markets and the progressive *saturation* of the needs of the core market.

■ Increased *internationalization* of markets as a result of the progressive lifting of barriers to international trade.

We shall examine these three factors of change successively, as well as their implications for the marketing function in the firm.

Technological progress

One of the significant features of the period between the Marshall Plan (1947) and the creation of the OPEC (1973) is the extraordinary diffusion of technological progress that penetrated and influenced most industrial sectors within a few years. As a result, we saw, during 25 years of continuous growth, a real explosion of new products and new industries, both quantitatively and qualitatively. A large number of products that we now use daily did not exist a few years ago. Frequently it is observed that in successful companies, 40–60 per cent of their turnover comes from products that did not exist five years ago.

> At Hewlett-Packard, for instance, more than 50 per cent of the turnover is generated by products launched into the market during the last three years and more than 500 projects of new product are currently in the process of development. (House and Price, 1991)

As far as technological progress is concerned, this period was more a period of innovation than of invention. The distinction between innovation and invention is important. Invention is the creative act underlying an innovation. Innovation is the creative and successful implementation of a concept, a discovery, or a progressive invention. Innovation is therefore the result of an explicit will to change and not the simple consequence of a stroke of good fortune. Although the pace of technological penetration accelerated rapidly during the 25 years after the Second World War, technology itself followed the path that had already been drawn previously. The new technologies of the 1950s, 1960s and 1970s, were mostly based on science and knowledge developed before the First World War, with two major exceptions: computers and antibiotics. When we talk about technological progress in this period, we are essentially talking about technological extensions, developments and modifications and not about structural technological change, which is the case at the present time.

The diffusion of technological progress results from acceleration, generalization and a systematic approach in scientific research.

■ The diffusion of technological progress is *accelerated*. By this we mean that we observe an increasing rate of innovation and a shorter time frame is required to pass from development to commercial exploitation on a large scale. This evolution implies a shorter technological life of

TABLE 1.2 *Shortening of the product life cycle: the computer market*

Development phases	Average duration (months)			
	1981	1984	1988	1991
R&D	24	20	18	8
Market research	9	7	4	2
Expected life	88	48	24	12

Source: *Dataquest*, April, 1992, SVM 25

products and, hence, the time available for recovering R&D costs. Table 1.2 illustrates this point in the computer market sector.

- The spread of technological progress is *generalized* throughout sectors, firms and countries. Few sectors have been sheltered from technological innovations, some of which are 'destructive' (Schumpeter, 1949); that is, they menace or eliminate existing industries. Basic sectors such as steel, leather, textiles, paper, have always been threatened by substitutes coming from industries that are technologically very distant. This evolution calls for a closer scrutiny of the technological and competitive environment.

- The spread of technological progress is *systematic*, in the sense that, unlike the days when scientific research was carried out by more or less isolated individuals, it has now become institutionalized in firms, universities and private or public specialized centres. Governments play a significant role in this domain, by allocating important resources to help scientific and industrial research. Technological innovation no longer depends on the chance of inventions. An innovation is the outcome of a concerted and planned effort, which itself is directed by some theoretical representations. There is continuity in the elaboration of theoretical tools, which is the job of fundamental research, and the implementation of methods that can be directly used in the production of goods and services. Research itself is planned according to tested methods and in terms of objectives laid out in advance.

This technological evolution has a direct bearing on product policy and forces the firm, for example, to review the structure of its product portfolio at a much faster rate than before. Therefore, this increased dependence on the technological environment requires a strengthening of the role to be played by market analysis and environment monitoring.

Saturation of the core market

The rapid expansion of the economy during the 1960s led to a saturation of demand for products corresponding to the basic needs of the market, and this evolution is a second significant change that has contributed once again to the modification of the role of marketing in the firm. This change manifested itself with the appearance of a potential demand for products adapted more specifically to the needs of distinct groups of consumers and buyers. This evolution, which appeared at different times in different sectors, leads to market *fragmentation* and strategies of *segmentation*. As an example, let us examine the following fictitious case.

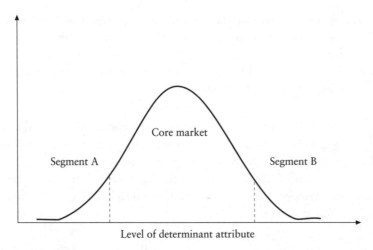

FIGURE 1.6 *The majority fallacy*

A firm is contemplating the launching of a new aperitif in the market and is wondering about the preference of potential consumers as to the degree of bitterness of the aperitif. Various tests are organized showing that the majority of consumers prefer a medium level of bitterness, as shown in the preference distribution of Fig. 1.6.

The tests also show that some consumers, fewer in number, prefer a higher degree of bitterness and others a lower degree of bitterness. A situation of *diffused preferences* is typical of a latent market and the firm must decide how to position its product with respect to this dominant feature (Kuehn and Day, 1962).

The natural tendency is to follow the *majority rule* and develop a product at a medium level (say level 4) of a significant product characteristic, so as to correspond to the preferences of the core of the market and thus minimize total dissatisfaction and fulfil the expectations of the greatest number. The pioneering firm thus finds access to the most important potential market and also benefits from economies of scale in production and distribution. At this stage, the firm will be exercising operational marketing to penetrate the market as rapidly as possible.

Market choices will therefore crystallize over products designed to meet the expectations of the majority. Peripheral preferences will not be met and this group of consumers will have to accept compromises. If successful, the pioneer will soon be followed by many imitators and the situation will progressively lead towards the *majority fallacy*, whereby all competing brands are clustered at the same medium level of the relevant product characteristic (Kuehn and Day, 1962).

The *active marketing* stage appears when the needs of the core market are saturated as a result of this situation, where a large number of competitors are making similar offers. At this stage it becomes worth while to rediscover the neglected differences in preferences and pay attention to the peripheral segments by launching products specially conceived to meet their needs.

In the above example, the latecomer on the market analysing consumers' preferences makes the same observations as before. However, by launching one very smooth (level 2) and simultaneously one very bitter aperitif (level 6), the alert firm can hope to gain a total market share well over what it would gain if it launched a similar product (a 'me too') to the existing ones at level 4, where all the competing brands are clustered.

These segments are certainly smaller, but nevertheless they constitute an unexploited potential, given that these consumers have never found a product in the market corresponding to their real preferences. The firm will adopt a *segmentation strategy* (based here on taste) and the market will subdivide into segments which correspond to the differentiated products. This stage, called the *segmentation stage*, requires the firm to have a finer understanding of the market and of the benefits sought by different groups of buyers.

At this maturity stage of the market, product policy must therefore be increasingly based on the analysis of needs and the services expected from products. In industrialized economies, most markets adequately meet basic needs. Finding growing segments is not an easy task, but requires a deep understanding of markets, needs, users and the use of products. This knowledge can only be achieved by strengthening the 'analytic' aspect of marketing—that is, by using strategic marketing and by adopting a customer orientation.

Internationalization of markets

The period now referred to as the 'Golden Sixties' corresponds to the beginning of the internationalization of markets, a process that has continued up to the 1990s. At the European level, internationalization took the form of the creation of the Common Market; at the world level it took the form of GATT (General Agreement on Tariffs and Trade) and the resulting progressive liberalization of trade, the end of the Cold War and the expansion of East–West trade. All these factors contributed to the widening markets, and, in general, to the intensification of competition and the reappraisal of established competitive positions.

1.4.4 Organization of the marketing function

The three groups of changes we have just examined all imply a consolidation of strategic marketing in the firm. As far as the organization of the firm with an 'active marketing' orientation is concerned, the significant change will be in regard to *product decisions*, which will henceforth be the responsibility of the marketing department in close liaison with the R&D department and the manufacturing department. This means that, in actual practice, strategic marketing regulates product policy and decides whether products are economically viable. The idea of new products may come from anywhere—manufacturing, R&D, or any other source—but it must first pass through the test of strategic marketing before adoption and manufacturing.

Firms that have adopted the marketing concept will have a marketing department (see Fig. 1.7) whose responsibilities will comprise all the tasks that flow from operational marketing and strategic marketing, including the choice of product markets. At this stage, the market-oriented firm has an *outside-in* perspective and places priority emphasis on customers' expectations as a starting point for its product policy.

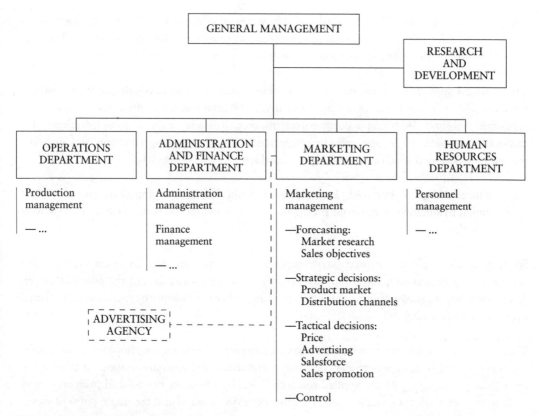

FIGURE 1.7 *The traditional marketing department*

1.4.5 Limitations of the traditional marketing concept

The implicit assumption at the root of the marketing concept is that *satisfying buyers' needs* is the prime objective of the firm, not because of altruism, but because it is the best way for the firm to achieve its own profit and/or growth objectives.

As in the case of the product concept and the selling concept, the marketing concept has its own limitations, of which one should be aware. An overenthusiastic adoption of the marketing concept can lead the firm to put too much emphasis on products in high demand, or *market-pull*, at the expense of products yet unknown but *pushed by technology*. A marketing strategy exclusively guided by market wishes inevitably tends to favour minor and less revolutionary innovations than those proposed by the laboratory. Such innovations, which correspond to needs felt and expressed by the market, are by this token less risky and are therefore seen as more attractive to the firm. On the other hand, a strategy based on technological advance is more likely to lead to a breakthrough innovation and hence ensure that the firm has a long-term competitive advantage that is difficult to equal (Bennett and Cooper, 1981). Most breakthrough innovations, in fact, originate from the laboratory and not from the market. It is therefore important to maintain a balance between these two strategies of product development: technology-push and market-pull.

Irrespective of the origin of the new product, however, the test of strategic marketing remains essential and must take place very early in the process of new product development. The high rates of failure in products convincingly prove this assertion (Urban et al., 1987, p. 41).

The practical application of the marketing concept in new product development is not without difficulty. When a new product is very innovative, potential users are often poor judges of its economic viability. Analysing a conventional market, it is very hard to establish clearly the distinction between a reaction reflecting scepticism about something too new and one that translates lack of real need or interest for the product.

> The president of Polaroïd, E. Land, was in the habit of saying that, given the very innovative nature of Polaroïd products, conventional methods of market analysis were insufficient.

Strategic marketing does not necessarily suppose immediate approval by users. The guiding principle must be a *knowledge* and *understanding* of the needs and uses of the potential buyer. There are many ways of acquiring this understanding other than simply by questioning potential users (see Chapter 5 below).

This is particularly important when it comes to commercializing high-technology products. At the fundamental stage, research can be done without any preoccupation about marketing or immediate profitability. At the applied research stage, on the other hand—and preferably very early in the development process—the firm must consider demand and the users' point of view.

> We can establish the same kind of distinction in the field of art marketing. It is clear that an artist is not concerned about the marketing problem; he creates without worrying whether his work will please or not and this is his social function. On the other hand, the artistic director of a cultural organization has the task of detecting and presenting those creations that meet the expectations of the target public that he has chosen to reach, whoever this public may be. (Searles, 1980)

Contrary to some interpretations, the application of the marketing concept does not mean that the firm should necessarily be led simply by demand expressed by the market and buyers, given that this demand is often for short-term and largely known requirements. If the firm were to adopt this kind of vision, it would always avoid *breakthrough innovations*, which are precisely the ones with greatest growth and profitability.

In practice, the marketing concept is integrated differently in different firms, even if most claim to be inspired by it. In fact, as we mentioned earlier, the marketing concept is an *ideal* to be reached; it is rarely fully realized, but should nevertheless guide all the activities of the firm.

1.4.6 The risk of a new form of marketing myopia

The necessity to adopt the marketing concept and to integrate the strategic dimension of marketing is perceived when (1) markets reach maturity, (2) segmentation and positioning strategies become key issues, (3) competition intensifies and (4) the pace of technological innovation accelerates. In this environment, the role of marketing is not simply to exploit an existing market through mass-marketing techniques. The priority objectives are to detect new segments or niches having a growth potential, to develop new product concepts, to diversify the firm's product portfolio, to find a sustainable competitive advantage and to design a marketing strategy for each business unit. The 'analysis' component of the marketing concept becomes the critical management skill. Its role is to select solid strategic options on which more efficient operational marketing programmes will be based.

The integration of the marketing concept has taken place at different periods according to sectors depending on the development stage reached by the market. The firms operating in the fast-moving consumer goods (FMCG) sectors were among the first to adopt the strategic dimension of the marketing concept. Other sectors, like the computer and the petroleum industries that were suddenly exposed in the 1990s to a structural slowing down of demand, have discovered more recently the necessity to become more market-driven.

From an organizational viewpoint, the implementation of the marketing concept has been achieved by the creation of powerful marketing departments (see Fig. 1.7) in charge of both strategic and operational marketing. Brand and product management played a key role in these organizational structures. A brand manager is concerned with the strategic issues such as R&D and product innovation, branding policies and communication, business analysis and forecasting. His or her task is also to organize a dialogue with the other functions within the firm and to co-ordinate and control all the operations or activities related to the brand. A separate sales department is responsible for the sales tasks and for getting products onto retailers' shelves. This system, adopted by most consumer goods companies and also by many industrial firms, contributed to establishing manufacturers' brand dominance in the market.

The negative side of this organizational structure, in addition to its high cost, is to confine *de facto* the market orientation to the marketing department, thereby giving birth to a new form of myopia, a *marketing myopia*, whereby market informations and market changes are perceived and decoded through the filter of the marketing department. Thus, the 'culture' component of the marketing concept is not diffused at all levels in the organization. As stated by Webster (1994, p. 25),

> Having marketing as a separate function let the rest of the organization 'off the hook' in terms of customer satisfaction. Other functional managers could follow the mandates of their own disciplines, not the customer's requirements. If the marketing department is going to worry about the customer, the other departments can go about their own business.

Today, more and more firms are questioning the existence of traditional marketing departments which, in the 1990s, do not match up to expectations. A recent study by Coopers & Lybrand (1994) concluded that '... there is a gap between what marketing should be and what is being done in marketing departments'. A similar conclusion is reached by McKinsey (Brady and Davis, 1993) who consider that '... the environment has changed so dramatically that marketers are simply not picking up the right signals anymore.'

As discussed in the following chapter, in the turbulent environment of the 1990s, dynamic firms are moving from a *marketing-oriented* to a *market-oriented* management style and are reinventing the marketing organization (George *et al.*, 1994).

SUMMARY

Marketing is both a business philosophy and an action-oriented process. One can identify three components in the marketing concept: *action*, *analysis* and *culture* (principle of consumer sovereignty). The ideological foundations of marketing are deeply rooted in the principles which govern the functioning of a market economy. Within the firm, marketing's function is two-fold: (a) to lead the firm towards market opportunities adapted to its resources and know-how and which offer a potential for profit and growth (*strategic marketing*); (b) to be the firm's commercial arm for achieving a targeted market share through the use of tactical means related to product, distribution, price and communication decisions (*operational marketing*). The role of marketing in society is to organize exchange and communication between sellers and buyers thereby assuming an efficient matching of supply and demand. This role is of an increased complexity in modern economies and determine the productivity of the entire market system. The priority role of marketing has evolved with the complexity of the economic, technological and competitive environment. In the current marketing practice, one can identify three levels of implementation of the marketing concept: *passive marketing*, *organizational marketing* and *active marketing*. Each of these business philosophies has its own limitations. To remain competitive in the environment of the years 2000, excellent companies are going one step further and are moving from a *marketing-oriented* to a *market-oriented* culture.

QUESTIONS AND PROBLEMS

1. 'Marketing is both a business philosophy and an action-oriented process which is valid for every organization in contact with its constituency of users.' Select a non-profit organization (university, hospital, museum, etc.) and discuss this proposition by reference to Figs 1.2 and 1.4. As a support for your analysis, read Sheth (1993).
2. Is marketing applicable in a firm operating in a developing country? How would you describe the priority objectives of strategic marketing in this type of environment? What would be the relative importance of each marketing instrument (the four P's)?
3. Compare and contrast market orientation, sales orientation and product orientation. What are the organizational implications for each of these three business philosophies?
4. Referring to your personal experience as a consumer, give examples of wild marketing practices. Which remedies would you suggest to deter companies from using these practices?
5. You have to audit the marketing function of a firm operating in a high-tech industrial market. To assess the degree of customer orientation of this firm, prepare a set of questions to be discussed with the general management of the firm.
6. How would you proceed to introduce strategic marketing in a small- or medium-sized company which has limited financial and human resources?

REFERENCES

Ames, B.C. and J.D. Hlavacek (1989), *Market Driven Management*. Homewood, Illinois: Dow Jones-Irwin.

Bennett, R.C. and R.G. Cooper (1981), 'The Misuse of Marketing: An American Tragedy', *Business Horizons*, November–December, pp. 51–60.

Booz Allen and Hamilton, Inc. (1982), *New Product Management for the 1980's*. New York.

Brady, J. and I. Davis (1993), 'Marketing in Mid-life Crisis', *The McKinsey Quarterly*, no. 2, pp. 17–28.

Cooper, R.G. (1979), 'The Dimensions of Industrial Product Success and Failure', *Journal of Marketing*, vol. 43, Summer, pp. 93–103.

Cooper, R.G. (1993), *Winning at New Products*, 2nd edn. Reading, Mass.: Addison-Wesley Publishing Company.

Coopers & Lybrand (1994), Marketing is Increasingly Living a Lie in my Organization, *Marketing at the Crossroads*. London.

Drucker, P. (1973), *Management, Tasks, Responsibilities and Practices*. New York: Harper & Row.

Friedman, R. and M. Friedman (1980), *Free to Choose*. New York: Avon Brooks Science Institute.

George, M., A. Freeling and D. Court (1994), 'Reinventing the Marketing Organization', *The McKinsey Quarterly*, no. 4, pp. 43–62.

House, C.H. and R.L. Price (1991), 'The Return Map: Tracking Product Teams', *Harvard Business Review*, vol. 69, January–February, pp. 92–100.

Kotler, P. (1991), *Marketing Management*, 7th edn. Englewood Cliffs: New Jersey, Prentice Hall Inc.

Kuehn, A.A. and R.L. Day (1962), 'Strategy of Product Quality', *Harvard Business Review*, vol. 40, November–December, pp. 100–110.

Lambin, J.J. and R. Peeters (1977), *La gestion marketing des entreprises*. Paris: Presses Universitaires de France.

Lambin, J.J. (1996), 'The Misunderstanding about Marketing', *CEMS Business Review*, vol. 1, no. 1, March.

Levitt, T. (1960), 'Marketing Myopia', *Harvard Business Review*, vol. 38, July–August, pp. 24–47.

de Maricourt, R. (1987), 'Les principes et les techniques du marketing sont-ils applicables aux pays en voie de développement?', *Revue Française du Marketing*, March–April, pp. 5–17.

Miller, R.B. and S.E. Heiman (1987), *Conceptual Selling*. Berkeley, California: Heiman-Miller Inc.

Narver, J.C. and S.F. Slater (1990), 'The Effects of Market Orientation on Business Profitability', *Journal of Marketing*, vol. 54, October, pp. 20–35.

Pirot, R. (1987), 'Plaute, ancêtre du marketing', *Revue Française du Marketing*, no. 114, pp. 83–88.

Schumpeter, J.A. (1949), *The Theory of Economic Development*. Cambridge, Mass.: Harvard University Press.

Searles, P.D. (1980), Marketing Principles and the Arts, in M. P. Mokwa *et al.* (eds), *Marketing the Arts*. New York: Praeger.

Sheth, J.N. (1993), User-oriented Marketing for Non-profit Organizations in Hammack D.C. and Young D.R. (eds), *Nonprofit Organizations in a Market Economy*. San Francisco: Jossey-Bass Publishers.

Smith, A. (1776), *The Wealth of Nations*. London: Methuen.

Urban, G.L., J.R. Hauser and N. Dholakia (1987), *Essentials of New Product Management*. Englewood Cliffs, New Jersey: Prentice Hall Inc.

Webster, F.E. (1994), *Market-Driven Management*. New York: John Wiley & Sons, Inc.

CHAPTER 2

FROM MARKETING TO MARKET-DRIVEN MANAGEMENT

LEARNING OBJECTIVES

After reading this chapter, you should be able to understand:

■ the major structural changes in Western economies and their marketing implications for the firm

■ the nature and threats of newly emerging competitive forces

■ the changing behaviour of consumers and the emergence of new societal needs

■ the 'accountable' marketing concept based on corporate ethical behaviour

■ the globalization process of the European and World economies

■ why and how firms have to reinforce their level of market-

orientation to remain competitive in the current turbulent
environment

■ how to measure the level of market orientation of a firm.

*E*ver since the first oil shock of October 1973, firms have operated in a restrictive, highly competitive environment of economic and social turbulence, in which change is no longer accidental, but has become systematic, intermittent and very largely unpredictable. What Peter Drucker (1980) calls an *Age of Discontinuity* is increasingly revealing itself, at least in Western Europe, as a structural transformation of the economic, competitive and sociocultural fabric. These deep modifications have forced firms to review their strategic options, to redefine their priorities and to change their managerial style. Marketing, which has also developed since the period of continuous growth of the Golden Sixties, is not immune to this reappraisal. In this chapter we shall describe the main environmental changes observed on the European scene and their implications for the marketing function in the years 2000.

2.1 THE NEW MACRO-MARKETING ENVIRONMENT

The underlying causes of the new challenges to be faced at the end of this century in Western Europe can be traced to several changes due to structural modifications of technology, the economy and markets, coupled with a realignment of social priorities. Today, at the end of the 1990s, change continues at a pace which makes it safe to predict that the current escalation of turbulence will persist in the years to come. The successive oil crises of the 1970s, the stock market crash of 1987, the reunification of the two Germanies, the turmoil in Eastern Europe, the Gulf War, the second Russian revolution, the European Single Market and the creation of the European Union in Maastricht are all examples of major modifications in a firm's macro-marketing environment. We shall briefly describe here the three major environmental changes: technological, economic and competitive.

2.1.1 The new technologies

Increasingly, firms are confronted with *innovation competition*, based on technical progress, which is used more and more as an offensive weapon to conquer markets. The effect of *creative destruction*, in the Schumpeter sense (1949), is well known. What is new is its acceleration and geographical generalization.

The growth rate of an economy is closely related to the number of new technologies and the number of new industries that can be created with the new technologies. Unfortunately, new technologies do not appear at regular intervals. In the absence of important innovations, an economy can stagnate. This was the case during the early 1980s in Western economies and especially in Europe. Industries that served the basic needs have reached saturation. These industries did not necessarily decline, but their growth slowed down. New industries emerged that cater to the affluent consumer in the form of luxury goods, recreation, travel and services. In addition to these, high-technology sectors have also developed, which constitute highways towards economic expansion. These growing markets are the stakes for which the world is engaged in battle.

Waves of inventions and innovations

We saw in the previous chapter that the growth of the last 25 years was in fact due to innovations which had been developed earlier, during the years preceding the First World War. The historical analysis of the pace at which inventions and innovations appear shows that they surge in waves with a given configuration and frequency: waves of innovation following waves of invention with a time lag.

Marchetti (1982) studied the various innovations that have taken place in the world industry during the last 200 years. His results are summarized in the graphs of Fig. 2.1. The lines represent the cumulative number of inventions and innovations as a function of time. The y-axis has a logarithmic scale so that the logistic function of time can be represented by a straight line in order to facilitate visual comparison. Marchetti identifies three successive waves: the 1802 wave, from

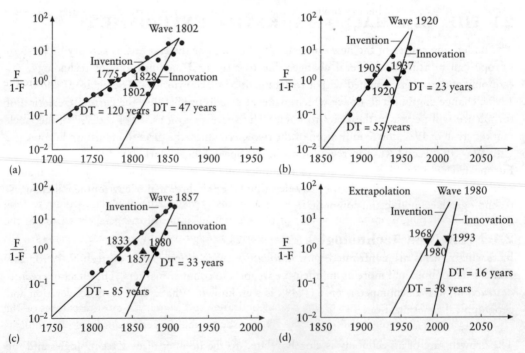

FIGURE 2.1 *The waves of inventions and innovations* (Source: *Marchetti, 1982*)

1775 to 1828, with 21 inventions and innovations; the 1857 wave (1833-80) with 40 observations; and the 1920 wave (1905–37), with 51 data points. Comparison and analysis of the three waves highlights the following points:

- Both the sets of inventions and those of innovations are similar, in that they are *ordered*: in each wave, inventions become innovations according to the 'first come, first served' rule.

- The lag between waves, measured by the time distance between the central points of each wave, has remained constant, of the order of 55 years for innovations and 63 years for inventions. This corresponds to the periodicity of long cycles observed by the Russian economist Kondratiev (1935).

- The lag between the central points of inventions and innovations in each wave tends to become shorter: 52 years, 47 years and 33 years respectively. This reveals an *acceleration* in the passage from the laboratory to industrialization.

- The phases of inventions and innovations also tend to accelerate and cover a shorter period. For inventions, the duration of each wave has evolved as 120, 85 and 55 years; and for innovations the duration is 47, 33 and 23 years.

By extrapolating the observed regularities, Marchetti estimates the next wave to span the period from 1968 to 1993, with the mean point in 1980. The phase is 38 years for inventions and 16 years for innovations. According to Marchetti, we are therefore at the centre of a new industrial era. As shown by the curve forecasting the 1980 wave, most of the inventions which should participate in the next great strides have already taken place.

Analogy with economic history obviously has some limits, but it is better than reading tea leaves or extrapolating the recent past.

The Kondratiev long cycle revisited

The observations on technological evolution are especially interesting since they corroborate the existence of long economic movements put forth by many economists, notably by the Russian economist Kondratiev (1935), who is considered to be the pioneer in the identification of long cycles (see Box 2.1.).

The theory of long cycles is far from being unanimously accepted by economists. Some economists, like Samuelson for instance, believe that it is based on science fiction. Other economists, like Marchetti (1982), consider it a means of visualizing over the medium to long term, while keeping in mind the benefit of placing oneself in a historic perspective and at the same time being aware of the danger in extrapolating a recent past. In recent years, many studies have added empirical support to the ideas of Kondratiev—see Pruden (1978) and Bossier and Hugé (1981) among others.

Independently of the regularities observed by Kondratiev and Marchetti, most researches on the interpretation of the economic crisis of the 1980s associate the greatest majority of the problems in Western economies over the last decade with modifications in the rate and form of technological change.

BOX 2.1

The Kondratiev long wave

In 1926, the Russian economist Nicolas D. Kondratiev published an article, which was translated nine years later in *Review of Economics and Statistics* (November 1935). In this article, Kondratiev published a study of the capitalist economies of the UK, France, the USA and Germany, looking at the wholesale price level, interest rates, wages, foreign trade and the production and consumption of coal and pig iron, and the production of lead. The data permitted a study back to the early 1800s.

Kondratiev identified three long waves ranging from 48 years to 60 years. Updates and extrapolations of the Kondratiev wave theory identified a fourth wave with a peak in 1975. The four long waves are:

	Rise	*Decline*	*Duration*
First wave	1785–1815	1815–1845	60 years
Second wave	1845–1870	1870–1895	50 years
Third wave	1895–1915	1915–(1945)	(60 years)
Fourth wave	(1945–1975)	(1975–2005)	(60 years)

Numerous other factors have been correlated with various phases of the Kondratiev wave.

1. During the rise of the long waves, years of prosperity are more numerous, whereas years of depression predominate during the downswing.
2. During the decline of the long waves, agriculture, as a rule, suffers an especially pronounced and long depression.
3. During the decline of the long waves, an especially large number of important discoveries and intentions in the techniques of production and communications are made, which, however, are usually applied on a large scale only at the beginning of the next long upswing.
4. At the beginning of a long upswing, gold production increases as a rule, and the world market for goods is generally enlarged by the assimilation of new and developing countries.
5. It is during the period of the rise of the long waves (i.e. during the period of high tension in the expansion of economic forces) that, as a rule, the most disastrous and extensive wars and revolutions occurs.

On the whole, the post-war economic conditions are sufficiently close to the Kondratiev scenario to suggest that Western economies are in the middle of the decline phase of a fourth Kondratiev wave.

The 1980s mark the end of a growth cycle, due to the fact that the major innovations which had sparked this growth are reaching maturity; after the era of steel, the steam engine and railways, after the era of electricity, chemistry and the internal combustion engine, here we are in the era of the silicon, synthetic materials, robotics, computers, astronautics, biotechnology, etc. The passage from one cycle to the next is discontinuous and is characterized by a transitory period of crisis which can be fatal to those firms unable to adapt.   (Maïsseu, 1984, p. 45)

The economic situation that we are going through corresponds to a deep-rooted phenomenon provoked essentially by the wearing out of the effects of conventional technologies. For most economic analysts, the only way out of the crisis is the generation of a new wave of innovations which could act as the driving force of a new expansion.

2.1.2 The new European economy
The effects of the technological changes on industry can be clearly seen in the light of the following facts regarding the countries in the European Union (OECD, 1995).

■ *Slowed down growth*, hardly over 2 per cent per year from 1973 to 1991, compared to more than 4.5 per cent on average before 1973; growth reduced to less than 1 per cent from 1992 to 1993 and expected to be around 2.5 in 1995 and 1996.

■ The *unemployment rate*, which had only reached about 3 per cent of the active population in 1973, went up to 10 per cent in 1983 in the seven largest industrial countries. In 1995, it was still around 11 per cent in OECD Europe.

■ Double digit *inflation* occurred in the European Community from 1973 to 1980, and then fell to below 3 per cent since 1993.

■ *Budget deficits* have reached such proportions that they seem to forbid any new increase in public spending, especially in the USA, Italy, UK and Belgium.

■ *The commercial influence* of the European Community countries has weakened. This can be witnessed in the decline in growth of exports. As a result, Western Europe's share of world trade in manufactures is in decline; from 54.1 per cent in 1986 to 46.6 per cent in 1995.

From now on, European firms must operate in a much more difficult economic environment. The profound changes in the economy imply very rapid and harsh penalties for management errors, as witnessed by the spectacular rise in the number of firms going bankrupt.

The European Single Market
To this macroeconomic analysis we must add a major political fact in Western Europe: the agreement of the twelve member states of the European Community to create a single market. This unique European Act, adopted by the heads of state in December 1985 and complemented in 1993 by the Maastricht treaty ratified by national Parliaments, creates a European Union extending over the whole of the Community by eliminating all non-tariffs barriers between the twelve national members by the end of 1992 and by creating a European currency.

The creation of this large market should not only allow for the elimination of a whole series of constraints affecting the performance of firms today, but will also result in a great shake-up by intensifying competition. According to a group of Community experts, the elimination of barriers and the resulting increased competition should have five major consequences (Cecchini *et al.*, 1988, p. 73):

■ Significant reduction in costs, due to the suppression of non-tariff barriers and to better exploitation of economies of scale.

■ Increased efficiency within firms and a decrease in prices as a result of competition.

■ Demand increase due to lower prices and further exploitation of economies of scale.

■ Adjustments between industries, with comparative advantages of some firms becoming more effective in an integrated market.

■ A flow of innovations, new products and processes generated by the dynamics of the internal market.

Figure 2.2 describes the mechanisms by which such effects are to be realized. It is important to note that the gains are essentially supply-side generated. The improvements in performance would result from a response by companies reacting to changes in cost and increased competition. The increase in demand that is assumed to occur is contingent on prices falling (Catinat and Jacquemin, 1990).

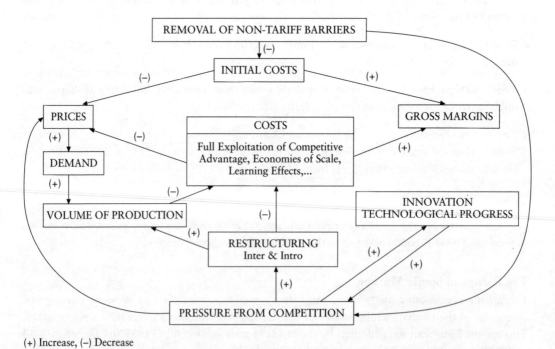

(+) Increase, (–) Decrease

FIGURE 2.2 *Micro-economic effects triggered by EC market integration (Source: Catinat and Jacquemin, 1990, p. 213)*

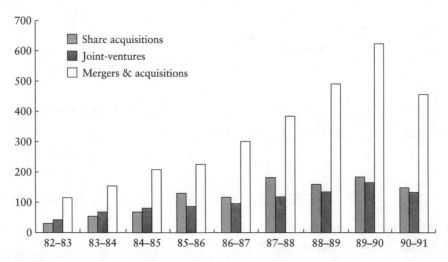

FIGURE 2.3 *Concentration and alliances among European firms*

A Community-wide survey of firms was conducted in 1988, i.e. several years before the introduction of the Single Market, to analyse how European firms perceived the opportunities presented by the completion of the internal market. This study revealed that European firms:

■ Believed that the suppression of barriers would bring costs down.

■ Expected their sales to go up in other countries of the Community.

■ Planned to take a series of measures to improve productivity.

■ Intended to increase the number of agreements of international co-operation with firms in other member states of the Community (*Economie Européenne*, No. 35, March 1988, pp. 139–143).

Thus, the expectations of firms facing the challenge of the internal market were positive with regard to the realization of a European single market and its expansion (see Fig. 2.3). *What is the situation today, in 1996, four years after the opening of the Single Market?* Several facts can already be pointed out.

■ Both from an economic and political standpoint the European Single Market is becoming a reality. As such it seems to be irreversible unless the European Union should be dissolved.

■ Companies have reacted to the Single Markets incentives as shown by (a) the significant development of intra-Community trade and (b) by the spectacular growth of agreements, alliances, mergers and acquisitions among European firms.

■ Competition increased following the progressive deregulations introduced into key sectors, such as telecommunication and air transportation.

■ Productivity gains due to restructuring and price decreasing due to intensified competition have already been observed in many sectors.

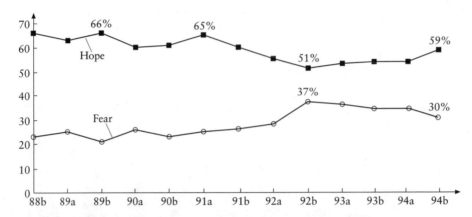

FIGURE 2.4 *Popularity of the European Single Market 1988–95 (Source:* Eurobaromètre, *no. 42, Spring; Fieldwork, December, 1994)*

It is important to realize, however, that many directives concerning the development of the Single Market have not yet been integrated into the national law of all member states. This delay can be explained by the fact that this major European restructuring coincided, in 1993–94, with a period of deep economic recession. As Fig. 2.4. shows, the popularity of the Single Market decreased during this period.

> Before 1991, the European Single Market was welcomed with great expectations by most Europeans (66 per cent). Later on, some of them were worried by certain points, especially those concerning competition, unemployment, free circulation of individuals, loss of national identity and the welfare dimension part of the project. People who were looking forward to the European Single Market were only 51 per cent in the fall of 1992 and 37 per cent of them were afraid of this perspective. ... One may note, in 1994, a significant renewal of hopefulness (59%) and a decline in 'fearfulness' (30%) for the first time since 1992.   (*Eurobaromètre*, No. 42, Spring 1995, p. 51)

Whatever the political, economic and social difficulties that would inevitably accompany such an ambitious plan, every day the Single Market becomes a reality which is both an opportunity and a major challenge for European companies. The ability to master the rules of this new game obviously depends on the capacity of firms to *think globally* at the European level and to adapt their management (marketing in particular) accordingly.

Eastern Europe: the new frontier

Suddenly, within a few months, extraordinary political and economic reforms swept Eastern Europe and the Soviet Union, focusing attention on this area. The disappearance of the Iron Curtain, the reunification of Germany, the split-up of the former Soviet Union, the autonomy of its republics are just examples of major changes, some of which are still on-going and for them it is therefore difficult to measure their impact. In any case, significant for the world economy is the fact that there is a new potential market of 430 million people. Many firms, be they European, American or Japanese, see it as a great opportunity. For example, IBM estimates its sales potential at the Russian market to reach US $1 billion by the end of the twentieth century (*Financial Izvestiya*, 11.05.95). Such long-term opportunity is of particular importance for European companies who have close cultural links going back over the centuries with these countries.

It is still difficult, even in 1996, to forecast accurately how things will evolve in the coming years even if there are significant trends that can be observed.

- The first thing to remember is the *diversity of Eastern Europe* which cannot be viewed as a monolithic economic bloc similar to the Western Europe. These countries are very different both economically and socially.

- The switch to a market economy, even if it is regularly subject to criticisms, is *irreversible* and according to public opinion in Eastern Europe, Communism and Socialist management are dead.

- This change-over will, however, take a long time and be accompanied by both political and social *turbulence*, as we can see today in Russia for instance.

- The legal and institutional framework of these countries will remain uncomplete, fuzzy and unstable for a long time, which means that direct investments will remain risky and will demand a strong sense of pionneering and entrepreneurship.

- In the long term, there is no doubt that, along with China, Eastern Europe will be the new launching pad for many industries.

It is more difficult to know how to react in the short term and how to position oneself in these markets. In fact, Eastern Europe offers three very *contrasting strategies* (see Pitt-Watson and Frazer, 1991).

(a) *Make it here, sell it there*   This is the strategy which spontaneously comes to mind as, in these countries, there is a great shortage of goods. Almost all foreign entrants, companies such as Coca-Cola, Philip Morris, Volvo, TetraPak, Sony, Philips, etc., have imported their products first—an opportunistic strategy that exploits demand based on novelty and scarcity. The most critical problem faced by these exporters is how to get money out of the country and into hard currency. If the products are not of strategic significance, barter arrangements are the only possible solution. Such arrangements are not always attractive since the products offered in exchange generally do not have a market.

This import strategy is not always sustainable in the long term and, as the market grows, companies tend to opt for some sort of local production, often to guarantee supplies as well as to control overall costs and the uncertainty of import duties. Since 1993, an increasing number of international companies have decided to make direct investments in Eastern Europe, including Russia. Among these are IBM, Honeywell, Baskin Robbins just to mention a few. For ABB Eastern Europe became one of the top priority fields for strategic expansion.

During 1990–1994 period ABB created a network of 60 companies covering 13 East European countries and Kazakhstan and employing more than 30,000 people. While total costs of establishing this network did not exceed 300 million US dollars, the orders ABB received in 1994 amounted to more than 1.4 billion and are expected to reach 2.3–3.3 billion in 2000.   (*Financial Izvestiya*, 16.01.96)

(b) *Make it there, sell it there*   The strategy of direct investment in Eastern Europe with the intention of selling in Eastern Europe remains a risky alternative. With the exception of Russia and the Ukraine, each republic is a small domestic market, and contrary to what happens in Western Europe the barriers between these countries tend to be reinforced today because of nationalistic pressures and/or because of the Russian big brother's rejection. Furthermore, there are many operational problems that need to be overcome: shortages of quality raw materials, complex bureaucracy, weak distribution and logistic channels, difficult transportation and stocking facilities, inefficient pricing mechanisms and, last but not least, a total lack of market orientation.

To establish local production, a newcomer can opt (generally in a joint venture) to buy or refurbish an existing facility, a so-called 'brownfield' development. Alternatively, it can select to invest in a new 'greenfield' site. The *brownfield* approach has the advantage of utilizing an established operation that may offer some protection in an unknown environment. Alcatel founded several communications companies in Russia as well as two joint ventures, one of which (LenBell) is active in manufacturing and servicing telephone stations (*Financial Izvestiya*, No. 21, 28.03.95). Pripps/Hartwalls' joint venture investment in the Baltica brewery in Saint Petersburg is an example. On the other hand, investment in a *greenfield* site means superior efficiency and productivity, but entails greater outlay, as Coca-Cola and Master Foods have discovered. A mixed strategy with fewer risks is to acquire and to adapt Russian brands—a strategy pursued by manufacturers keen to capture local tastes and to build on loyalty to existing national brands (Jenk *et al.*, 1995).

(c) *Make it there, sell it here*   It seems that a third opportunity for many companies is to use Eastern Europe as a possible production base for sales in the West, to exploit the skills of an East European workforce and sell the output through existing marketing channels. The Lada success in certain countries of the European Union, in Belgium in particular, is an example of the successful application of this strategy.

It follows that significance of Eastern Europe's entry into world trade is not limited only to the markets that are opened up. Also important are the competitive industries which will develop in those countries, particularly those which can be better developed without outside assistance. This could mean new competition for Western European companies and a pressure towards protectionist measures within the European Union. Just such a situation has already formed in relation to metals and textile goods exported from Russia into Europe (*Financial Izvestiya*, No. 13, 8.02.96).

2.1.3 The new competition

To the profound economic changes discussed above, we must add changes in competitiveness resulting from the *internationalization of reference markets* at the world level in an increasing number of industrial sectors. Once again, this evolution has come about from the application of technological progress to means of transport and communication. The elimination of distances, or at least the elimination of time cost or transport cost due to geographical distance, has taken us to the stage of competitiveness at the global level in markets, products, labour costs and prices.

The new competitors

Consequently, the comparative advantages between certain regions have been reversed: between world regions, between industrialized and developing countries, between market economies and centralized economies. These reversals have given rise to the appearance of *new competitors* for firms in industrialized countries:

- *Newly industrialized countries* (NIC) now hold important positions in basic sectors dominated in the past by industrialized countries (steel, chemistry, textiles, etc.).

- *Eastern European countries* are actively in competition with Western European firms in markets for basic industrial products, through barter and compensatory purchases in order to overcome shortages of hard currency. Recent changes in these countries will reinforce this trend, while at the same time presenting new opportunities for Western Europe.

- *Japanese firms*, such as Sony, Toyota, Canon, Seiko, Nikon and many others have acquired substantial market shares all over the world in sectors which are in high demand and often have aggressive commercial policies (Kotler *et al.*, 1985).

- *Large retailers and distributors*, like Ikea, Aldi, Sainsbury, Marks & Spencer, are discovering strategic marketing and are adopting product policies to compete directly with branded products (private and generic brands) more and more on the international scene.

In terms of a number of important sectors, these new rivals are in a better position for products that were traditionally part of the product portfolio of firms operating in industrialized countries.

It is within the context of such profoundly changing competition that firms must reposition themselves and find new market segments. These new market segments must provide the firm with higher value added, be better adapted to their capacities and technological edge and allow them to build a sustainable competitive advantage.

The revolution in the food retail sector

In the performance of the tasks of exchange and communication described in Fig. 1.1, the initiative was until recently on the suppliers' side who, specifically in the fast-moving consumer good (FMCG) sector, have developed dynamic branding policies supported by strong *pull communication* strategies targeted to the end-consumer. Branding policy has always been a key factor in the marketing strategy of suppliers.

A significant change of the last ten years in Europe, and also in the United States, is the growing power of the retailers. From passive intermediairies in the channel, retailers are now active marketers developing new store concepts and own-label brands designed for well-targeted segments. They are now directly competing with manufacturers' brands; they have the power to dictate terms to their suppliers and to push their brands off the shelves if they are not leaders in their product category. Several factors explain this shift of power from manufacturers to retailers.

- The high *concentration rate* of retailers, specifically in the FMCG sector in the UK, the Netherlands, Belgium and Germany; approximately 50 per cent of the market is accounted for by the top ten retailers.

- The creation, at the European level, of powerful *purchasing centres* which give retailers a strong bargaining power over suppliers.

- The development of *computerized systems* for recording sales at retail checkouts, which not only gives retailers full market information but also has important logistics implications for the optimization of the grocery supply chain, minimizing inventory levels and optimizing product availability.

- The adoption by retailers of sophisticated *store brand policies* targeted to segments often neglected by manufacturers and the growth of private labels.

- The emergence of new breed of retailers, the *hard discounters*, who, in warehouse stores, charge very low prices on their own private brands while excluding suppliers' brands from their shelves.

These new developments, to be reviewed in more detail in Chapter 12, modify considerably the European grocery retail and its power relationship with suppliers. They reinforce the necessity of strong strategic analysis by the suppliers and the distributors.

Global competitiveness

Competition is now global for a whole series of activities. This is obvious in products of a global 'nature', such as high-technology equipment (aerospace, aviation, telecommunication, etc.) or raw materials (basic products, etc.). It is less so in 'universal' consumer goods, whether durable or non-durable (hi-fi, video, cameras, drinks, hamburgers, jeans, etc.), and even less so in services (credit cards, tourism, rentals, databanks, advisory services, recruitment, etc.).

The industrialized countries, comprising Western Europe, North America and Japan—*the Triad*—form the natural reference market for firms operating in global sectors. This market includes more than 700 million inhabitants. However, as shown in Table 2.1, this represents only 15 per cent of the world population, but two-thirds (66 per cent) of gross world production, about 85 per cent of world discretionary purchasing power, and 90 per cent of the world's high-tech production (Ohmae, 1987, p. 10).

Competitive advantage must be defined at the Triad level. It is no longer enough just to do well at home; the firm must also perform well internationally in order to get a *leverage effect*. Many

TABLE 2.1 *The triadic countries*

Country/area	Population (million)
Western Europe	340
North America	250
Japan	120
	710 total

Source: Ohmae, 1987.

reasons can be cited for the globalization of competition (de Woot, 1990, pp. 16–17; Ohmae, 1987, pp. 10–14).

■ The 700 million consumers begin to form a *more homogeneous market* as a result of communication, transport and travelling. The progressive uniformity in needs and wants is favourable to the development of a potential market for 'global products', which is very attractive to firms because of economies of scale in production, distribution, advertising, etc.

■ *Diffusion of technical progress* has become so fast that it is necessary to introduce an innovation in the three large triad markets simultaneously. A delay in one of the markets exposes the firm to the possibility of being beaten by a rival who can launch a similar product and thus achieve a dominant position, which is difficult to overturn.

■ The *development cost* of some equipment goods is so high that it can only be recovered at the world level.

■ The *industrial fabric* has become more homogeneous, in the sense that for many goods and services, 70 to 80 per cent of production and consumption takes place in the countries of the triad.

To these major trends in the world economy one must add the European Single Market which, as discussed above, becomes ever more of a reality.

Warfare marketing

Another consequence of the appearance of new competitors is a reinforcement of the harshness of the competitive struggle and the necessity of a more systematic and thorough analysis of the competitive forces present. *Competitor analysis* is now a central preoccupation of strategic marketing (Porter, 1985); hence the origin of the expression *warfare marketing*. Ries and Trout (1986) emphasize the idea that beating competition has become the main objective of strategic marketing. Many factors explain this evolution:

■ In industrialized economies, firms are increasingly facing saturated and stagnant markets.

■ In these markets, the classical marketing concept is better integrated in firms and a knowledge of buyers' needs is no longer a sufficient competitive advantage.

■ Products available are often of similar quality and the differences are hardly perceptible.

■ Counteracting competitors' manoeuvres is therefore a key factor of success.

Warfare marketing advocates a reinforcement of the *competitor orientation* within the market-driven firm, a systematic analysis of competitive forces, and a development of attack and defence strategies, including flank and guerilla attacks inspired by military strategy. Creation and systematic exploitation of a sustainable competitive advantage have become just as necessary as the understanding of buyers' needs.

2.2 THE NEW CONSUMER

The mass-marketing era lifted the aspirations of consumers from the materialistic needs of comfort and safety to a drive for new values. Satisfaction of 'good living' needs coupled with growth in discretionary income have changed consumer demand patterns. Having 'filled their bellies', as Ansoff (1984, p. 7), put it, individuals begin to aspire to higher levels of personal satisfaction. They become increasingly discriminating in their demand for more customized services and complete information about their purchases, as well as for post-sales responsibility from the manufacturer and ecologically friendly products. They challenge the firm directly through consumerism and put pressure on governments for increased controls.

2.2.1 The coming of age of mass marketing

The nature of operational marketing has been changing rapidly in recent years owing to the profound changes observed in industrialized countries. This trend sets the stage for new directions in distribution, selling methods and communication. Among the most critical changes are:

■ Changing demography, with more single households, an increase in women in the workforce, two-income families, people staying healthier and living longer, etc.

■ Proliferation of weakly differentiated brands and products.

■ Weakening of advertising effectiveness.

■ Decline in brand loyalty.

■ Rising costs of personal communication.

■ Overcrowding of shopping malls and stores.

■ Escalation in self-defeating promotions.

These changes have contributed to the weakening of the foundations of traditional mass-marketing methods. They are simply no longer working very well. Rapp and Collins (1990) argue for a major turnaround in marketing, and predict that individualized marketing—we prefer to use the term *customized marketing*—should be substituted for mass or segment marketing.

The coming of age of mass marketing also implies placing more importance on close involvement with identified prospects and customers and replacing the marketing monologue which prevails in many market situations by a *marketing dialogue*. This can be achieved through direct marketing, interactive communication, response advertising, etc. These new developments in operational marketing will be reviewed in detail in Chapter 12.

Economic and competitive changes have been accompanied by sociocultural changes. These changes, which were the socio-economic, cultural and social consequences of some marketing practices, have in turn given rise to a reappraisal of the classical marketing concept. The starting point of this evolution goes back to the 1970s in Europe, and it can be traced to two different movements: *consumerism* and *environmentalism*.

2.2.2 Consumerism

Consumerism was born out of the growing consciousness of the excesses of operational marketing, or the practice of wild marketing (see p. 20) which attempts to mould demand to meet supply requirements rather than adapt supply to demand expectations. Consumerism is the consequence of the relative failure of the marketing concept. As stated by Drucker (1980, p. 85), '. . . consumerism is the shame of marketing'.

The main arguments of the consumerist critique are as follows:

■ Marketing tries to satisfy consumers' *short-term needs* at the expense of their *long-term well-being*.

■ Products are developed in order to *favour the profit objective* of the firm rather than the objective of satisfying needs.

■ Marketing favours the *symbolic value* of products (affective and emotional values) at the expense of their functional value.

■ There is a fundamental *imbalance* between buyers' and sellers' legal rights.

It is important to emphasize that consumerism does not fundamentally question the marketing concept, but rather demands its full application.

In fact, the consumerist movement reveals a phenomenon of *socialization* or of *unionization* of demand, similar to the workers' movement at the beginning of the century. This is an important fact for the firm, as it confronts ever more involved consumers who react to its actions in an organized manner and are better informed thanks mainly to consumer associations. The economic role of consumer unions is summarized in Box 2.2.

Due to its countervailing power, consumerism has undoubtedly contributed to the improvement of the ethical level of marketing practice. It forms a pressure group that firms can hardly ignore. Nevertheless, the objectives of consumerism have evolved clearly, owing to the pressure of change in the general economic situation. For more about the history of consumerism, see Aaker and Day (1982).

2.2.3 Environmentalism

The *environmentalist movement* reflects the new awareness of the scarcity of natural resources and reveals a change of outlook regarding consumption. Environmentalists question the impact

BOX 2.2

Economic analysis of consumerism

- On the graph presented below, the marginal return of an information search made by a consumer is depicted as a function decreasing with the level of information required by the consumer on the relevant product characteristics used as choice criteria. Thus, we have the R curve.
- Similarly, the *marginal cost of this search* is supposed to be independent of the level of information required. Thus, we have the straight line C.
- Point A represents the optimal stopping point for the consumer. To continue his or her search beyond this point would cost more than the expected return due to additional information.

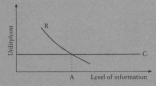

- Economic growth and prosperity have modified the situation in the following ways:

  - The perceived cost of personal time has increased.
  - The number of products with internal qualities difficult to assess and compare has also increased.
  - The number of weakly differentiated brands has increased.

- These changes have induced, first, a cost increase of an information search (C moves to C') and, second, an increased complexity of personal choices and therefore a decrease of the marginal return of an information search (R moves R').

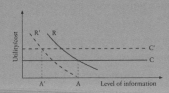

- The optimal stopping point of the consumer moves from A to A', which corresponds to a level of required information lower than the one prevailing before.
- Thus, economic growth leads to a certain loss of consumer sovereignty by making consumers more dependent on commercial informations controlled by the firm.
- It is therefore in the interest of individual consumers to participate in consumer associations to complement the information provided by the seller by the information provided by the consumerist organizations and distributed at a low cost. Consumers can therefore reach a higher level of information.

Source: Adapted from Lepage (1982).

BOX 2.3
Economic analysis of environmentalism

In 1972, the Meadow report of the Club de Rome called the attention of the economic and social world to the limits of economic growth, the risk of exhausting non-renewable resources, the destruction of the environment and the uncontrolled growth of waste. This new awareness led public authorities and political movements to listen to the recommendations made by economists.

To the economist, the environment is part of the economy and the best way to protect the environment is to assign a price to its use instead of considering it as a free public good, in contrast with the other goods found in a market economy.

If there is no market price, consumers and manufacturers are motivated to use the environment as a *free reservoir* even if the social costs generated by their polluting behaviour are high, since these costs are not assessed by the market. Thus, those who generate these social costs do not pay for them and are not held responsible for the costs involved by their elimination.

The solution proposed by the economists is to set a price on the use of the environment. This price should be equal to the sum of the total social costs generated by pollution as they are evaluated by the polluted parties. Given this price, polluters would use the environment only to the extent to which the expected benefits of this use are higher than the price they would have to pay. This way, the polluters would assume the social cost of pollution. This is the idea behind the principle '*who pollutes pays*'.

The economic instruments used to set a price on the use of the environment generally take the form of a direct tax on the polluting activities, either in a prevention (eco-taxes) or in a repairing (eco-fees) perspective. For a comparative analysis of the legislation in Europe, see Laurent (1994).

of consumption and of marketing on the environment, as summarized in Box 2.3. The reasoning is as follows:

> Each consumption has positive and negative utilities. By insisting on increasing consumption quantitatively, marketing is instrumental in neglecting the impact of negative consequences. These negative consequences have a high social cost, which is also a neglected cost. Given the scarcity of resources, it is necessary to allow explicitly for the social cost of consumption.

The data of Table 2.2 illustrate the relevance of the environmentalist reasoning in the personal transportation sector.

TABLE 2.2 *Socio-economic costs of personal transportation modes*

Personal transportation modes	Indirect social costs*			Total	Ratio
	Accidents	Noise	Pollution		
Cars (petrol)	1017.0	55	213	1285.0	36.4
Cars (diesel)	1017.0	55	75	1147.0	32.5
Buses	95.0	11	148	254.0	7.2
Electric trains	2.3	33	0	35.3	1.0
Diesel Trains	2.3	33	44	79.3	2.2

*In Belgian francs per 1000 traveller kilometres (i.e. 1 traveller over 1000 km or 20 travellers over 50 km); traffic jam costs not included. The last column shows the ratio of each transportation mode. The train has an indirect social cost of 1 franc and the petrol-driven car has a cost of BF36.4. (*Source: Le Soir*, Brussels, 16 December, 1987.)

In contrast with consumerists, environmentalists do not accept the principle of consumer sovereignty if the application of this principle leads to the destruction of the environment. They feel that the aim of the economic system should not be the satisfaction of the consumer as such, but rather the *improvement in the quality of life*. Their main concern is to protect and enhance people's living environment. The environmentalist movement has had a great impact in many industries and is undoubtedly a factor that will deeply affect economic and industrial life.

Only few years ago, the idea of paying taxes to collect and recycle packages and solid wastes was unthinkable. In 1996, it is now common practice in most countries of Western Europe to have

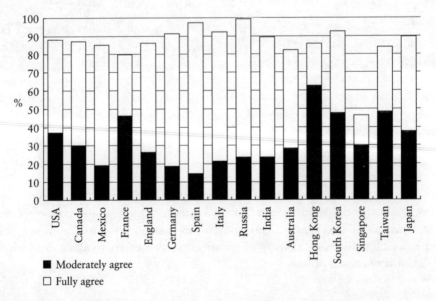

■ Moderately agree
□ Fully agree

FIGURE 2.5 *Worldwide environmental concern* (Source: CNN/Angus Reid Group World Poll, 1992)

government-sponsored programmes designed to focus on pollution control. These programmes are financed by *eco-fees* paid by manufacturers per package used to cover the cost of collection, selection processing and recycling of waste. The *eco-taxes system* adopted in Belgium embraced the concept of pollution prevention and is targeted directly to the end-user to induce him or her to use environmentally sound products.

Two fundamentally different approaches have evolved in assessing what constitutes an 'environmentally friendly' product. The first, the *incremental approach*, is one in which any environmental improvement to a product, however minor, is considered valid and can be labelled as 'environmentally friendly'. The second, the *cradle to grave approach*, also called the *life cycle inventory approach*, is one in which the total impact on the environment must be evaluated before the product can be labelled 'environmentally friendly'.

> Life cycle inventory (LCI) is a process that quantifies the use of energy, resources and emission to the environment associated with a product throughout its life cycle. It accounts for the environmental impact of raw materials procurement, manufacturing and production, packaging, distribution and in-use characteristics straight through to after-use and disposal.   (Ottman, 1993, p. 104).

Table 2.3 highlights the results of an LCI study commissioned by Procter & Gamble comparing the relative environmental impacts of cloth versus paper disposable diapers.

Obviously these two approaches—incremental versus life cycle—are very different viewpoints that are difficult to reconcile. Not surprisingly, businesses usually take the incremental approach while environmental groups prefer the 'cradle to grave' approach.

The environmental concern is the expression of new needs within society. It is not a fad or a protest trend, like the hippies in the late 1960s and early 1970s. It is a way of life which has and will spread throughout all levels of society. Satisfaction of these societal needs will certainly imply new constraints for many firms; for other firms, these new needs constitute an emerging market with new opportunities such as anti-pollution products, environmentally sound products, energy-saving products, recycled products, etc. Two examples of companies having

TABLE 2.3 *Example of life cycle inventory: cloth versus disposable diapers*

	Cloth	Disposable
Raw material consumption (lbs)	3.6	25.3
Water consumption (gals)	144	23.6
Energy consumption (BTUs)	78 890	23 920
Air emission (lbs)	0.860	0.093
Water pollution (lbs)	0.117	0.012
Solid waste(lbs)	0.24	22.18

Source: Ottman (1993, p. 105); *The New York Times*, 14 July, 1990.

successfully taken advantage of the environmental concern are the Body Shop Company, a speciality retail chain of natural cosmetics and toiletries, and Ecover, a firm which manufactures an all-natural, concentrated laundry detergent and line of houshold cleaning.

2.2.4 Green marketing

One impact of the environmentalist movement is the emergence of a new breed of consumerists, the *green consumerists*. Green consumerists have realized that it is possible to change what they consume in a way which benefits the environment and themselves. As a result, green consumerism is putting pressure on distributors and manufacturers to switch to food products and household goods that are healthier and environmentally friendly. They also put pressure on governments to act. Areas that seem likely to develop modified products which environmentally safe are: Personal hygiene, household cleaning products (phosphate-free), food items (organic farming), recycling (paper, glass, tin, etc.), toiletries and cosmetics (CFC-free sprays), recycled paper products (for household and office), packaging materials, energy-efficient equipment, petrol and automobiles (lead-free petrol, catalytic convertors).

The satisfaction of these needs will pose new restrictions on many firms. For others, it represents new opportunities as alert or proactive manufacturers are realizing that they can gain a competitive advantage over their rivals by adapting their products and packages in a way that is environmentally friendly.

> For several years, Rank Xerox has been developing an ambitious programme, called Renaissance, for reusing photocopying machine parts. These photocopiers are made of 80 per cent of recycled parts and are sold at a price that is 20 per cent less than the price charged for brand new machines. Today 40 per cent of company sales come from the Renaissance product category. Thus, the comment made by Rank Xerox Environment Manager '... within 10 years, brand new products will be non-existent'.
>
> (translation of article in *La Libre Entreprise*, 20 November 1993, p. 27)

Green marketing is the industry response to these new requirements of the market and many corporations and distributors have hurried to create ostensibly green products. However, in doing so they have often generated a great deal of confusion and, in some cases, an actual backlash towards the very products they are developing.

> According to a study by UK-based Marketing Intelligence Ltd, green products have multiplied 20 times faster than all other new packaged goods since 1986. As a result, product claims such as 'degradable', 'biodegradable', 'recyclable', 'CFC-free', 'ozone-friendly', 'environmentally friendly or safe' are appearing widely in ads and on packages.
>
> (*Business International Weekly Report*, 28 January 1991)

These terms are often used by marketers in positioning their products and are then disputed by environmentalists. Because of claims and counterclaims many consumers became confused, sceptical and questioning. This situation was created by the different approaches taken to assessing 'environmentally friendly' products, the incremental or the life-cycle approach.

BOX 2.4

The McDonald's restaurants' case

A good example illustrating the complexity of environmental issues is the McDonald's restaurant's case. Late 1990, the decision was made to wrap hamburgers in waxed papers instead of polystyrene foam. This decision was made in response to considerable consumer pressure (boycott, sit-ins, etc.) and publicity based on the impression that foam boxes were bad for the environment. Consider, however, the following:

- Polystyrene foam containers satisfy health regulations, keep the food warm, but are made from nonrenewable fossil fuels, are rarely recycled, and usually end up in garbage dumps where they remain intact for generations.
- Paper wrappers are made from renewable forest resources, are theoretically decomposable, but are made in an energy-intensive industry notorious for relaxing toxic chemicals into the environment; they are not recycled and also end up in garbage dumps, where they also remain for long period of time.
- One environmental group has calculated that foam containers consume 70 per cent more energy, produce 70 per cent more air pollution and 80 per cent more water pollution than the paper wrappers. Another environmetal group claims these calculations ignored the issue of whether toxics produced by making the foam were beter or worse than toxics from paper production.

McDonald's has researched the foam box issue three years previously and concluded that the boxes actually were more recyclable than paper. However, the real issue facing McDonald's was not the use of polystyrene; it was that the clam shell container had become a public symbol of a wasteful society.

Source: McDougall (1993, pp. 80–1).

Green consumerists argue that the lack of objective and uniform standards as to the meaning of green labels has left the environmentally conscious buyer uncertain and sceptical about green marketing in general. Green advertising campaigns are viewed as merely attention-getting devices for '... companies trying to hitchhike on the green bandwagon'. It is clear that a 'going green' policy should cover the entire manufacturing process and not just the advertising of the end-product. As discussed in Chapter 12 of this book, a going-green policy should start at the stage of the product concept design, in the laboratory with R&D people and not with advertising people. Firms that position themselves as 'environmentally friendly' must be in a position to prove their environmental credentials. Thus, companies adopting the incremental approach face the possibility of attacks by environmental groups who prefer the cradle-to-grave approach.

The first challenge facing the firm is to define what constitutes 'green' in its specific product category. According to Ottman (1993, p. 49), green products are typically durable, non-toxic, made from recycled materials and minimally packaged. Of course there are no completely green products, for they all use up energy and resources and create waste and pollution during their manufacture, distribution, consumption and after-use and disposal. So *green is relative, describing those products with less impact on the environment than alternatives*. The McDonald's restaurants' case summarized in Box 2.4 illustrates the complexity of environmental issues and the lack of agreement upon methods to measure the precise environmental impacts of a product against alternatives.

Firms that position themselves as 'environmentally friendly', particularly consumer product companies, should consider adopting a 'cradle-to-grave' approach in assessing the environmental impact of their products. Through this environmental audit, the firm can better assess the risk of scrutiny and possible attack by environmentalists. Seeking assistance and advice of environmentalist groups can also sensitize the firm to their concerns. Another benefit is that the firm gains expertise in a complex evolving area that is likely to become an important source of competitive advantage in the future.

To clarify the situation, national governments are introducing special product labels—*eco-labels*—to identify environmentally sound products for consumers and to encourage industry to design goods meeting these requirements. West Germany was the first country to introduce (in 1978) its official eco-labelling scheme (Blue Angel). These labels are criticized today by environmentalists because they are not based on a complete life-cycle analysis. It seems that a European eco-label will progressively replace the national eco-labels.

2.3 IMPLICATIONS FOR MARKETING MANAGEMENT

The arrival of affluence casts doubt on economic growth as the main instrument of social progress. In Western European countries, as well as in the USA, social aspirations have shifted from 'quantity' to 'quality' of life. The firm is now expected to be able to assume 'social accountability' as well as maintain affluence under severe constraints. The slogan, largely accepted until recently by the business community—*the business of business is business*—is no longer acceptable and the firm cannot remain immune from societal interference.

2.3.1 The accountable marketing concept

The consumerist and environmentalist movements have forced some marketing theoreticians to widen their classical marketing concept in a way that puts the emphasis on the necessity to develop an increased consciousness within the firm of the sociocultural side-effects of its economic and, especially, its marketing activity. Thus Kotler (1991, pp. 76–86) proposed the adoption of the *societal marketing concept*.

> The societal marketing concept holds that the organization's task is to determine the needs, wants and interests of target markets and to deliver the desired satisfactions more effectively and efficiently than competitors in a way that preserves and enhances the consumer's and the society's well-being.   (Kotler, 1991, p. 25)

This concept is based on three implicit assumptions:

- Consumers' wishes do not always coincide with their long-term interests or those of the public at large.

- Consumers prefer organizations that show real concern for their satisfaction and well-being as well as the collective well-being.

- The most important task of the organization is to adapt itself to the target markets in such a way as to generate not only satisfaction, but also individual and collective well-being, in order to attract and keep customers.

Two key ideas distinguish the concept of societal marketing from that of the classical marketing concept: (a) marketing must be concerned with the *well-being of buyers* and not simply with the satisfaction of their short-term needs; (b) the firm must pay attention to the side-effects of its economic and industrial activity in order to ensure the *long-term well-being of society as a whole* and not only that of individual consumers. By adopting this wider outlook, the firm will better achieve its own growth and profit objectives.

2.3.2 Ethical marketing

The firm embracing the accountable marketing concept has to define clearly the rules of ethics it intends to follow in its relationships with the market. If, in recent years, one has observed improved marketing conduct, it is largely the outcome due to strong countervailing powers, like the consumerist and environmentalist movements, which, in a way, forced companies to improve their ethical conduct. Nothing is more convincing than the fear of punishment to induce good citizen behaviour. The accountable firm must go beyond this and publicly confirm its commitment to promote ethical decisions and to create a corporate culture conducive to ethical behaviour.

In business, marketing is the most visible functional area because of its interface with the different market players: consumers, distributors, competitors and public opinion. Advertising and selling activities are the most noticeable and close to the public view and, therefore, it is not surprising that marketing is the subject of considerable societal analysis and scrutiny. Marketers, more than any other functional managers, are likely to be confronted with ethical dilemmas at some point in their careers. We believe that marketing managers need guidance from their firm to deal with ethically troublesome issues. This should not prevent managers from forming their own personal philosophy.

The costs of unethical conduct

An ethical dilemma occurs when a manager is confronted with a decision that involves the trade-off between lowering one's personal values in exchange for increased organizational or personal profit. In other words, marketers sometimes feel compelled to do things that they feel ought not to be done to achieve some organizational objectives, like increased sales, market share or short-term profit. The firm should attempt to foster ethical decisions, not only because it is simply the proper thing to do but also because it is its well-understood self-interest in the long term, since unethical behaviour can generate significant personal, organizational and societal costs (Laczniak and Murphy, 1993).

- *Personal costs*. When unethical actions become known, the outcome for the manager who engaged in the transgression is a reprimand or job termination. Even when superiors concede privately that organizational pressures may have contributed to a manager's unethical action, they will never admit this publicly. Unethical managers, believing that their companies will support them, are typically mistaken.

- *Organizational costs*. Substantial costs, like legal penalties or loss of goodwill, can result for the firm when ethical transgressions by a company become public. Two cases in point are the Nestlé powder milk infant formula promoted in less-developed countries and the Drexel Burnham with the junk bonds trading.

- *External costs*. More difficult to assess, those societal costs may be very important: excess economic costs, wastefulness and pollution costs that have to be assumed by the taxpayer or by the state.

More generally, unethical actions can undermine the functioning of a free market economy where the efficient firm, and not the dishonest fim, is supposed to be rewarded. Also, unethical marketing practices damage the thrust in the existing free-market system among the general public and generate authoritarian regulations from public authorities.

Models of ethical behaviours

To what extent are firms attempting to balance the drive for profits with ethical considerations? Reidenbach and Robin (1991) have identified five types of organizational ethical behaviours forming a hierarchy, from the lowest to the highest level of corporate moral development.

- *Stage 1: Amoral*. This is the lowest level. Owners and managers are the only important stakeholders. The prevailing philosophy is to maximize profit at almost any cost.

- *Stage 2: Legalistic*. Being ethical means simply obeying the law. The only obligations that a firm of this type recognizes are legal obligations.

- *Stage 3: Responsive*. The firms that reach this level begin to develop some ethical concern. They recognize that a good relationship with the community is important. The responsive firm usually behaves ethically, if only for self-serving reasons.

- *Stage 4: Emerging ethical*. These firms make explicit recognition that the cost of being ethical may sometimes involve a trade-off with profits. Concern for values is explictly mentioned in the corporate mission statement or in the code of ethics.

- *Stage 5: Developed ethical*. These organizations have clearly articulated value statements communicated, accepted and implemened by every one in the organization. These companies are at the peak of the ethical hierarchy.

In Western Europe, according to Bloon *et al*. (1994), most companies have reached stage 3 of the hierarchy. The number of companies at stages 4 and 5 is growing, however.

Ideas for ethical action

What constitutes the best ethical resolution of an issue? Laczniak and Murphy (1993, p. 49) suggest that one should proceed through a sequence of questions that tests whether the contemplated action is ethical or has possible ethical consequences. The questions Laczniak and Murphy asked are:

1. *The legal test*. Does the contemplated action violate the law?
2. *The duties test*. Is this action contrary to widely accepted moral obligations such as fidelity, gratitude, justice, non-maleficence, beneficence?
3. *The special obligation test*. Does the proposed action violate any other special obligation that stem from the type of marketing organization at focus (pharmaceutical firms, toy manufacturers . . .)?
4. *The motive test*. Is the intent of the contemplated action harmful?
5. *The utilitarian test*. Is there a satisfactory alternative action that produces equal or greater benefits to the parties affected than the proposed action?
6. *The rights test*. Does the contemplated action infringe upon property rights, privacy rights, or the inalienable rights of the consumer (such as the right to information, the right to be heard, the right to choice and the right to remedy)?
7. *The justice test*. Does the proposed action leave another person or group less well-off?

The main difficulty in implementing this test to a specific situation is to resolve the conflicts of interest that may exist among the different stakeholders of the firm.

> For example, there is fiduciary responsibility on the part of managers to render stock-holders a fair return. At times, this might involve taking steps that are clearly counter-productive to another stakeholder group, such as employees. The judgmental difficulty then comes in deciding which of the two duties take precedence.
>
> (Laczniak and Murphy, 1993, p. 50)

An interesting observation made in a recent American study is that the general public seems to be far more pessimistic about the ethical climate of business than are members of top management (Laczniak *et al.*, 1995, p. 40):

> In this study, 44 per cent of the CEO surveyed viewed business ethics as having improved in the last five years, whereas only 16 per cent of the consumers polled agreed with this sentiment. In contrast, 56 per cent of consumers saw corporate ethics as having deteriorated, versus only 28 per cent of the executives willing to agree that this is the case.

Both sets of respondents, CEO and consumers, were also asked about the ethicality of a series of issues facing business on a daily basis. Both groups most often characterized the same seven issues as '*always wrong*'. The full list of issues is presented in Table 2.4.

Firms are rapidly embracing the accountable marketing concept, as suggested by the increasing number of companies adopting code of ethics.

TABLE 2.4 *Management practices 'always' considered wrong*

Issues	Consumer (%)	CEO (%)
■ Misleading advertising or labelling	87	91
■ Causing environmental harm	86	76
■ Poor product or service safety	84	85
■ Padding expense account	79	98
■ Insider trading	78	95
■ Lack of equal opportunities for women or minorities	77	85
■ Dumping banned or flawed products in foreign markets	74	74
■ Overpricing	65	46
■ Hostile take-overs	52	19
■ Moving jobs overseas	45	2
■ Using nonunion labour in a union shop	35	11
■ Closing the plant	25	1

Source: Laczniak *et al.* (1995, p. 43).

2.3.3 From international to transnational marketing

The end of the 1980s is characterized by the completion of the process of internationalization of the world economy through *globalization*. In a growing number of activities, the geographic reference market is no longer a country or a continent, but the large industrialized countries, i.e. the Triad market. Competitive advantage must now exist at this level.

Internationalization is not a new phenomenon for marketing; it has been developing since the end of the Second World War. What is new is the *interdependence of markets* as a result of globalization. Markets are no longer considered as separate entities, but more and more as a single market. In this section, we shall examine the implications of the globalization of competition for the firm's marketing management.

Standardization versus customization

Every firm must face the question of knowing how to organize in order to confront the global market in such a way as to maintain a sustainable competitive advantage. When approaching this question, two very distinct attitudes may be adopted: one which promotes the standardiza-tion of marketing activity in all markets, thus giving priority to internal performance objectives, and another which, on the contrary, gives priority to *customization* of products, thus marketing to specific needs of different markets.

A *customization strategy* pinpoints existing differences between markets and does this in the spirit of the marketing concept. Three groups of factors help to differentiate markets:

■ Differences in *buyer behaviour*, not only in terms of socio-demographics, income, or living conditions, but especially in terms of consumption, habits, customs, culture, etc.

■ Differences in *market organization*, including the structure of distribution networks, the availability of media, regulations, climatic conditions, means of transportation, etc.

■ Differences in *competitive environment*, in terms of the degree of concentration of competition, the presence of domestic rivals, the competitive climate, etc.

It is clear that there are important differences among markets and that these differences will persist in the future. These differences will have implications for the marketing strategy to be adopted.

Believers in *the standardization strategy* underline the advantages that can result from a strategy based on what is similar between markets rather than what differentiates them. The *standardization thesis*, upheld by Levitt (1983) and Ohmae (1987), is based on three hypotheses:

■ World needs will become *homogenized* thanks to technology, transportation and communication.

■ Consumers are prepared to forgo specific preferences in order to benefit from products with *lower prices* and good quality.

■ Standardization resulting from homogenization of world markets brings about *economies of scale*, thus reducing the cost.

To support his thesis, Levitt mentions examples of products with high profiles such as: McDonalds, Coca-Cola, Pepsi, Revlon, Kodak, Sony, Levi's, etc., in addition to high-technology products which are naturally universal.

A false dilemma?

If homogenization of needs is indeed real, this does not mean that standardization is the only alternative open to the global firm. Levitt (1983) reduces global marketing to a standardization strategy. Many counterarguments can be put forth, however, which alter Levitt's arguments substantially:

■ Although it is true that needs are becoming homogenized throughout the world, we are only talking about 'segments', which are found in all triad countries, with the same expectations and with slight variations. Parallel to these world segments, we also observe a 'demassification', or a 'personalization of consumption' giving rise to segments which are more and more specialized and which vary greatly between countries because of the greater importance and regional values.

■ There is no evidence to show that consumers are becoming universally more sensitive to prices. Products such as Cartier watches, Louis Vuitton bags, Hermès scarves or Canon cameras—which are recognized as global products—are great commercial successes; but they are not particularly known for low prices.

■ It is no longer true that economies of scale go hand in hand with frantic standardization. New production technologies have now taken industry out of the Taylor era of large manufacturing chains which produced a single product at high speed. There are now new flexible workshops with instantaneous command change and lagged differentiation techniques, which can retain the advantages of standardization and, at the same time, are able to customize according to personalized requirements.

However, the problem of technical norms remains a major handicap for standardization. In Europe, each country still has its own particular norms which force firms to manufacture many variations of the same product. The 'crude' theory of standardization is therefore very doubtful and many authors have already discussed its limitations.

In reality, the dilemma of standardization versus customization is a false dilemma, in the sense that it poses the question of internationalization as 'all or nothing'. As suggested by Takeuchi and Porter (1986), the real question is how to reconcile the two approaches. One can concentrate on the similarities that exist between markets, which will probably develop more and more, without forgetting their differences and the corresponding need to customize. Most cases of international blunders are the outcome of a lack of cultural sensitivity and acknowledgment of values and attitudes, which means that a successful strategy in one country may prove to be bad in another.

Typology of international environments

The necessity for the firm to adopt a global approach in international marketing is dependent upon the characteristics of its market environment. Goshal and Nohria (1993) suggest an analysis of the international environment by reference to two dimensions.

■ *Local forces* like local customers, tastes, purchasing habits, governments and regulatory agencies which create strong needs for and local responsiveness and adaptation.

■ *Global forces* like economies of scale, uniform customer demands, worldwide competition, product uniformity, are powerful incentives for global integration and standardization.

For each of these two dimensions, Goshal and Nohria (1993) identify two levels (weak and strong) and broadly distinguish among four environmental conditions faced by multinational companies, as illustrated in Figure 2.6.

■ In the *global environment* forces for global integration are strong and local responsiveness weak. In such markets, structural uniformity in the organization is best suited to these conditions. It is the situation observed in many high-technology markets where local forces are non-existent and inoperative. The trend is towards standardization and centralization of responsibilities.

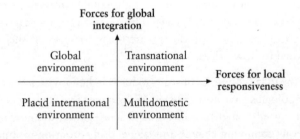

FIGURE 2.6 *Typology of international environments* (Source: *adapted from Goshal and Nohria, 1993*)

- In the *multinational* (or *multidomestic*) *environment*, on the contrary, the forces for national responsiveness are strong and the forces for global integration weak. In this type of market, adaptation to local conditions is a key success factor and companies tend to adopt different governance modes to fit to each local context. Many food companies fall into this category, where taste and culinary habits are important determinants of preferences and of purchase behaviour.

- In the *placid international environment* both forces are weak. The business of producing cement is an example.

  > Cement products are highly standardized and distribution systems are similar across countries. Thus demands for local responsiveness are weak. However, the trade-offs between the economics of cement production and transport costs are such that global integration is not attractive.
  > (Goshal and Nohria, 1993, p. 26)

- In the *transnational environment* both forces, local and global, are strong. It is the most complex situation where some degree of standardization and centralization is necessary, while maintaining the capacity to respond to local situations is also required.

An example of the transnational environment can be seen in a product such as Carlsberg, which has all the characteristics of a global brand. Distributed in 130 countries throughout the world, its taste, logo and bottle design are identical. Nevertheless, the 'beer culture' is very different from one country to the other, even within Europe. Thus a transnational organization combining centralization and local (or regional) adaptation is better suited to this brand.

Another example is the case of Volvo Truck (Lambin and Hiller, 1990). Trucks are designed upfront for the world market and are identical with few minor adaptations. But a key success factor in any market remains the role played by the local dealer who is in charge of after-sales-service and of the warranty. A highly centralized organization would not suit this market environment.

The global marketing concept

Compared to the multidomestic approach, globalization differs in these three basic ways:

- The global approach looks for *similarities* between markets. The multidomestic approach ignores similarities.

- The global approach actively seeks *homogeneity* in products, image and advertising messages.

- The global approach asks: 'Should this product or process be for the world market?' The multidomestic approach, relying solely on local autonomy, never asks the question.

Globalization also requires many internal modifications. By design, globalization calls for more centralized decision making.

Several years ago, the popular slogan *'think global, act local'* was supposed to describe the strategy of the global firm. Faced with the internationalization of markets, the transnational or the global firm should:

– think globally in its strategic marketing
– act locally in its operational marketing.

Global marketing would imply a two-stage process. At the first level, global thinking would imply the search for transnational segments of customers over a wider geographical market, no matter how narrow these new segments may be. The firm would then develop products targeted to these transnational segments. Their total market representation on the regional and international scale may constitute an important volume capable of generating economies of scale for the company. Globalization in this sense would apply essentially to the product concept and not necessarily to the other tools of marketing, such as communication, price and distribution, which would remain customized to local characteristics. Thus, customization would constitute the second level of consideration. 'Windows', 'Word', 'Exel' and other popular software products of Microsoft can serve as examples of global products adapted to local conditions. They exist in a multitude of national versions; in addition there exists even a special English version for Central and Eastern Europe (*Business Central Europe*, 1994, No. 9, p. 10).

This traditional vision of transnational marketing is criticized by several international companies because the slogan 'think global, act local' suggests that a firm has the capability to develop product concepts independently of local needs analysis and then to impose those products on the rest of the world by means of heavy communication. This is the reason why Procter & Gamble decided to place its international action under the slogan '*think global and local*' (Cerfontaine, 1994), thereby emphasizing that product development should be considered simultaneously on the local and global levels. Thus, we have a four-stage process:

■ Analyse local needs in a given country.

■ Globalize the product concept developed locally.

■ Customize the product to each local environment.

■ Use operational marketing to implement the chosen strategy.

As far as marketing management is concerned, the most important implication of globalization is the necessity for the firm to define its geographic reference market as the Triad countries and to elaborate active or defensive strategic options which take the new interdependence of markets into account.

It is important to realize that the global marketing concept concerns all firms and not only the large internationals. The small or medium-size firm operating in a global market must also be internationalized in such a way as to confront other competitors through a defensive tactic.

2.4 MARKET-DRIVEN MANAGEMENT

We have seen in this chapter that, during the 1990s, the macro-marketing environment of the firm has changed dramatically. What was the overall performance of the traditional marketing function in its confrontation with the above changes? The main reproaches or criticisms about marketing's performance are the following.

- To have confined market orientation to the marketing department, thereby preventing the development of a market culture within the organization.

- To be a big spender and to have failed to develop objective and quantified measures to judge its own overall performance.

- To have privileged tactical marketing instruments over strategic ones, by giving precedence to advertising and promotions over product innovations.

- To be risk-adverse by placing more emphasis on minor market-pull innovations over more revolutionary (but more risky) technology-push innovations.

- To have responded to environmentalism by green advertising unsupported by prior product redesign, thereby undermining the credibility of green marketing.

- To have neglected the 'fewer frills, low price' segments, thereby opening the door to private labels development.

- To have created confrontational rather than collaborative relationships with large retailers and to lose the battle of the brand in several product categories.

- To lose contact with the new consumer and to have failed to develop a long-term relationship with the customer base.

An increasing number of firms now believe that the marketing function must reinvent itself in a way which reinforces the *overall market orientation* of the firm. Thus the problem is not with marketing, but rather with the marketing function. In the new competitive environment, marketing has become too important to be left to the sole marketing function.

2.4.1 The cost of a weak market orientation
The absence of a strong market orientation culture may have significant impact on the competitiveness of the firm. Several potential problems may arise.

Environment monitoring   If the marketing function is the only one in charge of managing the interface between the firm and its environment, is there not a risk to see the announced changes underestimated by the other functions within the organization? Does marketing have enough credibility and enough weight to induce major changes within the the firm? For example, it is amazing to see how the chemical industry was unprepared, and taken almost by surprise, when new legislation suddenly imposed severe restrictions for one-way plastic bottles, while this environmentalist issue had been a much debated question for more than 20 years.

The links between R&D and innovations   If the market orientation is confined within the marketing department, the dialogue between R&D and strategic marketing will be more difficult and the link between inventions and innovations weaker. As a consequence, R&D activities will give rise to fewer successful implementations of inventions. According to a recent European study, it seems that fundamental research in Western Europe is indeed less productive than in the

USA and Japan. An analysis of the metallurgic sector in Belgium confirmed this observation (Theys, 1994).

New product development process   Developing a new product is typically a cross-functional effort which involves not only the marketing department but all other functions as well. In companies where the dominant culture is not the market orientation, new product development processes are generally sequential and the project is passed from one specialist to another. This process ends up with a desirable 'target price' reflecting the successive internal costs, which becomes the market price suggested to (or imposed upon) sales personnel. In a market-driven company, on the other hand, it is the *'acceptable market price'* which is identified upfront and which becomes the constraint to be met by R&D and production staff. The success rate of new products is much higher in this second case (Cooper, 1993).

Competitive advantage and the value chain   The definition of a sustainable competitive advantage is a major responsibility of strategic marketing. As shown by Porter (1985), the value chain is a basic tool for diagnosing competitive advantage and finding ways to create and sustain it. Thus, a firm must define its competitive advantage by reference to the different value activities—primary and support—that are performed. Each of these value activities—and not only the marketing activities—can contribute to a firm's relative cost position and create a basis for differentiation. If the firm is not market-oriented, it is not easy to induce the non-marketing activities to participate in the search of a sustainable competitive advantage. The risk is then to base competitive positioning on minor points of differentiation of low added value to the buyer.

Financial implication of sales promotions   A good indicator of performance for the marketing department is an increase in sales revenue which, in non-expandable markets, implies a market share increase. An easy but short-sighted way to achieve this objective is to embark on trade promotions and coupon offers which are in fact a *disguised form of price-cutting*. These promotional actions, because of their effectiveness, generate strong retaliatory actions from competition who respond by more promotions or coupon offers. This escalation leads to a situation of almost permanent promotions which eventually undermine brand loyalty and profitability. As a result of this 'marketing myopia', marketing activities are under increasing challenge and control from the finance department who questions the wisdom of this type of action.

Transactional versus relationship marketing   Finding new customers is traditionally an important objective of transactional marketing which is mostly interested in immediate sales results. In mature markets, this objective is losing relevance and cultivating the existing customer base becomes the priority goal. In business-to-business marketing, the repeat purchase rate of satisfied customers is around 90 to 95 per cent (Goderis, 1995) and therefore, attracting new customers is viewed as an intermediate objective. Relationship marketing tries to create and maintain a long-term mutually profitable relationship with customers. This customer satisfaction objective, however, is not the responsibility of the sole marketing function, but again of all other functions participating in the process of value creation for the customer. Thus, the customer satisfaction objective must be shared by everyone in the organization.

In conclusion It appears that the lack of market orientation of a given firm may seriously undermine its capacity to meet the challenges of the new macro-marketing environment. The next step is to define, in operational terms, what it really means to be market-oriented.

2.4.2 The components of a market orientation

In recent years, increasing attention has been given to market orientation as a business philosophy within academic literature. For a review, see Lambin (1995). The most significant contributions come from Kohli and Jaworski (1990) who have provided a conceptual definition of the construct, and from Narver and Slater (1990) who examined the relationship between market orientation and business profitability empirically.

In contrast with previous works, these authors have enlarged the marketing concept by defining the market orientation by reference to three components: customer orientation, competitor orientation and interfunctional co-ordination. So, for these authors, the construct of 'market orientation' is broader than the traditional concept of 'customer orientation'. In this book, we go a step further by proposing that market orientation is a business philosophy *involving all participants in the market and at all levels within the organization* (Lambin, 1995).

Thus, as illustrated in Fig. 2.7, we define market orientation in terms of five components: end-customers, distributor-customers, competitors, socio-economic climate and interfunctional co-ordination.

- *End-customer orientation.* End-customer focus is the central element of a market orientation and is at the core of the marketing concept. It implies the commitment to understand customer needs, to create value to the customer and to anticipate new customers' problems.

- *Distributor-customer orientation.* The shift of power from suppliers to distributors in some sectors, and particularly in the fast-moving consumer good sector, requires the adoption of much more proactive strategy *vis-à-vis* distributors who should be viewed as customers and not simply as partners.

- *Competitor orientation* includes understanding of competitor strengths and weaknesses, anticipation of competitors' strategies and speed of response to competitors' actions.

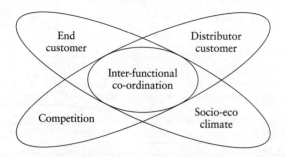

FIGURE 2.7 *The components of market orientation* (Source: *Lambin, 1996)*

- *Environment monitoring* is the continuing analysis of substitute technologies, social changes and government regulations which might constitute opportunities or threats for the firm.

- *Interfunctional co-ordination* refers to the dissemination of market information within the organization, functional integration in strategy formulation and use of the perspectives and skills of departments other than the marketing department to assess customers' needs and problems.

Thus market-driven management covers a field which is much broader than the traditional domain of marketing management, since it includes the organizational culture and climate that most effectively encourages the behaviours that are necessary for the successful implementation of a market orientation.

2.4.3 Market orientation and economic performance

As stated above, marketing theory suggests that there is a relationship between market orientation intensity and economic performance. Thus, the hypothesis is: *a firm which becomes more market-oriented will, in the long term, improve its economic and competitive performance.* Several theoretical and empirical observations support this proposition.

- Market-oriented companies have a large number of satisfied customers and therefore a higher rate of repeat purchase (Lash, 1990; Goderis, 1995) and lower selling costs (Dwyer *et al.*, 1987).

- A market-oriented firm gives faster response to changing needs by launching new or improved products, thereby maintaining a good balance between growth and profit objectives in its product portfolio (Cooper, 1993).

- A market-oriented firm brings more value to customers and therefore has a lower price sensitivity and higher market-acceptable prices (Nagle, 1987).

- A market-oriented firm is in a better position to identify a sustainable competitive advantage and to increase or defend its market share (Porter, 1985).

These conditions, when met, directly or indirectly, contribute to the firm's long-term economic performance. Various indicators of economic performance can be used: return on capital, sales or market share growth, success rate of new products, etc.

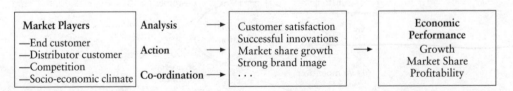

FIGURE 2.8 *Hypothetical relationship between market orientation and economic performance* (Source: *Lambin, 1996*)

2.4.4 Measuring market orientation

The basic hypothesis is that market-oriented firms allocate human and material resources to collect information about the expectations and behaviours of the different market participants. This information is then used to design market-oriented action plans which are implemented by involving all levels of the organization. Thus, to build a valid measure of market orientation two sets of indicators will be defined for each of the four market participants: '*analysis*' and '*action*' indicators, and one set of indicators for measuring the level of '*interfunctional co-ordination*'.

For each of these five components, we have identified a set of indicators with the objective of deriving a valid measure for each component and of analysing their relationships with various measures of business performance. These indicators are summarized in Table 2.5. The selection of these indicators has been made on the basis of an extensive review of the literature on the determinants of economic performance made by Rivera (1995). These indicators are presented here in general terms and they must be adapted in each case to reflect the characteristics of a specific sector.

2.4.5 Reinventing the marketing organization

The developments in the macro-marketing environment and the wide adoption of a market orientation at all levels of the firm have had several implications on the marketing function. First, the brand management system so successfully adopted by many companies during the last 30 years seems, today, unable to face the complex challenges of the new environment.

As put by McKinsey,

> ... brand managers (today) are not really mini general managers (as they were supposed to be). They are usually too junior, too inexperienced and too narrowly centred on marketing to provide the cross functional leadership and strategic thinking required to navigate through today's complex marketing landscape. They are too removed from the the sources of value added (which are not just advertising based), too overwhelmed with day-to-day tasks (like developing trade promotions in packaged goods, or staying on stock plan and taking markdowns in retailing) and too focused on implementing quick-fix solutions that will get them promoted in 18 months. (George *et al.*, 1994, p. 46)

Second, as the market orientation concept becomes more and more accepted and increasingly implemented across all functions within the firm, namely as a result of the 'total quality' movement often initiated by operations management, the specific role of marketing as a separate function has come under question and has to be reassessed. There is accumulating evidence that the new macro-marketing environment is forcing many companies to review the role to be played by the traditional marketing department in the corporation. Several dramatic organizational changes are reported in the professional literature and in the economic press (see *The Economist*, 9 April 1994) which confirm this evolution and for example,

> ... the abolition of chief marketing executive posts and the closure of marketing departments by major international companies like Unilever, Elida Gibbs and Pillsbury

TABLE 2.5 *Indicators of market orientation*

ANALYSIS Market intelligence available on:	ACTION Adopted behaviours:

END-CUSTOMER

■ Present and future needs of end-customers ■ Identification of emerging segments ■ Factors influencing the buying decision ■ Roles of the participants in the buying decision ■ Attitude and image measures of products ■ Added value of our products to customers ■ Acquisition cost of our products ■ Choice and preference criteria ■ In-use problems with our products ■ Measures of satisfaction/dissatisfaction ■ Measures of profitability by customer	■ Offer of a complete solution to the problem ■ Development of new product concepts ■ Launching of new or improved products ■ Fast response to changing needs ■ Fast response if dissatisfaction ■ Adapted products to each target segment ■ Training to ensure optimal use of the products ■ Pricing based on the value added to customers ■ Help for installation and operation ■ Communication targeted by segment ■ Co-ordinated and consistent marketing plan ■ Abandonment of unprofitable segments

DISTRIBUTOR-CUSTOMERS

■ Objectives pursued by distributors ■ Changing needs of distributors ■ Compatibility of our strategy with their goals ■ Measures of satisfaction/dissatisfaction ■ Problems and difficulties with our products ■ Value of our products (brands) for them ■ Image and attitude of our products (company) ■ Image of distributors perceived by end-customers ■ Profitability per distributor	■ Distributors' satisfaction objective ■ Sharing of information about our strategy ■ Consultations when new activities ■ Administrative and managerial support ■ Sales training sessions of our products ■ Adapting of our product to their needs ■ Direct contacts with top management ■ Fast response if dissatisfaction ■ Advertising and promotion support

COMPETITORS

■ Strengths and weaknesses of competitors ■ Characteristics of their products ■ Objectives and strategies of priority competitors ■ Measures of competitors 'performance' ■ Key components of their marketing strategy ■ Threats from substitute products	■ Strategy definition based on competition analysis ■ Well-defined competitive behaviour ■ Fast reaction to hostile moves ■ Comparison of performances ■ Capacity to anticipate competitive actions ■ Monitoring of their marketing strategies ■ Presence of well-differentiated products

SOCIO-ECONOMIC CLIMATE

■ Environment monitoring system ■ Identification of vulnerabilty or risk factors ■ Availability of early warning indicators	■ Involvement in professional networks ■ Active lobbying practices ■ Use of the scenario method in planning ■ Existence of crisis recovery plans

INTERFUNCTIONAL CO-ORDINATION

■ Formal dissemination of market information at all levels
■ Informal dissemination of market information
■ Direct interaction with customers at all levels of the firm
■ Interdepartmental meetings to discuss market trends
■ Concerted elaboration of marketing strategies
■ Measure of the contribution of each function to the customers' satisfaction
■ Good co-ordination of each department's activities and consistent image
■ Customers' satisfaction objective shared by everyone

Source: Lambin (1996).

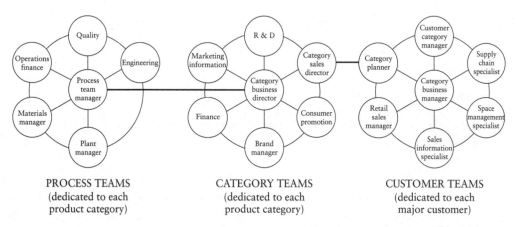

PROCESS TEAMS
(dedicated to each
product category)

CATEGORY TEAMS
(dedicated to each
product category)

CUSTOMER TEAMS
(dedicated to each
major customer)

FIGURE 2.9 *Managing through teams at Kraft* (Source: *Freeling and Court, 1995, p. 59*)

(Grand Metropolitan), AT&T and their replacement by business groups, customer development teams, customer focus teams, multidisciplinary teams and category rather than brand management.   (Piercy and Cravens, 1995, p. 12)

According to McKinsey (1995), tomorrow's marketing organizations will be organized around two roles, integrators and specialists, linked together through teams and processes rather than functional or business unit structures.

■ *Integrators* (or *process managers*) will play the critical role of guiding activities across the firm's entire value chain; identifying the market segments in which to compete and the levers to pull to maximize long-term profitability. They will be charged with tearing down the walls that divide function from function and with leading cross-functional teams for executing these strategies. Typically, they will be responsible for maketing strategy development (see Part 3 of this book). Integrators can be responsible for a distinct end-user segment (consumer integrators) or specific group of business customers like giant retailers (customer integrators) or be responsible for a process, like new product development (process integrators).

■ *Specialists* will provide the technical and specialized skills required to implement successfully the marketing strategy in the different disciplines such as marketing research, business intelligence, pricing strategy, advertising, promotion, direct marketing, etc. The trend will also be towards subcontracting to outside specialists marketing activities such as market research and analysis, database management, and even the execution of some operational marketing tasks.

In the new organizational context, the fifth component of market orientation—*interfunctional co-ordination*—is particularly important because it implies the involvement of all levels in the firm's organization. The key idea here is to consider that market orientation is the business of everyone and not only of marketing people. The literature, both academic and professional, concerning the implementation of the marketing concept has described how companies became or are becoming more market-oriented. For a review, see Lichtenthal and Wilson (1992). Masiello (1988) describes four reasons why many companies are not market-oriented:

- Functional areas do not understand the concept of being market-driven

- Most employees do not know how to translate their classical functional responsibilities into market/customer responsive actions

- Most functions do not understand the role of other functions

- Employees in each functional area do not give meaningful input to the marketing direction of the company.

In addition to these organizational problems, two other factors should be kept in mind. First, managers in other functions have constituencies other than customers—for example, share-holders, suppliers, personnel, scientists, etc.—that must be served and satisfied and the trade-offs between these potentially conflicting interests must be co-ordinated and managed. Second, managers in other functions may honestly believe that they are putting the customer's interest first when they look at things from their own internal company perspective, and it is easy for them to refuse to be guided by the information provided by the sole marketing department.

Thus, dissemination of market information, both formally and unformally, interfunctionally prepared decisions, co-ordination of activities, regular contacts with customers, etc., are the key remedies to use in order to instil a sense of market orientation regardless of functional boundaries. The selected set of indicators to measure the degree of interfunctional co-ordination is summarized in the last section of Table 2.5.

2.5 THE NEW MARKETING PRIORITIES

The evolution of the changing priority role of marketing is summarized in Box 2.5. The environmental changes mentioned above all imply a reinforcement of the market orientation for companies operating in highly industrialized markets. Companies need to review their strategic options in order to face the new challenges presented by the economic, competitive and sociocultural environment and by the internationalization of the world economy.

BOX 2.5
Evolution of the priority role of marketing

- *Passive marketing* The firm is 'product-oriented' and has an '*inside-in*' perspective.
- *Organizational marketing* The firm is 'sales-oriented' and has an '*inside-out*' perspective.
- *Active marketing* The firm is 'customer-oriented' and has an '*outside-in*' perspective.
- *Market-driven management* The firm is 'market-oriented' and has a *societal* perspective.
- *Global marketing* The firm is 'world market-oriented' and has a *transnational* perspective.

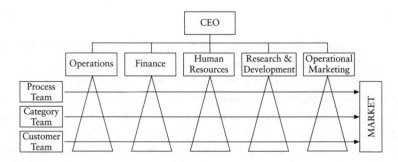

FIGURE 2.10 *Organization of a market-oriented company*

One can identify nine new priorities in strategic marketing:

1. *Market-driven management.* Successful implementation of the marketing concept within the firm requires cross-functional co-ordination and a corporate culture which encourages the adoption of a strong market orientation at all levels of the organization, as illustrated in Fig. 2.10.
2. *Customized marketing.* In affluent societies, sophisticated consumers expect to find tailor-made solutions to their problems and it is up to the firm to meet these expectations through direct response segmentation and interactive communication.
3. *Green marketing.* Environmentalism is the expression of a new societal need revealing deep change of outlook regarding consumption. Green marketing should start in the laboratory at the stage of the product concept design—a responsibility which goes far beyond the sole marketing function.
4. *Trade marketing.* There is a shift of power in the marketing channels, particularly in the field of fast-moving consumer goods. New types of relationships must be developed between suppliers and distributors who should be viewed as customers on their own right.
5. *Competition orientation.* In stagnant and mature markets, the capacity to anticipate competitors' actions and be more astute than rivals is a key factor of success. This capacity implies the existence of a competition-monitoring system.
6. *Development of foresighting systems.* In a turbulent environment, traditional sales forecasting methods are ineffective and the firm must develop organizational flexibility and contingency planning systems.
7. *Transnational marketing.* There is a growing interdependence among the countries of the triad where the industrial and cultural fabric becomes more homogeneous. Supranational segments appear which constitute market opportunities for the firm.
8. *Product portfolio restructuring.* To meet new competition's challenges, Western European companies must diversify their product portfolio by evolving towards higher value added activities, based either on technological advances or on organizational know-how.
9. *Accountable marketing.* New social needs are emerging in society which call for environmentally friendly products. Firms are beginning to show concern for both the individual and the collective well-being of society, instead of simply satisfying short-term needs.

In the following chapters, we shall examine the 'how to. . .?' issues raised by these new priorities.

SUMMARY

The macro-marketing environment of the firm has changed dramatically during the 1990s. A key change is the acceleration and generalization of the technological progress which shorten product life cycles and force companies to renew their product portfolio faster than previously. The internationalization of the world economy, the creation of the European Single Market, the opening of Eastern Europe and the appearance of new competitors are critical challenges which also imply redeployment and/or restructuring of current activities. In affluent societies, consumers are better educated and more demanding and mass-marketing techniques are coming of age. Customized marketing is the new market expectation. New societal needs also emerge, advocated by the consumerism and environmentalism movements, which call for the firm's greater sensitivity to the sociocultural fallouts of its economic action. Green marketing based on eco-designed products and accountable marketing based on corporate ethical behaviour are the appropriate industry responses. At the international level, the growing interdependence of markets raises the issue of standardization versus customization. To remain competitive, the adoption of global or transnational marketing is the appropriate strategy in market environments where local forces are weak. All these environmental changes call for a reinforcement of the level of the firm's market orientation. In today's turbulent environment, market orientation is too important to be left to the sole marketing department. The market culture should be diffused at all levels within the organization through interfunctional co-ordination. In this new context, marketing is more important than ever but the marketing department as a separate function is critically questioned and should reinvent itself. Marketing should be viewed as a process integrating the different functions and not a separate entity within the organization.

QUESTIONS AND PROBLEMS

1. Which factors explain the development of global marketing?
2. What are the strategies and/or policies to be adopted by firms operating exclusively on their domestic market, to reinforce their competitiveness within the enlarged European market?
3. Does the growing environmental concern represent a threat or an opportunity for the firm? How would you proceed to answer this question in your own company?
4. Are you personnally in favour of the legal application of the 'Who pollutes pays' principle? Compare the marketing and social impact of eco-taxes versus eco-fees.
5. Assuming that you are in favour of the accountable marketing concept, to what extent will this state of mind, new for your company, affect your marketing strategy and your practices regarding product, distribution, communication and pricing policies?
6. Is green marketing the right answer from the firm to meet society's environmental concern? Examine what green marketing means for each component of the marketing mix.
7. What difference(s) do you see between the following three business philosophies: 'marketing orientation', 'customer orientation' and 'market orientation'?
8. Select a company you know well and measure its level of market orientation, using the indicators presented in Table 2.4. Construct an aggregate score of market orientation and a

separate score for the 'analysis', 'action' and 'interfunctional co-ordination' components. Interpret the results and formulate recommendations.

REFERENCES

Aaker, D.A. and G.S. Day (1982), *Consumerism: Search for the Consumer Interest*, 4th edn. New York: The Free Press.

Ansoff, H.I. (1984), *Implanting Strategic Management*. Englewood Cliffs, NJ: Prentice-Hall.

Bloon, H., R. Calori and P. de Woot (1994), *EuroManagement: A New Style for the Global Market*. Kogan Page.

Bossier, R.C. and P. Hugé (1981), Une vérification empirique de l'existence de cycles longs à partir de données belges, *Cahiers économiques de Bruxelles*, no. 9, second trimester.

Drucker, P. (1980), *Managing in Turbulent Times*. New York: Harper Row.

Dwyer, F.R., P.H. Schurr and O. Sejo (1987), 'Developing Buyer–Seller Relationships', *Journal of Marketing*, vol. 51, April, pp. 11–27.

Cecchini, P. *et al.* (1988), *1992 :The Benefits of a Single Market*. Wildwood House, Gower: Aldershot.

Cerfontaine, B. (1994), *Le marketing global chez Procter & Gamble*. Conference given at IAG, Louvain-la-Neuve, March.

Cooper, R.G. (1993), *Winning at New Products*. Reading, Mass: Addison-Wesley.

Eurobaromètre, L'opinion publique dans la Communauté Européenne, no. 39, June 1993.

George, M., A. Freeling and D. Court (1994), 'Reinventing the Marketing Organization', *The McKinsey Quarterly*, no. 4, pp. 43–62.

Goderis, J.P. (1995), Les mesures de satisfaction/insatisfaction des acheteurs. Conference given at IAG, Louvain-la-Neuve, Belgium.

Goshal, S. and N. Nohria (1993), 'Horses for Courses: Organizational Forms for Multinational Corporations', *Sloan Management Review*, winter, pp. 23–35.

Jenk, J., C.H. Michel and V. Margotin-Roze (1995), 'The Russian Consumer Revolution', *The McKinsey Quarterly*, no. 2, pp. 35–40.

Kondratiev, N.D. (1935), 'The Long Waves in Economic Life', *Review of Economics and Statistics*, vol. 27, pp. 105–15.

Kotler, P. (1991), *Marketing Management*, 7th edn. Englewood Cliffs, New Jersey: Prentice Hall Inc.

Kotler, P., L. Fahey and S. Jatusripitak (1985), *The New Competition*. Englewood Cliffs, New Jersey: Prentice Hall Inc.

Laczniak, G.R. and P.E. Murphy (1993), *Ethical Marketing Decisions*. Boston: Allyn & Bacon.

Laczniak, G.R., M.W. Berkowitz, R.G. Brooker and J.P. Hale (1995), 'The Ethics of Business; Improving or Deteriorating?' *Business Horizons*, January–February, pp. 39–47.

Lambin, J.J. (1996), 'The Misunderstanding about Marketing', *The CEMS Business Review*, no. 1, June.

Lambin, J.J. and T.B. Hiller (1990), 'Volvo Trucks Europe: A Case Study', in Quelch, J.A. *et al.* (eds), *The Marketing Challenge of 1992*. Reading, Mass.: Addison-Wesley Publishing Co.

Lash, M.L. (1990), *The Complete Guide to Customer Service*. New York: John Wiley & Sons.

Laurent, J.L. (1994), La problématique des écotaxes dans le secteur des eaux minérales et des eaux de source. IAG, Louvain-la-Neuve (mémoire non publié).

Levitt, T. (1983), 'The Globalization of Markets', *Harvard Business Review*, vol. 61, May–June, pp. 92–102.

Lichtenthal, J.D. and D.T. Wilson (1992), 'Becoming Market Oriented', *Journal of Business Research*, vol. 24, pp. 191–207.

McDougall, G.H.G. (1993), 'The Green Movement in Canada: Implications for Marketing Strategy', *Journal of International Consumer Marketing*, vol. 5, No. 3, pp. 69–87.

Maïsseu, A. (1984), Une issue à la crise: le redéploiement des entreprises, *Futuribles*, November, pp. 44–54.

Marchetti, C. (1982), 'Invention et innovation: les cycles revisités', *Futuribles*, no. 53, March, pp. 43–58.

Masiello, T. (1988), 'Developing Market Responsiveness throughout Your Company', *Industrial Marketing Management*, vol. 17, pp. 85–93.

Nagle, T.T. (1987), *The Strategy and Tactics of Pricing*. Englewood Cliffs, NJ: Prentice Hall Inc.

OECD (1995), *Main Economic Indicators*, September.

Ohmae, K. (1987), 'The Triad World View', *The Journal of Business Strategy*, vol. 7, no. 4, pp. 8–19.

Ottman, J.A. (1993), *Green Marketing: Challenges & Opportunities for the New Marketing Age*. Lincolnwood, Illinois: NTC Business Books.

Piercy, N.F. and D.W. Cravens (1995), 'The Network Paradigm and the Marketing Organization', *European Journal of Marketing*, vol. 29, no. 3, pp. 7–34.

Pitt-Watson, D. and S. Frazer (1991), 'Eastern Europe: Commercial Opportunity or Illusion?', *Long Range Planning*, vol. 24, pp. 17–22.

Porter, M.E. (1985), *Competitive Advantage*, New York: The Free Press.

Pruden, H.O. (1978), 'The Kondratieff Wave', *Journal of Marketing*, April, pp. 63–70.

Rapp, S. and T. Collins (1990), *The Great Marketing Turnaround*, Englewood Cliffs: New Jersey, Prentice Hall Inc.

Reidenbach, R.E. and P. Robin (1991), 'A Conceptual Model of Corporate Moral Development', *Journal of Business Ethics*, April, pp. 265–274.

Ries, A. and J. Trout (1986), *Warfare Marketing*. New York: McGraw-Hill.

Rivera, J. (1995), L'orientation-marché: une strategie concumientielle performante. Unpublished doctoral dissertation, IAG: Louvain-la-Neuve, Belgium.

Takeuchi, H. and M.E. Porter (1986), Three Roles of International Marketing in Global Strategy, *Competition in Global Industries*. Boston: Harvard Business School Press.

Theys, F. (1994), Succès et échec de l'innovation dans l'IFME, unpublished term paper. Louvain-la-Neuve, IAG, Belgium.

de Woot, P. (1990), *High Technology Europe*. Oxford: Basil Blackwell.

FURTHER READING

Barwise, P. (1995), 'Marketing Today and Tomorrow', *Business Strategy Review*, vol. 6, no. 1, pp. 45–59.

Buzzell, R.D. (1968), 'Can you Standardize Multinational Marketing?', *Harvard Business Review*, vol. 46, November–December.

Catinat, M. and A. Jacquemin (1990), 'Europe et marché unique', in *Encyclopédie economique*, eds. X. Gresse, J. Maicesse and L.L. Reiffers. Paris: Economica.

Forrester, J. (1961), *Industrial Dynamics*. Cambridge, Mass.: MIT Press.

Group of Lisbon (1994), *Limits to Competition*. Gulbenkian Foundation.

Picardi, M. (1987), 'Globalisation: théorie et pratique', *Revue Française du Marketing*, pp. 83–8.

Potargent, G. (1991), *Le marketing des produits verts: recommandations pour l'annonceur*. Louvain-la-Neuve, IAG.

Quelch, J.A. and E.J. Hoff (1986), 'Customizing Global Marketing', *Harvard Business Review*, vol. 64, May–June, pp. 59–68.

Quelch, J.A., R.D. Buzzell and E.R. Salama (1991), *The Marketing Challenge of Europe 1992*. Reading, Mass.: Addison-Wesley Publishing Company.

Schumpeter, J.A. (1949), *The Theory of Economic Development*, Cambridge, Mass: Harvard University Press.

Schmeder, G. (1984), 'Les interprétations économiques de la crise', *Critiques de l'Économie Politique*, January–June.

Smith, C.N. and J.A. Quelch (1993), *Ethics in Marketing*. Homewood, Illinois: Irwin.

Theys, F. (1994), 'Innover, l'est gagnes', *FABRIMETAL*, no. 12, Dec.

PART 2

Understanding Buyer Behaviour

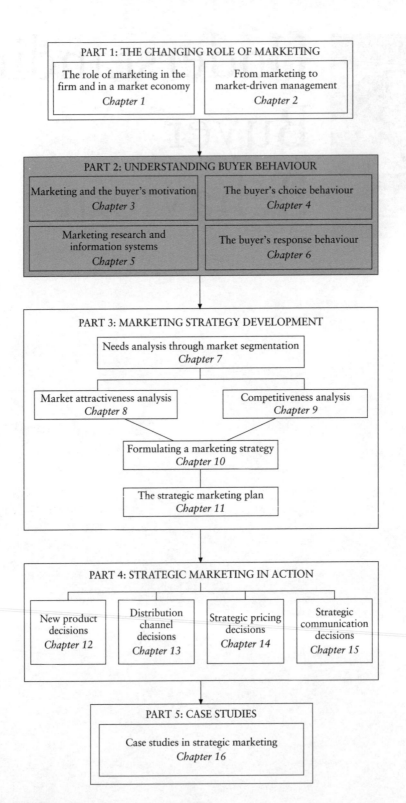

FIGURE PT2.1 *The structure of this book*

CHAPTER 3

MARKETING AND THE BUYER'S MOTIVATION

LEARNING OBJECTIVES

After reading this chapter, you should be able to understand:

■ the nature and diversity of individual needs

■ the concept of value as the motivational force of the individual buyer

■ the difference between consumer and business marketing

■ the main characteristics of the demand for industrial goods

■ the nature of organizational buying.

T he satisfaction of buyers' needs is at the heart of a market economy and of marketing. This chapter aims to make clear such basic conceptions of the needs theory as generic versus acquired and absolute versus related needs, needs classification and needs hierarchy. We shall also discuss the possibility of saturation in relation to different kinds of needs. The importance of strategic marketing in adapting the firm to the constant development in needs satisfaction will be pointed out. We shall also examine the main positions of economics and marketing theoreticians concerning the role marketing plays in creating or intensifying needs. Then we shall turn to psychology and, in particular, to the contributions experimental psychology has made in the study of human motivation. Finally, we shall analyse the motivation of the organizational or industrial customer which must be examined within a totally different framework from that of individual consumers.

3.1 HUMAN NEEDS IN ECONOMIC THEORY

The notion of need is a term that creates endless polemic because it contains elements of subjective judgement based sometimes on morality or ideology. Beyond the vital minimum that everyone accepts—but which no one tries to define—is it really necessary to vary one's food to satisfy taste, to travel out of curiosity or to have different hobbies? We must admit that, at least as far as consumer markets are concerned, these questions are not irrelevant, especially in view of the following facts: (a) the uninterrupted arrival of new products and brands on the market; (b) the continuous and spectacular presence of advertising in increasingly varied forms; and (c) the relative stability of the level of consumer satisfaction, despite the undisputed improvement in standard of living. These facts then raise the following questions:

- Do all these new products and brands really correspond to pre-existing needs?

- Would producers accept such high advertising expenditures if consumers were not allowing themselves to be influenced?

- Is the growth and economic development that marketing claims to encourage useful in the long term?

Economic theory does not help answer these questions. Economists believe it is not part of their discipline to worry about what motivates an action, or to enter into an introspection, which is always difficult, or especially to formulate a value judgement. It is useless to say that people strive for pleasure and avoid pain; it suffices to see that this indeed is the essence of the 'want to use' to justify its utility. The driving force, economic or otherwise, that makes an individual take an economic action is outside the scope of economics; only the results are important. The wish to be satisfied is the only acknowledged cause of behaviour.

A need must be felt before a choice is made, which means that the scale of preferences logically precedes effective choices. If an individual is intellectually adult and reasonable, it should be possible to predict the person's behaviour, which results from rational calculation.

> The consumption choices of an individual which express his needs can be described a priori completely, without experimentation and on the condition that a rational

behaviour, summarized by five axioms called the axioms of rationality, can be assumed.

(Jacquemin and Tulkens, 1988, p. 50)

The economic theory of consumer behaviour is therefore limited to the analysis of the logical implications of the hypothesis of human rationality. The problem of motivation is totally avoided, since economists believe that *the real behaviour of the consumer reflects his or her preferences and inversely that the consumer's preferences are revealed by his or her behaviour.*

The weakness of the basic assumptions in economics has been underlined on many occasions. In economic theory, the concept of *rationality* is defined as equivalent to the concept of *coherence*. However, the predictive value of coherence conditions depends mainly on the existence of well-known and stable preferences in the mind of the decider. But this is far from being satisfied if the original motivations are ignored, poorly known or simplified to the extreme, as is the case in economic models. How can we then be surprised by the observed difference between the 'economic person' and the 'real person'? We should nevertheless mention that serious efforts have been made to enrich the abstract psychology of the economic person and to come closer to the real person. Some examples are the work of Katona (1951), Abbott (1955), Becker (1965) and Lancaster (1966).

3.1.1 Generic versus derived needs

According to the dictionary, *a need is a requirement of nature or of social life*. This definition distinguishes two kinds of needs: *innate needs*, which are natural, generic or inherent in nature or in the organism, and *acquired needs*, which are cultural and social and depend on experience, environmental conditions and the evolution of society.

In the frame of strategic marketing analysis it is practical to view generic needs as problems of potential buyers who try to solve them by acquiring different products of services (this problem-solving approach will be discussed in Chapter 4). If we take this view, then following Abbott (1955, p. 40) we can define a *derived need* as a particular technological response (the product) to the generic need, as well as being the object of desire. For example, the car is a derived need with respect to the generic need of autonomous individual means of transportation. The same is true of the personal computer with respect to the need to process information.

A generic need cannot be saturated as saturation relates only to derived needs—in other words, to the dominant technological response at the time. At a given point, one may detect a tendency towards the saturation of the derived need, because of increased consumption of the good at a particular stage in its life cycle. The marginal utility of the derived need tends to diminish. But the basic problems (transportation, communication, protection, etc.) do not disappear, which means that generic need remains insatiable. Thanks to the impulse given by technological progress, it simply evolves towards higher levels owing to the arrival of improved products and, therefore, new derived needs.

The production of goods for the satisfaction of generic needs will therefore be incessantly subject to the stimulus of its own evolution. The latter will encourage the arrival of new products on the market which are more suitable to satisfying the new level of needs. These derived needs will be saturated in their turn and be replaced by new, more developed, products. The phenomenon of relative saturation brought about by technological progress, which is the basis of the model of product life cycle discussed later in this book, is observed for most goods and at two levels: first, in the improvement of technological performance of products themselves (more economical cars, more powerful computers, etc.); and, second, in the pure and simple substitution of a particular technological answer by another with higher performance (compact disc replacing long-playing records, fax replacing telex, etc.). The latter form of innovation, or *destructive innovation*, is becoming ever more important owing to the generalization of technological progress in all sectors, as we mentioned before.

Furthermore, it seems that the move to a product which is hierarchically superior tends to increase the marginal utility yet again. The decline of the marginal utility is interspersed with sudden peaks. Goods are often desired for their novelty features and the privilege of owning them, even if little is added to their performance.

Therefore, the distinction between generic and derived needs makes it clear that, although there can be no general saturation, it is perfectly possible to detect sectoral saturation. An important role for strategic marketing is thus to encourage the firm to adapt to this observed development in needs satisfaction. In this framework, it is better for the firm to define its mission by reference to generic needs rather than derived needs, given that the latter are saturable while the former are not. These are the basics of the *marketing concept*, described in the previous chapter.

3.1.2 Absolute versus relative needs

Going further into analysis of derived needs, Keynes discovered that saturation is possible only for a certain part of them. In fact, Keynes (1936, p. 365) had established an important distinction between

> ... those needs which are absolute in the sense that we feel them whatever the situation of our fellow human beings may be, and those which are relative in the sense that we feel them only if their satisfaction lifts us above, make us feel superior to our fellows.

Absolute needs are satiable, while relative needs are not. Relative needs are insatiable, because the higher the general level, the more these needs tend to surpass that level. In such conditions, producing to satisfy relative needs is tantamount to developing them. This is how individuals—even when they have in absolute terms enjoyed net improvements in their standard of living—often tend to think that their situation has deteriorated if those who normally serve as the yardstick have improved more relative to them. Cotta (1980, p. 17) writes, '... others' luxury becomes one's own necessity'. The distance between reality and the level of aspiration tends to move continuously with growing dissatisfaction.

The distinction between absolute needs and relative needs is in fact far from being as clear cut as one might at first think. One could say, for example, that anything essential to survival is infinitely more important that any other consumption. This idea is inexact.

To live is certainly an important objective for each of us, but suicide exists. Heroic acts too. More generally, every consumer, in his day to day search for satisfaction of various needs, takes risks that put his life in danger either immediately or in the long run. Smoking, overeating, driving, working too hard or not looking after one's health properly, travelling: these are all activities that one should avoid if survival is placed above all else.

(Rosa, 1977, p. 161)

Needs of a psycho-sociological origin may be felt just as strongly as the most elementary needs. For example, being deprived of intimacy and attention may provoke death or serious deficiencies in psychic and social functioning in the more extreme cases.

Despite a lack of clarity, the distinction between absolute needs and relative needs remains interesting in two respects. On the one hand, it shows that relative needs can be just as demanding as absolute needs. On the other hand, it brings to the fore the existence of a dialectic of relative needs which leads to the observation of the general *impossibility of saturation*. Even the tendency towards material comfort cannot objectively define a state of satisfaction. When an individual reaches a predefined level, he or she can then catch a glimpse of a new stage of possible improvement.

3.1.3 Needs, wants and demand

Though the notions of generic and derived needs seem productive and easy to understand, somewhat different terminology is also employed. For example Kotler establishes a distinction between needs, wants and demands (1991, p. 4). He defines need as '. . . a state of felt deprivation of some basic satisfaction'. This essentially coincides with the definition of a generic need.

Wants are specific satisfiers of deeper needs. While generic needs are stable and few, wants are many, changing and continually influenced by social forces. It is clear that wants is just another name for derived needs. According to Kotler, wants become *potential demands* for specific products when backed by an ability and willingness to buy.

The distinction between needs, wants and demand is important, but the needs–want relationship remains rather controversial. For example, Attali and Guillaume (1974) reject the described relationship between needs and wants. In direct opposition to Kotler's view, they believe that *needs are generated by wants*, things that have become normalized. They include things which no longer give pleasure, but that would be unacceptable to do without because they fall in the domain of the normal (Attali and Guillaume, 1974, p. 144). It is the dynamics of wants that explains the accumulation of needs.

Taking into account this controversy, the use of terms *generic* and *derived needs* seems preferable. However, the interesting point about the above analysis is possibly the fact that it puts forth the cultural and social origin of our needs.

3.1.4 Marketing and creation of needs

The criticism frequently levelled at modern marketing is that it has changed the market into a mechanism that creates needs rather than satisfies them. As we already know, the answer to this criticism given by economists is incomplete: they content themselves with the assumption that what consumers choose suits them, and they are unable to explain the real nature of consumption phenomena. But for strategic marketing, the role that society as a whole and marketing in particular play in creating needs is an important issue. It cannot be evaded because it is diametrically opposed to the classical analysis of consumer sovereignty, which is the keystone of the market economy.

We can now answer the question, drawing on results of analysis of the needs structure described above. One can easily imagine a generic need that corresponds to each of the tendencies governing the life of individuals, these tendencies being necessarily limited in number. Such generic need is therefore related to human nature and, hence, not created by society or by marketing; it exists before demand, whether latent or expressed. Marketing, however, can exacerbate needs, even if they existed before.

Nevertheless it is true that a great majority of our needs are cultural by origin. Hence there is a *dialectic of needs*, caused by the social and cultural environment and by technological development. Like all other social forces, marketing contributes to this dialectic.

According to Kotler (1991, p. 4), marketing tries to influence wants (or derived needs) and demands by making the product attractive, affordable and easily available:

> Marketers, along with other influences in society, influence wants. They suggest to consumers that a Cadillac would satisfy a person's need for social status. Marketers do not create the need for social status but try to point out how a particular good would satisfy that need.

If we admit that marketing creates or, more precisely, participates in the creation of at least some derived needs, much more serious problem arises: what social role—positive or negative—does marketing play in the modern society? This problem was and still is in the focus of interest of marketing theoreticians.

One of the extreme views was put forward by Attali and Guillaume (1974). They believe (p. 146) that producers exploit the dynamics of wants to find markets allowing them to preserve their economic power.

> If social demand, which dialectically results from needs, wants and social supply, is so restricted by the constraints of the productive system, shouldn't the political control of the production of needs logically precede that of production?

This viewpoint is obviously contrary to that of orthodox economists. Rosa (1977) notes that this analysis makes the implicit assumption that there are *real* needs and *false* needs and that the false needs are created by society and by the producer.

> In this school of thought, there is a fundamentally unequal exchange relationship between a dominated consumer and a dominant producer; society corrupts the individual by

creating artificial wants in order to better subjugate and alienate him. The conclusion that follows is simple; it suffices to make the 'good' political choice to get 'good' structures which will necessarily develop the flourishing and expression of 'real' needs'.

(Rosa, 1977, p. 176)

This analysis, which was widespread among so-called 'left intellectuals' in Europe at one stage, has one important weakness in that it never indicates how to distinguish true needs from false needs. Given that the vast majority of our present wants are indeed of a cultural origin, where should we draw the line, and especially who will be the enlightened dictator of consumption? Clearly, it is very difficult to answer these questions objectively.

> . . . to substitute the disputed sovereignty of the consumer for the questionable sovereignty of a bureaucrat or of an intellectual can only create more problems that it can ever hope to resolve. (Rosa, 1977, p.159)

It should also be added that the hypothesis of consumer impotence is daily rejected by facts such as the figures available on the rates of failure of new products; more than one in two products fails to enter the market successfully. The discretionary power of the consumer is a reality and firms know it well. We must therefore recognize that the debate of 'true' versus 'false' needs is in the first place an ideological debate. Economists refuse to enter this debate because they know it cannot be reconciled with a scientific approach.

Galbraith's analysis (1971) falls in this framework. As far as he is concerned, if a need is really felt, the production of a good to satisfy this need is useful, even if the need is perfectly ridiculous. But if the wants emerge with the production, then the urgency of the wants can no longer be used to defend the urgency of production. Production only fills a void that it has itself created and then this is proof that the need is artificial and the satisfaction it will bring can only be insignificant. This is how Galbraith illustrates what he calls the 'dependence effect':

> For then the individual who urges the importance of production to satisfy these wants is precisely in the position of the onlooker who applauds the efforts of the squirrel to keep abreast of the wheel that is propelled by his own efforts.   (Galbraith, 1971, p. 147)

Galbraith maintains that saturation of needs is real and it is advertising that is responsible for the creation of artificial needs, '. . . to bring into being wants that previously did not exist'.

In fact, Galbraith confuses needs and demands in his analysis. Advertising can help discover an already existing generic need, which cannot become a demand because the product aimed at satisfying it does not yet exist. We can indeed accept that a need may exist without there being any good to satisfy it. This is the case of a *latent market*, to which we referred in the previous chapter. By making the need known, advertising creates demand, but it does not create the need. In other words, advertising can create a demand for a pre-existing but unidentified need.

Similarly, the notion of *'artificial' need*, used by Galbraith, leads to a judgement on the degree of marginal utility of needs. The need to acquire superior products for the sake of conspicuous consumption takes on a life of its own owing to the contagious effect which characterizes this kind of need. In these conditions, we end up with a hypothesis of *the impossibility of saturation of needs* rather than a saturation hypothesis. Therefore, all that is left of Galbraith's analysis is a judgement over the degrees of marginal utility of new 'artificial' needs. Thus utility may be slight but it still exists. If one tries to avoid value judgements—which takes us back to the distinction between true and false needs—then the appearance of new needs can always be defended.

On the other hand, we should not forget that creating desires or wants (or derived needs) that cannot be turned into demand due to a lack of purchasing power can become an important source of frustration and malfunctioning in an economy. The responsibility of marketing is directly implicated here, which explains the duty to exercise restraint in its application. Various self-disciplinary movements have seen the light of day in the USA as well as in Europe, acknowledging the need for restraint and self-discipline.

To conclude this overview of economists' and marketing theoreticians' points of view, let us bear in mind the following propositions:

1. The economist is not concerned with the problem of motivation. There are only wants and preferences. The real question, as far as he is concerned, is to know whether or not the consumer has *autonomy of action and decision* and whether his preferences have some stability or, on the contrary, are malleable (Rosa, 1977, p. 162).
2. The problem is not to know whether there are true or false needs, because, on the one hand, it is impossible to establish the distinction objectively, and, on the other, economists refuse to make a judgement on the frivolity of choices. They consider the *structure of preferences as given*.
3. It is true that a great majority of our needs are cultural by origin. There is hence a *dialectic of needs* caused by the social and cultural environment and by technological development. Like all other social forces, marketing contributes to this dialectic.
4. The relative nature of many needs means that the wish to acquire superior products has a particular life of its own. *There can therefore be no general saturation.* Saturation is alien to the nature of relative needs. Their objectives are almost unlimited. By satisfying them, they become activated rather than fulfilled.
5. *Technological progress* and the resulting constant renewal of products also leads to a hypothesis of impossibility of saturating generic needs, to the extent that innovations make it possible to meet these needs more and more effectively.

To be able to distinguish between necessary needs and superfluous needs, one ought to define what should be the organic and social life of individuals and know the structure of their motivation. We therefore need to turn to theories of human motivation in order to make some progress.

3.2 MOTIVATION OF THE INDIVIDUAL BUYER

Economists, as we saw, make no distinction between what consumers choose and what suits them, and never consider the process of needs formation. What do individuals seek in their quest for well-being? How does this state of well-being come about? These two questions are never tackled by economic theory. Yet it is clear that a more thorough analysis of consumer behaviour and the structure of their motivation would make it easier to understand the links that both economists and marketing try to establish between supply and demand. Experimental psychology has made enlightening contributions in this field and helps us discover a whole range of general motivational orientations that determine various individual behaviours. This section is based on the works of Hebb (1955), Duffy (1957), Berlyne (1960), Scitovsky (1976) and Nuttin (1980).

3.2.1 The 'stimulus–response' theory

A central preoccupation of the theory of motivation has been to study why the organism moves into a state of activity. Motivation here becomes *energy mobilization*. Originally, experimental psychology was mostly interested in needs and drives of a purely physiological nature, such as hunger, thirst, sex, etc. In this scheme, called the 'stimulus–response theory' (or S–R theory) the stimulus is considered as the active starting point of the organism's reaction. One then speaks of *homeostasy*, which is a mechanism whereby a disorder creates an urge giving rise to activity which restores equilibrium and thus removes the urge. In this framework, the organism is basically assumed to be reactive: in other words, it responds in specific ways to stimuli. This more or less repudiates the problem of motivation. Inactivity is supposedly the natural state of the individual.

We observe, however, that the organism does not always react to the stimulus presented by its surroundings. Furthermore, it is a common occurrence to find individuals embarking on activities that disrupt equilibrium and setting up states of tension that would be hard to explain if one believed the S–R theory. This theory reduces the mechanism of motivation to a process of reducing tension and practically ignores *the ascending phase of motivation*, that is, the process by which new tensions or conflicts are worked out. However, this type of behaviour is frequently observed, especially in affluent societies, where basic needs are mostly met. A need, seen as a homeostatic need, cannot totally explain individual behaviour.

> More mysterious than the process of discharge is the process that can be called recharging; and more central than the reduction of tension is the act by which man seeks increased responsibilities, takes bigger risks and finds himself new challenges.
>
> (Nuttin, 1980, p. 201).

Today, experimental psychology emphasizes more and more the spontaneous activity of the nervous system and considers behavioural activity to be tied to the organism's being, in much the same manner as physiological activity.

3.2.2 The concept of arousal

Motivation theorists now tend to explain behaviours in a new way, particularly because of the fact that neurophysiologists have considerably improved their knowledge of the way the brain functions and now have a completely different viewpoint. Hebb (1955, p. 246), for instance, formulates a hypothesis that is based not on reactivity but on the natural activity of the nervous system. Contrary to the beliefs held until then, the brain does not have to be excited from outside in order to be active and to discharge. It is not physiologically inert and its natural activity constitutes a system of self-motivation. Hebb, and also Duffy (1957, p. 267), put forth the idea that the general state of motivation can be equated with arousal, or the activity emanating from the reticular formation of the brain stem. Activity level depends on the degree of organic energy mobilized—that is, on the variation in the level of arousal and vigilance. The level of arousal is measured by the variations in electric current controlled with an electroencephalogram (EEG). These variations show up as waves in the EEG; the faster the electric discharge of neurones, the higher the level of arousal and the higher the frequency of oscillations in the EEG, measured in periods per second.

Scitovsky (1976, p. 19) underlines the importance of the concept of arousal in understanding the reasons for a given behaviour.

> A high arousal is associated with vigilance and quick response; it makes the senses more sensitive to stimuli, increases the brain's capacity to process information, readies the muscles for action, and so shortens the total reaction time that elapses between an incoming sensation and the response through action. It makes you feel excited, emotional, anxious and tense. On the other hand, when you feel slow, less than vigilant, lax and drowsy, you are in a state of low arousal.

The increased level of arousal increases the organism's state of vigilance, thus providing favourable ground for the cerebral mechanism of stimulus–response to function rapidly and directly. The psychological measures of the level of arousal therefore provide a direct measure of the *motivational and emotional (drive) force* of a given situation for the individual (Duffy, 1957, p. 267). Also, this description of the concept of arousal suggests the existence of a continuum in the individual's level of activation.

3.2.3 Well-being and the optimal level of arousal

It is clear that the level of arousal has a great influence on the feeling of well-being or discomfort felt in general by people, and consequently bears on the determination of a person's behaviour. Excessive stimulation provokes tension, anxiety, nervousness, worry, frenzy, even panic; on the other hand, stimulation which is too weak, or non-existent, brings about boredom, or a certain degree of displeasure, and creates the desire for a bigger stimulation. A job that is too simple or too monotonous can become painful if one is forced to pursue it without interruption over a long period of time. In fact, psychologists (Hebb, 1955, p. 250) accept that there is an *optimal level of arousal and stimulation*, optimal in the sense that it creates a feeling of comfort and well-being. Deviations below the optimum provoke a feeling of weariness, and deviations above the optimum provoke a sensation of fatigue and anxiety. Experimental observations show that, on the whole, individuals try to maintain an intermediary level of activation (Berlyne, 1960, p. 194).

We can identify here a first aspect of the general direction of motivation in individuals: *ensure comfort and prevent discomfort*. This motivation implies, on the one hand, the *reduction of tensions* that satisfies various corporal and mental needs and reduces the level of arousal, which may be too high; on the other hand, it implies a *battle against boredom*, a behaviour that looks for stimulation and thus increases the level of arousal, which might be too low. These two types of behaviour have one thing in common; both try to fill a gap and to ensure a 'negative good', i.e. to stop pain, inconvenience and discomfort (Scitovsky, 1976, p. 69).

For economists, the reduction of arousal and tension is particularly important because, as far as they are concerned, almost all human activity, including consumption, is based on this process. We find here the notion of need defined by economists as simply a state of deficiency. However, the other type of behaviour—i.e. the raising of a level of arousal that is too low—is ignored by economists. This is commonly observed in more affluent economies, where prosperity has largely eliminated discomfort caused by tension, but where the search for stimulation, novelty and change is becoming ever more important.

> The new consumer is also a dreamer. He buys a product, certainly to use it, but even more for the magic it offers him as premium. (Séguéla, 1982, p. 50).

In some situations, finding sufficient stimulation to combat boredom can be a matter of life or death. This is true for old people, for example. It is also well known that longevity is strongly related to having been able to keep a satisfying job late in life.

3.2.4 The need for stimulation

Berlyne's work in this area is interesting, especially because it is based on solid experimental ground. Berlyne shows that novelty (meaning anything surprising, different from past events and from what one expected) attracts attention and has a stimulating effect.

> Novelty stimulates and pleases especially when it creates surprisingness change, ambiguity, incongruity, blurredness and power to induce uncertainty. (Berlyne, 1960, p. 290)

It is as if the incongruence of the new event produces a dynamic effect which sets in motion exploratory actions.

It must, however, be made clear that the new and surprising is attractive only up to a limited degree, beyond which it becomes disturbing and frightening. Attractiveness first increases, then diminishes with the degree of newness and surprisingness. This relationship takes the shape of an inverted U-curve, known as *the Wundt curve* (Wundt, 1874, in Berlyne, 1960), shown in Fig. 3.1. What is not new or surprising enough is boring, and what is too new is bewildering. An intermediate degree of newness seems to be the most pleasing.

The stimulation provoked by the collative properties of goods forms an important source of satisfaction for individuals. Much of the activity of marketers, such as new product policies, segmentation and positioning, communication and promotion, focuses on meeting this expectation. For better or for worse, goods act as stimuli over the nervous system, a little bit like toys for children. The intelligence of a child can become stagnant with lack of adequate toys. In the same manner, an adult deprived of all the stimuli, provided notably by the consumer society, can be overcome with boredom, depression and alienation.

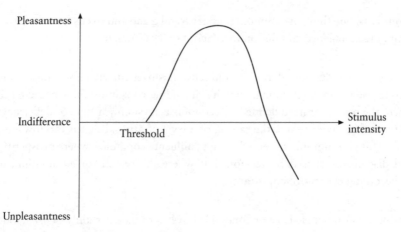

FIGURE 3.1 *The Wundt curve*

> Many people feel younger when they purchase a brand new car and associate the age of their car with that of their own body. Thus buying a new car takes on symbolic proportions by representing physical rejuvenation.   (Valaskakis *et al.*, 1978, p. 167).

Therefore, the organism needs a continuous stream of stimuli and different experiences, just as it needs air and food. *Human beings need to need.* This basic motivation, as well as the more obvious motivation of reducing tensions, explains a large variety of individual behaviour which can only elude the deductions made by economists. The theory of 'novelty seeking' provides an explanation for consumers' actions, which introduce change, variety and novelty into their lifestyle.

3.2.5 The need for pleasure

The sensation of comfort or discomfort is related to the level of arousal and depends on the situation of this level with respect to the optimum. Experimental psychologists have now proved that pleasure exists as a phenomenon different from absence of suffering or presence of comfort. The sensation of pleasure begins with variations in the level of arousal, in particular when a level of arousal that is too low or too high is approaching its optimum (Berlyne, 1960, p. 187).

Two sources of pleasure can be identified: one results from the satisfaction of a need and the resulting reduction in tension; the other comes from the stimulation itself. Satisfaction of a need is pleasant in itself and drives the organism to pursue its activity to the point of satiation, and even beyond.

> In very poor communities, families often plunge into debt for the sake of a funeral feast or a wedding celebration. Such behaviour horrifies economists of the not-so-poor countries. ... Yet the very universality of the custom of feasting among the poor people of so many different cultures is evidence that the pleasures of a good meal for those who seldom taste one are very great and weigh heavily against the biological needs of survival.
> (Scitovsky, 1976, p. 66).

The economic theory of the rational behaviour of consumers implies a judicious balance between different needs and does not take into account pleasure, which can lead the individual to an allocation different from the one predicted by economic theory. It is in fact frequently observed that people behave so as to have full satisfaction from time to time, and they properly space out the moments or periods during which they completely fulfil their wants. This type of behaviour is frequently observed in industrialized countries, in the leisure sector for example, and in particular in holiday expenditure.

Note that the pleasure inherent in the satisfaction of a need implies that discomfort must precede pleasure. This common-sense rule is very old and was debated by the ancient Greeks. Psychiatrists call it the *Law of Hedonic Contrast*. It follows from the rule that too much comfort may preclude pleasure (a child who is nibbling all day long cannot appreciate a good meal). This fact can explain the malaise observed at times in affluent societies, when satisfaction of needs does not bring about any pleasure. By eliminating simple joys, excessive comfort forces us to seek strong sensations.

At this stage the second source of pleasure, the one resulting from the *stimulation itself*, becomes evident. Here the object of the need is not to make up for a shortage but to contribute to the development of the individual. To quote Nuttin (1980), this is the *ascending phase of motivation*; a phase in which new tensions and discordances are established, giving individuals the *will to progress and surpass themselves*. People take pleasure in excitement. They get more satisfaction from the struggle to reach an objective than they get when they actually reach it. Once individuals have passed the moment of triumph, they almost regret having reached their goal. Most people then give themselves an even more distant objective, probably because they prefer to act and fight rather than passively observe their success (Nuttin, 1980, p. 201). In this way, individuals force their environment to stimulate them or to continue to stimulate them.

The pleasure of this type of stimulation results from the temporary tension it creates. Such pleasure is more constant than the pleasure of comfort and outlasts it, because these stimulations leave more room for imagination and creativity to the individual.

> ... the object of these stimulations is almost unlimited. By meeting them, tension goes up rather than down. Thus the tendency persists beyond the point where the objective is reached.
>
> (Nuttin, 1980, p. 202)

Here, we are now talking about *insatiable* needs. It is in the nature of *self-development* needs to know neither the saturation nor the periodicity of homeostatic needs.

> We see here what pleasure is and its relation to comfort: the former is the variation of the latter. If happiness is simply comfort, then it depends on the intensity of satisfied wants. Pleasure is complete when the want is a little or much more satisfied than it was. If happiness is not comfort but pleasure, then it is condemned to only live some privileged moments, prolonged with the help of memory.
>
> (Cotta, 1980, p. 11–12)

From the psychologist's point of view, seeking pleasure is an important factor in human behaviour, and it is a fundamental motivational force which must be taken into account in any analysis of individual buying behaviour.

3.2.6 Determinants of consumer's well-being

An overview of the major contributions of experimental psychology to the study of human motivation finally arrives at a much wider understanding of the notion of need. We started from the point of view of economists, for whom need is essentially a 'state of shortage' revealed by the buying behaviour, without any explanation of the origin or the nature of motivations at the root of this state of deficiency. The absence of theory about motivations leads economists to make normative recommendations which have as much value as their starting assumptions, but which have little to do with actual observed behaviour.

Research by psychologists makes it possible to retain three general motivational directions, which can explain a large variety of behaviours and which appear to be factors that explain the individual's general well-being. These determinants can be regrouped as *comfort, pleasure* and *stimulation*. Figure 3.2 explains diagrammatically the relations between these three determinants on the one hand, and their relation to individual well-being on the other.

The *three motivational forces*, determining individual well-being, can be briefly described as follows:

■ The search for *comfort* results from two kinds of behaviour: one that reduces tensions by satisfying homeostatic needs; and one that struggles against boredom with the help of stimuli such as novelty, change, incongruity, uncertainty, risk, etc.

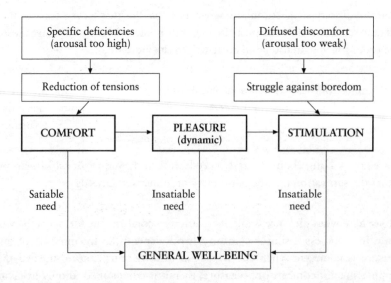

FIGURE 3.2 *The determinants of well-being*

- The search for *pleasure* also results from two sources: pleasure inherent in the reduction of tensions and pleasure obtained from stimuli.

- The search for *stimulation*—not only as a means to combat boredom but as a goal in itself without any other objective in mind but the tension it arouses—generates pleasure and creates the opportunity of development and actualization for the individual.

The search for comfort aims to make up for a deficiency and thus to ensure a *defensive good*; pleasure and stimulation aim to ensure a *creative good*.

By relying on this description of the major motivational forces we are in a better position to answer the questions facing marketing mentioned at the beginning of this chapter. The increased use of marketing—which takes the form of products being continually renewed, more and more subtle differentiation, sophisticated perceptual positioning, advertising suggesting elaborate life styles, etc.—in reality only responds to the rise in needs of pleasure and stimulation observed in richer societies, where basic needs are well met, but where, on the other hand, needs such as novelty, surprise, complexity, and risk have become vital necessities.

The needs to try varied experiences, to live different lifestyles, and the possibility to try new products and to have new sources of satisfaction form an important subject matter in this type of society. This search is endless, because there is no possible saturation in this type of need.

Some philosophers advocate rising above all wants in order to escape this endless escalation, which, far from bringing internal peace, causes worry and creates an infernal cycle. The wise Hindu, Sarna Lakshman, writes:

> Desire tells us: get this and then you will be happy. We believe it and we try to acquire the relevant object. If we don't get it, or if we don't get enough, we suffer. If we get it, then desire immediately suggests another objective, and we don't even see that we have been fooled.
>
> (Quoted by Boirel, 1977)

These philosophers are advocating the *ideal of ataraxy*; that is, the absence of turmoil as a result of the extinction of desire. The alternative to this extreme solution is *creative consumption*; that is, consumption that encourages ascending motivations of progress, self-actualization and excellence. If it is true that 'man prefers hunting to the catch', as Pascal said, then want, as being the driving force of activity, can be the first cause of satisfaction brought about by creative consumption.

3.3 TOWARDS A COMPREHENSIVE THEORY OF CONSUMPTION

The contributions of motivation theory help us to identify more general motivational orientations in human beings. These orientations govern a large variety of individual behaviours. These disciplinary contributions, however, provide only a general description of the needs structure, with little attempt at operationalization and no explicit reference to buying behaviour. More-over, they tend to focus on one dimension of behaviour (economic, social, psychological, etc.) and do not propose a comprehensive framework which integrates the concepts used in each contributing disciplines. Several attempts have been made to develop a comprehensive, multi-disciplinary description of behaviour, namely by compiling lists of needs.

3.3.1 Typologies of human needs

Well-being means having a product or service to satisfy each need, so a natural approach is to develop a list of needs and to compare it with available goods. The word 'goods' has here a special meaning. They are not only physical entities or services, but may be abstract, social or psychological entities, such as love, prestige, etc. The seminal works of Murray (1938), Maslow (1943), Rokeach (1973) and more recently Sheth *et al.* (1991) are representatives of this approach.

Murray's inventory of human needs

Murray calls a need a hypothetical construct because it is of a physiochemical nature that is unknown. It resides in the brain and is thus in a position to control all significant behaviour. In Murray's words:

> A need is a hypothetical construct that stands for a force in the brain region that organizes and directs mind and body behaviour so as to maintain the organism in its most desirable state.   (Murray, 1938, p. 123)

Murray gives a rather systematic inventory, classifying individuals' needs into four dimensions: *primary* (viscerogenic) *and secondary* (psychogenic) needs, according to whether they are of physiological origin or not; *positive and negative* needs, depending on whether or not the individual is attracted by the object; *manifest or latent* needs, according to whether or not the needs drive the individual to a real or imaginary behaviour; and *conscious or unconscious* needs, according to whether or not they drive the individual to take introspective steps. Murray lists 37 needs covering these categories.

Murray believes that all people possess the same needs, but he recognizes that the expression of these needs will differ from one person to another because of differences in personality and in environmental factors. Needs could be provoked by either internal or external stimuli, and they could be weak or strong at any particular time. A need exists in three different states: (1) refractory, in which no incentive will arouse it; (2) inducible, in which the need is inactive but susceptible to excitation; and (3) active, in which the need is determining the behaviour of the organism (Murray, 1938, pp. 85–6). Thus, marketing activities could have a direct impact on inducible needs.

Maslow's needs hierarchy

Maslow (1943) adopts a similar approach, grouping fundamental needs into the five categories—physiological, safety, social, esteem and self-actualization—described in Box 3.1. Maslow's analysis, however, goes further and is not limited to a simple classification. Maslow postulates the existence of a *hierarchy of needs*, which depends on the individual's state of development.

BOX 3.1

Maslow's hierarchy of needs

- *PHYSIOLOGICAL NEEDS* These are fundamental; once satisfied, they cease to be determinant factors of motivation and no longer influence behaviour.
- *SAFETY NEEDS* Physical safety, preservation of the physical structure of the organism, psychological safety, conservation of the psychic structure of personality. Need for own identity, to feel in charge of one's destiny.
- *SOCIAL NEEDS* People are social animals and feel the need to fit into a group, to associate with their fellows, they feel the need to love and be loved. Mutual help, belonging and sense of community are also social needs.
- *SELF-ESTEEM NEEDS* Self-esteem, personal dignity, confidence in oneself and one's own competence. The feel that one's objectives are valid. The esteem that others feel for us. The need for recognition, to be respected, to have a social status.
- *SELF-ACTUALIZATION NEEDS* Those needs are at the top of the scale of human needs, and include self-realization and development; the need of people to surpass themselves; to use all their capacities and push their limits; and to give a meaning to things and find their *raison d'être*.

Source: Maslow (1943).

According to Maslow, there is an *order of priorities* in needs, in the sense that we begin to try to satisfy dominant needs before going to the next category. Once the needs of a lower order have been satisfied, they allow needs of the higher order to become motivators and influence our behaviour. There is a progressive abatement in the intensity of needs already met and an increasing intensity of needs of a higher order not yet satisfied. We observe an evolution of the structure of needs depending on the individual's development as he or she goes from an overall objective of survival or living standard towards more qualitative objectives regarding lifestyle or quality of life.

Maslow's analysis is interesting because it puts forth not only the *multi-dimensional structure* of needs, but also the fact that needs have different degrees of intensity in different individuals. In reality, there is always some coexistence of these categories of needs, with one category or another becoming more important according to the individual, or according to the circumstances of one particular individual.

Products to be developed for satisfying needs must therefore be planned accordingly. A good or product may have more than one role or function beyond just the basic one. Individuals use goods not only for practical reasons, but also to communicate with their environment, to show who they are, to demonstrate their feelings, etc. It is important for marketing to be aware of the role played by goods and brands (Baudrillard, 1968), not simply for their functional value but also for their emotional or symbolic values. We shall see later in this chapter that the multi-dimensional structure of needs also exists with the organizational customer.

Rokeach's list of values

Human values research stresses the important goals which most people seek. Values are closely linked to human needs, but exist at a more realistic level. They are the *mental representations of underlying needs*, not only of individual needs but also of societal and institutional needs. In other words, values are our ideas about what is desirable.

> A value is an enduring belief that a specific mode of conduct or end-state of existence is personally or socially preferable to an opposite or converse mode of conduct or end-state of existence. A value-system is an enduring organization of beliefs concerning preferable modes of conduct or end-states of existence along a continuum of relative importance.
>
> (Rokeach, 1973, p. 5)

There are two types of values: (1) terminal and (2) instrumental. Terminal (or end-state) values are beliefs we have about the goals or end-states for which we strive (e.g. happiness, wisdom, etc.). Instrumental (or means) values refer to beliefs about desirable ways of behaving to help us attain the terminal values (e.g. behaving honestly or accepting responsibility).

Since values are transmitted through cultures, most people in a given society will possess the same values, but to different degrees. The relative importance of each value will therefore be different from one individual to another and these differences can be used as market segmentation criteria, as shown in Chapter 6 of this book. The prominence of different values can also change over time. Rokeach postulates that the total number of values that a person possesses is relatively small. In his empirical work, Rokeach (1973, p. 28) identifies 18 terminal and instrumental values.

In recent years, researchers have been working to develop a short list of values that can be measured in a reliable manner. Kahle (1983) has identified eight summary terminal values.

- Self-respect
- Security
- Warm relationships
- Sense of accomplishment
- Self-fulfilment
- Being well respected
- Sense of belonging
- Fun/enjoyment/excitement.

Several researchers have found that those values relate well to various aspects of consumer behaviour or to social change.

> For example, people who value fun and enjoyment may desire a cup of coffee for its rich taste, whereas people who value a sense of accomplishment may wish to use coffee as a

mild stimulant to increase productivity; and people who value warm relationships with others may want to share a cup of coffee as an aspect of a social ritual.

(Kahle *et al.*, 1988)

The logic of this methodology can be summarized as follows: to understand individuals' motivation, one place to start is to try to understand their values, particularly with products that involve consumer value. Also, an understanding of the way values are changing in a given society will facilitate the development of effective strategies for dealing with the dynamics of societal change.

3.3.2 The Sheth–Newman–Gross theory of consumption values

Applying the concept of 'value' to buying behaviour, Sheth, Newman and Gross (1991, pp. 18–25) describe market choice as a multidimensional phenomenon involving multiple values: functional, social, emotional, epistemic and conditional. They define these values as follows.

1. *Functional value.* The perceived utility acquired by an alternative as the result of its ability to perform its functional, utilitarian or physical purposes. Alternatives acquire functional value through the possession of salient functional, utilitarian or physical attributes.
2. *Social value.* The perceived utility acquired by an alternative as a result of its association with one or more social group. Alternatives acquire social value through association with positively or negatively stereotyped demographic, socio-economic and cultural ethnic groups.
3. *Emotional value.* The perceived utility acquired by an alternative as a result of its ability to arouse feelings or affective states. Alternatives acquire emotional value when associated with specific feelings or when they facilitate or perpetuate feelings.
4. *Epistemic value.* The perceived utility acquired by an alternative as a result of its ability to arouse curiosity, provide novelty and/or satisfy a desire for knowledge. Alternatives acquire epistemic value through the capacity to provide something new or different.
5. *Conditional value.* The perceived utility acquired by an alternative as a result of the specific situation or the context faced by the choice-maker. Alternatives acquire conditional value in the presence of antecedent physical or social contingencies that enhance their functional or social value, but do not otherwise possess this value.

These five values make *differential contributions* to specific market choices in the sense that some values can contribute more than others. Those values are also independent. They relate additively and contribute incrementally to choice. Although it is desirable to maximize all five values, users are often willing to accept less of one value to obtain more of another. That is why buyers are willing to trade off less salient values in order to maximize those that are most salient (Sheth *et al.*, 1991, p. 12).

Considerable overlaps are observed when comparing these summary values with the different need categories proposed by diverse disciplines. The functional value corresponds to the general motivation for comfort in Murray's viscerogenic needs and in Maslow's safety and physiological needs. The social and emotional functions correspond with Maslow's social needs of belonging-ness and love, with Rokeach's values of 'social recognition' and 'true friendship' and with the more general motivation for stimulation. The epistemic value is similar to Maslow's need for 'self-actualization', to the Rockeach's values 'exciting life' and 'pleasure' and also to the general need for stimulation and pleasure. Previous contributions did not include the conditional value construct, which is particularly well adapted to the situation of buying behaviour. In addition, Sheth *et al.* (1991; see Chapter 5) have operationalized their theory by developing a generic questionnaire and a standardized procedure for adapting the analysis to any specific market situation.

The 'value' approach provides the market analyst with a simple but comprehensive framework for analysing the need structure of the individual buyer and for segmenting markets. For an application of this approach see Gale (1994). The five summary values proposed by the Sheth–Newman–Gross theory will be used in the following chapters as a basis for designing operational market analysis and measurement.

3.4 MOTIVATION OF THE INDUSTRIAL BUYER

So far, our analysis has concerned only the needs and motivations of the individual as a buyer. But a large part of commercial activity, in any economy, is made up of transactions between organizations. This includes firms selling equipment, goods, intermediary products, raw materials, etc., to other firms using these products in their own manufacturing process. Although the principles governing marketing are just as pertinent for firms selling industrial goods as for firms selling consumer goods, the concrete manner in which these principles are implemented may appear very different.

Box 3.2 describes the main characteristics of business-to-business marketing or of organizational marketing, grouped into three categories according to whether they relate to demand, to the industrial client or to the product. By far the most significant feature, at least from the aspect of motivation, is the fact that the industrial customer, whose needs must be met by the supplier, is represented by a group of people called the *buying centre*. Furthermore, this collegiate structure of the industrial customer can be found at any stage of the *industrial chain* in which the customer is inserted. This is a second important feature specific to industrial marketing. The firm selling industrial goods therefore faces a double diversity of needs: those specific to the buying centre and those specific to each of the levels of the industrial chain.

3.4.1 The demand for industrial goods

Demand for industrial goods has the particularity of being a *derived demand*. It is demand expressed by an organization which uses the purchased products in its own manufacturing process in order to meet the demand of other organizations or of the final consumer. It therefore expresses a demand dependent on one or many downstream demands.

> The firm Polypal manufactures and sells metallic storage equipment. Such installations are purchased by firms investing in new production capacity or extending existing capacity in order to meet demand in their own markets. It is therefore in Polypal's interest first to identify developing sectors, and then to address the firms supplying the markets which would be likely to invest in storage equipment.

BOX 3.2

Distinctive characteristics of business marketing

THE NATURE OF DEMAND

- Industrial demand is a *derived demand*, that is, a demand expressed by an organization which uses the products purchased in its own manufacturing process, in order to meet either the demand of other organizations or the demand of the end-buyer. Thus, industrial demand is part of a chain (a supply chain) which depends on a downstream demand and is ultimately 'derived' from the demand of consumer goods.
- Industrial demand, and particularly capital equipment demand, is *highly fluctuating* and reacts strongly to small variations in final demand (the acceleration principle).
- Industrial demand is often *price inelastic*, insofar as the product represents a key component, perhaps made to exact specifications. The product is more of a necessity and there are fewer substitutes available.

THE INDUSTRIAL CUSTOMER

- The industrial firm faces *multiple customers:* its direct customers and the customers of its direct customers also participating in the supply chain.
- The organizational customer has a *collegiate structure* at each level of the industrial chain: a group of individuals, the buying centre, who exercise different functions and roles and have distinct competences and motivations.
- The customer is a *professional buyer,* technically competent; the purchase decision involves a degree of formalization not found in consumer purchasing.

PRODUCT CHARACTERISTICS

- The product sought is generally *well defined* by the customer who knows what is wanted; specifications are clearly defined and the supplier has little room for manoeuvring.
- Industrial products enter into the manufacturing process of the industrial customer and thus have a *strategic, if not vital*, importance.
- Industrial products often have a very *large number of different uses*, unlike consumer goods which are almost inevitably for a specific use.

The demand for an industrial good is even more complex to analyse when a product is at the start of the transformation chain, far from the final demand on which it nevertheless depends. Thus it faces many echelons of successive demand, each with differentiated needs structures.

The notion of an industrial chain goes beyond a list of names by branch or by sector and makes the conventional division of the economy into primary, secondary and tertiary sectors out of date. An industrial chain consists of all the stages of production, from raw materials to satisfying the final need of the consumer, irrespective of whether this final need concerns a product or a service. There is a hierarchy of industries which are either clients or suppliers of a given firm according to whether they are upstream or downstream. The strategic force of an industrial client depends, among other things, on the client's ability to anticipate and control the end market of the chain in which he or she participates.

The following list describes the structure of a typical industrial demand (see Fig. 3.3.). Clearly the chain of demands may be much longer and more complex in some cases. Without claiming this to be an exhaustive list, the following distinctions can be established.

1. *First transformation*. Demand is for processed materials that are transformed into semi-finished goods, for instance, steel bars, sheets, chemicals, leather, etc.

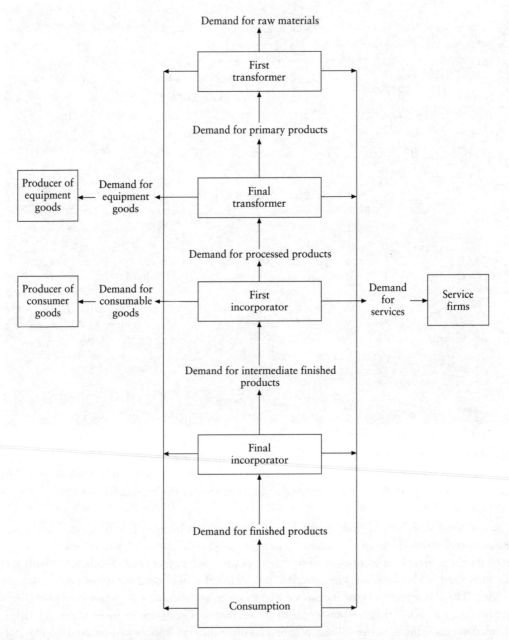

FIGURE 3.3 *Typical structure of an industrial supply chain*

2. *Final transformation*. Demand is for primary products that will be transformed into more elaborate processed products. For example, transformation of raw sheet metal into rust-proof sheet metal, either plated of pre-painted. Bekaert transforms raw steel into wires of different diameters.

3. *First incorporation*. Demand is for finished goods used to manufacture more complex products that are themselves components of other products. For example, pre-painted sheet metal is used to manufacture radiators; wires are used to manufacture radial tyres.

4. *Final incorporation*. Demand is for finished products incorporated in manufacturing finished products for final demand, for example, tyres and batteries, spark plugs, TV tubes, automobile windscreens, etc.

5. *Assemblers*. Demand is for a large variety of products that will be put together to form systems or large compounds. For example, radiators are placed with other products to form a heating system. Similarly, a system of public transport, such as an underground rail system, brings together a tremendous variety of different products.

In addition to these successive demands which follow one another in a chain, there are also lateral demands of capital equipment goods, consumable items (fuel, wrapping materials, office supplies, etc.) and services (maintenance and repair, manufacturing and business services, professional services).

Therefore the industrial firm in the position of the beginning of the production chain is faced with a sequence of independent demands which finally determine its own demand. It faces two categories of clients: its *direct customers* and the *customers of its customers*. In order to apply active marketing, the firm must take into account the specific demands of its direct customers, of the intermediary customers and of those who express final demand at the end of the chain. Figure 3.4 gives example of the successive customers, direct and indirect, facing a manufacturer of heat pumps.

3.4.2 The buying decision centre

In an industrial firm, buying decisions, and especially the more important ones, are mostly taken by a group of people called the *buying group* or the *buying centre*.

> The buying centre is defined as consisting of those individuals who interact for the specific purpose of accomplishing the buying task. . ... These persons interact on the basis of their particular roles in the buying process. The buying group is characterized by both a pattern of communication (interaction) and a set of shared values (norms) which direct and constrain the behaviour of the individual within it.　(Webster and Wind, 1972, p. 35)

There are several distinct roles in the buying centre: users, influencers, purchasers, deciders and gatekeepers. These individuals are either involved in the purchase itself or are concerned about its possible consequences on the firm's activity, and thus participate in some form in the purchase decision-making process. Understanding those roles will help one to understand the nature of interpersonal influence in the buying decision process. The buying centre comprises individuals with different functions and therefore with different goals, motivations and behaviours. Hence

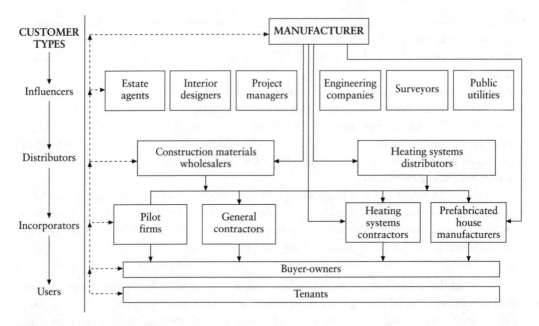

FIGURE 3.4 *Vertical structure of the domestic heat pump market* (Source: *adapted from FNGE, ESC, Lyon, 1976)*

many purchase decisions are conflicting, and they follow a complex process of internal negotiation.

In general, the buying centre includes the following five roles, which can be occupied by one or several individuals.

■ *Purchasers* have formal authority and responsibility for selecting alternative brands and suppliers and for determining the terms of purchase and negotiating contracts. This is usually done by the purchasing manager.

■ *Users* are the persons who use the product: the production engineer or the workers. The users can formulate specific purchase requirements or refuse to work with some materials. Generally speaking, users are better placed for evaluating the performance of purchased goods and services.

■ *Influencers* do not necessarily have buying authority but can influence the outcome of a decision by defining criteria which constrain the choices that can be considered. R&D personnel, design, engineering and consultants, etc., typically belong to this category.

■ *Deciders* have formal authority and responsibility to determine the final selection of brands or vendors. There is generally an upper limit on the financial commitment they can make, reserving larger decisions for other members of the organization—for instance, the board of directors.

■ *Gatekeepers* are group members who control the flow of information into the group and can exercise indirect influence on the buying process.

The composition of the buying centre will vary with the complexity and the degree of uncertainty of decisions in the firm. One can distinguish three kinds of situation:

■ *New task*: the purchase of a new product in a new class of products for the client organization.

■ *Modified rebuy*: problem and product are known, but some elements of the buyers' specifications are modified.

■ *Straight rebuy*: purchase of a known product, not modified and with which the firm has extensive experience.

In the first two cases the buying centre intervenes totally. One can see that it is vital for the supplier to identify all those involved in the purchasing process, because it must identify the targets of its communication policy. It is equally important to understand how these participants interact among themselves and what their dominant motivation is (Valla, 1980, p. 28).

3.4.3 Needs of the buying centre

The industrial customer is therefore identified with the 'buying centre' which comprises persons from different functions in the organization, who thus have distinct personal and organizational motivations. The notion of need in industry goes beyond the conventional idea of rational choice based only on the quality–price criterion. Choices are rational, as in the case of the individual consumer, insofar as all motivations and constraints with a bearing on purchase decisions are taken into account: personal motivations, interpersonal relations, economic and organizational constraints, environmental pressures, etc. As in the case of the individual consumer, need therefore has a multidimensional structure. The *overall need of an industrial customer* can be described with reference to at least five values.

■ *Technology*: product specifications, state-of-the-art technology, up-to-date and constant quality, just-in-time delivery, etc.

■ *Finance*: price competitiveness, transfer costs, installation and maintenance costs, payment terms, delivery reliability, etc.

■ *Assistance*: after-sales service, help for installation and operation, technical assistance and servicing, etc.

■ *Information*: communication, qualified sales personnel, priority access to new products, training, business intelligence, etc.

■ *Psycho-sociology*: reciprocal relations, compatibility of organizational forms, brand or company reputation, etc.

The following (Valla, 1980, p. 25) illustrates the multidimensional nature of the industrial customer's need. The statement from the purchase manager, 'No, we won't work with this supplier any more, they are not reliable', may have different meanings:

- The quality of their products is not constant (technical value).

- Their prices are whimsical (financial value).

- They were supposed to have repaired a machine two months ago (assistance value).

- They have promised to send one of their engineers to tell us about new products being developed; we have called many times and they still haven't done it (information value).

- They treat us as insignificant (psycho-sociological value).

We note that the determinants of well-being for the industrial client are of a very different nature from those governing the well-being of the individual consumer. The structure of motivations of the industrial customer is both more complex and more simple. It is more complex because it involves an organization and different individuals operating in the organization; it is more simple because the main motivations are more objective and thus easier to identify. However, despite the real differences that exist between the two areas, the basic ideas of marketing have the same relevance in the industrial market as they have in the consumer market: *to adjust supply to the overall need of the customer*. If this principle is not implemented, the penalty in the industrial market is probably paid more rapidly because of the buyer's professionalism and the fact that needs are more clearly defined.

3.4.4 The industrial buying process

The analysis of the buying process basically consists of identifying the specific roles played by each member of the buying centre at different stages of the decision-making process, their choice criteria, their perceptions of the performance of products or firms in the market, the weight given to each point of view, etc.

As in the case of the buying decision of the individual consumer, the industrial buying process can be divided into several stages. As illustrated in Table 3.1, Webster and Wind (1972, p. 80) suggest six phases in the process:

1. Anticipation and identification of need.

TABLE 3.1 *Decision stages and roles of the buying centre*

Stages in the buying process	Composition of the buying centre				
	User	Influencer	Buyer	Decider	Gatekeeper
Identification of need	*				*
Establishing specifications	*	*			*
Identifying alternatives			*		*
Evaluating alternatives	*	*	*	*	*
Selecting the supplier			*	*	*
Evaluation of performances	*				

Source: Webster and Wind (1972).

2. Determination of specifications and scheduling the purchase.
3. Search for buying alternatives.
4. Evaluation of alternative buying actions.
5. Selection of suppliers.
6. Performance control and appraisal.

Clearly, the decision of an industrial client does not always follow this process. The complexity of the decision and its degree of risk or novelty determine how formal the buying process will be. Furthermore, the decision-making and organizational processes can also vary according to the firm, both in terms of its size and its fields of activity.

One can imagine that the roles of the members of the buying centre are different at each stage of the decision-making process. The analysis of the buying process must answer the following questions:

■ Who is a major participant in the decision-making process of buying a given industrial product?

■ Who are the key influencers intervening in the process?

■ What is the level of their influence?

■ What evaluation criteria does each decision participant use?

■ What is the weight given to each criterion?

etc.

This information is usually collected by survey. It helps to clarify the issue, particularly when it comes to training salespeople by giving them a better understanding of the mechanism of the industrial buying process.

Valla (1980, p.27) emphasizes the fact that training salespeople to understand this type of analysis particularly helps them to:

■ understand better the buyer's role as well as the system of motivations and constraints within which the buyer operates

■ go beyond mere contact with the purchaser by identifying other possible communication targets within the industrial client's organization

■ determine better when is the best moment to directly intervene *vis-à-vis* appropriate targets in order to increase efficiency of contacts

■ be in a better position to take advantage of opportunities when they present themselves, owing to broader relations with all members of the buying centre.

We will see in Chapter 7 that the way the buying centre functions is an important segmentation criterion in industrial markets.

SUMMARY

The satisfaction of buyers' needs is at the heart of a market economy, yet it is popular in some quarters to claim that marketing creates needs. The notion of need generates controversy because it contains value judgement based on morality or ideology. Apart from the ethical or social rules imposed by society, marketing is pluralist and respects the diversity of tastes and preferences. The distinction between absolute and relative needs brings to the fore the existence of a dialectic of relative needs which leads to the general impossibility of saturation. Similarly, the distinction between generic and derived needs shows that saturation does not relate to generic needs but only to derived needs, i.e. the dominant technological response at the time. Experimental psychology has proposed a range of motivational orientations. Particularly useful are the conceptual frameworks proposed by the Stimulus–Response theory, Maslow's needs hierarchy and the Sheth–Gross–Newman theory of consumption values. If the principles governing organizational or business-to-business marketing are the same as for consumer marketing, two major differences do exist. First, the industrial firm is faced with a supply chain, made up of interdependent firms, which eventually determines its own demand, called derived demand. Thus the industrial firm faces two categories of clients: its direct customers and the customers of its customers. Second, the industrial customer is represented by a group of individuals, called the buying centre, who exercise different functions and have distinct motivations. The understanding of the needs and of the role played by each member of the buying centre in the buying decision process, at each stage of the chain, is a key input for the development of marketing strategy.

QUESTIONS AND PROBLEMS

1. What are the implications of Galbraith's criticism of marketing as the creator of artificial needs? Analyse this theory using a concrete example based on your personal experience as a consumer.
2. By reference to typology as proposed by either Maslow or Sheth, Newman and Gross, explain the success of products such as Coca-Cola, Club Med, Swatch. Choose a product to illustrate your answer.
3. Describe needs of an individual consumer and those of an industrial customer. Identify the main similarities and differences resulting from the complex structure of an industrial customer's need.
4. Describe the needs of each member of a buying decision centre in a company which produces high-tech goods.
5. Is it possible to imagine a point of complete saturation of consumption?

REFERENCES

Abbott, L. (1955), *Quality and Competition*. New York: John Wiley & Sons.
Attali, J. and M. Guillaume (1974), *L'anti-économique*. Paris: Presses Universitaires de France.
Baudrillard, J. (1968), *Le système des objets*. Paris: Gallimard.
Becker, G.S. (1965), 'A Theory of the Allocation of Time', *The Economic Journal*, September, pp. 494–517.

Berlyne, D.E. (1960), *Conflict, Arousal and Curiosity*. New York: McGraw-Hill Book Company.

Boirel, M. (1977), *Comment vivre sans tension?* Brussels: Marabout.

Cotta, A. (1980), *La société ludique*. Paris: Grasset.

Duffy, E. (1957), 'The Psychological Significance of the Concept of Arousal and Activation', *The Psychological Review*, vol. 64, September, pp. 265–75.

Galbraith, J.K. (1971), *The affluent society*, 2nd edn, Boston: Houghton Mifflin.

Gale, B.T. (1994), *Managing Customer Value*. New York: The Free Press.

Jacquemin, A. and H. Tulkens (1988), *Fondements d'économie politique*, 2nd edn. Brussels: De Boeck-Weesmael.

Hebb, D.O. (1955), 'Drives and the CNS (Conceptual Nervous System)', *The Psychological Review*, vol. 62, July, pp. 243–54.

Kahle, L.R. (ed.) (1983), *Social Values and Social Change: Adaptation to Life in America*, New York: Praeger.

Kahle, L.R., B. Poulos and A. Sukhdial (1988), Changes in Social Values in the United States during the Past Decade, *Journal of Advertising Research*, February–March, pp. 35–41.

Katona, G. (1951), *Psychological Analysis of Economic Behavior*. New York: McGraw-Hill.

Keynes, J.M. (1936), Essays in Persuasion—Economic Possibilities for our Grandchildren. *The Collected Writings of J.M. Keynes*, vol. 9, London: The Macmillan Press Ltd.

Kotler, P. (1991), *Marketing Management*, 7th edn. Englewood Cliffs, New Jersey: Prentice Hall Inc.

Lancaster, K.J. (1966), 'A New Approach to Consumer Theory', *The Journal of Political Economy*, Vol. 74, April, pp. 132–57.

Maslow, H. (1943), 'A Theory of Human Motivation', *The Psychological Review*, Vol. 50, pp. 370–96.

Murray, H.A. (1938), *Explorations in Personality*. New York: Oxford University Press Inc.

Nuttin, J. (1980), *Théorie de la motivation humaine*. Paris: Presses Universitaires de France.

Rokeach, M.O. (1973), *The Nature of Human Values*. New York: The Free Press.

Rosa, J.J. (1977), 'Vrais et faux besoins', in Rosa J.J. and Aftalion F. (eds), *L'économique retrouvé*. Paris: Economica.

Scitovsky, T. (1976), *The Joyless Economy*. Oxford: Oxford University Press.

Séguéla, J. (1982), *Hollywood lave plus blanc*. Paris: Flammarion.

Sheth, J.N., B.I. Newman and B.L. Gross (1991), *Consumption Values and Market Choices: Theory and Applications*. Cincinnati: South Western Publishing Company.

Valaskakis, K. *et al.* (1978), *La société de conservation*, Montréal: Les éditions Quinze.

Valla, J.P. (1980), Le comportement des groupes d'achat, in *L'action marketing des entreprises industrielles*, Paris: Collection Adetem, pp. 22–38.

Webster, F.E. and Y. Wind (1972), *Organizational Buying Behavior*. Englewood Cliffs, New-Jersey: Prentice Hall Inc.

FURTHER READING

Aaker, D.A. and G.S. Day (eds) (1982), *Consumerism: Search for the Consumer Interest*. New York: The Free Press.

Berlyne, D.E. (1968), The Motivational Significance of Collative Variables and Conflict, in Ableson, R.P. *et al.* (eds), *Theories of Cognitive Consistency: A Sourve Book*. Chicago: Rand McNally & Co.

Galbraith, J.K. (1961), *L'ère de l'opulence*. Paris: Calman Lévy.

Planchon, A. (1974), *Saturation de la consommation*. Paris: Mame, Collection Repères-Economie.

Stoffaès, C. (1980), Filières et stratégies industrielles, *Annales des Mines*, January, pp. 9–20.

THE BUYER'S CHOICE BEHAVIOUR

LEARNING OBJECTIVES

After reading this chapter, you should be able to understand:

■ the different decision-making processes adopted by the buyer

■ the rationale presiding over the buying decision process

■ what represents a 'product' (or a service) to the buyer

■ the type of information processed by the buyer in comparing buying alternatives

■ the information sources used by the buyer in his (or her) decision-making process

■ the role of advertising information.

*H*aving identified the key values influencing the individual consumer's choice behaviour, as well as the multidimensional need structure of the organizational customer, we shall now analyse the way in which buyers make purchasing decisions. During the last decade, there have been many theoretical and empirical contributions by diverse disciplines relevant to the understanding of buying behaviour. Market analysts have models and conceptual frameworks at their disposal to help them to organize the market information collected by the firm. This information is not always for the sake of scientific knowledge *per se*, but rather to gain a better understanding of market choice behaviour and to enhance marketing efficiency. The objective of this chapter is to review the major theoretical and conceptual contributions which could be applicable to individual as well as organizational buying decisions.

4.1 THE BUYER AS AN ACTIVE DECISION MAKER

From the marketing point of view, buying behaviour covers all activity preceding, accompanying and following purchase decisions. The individual or the organization actively takes part in the decisions in order to make choices in a systematic way, as opposed to random or stochastic selections. The purchasing behaviour is seen as a *process of problem solving*. All possible steps that may have something to do with the resolution of the problem are therefore part of the buying process. They can be grouped into five stages:

1. Problem recognition
2. Information search
3. Evaluation of alternatives
4. Purchase decision
5. Post-purchase behaviour.

This view of an active buyer is in total contrast with that of the passive buyer who is dominated by the unconscious and is defenceless against the selling activities of the firm and advertisers. The complexity of the decision process varies, however, with the type of buying decisions and with the risk implied by the choice.

4.1.1 Importance of the perceived risk

Not every purchase decision requires a systematic information search. The complexity of the approach to problem solving depends on the importance of the *perceived risk* associated with the purchase—in other words, on the uncertainty about the scope of the consequences of a particular choice. There are four kinds of risk or unfavourable consequences normally perceived by the buyer (Bauer, 1960):

■ A *financial loss*, when the product is faulty and needs replacement or repair at one's own expense.

■ A *loss of time*, due to hours of making complaints, returning to distributors, repairs, etc.

■ A *physical risk*, due to the consumption or use of products potentially harmful to one's health or the environment.

■ A *psychological risk*, when a bad purchase leads to loss of self-esteem or creates general dissatisfaction.

Market research shows that buyers develop strategies and ways of reducing risk that enable them to act with relative confidence and ease in situations where their information is inadequate and the consequences of their actions are incalculable (Bauer, 1960, p. 120).

To reduce the perceived risk before the purchase decision, the buyer can use various forms of information, such as personal sources (family, neighbours, friends), commercial sources (advertising, salespersons, catalogues), public sources (comparative tests, official publications) and experimental sources (product trials, inspection). The higher the perceived risk, the more extensive the information search will be.

Problem-solving approaches

Three types of approach to problem solving can be distinguished: routine response behaviour, and limited and extensive problem-solving behaviours (Howard and Sheth, 1969).

- *Extensive* problem solving is adopted when the value of information and/or the perceived risk are high. For example, this happens in situations where the buyer is confronted with an unfamiliar brand in an unfamiliar product class. The choice criteria by which alternatives are assessed will be weak or non-existent and an intensive information search will be necessary to identify the relevant criteria.

- *Limited* problem solving applies to the situation of a buyer confronted with a new, unfamiliar brand in a familiar product class, usually where existing brands do not provide an adequate level of satisfaction. Choice criteria already exist, but there will still be a certain amount of search and evaluation prior to purchase.

- Finally, *routine* response behaviour is observed in the case where the consumer has accumulated enough experience and knowledge and has definite preferences about one or more familiar brand within a familiar product category. Here the process of choice is simplified and repetitive, with little or no prior information search. Under this situation of low involvement, considerable consumer inertia and/or brand loyalty would be expected.

Note that routine response behaviour is also observed for low-cost, frequently purchased items, be they familiar or not to the buyer. For this product category, the best information comes from buying the product, because the cost of experimenting is low. If there is dissatisfaction, the consumer will simply not buy the brand at the next purchase occasion. Given the low cost of error, there is no need to search diligently for information. The fields of consumer behaviour analysis are summarized in Fig. 4.1.

The buyer's involvement

In recent years, the concept of *consumer involvement* has received considerable attention in the marketing literature. Involvement can be defined as '. . . a state of energy (arousal) that a person experiences in regard to a consumption-related activity' (Wilkie, 1990, p. 220). Thus involvement implies attention to something because it is somehow relevant or perceived as risky. High involvement requires high levels of prior deliberation and strong feelings, while low involvement will occur when consumers invest less energy in their thoughts and feelings. The concept of involvement, which overlaps somewhat with the above Howard and Sheth classification of

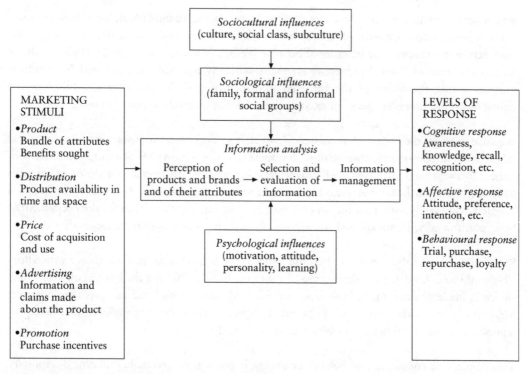

FIGURE 4.1 *The fields of consumer behaviour analysis*

problem-solving situations, is useful for analysing consumer behaviour at different levels of involvement and for deciding on the type of communication strategy to adopt in each situation. We shall return to this concept in the following chapter.

4.1.2 A rational approach to problem solving

In this framework, purchasing behaviour is neither erratic nor conditioned by the environment. It is rational in the sense of the *principle of limited rationality*, which means within the bounds of individuals' cognitive and learning capacities. The implicit assumptions are:

1. Consumers make choices after *deliberation*, the extent of which depends on the importance of the perceived risk.
2. Choices are based on *anticipation of future data* and not only on short-term observations.
3. Choices are also guided by the *principle of generalized scarcity* according to which any human acts. Any decision has an opportunity cost.

We live in an environment where everything is scarce: not only money and goods, but also information and especially time, our scarcest resource because it is perfectly inextensible.

This approach is called a *rational approach to problem-solving*. The use of the term *rational* is not in contrast with the term *emotional*, which implies a value judgement on the quality of the choice. The steps undertaken are considered to be rational as long as they are *consistent* with the set objectives, whatever these objectives may be. For example, an individual, for whom the social value or status effect is important is prepared to pay more for a product with the same quality. Such action is considered to be rational because the behaviour is consistent. In other words, as long as information about the objective is sought, critically analysed and processed, behaviour is rational within the limits of the gathered information and the cognitive capability of the individual. This, however, does not exclude the existence of another 'better' choice.

We are using here the notion of 'consistency' which is so dear to economists, with a fundamental difference. The consumer is consistent with respect to his or her own set of axioms, and not with respect to a set of axioms defined with no reference to specific situational context or preferences structure. Rational behaviour does not exclude *impulsive* behaviour. As long as the latter is adopted deliberately, either for the simple pleasure of acting impulsively, or for the excitement of being confronted with unexpected consequences, the behaviour is said to be rational.

Rationality here implies no more than the adoption of a kind of systematic choice procedure. This could be defined as the coherent use of a set of principles forming the basis of choice. When choice is made at random, behaviour is unpredictable and erratic, and analysis is impossible. Marketing accepts the existence of the latter type of behaviour, but believes that it is not representative of actual behaviour observed in most real-life situations.

This concept of consistency of behaviour makes it possible to reconcile different disciplinary approaches (economic, psychological, sociological) in the study of buying behaviour. Marketing is interested in the real person, the individual with all his or her diversity, as illustrated by the list of values described in the previous chapter. Actual choices are influenced by several values, but the individual or the organization may very well accept a suboptimal level of functional value, for example, in order to maximize social or epistemic value. This type of choice will be termed *rational* because it is consistent with the personal set of values prevailing in the specific choice situation (conditional value).

4.1.3 Consumer behaviour in a macroeconomic perspective

Macroeconomists considered for a long time that the consumers adjusted their consumption behaviour in terms of factors registered over a short period, with no explicit reference to time. However, observation of behaviour reveals that consumption is a question of habit more than anything else, its domain being certainly that of inertia, but also of expectations, predispositions and anticipations formulated in terms of longer horizons. In other words, there exists a *dynamics of behaviour* which must be taken into account when analysing and forecasting market development.

The permanent income hypothesis

A revealing example is the change of views regarding the macroeconomic theory of consumption and saving, which, until the mid-1940s, was dominated by the Keynesian theory. According to Keynes, total consumption tends to increase with increased income, but the increased income brings about a lesser increase in consumption. In an economy where income is increasing continuously, the *average propensity to consume*—that is, the share of income going to consumption—goes up at an increasingly slower rate. Logically, there should be a tendency towards saturation. In the short run, this tendency is supposedly the result of the passive behaviour of consumers, who tend to keep their old consumption habits (Keynes, 1936, pp. 96–7). Although the economy is growing, demand stagnates in traditional sectors at consumption levels previously reached, and rejects consumption of new products. Keynes considered this consumption function to be valid in the long run too, and thus formulated his *theory of long-run stagnation* which was widely accepted during the 1940s, and he advocated using public expenditure to sustain economic growth.

Econometric studies of the consumption function, such as that of Kuznets (1946) in the USA, later contradicted the Keynesian theory and showed that the propensity to consume was constant in the long run. Given that the theory of general saturation went uncorroborated, some economists began to question the basic assumptions of the Keynesian consumption function. Such efforts culminated, in the *permanent income hypothesis* (Friedman, 1957) which views consumption behaviour from a totally different perspective.

Like Keynes, Friedman accepts that the level of consumption is related to the level of income. However, he establishes a distinction between permanent and transitory income on the one hand, and permanent and transitory consumption on the other. Friedman considers that observed income and consumption are only homogeneous in appearance. They must be divided into two parts, as follows:

$$(\text{Observed income}) = (\text{Permanent income}) + (\text{Transitory income})$$

and

$$(\text{Observed consumption}) = (\text{Permanent consumption}) + (\text{Transitory consumption})$$

Permanent income is the income considered to be normal for the individual. It can be defined as follows:

> The constant stream of income having exactly the same present value as the variable stream of income expected by the individual within the limits of his or her planning horizon; in other words, the perpetual income stream that households expect their wealth can support.

One can imagine that permanent income is growing constantly. Transitory income, on the other hand, ensues from occasional variations in income (special economic conditions, gifts, inheritances, dividends, etc.). Permanent income is not based on past data, but on an expectation of income over a given period of time. Transitory income intervenes in the short run. Indeed, over the long run, the factors that could increase it begin to reverse their effects, and must cancel out.

According to Friedman, income and consumption can only be related when the increase in income is due to an increase in permanent income. If the increase is due to transitory income, then there can be no relation between the two variables. Econometric studies in various countries have confirmed this hypothesis and have shown that consumption increases in proportion with permanent income, and hence the hypothesis that the average propensity to consume is stable can also be accepted, at least over the long run.

For example, in the 13 largest countries of the OECD, households' net savings as a percentage of national disposable income (BIS, 1989, p. 36 and 1995, p. 28) display the following pattern:

> 1960–74: 8.6%   1975–79: 9.8%   1980–89: 8.8%   1992–94: 12.6%

It should be noted that this parallel development has continued despite major changes in the growth of purchasing power, given that before 1973 income and consumption were growing at an annual rate of 5–6 per cent, whereas since 1974 this growth rate has gone down to 3 per cent or even less. However, during the 1980s, a declining trend in private savings has been observed in most industrialized countries (BBL, 1989).

The buyer as an active decision maker

The permanent income hypothesis is interesting from our point of view because of its assumptions about consumption behaviour. This hypothesis shows that the way in which individuals manage the allocation of their resources is not affected by deviations in current income over a short period. In reality, it seems that consumers adjust their consumption and saving behaviour as a function of their personal career, expected family events (weddings, births, children going away, retirement) and the way in which they perceive the development of their property and not in relation to immediate risks.

> For the first time in neo-classical economic theory, the consumer is no longer pictured as a relatively passive being whose activity is limited to selective and timeless trade-off over essentially material choices, but as an individual whose rationality also integrates inter-temporal decisions based on expectations of future events. The consumer assumes his full role as an economic agent capable of rational choice and trade-off which goes beyond the narrow sphere of strictly market and monetary choices.   (Lepage, 1982, p. 15)

It is worth underlining the convergence in the points of view of behavioural theoreticians analysing the individual buying process on the one hand, and the macroeconomic analysis of aggregate consumption on the other. Both approaches lead to the same vision of the consumer: an *active decision-making agent* who makes consumption decisions on the basis of prior deliberation and of anticipations extending over a long horizon.

4.2 THE BUYER AS A PRODUCER OF SATISFACTIONS

In Chapter 3 we saw that individuals use goods to meet their needs and wants, which are expressions of their basic motivations. Let us recall that it is important that the notion of a good or a product should not be limited to physical objects only. Any entity likely to provide satisfaction can be called a good. This includes people, ideas, organizations and services in addition to objects.

In his search for well-being, the consumer behaves like an individual facing a decision problem and actively intervenes to solve it. Strategic marketing uses the new economic theory of consumer behaviour (Abbott, 1955; Becker, 1965; Lancaster, 1966) as its conceptual framework. According to this theory, consumption is an activity where the individual chooses goods, either singly or in combination, to 'produce' services which provide utility. From this viewpoint, goods are seen as bundles of characteristics, or *bundles of attributes* or *packages of benefits*, and the consumer as a producer of final satisfaction.

The notion of a product seen as a bundle of attributes is of central importance in strategic marketing. We shall put it in operational terms in section 4 of this chapter. The basic ideas of this model are very simple but extremely fertile; they constitute the theoretical foundations of benefit segmentation (Haley, 1968) and of positioning, as well as the corresponding product policies (Ratchford, 1975).

4.2.1 The multi-attribute product concept

The buying behaviour of consumers reflects the fact that they are motivated to seek rewarding experiences and satisfactions. The basic idea in marketing, as well as in the buyer behaviour theory, is the belief that *what the buyer is looking for is not a good, but the service or the solution to a problem that the good is likely to provide*. This simple but critical idea has important implications as far as product policy is concerned. The practical scope of the notion of product-service will become clearer in the light of the following propositions.

> PROPOSITION 1: *No one buys a product per se. Customers buy the product or the service for what they think it will do for them.*

Obviously, a car is not bought for its own sake, but for the service or the function it fulfils, namely autonomous individual transport. We are back to the distinction between a generic need and a derived need, seen in the previous chapter; one is not saturable, while the other is, particularly because of technological progress. Therefore, it is in the firm's interest to delimit its reference market with respect to the generic need or core function expected by the market when defining its mission, and not to a particular technology. For example, telex is disappearing from the market, but the need for fast communication is unchanged; nowadays it is better served by a fax. Similarly, integrated circuits today fulfil the same functions as lamps and transistors did not so long ago, only more efficiently.

This first proposition therefore advocates a *market* orientation rather than a *product* orientation, which carries the risk of myopia, as we saw in Chapter 1.

> PROPOSITION 2: *Different products can meet the same need.*

In order to meet a particular need or fulfil a particular function, the buyer usually has the possibility of choosing among different products. For example, if the basic function required is interior home decoration, there are at least four substitute alternatives: wallpapers, paint, wall textile, wood panels.

Substitute products are part of the reference market, although they may at times originate from sectors which are technologically very different. Only an analysis of the possible use of different products will allow the identification of the range of products the consumer may buy for a particular function. It is also essential to keep a close eye on the technological environment.

PROPOSITION 3: *Every product is a bundle of attributes or characteristics.*

Whether it is a product or a service, every good has a basic functional value or utility—*the core service*—to which *additional services*, generating secondary utilities of various nature, may be added. Such features may include brand image, after-sales service, etc., which improve or complete the core service. For instance, the basic function of toothpaste is to meet the need for dental hygiene, but it can also bring one or many additional utilities, such as decay prevention, gum protection, pleasant taste, etc. Similarly, a particular model of a car may present flexibility in its use, so that the car may serve both professional as well as leisure purposes.

These additional values or *added* services, may be objective or even simply perceptual; in the latter case they result from a brand image or from an advertising positioning which creates an effect of status or esteem. Some groups of buyers may prefer a particular brand simply because it offers this type of distinctive feature which they perceive as important, especially when different competitors cater to the core function equally well. In this kind of situation, it is often the secondary features which play a determining role in the formation of preferences. A firm can therefore choose to position itself with respect to one or the other of the sought attributes, and thus to address itself to a particular group of buyers.

PROPOSITION 4: *The very same product can meet different needs.*

Given that a good has many different attributes, one can imagine that the same good can meet the different needs of distinct groups of buyers, and thus fulfil different basic functions. This fact is often observed with industrial goods, which, contrary to consumer goods, often have a large number of different uses. Some examples are stainless steel, electric engines and petroleum products. The same microcomputer can meet a variety of needs of many groups of users: scientific calculations, word processing, video games or management of a small business firm. To each group of customers there corresponds a different core function. Hence, we have as many different product markets or segments as functions.

Levitt (1985, pp. 85–90) distinguishes between the notions of generic product, tangible product, augmented product and potential product:

- the *generic* product is the main service provided by the product

- the *tangible* product is all that normally goes with the generic product (delivery times, service, image)

- the *augmented* product is the extras offered by the vendor and the things that give the product its distinctive features compared to its competitors

- the *potential* product is all that is potentially feasible for attracting and keeping customers.

Therefore this is similar to the notion of the product concept which views products as a bundle of attributes.

The strategies of *benefit segmentation* (Haley, 1968) consist of a systematic search for new bundles of attributes for which there is no competing offering in the market, but which meet the expectations of a specific group of buyers. A market segmentation strategy therefore begins with the identification of the benefits sought by different groups of buyers; it then goes on to the development of product concepts aimed at meeting the specific requirements or expectations of the target group of potential buyers.

Several methods have been developed to operationalize the multi-attribute product concept. The most popular method is Conjoint Analysis (Green and Wind, 1975) which allows the measurement of the partial utilities that the potential buyer associates with each of the characteristics or attributes. On the basis of this information, the firm can then identify the set of attributes which best corresponds to the requirements of each market segment.

4.2.2 The dilemma of 'productivity versus diversity'

The notion of a product as a solution to a problem is therefore important for understanding segmentation strategies and the resulting proliferation of products and brands. In industrialized economies, the *logic of marketing* is based on the intensified need for novelty and change and on the growing personalization of behaviour. Taken to its extreme, the logic of marketing leads to products which are as diverse as market needs, even to the development of products tailor-made for personal preferences.

However, there exists an obvious limit to the phenomenon of segmentation which is imposed by the *logic of production*. Multiplying the models of the same product in order to meet diverse needs endangers the productivity of the production system by reducing the economies of scale obtained in mass production. The 'productivity versus diversity' dilemma may find a solution in new production technologies, such as flexible production systems, computerized production, robotics or new product concepts (Tarondeau, 1982) which are increasingly opening the way for reconciling these two requirements of successful management. The management of the interface between marketing, R&D and operations becomes of crucial importance in solving this kind of problem.

4.2.3 The domestic production function

The notion of a product as a solution to a problem underlines the fact that buyers' preferences are based directly on the satisfactions provided by goods; the overall utility level is itself derived from these satisfactions. If U_j denotes the utility function of buyer j, then we can write:

$$U_j = U_j \, [S_{1j}, S_{2j}, \ldots, S_{ij}, \ldots, S_{nj}] \tag{4-1}$$

where S_{ij} refers to the level of satisfaction i for each buyer. We said earlier that economic theory does not clarify the nature of these satisfactions; as far as the economist is concerned, the choices made simply reveal them. In the previous chapter, we examined the contributions made by theories of human motivation, suggesting three main motivational orientations which can explain a wide range of behaviour. Thus, from the marketing point of view, when we speak of the consumer's utility function, we mean the satisfactions sought by individuals. We therefore have:

$$U_j = U_j \text{ [functional, social, emotional, epistemic, conditional values]} \tag{4-2}$$

Buyers will look for defensive and creative goods, in order to maximize their utility. Similarly, when defining its product policy, the firm will endeavour to develop goods that can generate the satisfactions sought by the market, so as to best realize its own objectives.

Individual consumers seek the satisfactions provided by the services of a good and, guided by their basic motivations, they actively take part in this search. Based on these ideas, the theory of domestic production, due mostly to Becker (1965) and Lancaster (1966), explains the buying behaviour by treating consumers as economic agents who produce their own final satisfactions by combining time and commodities. The uniqueness of this theory lies in the fact that in the analysis of individual choice, time (t) is also treated as a scarce resource, like all the other factors entering into the production function.

We saw that preferences relate to satisfactions which provide an overall level of utility. Let us recall expression (1),

$$U_j = U_j \, [S_{1j}, S_{2j}, \ldots, S_{ij}, \ldots, S_{nj}]$$

Many satisfactions are sought, and they vary with the individual j. These satisfactions are 'produced' by the consumers themselves, through a series of personal production activities, i.e. the buying behaviour, which involves the use of commodities (x) as well as personal time (t). The productive efficiency of this domestic production depends on personal and on situational factors (E), such as the individual's competence, his or her cognitive capabilities, etc., or what we called the conditional value. Therefore, the domestic production function S_{ij}, corresponding to a particular satisfaction S_i sought by individual j, can be written

$$S_{ij} = S_{ij}[x_1, x_2, \ldots, t, E] \tag{4-3}$$

where x is the commodity, t is personal time and E denotes situational factors. In this expression, commodities and time are simply *inputs*, i.e. part of the means of production, just as raw materials are part of an industrial product.

> Thus, the objective of preparing a meal is to achieve culinary satisfaction and this necessitates the use of foodstuffs in various quantities (the x's) and of time spent for shopping, preparing, actual consumption of the meal and cleaning up. The variable E, for instance, may represent the cook's culinary competence, the presence of friends to share the meal (thus increasing the consumer's satisfaction) and a possible change in technology.   (Rosa, 1977, p. 164)

Note that, in this example, the meal may generate types of satisfaction other than just culinary: for example, the quality of the conversation exchanged during the meal may provide intellectual satisfaction. In fact, some of the participants may feel the latter more intensely than the culinary satisfaction. This brings us back to the idea that the same good can meet different needs and that individuals look for different satisfactions in the same good.

The theory continues as follows: consumers try to maximize their utility function subject to their monetary budget constraints and their time budget constraints. The monetary budget constraint of individual j can be written

$$R = \sum_{i=1}^{n} p_i . x_i \tag{4-4}$$

where R is monetary income and is the market price of good i. The constraint simply implies that the total monetary expenditure resulting from the purchase of good i should not exceed the individual's total monetary income from wages or other sources.

The time factor is taken into account because *time is our scarcest resource*, given that it cannot be expanded. Time is therefore not free in the sense that the time spent on domestic production activities is no longer available for other activities of leisure or work. There is an *option* or *opportunity cost*. When consumers spend time consuming, they cannot do other things. Economists measure this opportunity cost by the income forgone per unit of time consumed— that is, by the wages the individual could have earned in employment, given his or her abilities.

Let T denote total available time (24 hours a day). The time budget constraint may be written as follows:

$$T = t(w) + \sum_{i=1}^{n} t_i \tag{4-5}$$

where $t(w)$ is working time outside the home and t_i denotes various times of 'non-work' devoted to leisure and domestic production. The sum of the times devoted to each of these activities cannot exceed the total time budget. Therefore, consumer j tries to maximize the following utility function:

$$U_j = U_j[S_{1j}(x, t, E), S_{2j}(x, t, E), \ldots, S_{nj}(x, t, E)] \tag{4-6}$$

subject to the constraints (4) and (5) above.

The satisfactions included in the utility function may be very diverse; they depend not only on the individual's motivations, but also on the value they place on their time, as well as their ability to generate the satisfactions they seek efficiently. The nature of the satisfactions is not to be subjected to a value judgement. Marketing is *pluralist* in its approach, in the sense that it respects the diversity of tastes and preferences. Its only reservation is that certain constraints, imposed by the social, political, and moral environment which are the result of choices made by society, must be respected.

The introduction of the time factor in the domestic production function facilitates the analysis of consumption behaviour observed in opulent societies.

> In an economy, when the *per capita* income increases relative to the available volume of goods (because of increased labour productivity), the value of time also increases compared to the value of these goods. The increase in the relative value of time then leads to substitution effects in the domestic production function, such that the consumer is driven to using his time more economically.   (Rosa, 1977, p. 165)

Further analogy with production shows that it is rational for producers to save on a more costly resource and to alter their manufacturing process in such a way that the same final product is obtained with a lesser quantity of the resource which has an increased relative cost. Similarly, consumers will try to realize their preferences by means that are less time consuming.

> This is how the demand for ever faster means of transportation in rich countries is explained. Numerous services help to save time, such as those provided by fiscal experts, doctors, professors, garage owners, cookery books, frozen food, vacuum cleaners and television. Generally speaking, as the price of goods diminishes relative to time, the modern consumer uses more goods per unit of time.   (Rosa, 1977, p. 166)

Contrary to what some may suggest, the tendency to accumulate objects can be avoided, since these are individual choices and other forms of consumption are possible. The extreme case is the individual who, by choice lives in a state of ataraxy, i.e. using no objects, and is devoted to meditation and contemplation; the domestic production function for such a person will depend only on factors of circumstance (E) and on time (t).

The proposed conceptual framework is therefore quite broad and forms the *foundation of a theory of individual choice*, which can explain a wide range of behaviour from the most pronounced materialism to extreme frugality. The observed differences in the actual behaviour of individuals simply reflect differences in motivations and in the scales of personal values. To conclude this section, we shall quote the following from Abbott (1955, p. 41):

> What people desire are satisfying experiences. What is considered satisfying is a matter of individual decision; it varies according to one's tastes, standards, beliefs, and objectives— and these vary greatly, depending on individual personality and cultural environment. Here is a foundation for a theory of choice broad enough to embrace Asiatic as well as Western cultures, cynics, roisterers, religious fanatics, dullards and intellectual giants alike.

Consumers are viewed as people with their own objectives and their own scale of values, but this doesn't rule out the possibility that they might be influenced by their cultural, social and political environment.

4.3 MODELLING THE MULTI-ATTRIBUTE PRODUCT CONCEPT

We have seen that, from a buyer's point of view, a product or a brand can be defined as a 'bundle of attributes' which provides the buyer with the functional value or 'core service' specific to that class of product, as well as a set of secondary values or utilities that may be necessary or added. These additional services differentiate the brands and may have a determining influence on buyers' preferences. Here, we shall first discuss the different elements of this bundle and then conclude with a formal model of this notion.

4.3.1 The core service

The core service provided by a brand corresponds to *the functional value of its class of product*; it is the basic and generic benefit provided by each of the brands in a given product category. For a compressor, the core service is the production of compressed air; for a toothpaste, dental hygiene; for a watch, it will be time measurement; for an airline company, the transportation from Paris to New York; for wallpaper, home decoration, etc.

As underlined earlier, the core service defines the reference market in generic terms by providing an answer to the question: 'What business are we in?' The rationale is the following:

1. The buyer is not looking for a product as such, but for the core service it provides.
2. The buyer can get the same core service from technologically different products.
3. Technologies are moving and changing rapidly and profoundly, whereas the needs to which the core service responds, remain stable.

Levitt (1985) states that in order to avoid the risk of myopia, it is in the firm's best interest to define its *reference market* with respect to the core service provided, rather than to a particular technology. This allows the consumer to identify the alternative solutions likely to be considered when they are confronted with a choice problem.

All brands in the same reference market provide the buyer with the same core service in a way that tends to become uniform, given that competition and the diffusion of technological progress balance out technological performance. Consequently, in a significant number of markets, the core service by itself is no longer a determining factor in the buyer's decisions. The way in which the core service is provided or delivered becomes more of a deciding factor.

4.3.2 The peripheral services

In addition to the basic functional utility, a brand provides a series of other utilities or *peripheral services*, which are secondary compared to the core service, but which may prove to be decisive when competing brands tend to have even performances. These peripheral services may be of two kinds: 'necessary' services and 'added' services.

Necessary services identify with the mode of production of the core service (fuel efficiency, roominess, noise, etc.) and all that normally accompanies the core service (packaging, delivery, payment terms, after sales service etc.). For example, Atlas-Copco 'oil-free' compressors produce compressed air which is totally free of oil particles; Epson printers are particularly quiet; Japanese cars are well known for their reliability; Apple microcomputers are very user-friendly; Bang & Olufsen products have an outstanding design; Swatch has a large variety of designs, and so on.

Added services are utilities unrelated to the core service, which the brand provides as extras. Hence they constitute an important source of differentiation. For instance, Singapore Airlines offers free movies and drinks on board in economy class; some makes of cars include radio equipment in their basic price; some credit cards give the right to preferential conditions in five-star hotels; etc.

These peripheral services themselves, whether necessary or added, form attributes which generate *satisfaction* for the buyer. These attributes may differ greatly according to the brand and can thus be used as choice criteria. Furthermore, one can imagine that different buyers attach different degrees of importance to the presence of some attributes. Thus, a brand can be defined as a bundle of attributes which produce the core service plus the peripheral services, necessary or added, whose importance and performance can be differently perceived by potential buyers.

Note that any brand has at least one unique feature (generally more than one), which is simply its brand name. The buyer's global perception of a brand is commonly referred to as *the brand image*.

4.3.3 The multi-attribute product model

Based on the above general observations, we can proceed to operationalize the multi-attribute product concept, attempting to provide predictive value as well as descriptive and explanatory value of actual buying behaviour. Table 4.1 shows the various elements which enter into the

TABLE 4.1 *Modelling the multi-attribute product concept*

Objective characteristics	Attributes	Evaluation of attributes		Partial utilities	Total utility
		Importance	Performance		
$\ldots C_{1i} \ldots$	A_1	W_1	X_1	u_1	
$\ldots C_{2i} \ldots$	A_2	W_2	X_2	u_2	U
$\vdots$	$\vdots$	$\vdots$	$\vdots$	$\vdots$	
$\ldots C_{ni} \ldots$	A_n	W_n	X_n	u_n	
Reality	Bundle of attributes	Priorities	Beliefs	Value system	
Technical specifications	Exploratory study	Ratio scale	Interval scale	Integrative model	

Source: Lambin (1989).

model. Combining these elements, we can derive a measure of the total utility perceived from a particular brand for a given buyer.

Let us now consider in detail the various elements that determine the global perception of a brand by an individual. The following discussion is mostly based on theoretical work by Rosenberg (1956) and Fishbein (1967).

The notion of attribute

The term *attribute* refers to the benefit sought by the buyer; it is the attribute that 'generates' the service and the satisfaction and thus is used as a choice criterion. Using the previous examples, it is the 'design' of a watch, the 'reliability' of a car, the 'quietness' of a printer, the 'status effect' of garments, the 'purity of compressed air' produced by a compressor, etc.

As we mentioned before, the buyer generally takes many attributes into account. The overall evaluation of a brand is based on the combination of the evaluations of each attribute. These attributes can be of a functional nature (power, roominess), but also emotional or aesthetic in nature. It must be emphasized that only *relevant attributes* should be considered. Most products typically feature many functional attributes that are not pertinent to buyer decision making in that they do not suggest meaningful benefit to the user.

Given that the desired service may have many dimensions, one should avoid defining attributes in terms that are too general. For instance, the attribute of 'economical' is often mentioned by potential buyers, but it is too vague a criterion and may in fact combine other attributes. When talking about a car, the advantage of being 'economical' may result from at least three micro-attributes: low price, low running costs and low maintenance costs. Each brand can be evaluated differently on each of the micro-attributes, and it is therefore important to consider each separately.

This is also the case of the attribute 'quality', which is a *macro-attribute* covering a large number of dimensions. An attribute is in fact a discrete variable, that is, it can take on different values according to the degree of presence of the attribute in the brand being evaluated. One then considers the *level* of an attribute. Each brand constitutes a specific bundle of attributes due to the fact that the latter are present at specific levels.

The objective characteristics   These characteristics are what precede the attributes, i.e. the technical features that generate or produce the attribute. They correspond to the technical specifications of the brand or product. In general, several combined characteristics are required to generate the attribute. For example, comfort in a car results from the presence of many characteristics: independent 'four wheel' suspension, roominess of the cabin, seat structure, etc. Similarly, a supermarket is 'convenient' not only for its location, but equally for its ease of access, parking space, queuing time at cash registers, etc.

If evaluation is to cover objective characteristics, it is important to avoid those which are redundant, given that some characteristics are related. For example, the 'power' of a car depends on the size of its engine, which, in turn, contributes towards increasing its weight and dimensions; these characteristics are therefore intercorrelated, and a judgement on one of them is enough to evaluate the others.

In general, a potential buyer is not very interested in objective characteristics, except when these reinforce the performance of the brand in the production of one of the benefits sought, or when they increase the credibility of an expected performance. For example, the plasma screen of portable microcomputers is a technical characteristic which provides the user with reading comfort; the presence of fluorine in toothpastes helps to reinforce the credibility of the function 'preventing tooth decay'; the logo of a great fashion designer is enough to create the prestige or status effect sought by some groups of buyers.

Knowledge of buyers' requirements and/or expectations gives an important incentive to research and development (R&D). Its role is to find technical characteristics which help meet market expectations that are as yet unsatisfied, or improve performance of existing products thus creating competitive advantage for the pioneering firm. Gore-Tex is a good example in this respect. This is a microporous membrane in expanded PTFE used in the production of sports garments, among others things. This material is ventilated and permeable with respect to perspiration, but doesn't let rain or wind through, and thus gives the user a level of comfort which is superior to any other material. The brand uses the following advertising theme: 'Waterproof garments that breath like your skin.'

The interface between R&D and strategic marketing is crucial at the stage of product concept development. This search for distinctive qualities could potentially give a new product a competitive edge.

Evaluation of attributes
Buyers evaluate attributes or characteristics on the basis of two kinds of consideration: the degree of importance of each attribute and the beliefs about where each compared brand or product stands on each attribute.

Importance of attributes   All attributes do not have the same importance in the eyes of the buyer. For an individual, *attribute importance* reflects the values and priorities that he or she puts on each of the benefits provided by the brand.

Any reasonable person wishes to obtain more in exchange for less: best service, best performance, lowest price, minimum search time, complete information, etc. Since these objectives are generally irreconcilable, individuals are forced to arrive at compromises and to decide, in each specific situation, what is more important, given the ever-imperfect information at hand.

Attributes may be important but not determinant in the choice process. *Determinant attributes* are those which permit discrimination among brands. An attribute that is equally present in all the brands being compared, does not help in their differentiation and hence cannot be determinant in the choice (Myers and Alpert, 1976). The price is always an important criterion but not necessarily determinant, when, for example, all competing brands have exactly the same price.

Salient attributes are those that come spontaneously to a consumer's mind when asked to think of product attributes. These are not necessarily the most important attributes to the consumer. Attribute importance and determinance are more significant concepts than attribute salience.

The firm's knowledge of the expectations of different groups of buyers can lead to the development of new products which constitute new or improved bundles of attributes specifically designed to meet these expectations.

- Bang & Olufsen offers products designed for buyers who are particular about aesthetics and are willing to pay the price.

- Fluocaril, a brand of toothpaste, emphasizes the aspect of tooth decay prevention and addresses consumers who are sensitive to medical prevention.

- The 'oil-free' compressors of Atlas-Copco are particularly suitable for manufacturing sectors where the purity of the compressed air is important in the manufacturing process (pharmaceutical products, fine textiles, etc.)

- The design of Swatch watches suits buyers who like to follow the latest fashion.

Therefore, the knowledge of the attributes' relative importance can enable firms to develop *segmentation strategies*. The objective is to stick to the diversity of needs as well as possible, and avoid a situation where buyers are forced to be content with products of average performance with respect to each of the attributes.

Potential buyers are able to conceptualize the importance level of attributes and to communicate their perceptions in surveys. Ideally, the importance score of an attribute should be measured on a constant sum scale (from 0 to 100). When the number of attributes is too large, the respondent's task becomes difficult and an importance scale (from 1 to 5) will be used instead. Example of scales are presented in Appendix 5.1.

Perceived presence of an attribute   A buyer may feel that a particular attribute is very important, but at the same time perceive a particular brand as not exhibiting that attribute well enough. Hence, measures of importance need to be complemented with measures of beliefs as to the presence of attributes, also called *performance scores*.

People's perceptions are selective and relative. They are *selective* because attention is selective, given that individuals tend to filter the information to which they are exposed; some elements are retained because they fit in well with a current need or experience; others are distorted when they contradict the established framework; finally, others are rejected because they are worrying or simply disturbing (Pinson *et al.*, 1988). Furthermore, perceptions are *relative* because individuals' experiences and expectations are varied. Hence, the degree of presence of attributes is perceived differently.

Therefore individuals have perceptions about the presence of attributes in brands. These perceptions may be based on experience, collected information, friends' or neighbours' opinions, advertising or purely personal impressions. It doesn't really matter. Although they may not correspond to the brand's real nature, they do constitute the components of the brand image and of the brand equity. These perceptions form the reality with which the firm must deal, even if the true nature of the brand is different. Market research shows that respondents are able to express their views about the brands they know, and that these perceptions are measurable.

To recognize a brand, the consumer uses not only the brand name, but also other observable signals, such as packaging, design, logo, colour codes, etc. These externally visible signals form an integral part of the brand's equity, given that they are used by buyers to classify brands in terms of the type of promise they represent.

Any policy of systematic imitation of the observable characteristics, aimed at maximizing similarities in order to convince buyers that the bundle of attributes and services provided is identical to those of the imitated brand, is a form of market intoxication which, from a societal point of view, is as reprehensible as false advertising or forgery. These practices, which are sometimes adopted by private brands, create confusion in the market and complicate the process of well-informed choice desired by the buyer.

4.3.4 Estimating values and partial utilities

The value of an attribute to an individual depends on the association of two factors entering into the evaluation. These two factors are: the importance of the attribute and its perceived degree of presence. This value is referred to as the attribute's *partial utility*; each attribute will have such a subjective value attached to it. These values are the product of the perceived degree of presence of an attribute and its importance.

A brand's *total utility* for a given buyer is then assumed to be either the sum, or the product of the partial utilities he or she attaches to each attribute.

$$U = u_1(x_1) + u_2(x_2) + \cdots + u_i(x_i) + \cdots + u_n(x_n)$$

where U is the brand's total utility, u_i is the partial utility of attribute i and x_i is the perceived level of attribute i. In order to determine total utility, a model of integrating partial utilities is required. The model most often used is *compensatory and additive*:

- compensatory, because a low mark given to an attribute can be compensated by a high mark given to another

- additive, because it is assumed that there is no interaction between attributes.

In the following chapter, we shall see that other models of integrating partial utilities can be adopted, namely *non-compensatory models* which are applicable when the buyer privileges one or several attributes (disjunctive model) or when minimal values are imposed on the attributes' performance scores (conjunctive model).

4.3.5 Measuring the multi-attribute product concept

To estimate a brand's total and partial utilities, two estimation procedures are possible: 'compositional' or 'decompositional'. The *compositional* approach consists of constructing the total utility score on the basis of measures of importance and beliefs on determinant attributes, obtained through surveys. Using a compensatory or non-compensatory integration model to combine these measures, a total utility score is obtained which synthesizes individuals' partial evaluations and thus reveals their preferences.

In the *decompositional* approach, respondents react to a set of product concepts, described generally in terms of characteristics. The information to be collected from respondents is limited to a ranking of preferences for the proposed product concepts. The analyst's job is then to derive the partial utilities of each characteristic level. Starting from the preferential ranking of different bundles, the underlying partial utilities are estimated by statistical inference, with the necessary constraints to reconstruct best the original preferences ranking.

In this approach, one directly estimates partial utilities which combine importance and beliefs, without being able to identify them separately. Therefore, a high level of utility can result from either a very high level of importance and a low level of perceived degree of presence, or from a low level of importance compensated by a high level of perceived degree of presence. Various other estimation methods exist. The most common and most reliable method is econometric estimation with binary variables (0, 1). The next chapter will present a more detailed discussion of these methods.

The estimation of utility functions enables us to make predictions about individuals' choices when they face different brands, or different bundles of attributes. Irrespective of the approach adopted, it is important to emphasize the fact that buyers' preferences are observable and measurable, and tests of their predictive power have proved to be conclusive on the whole (Wittink and Walsh, 1988).

4.4 THE BUYER AND THE NEED FOR INFORMATION

The theory of domestic production suggests that consumers do not buy a product but a set of satisfaction-generating attributes, and, furthermore, that they actively participate in the production of the benefits sought. However, they still need to be aware of the existing possibilities for solving the problem they face. Yet, due to the constant increase in the number of products and brands available in the market, the ratio of the information held by the average individual to total available information continues to decrease. In most cases, therefore, consumers must necessarily make decisions based on incomplete information and on the limited number of options they can perceive.

The *evoked set* (Fig. 4.2) is the set of all alternatives that the individual takes, or can take, into consideration at the time of purchase (Howard and Sheth, 1969, p. 26). The evoked set can be very different from the overall set, which includes all available alternatives. The extent of the

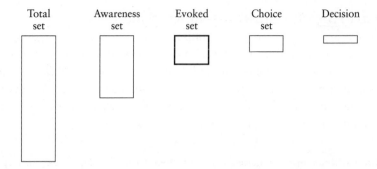

FIGURE 4.2 *The notion of evoked set* (Source: *Howard and Sheth, 1969*)

evoked set varies with the perceived risk associated with the purchase decision and according to the individual's cognitive abilities.

Given that the choice of the consumer can only be over a limited number of alternatives which can be perceived at any given moment, it is clear that the structure of the consumer's preferences changes necessarily as his or her experiences reveal new characteristics and new possibilities of choice that were previously unknown to the individual. However, this improved perception of products and their distinctive qualities does not come freely; it requires some research, which takes time and implies some information cost. In this section, we shall examine the types of information sought by consumers and the way in which they use information from advertising.

4.4.1 The cost of information

An individual facing a problem of choice, undertakes the search for information mainly to reduce uncertainty about available alternatives, their relative values and the terms and conditions of purchase. We can classify the various costs incurred by this information search into three categories (Lévy-Garboua, 1976).

- *Inspection costs*, implied by studying different markets and defining the range of possibilities (including substitutes) that the buyer could include in the set being contemplated.

- *Perception costs*, borne in view of identifying the relevant characteristics of goods included in the choice set, as well as the terms of exchange (places of purchase, price, guarantee, etc.).

- *Evaluation costs*, resulting from the evaluation of how often the sought attributes are present and how authentic the market signals are about the quality of goods.

These costs are mainly in the form of time spent. But the cost of time—measured by its opportunity cost—varies from individual to individual; it also varies with factors of circumstance. For example, the cost of time is not the same during a holiday as it is during a period of work. Therefore, it is not always in the consumer's interest to prolong the information search beyond a certain level. The extent of searching efforts will also vary with the degree of perceived risk in the buying decision under consideration.

TABLE 4.2 *Information search intensity per product category*

Product category	Percentage of purchases by number of stores visited		
	One store	Two stores	Three stores or more
Toys	87.4	6.1	6.5
Small electrical appliances	60.0	16.0	22.0
Refrigerators	42.0	16.0	42.0
Living room furniture	22.8	13.4	62.1
New cars and major appliances	49.0	26.0	23.0

Source: Loudon and della Bitta (1984, p. 620).

The economic theory of information helps to formalize this problem, i.e. a situation where the only question is that of possible financial loss as a result of too high a purchase price. Denote by ΔI the additional information, Δp the resulting decrease in price, q the volume of purchase and Δc the change in costs allocated for obtaining this information. New information can be justified as long as the following condition is satisfied,

$$q(\Delta p/\Delta I) \geqslant \Delta c$$

in other words, as long as the expected gain is higher than the cost of obtaining the information. From this relationship, we can deduce the following propositions (Farley, 1964):

1. As the size of the purchase increases, whether in quantity or in value, the importance of additional information will also increase.
2. There will be a tendency to observe less inertia among large buyers than small ones.
3. There will be less call for information among consumers who put a higher value on their time and assign a higher cost to extra information.

These propositions are simply the interpretation of the marginalist logic whereby the individual does a cost–benefit analysis and chooses the most satisfactory solution. Farley (1964) and Roselius (1971) have observed this kind of behaviour experimentally.

The data in Table 4.2 are from various surveys in the United States. It describes the number of retail stores visited before the actual purchase in terms of the type of product. We see that for goods with low unit costs, most buyers are happy with visiting a single salespoint; for products of a higher value, the number of places visited increases.

4.4.2 The sources of information

The cost of perceiving attributes varies with the observable nature of products. Nelson (1970, p. 214) establishes a distinction between goods with external qualities and those with internal qualities. For the first category, the product attributes can easily be checked before purchase by simple inspection; these are products such as clothing, furniture and toys for which the choice criteria can easily be verified with little cost. For products with internal qualities, however, the most important characteristics are only revealed with use, after purchase. Examples of this type of product are books, medicines, cars and computers. For this type of product, perception costs can be very high for a single individual, but the efficiency of surveying can be improved by using different sources of information, which have various degrees of reliability:

■ Information sources *dominated by the producer*; in other words, advertising, opinions and advice given by sellers and distributors, displays and brochures. The advantage of this kind of information is that it is free and easily accessible. The information is, however, incomplete and biased, in the sense that it emphasizes the positive qualities of the product and tends to overshadow others.

■ Personal information sources, *dominated by consumers*; this is information communicated by friends, neighbours, opinion leaders, and is better known as 'word of mouth'. This kind of information is often well adapted to the needs of the future buyer. Its reliability obviously depends on that of the person transmitting the information.

■ Information sources that are *neutral*, such as articles published in newspapers and reviews specializing in housing, furnishing, hunting, audio-visual and automobiles. Such publications often provide a lot of information at a relatively low cost. This category also includes publications such as official reports or reports of specialized agencies, laboratory tests and comparative tests initiated by consumer associations. The advantage of this source of information is its objectivity, its factual nature and the competence of the opinions reported.

It is worth emphasizing here the specific role played by *consumer associations*. In a situation where the perception of the attributes of a product is particularly costly, it is in the interest of the individual consumer to regroup with other consumers in order to proceed with a thorough analysis that would be impossible for an individual alone. This is a form of unionization of consumers, which constitutes a countervailing force *vis-à-vis* the firm, and has the reduction of the cost of information to the consumer as its main objective.

The most important limitation of the consumerist information is that the comparative tests generally concentrate only on criteria which determine the basic function of a product, without considering any secondary criteria such as aesthetics, attractiveness, ease of use, etc. Consumerist surveys implicitly assume that only the functional value matters and not the other values that accompany it. This is a value judgement which ignores the fact that goods can generate many different satisfactions and, in particular, 'pleasure and stimulation' to their buyer.

> ... and what shall we say about a decorative vase, one that graces a living room even when it is empty of flowers? Can the very shape that gives it beauty be said to 'interface with its uses'? The idea that efficiency is concerned only with practical uses and not with aesthetic ones, is in itself a value judgement.   (Abbott, 1955, p. 45)

Despite this limitation, the use of consumerist information is becoming the second best choice for an increasing number of consumers in affluent societies, particularly as the cost of time increases continuously and as the number of weakly differentiated products multiplies.

4.4.3 The role of advertising information

In Europe, in 1994, total media advertising expenditures represented 0.82 per cent of the gross domestic product (GDP). This is an average rate calculated over 16 European countries. Obviously, this rate varies from one country to another, as shown in Table 4.3. This average rate of advertising intensity is significantly lower than the one observed in the USA, which is 1.41 per cent of GDP.

On the whole, advertising expenditure has followed the growth rate of GDP, and this regular increase in expenditure suggests the efficiency of advertising for the producer. It is indeed difficult to accept that firms would comply with expenditures of this size over long periods if it were not profitable. Consequently, we are drawn to formulating the assumption that advertising also has utility for consumers, because they clearly use advertising information in some form in their buying process.

Of course, it can be said that advertising encourages waste and can make people buy anything. If this were really the case, the share of advertising in the GDP would be much higher, since it would be possible to sell more by advertising more. Firms which use advertising intensively are quite aware of the deceptiveness of this argument. Empirical studies done to measure the extent of the economic efficiency of advertising (see Lambin, 1976) also contradict this argument. Furthermore, the theory of encouragement to waste is also in contradiction with the conclusions of macroeconomic studies which show that, in the long run, the propensity to save has proved very stable in industrial economies despite the growth of absolute advertising intensity.

TABLE 4.3 *Indicators of advertising intensity in Europe (1994)*

	Total expenditure (in million ECU)	Per capita expenditure (current prices, ECU)	Advertising as percentage of GDP (at market prices)
Austria	1243	155.8	0.75
Belgium	1142	113.2	0.59
Denmark	995	191.5	0.80
Finland	704	138.4	0.85
France	7369	127.8	0.66
Germany	15 476	190.2	0.90
Greece	815	78.3	1.01
Ireland	390	109.0	0.88
Italy	4207	73.6	0.49
The Netherlands	2514	163.9	0.90
Norway	717	165.1	0.77
Portugal	593	60.1	0.80
Spain	3570	91.2	0.88
Sweden	1332	152.3	0.80
Switzerland	1831	291.6	0.98
UK	9692	166.3	1.13

Source: European Associations of Advertising Agencies (EAAA), Brussels (1995).

The utility of advertising, as far as the consumer is concerned, becomes more evident when one considers the objectives of communication pursued by producers who use advertising or any other form of communication with the market, such as the salesforce, for example. For the producer, advertising is a factor of production, like expenditures on raw materials and transport. Its purpose is to inform consumers and make them conscious of the existence of alternative solutions to their problem of choice—solutions which constitute different bundles of attributes or distinctive characteristics. As explained by Kirzner (1973, p. 155): '. . . the aim of advertising, and of sales costs in general, is to produce knowledge for consumers, in order to create demand for the product.'

It makes no sense to speak of demand for a product whose existence is unknown to consumers. The producer cannot simply develop a new product; this product will only really exist when consumers have been informed of its existence. Without advertising information, the product continues not to exist, in the same way that the American continent did not exist for centuries, as far as the peoples of the Western hemisphere were concerned, simply because its reality was unknown.

Information is therefore inseparable from the product itself. But informing is not sufficient; there must be communication. No matter how complete information may be, it does not exist, as far as the consumer is concerned, as long as it has not been perceived, understood and memorized. This explains why advertising must be attractive. In a situation where the individual is exposed to a lot of information and is constantly bombarded with advertising messages that are varied and often contradictory, the advertiser might resort to more and more aggressive means to ensure that an advertising message is perceived, understood and memorized. These may include an appeal to the imagination, to humour or to dreams, the use of slogans or images with a strong psychological content, or may even call upon theatre or sports personalities to broadcast the message. All these means, which often upset the observer, are designed to make the message forceful, to cut through the public's wall of indifference and thus make information more striking. Kirzner (1973, p. 162) underlines this notion as follows:

> It is not so much, perhaps, that effective communication needs to be persuasive as that it needs to be eye-catching, mind-catching, and reinforced by constant repetition.

In other words, the specific forms adopted for advertising information should not obscure the nature of its purpose, which is to reduce the perception costs to the consumer.

The value of advertising information
Given that advertising information is an information source dominated by the producer, it does not have the same value as other sources of information in the eyes of the consumer. It is indeed a *sales appeal*, which generates information designed to emphasize the positive aspects of the product. However, as far as the consumer is concerned, the utility of this type of information is two-fold:

1. On the one hand, the consumer can *get to know the distinctive qualities* claimed by the producer and can see if the product's 'promises' correspond to what the consumer is seeking.

2. On the other hand, it helps to *save personal time*, since the consumer obtains the information without having to collect it.

Lepage (1982, p. 53), underlines the fact that the important point for the consumers is that the efficiency of the advertising message intended to reach them should be higher than it would have cost them to collect the same information by other means—for example, by displacing themselves. These two services performed by advertising have the effect of helping the consumer to perceive opportunities of choice and of new potential forms of satisfaction at a minimum cost.

Nevertheless, one question needs to be asked: What confidence can one have in advertising information? The credibility that the consumer attaches to information from the producer differs according to the type of product. Earlier, we saw the distinction made between goods with external and internal qualities (Nelson, 1970).

For products with *external* qualities, advertising can provide credible information for consumers, because they know that the information can be objectively verified before purchase. Both consumers and advertisers know that, for this type of product, there is no room for advertising that is misleading or deceptive, because the penalty of the market is almost immediate. The same reasoning applies to products that are purchased repeatedly and have a low price; since the cost of an error of a test purchase is low, one might as well trust the advertising and follow its advice. If the product does not meet with expectations, it will not be bought again; the penalty is immediate.

For products with *internal* qualities, things are less evident, particularly in the case of durable goods with a long economic life where the possibility of deceiving the consumer is real. The question is to know whether the producer remains non-liable in the case of deceptive advertising. In fact, as Nelson explains, this is a double-edged weapon. If a well-known product proves to be of bad quality, it also becomes well known for being so. The misfortunes of some brands which have been placed on the blacklist by consumer associations show how difficult it is to regain the confidence of consumers once they have had bad experiences with a particular brand.

The role of advertising for products with internal qualities is therefore to link correctly the brand to its function and thus provide indirect information, for instance, on the firm's reputation. As far as the consumer is concerned, the interesting information is to know that a given firm is advertising, hence claiming publicly the market's penalty for its products. Quoting Nelson (1974, p. 732):

> The minuscule amount of direct information from advertising for experience qualities gives the consumer an incentive to extract any conceivable indirect information that would help. Such indirect information is available from advertising. The consumer can learn what the brand advertises. I contend that this is the useful information that the consumer absorbs from the endorsements of announcers, actors, and others who are paid for their encomiums, etc. Their total informational role—beyond the relation of brand to function—is simply contained in their existence. The consumer believes that the more a

brand advertises, the more likely it is to be a better buy. In consequence, the more advertisements of a brand the consumer encounters, the more likely he is to try the brand.

It seems logical indeed to assume *a priori* that the brand offering the best guarantee is the one that has invested the most in advertising, particularly if it is a good which is bought repeatedly and for which it is crucial, therefore, to have a high degree of loyalty.

This behaviour, which contradicts the saying '*à bon vin point d'enseigne*', is however, not the only possible behaviour of a consumer. It is observed that in practice, consumers tend to use many sources of information when dealing with products with internal qualities (Bucklin, 1965; Newman, 1979). It is equally for this type of product that consumerist information is mostly justified.

SUMMARY

The individual or the organization actively takes part in buying decisions in order to make choice in a systematic way. Purchasing behaviour is seen as a process of problem solving, the extent of which depends on the importance of the perceived risk associated with the purchase. Purchasing behaviour is rational within *the principle of limited rationality*, i.e. within the bounds of individuals' cognitive and learning capacities. From the buyer's point of view, the product is seen as a solution to a problem and as a package of benefits which provides the buyer with a functional value or 'core service' specific to that class of product as well as a set of secondary values or utilities. This product concept is formalized in the utility theory by the domestic production function and by the multi-attribute product model which can be empirically estimated through two distinct estimation procedures, the *compositional* and/or the *decompositional* approach, both currently used in marketing research. The individual or the organization facing a problem of choice undertakes the search for information to reduce uncertainty about the available alternatives, their values and conditions of purchase. The extent of the information search is also dependent on the perceived risk associated with the buying decision. Different sources of information of various degrees of reliability are available. Advertising information provides the buyer with (1) knowledge of the distinctive qualities claimed by the seller for the product and (2) a saving in personal time since the information is obtained at low cost. The credibility of advertising information differs, however, according to products with external or internal qualities.

QUESTIONS AND PROBLEMS

1. Marketing describes buying behaviour as a rational problem-solving process. Develop this proposition by describing the process of consumer decision making in situations of various degrees of risk and complexity.
2. You have invited a close friend to dine out and are hesitating over five restaurants you know well which are all in the price range. Think about this for a moment and make an instinctive decision. Write down your choice. Next, using the multi-attribute product model, calculate

the utility scale for each restaurant. Check to see if the restaurant with the highest utility score is the one you have chosen earlier. How would you proceed if the restaurants had not all been within the same price range?

3. Think about the recent purchase of a durable good (TV, camera, microcomputer, . . .). Try to recall the actual decision process that led you to buy it. Identify the information channels used and your type of problem-solving behaviour.

4. Select two advertisements from newspapers or magazines, one emphasizing the external qualities of a product, and the other emphasizing the internal qualities. Compare the content of the messages as well as the quantity of information provided in each case. In your opinion, what is the communication objective of these advertisements?

5. Pick out a product or a service which you know well as a user and for which you feel that you have a good level of expertise. Identify the characteristics or attributes that you consider to be most important and compare them with the attributes that are highlighted in advertising for this kind of product. What advice would you give to someone who might be interested in buying this type of product?

6. Consider the following products or services: an airline trip, a dishwasher, a stereo set, a heavy-duty truck. Identify the core service, the peripheral services, necessary and added, for each product.

REFERENCES

Abbott, L. (1955), *Quality and Competition*. New York: Columbia Press.

BIS, (1990), *60th Annual Report*, Basle: Bank for International Settlements.

Bauer, R.A. (1960), Consumer Behaviour as Risk Taking, in Hancock A.S. (ed.), *Proceedings of the Fall Conference of the American Marketing Association*, June, pp. 389–98.

Becker, G.S. (1965), 'A Theory of the Allocation of Time', *The Economic Journal*, September.

Bucklin, L.P. (1965), 'The Informative Role of Advertising', *Journal of Advertising Research*, vol. 5.

BBL (1989). 'Taux d'épargne et endettement des ménages', *Bulletin Financier*, 2233, September–October.

Farley, J.V. (1964), 'Brand Loyalty and the Economics of Information', *Journal of Business*, vol. 37, October, pp. 370–81.

Fishbein, M. (1967), Attitudes and Prediction of Behaviour, in Fishbein M. (ed.), *Readings in Attitude Theory and Measurement*. New York: John Wiley & Sons.

Friedman, M. (1957), *A Theory of the Consumption Function*. Princeton: Princeton University Press.

Green P.E. and Y. Wind (1975), 'New Ways to Measure Consumers' Judgments', *Harvard Business Review*, July–August, pp. 107–17.

Haley, R.I. (1968), 'Benefit Segmentation: A Decision-Oriented Research Tool', *Journal of Marketing*, July, pp. 30–5.

Howard, J.A. and J.N. Sheth (1969), *The Theory of Buyer Behaviour*, New York: John Wiley and Sons.

Keynes, J.M. (1936), *The General Theory of Employment, Interest and Money*. London: Macmillan & Co. Ltd.

Kirzner, I.M. (1973), *Competition and Entrepreneurship*. Chicago: The Chicago University Press.

Kuznets, S. (1946), *National Product Since 1869*. New York: National Bureau of Economic Research.

Lambin, J.J. (1976), *Advertising, Competition and Market Conduct in Oligopoly Over Time*. Amsterdam: North Holland Publishing Co.

Lambin, J.J. (1989), La marque et le comportement de choix de l'acheteur, in Kapferer J.N. and Thoenig J.C. (eds), *La marque*. Paris: Ediscience International.

Lancaster, K.J. (1966), 'A New Approach to Consumer Theory', *The Journal of Political Economy*, Vol. 74, April, pp. 132–57.

Lepage, H. (1982), *Vive le commerce*. Paris: Dunod, Collection l'Oeil Économique.

Levitt, T. (1985), *L'imagination au service du marketing*. Paris: Economica.

Lévy-Garboua, L. (1976), La nouvelle théorie des consommateurs et la formation des choix, *Consommation*, no. 3.

Loudon, D.L. and A.J. della Bitta (1984), *Consumer Behaviour: Concepts and Applications*, 2nd edn. New York: McGraw-Hill Book Co.

Myers, J.H. and M.L. Alpert (1976), Semantic Confusion in Attitude Research: Salience versus Importance versus Determinance, in Perreault, W.D. (ed.), *Advances in Consumer Research*, Proc. 7th Annual Conference of the Association of Consumer Research, October, pp. 106–10.

Nelson, D. (1970), 'Information and Consumer Behaviour', *The Journal of Political Economy*, vol. 78, March–April, pp. 311–29.

Nelson, D. (1974), 'Advertising as Information', *The Journal of Political Economy*, vol. 82, July–August, pp. 729–54.

Newman, J.W. (1979), 'Consumer External Research: Amounts and Determinants', in Bettman, R. (ed.), *An Information Processing Theory of Consumer Choice*. Reading, Mass.: Addison Wesley.

Pinson, C., N.K. Malhotra and A.K. Jain (1988), 'Les styles cognitifs des consommateurs', *Recherche et Applications en Marketing*, vol. 3, No. 1, pp. 53–73.

Ratchford, B.T. (1975), 'The New Economic Theory of Consumer Behaviour', *Journal of Consumer Research*, vol. 2, September, pp. 65–78.

Rosa, J.J. (1977), 'Vrais et faux besoins', in Rosa J.J. and F. Aftalion (éds), *L'économique retrouvé*. Paris: Economica, pp. 155–92.

Roselius, T. (1971), 'Consumer Rankings of Risk Reduction Methods', *Journal of Marketing*, vol. 35, January, pp. 56–61.

Rosenberg, M.J. (1956), 'Cognitive Structure and Attitudinal Affect', *Journal of Abnormal and Social Psychology*, vol. 53, pp. 367–72.

Tarondeau, J.C. (1982), Sortir du dilemme flexibilité-productivité, *Harvard–L'Expansion*, Spring, pp. 25–35.

Wilkie, W.L. (1990), *Consumer Behaviour*, 2nd edn. New York: J. Wiley & Sons.

Wittink, D.R. and J.W. Walsh (1988), *Conjoint Analysis: Its Reliability, Validity and Usefulness*. Proc. Sawtooth Conference, April.

CHAPTER 5

MARKETING RESEARCH AND INFORMATION SYSTEMS

LEARNING OBJECTIVES

After reading this chapter, you should be able to understand:

■ the importance of market information in a market-driven company

■ the structure of a market information system

■ why marketing research must be scientifically conducted

■ the differences between exploratory, descriptive and causal research

■ the characteristics of the methods for collecting primary data.

*T*he central problem confronting a market-oriented organization is how to monitor the needs of the marketplace and the macro-marketing environment in order to be able to anticipate the future. In response to this need for information, the concept of a formalized market information system (MIS) has emerged to acquire and to distribute market data within the organization and to facilitate market-oriented decisions. The objective of an MIS is to integrate marketing data (internal accounting data, salespeople's reports, marketing services data, marketing research studies and so on) into a continuous information flow for marketing decision making. Within an MIS, marketing research has mainly an *ad hoc* data-gathering and analysis function to perform. Marketing research can supply information regarding many aspects of the marketplace. In this chapter, we shall review the main tasks and preoccupations of marketing research.

5.1 STRUCTURE OF A MARKET INFORMATION SYSTEM

Few managers are happy with the type of market information they receive. The usual complaints are:

- Available information is very often not relevant to decision needs.

- There is too much information to be used effectively.

- Information is spread throughout the firm and is difficult to locate.

- Key information arrives too late to be useful or is destroyed.

- Some managers may withhold information from the other functions.

- The reliability and accuracy of information is difficult to verify.

The role of MIS is to study information needs carefully, to design an information system to meet these needs, to centralize the information available and to organize its dissemination throughout the organization. A marketing information system has been defined as follows:

> A marketing information system is a continuing and interacting structure of people, equipment and procedures to gather, sort, analyse, evaluate and distribute pertinent, timely and accurate information for use by marketing decision makers to improve their marketing planning, implementation and control.
>
> (Smith *et al.*, 1968, quoted by Kotler, 1984, p. 188)

The importance of a market information system (MIS) has already been mentioned in Chapter 2 (see Section 2.4.4). The structure of an MIS is illustrated in Fig. 5.1. The figure shows the macro-marketing environment to be monitored by management. These flows of information are captured and analysed through three subsystems of data collection: the internal accounting

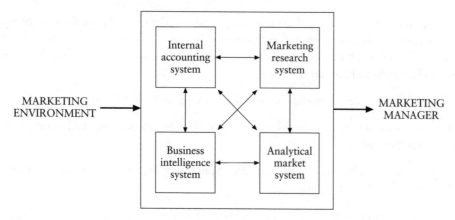

FIGURE 5.1 *Structure of a market information system*

system, the business intelligence system and the marketing research system. A fourth subsystem—the analytical market system, which is in charge of the data processing and transfer of information to management as aids to understanding, decision and control—will be discussed in Chapter 6.

Thus, viewed in this perspective, marketing research appears as only one component of a market information system. Marketing research's role is punctual and confined to a specific decision problem, while the role of an MIS is much broader and is organized on a permanent basis.

5.2 INTERNAL ACCOUNTING SYSTEM

All organizations collect internal data as part of their normal operations. These data, which are collected for purposes other than research, are called *internal secondary data*. Sales data are recorded within the 'order–shipping–billing' cycle. Cost data are recorded, sales reports are submitted by sales representatives and dealers, advertising and promotion activities are recorded, research and development and manufacturing reports are made. These are but a few of the data sources available for research in a modern organization. Sales records should allow for classification by type of customer, payment procedure, product line, sales territory, time period and so forth.

By way of illustration, a monthly sales statement classified by product, customer group, and sales territory will permit the following analyses:

- Comparison of year-to-date sales in volume and value.

- Analysis of the product mix structure of the total turnover.

- Analysis of the concentration rate of the turnover per customer.

- Evaluation of the sales efficiency by comparing territory sales, number of sales calls, average revenue per sales call and so forth.

- Analysis of the market penetration per territory by reference to buying power indices.

Many companies do not collect and maintain sales and cost data in sufficient detail to be used for research purposes. These data, stored and processed by the market analytical subsystem, should constitute a database of time series useful, namely, for forecasting purposes. The types of analyses to be conducted are, for example:

■ Graphic analyses to identify trends, seasonality patterns and growth rates.

■ Short-term sales forecasts based on endogenous sales forecasting techniques, such as exponential smoothing.

■ Correlation analyses between sales and key explanatory factors such as distribution rates, advertising share of voice, relative price.

■ Multi-variables or multi-equation econometric models.

These forecasting techniques will be discussed in more detail in Chapter 8.

The generalized use of computers has greatly facilitated the development of internal accounting systems. A certain number of attributes should be met in designing a reporting system.

■ *Timeliness*: the information must be available when needed and not reported too late.

■ *Flexibility*: the information must be available in varied formats and detail such that the specific information needs of alternative decision situations can be served.

■ *Inclusiveness*: the reporting system must cover the entire range of information needs, while avoiding the risk of information overload.

■ *Accuracy*: the level of accuracy should fit the needs of the decision situation, and the information should not be presented in too much detail.

■ *Convenience*: the information must be easily accessible to the decision maker and presented in a clear and usable manner.

Data from the internal accounting system originate within the organization and are available at minimal cost. They constitute the backbone of the MIS.

5.3 BUSINESS INTELLIGENCE SYSTEM

The data provided by the internal accounting system must be complemented by information about the macro-marketing environment and about competition. It is the role of the business intelligence subsystem to gather information about developments in the environment, to enable management to monitor the strengths and weaknesses of the firm's competitive position. A detailed description of the type of information to collect is presented in Chapter 11.

Several methods can be used to collect business intelligence information: the casual method, the use of the salesforce, the establishment of information centres or the purchase of data from syndicated services.

- The *casual method* is the informal search for information carried on by managers on their own through reading newspapers and trade publications, talking to suppliers, distributors, customers, or by participating in professional meetings, trade shows, etc.

- The *sales force* is often in a good position to provide data regarding many aspects of the market situation and to spot new market developments or new competitive actions. Sales representatives should be trained and motivated to report market information.

- Some companies have established *information or documentation centres* where the staff systematically scans and analyses major trade industrial or professional publications. For example, much can be learned about competition through reading competitors' published reports. News letters or bulletins are then published and disseminated within the company.

- Most companies also purchase *syndicated* data from outside firms which collect and sell standardized data about market shares, retail prices, advertising expenditures, promotions, etc.

Besides internal accounting information and market intelligence, marketing management also requires studies on specific problems or opportunities, such as a product concept test, a brand image study or a sales forecast for a particular country or region. It is the role of marketing research to conduct these types of focused studies.

5.4 MARKETING RESEARCH SYSTEM

The role of marketing research is to provide market information data that will help management to adopt and implement a market orientation. Its role can be defined in the following terms:

> Marketing research involves the diagnosis of information needs and the selection of relevant interrelated variables about which valid and reliable information is gathered, recorded and analysed. (Zaltman and Burger, 1975, p. 3)

According to this definition, marketing research has four distinctive functions to perform:

- The *diagnosis of an information need*, which supposes a good interactive relationship between the decider and the market analyst.

- The *selection of the variables* to be measured, which implies the capacity to translate a decision problem into empirically testable research questions.

- The responsibility of the *internal* and *external validity* of the collected information, which implies a good command of the research methodology.

- The *transfer of information* to management as an aid to understanding, decision and control.

The role of the market analyst is not confined, therefore, to the technical aspects linked to the execution of a research project. He or she has to participate actively in the research problem definition, the design of the research plan and the interpretation and exploitation of the research results.

5.4.1 Managerial usefulness of marketing research

Marketing research has its usefulness for strategic and operational marketing decisions. Three types of objectives can be identified:

- *Understanding aid:* to discover, describe, analyse, measure and forecast market factors and demand.

- *Decision aid:* to identify the most appropriate marketing instruments and strategies and determine their optimal level of intervention.

- *Control aid:* to assess the performance of the marketing programmes and evaluate results.

The first objective is more directly linked to strategic marketing decisions and has an important creative component: to discover new opportunities and/or untapped market potential. The other two objectives are felt more directly by operational marketing people.

Marketing research often has important implications for functions other than marketing. For example, research results on the changing mood of the market *vis-à-vis* ecology may induce R&D and production staff to develop environmentally sound products. Similarly, sales forecasting is a key input for financial analysis and for distribution planning and logistics.

A key question for a manager faced with a decision problem is to decide whether or not a specific marketing research study should be conducted. Several factors must be considered in examining this question.

1. *Time constraint.* Marketing research takes time, and in many instances decisions have to be taken rapidly even if the information is incomplete. The time factor is crucial and the urgency of the situation often precludes the use of research. This factor reinforces the importance of the MIS which is a permanent information system.
2. *Availability of data.* In many instances, management already possesses enough information and a sound decision may be made without further research. This type of situation will occur when the firm has a well-managed permanent MIS. Sometimes, marketing research is nevertheless undertaken to prevent the criticism of ill-prepared decisions. Marketing research here takes the form of an insurance that will be useful if the decision taken happens to be the wrong one.
3. *Value to the firm.* The value of marketing research will depend on the nature of the managerial decision to be made. For many routine decisions, the cost of a wrong decision is minimal and substantial marketing research expenditures are difficult to justify. Thus, before conducting a research, managers should ask themselves: '*Will the information gained by marketing research improve the quality of the marketing decision to an extent large enough to warrant the expenditure?*' In many cases even a modest marketing research study may substantially improve the quality of managerial decisions.

Frequently, marketing research projects are not directly linked to a particular decision but are purely exploratory. The objective is then to improve the understanding of a market or to search for opportunities in a new unknown market. This type of research is likely to improve the choice of strategic options by the firm.

5.4.2 Marketing research and the scientific method

If nobody questions today that management is much more of an art than a science, it is important to state clearly that marketing research must be scientific. It is important because marketing research has to deal with *accredited* (or *certified*) *knowledge*, and without accredited knowledge good management decisions cannot be made (Zaltman and Burger, 1975, p. 7). The implication of this statement is that the scientist attempts to uncover objective 'truths'. Because management is primarily interested in making decisions based on accurate and unbiased data, it is clear that the market researcher must follow a scientific procedure in order for data to be collected and analysed properly.

The rules of the scientific method are designed to provide two types of validity: internal and external.

■ *Internal validity* is concerned with the question of whether the observed effects of a marketing stimulus (price, advertising message, promotion, etc.) could have been caused by variables other than the factor under study. Is the relationship established without ambiguity? Without internal validity the experiment is confound and the causal structure is not established.

■ *External validity* is concerned with the generalizability of experimental results. To what populations, geographic areas, treatment variables can the measured effects be projected?

This problem of scientific reliability is fundamental because, on the basis of marketing research results, management will make highly risky decisions, such as the launch of a new product, modification of a price or adoption of a specific advertising theme.

Characteristics of scientific knowledge

The understanding of the main features of science is essential to performing marketing research scientifically, and therefore we shall now briefly review the main features of the scientific method (Zaltman and Burger, 1975, pp. 26–30).

1. *Scientific knowledge is factual*. Science starts by establishing facts and seeks to describe and explain them. Established facts are empirical data obtained with the aid of theories and, in turn, help to clarify theories.
2. *Science goes beyond facts*. The market analyst should not confine his or her work to facts that are easily observed and already in existence. Thus qualitative research is an integrated part of the research process. The market analyst may want to find new facts, but new facts should be authentic and lend themselves to empirical verification or falsification.
3. *Scientific knowledge is verifiable (or falsifiable)*. Scientific knowledge must be testable empirically through observational or experimental experiences. This is one of the basic rules of a science. It must be possible to demonstrate that a given proposition or theory is false. The scientist can only say: 'I have a theory which I have objectively tested with data and the data are consistent with my theory.'
4. *Science is analytic*. The market researcher tries to decompose the buying decision process into its basic parts to determine the mechanisms which account for the way the process functions. After analysing the component parts separately and also in their interrelationships, the market researcher is then able to determine how the whole decision process emerges. An

illustration of this analytic process is given in the next chapter in the discussion of the concept of attitude.

5. *Scientific knowledge is clear and precise.* Scientific knowledge strives for precision, accuracy and reduction of error although it is almost impossible to achieve these completely. The researcher attempts to reach these objectives by stating questions with maximal clarity, giving unambiguous definitions to concepts and measures and recording observations as completely and in as much detail as possible.

6. *Scientific knowledge is communicable.* Research must be in principle communicable—that is, it must be sufficiently complete in its reporting of methodologies used and sufficiently precise in the presentation of its results to enable another researcher to duplicate the study for independent verification or to determine if replication is desirable.

7. *Scientific knowledge is general.* The market researcher should place individual facts into general patterns which should be applicable to a wide variety of phenomena. This provides generalizations that can guide marketing decisions. The market analyst is concerned with learning not just what an individual buyer does, but rather what that buyer does that others are also likely to do in the same situation.

The manager–researcher interface

The managerial value of marketing research is largely determined by the quality of the interface between the market analyst responsible for the research project and the decision maker who has to use the research results. In many instances, market researchers are not sufficiently management-oriented and many managers are not sufficiently research-oriented. To overcome this difficulty of communication, the manager and the researcher's responsibilities should be clearly defined and accepted by both parties.

The *user of the research* should keep the market researcher informed on:

- The precise problem faced by the firm and the way that a decision is going to be made.

- The background of the problem and its environment.

- All limitations on costs and time for doing the study and on the courses of action that the company can realistically consider.

- What data will be provided by the firm and where to obtain it.

- Any changes in the situation that arise as the study is under way.

Similarly, the *responsibilities of the researcher* are:

- Being honest and clear regarding the meaning and any limitations of the expected findings.

- Being of maximum help in presenting and explaining the conclusions and aiding the decision maker's application.

- Demanding that the decision maker provide the information needed to plan and conduct the study.

■ Insisting that valid and full reporting be made of the findings.

■ Refusing to distort or abridge them on behalf of the user's biases and prejudices.

In reporting research findings some researchers fail to recognize that their role is advisory; they are not being asked to make the decision for management. Similarly, some managers operate as if the researcher is clairvoyant regarding the nature of the decision situation and the information needed to reduce the decision uncertainty. Consequently, many research projects are not decision-oriented because of the manager's poor communication skills.

5.4.3 Stages in the research process

Systematic inquiry requires careful planning in an orderly investigation. Marketing research, like other forms of scientific research, is a sequence of interrelated activities. The five stages of the research process are presented in Fig. 5.2.

1. *Problem definition.* The first step in research calls for the manager (the user of the research result) and the market analyst (the researcher) to define the problem carefully and to agree on the research objective. In marketing research, the old adage, '*a problem well defined is a problem half solved*' is worth remembering. Another way to express the same idea would be: '*. . . if you don't know what you are looking for, you won't find it.*' Thus, at this stage a working interface 'decider–analyst' is essential and the research objective should state, in terms as precise as possible, the information needed to improve the decision to be made.

2. *Research design.* The research design is a master plan specifying the methods and procedures for collecting and analysing the needed information. It is a framework for the research plan of action. This is typically the responsibility of the market analyst. The research plan should be designed professionally and specify the hypotheses and the research questions, the sources of information, the research instrument (focus groups, survey or experimentation), the sampling methodology, the schedule and the cost of the research. The decider should approve the research plan to ensure that the information collected is appropriate for solving his or her decision problem.

3. *Collection of the information.* Once the research design is approved, the process of gathering the information from respondents may begin. In many cases, the data collection phase is subcontracted to a specialized market research company. Data collection methods are rapidly

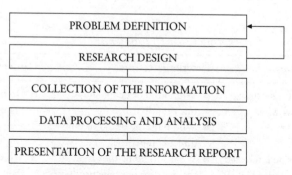

FIGURE 5.2 *The stages of a research process*

changing under the impact of telecommunication and computer. Telephone interviews combined with data-entry terminals, computer-assisted interviews, interactive terminals in shopping malls, fax interviews, electronic cash registers using the Universal Product Code (UPC) are new techniques which accelerate the data-gathering process and also eliminate the risks of errors. There are generally two phases in data collection: pre-testing and the main study. The pre-test phase, based on a small subsample, is used to determine whether the data-gathering plan for the main study is appropriate.

4. *Data processing and analysis.* Once the data have been collected, they must be converted into a format that will answer the manager's questions. This stage implies editing the data, coding, tabulating and developing one-way or two-way frequency distributions. These tasks are also generally subcontracted to specialized agencies and strict controls should be made on the rules and procedures adopted. Statistical analysis techniques will be used to summarize the data, to present them in a more meaningful way, to facilitate the interpretation or to help discover new findings or relationships. Advanced multi-variate statistical analyses should be used only if they are relevant for the purpose of the study.

5. *Presentation of the research report.* The final stage in the research process is that of interpreting the information and making conclusions for managerial decisions. The research report should communicate the research findings effectively, i.e. in a way which is meaningful to a managerial audience. The risk here is to place too much emphasis on the study's technical aspects, even if any responsible manager will want to be convinced of the reliability of the results, otherwise he or she will not use them. Thus again a close interaction between the manager and the researcher is key success factor.

This research process is of general application even if the stages of the process overlap continuously. The relative importance of each phase also varies with the nature of the market research.

5.4.4 Types of marketing research

Marketing research studies can be classified on the basis of techniques or on the basis of the nature of the research problem. Surveys, experimentations or observational studies are the most common techniques. The nature of the problem will determine whether the research is exploratory, descriptive or causal. Examples are provided in Table 5.1.

TABLE 5.1 *Types of marketing research problems*

Exploratory research	Descriptive research	Causal research
■ Sales of brand A are declining and we don't know why.	■ What kind of people buy our brand? ■ Who buys the brand of our direct competitor?	■ Do buyers prefer our product in an 'eco-design' package?
■ Would the market be interested by our new product idea?	■ What should be the target segment for our new product?	■ Which of the two advertising themes is more effective?

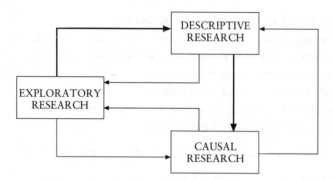

FIGURE 5.3 *The different sequences of research* (Source: *Churchill, 1987*)

- *Exploratory research* is conducted to clarify the nature of a problem, to gain better understanding of a market situation, to discover ideas and insights and to provide directions for any further research needed. It is not intended to provide conclusive evidence from which to determine a particular course of action. The methods used are desk research and qualitative studies.

- *Descriptive research* seeks to determine answers to 'who', 'what', 'when', 'where' and 'how' questions. Descriptive research is concerned with determining the frequency with which something occurs or the relationship between two variables. Unlike exploratory research, descriptive studies are based on some previous understanding of the nature of the research problem. Descriptive information is often all that is needed to solve a marketing problem. The methods used are typically secondary data, observation and communication. Most marketing research studies are of this type.

- *Causal research* is the most ambitious form of research and is concerned with determining cause-and-effect relationships. In causal studies, it is typical to have an expectation of the relationship which is to be explained, such as predicting the influence of price, packaging, advertising. Causal studies usually take the form of controlled experiments.

In principle, exploratory and descriptive research precede cause-and-effect relationship studies and are often seen as preliminary steps, as illustrated in Fig. 5.3. But other sequences may also exist. For example, if a causal hypothesis is discovered, the analyst might need another exploratory or descriptive study. In the following sections, we shall analyse in more detail the objectives and the methods used in these three types of market research studies.

5.5 EXPLORATORY RESEARCH STUDIES

Marketing research is of an exploratory type when the emphasis is placed on gaining insights and ideas rather than on formally testing hypotheses derived from theory or from previous research studies. This type of study is very popular among firms because of its low cost, speed, flexibility and emphasis on creativity and on the generation of ideas.

5.5.1 Objectives of exploratory research

The need for exploratory research typically arises when the firm is confronted with ill-defined problems such as: 'Sales of brand X are declining and we don't know why' or 'Would people be interested in our idea for a new product?' In these two examples, the analyst could guess a large number of possible answers. Since it is impractical to test them all, exploratory research will be used to find the most likely explanation(s) that will then be tested empirically. Thus, the main objectives of exploratory research are the following:

■ To give a rapid examination of the threats of a problem or the potential of an opportunity.

■ To formulate a poorly defined problem for more precise investigation.

■ To generate hypotheses or conjectural statements about the problem.

■ To collect and analyse readily available information.

■ To establish priorities for further research.

■ To increase the analyst's familiarity with a problem or with a market.

■ To clarify a concept.

In general, exploratory research is appropriate to any problem about which little is known.

Hypotheses development

Exploratory research is particularly useful at the first stage of a research process at the problem formulation phase, to translate the research problem into specific research objectives. The objective is to develop testable hypotheses. Hypotheses state what we are looking for; they anticipate the possible answers to the research problem and add a considerable degree of specificity. Normally there will be several competing hypotheses, either specified or implied.

How does the analyst generate hypotheses? The process of hypothesis development is illustrated in Fig. 5.4. Four main sources of information can be identified: (1) theory from such disciplines as economics, psychology, sociology or marketing; (2) management experience with related

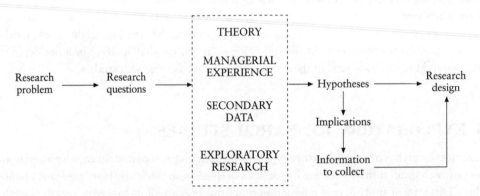

FIGURE 5.4 *The process of hypothesis development*

TABLE 5.2 *From a research problem to research questions*

Research problem: Why is the penetration rate of cable TV in private homes far below average in several geographic areas?

Hypotheses	Research questions
1. Good TV reception is available without cable.	1. How is the quality of TV reception without cable?
2. Residents are illegally connecting their sets to the cable network.	2. Is it technically possible to be illegally connected?
3. There is a very transient population in these regions.	3. What is the mobility rate in these regions?
4. Residents have had poor experience with cable services.	4. What is the corporate image of the cable company in the regions?
5. The price is too high, given the level of income in the region.	5. How different are income statistics among regions?
6. The salesforce coverage has been inadequate.	6. How active was the salesforce in the regions?
7. A large part of the residents are in age or social class groups that seldom watch TV.	7. Analyse demographic and social class statistics per region.

problems, (3) the use of secondary data (see below), or (4) exploratory research when both theory and experience are lacking.

After an exploratory research, the market analyst should know which type of data to collect in order to verify or falsify the competing explanations. An example is presented in Table 5.2, concerning the low level of market penetration of cable TV in some regions. The exploratory study has identified seven possible explanations (or hypotheses). The derived research objectives clearly indicate the type of data required to verify these tentative explanations.

5.5.2 Techniques used for exploratory research

Since the objective of exploratory studies is to find new ideas, no formal design is required. Flexibility and ingenuity characterize the investigation. The imagination of the researcher is the key factor. The techniques used are the study of secondary data, key informant survey, analysis of related cases and qualitative research through focus groups.

Use of secondary data

Secondary data are previously published data collected for purposes other than the specific research needs at hand. Primary data, on the other hand, are collected specifically for purposes of the investigation. The main sources of secondary data, internal and external, are presented in Fig. 5.5.

FIGURE 5.5 *Sources of marketing data (Source: Aaker and Day, 1980, p. 71)*

Secondary data can be classified as coming from internal sources or external sources, the former being available within the organization and the latter originating from outside. Internal data are centralized in the internal accounting system described in the first section of this chapter. External data come from an array of sources such as government publications, trade association data, books, bulletins, reports and periodicals. Data from these sources are available at minimal cost or free in libraries. External sources not available in a library are usually standardized marketing data which are expensive to acquire. These syndicated data sources are consumer panels, wholesale data, media and audience data, etc.

To start with secondary data is the most logical thing to do and their usefulness should not be underestimated. The primary *advantage* of secondary data is that it is always faster and less expensive to obtain them than to acquire primary data. Also they may include information not otherwise available to the researcher. For example, trucks and car registrations are secondary data published by the Car Registration Administration. A competent market analyst should be familiar with the basic sources pertaining to the market studied.

Secondary data, however, present a certain number of *disadvantages* and the market analyst should examine their relevance thoroughly. The most common problems associated with secondary data are: (1) outdated information, (2) variation in definition of terms, (3) different units of measurement. Another shortcoming is that the user has no control over the accuracy of secondary data. Research conducted by other persons may be biased to support the vested interest of the source. Also, the user of secondary data must critically assess the data and the research design to determine if the research methodology was correctly implemented. The following rules should be followed in the use of secondary data:

1. Always use the primary source of secondary data and not the secondary source that secured the data from the original source.
2. Assess the accuracy of the secondary data by carefully identifying the purpose of the publication.
3. Examine the overall quality of the methodology; a primary source should provide a detailed description of how the data were collected, including definitions, collection forms, sampling and so forth.

The above is not to say that such data cannot be used by the analyst. Rather, it is simply to suggest that such data should be viewed more critically.

Key informants survey

After having explored secondary sources, additional insights and ideas can be gained by talking with individuals who have special knowledge and experience regarding the problem under investigation. These knowledgeable persons may be 'players' or 'experts'. By 'players' we mean anyone participating in the market situation, such as the personnel within the firm, wholesalers, retailers, suppliers or consumers. By 'experts' we mean anyone having privileged information due to their function, such as civil servants, economists, sociologists, R&D personnel, members of a professional organization and so forth.

> For example, a publisher of children's books [who is] investigating a sales decrease gained valuable insights by talking with librarians and school teachers. These discussions indicated that an increased use of library facilities, both public and school, coincided with the product's decline in sales. These increases were, in turn, attributed to a very sizable increase in library holdings of children's books resulting from federal legislation that provided money for this purpose. (Churchill, 1987, p. 78)

No attempt should be made to have a probability sample in this type of survey, but it is important to include people with different points of view. The interviews are informal and do not use structured questions, such as those on a questionnaire. Rather, very flexible and free-flowing situations are created in order to stimulate the search for ideas and to uncover the unexpected. Various hypotheses may be presented to these individuals to test their reaction and see whether reformulation is necessary.

Analysis of selected cases

A third method currently used in exploratory research is the detailed analysis of cases that are similar to the phenomenon under investigation in order to seek explanations or to gain ideas for actions. For example, in many situations the United States are ahead of Europe and it is interesting to analyse the US situation to understand the problems that might occur in the European market.

For example, convenience stores in petrol stations have been in operation in the USA for many years. The same concept has recently been adopted by petroleum companies in Western Europe. A detailed study of selected stores in the USA proved to be very useful when determining the types of assortment, the opening hours, and the layout of these convenience stores.

Some situations are particularly productive of hypotheses—namely, cases reflecting abrupt changes or cases reflecting extreme behaviour.

Focus group discussions

The focus group interview is a more elaborate exploratory study. A focus group interview is an unstructured, free-flowing interview with a small group of 8 to 12 people. It is not a rigidly constructed question-and-answer session but a flexible format discussion of a brand, an advertisement or a new product concept. A focus group functions as follows.

> The group meets at a location at a predesignated time; it consists of an interviewer or moderator and 8 to 12 participants; the moderator introduces the topic and encourages group members to discuss the subject among themselves; focus groups allow people to discuss their true feelings, anxieties and frustrations as well as the depth of their conviction.

The primary advantages of focus group interviews are that they are relatively rapid, easy to execute and inexpensive. In an emergency situation three or four group sessions can be conducted, organized and reported on in less than a week. From the first discussion the analyst invariably learns a great deal. The second interview produces more, but less is new. Usually, in the third and fourth sessions, much of what is said has been heard before and there is little to be gained from continuing. By way of illustration, the result of a group discussion about coffee consumption is presented in Box 5.1.

In addition to the advantage of time, Wells (1974, pp. 133–4) underlines the following *advantages* for group interviews:

- The group interview is a superb mechanism for generating hypotheses when little is known about the problem under study.

- The group method drastically reduces the distance between the respondent who produces research information and the client who uses it.

- Another advantage of the group interview technique is its flexibility, by contrast with survey interviewers who work from a rigid question schedule.

- The group interview has the ability to handle contingencies of consumer behaviour of the type: 'if . . .; otherwise', an answer unlikely to emerge in a survey.

- In a group discussion respondents stimulate one another and more information is spontaneously obtained than in individual interviews.

- Finally in a group interview study, the findings emerge in a form that most people fully understand.

BOX 5.1

The results of a group discussion: motivations for coffee consumption in Belgium

1. *Time and space structure.* Coffee gives a certain rhythm to your day; it is a ritual which punctuates the different parts of a day: morning, morning break, mealtime, after a meal, evening, weekend, afternoon break, etc. Each moment has its own identity, typical to its environment and conditions for the expected satisfaction for consumption.

2. *Social function.* Offering a cup of coffee is a typical sign of hospitality. A cup of coffee relaxes and welcomes, develops a feeling of harmony, a certain atmosphere. Coffee brings people together, is the excuse for bringing people together.

3. *Sensorial function.* Coffee is satisfying to the individual, catering as much to the emotions as to the senses. The sense of smell, taste, the appearance and the warmth of coffee are all involved.

4. *Function as a stimulant.* Coffee supposedly acts as both a physical and psychological stimulant. Even a restorative, curative function is attributed to coffee; it picks you up; it is an affective, emotional comforting tonic.

Source: MDA Consulting Group, Brussels.

The *limitations* of focus group interviews are important and should not be underestimated.

- The respondents are not representative of the target population given their number and the recruiting procedure. Thus, the external validity of the results is necessarily limited.

- The interpretation of the results is typically judgemental and highly dependent on the personality of the analyst. Given the absence of a structured questionnaire and the wealth of disparate comments usually obtained, the analyst can always find something which agrees with his or her view of the problem. The importance of this bias is difficult to measure, however.

- The risk always exists to see one participant dominating the session and to provoke negative reactions from the other members of the group.

- Evaluations by means of group interviews tend to be conservative. It favours ideas that are easy to explain and understand and, therefore, not very new.

- Very disturbing is the unethical practice of some market research firms specializing in focus groups to recruit 'professional respondents' to make the session go well.

Despite these limitations, focus group interviews are very popular, particularly among advertising agencies. A more recent development in the field of qualitative research is the use of interpretation models such as the Freudian or the Jungian models (Pellemans, 1995). The risk here is to privilege one scheme of interpretation. To avoid this trap, several interpretation models should be used simultaneously and their results confronted.

Projective techniques

Respondents are often reluctant or embarrassed to discuss their feelings but may be more likely to give a true answer (consciously or unconsciously) if the question is disguised. A projective technique is an indirect means of questioning that enables respondents to 'project' their beliefs or feelings into a third person when exposed to unstructured stimulus. Projective techniques are currently used in clinical and personality tests. The theory behind such a technique is that when a person is asked to structure or organize an essentially unstructured or ambiguous situation he can do so only by calling upon and revealing his own personality or attitudinal structure.

> ... the more unstructured and ambiguous a stimulus, the more a subject can and will project his emotions, needs, motives, attitudes and values.   (Kerlinger, 1973, p. 515)

The most common projective techniques in marketing research are picture–story association, sentence completion, word association, role playing. On this topic see Kassarjian (1974).

5.5.3 Limitations of exploratory research

Exploratory research cannot take the place of quantitative, conclusive research. Nevertheless, there is great temptation among many managers to accept small sample exploratory results as sufficient for their purpose because they are so compelling in their reality. The dangers of uncritical acceptance of the unstructured output from a focus group or a brief series of informal interviews are two-fold:

- First, the results are not representative of what would be found in the population and, hence, cannot be projected.

- Second, there is typically a great deal of ambiguity owing to the moderator's interpretation of the results.

In fact, the greatest danger of using exploratory research to evaluate an alternative advertising copy strategy, a new product concept and so on, is not that a poor idea will be marketed, because successive steps of research will prevent that; the real danger is that a good idea with promise may be rejected because of findings at the exploratory stage. In other situations, where everything looks positive in the exploratory stage, there is the temptation to market the product without further research (Adler, 1979).

In view of these pitfalls, these methods should be used strictly for insights into the reality of the buyer's perspective and to suggest hypotheses for further research.

5.6 DESCRIPTIVE RESEARCH STUDIES

Descriptive studies, as their name suggests, are designed to describe the characteristics of a given situation or of a given population. Descriptive studies differ from exploratory studies in the rigour with which they are designed. Exploratory studies are characterized by flexibility. Descriptive studies attempt to obtain a complete and accurate description of a situation. Formal design is required to ensure that the description covers all phases desired and that the information collected is reliable. The most popular technique used in descriptive research is the survey.

5.6.1 Objectives of descriptive studies

Descriptive research encompasses a vast array of research objectives. The purpose is to provide a graph of some aspect of the market at a point of time or to monitor an activity over time. The objectives of descriptive studies are:

- To describe the organization, the distribution channels or the competitive structure of a specific market or segment.

- To estimate the proportion and the socio-demographic profile of a specified population which behaves in a certain way.

- To predict the level of primary demand over the next five years in a given market using heuristic or extrapolating sales forecasting methods.

- To describe the buying behaviour of certain groups of consumers.

- To describe the way buyers perceive and evaluate the attributes of given brands against competing brands.

- To describe the evolution of lifestyles among specific segments of the population.

Descriptive research should be based on some previous understanding and knowledge of the problem in order to determine with precision the data collection procedure. As illustrated in the previous section, this should rest on one or more specific hypotheses. Three conditions must be met before beginning a descriptive research:

1. One or several hypotheses or conjectural statements derived from the research questions to guide the data collection.
2. A clear specification of the 'who', 'what', 'when', 'where', 'why' and 'how' of the research.
3. A specification of the method used to collect the information: communication or observation.

A specification of the information to collect is presented in Box 5.2.

Two types of descriptive studies can be identified: longitudinal and cross-sectional. *Cross-sectional studies* involve a sample from the population of interest and a number of characteristics of the sample members are measured once at a single point of time. *Longitudinal studies* involve panels; they provide repeated measurement over time, either on the same variables (panels) or on different variables (omnibus panels). The sample members in a panel are measured repeatedly, as contrasted to the one-time measurement in a cross-sectional study. The most common form of cross-sectional study is the sample survey.

BOX 5.2

Specification of the information to collect

A firm is considering the launch of new food product to be purchased by medium–high income family housewives. The questions that must be examined before the beginning of the field work are:

- *Who?*   Who is the target person? The buyer? The user? The prescriber?

- *What?*   What characteristics should be measured? The socio-demographic profile? The attitude? Preferences? Purchasing habits? etc.

- *When?*   When should we ask? Before or at the purchasing time? After the use of the product? How long after? etc

- *Where?* Where should we ask? At the place of purchase? At home? At the place of work? etc.

- *Why?*   What is the purpose of the study? What use will be made of the results?

- *How?*   How should we proceed? Face to face interview? Telephone? Mail? etc.

The answers to these questions are not obvious. The results of the exploratory study should be useful to reduce the sources of uncertainty.

5.6.2 Primary data collection methods

In Fig. 5.5 a distinction was made between three methods of primary data collection: observation, communication and experimentation. Experimentation differs from the other methods in terms of degree of control over the research situation. Experimentation is the method typically used in causal research and its characteristics will be discussed in the next section. The observation and the communication methods are used for cross-sectional and longitudinal studies.

Observation methods

Scientific observation is the systematic process of recording the behavioural pattern of people, objects and occurrences without questioning or communicating with them. The market analyst using the observation method of data collection witnesses and records information as events occur or compiles evidence from records of past events. At least five kinds of phenomena can be observed:

- Physical actions and evidence, such as purchases, store locations and layout, posted prices, shelf space and display, promotions.

- Temporal patterns, such as shopping or driving time.

- Spatial relations and locations, such as traffic counts or shopping patterns.

■ Expressive behaviour, such as eye movement or levels of emotional arousal.

■ Published records, such as analysis of advertisements or newspaper articles.

The most important advantage of the observational method is its *unobtrusive nature* since communication with the respondent is not necessary. The 'observer' may be a person or the data may be gathered using some mechanical device such as a traffic counter, TV audimeters placed in homes to record and observe behaviour, or optical scanners in supermarkets to record sales and purchase behaviour. Observational data are typically more objective and accurate than communication data.

Technological systems such as the Universal Product Code (UPC) have made a major impact on mechanical observations and, UPC consumer panels now provide companies with quick, accurate and dynamic data about how their products are selling, who is buying them and the factors that affect purchase.

Despite their advantages, observation methods have one crucial limitation; they cannot observe motives, attitudes, preferences, intentions. Thus, they can be used only to secure primary behavioural data.

Communication methods

Communication involves questioning respondents to secure the desired information, using a data collection instrument called a questionnaire. The questions may be oral or in writing and the responses may also be given in either form. There are three methods of collecting survey data: personal interviewing, telephone interviewing and mail or self-administered questionnaires:

1. *Personal interviewing*. This method is well suited for complex product concepts requiring extensive explanations or for new products. Information is sought in face-to-face question-and-answer sessions between an interviewer and a respondent. The interviewer usually has a questionnaire as a guide, although it is possible to use visual aids. Answers are generally recorded during the interview. Personal interviews get a high response rate, but are also more costly to administer than the other forms. The presence of an interviewer may also influence the subjects' responses.

2. *Telephone interviewing*. This is best suited for well-defined basic product concepts or specific product features. Questioning is done over the telephone. The information sought is well defined, non-confidential in nature and limited in amount. The method has the advantage of speed in data collection and lower costs per interview. However, some telephone numbers are not listed in directories, and this causes problems in obtaining a representative sample. Absence of face-to-face contact and inability to use visual materials are other limitations.

3. *Mail questionnaires*. These are used to broaden the base of an investigation. They are most effective when well-defined concepts are involved and specific limited answers are required. They are generally less expensive than telephone and personal interviews, but they also have a much lower response rate. Several methods can be used to encourage a higher response rate. Questionnaires by mail must be more structured than others.

A comparison of the advantages and disadvantages of these three methods is made is Table 5.3. Each method of data collection has its own merits. Often these methods can be used in combination; for example, the telephone can be used to introduce the topic and to secure co-operation from the respondent. If the attitude is positive, the questionnaire is then sent by mail with a covering letter. Through this procedure, reasons for refusal can be obtained and follow-up calls can be made to secure the needed response.

5.6.3 Questionnaire design

Good questionnaire design is the key to obtaining good survey results. A questionnaire is simply a set of questions selected to generate the data necessary for accomplishing a research project's objective. Developing questionnaires may appear to be simple, especially to those who have never designed one.

> A good questionnaire appears as easy to compose as does a good poem. The end product should look as if effortlessly written by an inspired child, but it is usually the result of long, painstaking work. (Erdos, 1970)

The function of the questionnaire is that of measurement. The questionnaire is the main channel through which data are obtained from respondents and transferred to researchers, who in turn will transfer this certified knowledge to managers for decision making. This channel has a dual communication role: (a) it must communicate to the respondent what the researcher is asking for, and (b) it must communicate to the researcher what the respondent has to say. The accuracy of data gathered through questionnaires will be greatly influenced by the amount of distortion or 'noise' that occurs in the two types of communication. A sloppy questionnaire can lead to a great deal of distortion in the communication from researcher to respondents, and vice versa.

> To assume that people will understand the questions is a common error. People simply may not know what is being asked. They may be unaware of the product or topic of interest; they may confuse the subject with something else, or the question may not mean the same thing to everyone interviewed. Respondents may refuse to answer personal questions. Most of these problems may be minimized if a skilled researcher composes the questionnaire. (Zikmund, 1986, p. 371)

Figure 5.6 shows that the questionnaire is at the interface of the four participants in any survey:

■ The *decider*, who requires specific information to solve a decision problem.

■ The *market analyst*, whose role is to translate the research problem into research questions.

■ The *interviewer*, who has to collect reliable information from respondents.

■ The *respondents*, who have to agree to communicate the information sought.

One important characteristic of a good questionnaire is its degree of standardization—a condition required to ensure that the answers obtained from different respondents and through different interviewers are indeed comparable and therefore lend themselves to statistical analysis.

TABLE 5.3 *Comparison of survey methods*

Type	Advantages	Disadvantages
Personal interview	1. Allows interviewer to gain additional information from his or her own observation. 2. Better control over the sequence of questions. 3. Allows more detailed information to be gathered. 4. Usually gets a higher percentage of completed answers, since interviewer is there to explain exactly what is wanted. 5. Can use visual aids (e.g. tables, charts, samples, prototypes) to demonstrate concepts. 6. Allows in-depth exploration of product attributes and how to solve problems. 7. Is flexible to allow interviewer to adjust questions to respondent's greatest interests. 8. Personal contact often stimulates greater co-operation and interest by respondents.	1. Can be costly when compared to other methods, especially when wide geographic areas must be covered. 2. Interviewer bias can seriously cause misleading responses and misrecording of answers. 3. Requires detailed supervision of data-collection process. 4. Time consuming to train interviewers and to obtain data. 5. May distract respondents if interviewer is talking and writing answers at the same time. 6. Different approaches by different interviewers make it difficult to standardize conduct of survey.
Telephone survey	1. Fast (e.g. quicker than personal or mail). 2. Inexpensive (e.g. cost of an equal number of personal interviews would be substantially greater). 3. Easier to call back again if respondent is busy at the time. 4. Usually has only a small response bias because of closed-end questions. 5. Has wide geographical reach.	1. Limited to number published in telephone directory. 2. Can usually obtain only a small amount of information. 3. Can usually provide only limited classification data. 4 Difficult to obtain motivational and attitudinal information. 5. Difficult for highly technical products or capital goods. 6. Can become expensive if long-distance calls are involved.
Mail survey	1. Can get wide distribution at a relatively low cost per completed interview. 2. Helps avoid possible interviewer bias; absence of interviewer may lead to a more candid reply. 3. Can reach remote places (e.g. drilling engineer on site in Saudi Arabia). 4. Unless a name is requested, the respondent remains anonymous and, therefore, may give confidential information that otherwise would be withheld. 5. Respondent may be more inclined to answer since his or her replies can be made at leisure.	1. Accurate, up-to-date mailing lists are not always available to ensure successful distribution. 2. As many as 80–90% may not return questionnaires. Respondents generally have stronger feelings about the subject than non-respondents. 3. Questionnaire length is limited. 4. Inability to ensure that questions are understood fully and answers are properly recorded. 5. It is difficult to lead respondents through questions one by one since the respondent can read the entire questionnaire before answering. 6. Time consuming. 7. Troublesome with certain highly technical products

Source: Adapted from Chase and Barasch (1973).

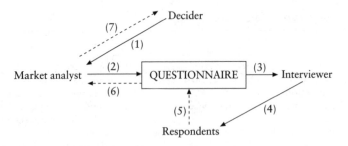

FIGURE 5.6 *The key role of the questionnaire in a survey*

Questionnaire design procedure

Although there are no rules for developing a flawless questionnaire, the collective experience of numerous researchers offer a broad set of guidelines for minimizing the likelihood and the severity of data validity problems in designing questionnaires. On this topic, an excellent reference remains Boyd and Westfall (1972). A seven-step procedure is proposed to assist the design of a questionnaire.

Step 1: Determine the information required.   Since the questionnaire is the link between the information needs and the data to be collected, the researcher must have a *detailed listing of the information needs* as well as a clear identification of the respondent group. This step is normally the result of exploratory research and the hypotheses development phases. The different forms of market response described in the preceding chapter will help the analyst to identify the concepts to be measured.

Step 2: Determine the type of questionnaire to be used.   Data collection can be made by personal interview, mail or telephone. The choice among these alternatives is largely determined by the type of information to be obtained. It is necessary to decide on the *type of questionnaire* at this point since the content and wording of the questions, the length of the questionnaire and the sequence of questions will all be influenced by this decision. A decision to use conjoint analysis, for example, would preclude the use of a telephone interview. Thus, at this stage the market analysis must specify precisely how the primary data needed will be collected and also the type of analysis to be made with the data.

Step 3: Determine the content of individual questions.   Once the information needed is known and the data collection method decided, the researcher is ready to begin formulating the questions. Several points should be reviewed systematically once the content of questions is determined.

■ *Is the question necessary?* Avoid including interesting questions which are not directly related to the information needed.

■ *Are several questions needed instead of one?* Some questions may have two or more elements and if these are left in one question, interpretation becomes impossible. This is typically the case for the 'why' question.

■ *Does the respondent have the information requested?* Three sub-questions can be examined: (1) is the point raised within the respondent's experience?; (2) can the respondent remember the information?; (3) will the respondent have to do a lot of work to get the information?

■ *Will respondents give the information?* Even though they know the answer, respondents will sometimes not answer questions because (1) they are unable to phrase their answer or (2) because they do not want to answer.

Step 4: Determine the type of question to use. In forming the actual questions, the researcher has the choice between three major types of question.

■ An *open-ended* question requires the respondents to provide their own answers to the question.

■ A *multiple-choice* question requires the respondent to choose an answer from a list provided with the question. The respondent may be asked to choose one or more of the alternatives presented.

■ A *dichotomous* question is an extreme form of the multiple-choice question which allows the respondent only two responses, such as yes–no, agree–disagree and so on.

Examples of questions are presented in Appendix 5.1.

In a multiple-choice question, when the proposed answers are ranked, the objective is not simply to identify a category as in a *nominal scale*, but rather to 'measure' a level of agreement, a degree of importance or a level of preference. Two types of scale can be used: an *ordinal scale* where the numbers possess the property of rank order or an *interval scale* which has all the properties of an ordinal scale and, in addition, the differences between scale values can be meaningfully interpreted. The distinction is important because the permissible mathematical operations are different with each type of scale. In practice, responses to questions on importance or preference are frequently assumed to form an interval scale.

Different scales are currently used. The most common are the *Likert scale* with descriptor labels attached to each category, the *semantic differential scale* using bipolar adjectives and the *constant sum scale*, where the respondent is instructed to allocate a given sum among two or more attributes on the basis of their importance to that respondent. This is the procedure used in Chapter 6 to measure a multi-attribute model (see Table 6.3) through the compositional method.

Step 5: Decide the wording of questions. The problem at this stage is to phrase the questions in a way that (1) can easily be understood by the respondent and (2) does not give the respondent a clue as to how he or she should answer. A certain number of questions are worth reviewing.

1. *Is the issue clearly defined?* Each question should be checked on the six points: who, where, when, what, why and how to be sure that the issue is clear.
2. *Should the question be subjective or objective?* A subjective question puts the question in terms of the individual while objective phrasing tends to refer to what people in general think. Subjective questions tend to give more reliable results.

3. *Use simple words.* Words used in questionnaires should have only one meaning, and that meaning should be known by everyone. There are many examples of misunderstanding of what seem to be everyday words. In particular, the technical jargon of marketing (brand image, positioning, etc.) should be avoided The pre-test of the questionnaire is very useful in overcoming this difficulty.

4. *Avoid ambiguous questions.* Ambiguous questions mean different things to different people. Indefinite words as *often, occasionally, frequently, many, good, fair, poor* and so on may have many different meaning. For example, *frequent* reading of *The Economist* may be six or seven issues a year for one person and twice a year for another.

5. *Avoid leading or one-sided questions.* A leading question is one that may steer respondents towards a certain answer. One-sided questions present only one aspect of an issue. A question should be constructed in as neutral a way as possible, by avoiding the name of a brand or a company or by presenting all the sides of an issue.

6. *Avoid double-barrelled questions.* A double-barrelled question is one that calls for two responses and thereby creates confusion for the respondents. In this case, two questions instead of one are necessary.

7. *Use split-ballot wherever possible.* There is no wording that is the only correct one for a question. When there are two wordings from which to choose, but no basis on which to select one in preference to the other, one wording can be adopted on half of the questionnaires and the other on the other half.

Step 6: Decide the sequence of questions. There are generally three major sections in a questionnaire: (1) the basic information sought; (2) the socio-demographic information useful in obtaining the profile of the respondent and (3) the identification section to be used by the interviewer. The general rule is to put the sections in that order: The body of the questionnaire in first position and the socio-demographic questions at the end, unless they serve as filter questions to qualify respondents for the survey. The researcher should also pay attention to the following points.

1. *Use simple and interesting opening questions.* If the opening questions are interesting, simple to comprehend and easy to answer, the respondent's co-operation will be gained.

2. *Use the funnel approach.* The funnel· approach involves beginning with a very general question on a topic and gradually leading up to a narrowly focused question on the same topic.

3. *Arrange questions in logical order.* The order should be logical to the respondent. Sudden changes in subject confuse the respondent and cause indecision.

4. *Place difficult or sensitive questions near the end.* Sensitive questions should be relegated towards the end of the questionnaire, once the respondent has become involved in the study.

A mail questionnaire raises specific sequence problems since it must sell itself. It is particularly important that the opening questions capture the respondent's interest. Questions should then proceed in logical order. In a mail questionnaire, it is not possible, however, to take advantage of sequence position in the same way as in personal interviews since it is the respondent who will decide the order of response. The layout and physical attractiveness is particularly important for a self-administered questionnaire.

Step 7: Pre-test the questionnaire.   Before a questionnaire is ready for the field it needs to be pre-tested under field conditions. Pre-testing involves administering the questionnaire to a limited number of potential respondents selected on a convenience basis but not too divergent from the target population. It is not necessary, however, to have a statistical sample for pre-testing. The pre-testing process allows the researcher to determine if the respondents have any difficulty in understanding the questionnaire or if there are ambiguous or biased questions. Tabulating the results of the pre-test is also very useful to ensure that all the needed information will be obtained.

5.6.4 Sampling methods

Once the market analyst has developed and tested the questionnaire, the next question is the selection of the respondents from whom the information will be collected. One way to do this would be to collect information from each member of the target population through a *census*. Another way would be to select a fraction of the population by taking a *sample* of respondents. The census approach is frequently adopted in industrial market research studies when the target population has a total size of 100 to 300 units. In most situations, however, the population sizes are large and the cost and time required to contact each member of the population would be prohibitively high. Thus, sampling can be defined as follows:

> Sampling is the selection of a fraction of the target population for the ultimate purpose of being able to draw general conclusions about the entire target population.

Sampling techniques can be divided into two broad categories of probability and non-probability samples:

■ In a *probability* sample, an objective selection procedure is used and each member of the population has a known, non-zero chance of being included in the sample.

■ In a *non-probability* sample, the selection procedure used is subjective and the probability of selection for each population unit is unknown.

These two sample selection procedures have their own merits. The main superiority of probability sampling is that there are appropriate statistical techniques for measuring random sampling error, while in non-probability samples the tools of statistical inference cannot be legitimately employed. If, as a general rule, a probability sample should be preferred, there are situations where non-probability samples are useful, namely because they are less costly and easier to organize.

Probability samples

The different types of probability samples are simple random samples, stratified samples (proportionate or disproportionate), cluster samples and multi-stage area samples.

■ A *simple random sample* is a sampling procedure that assures that each element of the population will have not only a known but an *equal chance* of being included in the sample. Different drawing procedures exist (random number, systematic sampling), which all presuppose the existence of a list of the population members.

■ In a *stratified sample* the target population is subdivided into mutually exclusive groups—based on criteria such as size, income or age—and random samples are drawn from each group, called 'stratum'. In a proportionate stratified sample the total sample is allocated among the strata in proportion to the size of each stratum, while in a disproportionate stratified sample, the total sample is allocated on the basis of the relative variability observed in each stratum.

■ In a *cluster sample* the target population is divided into mutually exclusive subgroups called clusters instead of strata, and a random sample of the subgroups is then selected. Thus, each subgroup must be a small-scale model (or a miniature population) of the total population. The difference between stratified and cluster sampling is illustrated in Fig. 5.7.

■ *Multi-stage area sampling* involves two or more steps that combine some of the probability techniques of cluster sampling. Instead of picking all the units from the randomly chosen clusters (or area), only a sample of units is randomly picked from each of them; the selected subclusters themselves can be subsampled. The main advantage of multi-stage area sampling is to permit probability samples to be drawn even when a current list of population is unavailable.

In general, probability sampling methods will be more time consuming and expensive than non-probability sampling methods because (1) they require an accurate specification of the population and an enumeration of the units of the population and (2) the selection procedure of the sample units must be precisely followed.

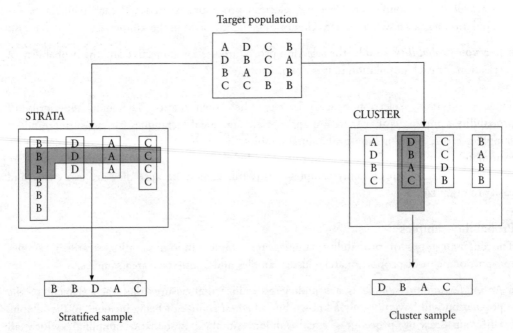

FIGURE 5.7 *The difference between stratified and cluster sampling*

Non-probability samples

Three types of non-probability sampling can be identified: convenience, judgemental and quota.

- *Convenience sampling* refers to a sampling procedure of obtaining the respondents who are most conveniently available for the market analyst.

- *Judgemental sampling* is a procedure in which the market analyst exerts some effort in selecting a sample of respondents that he or she feels most appropriate for the research objectives.

- *Quota sampling* resembles stratified random sampling and convenience sampling. The interviewer finds and interviews a prescribed number of people in each of several categories. The sample units are selected on a subjective rather than a probabilistic basis.

In general, the choice between probability and non-probability sampling involves a trade-off between the capability to generalize the sample results to the target population with a known degree of accuracy and lower time/cost requirements.

Errors in survey research

One of the main responsibilities of the market analyst in charge of a survey is to estimate the overall accuracy and reliability of the survey results. The total error associated with a survey can be subdivided into two broad categories: sampling error and non-sampling error, also called systematic bias. The different sources of error, sampling and non-sampling, are described in Fig. 5.8.

The size of the sampling error can be reduced by increasing the sample size or by improving the design of the sampling procedure. More difficult to control are the non-sampling errors which arise from a multitude of factors, such as poor questionnaire construction, ill-trained interviewers, errors from respondents or errors in coding responses. The best way to minimize non-sampling errors is to have strict control over the entire process of primary data gathering, coding, and analysis. If the survey research is subcontracted to a market research company, the market analyst should give precise instructions and closely supervise the field work.

5.6.5 Data analysis: from data to information

Once data have been collected, emphasis in the research process turns to analysis. The raw data collected in the field must be transformed into information that will help to answer the questions raised by the decider. The transformation of raw data into information is achieved in several steps: data conversion, descriptive analysis and inferential analysis.

- *Data conversion* implies data editing, coding, storing and tabulating, in order to obtain an organized collection of data records (called a data set or data bank) which lends itself to analysis.

- *Descriptive analysis* gives an initial idea about the nature of the data; it involves obtaining appropriate measures of central tendency and of dispersion of the data for all variables, frequency distribution, cross-tabulations, graphic representations and so forth. Multi-variate techniques like factorial analysis, can also be used to summarize data.

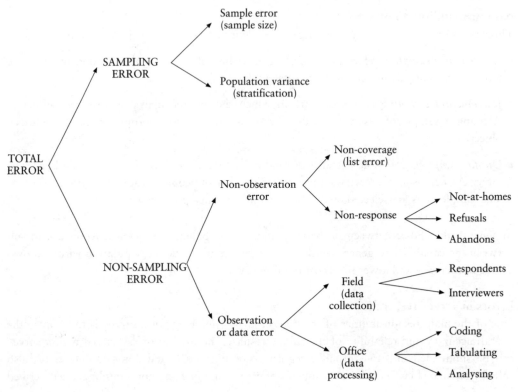

FIGURE 5.8 *Total error in survey research*

■ *Inferential analysis* aims at exploring the extent and nature of possible associations between pairs of variables, to test hypotheses about the target population or to examine the statistical significance of differences.

Attitude and *brand* (or *corporate*) *image* measurement is an important application of survey and will be discussed in Chapter 6. Several multi-variate data analysis methods presented there are based on survey data. These methods are used to extract meaningful information from primary data. The most popular ones are: simple and regression analysis, discriminant analysis, factorial analysis, multi-dimensional scaling and cluster analysis. For an overview of applications and problems of these techniques, see Jain *et al.* (1982).

5.7 CAUSAL RESEARCH STUDIES

The use of a two-way table to uncover a relationship between two variables is common practice in descriptive research. A frequent temptation when a two-way table shows evidence of a statistically significant relationship, especially if one variable is presumed to influence the other (as in regression analysis), is to view this result as conclusive evidence of a causal relationship. This temptation should be resisted unless the empirical evidence stems from an experiment in which the other variables that may influence the response variable were controlled. A *causal research design* is required to establish the existence of a causal link. A descriptive study can only suggest the existence of a causal link. The basic tool used in causal studies is the controlled experiment.

5.7.1 Objectives of causal studies

In descriptive studies it is impossible to entirely separate the effect of a given variable from the effect of the other variables. Causal studies overcome this difficulty by organizing the data-gathering procedure in such way as to permit unambiguous interpretation. Causal studies have three distinct, although very complementary, research objectives.

■ To establish the direction and intensity of a *causal link* between one or several action variables and one response variable.

■ To measure in quantitative terms the *rate of influence* of an action variable on a response variable.

■ To generate *predictions* of a response variable for different levels of the action variables.

These three objectives can be dissociated and several causal studies have the sole objective of establishing a cause-and-effect relationship in order to gain a better understanding of the phenomenon under study. In these cases, no quantitative estimates of the influence rate are sought.

Three rather intuitive types of evidence are relevant for evaluating causal relationships:

■ Evidence that the action variable *precedes* the response variable.

■ Evidence that a strong *association* exists between an action and an observed outcome.

■ Evidence that the influence of *other possible causal factors* has been eliminated or controlled.

This last condition is particularly demanding and requires that all extraneous variables are controlled in order to ensure that the experiment has not been confused. The most important threats to internal validity in an experiment are briefly described here:

■ *History*: events external to the experiment that affect the responses of the people involved in the experiment.

■ *Maturation*: changes in the respondents that are a consequence of time, such as ageing, getting hungry, or getting tired.

■ *Testing effect*: awareness of being in a test which can sensitize and bias respondents.

■ *Before-measure effect*: the before measure can also sensitize and bias respondents, therefore influencing both the after-observation and the respondent's reaction to the experiment treatment.

■ *Instrumentation*: the measuring instrument may change, for example, when there are many observers or interviewers.

- *Mortality*: respondents may drop out of the experiment.

- *Selection bias*: an experimental group may be systematically different in some relevant way from the target population.

An experimental design is specifically constructed by the market analyst to ensure that these extraneous factors are eliminated or controlled.

5.7.2 Experimentation defined

Experimentation is a scientific investigation in which the researcher manipulates and controls one or more action variables and observes the response variable(s) for variation concomitant to the manipulation of the action variable. *Treatments* are the action variables that are manipulated and whose effects are measured. The *test units* are the entities, respondents or physical units to whom the treatments are presented and whose response is measured.

An *experimental design* involves the specification of (a) the treatments that are to be manipulated, (b) the test units to be used, (c) the response variable to be measured and (d) the procedure for dealing with extraneous variables. Two types of experimentation can be distinguished:

- In a *laboratory experiment* the researcher creates a situation with the desired conditions (a trailer set up as a store or a survey situation) and then manipulates some variables while controlling others.

- A *field experiment* is organized in a realistic or natural situation (in-store test), although it too involves the manipulation of one or more action variables under carefully controlled conditions.

In general, field experiments are superior to laboratory experiments in terms of external validity.

Types of experimental design

In a typical experiment two groups of respondents (or stores) are selected in such a way that the groups have similar characteristics as far as the purpose of the study is concerned. The causal factor or the treatment (for example, advertising A) is introduced into one of the two groups, called the *experimental group*. No such factor is introduced in the other group, called the *control group*. If sales increase within the experimental group but not in the control group, it is inferred that the hypothesis is tenable, i.e. that advertising caused the sales increase. If no sales increase occurs in the experimental group, or if sales increase to the same extent in the control group, it is inferred that the hypothesis is not tenable (Boyd and Westfall, 1956, p. 82).

Within this general pattern, experimental designs vary in the manner in which experimental and control groups are selected and the degree of control that is exercised over the extraneous factors that affect the results. To illustrate this, two pre-experimental designs and two true experimental designs will be discussed briefly.

The 'one-shot' case study. A single group of test units is exposed to treatment (X) and an 'after' measurement (O) is then taken on the response variable. Thus we have:

$$X \quad O$$

This is not a true experimental design and it is clearly impossible to draw any meaningful conclusions from it. The observed level of O may be the result of many uncontrollable factors and in the absence of pre-treatment observation, it is impossible to conclude.

The one group 'before–after' design. In this design a 'before' measurement is made in addition to the 'after' measurement. Thus, we have:

$$O_1 \quad X \quad O_2$$

The difference between the 'after' and 'before' measurements $(X_2 - X_1)$ would be assumed to be the effect of the treatment. This assumption is questionable, however, because the difference between the 'after' and the 'before' measurements could very well be a measure of the treatment *plus* the changes caused by all the uncontrolled factors, such as history, maturation, testing effect and so on.

The 'before–after' design with control group. A true experiment is one where the researcher is able to eliminate all extraneous factors as competitive hypotheses to the treatment. An experimental and a control group are selected in such way that they are interchangeable for purposes of the experiment. The control group is measured at the same time as the experimental group, but no treatment is introduced. Thus, we have:

$$\text{Experimental group:} \quad O_1 \quad X \quad O_2$$
$$\text{Control group:} \quad\quad\quad O_3 \quad\quad O_4$$

Thus, the difference between the 'after' and the 'before' measurements of the control group $(O_4 - O_3)$ is the result of uncontrolled variables. The difference between the 'after' and 'before' measurements of the experimental group $(O_2 - O_1)$ is the result of the treatment *plus* the result of the same uncontrollable events affecting the control group. The effect of the treatment alone is obtained by subtracting the difference in the two measurements of the control group from the two measurements of the experimental group.

$$\text{True treatment effect} = [O_1 - O_2] - [O_4 - O_3]$$

All potential destroyers of internal validity are controlled by this design, except the testing effect in the experimental group which is not eliminated.

Thus, when the 'before' measurement is made in an undisguised way—for example, by interviewing respondents—the *interactive testing effect* is likely to be present and cannot be separated from the treatment effect. If the collection of the data is made without the knowledge of the individuals involved, this design is appropriate. In the other cases, a way to escape the problem of the testing effect is the 'after-only with control group' design.

'After-only with control group' design.   In this design, the experimental and the control groups are selected in such a way as to be equivalent. No 'before' measurement is made in either group and treatment is introduced in the experimental group.

$$X \quad O_1$$
$$O_2$$

The effect of the treatment is determined by computing the difference between the two 'after' measurements ($O_2 - O_1$). In this design, uncontrollable factors influence both the control and the experimental groups and there is no testing effect because no pre-measurements are made. The only weakness of this design is its *static nature* which does not permit an analysis of the process of change as in the 'before–after' design. A classic example of application of this design is the 'Instant Nescafé study' summarized in Table 5.4.

> The objective of the study was to determine the image of the housewife who uses instant coffee. Two comparable groups of housewives were shown similar shopping lists and asked to describe the housewife who prepared the list. On the list shown to the control group, one item was Maxwell House Coffee, a well-known drip grind coffee brand. On the list shown the experimental group, the item was replaced by Nescafé Instant Coffee, a relatively new concept at the time. The results measured were the percentages of the respondents who described the shopping list author as having various characteristics. The effect of the treatment (Nescafé Instant Coffee user) was the difference in the percentage ascribing each characteristic to the 'instant coffee woman' from the percentage ascribing the same characteristics to the 'drip grind' woman.   (Boyd and Westfall, 1972, p. 96)

The results of this experiment—a replication of a study conducted by Mason Haire in 1950—are summarized in Table 5.4. A chi-square test shows that there are no significant differences between the characteristics ascribed to the Maxwell shopper and those for the Nescafé shopper (Webster and von Pechmann, 1970, pp. 61–3).

TABLE 5.4 *Results of the instant coffee experiment*

Measurements	Experimental group		Control group	
Before measurement	No		No	
Treatment variable	Instant coffee (Nescafé)		Drip grind coffee (Maxwell)	
After measurements	Lazy	18%	Lazy	10%
	Thrifty	36%	Thrifty	55%
	Spendthrift	23%	Spendthrift	5%
	Bad wife	18%	Bad wife	5%

Source: Webster and von Pechmann (1970, p. 62).

A fundamental principle is implicitly assumed to be applicable in experimental design: the market analyst does not care what extraneous factors are operative *as long as they operate equally on all experimental and control groups*. Thus random selection of the test units and of the groups and random allocation of the treatments among the groups is a key condition of validity.

With the development of scanner systems in supermarkets, the organization of marketing experiments is greatly facilitated today.

SUMMARY

A market-oriented firm has to develop a market information system to monitor the changes in the macro-marketing environment. The role of marketing research is to provide market information data that will help management to implement a market-oriented strategy. Marketing research has to provide management with accredited (or certified) knowledge and, for this reason, has strictly to follow the rules of the scientific method. The development of a research project implies a sequence of interrelated activities which ensures a systematic and orderly investigation process. Three types of marketing research can be identified: *exploratory, descriptive* and *causal studies*. The objective of exploratory research is to generate hypotheses and to translate the research problem in research objectives. The techniques of exploratory research are: use of secondary data, key informant surveys, analysis of selected cases and focus group discussions. Group discussions, also called *qualitative research*, are particularly useful, but they should be used strictly to suggest hypotheses for further research and not as conclusive evidence. Descriptive studies attempt to obtain a complete, quantitative and accurate description of a situation and must follow a precise methodology. The techniques used are *observation* and *communication*. The most popular communication method is by far the survey method through personal, telephone or mail interviewing. Good questionnaire design is the key to obtaining good survey results and a seven-step procedure is proposed to help in designing a questionnaire. Sampling techniques can be divided in two categories: *probability* and *non-probability* samples. These two sampling techniques have their own merits. The two sources of error in survey research are *sampling* and *non-sampling* errors. To minimize non-sampling error the market analyst should have strict control over the entire data-gathering process. Causal research is used to establish the existence of a causal link between an action and a response variable. An experimentation is a scientific investigation in which the researcher manipulates and controls one or more action variables and observes the response variable for variation concomitant to the manipulation of the action variable. Different types of experimental designs exist which vary in the way the analyst controls extraneous factors.

QUESTIONS AND PROBLEMS

1. State (a) the complaints that managers typically have against marketing researchers and (b) the complaints that marketing researchers typically have against managers.

2. What is the difference between external and internal validity and which research procedure(s) will contribute towards an improvement in the validity of both?
3. Why is it important to determine research hypotheses before undertaking a survey research?
4. What is the basic difference between exploratory and conclusive research?
5. What are the general advantages and disadvantages associated with obtaining information by questioning or by observation?
6. What distinguishes a probability sample from a non-probability sample? Compare the merits and weaknesses of these two sampling procedures.
7. What are (a) an ambiguous question, (b) a leading question and (c) a double-barrelled question?
8. What are the main types of true experimental designs? What are the key issues or problems associated with each of these designs?

REFERENCES

Aaker, C. and G.S. Day (1980), *Marketing Research*. New York: John Wiley & Sons.

Adler, L. (1979), 'To Learn What's on the Consumers' Mind, Try Focus Group Interviews', *Sales and Marketing Management*, 9 April, pp. 76–80.

Boyd, H.W. and R. Westfall (1956 and 1972), *Marketing Research: Text and Cases*. Homewood, Ill.: R.D. Irwin, Inc.

Chase, C. and L.L. Barasch (1973), *Marketing Problems Solver*, 2nd edn. Radnur, Pennsylvania: Chiltern Book Company.

Churchill, G.A. (1987), *Marketing Research, Methodological Foundations*, 4th edn. Chicago: The Dryden Press.

Erdos, P.L. (1970), *Professional Mail Surveys*. New York: McGraw-Hill.

Ferber, R. (ed.) (1974), *Handbook of Marketing Research*. New York: McGraw-Hill Book Co.

Jain, A.K., C. Pinson and B.T. Ratchford (eds) (1982), *Marketing Research: Applications and Problems*. New York: John Wiley & Sons.

Kassarjian, H.H. (1974), 'Projective Methods', in Ferber R. (ed.), *Handbook of Marketing Research*. New York: McGraw-Hill Book Co.

Kerlinger, F.N. (1973), *Foundations of Behavioural Research*. London: Holt Rinehart & Winston Inc.

Kotler, P. (1984), *Marketing Management*. Englewood Cliffs, NJ: Prentice-Hall International.

Lambin, J.J. (1990), *La recherche marketing: analyser, mesurer prévoir*. Paris: Ediscience International.

Pellemans, P. (1995), Jungian Analysis as a Tool for new Qualitative Research Methods in Marketing, Unpublished Working Paper, IAG, Louvain-la-Neuve, Belgium.

Webster, F.E. and von Pechmann (1970), 'A Replication of the Shopping List Study', *Journal of Marketing*, Vol. 34, April, pp. 61–77.

Wells, W.D. (1974) 'Group Interviewing', in Ferber R. (ed.) *Handbook of Marketing Research*. New York: McGraw-Hill Book Co.

Zaltman, G. and P.C. Burger (1975), *Marketing Research: Fundamentals and Dynamics*. Hinsdale, Ill.: The Dryden Press.

Zikmund, W.G. (1986), *Exploring Marketing Research*, 2nd edn. Chicago: The Dryden Press.

APPENDIX 5.1

Examples of Questions

1. *Open-end question, unaided awareness*
   Which magazines do you know?

   ■.. ■.. ■..
   ■.. ■.. ■..

2. *Closed-end question: dichotomous: aided awareness*
   Here is a list of different magazines, which one(s) do you know?

Magazine A	YES/NO
Magazine B	YES/NO
Magazine C	YES/NO
Magazine D	YES/NO
Magazine E	YES/NO

3. *Closed-end question: multiple choice: qualified awareness*
   To what extent do you know the following magazines?

	Don't know	Know by name only	I read it regularly
Magazine A	......	......	......
Magazine B	......	......	......
Magazine C	......	......	......
Magazine D	......	......	......
Magazine E	......	......	......

4. *Agreement/disagreement scale: Likert itemized rating scale*
   Please indicate the amount of agreement/disagreement concerning the following statement:
   '*The following three magazines give well-documented and objective information*'

	Strongly disagree (1)	Disagree (2)	Neither agree nor disagree (3)	Agree (4)	Strongly agree (5)
A	.....	.....	.....	.....	.....
B	.....	.....	.....	.....	.....
C	.....	.....	.....	.....	.....

5. *Osgood rating scale with bipolar adjectives*
How adequate is the coverage of *contemporary issues* in the following three magazines:

	Very poor coverage (−3)	(−2)	(−1)	(0)	(+1)	(+2)	Very good coverage (+3)
A	......	......	......	......	......	......	......
B	......	......	......	......	......	......	......
C	......	......	......	......	......	......	......

6. *Importance scale*
In selecting a magazine, how important is the presence of TV programmes ?

Not at all important (1)	Not very important (2)	Somewhat important (3)	Very important (4)	Extremely important (5)

7. *Constant-sum scale: evaluation of the relative importance of an attitude*
Divide 100 points among each the following toothpaste characteristics according to how important each characteristic is to you when selecting a brand of toothpaste.

Cavity protection   ....
Breath freshening   ....
Taste and colour   ....
                                 100

8. *Evaluation scale: rating some attribute*
How would you rate the attribute 'clear editorial presentation' of Magazine A?

Very poor (1)	Fair (2)	Good (3)	Very good (4)	Excellent (5)

9. *Preference scale*
Divide 100 points among each of the following brands according to your preference for the brand.

Brand A: ....
Brand B: ....
Brand C: ....

10. *Two-by-two comparison: preferences*
Among the following 'pairs' of brands, which one do you prefer?

A ...   or   B ...
A ...   or   C ...
B ...   or   C ...

11. *Triad of preferences*
    Among the following brands: Brand A, Brand B, Brand C,

    - Which one would you prefer to buy? ....
    - If the one you prefer is not available, which one would you then prefer to buy? ....
    - And if none of these first two preferred brands is available, which one would you buy? ....

12. *Purchase intentions*
    How likely is it that you will purchase a compact disk player within the next three months?

I definitely will not buy	I probably will not buy	I might buy	I probably will buy	I definitely will buy
(1)	(2)	(3)	(4)	(5)

13. *Probability of purchase*
    How likely is it that you will buy a new car within the next 12 months?

0	10	20	30	40	50	60	70	80	90	100
Abso-lutely no chance		Slight prob-ability						Strong poss-ibility		Abso-lutely certain

14. *Measure of the behavioural component of an attitude (action tendency)*
    How likely is it that *you would* pay a 5% premium price to purchase an environmentally friendly brand in this particular product category?

Extremely unlikely	Very unlikely	Somewhat likely	Likely, 50–50	Somewhat likely	Very likely	Extremely likely
(1)	(2)	(3)	(4)	(5)	(6)	(7)

6

THE BUYER'S RESPONSE BEHAVIOUR

LEARNING OBJECTIVES

After reading this chapter, you should be able to understand:

■ the ways buyers respond to the marketing stimuli used by the firm

■ the difference between cognitive, affective and behavioural responses

■ the various paths of response observed among buyers

■ the different measures of the cognitive, affective and behavioural responses

■ the post-purchase behaviour of buyers

■ the behaviour of dissatisfied customers.

*T*he purpose of this chapter is to analyse how potential buyers choose and how they respond to marketing stimuli used by producers as part of their product distribution, pricing and communication policy. The information collected or received by buyers during their purchasing process helps them to identify the relevant characteristics in goods and to evaluate different products or brands in their evoked set. As a result of this evaluation phase, buyers rank their preferences and decide whether or not to buy, unless situational factors intervene. Having sampled the purchased brands, buyers feel either satisfied or dissatisfied. This feeling will determine their after-purchase behaviour. This process of preference formation is analysed in its entirety by marketing researchers and this enables the firm to adapt its offerings more effectively to market expectations. In this chapter, we shall review the main concepts and methods used to anticipate and to measure market response.

6.1 THE LEVELS OF MARKET RESPONSE

One can identify different ways in which potential buyers respond to perceived information and producer stimuli. Here, 'response' means *all mental or physical activity caused by a stimulus*. A response is not necessarily manifested in external actions, but may be simply mental.

Economic theory is only interested in the act of purchase *per se* and not in the overall behavioural process which leads to purchase. From the economist's point of view, as we saw earlier, preferences are revealed by behaviour and consumer's response is the same as the demand expressed by the market in terms of quantities sold. In reality, market demand defined in this way is an 'ex-post' or historical observation, often of little practical value to the decision maker. Market analysts hope to retrace and understand the process followed by the buyer so as to intervene in that process in a better informed manner and to be able to measure the effectiveness of marketing actions. Therefore, response behaviour is a much broader notion to the marketer than it is to the economist.

6.1.1 The 'learn–feel–do' hierarchy

The various response levels of the buyer can be classified into three categories: *cognitive response,* which relates to retained information and knowledge, *affective response,* which concerns attitude and the evaluation system and *behavioural* (or *conative*) *response,* which describes action—not only the act of purchasing, but also after-purchase behaviour. A brief description of the main measures currently used for each response level may be given as follows:

■ *Cognitive response* Saliency; awareness; recall; recognition; knowledge; perceived similarity.

■ *Affective response* Consideration set; importance; determinance; performance; attitude; preference; intention to buy.

■ *Behavioural response* Information seeking; trial; purchase; market share; loyalty; satisfaction/dissatisfaction.

It has been postulated by practitioners in communication that these three response levels follow a sequence and that the individual, like the organization, reaches the three stages successively and in this order: cognitive (learn)—affective (feel)—behavioural (do). We then have a *learning process* which is observed in practice when the buyer is heavily involved by his or her purchase decision, for example, when the perceived risk (Bauer, 1960) or the brand sensitivity (Kapferer and Laurent, 1983) is high.

The learning response model was originally developed to measure advertising effectiveness (Lavidge and Steiner, 1961) and later extended to include the process of adoption of new products (Rogers, 1962). Palda (1966) has shown that this model is not always applicable and that uncertainty remains as to the causal links and direction existing between the intervening variables. Moreover, the learning process hypothesis implies a well-thought-out buying process, observed only when the buyer is heavily involved in his purchase decision. Psycho-sociologists have also shown that other sequences exist and are observed, for example, when there is *minimal involvement* (Krugman, 1965), or when there is *cognitive dissonance* (Festinger, 1957).

Although the learning process hypothesis is not generally applicable, the 'learn–feel–do' model remains valuable in structuring the information collected on response behaviours, particularly when complemented with the concepts of 'perceived risk' and 'buyer involvement', discussed in the previous chapter.

6.1.2 The Foote, Cone and Belding (FCB) involvement grid

The various paths of the response process may be viewed from a more general framework which includes the degree of involvement and the perception of reality mode. Brain specialization theory proposes that anatomical separation of the cerebral hemispheres of the brain leads to specialized perception of reality: the left side of the brain (or the intellectual mode) and the right side (or the affective or sensory mode).

- The left side, or *intellectual mode*, is relatively more capable of handling logic, factual information, language and analysis, i.e. the cognitive *thinking* function.

- The right side, or *affective mode*, which engages in synthesis, is more intuitive, visual and responsive to the non-verbal, i.e. the *feeling* function.

In order to provide a conceptual framework which integrates the 'learn–feel–do' hierarchy with the consumer involvement and the brain specialization theory, Vaughn (1986) presented a grid in which purchase decision processes can be classified along two basic dimensions: 'high–low' involvement and 'think–feel' perception of reality. Crossing the degree of involvement with the mode of reality perception leads to the matrix in Fig. 6.1, in which we can see four different paths of the response process.

- Quadrant 1 corresponds to a buying situation where product involvement is high and the way we perceive reality is essentially intellectual. This situation implies a large need for information due to the importance of the product and mental issues related to it. Quadrant 1 illustrates the *learning process* described earlier, where the sequence followed was *learn–feel–do*.

  Major purchases with high prices and significant objective and functional characteristics, such as cars, electrical household goods and houses follow this process. Industrial goods also fall in this category. These factors suggest a need for informative advertising.

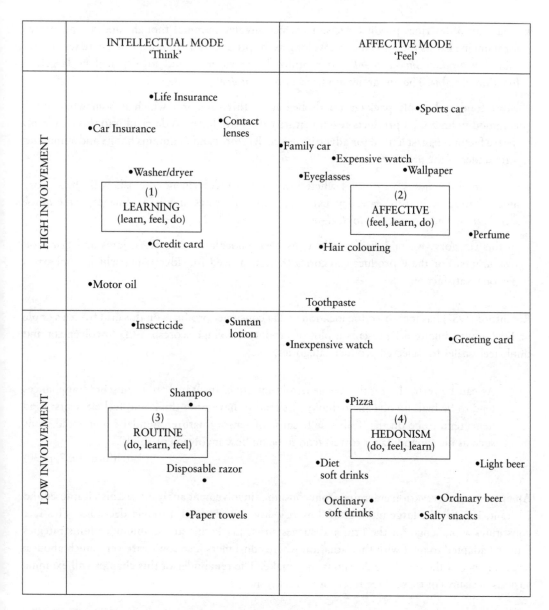

	INTELLECTUAL MODE 'Think'	AFFECTIVE MODE 'Feel'
HIGH INVOLVEMENT	•Life Insurance •Car Insurance •Contact lenses •Washer/dryer **(1) LEARNING** **(learn, feel, do)** •Credit card •Motor oil	•Sports car •Family car •Expensive watch •Eyeglasses •Wallpaper **(2) AFFECTIVE** **(feel, learn, do)** •Perfume •Hair colouring Toothpaste
LOW INVOLVEMENT	•Insecticide •Suntan lotion Shampoo • **(3) ROUTINE** **(do, learn, feel)** Disposable razor • •Paper towels	•Inexpensive watch •Greeting card •Pizza **(4) HEDONISM** **(do, feel, learn)** •Diet soft drinks •Light beer Ordinary • soft drinks •Ordinary beer •Salty snacks

FIGURE 6.1 *The Foote, Cone and Belding Involvement Grid* (Source: *adapted from Ratchford, 1987*)

■ Quadrant 2 describes buying situations where product involvement is also high. Specific information is, however, less important than an attitude or an *emotional arousal*, since the product or brand choice reveals the buyer's system of values and personality and relates to the buyer's self-esteem. The sequence here is *feel–learn–do*.

In this category, we find all products that have important social and/or emotional value, such as perfumes, clothes, jewellery and motorcycles. These factors suggest a need for emotional advertising.

- Quadrant 3 describes product decisions which involve minimal thought and a tendency to form buying habits for convenience. As long as the product fulfils the expected core service, we find *low product involvement* and routinized behaviour. Brand loyalty will be largely a function of habit. The hierarchy model is a *do–learn–feel* pattern.

  Most food and staple package goods belong in this category, which is somewhat like a commodity limbo. As products reach maturity, they are likely to descend into this quadrant. These factors suggest a need for advertising which creates and maintains habits and stimulates a reminder of the product.

- Quadrant 4 illustrates a situation where low product involvement co-exists with the sensory mode. Products in this category cater to personal tastes involving imagery and *quick satisfaction*. The sequence is *do–feel–learn*.

  In this category, we find such products as beer, chocolates, cigarettes, jams and fast food restaurants. For these product categories there is a need for advertising which emphasizes personal satisfaction.

Ratchford (1987) has measured the location of 254 consumer products on this grid from a sample of 1792 adults. Figure 6.1 presents a plot of products' average scores on the 'involvement and think/feel' scales for selected product categories.

> As can be seen, the results are generally intuitive. Insurance and household appliances tend to be high involvement/think; cars tend to have both think and feel elements; food items tend to be on the 'feel' side because of sensory nature; mundane household items such as bleach and paper towels tend to be on 'low involvement/think'.
>
> (Ratchford, 1987, p. 30)

An interesting observation emerging from consumer involvement analyses (see also Kapferer and Laurent, 1983) is the large number of 'low risk–low involvement' product decisions. This fact constitutes a challenge for the firm and suggests that marketing and communication strategies must be adapted to deal with this situation where consumers just don't care very much about a large number of the purchase decisions they make. The remainder of this chapter will examine various measures of these three levels of market response.

6.2 MEASURING THE COGNITIVE RESPONSE

Cognitive response relates to knowledge, i.e. the totality of information and beliefs held by an individual or a group. Individuals store this information, which influences their interpretation of the stimuli to which they are exposed. The quantity and nature of the information retained varies according to cognitive styles (Pinson *et al.*, 1988) and perceptual capacities. *Perception* (according to Berelson and Steiner, 1964, p. 88) can be defined as:

> The process by which an individual selects, organizes and interprets the information inputs to create a meaningful picture of the world.

Individuals will, in general, have different perceptions of the same situation, because of selective attention. Perception has a regulating function since it filters information. Some elements of information are retained either because they meet the needs of the moment, or because they come as a surprise: this is *selective perception and retention*. Other elements are perceived as altered when they contradict the specific framework of interest: this is *perceptual bias*. Finally, other elements are rejected because they are worrying or disturbing: this is *perceptual defence*. For example, a study done in the USA reveals that only 32 per cent of smokers have read newspaper articles suggesting a link between cigarette smoking and the development of cancer of the larynx, as opposed to 60 per cent of non-smokers.

Clearly, the first objective of producers must be to overcome perceptual resistance and to propagate knowledge about their products and about their claimed distinctive features. This first stage conditions the development of any market demand.

Several measures of the cognitive response have been developed. They can be grouped into three categories: brand awareness, advertising recall and perceived similarity.

6.2.1 Brand awareness

The simplest level of cognitive response is the knowledge of the existence of a product or a brand. Is the potential buyer aware of the brand existence within a given product category? Brand awareness can be defined as follows:

> The ability of a potential buyer to identify (recall or recognize) the brand with sufficient detail to propose, recommend, choose or use the brand to meet the need of a certain product category.

Thus, awareness establishes a link between the brand name and a product class. Information about brand awareness can easily be obtained by questioning potential buyers about the brands they know in the class of products under consideration. Three types of brand awareness can be distinguished:

1. *Brand recognition* implies that brand recognition precedes and leads to the need (I recognize brand A and I realize that I need such a product category). Recognition is a minimal level of awareness which will be particularly important at the point of purchase when choosing a brand.
2. *Brand recall* implies that the need for a product category precedes and leads to the brand (I need that product category; I shall buy brand A). Recall is a much more demanding test.
3. *Top of the mind awareness* refers to the first-named brand in a recall test. The brand is ahead of all the other competing brands that the person can think of.

Brand recall is measured by unaided awareness; brand recognition is measured by aided or qualified awareness. *Unaided awareness* refers to the case where the respondent is questioned about a brand but the question makes no reference to any brand. *Aided awareness* refers to a set of brand names from a given product class which are presented to respondents, who are asked to note the ones they have heard of before. In the latter case, respondents may also be asked to

TABLE 6.1 *Measuring brand awareness*

Unaided awareness	Aided or qualified awareness	
Which brands of laptop computers do you know ?	Among the following brands of laptop computers, indicate the brand(s) you know	
....		
....	Know very well:	....
....	Know by name only:	....
....	Don't know:	....

specify their level of familiarity with the brand on a scale of three or five positions, as illustrated in Table 6.1. We then have a measure of *qualified awareness*.

The responses to these simple questions provide useful information to allow the evaluation of the *capital of goodwill* (Nerlove and Arrow, 1962) or *brand equity* (Aaker, 1991) enjoyed by the brand or by the firm. The information provided by a brand awareness analysis is used as follows.

- To determine the *brand's share of mind*, i.e. the percentage of potential buyers who name the brand or the company as the first brand or company that comes to mind in the product category.

- To identify the *triplet of the best-known brands* which are in direct competition in the minds of potential customers, i.e. the number of times a brand is mentioned in an unaided recall test in first, second or third position.

- To compare the observed changes in the *recall versus recognition scores* in an unaided versus an aided recall test. Some brands or companies have a weak evocative power; a product may be easily recognized due to its obvious link with the product class, but in an unaided recall test the product scores low (see Krugman, 1972).

- To compare the correlation between the *awareness score* and *market share* of each brand with regard to the market average performance. Some brands enhance their awareness better than others and are situated above the market average (see Assael and Day, 1968).

- To construct a *one-dimensional interval scale*, based on the Law of Comparative Judgements (Thurstone, 1959). This method is used to obtain a ranking as well as measures of distance between brands in terms of awareness.

- To compare awareness scores (aided and unaided) between *different groups of buyers* and thereby identify zones of weakest awareness where remedial action should be taken.

It is worth remembering that a high awareness score is a key brand asset to the firm; it takes years to build and requires significant and repetitive advertising investments. Brand awareness is a key component of brand equity, even if it alone cannot create sales. On the concept of brand equity, see Aaker (1991).

In addition, apart from the identification of the brand itself, measures of knowledge may also relate to the identification of some of its characteristics, such as usual places of sale, current advertising themes and price levels.

6.2.2 Advertising recall

Advertising recall scores are commonly used as intermediate measures of advertising effectiveness. They are also used with different variations to measure new product acceptance. Various impact scores are available which measure the percentage of readers or viewers who correctly identify the advertisement or the message after an advertising campaign. There is a large number of variants of impact scores. The following three measures of print advertising effectiveness, obtained from interviews, recur regularly:

■ *Noted score*: the percentage of readers who say they previously saw the advertisement in the magazine (ad recognition).

■ *Saw-associated or Proved Name Registration (PNR) score*: the percentage of individuals who correctly identify the product and advertiser with the advertisement.

■ *Read most*: the percentage who say they read more than half of the written material in the advertisement.

These impact scores are collected after several exposures and are cumulative scores. Another useful impact score, called the '*beta (β) score*' (Morgensztern, 1983) or day-after score, is a more revealing measure. It is defined as:

> The percentage of individuals who, when exposed for the first time to a new message, memorize the brand and at least one of the visual or textual elements of the advertisement.

Comparisons of beta scores from different advertising campaigns show enormous fluctuations between campaigns with the same intensity within a medium as well as between advertising media (see Table 6.2). Companies specializing in this kind of analysis, such as Daniel Starch in the USA, also provide 'adnorms' showing the average scores for each product category for the year. This information enables advertisers to compare their advertisement's impact with those of competition.

The comparison of impact scores, obtained from a large number of advertisements, shows that:

■ The prior level of brand awareness has a significant effect on scores of advertising recall; the greater the brand awareness, the higher the impact of the message.

■ Some product categories benefit from a recall above average.

■ Recall measured in terms of 'saw-associated' scores is better among the upper social classes.

TABLE 6.2 *Comparing impact scores of media advertising*

Media	Beta scores (%)		
	Average scores	Minimum scores	Maximum scores
Television (30 seconds)	27	9	70
Dailies (1/4 page mono)	35	0	75
Dailies (1/2 page mono)	27	3	69
Magazines (colour page)	19	6	46
Magazines (d.p.s. colour)	27	6	46

Source: Carat, Belgium.

■ Creative factors, advertisement formats, use of colour and visualization of the product in the advertisement are factors that explained the variance of observed scores.

These scores are only intermediate measures of advertising effectiveness and give no indication about advertising's ultimate effectiveness, which should ideally help to produce sales. These intermediate measures are nevertheless useful since they enable advertisers to verify whether the advertisement has actually succeeded in breaking the wall of indifference of the target audience. Observed differences in recall scores can be explained by the attractiveness of the message, by the element of surprise, incongruity and originality. The comparison of qualitative scores (agreement, credibility, originality) shows that consumers perceive differences between advertisements by product category. These differences also exist between brands within the same class of products.

6.2.3 The remembering and forgetting of advertising

Studying the dynamics of recall scores provides some knowledge about the evolution of recall over time and allows the determination of optimal advertising scheduling given the communication objective.

Experiments done in this domain (Morgensztern, 1983) have established that the proportion of individuals retaining an induced opinion change decrease geometrically over time. The rates of depreciation of recall, however, vary largely with the contents to be retained. Figure 6.2, based on an experiment conducted by Watts and McGuire (1964), illustrates this point.

One can see that recall of the message topic drops sharply after one week (from 95 per cent to 60 per cent), but then continues at this level; on the other hand, recall of the arguments used in the message sees a much sharper drop in the first week (from 72 per cent to 28 per cent) and then continues to decay to reach approximately 20 per cent in the sixth week. One observes a similar but less abrupt pattern for recall of the message source. Thus, advertisers have very little time at their disposal to get the value of the investment on communication that they have made.

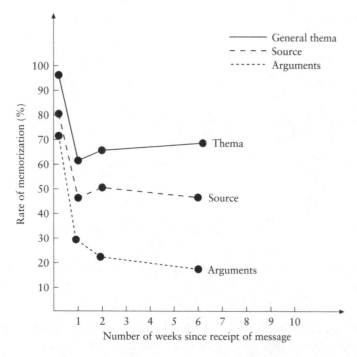

FIGURE 6.2 *Induced opinion change as a function of time* (Source: *Watts and McGuire, 1964*)

The repetition of the message clearly has an effect on people's ability to remember over time. Many experiments have been carried out, namely by Zielske (1958) and Zielske and Henry (1980), which have underlined the relation between the change in the recall rate and different advertising schedules. In his 1958 study, Zielske measured the impact on recall of two advertising campaigns of 13 newspaper advertisements each.

> The plan of this experiment was to expose one group of women to 13 different advertisements from the same newspaper advertising campaign at four-week intervals (staggered action). Every four weeks for a year an advertisement was mailed to women in this group. A second group of women received a total of 13 advertisements, mailed one week apart (intensive action). Recall of the advertising, aided only by mention of the product class, was obtained by telephone interviews throughout the study, with no single individual being interviewed more than once.

The recall of advertising by both groups, as reported by Zielske, is shown in Fig. 6.3. These data emphasize the nature of response rather than the interim decay.

The following observations emerge:

1. After 13 weekly exposures (intensive action), the rate of recall registered among exposed households was 63 per cent; after 13 monthly exposures, it was only 48 per cent in the other group subjected to the staggered action.

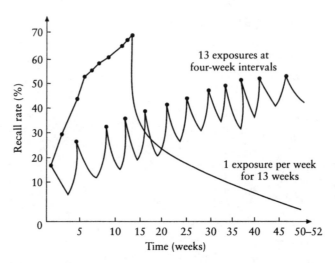

FIGURE 6.3 *Dynamic evolution of recall as a function of time and number of exposures* (Source: *Zielske, 1958*)

2. During the period of 52 weeks, however, the average percentage of households who could recall the advertising was 29 per cent in the case of the staggered action and only 21 per cent in the other group.
3. In the case of weekly exposures, four weeks after the end of the campaign the rate of recall dropped by 50 per cent, and six weeks later by 66 per cent.
4. The rate of forgetting decreased as the number of repetitions increased; three weeks after one exposure to the message, the recall rate dropped from 14 per cent to 3 per cent, that is a depreciation rate of 79 per cent; after 13 exposures, the recall rate dropped from 48 per cent to 37 per cent in three weeks, which is a depreciation rate of only 23 per cent.

Similar results were obtained with another experiment done in 1980 (Zielske and Henry) with television advertising, again involving actions with the same intensity but different schedules. The forgetting mechanisms are very powerful and memory loss is very rapid, implying the necessity for a sufficient number of repetitions of the message.

> A television campaign consisting of 6 repetitions in its first wave, and creating a 60 per cent rate of recall, should not be interrupted for more than three months if one doesn't want to see the rate drop below 20 per cent.   (Morgensztern, 1983, p. 210)

Large fluctuations will exist between different campaigns, according to their relevance and to the creative value of their messages. The same phenomenon of rapid forgetting is also observed with other media, the daily press in particular.

How to overcome the buyers' wall of indifference or perceptual defence is not obvious. Yet, if this condition is not met, nothing will happen where attitudes of behaviour are concerned. As long as advertising information is not perceived, understood and memorized, it doesn't exist for the potential buyer. Informing is not sufficient; one must also communicate.

6.2.4 Perceived similarity analysis

Multi-dimensional scaling of perceived similarity is a method used for understanding how a brand is positioned in the minds of potential buyers *vis-à-vis* competing brands. This is done through the construction of perceptual maps which give a visual representation of perceived similarities among brands without formulating any prior hypotheses concerning the causes of the perceived similarities or dissimilarities. Thus, the method is a *non-attribute-based approach* which does not ask respondents to rate the brands on designated attributes, but rather asks them to make some summary judgements about the brands' degree of similarity.

For this reason, non-attribute-based perceptual maps can be considered as a form of cognitive response, even though there exists an underlying evaluation in the comparative judgements provided by the respondent. Multi-dimensional scaling of perceived similarities is based on the following assumptions:

■ Any product or brand (any object) is perceived by the individual as a *bundle of characteristics* or *attributes*.

■ These characteristics are used as *criteria for comparing* brands which are part of their evoked set.

■ If each of the K characteristics is geometrically represented along one axis, i.e. by one dimension of a K-dimensional space, each brand or object will represent one point in this space and the co-ordinates of this point will be the evaluations of the product according to each characteristic.

■ In practice, it is observed that potential buyers' perceptions of products or brands are based on a small number of dimensions, rarely more than two or three, called macro-characteristics.

These privileged dimensions, or macro-characteristics, are identified and are used to compare the positioning of the different brands. Multi-dimensional similarity analysis finally leads to perceptual maps where each point represents a brand and the distance between points measures the approximate degree of similarity perceived by respondents. Box 6.1 succinctly describes the estimation procedure followed in such analyses.

Figure 6.4 is an example of a non-attribute-based perceptual map. It depicts the market for jams in Belgium in 1978. The analysis, based on a random sample of 400 respondents, brings to the fore the existence of two dimensions in respondents' perceived similarity.

■ The first dimension (horizontal) contrasts industrial jams with home-made jams. Price differences are significant between these two types of product.

■ The second dimension contrasts private brands (Sarma, GB and Delhaize) with manufacturers' brands. Note that these two groups of brands have more or less the same ranking on the first dimension, implying that respondents perceive them as similar as far as this characteristic is concerned.

We have a visual representation of perceived similarities between the brands according to two dimensions which summarize the market perceptions. These results may appear trivial, in that

BOX 6.1

Multi-dimensional scaling analysis: description of the estimation procedure

The objective is to develop a non-attribute-based multi-dimensional map to characterize the perceived relationships among a set of brands competing within a given market segment.

A representative sample of respondents is asked to rank all possible pairs of the studied brands according to their perceived degree of similarity. We thus have a triangular matrix where the entries are simple ranks, or ordered relationships by increasing dissimilarity. For N compared brands, we will have $N(N - 1)/2$ different entries.

The objective of the method is to seek a configuration of points of minimum dimensionality that most nearly matches the original order of perceived distances among brands. That is a geometric configuration in which the physical distances between points are monotonic (i.e. in the same order) with the original similarity judgements.

To find this configuration, generally the computer program operates iteratively. It starts with a given (arbitrary) configuration in $N - 1$ dimensions. It generates an initial solution and then assesses how well the ordering of the actual distances between the brands matches the original ranking of similarity and determines whether the fit can be improved. It then reduces the number of dimensions and repeats the process with the objective of finding the lowest dimensionality for which the monotonicity constraint is closely met.

Once the best configuration is identified, the last step is to interpret the retained dimensions and to discover the underlying macro-characteristics used by the respondents to compare the brands.

Source: Adapted from Churchill (1987).

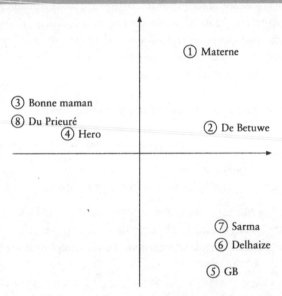

FIGURE 6.4 *An example of a non-attribute-based perceptual map: the market for jams in Belgium (Source: Brussels, MDA Consulting Group)*

they don't provide any new information to the manufacturer. Nevertheless, they are important because:

■ The analysis made it possible to identify the two dimensions spontaneously used by consumers when they mentally compare brands, in this example, the perception of 'industrial versus home-made' and the contrast of 'private brands versus manufacturers' brands'.

■ The analysis brings to the fore the structure of the market in each subgroup by identifying whether or not the brands are perceived as direct substitutes.

■ The analysis allows each firm to contrast the positioning perceived by the market with the positioning sought for the brand.

The method of multi-dimensional analysis does, however, have problems, which ought to be underlined.

■ When the number of brands to be evaluated becomes large, the task facing respondents is very tedious. If there are 7 brands to compare, 21 pairs of brands need to be ranked, which might overwhelm the cognitive abilities of respondents.

■ Interpretation of the axes is not always obvious and normally requires additional information.

Despite these difficulties, this method of structuring the market has the following advantages:

1. The method preserves the multi-dimensional nature of market perceptions.
2. The dimensions, or comparative criteria, are not *a priori* imposed.
3. Inputs are simple non-metric ranking data, which are in principle easy to obtain from respondents when the number of objects to compare is not large.

In order to be fully operational, multi-dimensional scaling analysis needs to be complemented with an attribute-based approach which relies on attribute-by-attribute assessments of the various brands. In general, this approach is the objective of affective response measurements (Green and Rao, 1972).

6.3 MEASURING THE AFFECTIVE RESPONSE

The affective response is evaluative. It is no longer based only on simple knowledge. It also includes feelings, preferences, intentions and favourable or unfavourable judgements about a brand or an organization. Several operational measures are also available to market analysts, with attitude as a central concept.

6.3.1 The consideration set

The brands identified in the product category by the respondent constitute the *evoked set* of brands, as mentioned in Chapter 4 (see Fig. 4.2). The choice or consideration set is more restrictive, because it only contains the brands which, from the buyer's perspective, have a non-zero probability of being purchased. The distinction is quite significant; a buyer may know a brand very well but may never consider purchasing it. To identify the consideration set, additional information is necessary: identification of brands that the buyer might consider for the next purchase.

In the consumer goods sector, it is believed that the average number of known brands may vary between 10 and 20 according to the class of products, whereas the average size of the consideration set is three to five brands (Jarvis and Wilcox, 1977). The notion of the consideration set is important; there is little chance that a brand will get adopted if it is not part of this set. It is in the producer's interest to know which brands or suppliers are on the short list of potential customers.

6.3.2 Definition of attitude

A central notion in affective response is the *concept of attitude*. A classical definition of attitude is the one given by Allport (1935):

> The mental process by which an individual—on the basis of past experience and stored information—organizes his perceptions, beliefs and feelings about a particular object and orientates his future behaviour.

In this definition, we find the three levels or components of market response defined in the first section of this chapter.

- Attitude is based on a *series of information* about the object being evaluated, which is progressively stored by the individual (cognitive component).

- Attitude is oriented and reflects feelings, positive or negative, or *evaluation* regarding the object (affective component).

- Attitude is dynamic and is a *predisposition to respond*; as such, it has predictive value (behavioural component).

Psycho-sociologists (see Fishbein, 1967) also consider that attitude is *persistent*, although it can be modified; is *structured*, in the sense that it has internal consistency and is based on evaluative criteria; and its *intensity* may vary widely or retain a state of neutrality.

Experimental studies in this area have shown that although measures of attitude are not infallible, they predict actual behaviours reasonably well. To be more precise, the following facts are generally accepted:

- When buyers' attitudes towards a brand become more favourable, its use tends to grow and, conversely, an unfavourable attitude heralds its decline.

- Consumers' attitudes help to explain market shares held by different brands (Assael and Day, 1968).

- As the number of competing products and brands increases, the firm needs to intervene to maintain and to reinforce favourable attitudes.

Since measures of attitude are likely to be taken before a purchasing decision, they are of great importance for market analysis, as concerns diagnosis, control and prediction.

- *Diagnosis*: knowledge of a brand's strengths and weaknesses helps identify opportunities and/ or threats facing a brand.

- *Control*: measures of attitudes taken 'before' and 'after' help evaluate the effectiveness of strategies aimed at changing the attitude towards the brand.

- *Prediction*: knowledge of attitudes helps predict the market response to a new or modified product, without having to rely on ex-post observations.

Given the importance of this notion, considerable attention has been given during the last 20 years to attitude measurement issues, not only in psycho-sociology research (Rosenberg, 1956; Fishbein, 1967), but also in marketing research (Wilkie and Pessemier, 1973).

6.3.3 The multi-attribute model

The multi-attribute product concept defined in the previous chapter serves as the conceptual basis for modelling attitude. As mentioned earlier, two estimation procedures can be used for measuring a multi-attribute model: the 'compositional' approach or the 'decompositional' approach. These two approaches will be examined successively.

The compositional approach

The multi-attribute product concept has been defined in the previous chapter. Let us briefly review the basic ideas of this notion, as they are summarized in Table 4.1.

1. Individuals perceive a brand or a product as a bundle of attributes.
2. Each individual does not necessarily attach the same importance to attributes.
3. Individuals hold certain beliefs about the degree of presence of attributes in each brand which is evaluated.
4. Individuals have a utility function for each attribute, associating the degree of expected satisfaction or utility with the degree of presence of the attribute in the object.
5. Individuals' attitude is structured, i.e. based on processing the stored information.

The most widely used multi-attribute model is the model developed by Fishbein (1967) and by Bass and Tarlarzyck (1969), which can be formalized as follows:

$$A_{ij} = \sum_{k=1}^{n} w_{jk} \cdot x_{ijk}$$

where A_{ij} is the attitude of individual j about brand i; w_{jk} is the relative importance to individual j of attribute k; x_{ijk} is the perceived degree of presence of attribute k in brand i by individual j (score) and n is the number of determinant attributes ($k = 1$ to n).

This formula is a weighted average of evaluation scores. To estimate this model, the market analyst needs an importance score for each attribute and an evaluation (or performance) score of the brand with respect to each attribute. A numerical example is given in Table 6.3, where five brands of laptop computer are evaluated according to five determinant attributes.

If the potential buyer evaluates brands in a linearly additive fashion, the selected laptop computer will not necessarily be the most compact, the most powerful, nor the one with the most readable screen, the most convenient keyboard, etc. The selected computer, however, will be that which is 'globally' best for this buyer, taking into account all the relevant attributes and their relative importance. In this example, the model suggests that brand D will be preferred by the market.

In this model, the multiplicative relations between importance and performance, the summation over all attributes and the nature of the scores show that it is a linear compensatory attitude model. This fact allows high scores in some attributes to compensate for low ratings in others.

Measuring attribute determinance   To measure attitude empirically, the attributes used as choice criteria by the target group must be identified. A distinction must be made between attribute 'salience', 'importance' and 'determinance' as already discussed in Chapter 4. Briefly,

- *Salience* corresponds to the fact that the attribute is in the respondent's mind at a given moment.

- *Importance* reflects the value system of the individual.

- *Determinance* reflects the ability of a particular attribute to discriminate among alternative brands.

Thus, determinance refers to important attributes which help differentiate among objects being evaluated. If an important attribute is equally represented in all competing brands, it clearly doesn't allow discrimination among them, and is not a determinant in the choice. Measuring determinance implies not only a measure of importance, but also a *differentiation score*, which is a measure of perceived difference between brands with respect to each attribute.

Determinance is then obtained by multiplying scores of importance and differentiation. Differentiation may be measured by a direct question about perceived differences between brands for each attribute using, for example, a scale of 1 (no difference) to 5 (great difference). A simpler method would be a measure of dispersion for differentiation score (such as standard deviation of evaluation scores), as illustrated in Table 6.3. This method would prevent the respondents' task from being too demanding.

Clearly, it is with respect to determinant attributes that it is interesting to situate different competing brands in the market. In the example of Table 6.3, global attitude scores are calculated first with the importance scores and then with the determinance scores. The model predicts that individual j will prefer computer D. But the ranking of computers B and C is modified, however, when the determinance scores are used.

TABLE 6.3 *A compositional multi-attribute model*

Brands of laptop computer	Compact-ness	Autonomy	Power	Keyboard	Screen	Mean	Adjusted
Brand A	6	8	9	8	7	7.50	7.68
Brand B	7	8	7	8	9	7.60	7.58
Brand C	5	9	9	8	8	7.55	7.86
Brand D	7	8	9	7	9	7.85	7.95
Brand E	8	8	5	6	7	7.00	7.08
Brand F	9	2	5	6	7	5.80	5.07
Importance	0.30	0.25	0.20	0.15	0.10	1.00	1.00
Differentiation*	1.41	2.56	1.97	0.98	0.98	—	—
Determinance†	0.25	0.38	0.23	0.09	0.06	1.00	1.00

Header spanning note: columns "Compact-ness" through "Screen" are under **Attribute**; "Mean" and "Adjusted" are under **Overall score‡**.

* Differentiation of a particular attribute is measured by the standard deviation of the scores on that attribute.

†Determinance is obtained by multiplying the importance score by the differentiation score and by standardizing those products to have a sum equal to 1.

‡The mean score is calculated using the importance scores, while the adjusted mean score is determined using the determinance scores.

The importance/performance matrix   An attribute can be considered as very important by a buyer and not be perceived as present in a particular brand. The problem then is whether to reinforce the attribute's presence in the product or to use better communication to increase awareness and/or conviction about the attribute's presence. To confront importance and performance scores, it is convenient to use a matrix similar to the one presented in Fig. 6.5 where the attributes of a brand are situated along two dimensions (Martilla and James, 1977). The horizontal axis indicates the importance of the attributes from low to high and the vertical axis represents their perceived performance from low to high. The placements of attributes on this two-dimensional grid suggest the suitable strategy for each.

■ In the upper-right quadrant are located the '*strengths*', i.e. attributes evaluated high in both importance and performance. The brand has a strong image for these criteria which must be highlighted in the communication.

■ In the quadrant just below are the brand '*weaknesses*': These attributes are rated high in importance but low in performance. In this case the firm has to act and make efforts to improve its performance.

■ In the upper-left quadrant are the '*false problems*', the criteria rated high in performance but low in importance. This implies that an overkill has occurred. Perhaps the resources committed to these attributes should be reallocated.

FIGURE 6.5 *The importance–performance matrix*

■ Finally, in the quadrant below are the *'false strengths'*: These attributes are rated low in both importance and performance. They are considered to be of low priority and, hence require no further action.

This analysis is useful to identify the components of a brand image and the communication programme to support this image. This matrix, as outlined above, has two weaknesses however, which limits its usefulness for identifying the brand's sustainable competitive advantage.

■ First, performance of the brand on a particular attribute is defined in absolute terms ignoring performance *vis-à-vis* competitors. In reality, buyers do not evaluate an object in a competitive vacuum but in comparative terms. Thus, *relative performance* scores should be determined for each attribute by reference to priority competitor(s).

■ Second, as discussed above, importance scores do not recognize the *determinance* of an attribute. Determinant attributes are those that discriminate well among competing brands and directly influence buyer choice. Thus, focusing solely on importance may misguide strategy definition (Yavas and Eroglu, 1995).

The extended 'importance–performance' analysis is designed to rectify these two weaknesses by incorporating a relative performance dimension and a determinance dimension. Three levels of determinance (high, medium, low) are combined with three levels of relative performance (competitive advantage, parity or disadvantage) as shown in the matrix of Fig. 6.6.

Attribute-based perceptual maps   The problem of *redundancy* remains as a final question about the relevance of attributes. Two attributes are said to be redundant when there is no difference in their significance. For example, in a study of the heavy trucks market in Belgium, the two criteria

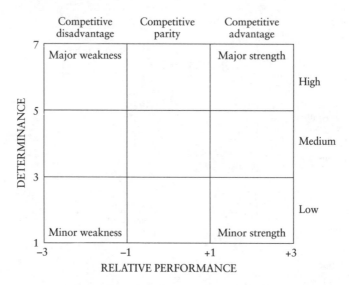

FIGURE 6.6 *Determinance versus relative performance analysis*

of 'loading capacity' and 'engine capacity' were spontaneously evoked as important attributes. The two criteria were being used interchangeably, neither existing without the other.

If two determinant attributes are retained, but they both indicate the same characteristic, this situation is equivalent to selecting only one attribute. The analyst should establish a list of determinant but non-redundant attributes.

The method used for this purpose is factorial analysis—for example, Principal Components Analysis (PCA). This method is a statistical technique which organizes and summarizes a set of data (the N determinant attributes in this case) into a reduced set of factors called the principal components or 'macro-characteristics', which are independent of each other and which contrast best the objects under study (see Hair *et al.*, 1992). The output of a PCA is an attribute-based perceptual map. Each brand is positioned along the two or three retained components which can be interpreted by the correlation observed between these principal components and each attribute. The interpretation of a perceptual map resulting from a PCA is as follows:

■ Two brands are close on the perceptual map if they are evaluated in the same way according to all retained attributes.

■ Two attributes are close if they lead to the evaluation of brands in the same manner.

Examples of PCAs are presented in Figs 6.4 and 6.7.

Brand image studies measure buyers' perceptions and help to discover market expectations. The perceptual map of Fig. 6.7 illustrates this point. This map is based on the rating scores of 12 attributes obtained from a sample of regular users of skin-care and make-up brands. A PCA of these scores identified two macro-attributes which summarize 83 per cent of the total variance.

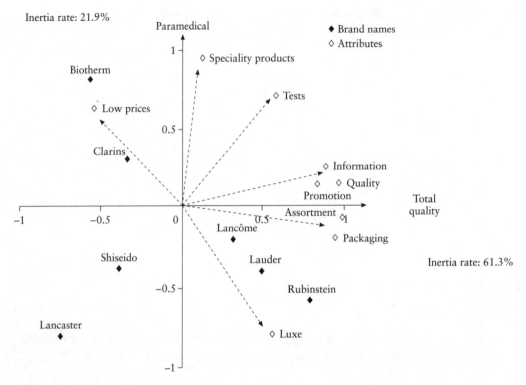

FIGURE 6.7 *Attribute-based perceptual map: the skin-care and make-up market* (Source: *van Ballenberghe, 1993*)

- The first axis is total quality as perceived by the respondents and includes the following micro-attributes: 'technical quality, 'extent of product line', 'quality of packaging', 'information', 'attractive promotions'. These attribute are mentally opposed to 'attractive prices'.

- The second axis is strongly correlated with the attributes 'medicare products', 'laboratory tests' and is opposed to 'luxury design'. This axis reflects the paramedical nature of these products.

In the map of Fig. 6.7, we can see that brand A is well positioned along the price dimension, but poorly placed on the total quality dimension—namely, because of its poor performance in providing assistance in use (information and services), which is a service 'added' by the most quality-oriented competitors. This analysis leads to the suggestion that brand A should modify its offering and reinforce the attribute 'assistance' which is part of the bundle of attributes expected by consumers of this type of product. Another approach to determining modelling preferences can be found in Box 6.2.

Non-compensatory models of attitude   We have seen that the Fishbein model is compensatory, i.e. low points on an attribute are compensated by high points obtained for other attributes. This way of evaluating brands is not necessarily the most effective and one can imagine that an individual may face an absolute constraint on a price level. In this kind of situation, evaluation is no longer compensatory because one criterion dominates.

BOX 6.2

Modelling preferences through the decompositional approach: the coffee market in Belgium

■ We have data of global preference rankings for 9 brands of coffee, as expressed by a sample of 811 respondents.

■ These 9 brands were then evaluated, on a 5-point rating scale, by the same respondents according to 11 micro-attributes.

■ A Principal Component Analysis (PCA) of these rating scores identified two macro-attributes which alone explained 89.6 per cent of the total variance.

■ The co-ordinates of the 9 brands on these two dimensions were then used as two explanatory variables of the global preference scores in a multiple regression model with the following results:

$$\text{Preferences} = 8.6 + 8.3 \text{ attribute #1} + 10.3 \text{ attribute #2}$$
$$[5.1] \qquad\qquad\qquad [2.9]$$
$$R^2 = 0.851 \qquad \text{F-test} = 17.1 \, [2.6]$$

■ The observed relationship is statistically significant and its coefficients have the expected signs, thereby suggesting that the selected set of attributes do explain the global preference.

The t-tests in square brackets are under the regression coefficients.

In Box 6.3 the major non-compensatory models of attitude are defined. The most common observation is a two-stage choice procedure. At the first stage, the potential buyer adopts a conjunctive model allowing products that do not satisfy his or her minimal requirements to be eliminated. At the second stage, the remaining products are subjected to compensatory evaluation or lexicographic ordering.

Strategies for changing attitude   Knowledge of the way consumers perceive competing products in a segment is important in determining the strategy to be adopted to modify an unfavourable position. Six different strategies may be considered (Boyd *et al.*, 1972):

1. *Modifying the product.* If the brand is not up to market expectations of a particular characteristic, the product can be modified by reinforcing the given characteristic.
2. *Modifying attribute weights.* Convince the market that more importance ought to be attached to a particular characteristic that the brand exhibits well.
3. *Modifying beliefs about a brand.* The market may be badly informed and underestimate some real distinctive qualities of the brand. This entails perceptual repositioning.
4. *Modifying beliefs about competing brands.* This strategy is to be used if the market overestimates some characteristics of competitors. It implies the possibility of using comparative advertising.

BOX 6.3

Non-compensatory decision and attitude models

- *Disjunctive model*   Instead of setting minimum standards on different attributes and rejecting alternatives that do not meet all those minima, the buyer sets a high standard for *one or a few attributes* and then considers buying only those brands meeting or exceeding the standards on these attributes only.

- *Conjunctive model*   The buyer has some *minimum cut-off level* in mind for each important attribute. He or she rejects alternatives that fall below the minimum on any one of those attributes. The buyer will favour the brand(s) that exceed the minimum requirements on all important criteria. A high score on one attribute will not compensate for a below minimum level on another.

- *Lexicographic model*   In a lexicographic model, the buyer first *ranks criteria* or *attributes* in order of importance. Next, all brands or choice alternatives are compared on the most important attribute. If one brand scores higher on the most important criterion than any other brands, then it is chosen. If not (suppose it is tied with two others), then the inferior brands are eliminated and comparisons are made among the tied brands using the second most important attribute. The procedure is continued until a final superior brand remains to be chosen or until no further brands can be eliminated.

5. *Attracting attention to neglected attributes*. This strategy usually involves the creation of a new benefit not yet considered by the target segment.
6. *Modifying the required attribute level*. It is possible that the market expects a quality level that is not always necessary, at least as far as some applications are concerned. The firm can try to convince the segment that the quality offered for that particular dimension is adequate.

The major advantage of multi-attribute models over simple overall attitude measure is in gaining an understanding of the attitudinal structure of the segment under study, in order to identify the most appropriate strategies of positioning and communication.

The decompositional approach

The compositional approach proceeds from evaluations of brands according to different attributes and builds a global utility score. The decompositional approach proceeds in the opposite direction and starts from the classification of preferences over different products or brands whose bundles of characteristics are described. From this classification, the underlying *partial utilities* of each characteristic are derived, which allows reconstitution of the respondent's order of preferences in the best possible way. Therefore, for a given buyer, the total utility of a brand is equal to the sum of its partial utilities.

In this approach, the partial utilities that buyers attach to attributes are directly estimated. These partial utilities reflect the subjective value associated with each attribute; in fact, they result from the perceived degree of presence of an attribute and its importance, without it being possible to separately identify them. Therefore, a high level of utility may be the result of either a high degree of importance and a low level of perceived presence, or a low degree of importance compensated by a high level of perceived presence. Table 4.1, discussed above (p. 120), sets out the complementarity between the compositional and decompositional approaches.

To derive partial utilities, various estimation methods are available, such as *conjoint analysis* (Green and Srinivasan, 1978) or *trade-off analysis* (Johnson, 1974). The simplest and most reliable estimation technique is the multiple regression method based on binary (or dummy) variables, as shown in Table 6.4.

6.3.4 Example of conjoint analysis

In this illustrative example, the objective was to measure and compare the price sensitivities of four brands competing in the blended cigarettes segment: Marlboro, Barclay, Camel and Gauloise Blonde. A cigarette brand can be defined as a bundle of seven characteristics: brand name, package content and stiffness, cigarette length, tar and nicotine content, cigarette diameter and price. The four studied brands are different only with regard to three of these characteristics: brand, tar (T) and nicotine (N) content, and price; only these characteristics are therefore determinant in the choice (Herwats, 1986).

Four levels were considered for each of these characteristics:

- Four brand names: Barclay, Camel, Marlboro and Gauloise Blonde.

- Four contents of tar and nicotine: Barclay: T = 1 mg, N = 0.2 mg; Camel: T = 4 mg, N = 0.4 mg; Marlboro: T = 9 mg, N = 0.7 mg; Gauloise Blonde: T = 15 mg, N = 1 mg.

- Four prices: BF57, 62, 67, 72, respectively.

Thus, altogether, the analyst can form 64 possible combinations of these components (4 × 4 × 4). Conjoint analysis is concerned with measuring the joint effect of these independent variables (the product components) on the ordering of a dependent variable, such as preference or intention-to-buy.

Given the total number of combinations, it would be too demanding a task to ask respondents to rank or rate all these combinations. The use of efficient experimental designs, such as fractional factorial designs, provides guidelines for selecting a reduced number of the 64 combinations. In this case a 4 × 4 latin square design was used and the respondents were asked to rank the 16 selected combinations from the most preferred to the least preferred. This design permits one to estimate all the main effects, while assuming the absence of significant second-order interactions among factors (Addelman, 1962). For example, bundle 6 (C-62–9/0.7) is defined as follows: the brand Camel, with a price of 62, with a tar content of 9 mg and a nicotine content of 0.7 mg. The analyst will normally use support material (pictures, logos, etc.) to help the respondent in his or her task.

As shown in Table 6.4, each combination of the *k* variables can be described by a set of *k*-1 binary variables (0,1) denoting the absence or presence of the levels of each characteristic. In a

TABLE 6.4 *Modelling preferences through the decompositional approach: the blended
cigarettes segment in Belgium*

Bundle of characteristics	Brands			Price			T/N Content			Rank-ing(y)
	C	M	G	BF62	BF67	BF72	4/0.4	9/0.7	15/0.1	
1. B-57–1/0.2	0	0	0	0	0	0	0	0	0	–
2. B-62–4/0.4	0	0	0	1	0	0	1	0	0	–
3. B-67–9/0.7	0	0	0	0	1	0	0	1	0	–
4. B-72–15/1.0	0	0	0	0	0	1	0	0	1	–
5. C-57–4/0.4	1	0	0	0	0	0	1	0	0	–
6. C-62–9/0.7	1	0	0	1	0	0	0	1	0	–
7. C-67–15/1.0	1	0	0	0	1	0	0	0	1	–
8. C-72–1/0.2	1	0	0	0	0	1	0	0	0	–
9. M-57–9/0.7	0	1	0	0	0	0	0	1	0	–
10. M-62–15/1.0	0	1	0	1	0	0	1	0	0	–
11. M-67–1/0.2	0	1	0	0	1	0	0	0	0	–
12. M-72–4/0.4	0	1	0	0	0	1	0	0	1	–
13. G-57–15/1.0	0	0	1	0	0	0	0	0	1	–
14. G-62–1/0.2	0	0	1	1	0	0	0	0	0	–
15. G-67–1/0.4	0	0	1	0	1	0	1	0	0	–
16. G-62–9/0.7	0	0	1	0	0	1	0	1	0	–

B = Barclay, C = Camel, M = Marlboro, G = Gauloise Blonde.

linear regression model, these binary variables are used as explanatory variables for the
preference ranking of each respondent. Table 6.4 shows the experimental design as well as data
of one respondent who ranked the 16 bundles of characteristics, with each bundle composed of a
specific combination of variables.

Box 6.4 shows the results obtained for two respondents, a Barclay smoker and a Gauloise Blonde
smoker. The regression results are globally statistically significant in both cases and most
regression coefficients have significant *t*-tests. In this case, the reference bundle is bundle #1
which has the following composition: the brand Barclay at the lowest price (BF57) and the lowest
tar and nicotine content (1/0.2). Given that the most preferred bundle is ranked 16th, the
regression coefficients must be interpreted in terms of ranks gained or lost compared to this rank.

- The *Barclay smoker* is obviously very satisfied with the reference bundle; any modification has
  a negative impact. Marlboro (−4.0) is the most acceptable brand, and Gauloise blonde
  (−12.0) is the least acceptable. This buyer is little affected by price. An increase in the price by
  BF5 has only a small impact (−0.25); a larger price increase induces a stronger reaction which
  remains small in absolute value. Similarly, the reactions to increases in tar and nicotine content
  are weak.

- The behaviour of the *Gauloise Blonde smoker* is very different. This individual seems to
  welcome a change in brand; after the usual brand, he or she would happily turn to Camel
  (+8.5) and then to Marlboro (+6.0). Compared with the other respondent, reactions to price
  increases are much stronger, as well as to changes in tar and nicotine content.

BOX 6.4

Comparing the utility functions of two respondents

■ *Utility function of respondent #17 (smoker of Gauloise Blonde)*
   Preference = 8.25 (Barclay, P = 57, T/N = 1 and 0.2)
                  + 6.0(Marlboro) + 9.5(Gauloise) + 8.5(Camel)
                    (4.8)   *(7.6)*   *(6.8)*
                  − 2.5(P = 62) − 3.5(P = 67) − 5.0(P = 72)
                    (2.0)   *(2.8)*   *(4.0)*
                  − 3.5(T/N = 4/0.4) − 4.0(T/N = 9/0.7) − 4.5(T/N = 15/1.0)
                    (2.8)   *(3.2)*   *(3.6)*
                              $R^2 = 0.860$ F-test = 11.3

■ *Utility function of respondent #86 (smoker of Barclay)*
   Preference = 16.0 (Barclay, P = 57, T/N = 1/0.2)
                  − 4.0(Marlboro) − 12.0(Gauloise) − 8.0(Camel)
                    (4.6)   *(13.9)*   *(9.2)*
                  − 0.25(P = 62) − 1.25(P = 67) − 1.50(P = 72)
                    (0.3)   *(1.4)*   *(1.7)*
                  − 0.75(T/N = 4/0.4) − 0.75(T/N = 9/0.7) − 1.50(T/N = 15/1.0)
                    (0.9)   *(0.9)*   *(1.6)*
                              $R^2 = 0.934$ F-test = 24.6

T-tests between brackets and in italics are under the regression coefficients.

Similar results obtained from larger sample of respondents allow the measurement of buyers' preferences, market segmentation with respect to price, and taste and guidelines for product development and pricing strategies.

6.4 MEASURING THE BEHAVIOURAL RESPONSE

The simplest and most direct measure of behavioural response is given by sales data for the product or brand, complemented by an analysis of the market share held within each segment covered. Other types of information are useful for interpreting sales data and formulating a valid diagnostic of the positioning of the product, i.e. information about purchasing habits and also information about after-purchase behaviour.

6.4.1 Analysis of purchasing habits

The aim of this analysis is to establish the profile of the buying behaviour by segment of consumers within the product category being studied. Information is required on three types of behaviour: *acquisition*, *utilization* and *possession*. Table 6.5 presents the main elements of information being sought. These elements vary by product category and must be adapted to each particular situation.

TABLE 6.5 *Information on purchasing behaviour*

Questions	Acquisition	Use	Possession
What?	■ Regular brand ■ Last brand purchased	■ Type of use ■ Substitute products	■ Brand now on hand
How much?	■ Quantity per purchase occasion (size, units)	■ Consumption per week ■ Most important use	■ Quantity owned now
How?	■ Purchasing situation	■ Mode of use	■ Mode of storage
Where?	■ Usual place of purchase	■ Usual place of use	■ Usual place of storage
When?	■ Date of last purchase ■ Interpurchase timing	■ Usual period of use	■ Length of storage
Who?	■ Person who buys	■ Person who uses	■ Person who holds

The description of buying behaviour is facilitated by using the following basic questions: what, how much, how, where, when and who.

■ '*What*' allows the definition of the evoked set of brands and identification of possible substitutes.

■ '*How much*' provides quantitative information on the volume of purchases and consumption and on storage habits.

■ '*How*' highlights different ways of purchasing (hire purchase, instalment plan) and different uses to which the product is put.

■ '*Where*' is important for identifying the main distribution networks used, places of consumption and storing of the product.

■ '*When*' helps to get knowledge about situational factors and consumption opportunities, as well as the rhythm of purchase and repurchase.

■ '*Who*' aims to identify the composition of the buying centre and the role of its members.

These questions are useful to guide the collection of market primary data and to build a market information system.

The family viewed as a buying decision centre
As mentioned before, the question of the *buying centre* and its structure is fundamental in industrial marketing. It is also important regarding consumer goods, since buying decisions are hardly ever made by isolated individuals and are mostly made within the family, which, in fact, constitutes a buying centre comparable to the one observed in an organization.

Knowledge of purchasing habits implies identification of the respective roles of the mother, the father and the children, and this by product category and at different stages of the buying process. These questions are important to marketers, who must adapt their product, price and communication policies to their real client (Davis and Rigaux, 1974), especially since the distribution of the roles and influence of spouses tends to change, due in particular to the rapidly changing role of women in society. One of the first proposed typologies suggests four allocations of roles (Herbst, 1952):

■ Autonomous decision by the husband or the wife

■ Dominant influence of husband

■ Dominant influence of wife

■ Synchretic decision, i.e. taken together.

The role of children is still to be taken into account. Comparison of the results of studies on the allocation of roles for various product categories shows that the influence of spouses varies greatly according to the type of product (Davis and Rigaux, 1974).

Pras and Tarondeau (1981, p. 214) emphasize that the aim of this kind of research is to define the strategies to be adopted due to a better understanding of the behaviour of the target group. Their relevance can be summarized as follows:

■ Properly choose the persons to be questioned.

■ Determine the content of advertising messages.

■ Choose the best adapted support material.

■ Adapt product conception to the needs of the person with greatest influence.

■ Choose the most appropriate distribution network.

Mastering this set of information about buying habits will contribute to a significant improvement in the firm's marketing practice and thus increase the impact of behavioural response.

6.4.2 Market share analysis

Company or brand sales, measured in volume or in value, are the most direct measures of the market behavioural response. A sales analysis can be misleading, however, since it does not reveal how the brand is doing relative to competing brands operating in the same reference market. An increase in sales may be due to a general improvement in market conditions and have nothing to do with the brand's performance, or the increase may be hiding a deterioration of the brand's position, for instance when it has grown, but less than its rivals. To be useful, a sales analysis must therefore be complemented by a market share analysis, ideally in volume within each segment covered.

Calculating market shares assumes that the firm has clearly defined its *reference market*, i.e. the set of products or brands with which it competes. The method of defining a reference market is described in Chapter 7.

Once the reference market has been determined, market share is simply calculated as follows:

$$\text{Market share} = \frac{\text{Brand A unit sales}}{\text{Total unit sales}}$$

The reason for measuring the market share is to eliminate the impact of environmental factors which exert the same influence on all competing brands and thus allow a proper comparison of the competitive power of each. Nevertheless, as suggested by Kotler (1991, p. 711), the notion of market share needs to be used with caution, keeping the following considerations in mind:

- The level of market share depends directly on the choice of the basis of comparison, i.e. on the *reference market*. It is important to check that this basis is the same for all the brands.

- The hypothesis that *environmental factors* have the same influence on all brands is not necessarily verified. Some brands may be better or less well placed with respect to some environmental factors.

- When *new brands* are introduced into a market, the share of each participant must necessarily drop, without there being any bad performance, even if some brands resist the entry of a new competitor better than others.

- Market shares can sometimes fluctuate because of *accidental* or *exceptional factors*, such as a large order.

- Sometimes a drop in market share may be *deliberately provoked* by the firm because, for example, a distribution network or a market segment is being abandoned.

Irrespective of the definition adopted for the reference market, various measures of market share can be calculated.

- *Unit market share* relates to the company or brand sales in volume expressed as a percentage of total sales of the reference market.

- *Value market share* is calculated on the basis of turnover rather than sales in units. A market share in value is often difficult to interpret because changes in market share reflect a combination of volume and price changes.

- *Served-market share* is not calculated relative to the total reference market, but relative to sales in the market segment(s) addressed by the firm. Note that the served-market share is always larger than the overall market share.

- *Relative market share* compares the firm's sales to that of its competitors, thus excluding the firm's own sales. If a firm holds 30 per cent of the market, and its top three competitors hold respectively 20, 15 and 10 per cent, and the 'others' 25 per cent, relative market share will be 43 per cent (30/70). If relative market share is calculated by reference to the top three competitors, then the firm's relative market share is 67 per cent (30/45). Relative market shares above 33 per cent are considered to be strong.

■ *Relative market share to leading competitor* is calculated by reference to the leading competitor's sales. In the previous example, the dominant firm has a relative market share of 1.5 (30/20). The relative market share of the other firms is obtained by dividing their market share by that of the leading competitor, i.e. 0.67, 0.50 and 0.33, respectively, in this example.

Measuring market shares can raise problems depending on the availability of the necessary information. To measure served-market share implies that the firm is in a position to evaluate total sales in each segment. Similarly, relative market share assumes knowledge of sales achieved by direct competition. Obtaining this information varies in levels of difficulty from sector to sector.

In the field of consumer goods, market shares are available through syndicated consumer or dealer panels or through scanning diary panels. In the other fields, in cases where government organizations and trade associations do not provide this information, it is up to the *marketing information system* to arrange how to purchase or to create this information, which is vital for tracking sales performance.

6.4.3 Quality of market share analysis

Quality market share analysis helps predict future performance. The critical question addressed is: *What makes up our market share?* Traditional market share measures in units or in value should be complemented by an analysis of the customer base, as shown in Table 6.6, where two competitors having the same market share are compared.

TABLE 6.6 *Quality market share analysis*

Company	Competitor A	Competitor B
Example (a)		
Overall market share	30%	30%
Composition of customer base:		
High profit	15%	5%
Switchable	15%	50%
Unprofitable	5%	15%
Loyal	65%	30%
Example (b)		
Overall market share	30%	30%
Composition of customer base:		
Growers	40%	20%
Maintainers	25%	30%
Decliners	35%	50%

Source: CDI Point of View (1992).

The question is: *Which 30 per cent market share is preferable?* Clearly, Competitor A has:

■ Less risk with fewer 'switchable' customers.

■ A stronger financial position fuelled by more 'high profit' customers.

■ Fewer 'unprofitable' customers draining its resources.

Competitor B's outlook is not so bright. With few 'high profit' customers and 50 per cent of its customer base at risk in 'switchables', we can anticipate declining sales and unattractive profitability.

Similar analyses of the customer base can be made, for instance, on how many customers are increasing, maintaining or decreasing their spend.

6.4.4 Market share movement analysis

Consumers' and dealers' panels provide detailed information on market shares by region, segment, distribution network, etc. Such data allow the implementation of more refined types of analysis, used to interpret gains or losses in market shares.

Parfitt and Collins (1968) have shown how to decompose market share into a number of components which help to interpret and to predict its development.

■ *Penetration rate* is the share of buyers, i.e. the percentage of buyers of brand x compared to the total number of buyers in the reference product category.

■ *Exclusivity rate* is defined as the share of total purchases in a product category reserved for brand x. This rate is a measure of the loyalty attached to brand x, given that buyers have the possibility of diversifying their purchases and acquiring different brands in the same product category.

■ *Intensity rate* compares average quantities purchased per buyer of brand x with average quantities purchased per buyer of the product category.

A brand's market share can then be calculated from these three components. Thus,

$$\text{Market share} = \text{Penetration rate} \times \text{Exclusivity rate} \times \text{Intensity rate}$$

Let x denote the brand and c the reference product category to which x belongs. Let us also adopt the following notations:

N_x = Number of buyers of x

N_c = Number of buyers of c

Q_{xx} = Quantity of x purchased by buyers of x

Q_{cx} = Quantity of c purchased by buyers of x

Q_{cc} = Quantity of c purchased by buyers of c.

It can be verified that

$$\text{Market share} = \frac{Q_{xx}}{Q_{cc}} = \frac{N_x}{N_c} \cdot \frac{Q_{xx}/N_x}{Q_{cx}/N_x} \cdot \frac{Q_{cx}/N_x}{Q_{cc}/N_c}$$

To express market share in value, a relative price index must be added: the ratio of the brand's average price to the average price charged by all competing brands. This definition of market share can be generally applied. It permits the identification of the possible causes of observed movements in market share. The following are possible explanations of a fall in market share:

■ The brand is losing customers (lower penetration rate).

■ Buyers are devoting a smaller share of their purchases of the product to this particular brand (lower exclusivity rate).

■ Buyers of the brand are purchasing smaller quantities compared to the quantities bought on average by buyers of the product (lower intensity rate).

By tracking these market indicators over time, the market analyst can identify the underlying causes of market share changes and suggest corrective measures accordingly.

Measures of market share can be used from two different perspectives, as an *indicator of competitive performance* or as an *indicator of competitive advantage*. In the first case, market shares should, as much as possible, be calculated over finer divisions, i.e. by segment, by distribution network or by region. In the second case, a more aggregate basis would be more suitable because it would better reveal the strength of the market power held by the firm and the possible existence of economies of scale or of learning curve effects.

6.4.5 Estimating marketing response functions

A marketing response function is a relationship that links buyers' response, expressed in terms of volume or market share, to one or more marketing variables. Response functions are generally obtained from historical data through econometric analysis. Quantitative estimation of response functions leads to *elasticity coefficients* measuring demand or market share sensitivity to a variation in one of the explanatory variables, such as price, advertising or household income. The notion of elasticity is defined in more detail in Appendix 6.1.

Response functions are useful because their estimations, based on observations on different markets, different segments or different product categories, improves one's understanding of buyers' response mechanisms. Thus one progressively builds a more rigorous basis for future marketing programmes (see Assmus *et al.*, 1984).

By way of illustration, Table 6.7 presents estimates of the elasticities of marketing variables for a sample of 127 brands operating on the European market and coming from 21 different product categories. These elasticity coefficients observed for the distribution, price and advertising variables are directly useful for forecasting and control. They constitute good starting points for

TABLE 6.7 *Selected estimates of elasticities of marketing variables*

Product categories	Number of brands	Advertising elasticities*	Price elasticities	Distribution elasticities†
Soft drinks	5	0.070	−1.419	1.181
Yoghurt	2	0.031	−1.100	−
Confectionery	2	0.034	−1.982	2.319
TV sets	4	0.122	−	−
Cigarettes	1	0.154	−1.224	−
Bank services	5	0.003	−	0.251
Cars transported by rail	1	0.184	−1.533	−
Coffee	1	0.036	−2.933	1.868
Fruits	1	0.095	−1.229	−
Electric shavers	18	0.219	−2.460	0.909
Gasoline	19	0.024	−0.600	0.923
Shampoos	11	0.036	−1.762	−
Insecticides	9	0.058	−	−
Deodorants	11	0.054	−	−
Detergents	6	0.084	−	−
Suntan lotion	11	0.300	−	−
Average: study 1976‡	N = 107	0.094	−1.624	1.243 ·
Female hygiene	6	0.010	−1.405	0.958
Dishwashers	2	0.029	−1.692	−
Detergent	1	0.049	−2.009	−
Jam	3	0.022	−2.672	2.757
Automobiles	8	0.093	−2.004	−
Average: study 1988§	N = 20	0.041	−1.956	−
Average: 1976 and 1988	N = 127	0.081	−1.735	1.395

Source: Lambin (1976, 1988).

*These are average elasticities.

†Based on Nielsen indices of distribution coverage.

‡The observation basis is the brand per country. The countries are: Belgium, France, Holland, West Germany, Denmark, Italy, Norway, Sweden.

§The observation basis is Belgium.

simulation exercises designed for analysing the implications of alternative marketing programmes (Lambin, 1972).

In consumer markets, the use of response functions is now largely facilitated by constant improvement in databases. This development is the result of technological innovation; the progressive but irreversible introduction of *scanning systems* in retail stores and increasing computerization of marketing information systems in firms (The Nielsen Researcher, 1981). Market analysts now have at their disposal more reliable information on market shares, selling prices, advertising, promotions, out-of-stocks, etc. The most important change in this area is in the frequency of data, which is now available weekly rather than on a bimonthly or monthly basis. This weekly frequency gives more timely and sensitive information to assist the market analyst in assessing competitive response and brand performance. Direct causal relationships between market shares and the marketing variables can also be established.

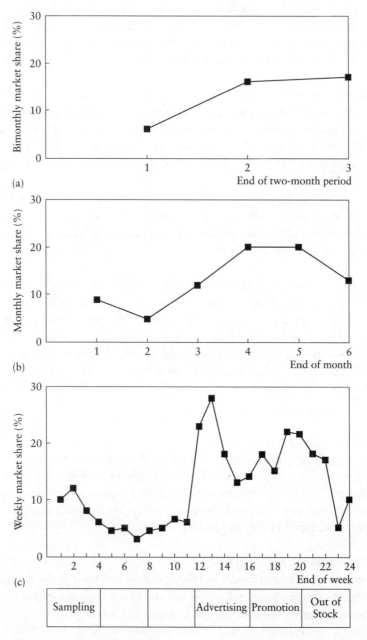

FIGURE 6.8 *Penetration curves of a new product (*Source: The Nielsen Researcher, *1981)*

Figure 6.8 presents the penetration curve of a new brand described successively in terms of bimonthly, monthly and weekly observations. Causal data, i.e. the marketing variables active during the launching period, are shown in the lower part of the graph, below the time scale. It is clear that bimonthly and monthly data completely mask the market response. The weekly observations, on the other hand, show the causal relationship very clearly.

6.4.6 Post-purchase behaviour

Having bought and used the product, the consumer or buyer develops a new attitude, based mainly on the degree of *satisfaction* or *dissatisfaction* that is felt after using the product. This positive or negative attitude will lead to a post-purchase behaviour which determines the product's acceptance and also the repeat purchase rate if it is a product that is bought repeatedly.

The buyers' satisfaction will be a function of the degree of concordance existing between their expectations of the product on the one hand, and their perception of its performance on the other hand. If the result conforms to their expectations, there is satisfaction; if it is higher, satisfaction is greater; if it is lower, there is dissatisfaction. The notion of expected result goes back to Lewin's (1935) *aspiration level theory*. Lewin's analysis is based on the following propositions:

> Every time someone feels the need or desire for something, he or she identifies (a) a level of satisfaction, called the *realization level*, perceived as already obtained; (b) a level of satisfaction expected by the purchase, the *aspiration level* and (c) the highest possible level of satisfaction, the *ideal level*.

Individuals' aspiration levels are formed on the basis of their experiences, as well as the promises made in the firm's advertising about its products' performances. Individuals' aspirations develop differently according to their personality. Some set their aspiration level at a *minimum* which they intend to surpass. This attitude describes risk aversion. Others set their level at a *maximum*, representing an objective they endeavour to approach, but do not expect to attain. Here, the aspiration level acts as a stimulus. Finally, others set their level roughly to the *average* of the results already obtained, reflecting an equality between the aspiration level and the realization level.

Aspirations are not static, but develop continuously. As emphasized in Chapter 3, individuals constantly seek stimulation and novelty. If successful, aspirations tend to amplify. They are also influenced by performances of other members of the group to which the individual belongs. Expectation theory therefore suggests adopting a communication policy based on the product's likely performances, and avoiding inconsiderate promises that can only create dissatisfaction, by contradicting or invalidating buyers' expectations.

6.4.7 Brand-switching analysis

A good indicator of consumer satisfaction in a competitive market is the buyers' loyalty rate. Brand-switching analysis is also useful to forecast the brand dynamic evolution. Consider the market share development of brands A, B and C shown in Fig. 6.9.

The stability of brand A's market share can be interpreted in two very different ways:

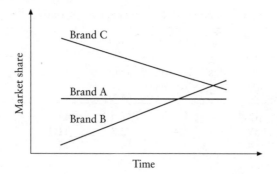

FIGURE 6.9 *The dynamics of market share movements (Source: Lambin and Peeters, 1977, p. 145)*

■ A fixed number of consumers buy the same quantity of brand A at regular intervals.

■ The number of consumers dropping brand A is equal to the number of consumers adopting brand A; entry rate then compensates exit rate exactly.

On the basis of aggregate market data, it is not possible to decide which is the true state. Similarly, one could give the following explanations for brand B's growth:

■ Brand B has a fixed number of loyal buyers to whom new buyers are added at a regular pace.

■ Entry rate is higher than exit rate.

■ The number of brand B's buyers remains unchanged, but some of them are purchasing an increased quantity per buying occasion.

Here again, the available information does not permit us to discriminate between these possible explanations.

To keep the analysis simple, let us limit ourselves to a market composed of two competing brands. As shown in Fig. 6.10, each particular purchasing act, viewed in a dynamic perspective, can be described in terms of three origins and three destinations. For each brand, we can thus define a loyalty rate and an attraction rate. These switching rates can be defined as follows:

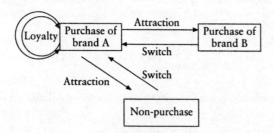

FIGURE 6.10 *The brand switching dynamic (Source: Lambin and Peeters, 1977, p. 146)*

TABLE 6.8 *Brand-switching analysis: the heavy duty truck market*

| Replaced brands in period (t) | Brands purchased in period (t + 1) | | | | | | Market share in t (%) |
	Daf (%)	Mercedes (%)	Renault (%)	Scania (%)	Volvo (%)	Others (%)	
Daf	56.2	15.3	1.3	2.3	11.4	13.5	7.6
Mercedes	8.2	59.5	2.4	2.3	11.1	16.5	16.3
Renault	9.0	9.2	53.0	5.0	1.2	22.6	3.2
Scania	8.1	13.3	0.0	65.6	6.1	6.9	3.3
Volvo	16.5	12.9	1.2	1.7	60.0	7.7	6.2
Others	11.7	17.1	4.8	2.9	10.3	53.2	63.4
Market share in t + 1	14.6	23.2	5.3	4.8	13.2	38.9	100.0

Source: MDA Consulting Group, Brussels.

- The *loyalty rate* is the percentage of buyers who, having purchased brand A in the previous period $(t - 1)$, continue to buy brand A in the current period (t).

- The *attraction rate* is the percentage of buyers who, having purchased a competing brand in period $t - 1$, purchase brand A in period t.

These proportions, called *transition probabilities*, can be estimated through survey or on the basis of panel data. To illustrate, the transition probabilities observed in the Belgian market among six makes of heavy trucks are presented in Table 6.8.

These transition probabilities allow the market analyst to explain market share movements over time, to describe the underlying competitive dynamics and to formulate predictions on market developments assuming that the observed transition probabilities will remain unchanged within a reasonable planning horizon.

If α denotes loyalty rate and β attraction rate, brand A's market share (MS) in a future period $t + 1$ will be,

$$MS(t + 1) = \alpha \cdot MS(t) + \beta[1 - MS(t)]$$

Brand A's long-run or equilibrium market share, MS(e), can be calculated from the expression

$$MS(e) = \frac{\text{Attraction rate}}{(1 - \text{Loyalty rate}) + \text{Attraction rate}} = \frac{\beta}{(1 - \alpha) + \beta}$$

Note that the equilibrium market share is independent of the initial market share. It describes the brand's trajectory, assuming constant transition probabilities. This type of dynamic analysis is particularly useful at the launching stage of a new product.

6.5 MEASURING SATISFACTION AND DISSATISFACTION

The buyer's satisfaction is at the heart of the marketing process and yet it is only recently that companies have begun to systematically measure the degree of satisfaction felt by consumers. Previously, analysis was restricted to internal measures of quality, such as ISO9000. The most obvious level of satisfaction would seem to be the level of sales or market share, just as the number of complaints would be the sign of dissatisfaction.

In fact, things are much more complicated and there can be a big difference between what the company thinks customers want and what the customers are really looking for. In other words, the gap between the designed and the expected quality may be very large, even if the customers never formally express their dissatisfaction. This is why it is necessary to interview customers directly to assess scientifically their level of satisfaction or dissatisfaction. The value of this type of study is also to permit international comparisons for the same brand from country to country and to allow longitudinal analyses to keep track of the changes in satisfaction over a certain period.

6.5.1 The behaviour of dissatisfied customers

Marketing research studies (Lash, 1990) of customers' post-purchase behaviours in different product categories have shown the following facts:

∎ Only 3 per cent of sales transactions result in complaints directly made to the company.

∎ On average, 15 per cent of transactions result in indirect complaints to the sales representatives, neighbours, friends, etc.

∎ In addition, 30 per cent of the transactions caused problems to customers but have not resulted in any kind of communication with the company.

There are two different explanations for this last group. Buyers have either minimized the problem or were pessimistic about the outcome of a complaint, given the dominant position of the supplier or because, in previous instances, a complaint has remained unanswered.

Thus, in total, 48 per cent of the transactions of an average firm may cause problems to customers—a level of dissatisfaction which is not well reflected by the tip of the iceberg, i.e. the 3 per cent of formal complaints.

Insofar as a complaint is efficiently handled by after-sales service, the negative consequences for the firm can be limited. On the other hand, a real problem remains with the 30 per cent group of dissatisfied customers who do not communicate with the supplier but who could really affect market share in the long run. This is why the adoption of a proactive attitude here is important by measuring regularly the level of satisfaction/dissatisfaction of different customer groups and identifying their causes. Remember that, in sectors where primary demand is non-expansible, 80 to 90 per cent of the turnover is due to existing customers. It is easy to understand why it is important to maintain satisfaction for this portfolio of existing customers.

An additional argument is provided by an analysis of the behaviour of dissatisfied customers whose complaints were well handled by the firm. Findings reported in studies made by Lash (1990) and TARP (1986)) have shown the following results:

- For satisfied customers, the average repeat purchase rate is 92 per cent.

- For dissatisfied customers who do not complain, the repeat purchase rate drops to 78 per cent, or a loss of 14 per cent.

- Among customers who had made a complaint but had received a poor response from the firm, the repeat purchase rate drops to 46 per cent.

- Of dissatisfied customers who had complained and had received an appropriate response from the firm, the repeat purchase rate was 91 per cent, about the same as that of satisfied customers.

The management of ICMA International, who has a broad experience in the field of satisfaction/ dissatisfaction studies, believe that this repeat purchase rate is even higher than the one observed for satisfied customers (Goderis, 1994).

Problem customers are (1) those who are dissatisfied but do not complain and (2) those who complain but are not happy with the way their complaint has been treated by the company. The loss of customers from these two groups constitutes a form of negative advertising by word-of-mouth; it is costly for the firm and is very difficult to control. Research findings (Rhoades, 1988) show that '... *dissatisfied customers will tell ten other people about their bad experience with a company or a brand.*'

Three important conclusions can be drawn from these various studies on the behaviour of dissatisfied customers.

1. The level of satisfaction/dissatisfaction is a key input data in the market information system of any company.
2. A complaint is not necessarily negative, because the customer will accept a problem as long as the company finds a good solution to that problem.
3. Complaints are important sources of information, allowing a company to better understand customer needs and their perception of the product quality.

Current complaint management is only one necessary but insufficient aspect of a total quality programme aiming towards complete customer satisfaction.

6.5.2 The satisfaction–loyalty relationship

As already emphasized, a high level of satisfaction leads to increased customer loyalty and increased customer loyalty is the single most important driver of long-term financial perfor-

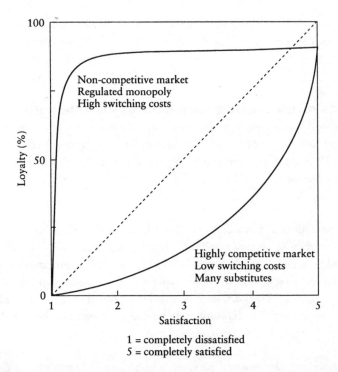

FIGURE 6.11 *The satisfaction–loyalty relationship* (Source: *Jones and Sasser, 1995*)

mance. The relationship between satisfaction and loyalty has been empirically established by Jones and Sasser (1995), as shown in Fig. 6.11.

According to conventional wisdom, the relationship between satisfaction and loyalty should be a simple linear relationship: as satisfaction increases, so does loyalty. A research conducted at Rank Xerox and replicated by Jones and Sasser (1995) showed a much more complex relationship.

The two extreme curves of Fig. 6.11 are representative of two different competitive situations.

■ *In non-competitive markets*—the upper left zone—satisfaction has little impact on loyalty. These markets are typically regulated monopolies like telecommunication, electrical or transportation utilities; or market situations where switching costs are very high. Customers in fact have no choice; they are captive customers. This situation can change rapidly, however, if the source of monopoly disappears, because of deregulation or the emergence of an alternative technology.

■ *In competitive markets*—the lower right zone—where competition is intense with many substitutes and low switching costs, a very large difference is observed between the loyalty of 'satisfied' (score of 4) and 'completely satisfied' (score between 4 and 5) customers. This was the discovery made at the Xerox Corporation:

> ... its totally satisfied customers were six times more likely to repurchase Xerox products over the next 18 months than its satisfied customers.   (Jones and Sasser, 1995, p. 91)

The implications are profound. Merely satisfying customers who have the freedom to make choices is not enough to keep them loyal. The only true loyal customers are totally satisfied customers.

6.5.3 Methods of measuring satisfaction/dissatisfaction

The conceptual model underlying satisfaction/dissatisfaction research is simply the attitude multi-attribute model discussed earlier in this chapter. The questions concern the importance of each attribute and the degree of perceived presence of the attribute (performance) in the evaluated product or service.

The interviewing procedure is in three steps. First, the overall level of satisfaction is obtained from the respondent; then importance and performance scores are requested for each attribute on a 10-point rating scale. Finally, repeat purchase intentions are measured. The typical questions used are presented in Box 6.5. This type of questionnaire is preferably administered by telephone, experience having shown that dissatisfied customers are the most likely to respond to a mail questionnaire, thereby undermining the representativeness of the sample.

This type of questionnaire can be given regularly to representative samples of customers of the same company in different markets, or to customers of different companies in the same market. In this latter case, there are syndicated studies that offer the advantage of allowing comparisons of competitors.

BOX 6.5

Typical questions used in a satisfaction/dissatisfaction study

1. *Overall evaluation* Generally speaking, how do you evaluate your overall degree of satisfaction concerning your supplier:

Overall satisfaction: 1 2 3 4 5 6 7 8 9 10

2. *Evaluation for each attribute* How do you evaluate the importance and your level of satisfaction regarding each of the following attributes:

Importance: 1 2 3 4 5 6 7 8 9 10

Performance: 1 2 3 4 5 6 7 8 9 10

3. *Repeat purchase intention* Would you buy your next product ABC from the same supplier?

Yes:...........   No:...........   Don't know yet:...........

Why:...........   Why:...........   Why:...............

6.5.4 Analysis of customer satisfaction

The first step is to calculate the average performance score for each attribute as well as its standard deviation. These scores are then compared with the average scores observed in the sector or with the scores obtained by priority competitors. This comparison will result in a good picture of how the market perceives the quality of the product, viewed as a package of benefits.

The performance scores obtained on the attributes are situated along two axes: on the horizontal axis are placed the average performance scores and on the vertical axis the standard deviations for these scores. A high standard deviation means that few respondents have the same opinion and a low standard deviation will, on the contrary, show that most customers share the same opinion.

The choice of a cut-off point for these two axes is always a sensitive problem. It is common practice to use the average score observed in the sector or the score of the priority competitor. The result is a two-by-two matrix defining four quadrants, as shown in Fig. 6.12.

■ In the lower right-hand quadrant, the attributes of brand or company X have an average score superior to the sector's average and also a lower than average standard deviation. This means that customers are generally satisfied and agree to say so. We have here a case of 'homogeneous satisfaction'.

■ In the top right-hand quadrant, the brand's attributes also have an above-average score, but the standard deviation this time is high, which means that customers have varying opinions. We thus have a situation of 'distributed satisfaction', which can be caused, for example, by a lack of consistency in the quality of the services provided. Identification of the dissatisfied

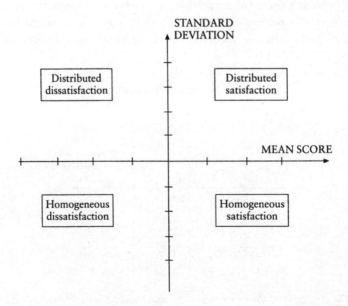

FIGURE 6.12 *The satisfaction–dissatisfaction matrix*

customers and of the causes of their dissatisfaction is a priority objective to adopt the individualized remedial actions before customers switch to competition.

- In the upper-left quadrant, the average is below the sectoral average and the standard deviation is high. This is a case of '*distributed dissatisfaction*'; most of the customers are dissatisfied, but some are less dissatisfied than others. This state of affairs can be explained by a product or service ill-adapted to some customer group(s).

- In the lower left hand quadrant, customers are dissatisfied and agree to say so. This is the most unfavourable situation of '*homogeneous dissatisfaction*'.

6.5.5 Analysis of the 'performance/importance' ratios

The satisfaction–dissatisfaction matrix remains very descriptive. Integrating the attributes' importance scores can now allow a tool to be developed for decision making. A comparison of importance and performance scores is useful as it can be used as a check on whether or not the package of benefits provided by the product or the service is adapted to customer expectations.

The degree of importance is normally higher than the degree of performance. If the performance score is greatly inferior, the product will be judged as inadequate by the customer. On the other hand, if the company offers a product or service of much higher quality than expected, we can have overkill. There is no sense in ensuring excellent quality for an attribute that is of little or no importance. On the other hand, a poor level of quality for an important attribute can have a very negative impact on the company's image. This is why it is essential to establish a ranking of attributes by order of decreasing importance in order to identify the main attributes on which to concentrate.

To measure the product's degree of adaptation, the performance/importance ratio will be used as shown in Fig. 6.13. The performance/importance ratios are shown on the horizontal axis; the vertical axis shows the standard deviations of the satisfaction scores. The cut-off point is fixed at

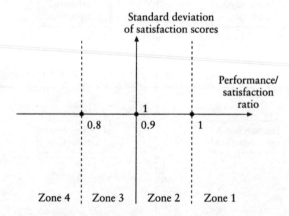

FIGURE 6.13 *Analysis of the performance/importance ratios (Source: ICMA International, 1994)*

a standard deviation of 1 and a value of 0.9 for the performance/importance ratios. The horizontal axis is subdivided into four distinct zones:

- *Zone 1*: the 'performance/importance' (P/I) ratio is above 100 per cent: performance is higher than the importance given to the attribute. This is the case of overkill where too much resources are allocated to a particular attribute.

- *Zone 2*: the P/I ratio is between 90 and 100 per cent; the level of satisfaction on important attributes is good.

- *Zone 3*: the P/I ratio is included between 80 and 90 per cent; the level of performance is insufficient as compared to the importance of the attributes.

- *Zone 4*: the P/I ratio is below 80 per cent; performance is much lower than the importance of the attributes.

This information is useful in identifying the weak points of a product and in identifying the actions to be taken by priority. For further information on the topic of customer satisfaction, see TARP (1979, 1986) and Rhoades (1988).

SUMMARY

Buyer's response means all mental or physical activity caused by a marketing stimulus. The various response forms of the buyer can be classified in three categories: *cognitive response*, which relates to retained information and knowledge; *affective response*, which concerns attitude and evaluation; and *behavioural response*, which describes the actions taken, not only at the moment of purchase but also after the purchase. A learning process supposes that the individual, like the organization, reaches these three stages successively and in this order: learn–feel–do. Other sequences of response are observed depending on the degree of the buyer's involvement and his or her mode of reality perception. The main measures of the cognitive response are *awareness*, *recall* or *recognition* and *perceived similarity*. Regarding the affective response, the concept of attitude is central. The multi-attribute product concept defined in Chapter 4 serves as a conceptual basis for modelling attitudes. Two estimation procedures can be used for measuring a Fishbein multi-attribute model: the *compositional* approach and the *decompositional* approach through conjoint analysis. Attitude measurements are summarized in the 'importance–performance' matrix and also in attribute-based perceptual maps. Non-compensatory models of attitude can be used in more complex cases. Measures of the behavioural response are purchasing habits analysis, market share movements analysis and econometric marketing response functions. Post-behaviour is based mainly on the degree of satisfaction–dissatisfaction of customers. A good indicator of customer satisfaction is the loyalty rate. For fast-moving consumer goods (FMCG), brand-switching analysis is also very useful.

QUESTIONS AND PROBLEMS

1. Look at Fig. 6.2. How would you rank electric razors, mustard, microcomputers, chocolates pralines, painkillers, garden hoses, costume jewellery? What kind of information would you use to justify your ranking?
2. Select a consumer product category you know well and prepare a questionnaire to measure unaided, aided and qualified awareness of the main competing brands within the category. How would you proceed to analyse the results?
3. Brand A has a 30 per cent penetration rate and a 60 per cent exclusivity rate. Buyers of this brand usually consume the same quantity of the product as do the buyers of competing brands. What is brand A's market share? If the exclusivity rate drops to 50 per cent, what will be its market share?
4. Two brands are competing in the same reference market. Brand A has a loyalty rate of 80 per cent and an attraction rate of 30 per cent. The market shares are, respectively, 30 per cent for brand A and 70 per cent for brand B. What are the expected equilibrium market shares of these two brands if the loyalty and attraction rates remain unchanged? What would you do if you are the brand manager of brand B?
5. Compare four makes of microcomputers using four attributes (A, B, C and D) having the following determinance rates : 0.40/0.30/0.20/0.10. The score obtained (on a 10-point rating scale) by the brands on the four attributes are: A = 10/8/6/4; B = 8/9/8/3; C = 6/8/10/5; D = 4/3/7/8. Compute a total utility score for each brand using these data. Compare and interpret the results.
6. In a brand image study, measures of perception of four brands (A, B, C and D) from the same product category were obtained from a sample of respondents. The importance scores of the four determining attributes are: 0.40/0.30/0.20/0.10. The performance scores for each brand are: A = 8/4/4/1; B = 8/3/5/3; C = 6/6/5/3; D = 5/9/6/5. Which brand will be preferred by the market if the buyers use (a) the compensatory model as a decision rule, (b) the disjunctive model, (c) the conjunctive model with a minimum of 5 required for each attribute, (d) the lexicographic model?

REFERENCES

Aaker, D.A. (1991), *Managing Brand Equity*. New York: The Free Press.

Addelman, S. (1962), 'Orthogonal main-effect plans for asymmetrical factorial experiments', *Technometrics*, vol. 4, No. 1, April, pp. 21–46.

Allport, G.W. (1935), 'Attitudes', in Murchison, C.A. (ed.), *A Handbook of Social Psychology*. Clark University Press, Worcester, Mass., pp. 798–844.

Assael, H. and G.S. Day (1968), 'Attitudes and Awareness, Predictors of Market Shares', *Journal of Advertising Research*, vol. 8, December, pp. 10–17.

Assmus, G., J.U. Farley and D.R. Lehman (1984), 'How Advertising Affects Sales: Meta-Analysis of Econometric Results', *Journal of Marketing Research*, vol. 21, February, pp. 65–74.

Bass, F.M. and W.W. Tarlarzyck (1969), 'A Study of Attitude Theory and Brand Preferences', *Journal of Marketing Research*, vol. 9, pp. 93–6.

Bauer, R.A. (1960), 'Consumer Behaviour as Risk Taking', in Hancock, A.S. (ed.), *Proc. Fall Conference of the American Marketing Association*, pp. 389–98.

Berelson, B. and G.A. Steiner (1964), *Human Behavior: An Inventory of Scientific Findings*. New York: Harcourt Brace Jovanovich.

Boyd, H.W., M.L. Ray and E.C. Strong (1972), 'An Attitudinal Framework for Advertising Strategy', *Journal of Marketing*, vol. 35, April, pp. 27–33.

CDI Point of View (1992), *Quality of Market Share*. Boston: Corporate Decisions Inc.

Churchill, G.A. (1987), *Marketing Research: Methodological Foundations*. Chicago: The Dryden Press.

Davis, H.L. and B.P. Rigaux (1974), 'Perceptions of Marital Roles in Decision Processes', *Journal of Consumer Research*, vol. 1, pp. 51–62.

Festinger, L. (1957), *A Theory of Cognitive Dissonance*. New York: Harper & Row.

Fishbein, M. (1967), 'Attitudes and Prediction of Behaviour', in Fishbein, M. (ed.), *Readings in Attitude Theory and Measurement*. New York: John Wiley & Sons, pp. 477–92.

Goderis, J.P. (1994), *Les mesures de satisfaction/insatisfaction des acheteurs*. Conference held at the IAG, Louvain-la-Neuve.

Green, P.E. and V.R. Rao (1972), *Applied Multidimensional Scaling*. New York: Holt, Rinehart & Winston.

Green, P.E. and V. Srinivasan (1978), 'Conjoint Analysis in Consumer Research: Issues and Outlook', *Journal of Consumer Research*, vol. 5, September, pp. 103–23.

Hair, J.F., R.E. Anderson, R.L. Tatham and W.C. Black (1992), *Multivariate Data Analysis*. New York: Maxwell Macmillan International Editions.

Herbst, P.G. (1952), 'The Measurement of Family Relationships', *Human Relations*, no. 5, pp. 3–35.

Herwats, B. (1986), *Etude de la sensibilité de la demande au prix des cigarettes blended*. IAG: Louvain-la-Neuve, Belgium.

ICMA International (1994), *Les mesures de satisfaction/insatisfaction des acheteurs*, Conference held at the IAG, Louvain-la-Neuve, Belgium.

Jarvis, L.P. and J.B. Wilcox (1977), 'Evoked Set, Some Theoretical Foundations and Empirical Evidence', in Howard J.A. (ed.), *Consumer Behaviour: Applications of Theory*. New York: McGraw-Hill Book Co.

Johnson, R.M. (1974), Trade-Off Analysis of Consumer Values, *Journal of Marketing Research*, vol. 11, pp. 121–7.

Jones, T.O. and W.E. Sasser (1995), 'Why Satisfied Customers Defect', *Harvard Business Review*, vol. 73, no. 6, November–December, pp. 88–99.

Kapferer, J.N. and G. Laurent (1983), *La sensibilité aux marques*. Paris: Fondation Jours de France.

Kotler, P. (1991), *Marketing Management*, 7th edn. Englewood Cliffs, New Jersey: Prentice-Hall Inc.

Krugman, H.E. (1965), 'The Impact of Television Advertising: Learning without Involvement', *Public Opinion Quarterly*, Autumn, pp. 349–56.

Krugman, H.E. (1972), 'Low recall and High Recognition of Advertising', *Journal of Advertising Research*, vol. 86, February–March, pp. 79–86.

Lambin, J.J. (1972), 'A Computer On-Line Marketing Mix Model', *Journal of Marketing Research*, vol. 9, May, pp. 119–26.

Lambin, J.J. (1976), *Advertising, Competition and Market Conduct in Oligopoly over Time*. Amsterdam: North Holland.

Lambin, J.J. (1988), *Synthèse des études récentes sur l'efficacité économique de la publicité*. CESAM Working Paper (unpublished), Louvain-la-Neuve, Belgium.

Lambin, J.J. and R. Peeters, (1977), 'La gestion marketing du enterprises'. Paris: Presses Universitaires de France.

Lash, M.L. (1990), *The Complete Guide to Customer Service*. New York: John Wiley & Sons.

Lavidge, R.J. and G.A. Steiner (1961), 'A Model for Predictions Measurement of Advertising Effectiveness', *Journal of Marketing*, vol. 25, October, pp. 59–62.

Lewin, K. (1935), *A Dynamic Theory of Personality*. New York: McGraw-Hill Book Co.

Martilla, J.A. and J.C. James (1977), 'Importance–performamce Analysis', *Journal of Marketing*, vol. 41, no. 1, January, pp. 77–9.

Morgensztern, A. (1983), 'Une synthèse des travaux sur la mémorisation des messages publicitaires', in Piquet, S., *La publicité, nerf de la communication*. Paris: Les Editions d'Organisation.

Nerlove, M. and K. Arrow (1962), 'Optimal Advertising Policy under Dynamic Conditions', *Economica*, vol. 29, pp. 131–45.

Nielsen Researcher (1981), *Utilizing UPC Scanning Data for New Products Decisions*, no. 1.

Palda, K.S. (1966), 'The Hypothesis of a Hierarchy of Effects', *Journal of Marketing Research*, vol. 3, pp. 13–24.

Parfitt, J.H. and B.J.K. Collins (1968), 'The Use of Consumer Panels for Brand Share Prediction', *Journal of Marketing Research*, vol. 5, May, pp. 131–45.

Pinson, C., N.K. Malhotra and A.K. Jain (1988), 'Les styles cognitifs des consommateurs', *Recherche et Applications en Marketing*, vol. 3, no. 1, pp. 53–73.

Pras, B. and J.-C. Tarondeau (1981), *Comportement de l'acheteur*. Paris: Editions Sirey.

Ratchford, B.T. (1987), 'New Insights about the FCB Grid', *Journal of Advertising Research*, vol. 27, pp. 30–1.

Rhoades, K. (1988), 'The Importance of Consumer Complaints', *Protect Yourself*, January, pp. 115–18.

Rogers, E.M. (1962), *The Diffusion of Innovations*. New York: The Free Press.

Rosenberg, M.J. (1956), 'Cognitive Structure and Attitudinal Affect', *Journal of Abnormal and Social Psychology*, vol. 53, pp. 367–72.

Thurstone, L.L. (1959), *The Measurement of Values*. Chicago: University of Chicago Press.

TARP (1979 and 1986), *Consumer Complaint Handling in America*. Washington, D.C.: US Office of Consumer Affairs.

Van Ballenberghe, A. (1993), Le comportement des consommateurs en période de promotion: analyse des perceptions des marques. Unpublished Memoir, IAG, Louvain-la-Neuve, Belgium.

Vaughn, R. (1980), 'How Advertising Works: A Planning Model Revisited', *Journal of Advertising Research*, vol. 20, February–March, pp. 57–66.

Watts, W.A. and J.W. McGuire (1964), 'Persistence of Induced Opinion Change and Retention of Inducing Message Content', *Journal of Abnormal and Social Psychology*, vol. 68, pp. 233–41

Wilkie, W.L. and E.A. Pessemier (1973), 'Issues in Marketing's Use of Multi-Attribute Attitude Models', *Journal of Marketing Research*, vol. 10, November, pp. 428–41.

Yavas, U. and D. Eroglu (1995), 'Assessing Competitive Edge: Exposition and Illustration of a Diagnostic Tool', *Journal of Consumer Marketing*, vol. 12, no. 2, pp. 47–59.

Zielske, H.A. (1958), 'The Remembering and the Forgetting of Advertising', *Journal of Marketing*, vol. 24, January, pp. 239–43.

Zielske, H.A. and W.A. Henry (1980), 'Remembering and Forgetting Television Ads', *Journal of Advertising Research*, vol. 20, April, pp. 7–13.

FURTHER READING

Axelrod, J.N. (1968), 'Attitude Measures that Predict Purchases', *Journal of Advertising Research*, vol. 8, March, pp. 3–7.

Beauduin, D. (1993), Les études de satisfaction de la clientèle: Une approche quantitative. Unpublished Memoir, IAG, Louvain-la-Neuve, Belgium.

Delta 2000 (1988), *L'impact de la presse quotidienne en Belgique*, May.

Evrard, Y. (1994), 'La satisfaction des consommateurs: état des recherches', *Revue Française du Marketing*, no. 144–45, pp. 53–65.

Kotler, P. and B. Dubois (1994), 'Satisfaire la clientèle à travers la qualité, le service et la valeur', *Revue Française du Marketing*, no. 144–45, pp. 35–52.

Lambin, J.J. (1989), 'La marque et le comportement de choix de l'acheteur', in Kapferer J.N. and J.C. Thoenig (eds), *La marque*. Paris: Ediscience International.

Myers, J.H. and M.L. Alpert (1976), 'Semantic Confusion in Attitude Research: Salience versus Importance versus Determinance', in Perreault, W.D. Jr (ed.), *Advances in Consumer Research*, Proceedings of the 7th Annual Conference of the Association of Consumer Research, October, pp. 106–10.

Rossiter, J.R., L. Percy and R.J. Donovan (1991), 'A Better Advertising Planning Grid', *Journal of Advertising Research*, October–November, pp. 11–21.

Servais, M. (1988), *Le marché du gant industriel de protection en Belgique*. IAG, Louvain-la-Neuve, Belgium.

Wittink, D.R. and J.W. Walsh (1988), *Conjoint Analysis: Its Reliability, Validity and Usefulness*. The Johnson Graduate School of Management, Cornell University.

Appendix 6.1

Defining the Notion of Elasticity

The elasticity of demand, with respect to a marketing variable, measures the responsiveness of the quantity demanded for a product or a brand to a change in the level of the marketing variable. Specifically, if we consider price (p) as the marketing variable under study, price elasticity is defined as the rate of percentage change in quantity (q) demanded relative to the percentage change in price, or

$$\varepsilon_{q,p} = \frac{\% \text{ change of } q}{\% \text{ change of } p} = \frac{dq/q}{dp/p} = \frac{dq}{dp} * \frac{p}{q}$$

For the generally assumed case, demand increases as price decreases.

Demand is said to be *elastic* with respect to price, if the ratio is greater than 1 in absolute terms; it is *inelastic* if price elasticity is less than 1. Elasticity is normally not the same at each level of the marketing variable.

When the response function is $q = a \cdot p^\beta$ the exponent β is the elasticity assumed constant between two levels (q_1, p_1) and (q_2, p_2). This can be determined as follows:

$$\varepsilon_{q,p} = \frac{\log(q_1/q_2)}{\log(p_1/p_2)}$$

If the response function is $q = a + \beta \ln s$, where s is the advertising expenditure, the elasticity coefficient is variable and is given by

$$\varepsilon_{q,s} = \frac{\beta}{q}$$

A distinction must be made between short- and long-term elasticity. If the dynamic advertising response function is

$$q = \alpha + \beta \sum_{i=0}^{\infty} \lambda^i s_{t-i}$$

the cumulative advertising elasticity is

$$\varepsilon_{q,s} = \frac{\beta}{1-\lambda} \cdot \frac{s}{q}$$

where λ denotes the rate of the implied geometric progression. Other forms of the response functions are, of course, possible.

PART 3

Marketing Strategy Development

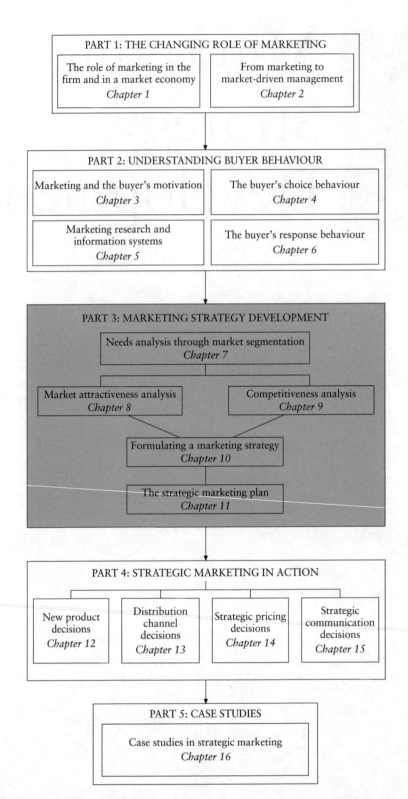

FIGURE PT3.1 *The structure of this book*

NEEDS ANALYSIS THROUGH MARKET SEGMENTATION

LEARNING OBJECTIVES

After reading this chapter, you should be able to:

■ identify a target market and the objectives of market segmentation

■ describe the advantages and disadvantages of the different segmentation methods

■ explain the requirements for effective segmentation

■ define the objectives of strategic positioning

■ discuss the different approaches to international market segmentation.

O ne of the first strategic decisions a firm has to make is to define its target market or, in other words, to choose which potential customers it is going to serve. This choice implies the splitting of the total market into groups of customers (called market segments) with similar needs and behavioural or motivational characteristics, and evaluation which of these segments constitute distinct market opportunities. A firm can elect to serve all possible customers or to focus on one or several specific segments within the defined market. This segmentation of the total market is generally done in two steps, corresponding to different levels of market disaggregation. The first step, called *macro-segmentation*, has the objective of identifying the 'reference market' (usually in the form of 'product markets'), while in the second step, called *micro-segmentation*, the goal is to uncover customer 'segments' within each product market previously identified. Using this mapping of the reference market, the firm will then evaluate the attractiveness of each product market and/or segment (see Chapter 8) and assess its own competitiveness (see Chapter 9). This chapter describes a general methodology for segmenting a market and also presents alternative ways of international segmentation.

7.1 MACRO-SEGMENTATION ANALYSIS

Any decision on a target market definition has to start from the presumption that different consumers have varying desires and interests. This variety stems from diverse buying practices and basic variations of customers' needs and the benefits they seek from products. As a consequence, even in respect of the same need it is often impossible to satisfy all customers with a single product or service. Increasingly, therefore, companies have found it essential to move away from mass marketing towards a target-marketing strategy, where the focus is on a particular group of customers. This identification of target customer groups is market segmentation, where the total market is disaggregated into subgroups, with similar requirements and buying characteristics. Knowing how to segment a market is one of the most important skills a firm must possess. Segmentation defines the business a firm should be in, guides strategy development and determines the capabilities needed in the business unit.

7.1.1 Defining the reference market in terms of 'solution'

Implementation of a market-targeting strategy should begin with a company's mission definition that reveals the true function or purpose of the firm in a customer-oriented perspective. The mission statement is the starting point for strategy development. It helps identify the customers to be served, the competitors to surpass, the key success factors to master and the alternative technologies available for producing the service or the function sought.

To define a company's mission, the following questions of major importance should be addressed:

■ What business(es) are we in?

■ What business(es) should we not be in?

Finding the answer to these two questions will bring better understanding of market structure, main market forces, opportunities and threats associated with its different parts. All this knowledge will be instrumental in solving the core issue of corporate mission:

■ What business(es) should we be in?

As was recommended in Chapter 3, the business(es) definition(s) constituting the base for the mission statement should be made in terms of generic needs, i.e. in terms of 'solutions' sought by the customers and not in technical terms, to avoid the risk of myopia. The rationale behind the *solution approach* has been explained in Chapter 4. It can be summarized as follows:

■ To the buyer, the product is what it does.

■ No one buys a product *per se*. What is sought is a solution to a problem.

■ Different technologies can produce the same function, or solution.

■ Technologies are fast changing, while generic needs are stable.

It is therefore important for the market-oriented firm to formulate its mission statement through references to generic needs, rather than in terms of a product. Here are some examples of mission definitions.

■ *Derbit Belgium* is operating in the European roofing market and manufactures membranes of APP-modified bitumen. The company defines its mission as follows: 'We are selling guaranteed waterproof solutions to flat-roofing problems in partnership with exclusive distributors and highly qualified roofing applicators.'

■ *Sedal*, a small French company manufacturing ventilation metallic grids, defined its business as the 'air and temperature control' business and expanded its offerings to air ventilation and air-conditioning systems.

■ *Automatic Systems* manufactures gates and doors, but defines its mission as the sales of 'access control solutions' and offers to its customers not only the hardware but also the software (security systems).

■ *IBM* defines its mission in the following terms: 'We are in the business to helping customers solve problems through the use of advanced information technology. We are creating value by offering the solutions, products and services that help customers succeed.'

Ideally, the business definition should be stated in terms narrow enough to provide practical guidance, yet broad enough to stimulate imaginative thinking, such as openings for product line extensions or for diversification into adjacent product areas. At the Grumman Corporation, the guidelines for the mission statement advise:

> We should be careful not to confine the market boundaries by our existing or traditional product participation. The market definition analysis is purposely meant to create an outward awareness of the total surrounding market, and of its needs and trends that may offer opportunity for, or on the other hand challenges to, our current or contemplated position.   (Hopkins, 1982, p. 119)

These guidelines clearly show that the mission statement is essentially a generalized definition of the firm's total market. As can be seen from the cited examples, this definition as a rule is too broad in the sense that it also covers customer groups which are too hard to reach (e.g. because of strong competition) or have low attractiveness to the company. That is why the next stage in a market-targeting strategy, called macro-segmentation, consists in selecting a *reference market*, corresponding to that part of the total market which offers the best advantages to the firm.

7.1.2 Conceptualization of the reference market

The reference market also must be described in the buyer's perspective and not only from the producer's point of view, as is too often the case. As suggested by Abell (1980), a reference market can be defined as a result of structuring the total market by answering the following questions:

- *Who* is being satisfied, or which customer group?

- *What* is being satisfied, or which customer functions or needs?

- *How* are customer needs being satisfied, or which technologies are used to meet the need?

We thus have a three-dimensional framework, as shown in Fig. 7.1. To segment the market, the first step is to identify the relevant criteria for describing each of these three dimensions.

Functions

We refer here to the need to be fulfilled, or to solution provided by the product or the service. Examples of functions would be: home interior decoration; international transportation of goods; waterproof roof protection; rust prevention; teeth cleaning; deep versus shallow drilling; diagnostic imaging; etc.

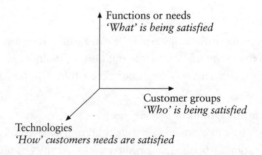

FIGURE 7.1 *Defining the reference market* (Source: *Abell, 1980*)

Solutions have to be conceptually separated from the way the function is performed (i.e. the technology); that is, the dividing line between 'functions' and their 'benefits' is not always clear as functions are narrowly subdivided or an assortment of functions is considered—for example, teeth cleaning *plus* decay prevention, shampoo *plus* anti-dandruff treatment. Thus, functions can also be defined as a package of benefits sought by different customer groups.

Customers

We describe the different customer groups that might buy the products offered at the total market. The most common criteria used for dividing customers into different groups are: households versus industrial buyers, socio-economic class, geographic location, type of activity, company size, OEM versus user, decision-making unit, etc.

At this level of macro-segmentation, only broad customer characteristics are retained. The more detailed criteria that are often necessary, especially for consumer goods (such as age group, benefits sought, lifestyle, purchase behaviour, etc.) are retained for the micro-segmentation stage.

Technologies

Technologies constitute the alternative ways in which a particular function can be performed for a customer. For example, paint or wallpaper for the function of home interior decoration; road, air, rail or sea for international transportation of goods; bitumen or plastic for roof protection; toothpaste or mouthwash for teeth cleaning; X-ray, ultrasound or computerized tomography for diagnostic imaging, etc.

As emphasized above, the technology dimension is dynamic, in the sense that one technology can displace another over time. For example, X-rays are displaced by ultrasound, nuclear medicine and CT scanning as alternative imaging diagnostic techniques. Similarly, electronic mail tends to displace printed material in the field of written communication.

7.1.3 Definitions of reference market boundaries

Using this framework, we may distinguish between three alternative definitions of the reference maket: a 'product market', a 'solution market' and an 'industry' (Fig. 7.2).

■ A *product market* is defined by a specific customer group, seeking a specific solution (function) or assortment of functions based on a single technology.

■ A *solution market* is defined by a specific customer group, seeking a specific solution (funtion) or assortment of functions including all the substitute technologies to perform those functions.

■ An *industry* covers several customer groups and several functions or assortments of functions based, however, on a single technology.

These alternative boundary definitions of the reference market correspond to different market coverage strategies, each having its own merits and weaknesses.

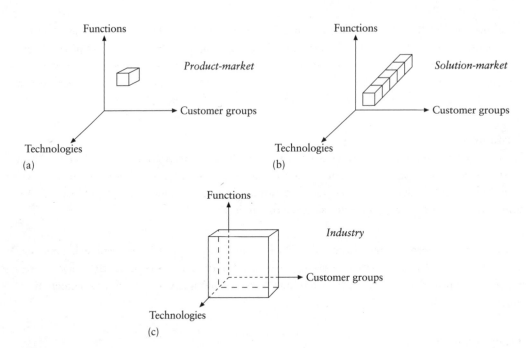

FIGURE 7.2 *Market boundaries definition*

The *industry* definition is the most traditional, but also the least satisfactory because it is supply-oriented and not market-oriented. From a marketing point of view, this definition is too general, since it includes a large variety of functions and customer groups.

The microwave industry, for example, would include microwave transmitter and microwave oven, two very different products in terms of growth potential and of customers' behaviour characteristics. However, most industrial and foreign trade statistics are industry-based and it is therefore difficult to avoid industry definitions completely.

The *solution market* (or simply the 'market') definition is very close to the generic need concept and has the merit of emphasizing the existence of substitute technologies for performing the same function. A technological innovation can dramatically change existing market boundaries. The monitoring of substitute technologies is enhanced by this reference market definition. The major difficulty stems from the fact that the technology domains involved may be very different.

> Customers with a need for a 6 mm hole will normally use a metal twist drill, but some segments are finding lasers or high-pressure water jets to be a better solution. Also, companies that refine cane sugar wrestle with this question often. Their product is a sweetener, but the needs of soft drink and candy manufacturers for sweetening can be satisfied with sugar made from corn (fructose) or sugar beet. Depending on market conditions, these alternatives may be cheaper. Should they offer all sweetening materials?
>
> (Day, 1990, p. 27)

The 'solution market' definition is very useful for giving directions to research and development and for suggesting diversification strategies.

The *product market* definition is the most market-oriented one. It corresponds to the notion of a strategic business unit (SBU) and is very close to the real world market. This market definition automatically dictates four key elements of the firm's strategic thrust.

- The customers to be served.

- The package of benefits to be provided.

- The competitors to surpass.

- The capabilities to acquire.

This partitioning of the total market into product markets will guide the market coverage decisions and determine the type of organizational structure to adopt. One shortcoming of this market definition is the difficulty of finding appropriate market measurements, most government statistics being industry-based and not market-based.

7.1.4 Development of a macro-segmentation grid

Once the relevant segmentation variables are identified, the next task is to combine them and develop a segmentation grid. To illustrate this process, let us consider the market of heavy duty trucks. The identified segmentation variables are as follows:

- *Functions*: regional, national and international transport of goods.

- *Technologies*: air, rail, water and road.

- *Customers*: types of activity—own account, professional transporters and renting companies; size of fleet—small (1–4 trucks), medium (5–10 trucks) and large (11+ trucks).

If we consider all possible combinations, we have here a total of 108 ($3 \times 4 \times 3 \times 3$) possible product markets. To refine our analysis in respect of regional transport, we shall subdivide it into three categories: distribution, construction and others. As this will further increase the number of combinations, for the purposes of simplification we shall limit further analysis to the road transportation, but establish a distinction between trucks below and above 16 tonnes and ignore truck-renting companies.

In this way we obtain 60 ($5 \times 2 \times 2 \times 3$) segments as shown in Table 7.1. Usually it is not necessary to consider each segment, as the pertinence analysis should demonstrate.

Pertinence analysis

In developing an operational segmentation grid, the following rules should be adopted:

1. The analyst should start with the longest list of segmentation variables to avoid overlooking meaningful criteria.
2. Only those variables with a truly significant strategic impact should be isolated.
3. The number of variables can be reduced by collapsing together variables that are correlated.

TABLE 7.1 *Macro-segmentation of the truck market (as a percentage of the total truck population)*

	Fleet size and weight						
	Small (1–4)		Medium (5–10)		Large (11+)		
Activity/functions	⩽16t	>16t	⩽16t	>16t	⩽16t	>16t	Total
Own account transporters							
Distribution	7.3	4.5	1.1	1.8	0.4	2.1	17.2
Construction	0.1	1.1	0.9	1.4	1.7	1.6	6.8
National	4.7	1.6	1.4	3.8	1.7	3.6	16.8
International	1.3	0.9	0.2	1.3	–	1.4	5.1
Others	–	0.6	0.3	–	2.5	–	3.4
Professional transporters							
Distribution	1.1	0.8	0.9	1.6	–	1.6	6.0
Construction	0.2	1.6	–	0.4	–	1.2	3.4
National	1.4	1.5	1.4	3.0	2.5	8.5	18.3
International	0.2	0.7	0.5	6.1	0.4	14.7	22.6
Others	–	0.4	–	–	–	–	0.4
Total	16.3	13.7	6.7	19.4	9.2	34.7	100.0

Source: Lambin and Hiller (1990).

4. Some cells are generally unfeasible combinations of segmentation variables and therefore can be eliminated.
5. Some segments can be regrouped if the differences among them are not really significant or their size is too small.
6. The segmentation grid should also include potential segments, not only segments that are currently occupied.

In this heavy-duty trucks example, the size of segments indeed varies widely as the figures in Table 7.1 show (these figures represent the percentage of registered license plates for trucks within each segment). Re-examination of the segmentation grid suggested a regrouping of similar segments that must be served together, eventually to retain four major segments which altogether represent 70.4 per cent of the total truck population in the Belgian market.

This is the most difficult phase. The task is to conciliate realism and operationality, two often contradictory objectives. When eliminating segments, one must eliminate only the unfeasible combinations of segmentation variables but keep the empty cells which, while currently unoccupied, could become potential segments in the future.

Testing the macro-segmentation grid

To verify the usefulness of the grid, customers of the company and its direct competitors should be located in the different segments. The objective is to evaluate the potential of each segment in terms of size and growth, and to measure the market share held by the firm within each segment. The questions to examine are:

- Which segment(s) display the highest growth rate?

- What is our present market coverage of the market?

- Where are our key customers located?

- Where are our direct competitors located?

- What are the requirements of each segment in terms of service, product quality, etc.?

The following questions can also help decide whether or not two products belong to the same strategic segment.

- Are the main competitors the same?

- Are their customers or groups of customers the same?

- Are the key success factors the same?

- Does divesting in one affect the other?

Positive answers to these four questions would tend to show that both products belong to the same product market (Ader, 1983, p. 8). The answers to these questions will also help the firm to define its market coverage strategy and to regroup segments having the same requirements and/ or the same competitors.

7.1.5 Finding new segments

Some segmentation variables are readily apparent as a result of industry convention or established norms for dividing buyers. Macro-segmentation analysis goes beyond conventional wisdom and accepted classification schemes and gives the opportunity for discovering new ways of segmenting the market. In searching for potential new segments, the following questions should be considered.

- Are there other technologies to perform the required functions?

- Could additional functions be performed by an enhanced product?

- Could the needs of some buyers be better served by reducing the number of functions and possibly lowering the price?

- Are there other groups of buyers requiring the same service or function?

- Are there new channels of distribution that could be used?

- Are there different bundles of products and services that could possibly be sold as a package?

Finding new ways to segment the market can give the firm a major competitive advantage over rivals (Porter, 1985, p. 247).

7.1.6 Reference market coverage strategies

Reference market coverage decisions will be made on the basis of the 'attractiveness/competitiveness' analysis of the different product markets (see Chapter 10). Different market coverage strategies can be considered by the firm.

1. *Focused strategy*. The market boundaries are defined narrowly in terms of functions, technology and customer groups. This is the strategy of the specialist seeking a high market share in a narrow niche.
2. *Functional specialist*. The firm serves a single or narrow set of functions but covers a broad range of customers. The market boundaries are defined narrowly by function, but broadly by customer group. Firms manufacturing intermediate components fall in this category.
3. *Customer specialist*. The market boundaries are defined broadly by function but narrowly by customer group. The focus is on the needs of a particular group of customers. Companies specializing in hospital equipment belong to this category.
4. *Mixed strategy*. The firm is diversifying its activities in terms of functions and/or customer groups.
5. *Full coverage*. The market boundaries are defined broadly by function and customer group. The firm covers the whole market. A steel company is a good example of this kind of market.

In most cases, market coverage strategies can be defined in only two dimensions, functions and customer groups, because in general only one technology is mastered by the firm, even if substitute technologies exist.

For example, jam is in direct competition with melted cheese and chocolate paste. Because manufacturing requirements are so different, none of the firms operating in the sector of fruit transformation also has industrial operations in these adjacent sectors. In some cases, however, firms define their businesses in terms of several substitute technologies, such as General Electric in the diagnostic imaging market (see Abell, 1980).

In a given sector of activity, business definitions may differ from one competitor to another. A firm specializing in a particular function can be confronted by a rival specializing in a particular customer group interested in the same function. The first competitor will probably have a cost advantage over the second, who will probably be more efficient in terms of distribution or customer service. The competitor analysis system should help identify the distinctive qualities of direct competitors.

Changes in market boundaries

Under the pressure of technological progress and changing consumption habits, definitions of market boundaries are constantly changing along any one of three dimensions: functions, technologies or customers.

- *Extension to new customer groups* through a process of adoption and diffusion; for example, adoption of microcomputers in the classroom.

■ *Extension to new functions* through a process of systematization and through the creation of products to serve a combination of functions; for example, telephone sets combined with a fax and with an automatic answering device.

■ *Extensions to new technologies* through a process of technological substitution; for example, electronic mail replacing printed mail.

These changing forces explain the changing profiles of product life cycles, a key criterion for assessing the attractiveness of product markets. (The product life cycle (PLC) model will be analysed in the next chapter.)

7.2 MICRO-SEGMENTATION ANALYSIS

The objective of micro-segmentation is to analyse in more detail the diversity of customers' requirements within each of the product markets (or macro-segments) identified during macro-segmentation analysis. Within a particular product market, customers seek the same core service—for instance, time measurement in the watches market. However, keeping in mind the multi-attribute product concept, the way the core service is provided and the secondary services that go with the core service can be very different. The goal of micro-segmentation analysis is to identify customer groups searching for the same package of benefits in the product. This can lead to a differentiation strategy to obtain a competitive advantage over rivals by doing a better job of satisfying customer requirements.

7.2.1 Market segmentation vs product differentiation

A distinction should be clearly made between the two key marketing concepts of segmentation and differentiation.

Product *differentiation* provides a basis upon which a supplier can appeal to selective buying motives. Chamberlin (1950, p. 56) has defined this concept in the following way:

> A general class of product is differentiated if any significant basis exists for distinguishing the goods (or services) of one seller from those of another. Such a basis may be real or fancied, so long as it is of any importance whatever to buyers, and leads to a preference for one variety of a product over another.

The products are differentiated if the consumer believes they are different.

While product differentiation is based on distinctions among products, market *segmentation* is based on distinctions among prospects that constitute the market (Smith, 1956). Recognition of the heterogeneity of customers has led firms to appeal to segments of what once might have been considered as a homogeneous market. Generally, segmentation is viewed as a process of market disaggregation. It may be useful to view it as a process of consumer aggregation.

The firm could consider each buying unit as a segment. However, at least some economies of scale should be possible if these buying units were clustered into fewer groups. Buying units are aggregated in segments in such a way that there is a maximum homogeneity of demand within segments and maximum heterogeneity of demand between segments. Continuation of the aggregation process eventually leads to the formation of a single segment: the market as a whole. The firm must determine the level of aggregation which will generate the optimal profits.   (Dalrymple and Parsons, 1976, p. 143)

Thus, product differentiation is a supply concept, while market segmentation is a demand concept.

7.2.2 Steps in market segmentation

The implementation of a micro-segmentation analysis consists of four basic steps.

- *Segmentation analysis*, or subdividing product markets into distinct groups of potential buyers having the same expectations or requirements (homogeneity condition) and being different from customers who are in other segments (heterogeneity condition).

- *Market targeting*, or selecting particular segment(s) to target, given the firm's strategic ambition and distinctive capabilities.

- *Market positioning*, or deciding how the firm wants to be perceived in the minds of potential customers, given the distinctive quality of the product and the positions already occupied by competitors.

- *Marketing programming*, aimed at target segments. This last step involves the development and deployment of specific marketing programme(s) specially designed for achieving the desired positioning in the target segment(s).

7.2.3 Segmentation analysis

The first step, segmentation analysis, can be implemented in four different ways:

- *Descriptive segmentation*, which is based on socio-demographic characteristics of the customer irrespective of the product category.

- *Benefit segmentation*, which considers explicitly the product category and the person's system of values.

- *Lifestyle segmentation*, which is based on sociocultural characteristics of the customer, irrespective of the product category.

- *Behavioural segmentation*, which classifies customers on the basis of their actual purchasing behaviour in the marketplace.

Each of these segmentation methods has its own merits and weaknesses, which will be discussed below.

Descriptive or socio-demographic segmentation

Socio-demographic segmentation is an indirect segmentation method. The basic assumption embedded in this buyers' classification is the following:

> People having different socio-demographic profiles also have different needs and expectations regarding products and services.

This is obvious in many fields. Women and men have different needs for products like clothes, hats, cosmetics, jewellery, etc., and similarly for teenagers or senior citizens, for low- and high-income households, for rural versus urban households, and so on. Thus, socio-demographic variables are used as proxies for direct needs analysis.

The most commonly used variables are: sex, age, income, geographic location, education, occupation, family size and social class—all variables which reflect the easily measurable vital statistics of a society.

Frequently, a socio-demographic segmentation combines several variables, as shown in Fig. 7.3. The case analysed here is a recently launched new brand in the food sector. The market response is described by reference to two dependent variables: the proportion of households having

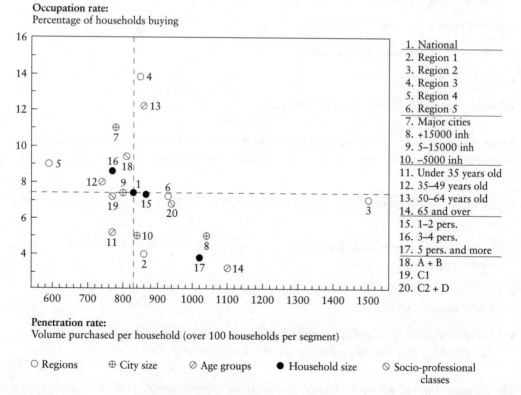

Occupation rate:
Percentage of households buying

	1. National
	2. Region 1
	3. Region 2
	4. Region 3
	5. Region 4
	6. Region 5
	7. Major cities
	8. +15000 inh
	9. 5–15000 inh
	10. –5000 inh
	11. Under 35 years old
	12. 35–49 years old
	13. 50–64 years old
	14. 65 and over
	15. 1–2 pers.
	16. 3–4 pers.
	17. 5 pers. and more
	18. A + B
	19. C1
	20. C2 + D

Penetration rate:
Volume purchased per household (over 100 households per segment)

○ Regions   ⊕ City size   ⊘ Age groups   ● Household size   ◌ Socio-professional classes

FIGURE 7.3 *Socio-demographic segmentation: the case of a food product* (Source: *Industry*)

purchased the brand (market occupation rate) and the average quantity purchased per household (market penetration rate). The national average is at the intersection of the two dotted lines, the other points describing the behaviour of different socio-economic subgroups.

For instance, one observes that the highest occupation rates are within the subgroups denoted respectively 4/13/7/18: (region 3), (age-group 50–64), (large cities), (classes A + B). Similarly, the market penetration rate is higher within the following subgroups: 3/14/8/17: (region 2), (age group 65 and higher), (middle size cities), (household composition: 5 persons and higher). This information is essential to verify whether the target group has been reached and, if not, to adjust the marketing programme accordingly.

Usefulness of socio-demographic data.   The *merits* of socio-demographic segmentation are its low cost and ease of application. In most markets, information on socio-demographic variables is readily available in published sources. In addition, consumer panels use these criteria in their monthly or bimonthly reports on a similar base across the main European countries.

Also, in recent years significant socio-demographic changes have been observed in industrialized countries. Among these changes are:

- Declining birth rate

- Increase in life expectancy

- Increasing number of working women

- Postponement of the age of marriage

- Increasing divorce rate

- Increasing number of single-parent families.

These changes all have direct implications on the demand structure and on consumer purchase behaviour. They create new market segments and new requirements in existing segments. Examples are:

- The *senior citizens* (over 65) segment for banking services, recreational activities, medical care, etc.

- The segment of *single-adult households*, i.e. the unmarried, divorced, widowed or single-parent families.

- The *dual-income households*, having higher discretionary income; also called the 'DINKS' (Double Income No Kids).

- The segment of *working women* for all time-saving goods and services, like microwave ovens, catalogue shopping, easy-to-prepare foods, fast-food restaurants, etc.

The changes observed during the last 20 years in the socio-demographic profile of the European Union are presented in Table 7.2.

TABLE 7.2 *Changes in the socio-demographic profile of the European Union*

	Past	Present and future
Total population	1980: 279 m	1990: 327 m
Persons aged 60 and over	1980: 17%	2010: 27%
Persons under 20 years old	1980: 30%	2010: 20%
Life expectancy (years)	1960: 67.3 (M); 72.7 (F)	1988: 72.0 (M); 78.6 (F)
Infant mortality rate		
(per 1000 live births)	1960: 34.8	1988: 8.2
Foreign population		Extra-EU: 2.5% or 7.9 m
		Intra-EU: 1.5% or 4.9 m
Number of households		111.5 m private households
		2.8 persons per household
Number of one-person households		22.3% of total households
Average age of first marriage	1950–70: 25.6 (M); 23.0 (F)	1987: 27.1 (M); 24.6 (F)
Number of divorces (× 1000)	1960: 125.3	1988: 534.2
Activity rate for women		
(% of active population)	1983: 46.6%	1988: 51.0%

Source: EUROSTAT (1991).

Several uses are currently made of socio-demographic data, namely:

■ To describe and better understand present customers

■ To have the ID profile of a target segment

■ To select media having a higher probability of reaching a target group

■ To identify prospective buyers of a new product.

Limitations of descriptive segmentation. Socio-demographic segmentation (as well as behavioural segmentation) is an *ex-post analysis* of the kind of people who make up specific segments. The emphasis is on describing the characteristics of segments rather than on learning what causes these segments to develop. This is the reason for the term *descriptive segmentation*.

Another major weakness is the *declining predictive value* of socio-demographic segmentation in industrialized countries as, increasingly, different persons adopt the same consuming behaviour with the growing standardization of consumption modes across social classes. In other words, the fact of belonging to the upper class no longer implies the existence of a purchase behaviour different from a middle-class person. Today, two consumers of the same age, same family structure and same income may have extremely different behaviours and attitudes, reflected in different buying habits, product preferences and sometimes completely opposite reactions to advertising. Socio-demographic segmentation must be complemented by other methods to understand and predict buyers' behaviour.

Benefit segmentation

In benefit segmentation, the emphasis is placed on differences in people's values and not on differences in socio-demographic profiles. Two individuals, identical in terms of socio-demographic profiles, may have very *different value systems*. Moreover, the same person can attribute different value scales to different kinds of products. For example, a person who buys a refrigerator because it is the cheapest available may want to buy the most expensive TV set simply because of its superior design. Or, the individual who pays a high price for a bottle of wine may own a very cheap watch.

Thus, as discussed in Chapter 3, the value or the benefit sought in purchasing a particular product is the critical motivational factor to identify. The objective of benefit segmentation is to explain differences in preferences and not simply to give ex-post descriptions of purchase behaviours.

A classic example of benefit segmentation analysis is due to Yankelovich (1964) in the watches market. His approach discloses three distinct segments, each representing different values attributed to watches by each of three different groups of consumers.

1. *Economy segment.* This group wants to pay the lowest possible price for any watch that works reasonably well. If it fails within a year, they will replace it (23 per cent of buyers).
2. *Durability and quality segment.* This group wants a watch with a long life, good workmanship, good material and good styling. They are willing to pay for these product qualities (46 per cent of buyers).
3. *Symbolic segment.* This groups wants useful product features and meaningful emotional qualities. The watch should suitably symbolize an important occasion. Here, a well-known brand name, fine styling, a gold or diamond case, and a jeweller's recommendation are important (31 per cent of buyers).

Without such an understanding, the demographic characteristics of the buyers were most confusing. For example, the most expensive watches are being bought by people with both the highest and the lowest incomes. On the other hand, some upper-income consumers are no longer buying costly watches, but are buying cheap, well-styled watches to throw away when they require servicing. Other upper-income consumers, however, continue to buy fine, expensive watches for suitable occasions (Yankelovich, 1964).

At one time, most watch companies were oriented almost exclusively towards the third segment, thus leaving the major portion of the market open to attack and exploitation. The US Time Company, with the brand Timex, took advantage of this opening and established a very strong position among buyers in the first two segments.

Required market data.   Benefit segmentation (Haley, 1968) requires detailed information on consumer value systems. Each segment is identified by the benefits it is seeking. It is the total package of benefits sought which differentiates one segment from another, rather than the fact that one segment is seeking one particular benefit and another a quite different benefit. Individual benefits are likely to have appeal for several segments. In fact, most people would like as many benefits as possible. However, the relative importance they attach to individual benefits when forced to make trade-offs can differ greatly, and, accordingly, can be used as an effective criterion in segmenting markets. Thus, opportunities for segmentation arise from *trade-offs* that consumers are willing to make among the benefits possible and the prices paid to obtain them.

Thus, the *multi-attribute product concept* (see Chapter 4) is the implied behavioural model in benefit segmentation. Its implementation requires the following information from a representative sample of target consumers.

■ The list of attributes or benefits associated with a product category.

■ An evaluation of the relative importance attached to each benefit.

■ A regrouping procedure of consumers with similar rating patterns.

■ An evaluation of the size and profile of each identified segment.

Thus, in the dental and mouth hygiene market, the attributes identified through consumer research were as follows: whiteness, freshness, good tasting, product appearance, decay prevention, gum protection and economy. The next question was to ask respondents to divide 100 points among each of the toothpaste attributes according to the importance they attached to each characteristic when selecting a brand of toothpaste. Four segments were identified, as shown in Table 7.3 (Haley, 1968): Supplementary information has also been collected about the people in each of these segments.

■ The *sensory* segment is particularly concerned with the flavour and the appearance of the product. In this segment, a large portion of the brand deciders are children. Their use of spearmint toothpaste is well above average.

■ The *sociables* segment comprises people who show concern for the brightness of their teeth. It includes a relatively large group of young married couples. They smoke more than average and their lifestyle is very active.

TABLE 7.3 *Benefit segmentation of the toothpaste market*

	Benefit segments			
Benefits sought	Sensory	Sociables	Worriers	Independents
Flavour, appearance	***	*	*	*
Brightness of teeth	*	***	*	*
Decay prevention	*	*	***	*
Low price	*	*	*	***

Source: Adapted from Haley (1968).
*** Most important.

■ The *worriers* segment contains a large number of families with children. They are seriously concerned about the possibilities of cavities and show a definite preference for fluoride toothpaste.

■ The *independents* segment is price-oriented and shows a dominance of men. It tends to be above average in terms of toothpaste usage. People in this segment see very few meaningful differences between brands.

Benefit segmentation has important implications for the product policy of the firm. Once marketing understands the expectations of a particular consumer group, new or modified products can be developed and aimed at people seeking a specific combination of benefits.

Limitations of benefit segmentation.   The greatest difficulty in applying this approach lies in the selection of the benefits to emphasize, mainly in the consumer goods markets. When market analysts ask consumers what benefit they want in a product, they are not likely to provide new information about product benefits, since they are not highly introspective. If direct market analysis is supplemented with information about consumers' problems, however, new insights can be obtained. For example, in the toothpaste market, protection of gums is a new benefit promoted by brands having adopted a paramedical positioning. This is the outcome of dental hygiene analysis conducted together with dental specialists.

There is another difficulty of benefit segmentation: if we are gaining in understanding of consumer preferences, we are losing in terms of knowledge of the socio-demographic profiles of different customer groups. How do we reach, selectively, the 'worriers'? Thus, additional information must be collected to be able to describe these segments in socio-demographic terms.

Benefit segmentation analysis requires the collection of primary data, which is always a costly exercise. In addition, sophisticated multi-variate measurement techniques (cluster analysis) must be used to identify the different customer groups. In some cases, however, interesting insights on benefits sought can be obtained through qualitative research, as illustrated in Box 7.1, in the hi-fi chains market.

Segmenting markets with conjoint analysis.   The method of conjoint analysis has been described and illustrated in Chapter 6. As explained, the focus of conjoint analysis is on the measurement of buyer preferences for product attribute levels and of the buyer benefits generated by the product attributes. Since measurements are made at the individual level, if preference heterogeneity exists, the market analyst can detect it and regroup individuals displaying the same utilities.

An empirical example will clarify the methodology. The application involves a bimonthly magazine which publishes new book reviews, book guidance and advice, book digests and short articles. The editor is considering three alternative modifications of the editorial content:

■ Concentrating on book reviews and analyses and dropping all the other editorial sections (*book review*).

BOX 7.1

Hi-fi chains market: benefit segments and principal benefits sought

The technicians
- Mean to enjoy high-fidelity sound in its technical aspects
- Look for the quality and purity of the sound
- Mostly interested by the technical features without being necessarily qualified

The musicians
- Mean to enjoy music
- Look for the spirit of the music, its musical space and colour
- Mostly interested by the musical interpretation without having necessarily a great musical culture

The snobs
- Mean to show their resources, taste and aesthetic sense
- Look for prestige, demonstration effects and social integration
- Often poorly informed, tend to buy what is known and safe

The others

- Concentrating on guidance and advice on a larger number of books using standardized evaluation grids (*reader's guide*).

- Limiting the number of book reviews, but adding a section on literary news with interviews of authors and special topical sections (*literary news*).

A 'do nothing' alternative is also considered, i.e. to keep the present editorial content unchanged. As to the selling price, three levels are considered: the present price of BF142, an increased price of BF200 and a decreased price of BF100, the number of pages remaining unchanged (30 pages). A questionnaire was mailed to 400 respondents selected among a group of readers, and 171 valid questionnaires were used to estimate the utility functions. A cluster analysis programme was then used to regroup the respondents having the same utilities. As shown in Table 7.4, four different segments were identified.

- In segment 1 the respondents seem to be happy with the present editorial content. They react very negatively to the first two alternatives, and positively, but without enthusiasm, to the 'literary news' concept.

- In segment 2 there is a clear preference for the 'book reviews' concept and a negative attitude towards the other two editorial concepts.

- In segment 3 the 'reader's guide' concept is preferred, the other two being clearly rejected.

TABLE 7.4 *Benefit segmentation through conjoint analysis: book review*

Attributes	Segment 1 (35.5%)	Segment 2 (21.0%)	Segment 3 (11.3%)	Segment 4 (32.2%)
Content				
Book review	−7.1	1.2	−6.2	−1.8
Book guide	−7.4	−7.9	2.9	−3.1
Present content	0	0	0	0
Literary news	0.3	−2.1	−6.8	−3.3
Range:	7.7	9.1	9.7	3.3
Price				
BF100	0.5	0.6	0.3	1.1
BF142	0	0	0	0
BF200	−0.7	−0.6	−0.4	−1.0
Range:	1.2	1.2	0.7	2.1

Source: Adapted from Roisin (1988).

■ In segment 4 the present editorial content is the best alternative, but the range of utilities is also the smallest.

Thus, in terms of benefits sought, the four segments are very different. As to the prices, the largest price sensitivity is observed in segment 4, as evidenced by the range, while segments 1 and 2 react in a very similar way, segment 3 being the least price sensitive. Analysis of the composition of these four segments showed that segment 4 was largely composed of librarians, while high school teachers were an important group in segment 3.

For a review of the contributions of conjoint analysis in market segmentation, see Green and Krieger (1991).

Behavioural segmentation

Usage segmentation attempts to classify consumers on the basis of their actual purchase behaviour in the marketplace. As such, it is also a descriptive and ex-post segmentation method. The criteria most commonly used are product usage, volume purchased and loyalty status.

1. *Product-user segmentation.* A distinction can be made between users, non-users, first users, ex-users, potential users, and occasional versus regular users. A different selling and communication approach must be adopted for each of these user categories.
2. *Volume segmentation.* In many markets, a small proportion of customers represents a high percentage of total sales. Often, about 20 per cent of the users account for 80 per cent of total consumption. A distinction between heavy, light and non-users is often very useful. Heavy users, or key accounts, deserve special treatment.

3. *Loyalty segmentation*. Among existing customers a distinction can be made between hard-core loyals, soft-core loyals and switchers. Markets like cigarettes, beers and toothpaste are generally brand-loyal markets. Keeping loyal customers is the objective of relationship marketing. Appropriate marketing strategies can be developed to attract competitors' customers or to increase the loyalty of switchers.

7.2.4 Sociocultural or lifestyle segmentation

As mentioned above, socio-demographic criteria are losing predictive value in affluent societies as consumption patterns become more and more personalized. Individuals from the same socio-demographic groups can have very different preferences and buying behaviour, and vice versa.

Sociocultural segmentation, also called *lifestyle* or *psychographic segmentation*, seeks to supplement demographics by adding such elements as activities, attitudes, interests, opinions, perceptions and preferences to get a more complete consumer profile. It attempts to draw human portraits of consumers adding detail at the less obvious levels of motivation and personality. Wells and Tigert make the following point:

> Demographics have been and continue to be extremely useful, but they are unsatisfying. They lack color. They lack texture. They lack dimensionality. They need to be supplemented by something that puts flesh on bare statistical backbone.
>
> (Wells and Tigert, 1971, published in Wells, 1974, p. 37)

The basic objective is to relate personality-type variables to consumer behaviour. Lifestyle descriptors are used as proxies for personality traits. 'Lifestyle' refers to the overall manner in which people live and spend time and money. A person's lifestyle (or psychographic profile) can be measured and described in a number of ways.

■ At the most stable and persistent level are the person's *value system* and *personality traits* which are, of course, more difficult to measure.

■ At an intermediate level, a person's *activities, interests* and *opinions* are revealing of her or his value system.

■ At a superficial level but directly observable level, consumers' lifestyles are reflected by the *products and services purchased* and by the way in which buyers are using or consuming them.

Valette-Florence (1986) suggests defining a person's lifestyle as the interaction of these three levels: the group of persons having a similar behaviour at each of these levels is homogeneous in terms of lifestyle. Thus *a lifestyle is the result of a person's value system, attitudes, interests and opinions (AIO) and of the individual's consumption mode*. It describes the sort of person he or she is and, at the same time, differentiates that person from others.

Lifestyle studies can be conducted at one of these three levels. The closer we are from actual purchase decisions, the easier are the measurements, but also the more volatile are the conclusions. The largest majority of empirical lifestyle studies have been conducted at the AIO level, where research measures:

TABLE 7.5 *Lifestyle dimensions*

Activities	Interests	Opinions	Demographics
Work	Family	Themselves	Age
Hobbies	Home	Social issue	Education
Social events	Job	Politics	Income
Vacation	Community	Business	Occupation
Entertainment	Recreation	Economics	Family size
Club membership	Fashion	Education	Dwelling
Community	Food	Products	Geography
Shopping	Media	Future	City size
Sports	Achievements	Culture	Life cycle

Source: Plummer (1974).

- People's *activities* in terms of how they spend their time.

- Their *interests*, i.e. what they place importance on in their immediate surroundings.

- Their *opinions* in terms of views of themselves and the world around them.

Also considered are some basic *demographic* characteristics such as their stage in the lifecycle, income, education and where they live. Table 7.5 lists the elements included in each major dimension of lifestyle.

Lifestyle studies provide a broad everyday view of consumers—a living portrait that goes beyond flat socio-demographic descriptions and helps understand actual consumer behaviour.

Lifestyle research methodology

In a typical lifestyle study, a questionnaire is developed containing a set of statements measuring the lifestyle dimensions relevant to the product category under study. Each dimension is measured by several statements or propositions to which respondents indicate the extent of their agreement or disagreement on a 5-point Likert scale ranging from 'definitely disagree' to 'definitely agree'. Some general lifestyle statements are presented here.

- I find myself checking the prices in the grocery stores even for small items (*price conscious*).

- An important part of my life and activities is dressing smartly (*fashion conscious*).

- I would rather spend a quiet evening at home than go out to a party (*homebody*).

- I like to work on community projects (*community minded*).

- I try to arrange my home for my children's convenience (*child oriented*).

Typically, several different statements are introduced into the questionnaire to measure the same concept. Approximately 200 to 300 AIO statements may be included. In addition to the AIO statements, information is also collected on product usage and demographic character-istics.

Armed with these three sets of data (AIO statements, product usage and demographics), the market analyst constructs user profiles. The analysis involves relating levels of agreement on all AIO items with the levels of usage on a product and with demographic characteristics. The procedure is as follows.

1. Factor analysis is used to reduce the set of statements to a summary set of factors.
2. Each respondent's scores on the factors are computed.
3. Respondents are then clustered into segments that are relatively homogeneous using a cluster analysis programme.
4. The clusters are then labelled by the factors which most typify each cluster.
5. Finally, the segments are cross-tabulated with demographic and usage variables to help to characterize the identified segments.

An example of general lifestyle segmentation of the European market is presented in Fig. 7.4.

Usefulness of lifestyle segmentation

The results of lifestyle studies are stocked and regularly up-dated. Factorial analyses are used to uncover principal components or macro-characteristics and meaningful clusters of answers, which correspond to *stereotypes* or '*socio-styles*' observed in society or within the specific group under study. Two kind of lifestyle studies can be made: general or product-specific.

General lifestyle studies classify the total population into groups based on general lifestyle characteristics, such as 'receptivity to innovation', 'family centred', 'ecological sensitivity', etc. Each subgroup represents a different pattern of values and motivations and the analyst can discern which types of consumers are strong prospects for their products, what other things appeal to these prospects and how to communicate with them in the most effective way.

The up-dating of lifestyle data keeps track of the changing weight of the different socio-styles and enables the company to keep up with the changes in motivation and behaviour of different social subgroups. The usefulness of lifestyle analyses is two-fold:

■ To identify emerging trends and sensitivities within society and to assess the opportunities and threats associated with these changes; this is the dynamic aspect.

■ To determine whether a particular subgroup is ahead or lagging a sociocultural trend; this is the more static aspect of the analysis.

Thus, this process shows up *leading indicators of changes*, or trends that will generate changes.

In Europe, Europanel (GFK) has developed a general typology of 16 European socio-style profiles. In the USA, the VALS programme was created by SRI International with eight consumer segments (VALS-2). The 16 Euro-styles identified in the European market by the Europanel group are presented in two dimensions on the map of Fig. 7.4.

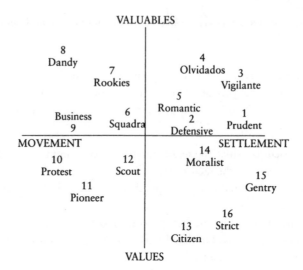

<FIGURE 7.4 *European life style segmentation* (Source: *Winkler, 1981*)

1. *Prudent*
   Retirees resigned to their fate;
   seeking security.

2. *Defensives*
   Younger inhabitants of small towns
   seeking protection and support in
   their traditional family structures.

3. *Vigilante*
   Frustrated blue-collar workers
   trying to preserve their identities.

4. *Olvidados (left out)*
   Retirees and housewives threatened
   and left out by society's growing
   complexity; seeking protection.

5. *Romantic*
   Sentimental, romantic young nest
   builders seeking modern progress
   and a secure life for their families.

6. *Squadra (team player)*
   Tolerant suburban young couples
   seeking a secure life of sports and
   leisure; smaller group gives feeling of
   security.

7. *Rockies*
   Working-class youth, excluded in
   their own eyes, seeking integration via
   money-making/consumption; frustrated
   by low education.

8. *Dandy*
   Hedonistic group 'show-offs'
   with modest income and concern
   for outward appearances.

9. *Business (sharks)*
   Spendthrift, well-educated,
   ambitious young wolves, seeking
   leadership in a competitive society.

10. *Protest*
    Intellectual young critics seeking
    to revolutionize society.

11. *Pioneer*
    Young well-off, ultra-tolerant
    intellectuals seeking social justice.

12. *Scout*
    Tolerant middle-aged conservatives
    seeking orderly social progress.

13. *Citizens*
    Community organizers seeking
    leadership in social activities.

14. *Moralist*
    Quiet, religious citizens seeking a
    peaceful future for their children.

15. *Gentry*
    Law and order conservatives belonging
    to old money established élite.

16. *Strict*
    Repressive puritans

FIGURE 7.4 *European life style segmentation* (Source: *Winkler, 1981*)

- The first dimension may be described roughly as the willingness to accept new ideas or to try new things: *movement versus settlement*.

- The second dimension opposes an orientation towards material goods (*valuables*) and ethics (*values*).

A third dimension opposing rational and emotional behaviour has been observed but is not represented here.

> Thus people in type 8 (Dandies), which is close to the upper left-hand corner of the map, are materialistic and adventurous. People belonging to type 16 (Strict), near the bottom right-hand corner of the map, are more interested in ethical issues than material considerations and are very conservative in attitude. (Winkler, 1991, p. 9)

Having this map, it is possible to overlay the pattern of product (or brand) usage or attitude and to compare the kinds of people being heavy users of the product category and/or the brand.

In *product-specific* lifestyle studies, the objective is to understand consumer behaviour related to a particular product or service. The AIO statements are then more product-specific. To illustrate, here are examples of AIO statements adapted to the credit cards market:

- I like to pay cash for everything I buy.

- I buy many things with a credit car or a charge card.

- In the past year, we have borrowed money from a bank or finance company.

- To buy anything other than a house or a car on credit is unwise.

Lifestyle research methodology also has some important advantages over motivation research and depth interviews: (a) samples are large; (b) conclusions do not rely heavily on interviewer interpretation of relatively unstructured responses; (c) data are easily analysed by a variety of well-understood statistical methods; and (d) less highly trained interviewers can be employed.

Problems in lifestyle research
Lifestyle research was at a time very popular in market research, particularly among advertising people, although several researchers have very early expressed considerable reservations as to its validity and predictive value. A certain number of methodological issues are still unresolved.

1. To date, there is *no explicit theoretical model* which specifies the key concepts of lifestyle to be explored and their hypothesized relations to purchase behaviour. In most cases, it is a trial-and-error procedure which is adopted.
2. As a consequence, the *selection of lifestyle dimensions* and indicators is largely based on intuition, hunches and the researcher's imagination. Lifestyle researchers do not agree on the variables that should be included. The end result is a very large number (up to 300) statements included in the questionnaire, a way out facilitated by increasing computer capacities.

3. Lifestyle analyses belong to the class of causal studies, since the objective is to explain why people behave as they do. To demonstrate the existence of a causal relationship requires a well-conceived experimental design and careful testing of the observed relationship are required. Evidence of a relationship does not necessarily imply causality. Spurious correlations as well as spurious non-correlations exist and the lack of prior research design can cause faulty interpretation of data.
4. Traditionally, the association between lifestyle data with such variables as product usage, brand loyalty, etc., are examined by direct cross-tabulations, while the multi-variate nature of data suggest the use of multi-variate statistical techniques.
5. Questions are also raised regarding the reliability of the measuring instrument. Can we expect reliable and valid responses from a questionnaire that takes several hours to complete and may lead to boredom or fatigue?

Several of the methodological issues raised here are critical and question the internal and external validity of general lifestyle studies. This means that its users must make special efforts to be careful in measurements, statistical analyses and interpretations of results if they are to uncover valid information on consumer behaviour. It is up to the market analyst to verify whether the basic validity conditions are indeed fulfilled.

These are basic questions to which every professional user has the right to receive precise answers, since they will determine the validity of lifestyle analyses. As underlined in chapter 5, marketing research has to deal with *accredited knowledge*, since management is primarily interested in making decisions on accurate and unbiased data. The absence of satisfactory answers to these methodological issues, combined with the data inaccessibility and with the secrecy of the questionnaire, explain the low degree of interest for these studies in the scientific community.

In spite of the methodological issues in lifestyle research, the sociocultural approach is both interesting and promising. It is an undeniable improvement over segmentation methods based on the sole economic and socio-demographic criteria. For a systematic analysis of the methodological issues raised by lifestyle research and for the remedies suggested, see Green and Wind (1974) and Valette-Florence (1986, 1988). For an empirical validation of lifestyle studies in the French market, see Kapferer and Laurent (1981).

7.3 SEGMENTATION OF INDUSTRIAL MARKETS

Conceptually, there is no difference between industrial and consumer market segmentation, but the criteria used to segment the market vary greatly. The same distinction between macro- and micro-segmentation can be made. The method of macro-segmentation described in section 7.1 of this chapter is of direct application. The micro-segmentation criteria tend to be different, however.

7.3.1 Benefit segmentation

As for consumer goods, *benefit segmentation* is the most natural method. It is based on the specific needs, in general well defined, of the industrial customer. In industrial markets, this means classifying the customers by type of industry or by end use. End-users are generally looking for different benefits, performance or functions in a product. Industrial products often have a wide range of possible uses—for instance, in electric motors, ball bearings, steel sheets, etc. The classification by industry type points out the priority needs and their relative importance.

By way of illustration, let us consider the case of company that specializes in manufacturing small electric motors, a product which has a very large number of possible uses. For each end use, beyond the core function, one or several product characteristics may be particularly important. This is the case for the following three industrial applications.

■ Motors incorporated in petrol pumps: security norms (spark free) are essential.

■ Motors incorporated into computers or in medical instruments used in hospitals: the response time must be instantaneous.

■ Motors incorporated in industrial sewing machines: resistance to frequent stopping and starting is important and fast reaction is secondary.

The functions of an industrial good and their importance in the customer's industrial process vary according to whether it is a major equipment good (turnkey factory, steel mill, alternator) or secondary equipment good (radiator, light trucks, typewriter); semi-finished intermediate products (coated steel sheets); parts to be incorporated (electric motors, gear shifts); finished goods (tools, oil); raw materials (coal, grease, polyurethane foam); services (engineering, industrial cleaning, maintenance). In each case, the customer's perceived economic value of the product will be very different.

It is important to recall that, in many industrial sectors, sales are based on orders with detailed specifications. In this type of market situation, the product is naturally adjusted to the particular needs of the customer.

7.3.2 Descriptive segmentation

Demographic or *descriptive segmentation* is based on criteria describing the profile of the industrial customer. These criteria generally concern activity, geographic location, size, shareholder composition, etc. Many companies chose to have separate sales service systems for large and small customers. Large customers are directly serviced by the company while small customers will be dealt with by distributors.

7.3.3 Behavioural segmentation

Behavioural segmentation is important for industrial markets. Its purpose is to develop a strategy for approaching industrial customers according to their structures and the way their buying decision centre operates. The way a buying decision centre works was discussed in Chapter 3, where we also saw that the buying process can be more or less formalized according to the complexity of decisions and organizational structures.

In some companies, buying is centralized and precise rules govern the purchase decisions. Other companies, on the contrary, decentralize buying and the approach to such a company will be similar to that used for a smaller firm. Other characteristics of the buying centre are also important: motivations of different members of the buying team, the different forces at play between the representatives of different functions, the degree of formalism and the length of time necessary for a decision. These behavioural characteristics are not usually directly observable and thus are often hard to identify. However, as seen above, these are important things for salespeople to be aware of.

Because of the complexity and variety of possible bases for the segmentation of industrial markets, Shapiro and Bonona (1983) have expanded the use of macro- and micro-segmentation into what is called a 'nested approach'. This method assumes a hierarchical structure of segmentation bases which move from very broad or general bases to very organization-specific bases. Rather than a two-step process, the nested approach allows three, four or five steps. The list of segmentation criteria is presented in Box 7.2.

The simplest way to segment industrial markets is to use broad descriptive characteristics, such as industrial sectors (NACE or SIC category), company size, geographic location or end-market served. This information is easily accessible since these data are readily available through government agencies, who publish detailed industrial classifications. Benefit segmentation is also easier in industrial markets than in consumer markets, because users are professional people who have less difficulty in expressing their needs and in qualifying the relative importance of different product attributes.

7.4 IMPLEMENTATION OF A SEGMENTATION STRATEGY

Having completed the market segmentation analysis phase we have a segmentation grid which describes the different existing segments. The next step for management is to make decisions regarding the segments to target and regarding the positioning to adopt within the targeted segments. The final stage is to define the type of marketing programme to adopt within each chosen segment. A preliminary question must be raised, however, to verify the extent to which the requirements for effective segmentation are met.

7.4.1 Requirements for effective segmentation

To be effective and useful a segmentation strategy should identify segments that meet four criteria: differential response, adequate size, measurability, and accessibility.

Differential response

This is the most important criterion to consider when choosing a segmentation strategy. The segments must be different in terms of their sensitivity to one or several marketing variables under the control of the firm. The segmentation variable should maximize the behavioural

BOX 7.2

Major bases for industrial segmentation: the nested approach

Organizational demographics
- Industry sectors
- Company size
- Geographic location

Operating variables
- Technology
- User–non-user status
- Customer capabilities

Purchasing approaches
- Decision centre organization
- Purchasing policies
- Purchasing criteria

Situational factors
- Urgency
- Application
- Size of order

Personal characteristics
- Motivation
- Buyer and seller relationship
- Risk perceptions

Source: Shapiro and Bonona (1983).

difference between segments (*heterogeneity condition*) while minimizing the differences among customers within a segment (*homogeneity condition*).

A key requirement is to avoid segment overlapping, the risk being the possibility of cannibalism among products of the same company but targeted to different segments. The more a product has distinctive and observable characteristics, the more homogeneous the segment will be.

We must, however, remember that segment homogeneity does not necessarily imply that all categories of buyers are mutually exclusive. An individual may of course belong to more than one segment. Products from different segments may be bought by the same person for different people within the household, for different use occasions or just for the sake of variety. Observation of shopping trolleys outside a supermarket often shows that brands from both the high and the low end have been purchased at the same time. One segment does not necessarily cover the buyers, but rather the products purchased by the buyers.

Adequate size

Segments should be defined so that they represent enough potential customers to provide sufficient sales revenue to justify the development of different products and marketing programmes.

Identified segments must represent a market potential large enough to justify developing a specific marketing strategy. This condition affects not only the size of the segment in volume and frequency of buying but also its life cycle. All markets are affected by fashion. It is essential to verify that the targeted niche is not temporary and that the product's life span will be economically long. Finally, the size requirement also implies that the added value of the product, because of its specificity, will be financially worth while, in the sense that the market price acceptable by the target segment is sufficiently rewarding for the firm.

Meeting this requirement often implies a trade-off between two logics: the logic of *marketing management*, which tries to meet the needs of the market through a narrow definition of segments in order to adapt the firm's offering to the diversity of market needs as best as possible, and the logic of *operations management*, which emphasizes the benefits of economies of scale through standardization and long production runs.

Measurability

Before target segments can be selected, the size, the purchasing power and the major behaviour characteristics of the identified segments must be measured. If the segmentation criteria used are very abstract, such information is difficult to find. For example, if the prospects are companies of a certain size, it would be easy to find information about their number, location, turnover, etc., but a segmentation criterion like 'innovativeness of companies' does not lend itself to easy measurement and the firm would probably have to conduct its own market survey. Abstract criteria are often used in benefit and lifestyle segmentations, while descriptive segmentation is based on more concrete and observable criteria.

Accessibility

Accessibility refers to the degree to which a market segment can be reached through a unique marketing programme. There are two ways to reach prospects.

- *Customer self-selection* involves reaching a more general target while relying on the product's and advertising's appeal to the intended target group. These consumers select themselves by their attention to the advertisements.

- *Controlled coverage* is very efficient because the firm reaches target customers with little wasted coverage of individuals or firms who are not potential buyers.

Controlled coverage is more efficient from the firm's point of view. This communication strategy implies a good knowledge of the socio-demographic profile of the target group, which is not always the case when using benefit or lifestyle segmentation. The main characteristics of each segment can be summarized in a segmentation grid, as shown in Table 7.6.

TABLE 7.6 *Comparative evaluation of segments*

	Segment 1	Segment 2	Segment 3	Segment 4
Demographics	———	———	———	———
Benefits sought	———	———	———	———
Buying behaviour	———	———	———	———
Success factors		*Importance of success factors*		
Product features	———	———	———	———
Price	———	———	———	———
Services	———	———	———	———
Delivery	———	———	———	———
Assistance	———	———	———	———
Economic factors				
Size in volume	———	———	———	———
Average price	———	———	———	———
Growth rate	———	———	———	———
Life-cycle phase	———	———	———	———

7.4.2 Market-targeting strategies

Having analysed the reference market's diversity, the next task is to decide on the type of market coverage strategy to adopt. The options open to the firm are of three types: undifferentiated, differentiated or focused marketing (Smith, 1956).

By adopting an *undifferentiated* marketing strategy, the firm ignores market segment differences and decides to approach the entire market as a whole and not take advantage of segmentation analysis. It focuses on what is common in the needs of buyers rather than on what is different. The rationale of this middle-of-the-road or standardization strategy is cost savings, not only in manufacturing but also in inventory, distribution and advertising. In affluent societies, this strategy is more and more difficult to defend as it is rarely possible for a product or a brand to please everyone.

In a *differentiated* marketing strategy, the firm also adopts a full market coverage strategy but this time with tailor-made programmes for each segment. This was the slogan of General Motors, claiming '... to have a car for every purse, purpose and personality'. This strategy enables the firm to operate in several segments with a customized pricing, distribution and communication strategy. Selling prices will be set on the basis of each segment's price sensitivity. This strategy generally implies higher costs, since the firm is losing the benefits of economies of scale. On the other hand, the firm can expect to hold a strong market share position within each segment. Differentiated marketing does not necessarily imply full market coverage. The risk may be to over-segment the market, with the danger of cannibalism among the excess brands of the same company.

In a *focused* marketing strategy, the firm is concentrating its resources on the needs of a single segment or on a few segments, adopting a specialist strategy. The specialization can be based on a function (functional specialist) or on a particular customer group (customer specialist). Through focused marketing, the company can expect to reap the benefits of specialization and of improved efficiency in the use of the firm's resources. The feasibility of a focused strategy depends on the size of the segment and on the strength of the competitive advantage gained through specialization.

The choice of any one of these market coverage strategies will be determined (1) by the number of identifiable and potentially profitable segments in the reference market and (2) by the resources of the firm. If a company has limited resources, a focused marketing strategy is probably the only option.

Hyper-segmentation versus counter-segmentation
A segmentation strategy can result in two extreme policies.

■ A *hyper-segmentation* policy, which develops made-to-order products tailored to individual needs, offering many options and a variety of secondary function along with the core function, and this at a high cost.

■ A *counter-segmentation* policy, offering a basic product with no frills or extras, few options and at much lower cost.

This is the *standardization–adaptation* dilemma mentioned in Chapter 2 which faces companies having to define a global or transnational strategy.

During periods of affluence of the golden sixties, in the field of consumer goods, companies tended to follow hyper-segmentation strategies by refining their segmentation strategies. The result was a proliferation of brands, an increase of production and marketing costs and eventually of retail prices.

The changes brought about during the period of economic and social turmoil described in Chapter 2 gradually led consumers to become more aware of the 'price/satisfaction' ratio in their purchasing decision process. More and more consumers behave like *smart buyers* and make a trade-off between price benefits and product benefits. The success of generic brands and of private labels in Western economies is an example of this evolution.

In several sectors, and namely in the fast-moving consumer goods (FMCG) sector, there is trend towards a return to 'voluntary simplicity', i.e. towards less sophisticated products, providing the core function without frills, but sold at much lower prices thanks to their high level of standardization. Thus, we have here a segmentation strategy based on the 'price/satisfaction' ratio, a segment too often neglected by manufacturers and very well covered by large retailers.

7.4.3 Product-positioning strategies
Once the market coverage decisions made, the next step is to decide on the positioning strategy to adopt within each target segment. Selection of the positioning strategy provides the unifying

concept for the development of the marketing programme. Positioning indicates how the firm would like to be perceived in the minds of target customers. Positioning can be defined as follows:

> Positioning is the act of designing and communicating the firm's offer so that it occupies a distinct and valued place in the target customers' mind!   (Ries and Trout, 1981)

Positioning is mostly relevant when coupled with a segmentation analysis which requires a positioning by segments instead of a single positioning for the total market. Positioning strategy is the operational way to implement a differentiation strategy. The typical questions to address are:

■ Which distinctive features and/or benefits, real or perceived, are considered to be the most important from the buyer's point of view?

■ Which are the perceived positions of the main competing brands according to these features and/or benefits?

■ Given the strengths and weaknesses of our brand and the positions already occupied by competing brands, what is the best positioning to adopt?

■ What is the most appropriate marketing programme for achieving the chosen positioning?

Thus, not all brand or product differences are meaningful to buyers. As will be discussed in Chapter 9 below, the source of differentiation should be unique, important to the buyer, sustainable, communicable and affordable.

Alternative bases for positioning

Wind (1982, pp. 79–80) has identified six alternative bases for positioning. These are:

■ Positioning on product features.

■ Positioning on benefits, on problem solution or needs.

■ Positioning for specific usage occasion.

■ Positioning for user category.

■ Positioning against another product

■ Product class dissociation.

Other positioning bases exist, such as, for example, lifestyle positioning.

Selecting a positioning basis

When selecting a positioning basis, a certain number of conditions must be carefully met.

■ To have a good understanding of the *present positioning* of the brand or firm in the customers' minds. This knowledge can be acquired through brand image studies, as described in Chapter 5.

- To know the present positioning of *competing brands*, in particular those brands in direct competition.

- To select one positioning and to identify the most relevant and credible *arguments* which justify the chosen positioning.

- To evaluate the potential *profitability* of the contemplated positioning, while being suspicious of false market niches invented by advertising people or discovered through an invalidated qualitative study.

- To verify whether the brand has the required *personality potential* for achieving the positioning in the minds of consumers.

- To assess the *vulnerability* of the positioning. Do we have the resources required to occupy and to defend this position?

- To ensure *consistency* in the positioning with the different marketing mix instruments: pricing, distribution, packaging, services, etc.

Once the positioning strategy is adopted and clearly defined, it is much simpler for marketing people to translate this positioning in terms of an effective and consistent marketing programme.

Attribute-based perceptual maps

When the number of benefits to consider is large, attribute-based perceptual maps are useful to identify the different packages of benefits and to describe the perceived positioning of the major competing brands. To illustrate, we refer to a study of the Belgian toothpaste market aiming to verify the way consumers perceive a brand extension of the brand Signal, called Signal-plus. In this analysis, 24 product benefits were identified through unstructured group discussions:

Good for children	Young	Economical
Protects gums	Medical	Unpleasant taste
Prevents decay	Humorous colours	For the whole family
Expensive	With fluoride	Strong taste
Sold in pharmacies	Traditional	Pleasant advertising
Much advertised	Prevents tartar	Friendly
Whitens teeth	Fresh breath	Less effective than claimed
Cavity protection	Pleasant taste	Attractive packaging

A representative sample of 130 respondents in the 12–30 age group were exposed to the 12 brands and asked to rate the 12 leading brands of toothpaste by simply noting their perceptions as to the absence or presence (0,1) of each particular benefit in each brand. These data were fed into a computer program called Factorial Correspondence Analysis (ANAFACO) to determine the association of the benefits with the brands. Three dimensions have been identified.

- The first axis confronts the paramedical aspect (medical, sold in pharmacy, expensive, bad taste) to the ludic aspect of the product (young, pleasant texture, attractive). This axis shows an inertia rate of 41 per cent and compares two distribution channels, the food and the drug networks.

- The second axis compares the attribute of the specific dental anti-cavities treatment (fluor, anti-cavities, children like it) with the more general attributes of dental hygiene (whitens teeths, strong taste, pleasant advertising). The inertia rate here is 21 per cent.

- A third axis also emerges which isolate a relatively new benefit sought: gums care opposed to the traditional cosmetic toothpaste. The inertia rate here is 13 per cent. In total, we thus have an explained variance of 75 per cent.

The two-dimensional map identified is presented in Fig. 7.5, which provides management with a picture of the market for all competing brands and for the benefits associated with the brands.

- Segment 1 regroups the medical brands perceived as giving 'gum protection', being 'sold in pharmacies', 'expensive' and with 'unpleasant taste'.

- Segment 2 regroups the cosmetic brands, emphasizing 'fresh breath', being 'friendly', with a 'pleasant taste', 'attractive packaging' and 'pleasant texture'.

- Segment 3 regroups the anti-cavity brands and emphasizes 'white teeth', 'good for children', 'humorous colours', 'with fluoride', 'pleasant advertising'.

The promise in segment 3 is more friendly than in segment 1 but is coupled with a more serious promise: cavity protection.

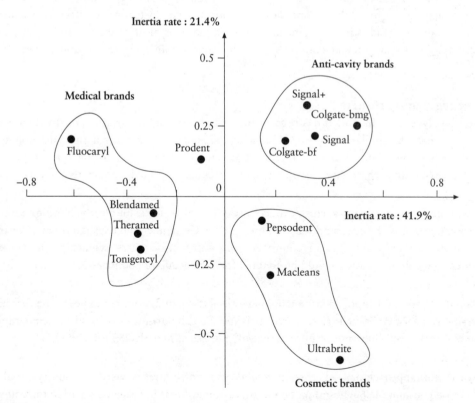

FIGURE 7.5 *Product positioning analysis: the toothpaste market in Belgium, 1985*

Thus, this type of perceptual map permits management to evaluate the way segments perceive the different brands and whether the intended positioning has been reasonably well achieved.

7.5 INTERNATIONAL SEGMENTATION

With the globalization of the world economy, opportunities are growing to create demand for universal products. International segmentation is a way in which a global approach can be adopted to sell a physically similar product world wide. The objective is to discover in different countries and/or regions groups of buyers having the same expectations and requirements *vis-à-vis* products, despite cultural and national differences. Those segments, even if they are small in size within each country, may represent in total a very attractive opportunity for the international firm. To adjust to local differences, the physical product can be customized through services, accessories or inexpensive product modifications. The potential for globalization is not the same for each product category and different approaches can be adopted. For a review of the literature on this topic, see Hassan and Katsanis (1991).

7.5.1 Identification of global market segments

Global market segmentation can be defined as the process of identifying specific segments, whether they be country groups or individual buyer groups, of potential customers with homogeneous attributes who are likely to exhibit similar buying behaviour. There are three different approaches for global segmentation: (a) identifying clusters of countries that demand similar products; (b) identifying segments present in many or most countries; and (c) targeting different segments in different countries with the same product (Takeuchi and Porter, 1986, pp. 138–40).

Targeting country clusters

Traditionally, the world market has been segmented on geographic variables, i.e. *by regrouping countries* that are similar in terms of climate, language, religion, economic development, distribution channel, etc. Products rarely require modification or tailoring for every single country, except for such things as labelling and the language used in the manuals and catalogues.

On the European scene, natural clusters of countries would be, for example, the Nordic countries (Denmark, Norway, Sweden and maybe Finland); the Germanic countries (Germany, Austria, part of Switzerland), the Iberian countries, etc. With this country segmentation strategy, products and communication would be adapted for each group of countries.

Within the European Union, an argument in favour of this country approach lies in the very high diversity of the different countries, as evidenced by the comparison of their socio-demographic profiles. See the social portrait of Europe recently published in EUROSTAT (1996).

However, this approach presents three potential limitations: (a) it is based on country variables and not on consumer behavioural patterns, (b) it assumes total homogeneity within the country segment and (c) it overlooks the existence of homogeneous consumer segments that might exist across national boundaries. With the growth of regionalism within Europe, the second assumption becomes more and more a limiting factor.

In fact, with the elimination of country boards, more and more European firms are defining their geographic market zones by reference to regions and not to countries.

Selling to universal segments across countries

As discussed in Chapter 2, several trends are influencing consumption behaviour on a global scale and many consumer products are becoming more widely accepted globally, such as consumer electronics, automobiles, fashion, home appliances, food products, beverages and services. Many of these products respond to needs and wants that cut across national boundaries.

Thus, even if product needs overall vary among countries, there may be a segment of the market with identical needs in every country. The challenge facing international firms is to identify these *universal* segments and reach them with marketing programmes that meet the common needs of these potential buyers. These universal segments are most likely to be high-end consumers, sports professionals, executives of multinational companies or, in general, sophisticated users, because these groups tend to be the most mobile and therefore the most likely to be exposed to extensive international contacts and experiences.

> A growing market segment on a global scale is composed of consumers aspiring to an 'élite life style'. This élite, in Tokyo, New York, Paris, London, Hong Kong, Rio de Janeiro, etc., is the target of brands that fit the image of exclusivity like Mercedes, Gucci, Hermès, American Express, Gold Card, Chivas, Godiva, etc.

Such high-end brands can be targeted internationally to this universal segment in exactly the same way they are currently positioned in their respective home market. This international segmentation strategy is illustrated in Fig. 7.6(a). The size of universal segments can be small in each country; what is attractive is the cumulative volume. For example, the Godiva pralines are present in 20 different countries all over the world, sometimes with modest market shares. It is nevertheless the world's leading chocolatier.

Targeting diverse segments across countries

Even if product needs vary among countries, the same product can sometimes be sold in each country but in different segments, by adopting different market positioning based on non-product variables such as distributive networks, advertising and pricing. This approach is illustrated in Fig. 7.6(b).

> The positioning adopted for the Canon AE-1 provides a good example of this international segmentation approach. The AE-1 was targeted towards young replacement buyers in Japan, upscale first-time buyers of 35 mm single-lens reflex cameras in the USA, and older and more technologically sophisticated replacement buyers in Germany. Three different marketing programmes were developed for Japan, the USA and Europe.
>
> (Takeuchi and Porter, 1986, p. 139)

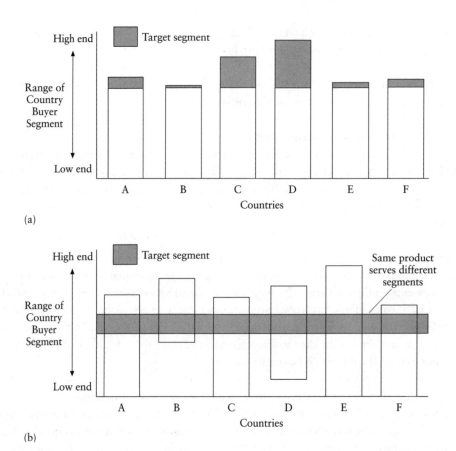

FIGURE 7.6 *International segmentation: two different market positioning strategies (Source: Takeuchi and Porter, 1986) (a) Universal segment positioning across countries (b) Diverse segment positioning across countries*

This approach requires important adaptations of communication and selling strategies which contribute to increasing costs or at least to preventing cost decreases as a consequence of standardization.

Of the three segmentation approaches, universal segmentation is the most innovative and also the most likely to give the firm a significant competitive advantage, because product and communication can be standardized and transferred among countries. This gives the brand a reputation and a coherence in image and positioning which is internationally reinforced. The diverse segmentation approach has the merit of taking into consideration differences in consumer behaviour among countries and of introducing adaptations to accommodate these differences. On the other hand, because of these country to country adaptations, the brand image in each country will probably be different.

7.5.2 The case of universal segments
The global approach in segmenting world markets looks for similarities between markets. The traditional international approach is multi-domestic, i.e. it tends to ignore similarities. The

global approach actively seeks homogeneity in product, image, marketing and advertising message, while the multi-domestic approach maintains unnecessary differences from market to market. The goal, however, is not to have a uniform product line world wide; rather the goal is to have a product line that is as standardized as possible, while recognizing that allowances for some local conditions are both necessary and desirable.

The case of Black & Decker provides a good illustration of this strategy (Farley, 1986). Black & Decker is established in 50 countries and manufactures in 25 plants, 16 of which are outside the USA. It has a very high level of brand awareness world wide, sometimes in the 80–90 per cent range. For Black & Decker the potential economies of scale and cost savings of globalization were considerable, and the following challenges had to be overcome.

■ Different countries have different safety and industry standards that make complete standardization impossible.

■ European and American consumers have very different responses to product design and even to colours.

■ Consumers use the products in different ways in different countries. For example, Europeans are more power-oriented in their electric tools than Americans (Farley, 1986, p. 69).

As a consequence of this diversity, the multi-domestic organization approach produced staggering product proliferation. The company had hundreds of products world wide and relatively few interchangeable among countries. As a result of the globalization approach implemented between 1980 and 1990, Black & Decker has developed global products. The rule now is that any new product must be designed for a world market. People within the organization are expected to think 'world product' first; anything else has to be justified.

Trade-off between standardization and customization
In the largest majority of market situations, some degree of adaptation will be necessary. The essence of international segmentation can be summarized as follows: *think of global similarities and adapt to local differences*. This perspective should help management to determine similarities across national boundaries while assessing within-country differences. The different strategies susceptible to adoption, depending on the diversity of expectations and cultural background, are presented in Table 7.7. Three types of product policy can be considered:

1. *Universal product*. The physical product sold in each country is identical except for labelling and the language used in the manuals.
2. *Modified product*. The core product is the same, but some modifications are adopted, such as voltage, colour, size or accessories, to accommodate government regulations or to reflect local differences in taste, buying habits, climate, etc.
3. *Country-tailored product*. The physical product is substantially tailored to each country or group of countries.

The financial and cost implications of these alternative product policies are, of course, particularly important.

TABLE 7.7 *Strategies of international segmentation*

| | Expectations of segments | | | | |
| | Homogeneous | | Similar | | |
Global marketing strategies	Same culture	Different culture	Same culture	Different culture	Different
1. Unchanged product and operational marketing	1	–	–	–	–
2. Unchanged product and adapted operational marketing	–	2	2	2	–
3. Adapted product and operational marketing	–	–	–	3	3
4. New product and specific operational marketing	–	–	–	–	4

Source: Blanche (1987).

Establishing a world brand

Every product has not the same global vocation, and some products may be easier than others to develop as world brands. There are some universally recognized world brands: Coca-Cola, Marlboro, Kodak, Honda, Mercedes, Heineken, Swatch, Canon, Gucci, Britsh Airways, Perrier, Black & Decker, Hertz, Benetton, McDonalds, Godiva and many others. It is worth noting that the popularity of these brands is independent of the attitude towards their country of origin.

In reality, the universal vocation of a product is closely linked to the universality of the benefit sought. To the extent that a product is a proven success in meeting the needs of a particular group of buyers in a given country, it is logical to expect a similar success with the same group of people in another country, provided of course the product is adapted to local consuming habits or regulations. In other words, as suggested by Quelch and Hoff (1986), the driving factor in moving towards global marketing should be 'the efficient world-wide use of good marketing ideas rather than scale economies from standardization'.

The closer the product is to the *high-tech/high-touch poles*, the more universal it becomes. These two product categories have in common the featues of (a) being high-involvement products and of (b) sharing a common language (Domzal and Unger, 1987, p. 28).

- *High-tech products* appeal to highly specialized buyers who share a common technical language and symbols. This the case among computer users, tennis players and musicians, who all understand the technical aspects of the products. This is true not only for heavy machinery, computer hardware and financial services, but also for personal computers, video equipment, skiing equipment, etc. The mere existence of a common 'shop talk' facilitates communication and increases the chance of success as a global brand.

■ *High-touch products* are more image-oriented than product features-oriented, but they respond to universal themes or needs, such as romance, wealth, heroism, play, etc. Many products, such as fragrance, fashion, jewellery and watches, are sold on these themes.

For these two product categories, buyers all over the world are using and understanding the same language and symbols. World-wide brand standardization appears most feasible when products approach either end of the high-tech/high-touch spectrum (Domzal and Unger, 1987, p. 27).

SUMMARY

In a market-oriented company, the target market is identified in the buyer's perspective, i.e. by reference to the 'solution' sought by the customer and not in technical terms. Given the diversity of buyers' expectations, the choice of a target market implies the partitioning of the total market into subgroups of potential customers with similar needs and behavioural characteristics. A first level of market segmentation, called macro-segmentation, splits the market by reference to three criteria: (a) solutions or functions performed, (b) groups of buyers and (c) technologies. A key output of this exercise is a segmentation grid which can help to decide on the market coverage strategy and can also be used as an instrument to discover new potential segments. The objective of micro-segmentation is to analyse the diversity of potential customer profiles in a more detailed way within each previously identified macro-segment. Four micro-segmentation methods exist which each have their own merits and weaknesses: socio-demographic, benefit, lifestyle and behavioural segmentation. Different market coverage strategies can be considered: undifferentiated or standardised marketing, differentiated or focused marketing. To be effective, a segmentation strategy must meet four criteria: differential response, adequate size, measurability and accessibility. Having selected one or several target segment(s), the next step is to decide upon a positioning strategy for each segment which will be communicated to the target group. International segmentation is a key issue in global marketing. The objective is to identify supranational or universal segments that can be reached with a standardized marketing programme.

QUESTIONS AND PROBLEMS

1. Use the macro-segmentation method based on the three criteria 'function/buyers/technologies' in one of the following industrial sectors: paint, fax, banking services, medical imagery. In each case, define the product markets, the market and the industry.
2. A European importer of a Japanese camera wishes to have a benefit segmentation analysis of the European market. Construct a segmentation grid that seems appropriate and propose a procedure to collect the required market data to verify the value of the proposed segmentation scheme.
3. Pick-up two magazines targeting a specific socio-demographic group (teenagers, seniors, housewives, ethnic group, ...). Select three or four advertisements and try to identify the positioning sought by the advertisers.

4. In affluent societies, consumers want more and more to find adapted solutions to their specific problems. To the firm the question is to know how far to go in segmenting a market. Analyse the factors in favour of a fine market segmentation strategy (hyper-segmentation) and the arguments, on the contrary, that suggest a standardized strategy (counter-segmentation).
5. In affluent societies, one observes a growing fragmentation of markets, with buyers requesting more and more products to be adapted to their specific needs. How can this fact be conciliated with the objectives of global marketing, which emphasizes a strategy of standardization of products and brands across the entire world?

REFERENCES

Abell, D.F. (1980), *Defining the Business: The Starting Point of Strategic Planning*. Englewood Cliffs, New Jersey: Prentice Hall Inc.

Ader, E. (1983), 'L'analyse stratégique moderne et ses outils', *Futuribles*, December, pp. 3–21.

Blanche, B. (1987), 'Le marketing global: paradoxe, fantasme ou objectif pour demain?', *Revue Française du Marketing*, no. 114.

Chamberlin, E.H. (1950), *The Theory of Monopolistic Competition*. Cambridge, Mass: Harvard University Press.

Dalrymple, D.J. and L.J. Parsons (1976), *Marketing Management: Text and Cases*. New York: John Wiley & Sons.

Day, G.S. (1990), *Market-Driven Strategy*. New York: The Free Press.

Domzal, T. and L.S. Unger (1987), 'Emerging Positioning Strategies in Global Marketing', *The Journal of Consumer Marketing*, vol. 4, no. 4, Autumn.

EUROSTAT (1996), *A Social Portrait of Europe*. Statistical Office of the European Communities.

Farley, L.J. (1986), 'Going Global: Choices and Challenges', *The Journal of Consumer Marketing*, vol. 3, no. 1, Winter.

Green, P.E. and A.M. Krieger (1991), 'Segmenting Markets with Conjoint Analysis', *Journal of Marketing*, vol. 55, October, pp. 20–31.

Green, P.E. and Y. Wind (1974), 'Some Conceptual, Measurement and Analytical Problems in Life Style Research', in Wells, W. (ed.), *Life Style and Psychographics*. Chicago: American Marketing Association.

Haley, R.I. (1968), 'Benefit Segmentation: A Decision-Oriented Tool', *Journal of Marketing Research*, vol. 32, July, pp. 30–5.

Hassan, S.S. and L.P. Katsanis (1991), 'Identification of Global Consumer Segments: A Behavioural Framework', *Journal of International Consumer Marketing*, vol. 3, no. 2, pp. 11–29.

Hopkins, D.S. (1982), *The Marketing Plan*. New York: The Conference Board.

Kapferer, J.N. and G. Laurent (1981), *Une analyse des relations entre les classifications socioculturelles et de style de vie et l'achat de produits courants*. Paris: Institut de Recherches et d'Études Publicitaires, 21st Journée de l'IREP.

Lambin, J.J. and T.B. Hiller (1990), 'Volvo Trucks Europe: A Case Study', in Quelch, J.A. *et al.* (eds), *The Marketing Challenge of 1992*. Reading, Mass: Addison-Wesley Publishing Co.

Plummer, J.T. (1974), 'The Concept and Application of Life Style Segmentation', *Journal of Marketing*, vol. 38, January, pp. 33–7.

Quelch, J. and E.G. Hoff (1986), 'Customizing Global Marketing', *Harvard Business Review*, vol. 64, May–June, pp. 59–68.

Ries, A. and J. Trout (1981), *Positioning: The Battle for your Mind*. New York: McGraw-Hill.

Roisin, J. (1988), *Etude du concept d'une revue littéraire: une application de l'analyse conjointe*. Louvain-la-Neuve, IAG.

Shapiro, B.P. and T.V. Bonona (1983), *Segmenting Industrial Markets*. Lexington, Mass: Lexington Books.

Smith, W.R. (1956), 'Product Differentiation and Market Segmentation as Alternative Strategies', *Journal of Marketing*, vol. 21, July, pp. 3–8.

Takeuchi, H. and M.E. Porter (1986), 'Three Roles of International Marketing in Global Industries', in Porter, M.E. (ed.), *Competition in Global Industries*. Boston: The Harvard Business School Press.

Valette-Florence, P. (1986), 'Les démarches de styles de vie: concepts, champs d'investigation et problèmes actuels', *Recherche et Applications en Marketing*, vol. 1, nos 1 and 2.

Valette-Florence, P. (1988), 'Analyse structurelle comparative des composantes des systèmes de valeurs selon Kahle et Rokeach', *Recherche et Applications en Marketing*, vol. 3, no. 1.

Wells, W. (1974), *Life Style and Psychographics*. American Marketing Association.

Wells, W.D. and D.J. Tigert (1971), 'Activities, Interests and Opinions', *Journal of Advertising Research*, vol. 35, pp. 27–34.

Wind, J.Y. (1982), *Product Policy: Concepts, Methods and Strategy*. Reading, Mass.: Addison Wesley.

Winkler, A.R. (1991), *Euro-styles in Panel Analyses*. Europanel Marketing Bulletin.

Yankelovich, D. (1964), 'New Criteria for Market Segmentation', *Harvard Business Review*, March–April, pp. 83–90.

FURTHER READING

Cathelat, B. (1984), 'Les styles de vie due C.C.A.: les mutations de 1984', *Futuribles*, October, pp. 30–4.

Cathelat, B. (1985), *Styles de vie*. Paris: Les Éditions d'Organisation, Tomes 1 and 2.

de Singly, F. (1987), 'Etudes de styles de vie', *Universalia* 1987, Paris, Encyclopedia Universalis.

Douglas, S.P. and P. Lemaire (1976), 'Le style de vie à travers les activités, les attitudes et les opinions', *Revue Française du Marketing*, May–June, p. 69.

Douglas, S.P. and Y. Wind (1987), 'The Myth of Globalization', *Columbia Journal of World Business*, Winter 1987.

Porter, M. (1985), *Competitive Advantage*. New York: The Free Press.

Shama, A. (1981), 'Coping with Stagflation: Voluntary Simplicity', *Journal of Marketing*, Summer, pp. 120–34.

Valette-Florence, P. (1994), *Les styles de vie: bilan critique et perspectives*. Paris: Editions Nathan.

Yorke, D.A. (1982), 'The Definition of Market Segments for Banking Services', *European Journal of Marketing*, vol. 16, no. 3.

CHAPTER 8

MARKET ATTRACTIVE-NESS ANALYSIS

LEARNING OBJECTIVES

After reading this chapter, you should be able to:

- describe the major concepts of demand analysis and their structure

- explain the structure of demand for consumer and industrial goods, for durable and non-durable goods and for services

- explain how to detect growth opportunities in a given market through gap analysis

- describe the product life cycle (PLC) model and its strategic implications at each phase of the PLC

- discuss the main demand forecasting methods, their respective merits and conditions for application.

T he output of a segmentation analysis takes the form of a segmentation grid displaying the different segments or product markets that belong to the reference market. The next task is to assess the business opportunity of each of these segments in order to decide which segment(s) to target. *Attractiveness analysis* has the objective of measuring and forecasting the size, life cycle and profit potential of each segment or product market. Measuring the sales potential of a market is the responsibility of strategic marketing. These market projections will then be used by general management to calibrate investments and production capacity. Market potential forecasting and measurement is a key input for these decisions. The objective of this chapter is to review the major concepts of demand analysis and to describe briefly the main sales forecasting methods.

8.1 BASIC CONCEPTS IN DEMAND ANALYSIS

At its simplest level, the demand for a product or service is the quantity sold. It is important to distinguish clearly between two levels of demand: primary demand, or total market demand, and company demand (also called selective demand).

> The primary demand for a particular product is the total sales volume bought by a defined customer group, in a defined geographic area, in a defined time period, and in a defined economic and competitive environment.

The term *product category need* or 'category need' is also commonly used. Thus, primary demand measurement implies prior definition of the segment or product market. Also, it is a function of both environmental and total industry marketing efforts.

> Company demand is the company or brand's share of primary demand.

It, too, is a *response function*. Its determinants are environmental factors and company (or brand) marketing factors. These demand determinants fall into two categories: the environmental factors that are outside the control of the firm and the factors under control, i.e. the marketing mix or the total marketing pressure exerted by the firm to support its brand.

8.1.1 The notion of market potential

Market potential represents the upper limit of demand in a defined period of time. The relationship between primary demand and total industry marketing efforts is depicted in Fig. 8.1(a). The response function is S-shaped with total demand on the vertical axis and total marketing efforts on the horizontal axis. The curve of Fig. 8.1(a) is defined for a constant macro-environment.

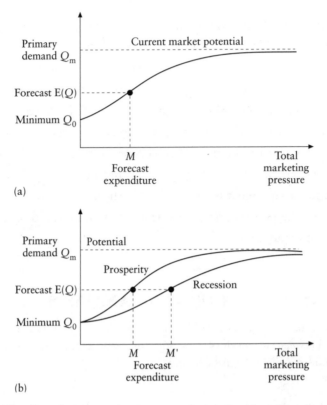

FIGURE 8.1 *The relationship between primary demand and total marketing intensity*

Typically, the relationship is not linear. Some minimum level of demand (Q_0) will occur at zero marketing effort; as the total marketing pressure on the market increases, sales also increase, but at a decreasing rate. Beyond a certain level of marketing intensity, primary demand reaches an upper limit (Q_m) called the saturation level or the *current market potential*.

The level of primary demand is influenced not only by the total marketing efforts made the firms operating in the segment, but also by environmental factors. A change in the socio-economic environment will move the response curve vertically, as illustrated in Fig. 8.1(b). A distinction must be made, therefore, between a movement along the reponse curve and a shift of the response curve itself.

Two scenarios (or market demand functions) are represented in Fig. 8.1(b): a scenario of *prosperity* and a scenario of *recession*. Under the prosperity scenario, the forecast or expected level of total sales is E(Q), assuming the level M for total industry marketing effort. If the recession scenario prevails, then to achieve the same sales volume, total marketing effort should be at the level M' and not M.

Firms cannot do much about the prevailing market scenario, except to try to anticipate future environmental conditions as accurately as possible. In the turbulent environment of the 1990s this is a particularly difficult task and many firms are systematically developing alternative scenarios to increase their capacity to react quickly to a sudden crisis in the environment.

In Fig. 8.1(b), the current market potential corresponds to the saturation level Q_m. This level is not static, however; it evolves over time under the influence of diffusion and contagion effects, and tends towards its upper limit, which is the absolute market potential.

8.1.2 Expansible versus non-expansible primary demand

The gap between the minimum (or present) level of primary demand and its maximum level reflects the size of the market opportunity. In the first part of the curve, demand is said to be *expansible*: i.e. the level of primary demand is easily affected by the size and intensity of total marketing efforts. Primary demand elasticity is high and each firm contributes to the development of the total market. In the upper part of the response curve, demand becomes inelastic and the market is said to be *non-expansible*. Further increases in marketing intensity have no impact on the size of the market, which has reached its maturity stage.

Thus, in a non-expansible market the size of the market is fixed. Any sales increase in favour of a particular firm necessarily implies a market share gain.

8.1.3 Absolute versus current market potential

A potential market may develop over a certain period, not only because of economic factors but also through the influence of cultural and social factors which tend to stimulate consumer habits. For instance, environmental concern is growing and this may encourage the demand for anti-pollution equipment. Similarly, the use of computers in small and medium-sized companies has grown under the influence of diffusion, learning and contagion phenomena, independently of the total marketing efforts made by the companies operating in the sector. Thus, there is a difference between the current market potential and the absolute market potential.

■ *Current market potential* is the limit approached by primary demand as total industry marketing efforts tend towards infinity, in a given environment and in a given time period.

■ *Absolute market potential* corresponds to the total sales level (in volume or value) that would be observed if every potential user consumed the product at the optimum frequency rate and at the full rate per use occasion.

Thus, the absolute market potential (AMP) defines the upper limit of the market size under the somewhat artificial assumption of optimum market coverage. The concept is useful, however, for assessing the size of a business opportunity and for estimating the growth opportunity in a particular market given the present level of demand. Three assumptions are made concerning usage of the product in order to derive the absolute market potential.

■ Everyone who could reasonably be expected to use the product is using it.

■ Everyone who is using it is using it on every use occasion.

■ Every time the product is used, it is used to the fullest extent possible (i.e. full dosage, full serving, etc.).

BOX 8.1

Estimating industry absolute market potential for mouthwash

Number of potential users
- Assume that everyone 5 years and older is a potential user.
- Approximately 90 per cent of the US population.
- US population: 222 million.
- Number of potential users: 90 per cent of 222 m = 200 million.

Number of use occasions per year
- Assume that each potential user can use mouthwash twice a day.
- Number of use occasion per year:
   200 million people × 2/day × 365 days
   = 146 billion use occasions per year.

Full use on each occasion
- Assume that full use (or full dosage) is 1 oz. per use.
- The absolute market potential is therefore: 146 billion oz. per year.
- An average of 16 oz. per bottle.
- Result: 9125 billion bottles per year.

Source: Weber (1976, p. 66).

An estimation of absolute market potential is presented in Box 8.1.

The current market potential is time-dependent, as illustrated in Fig. 8.2. Its evolution over time is caused by external factors like change in consumption habits, cultural values, disposable income, technological changes, level of prices, government regulations, etc. The firm has no direct control over these factors, yet they have a decisive influence on the development of the market. Occasionally, firms are indirectly able to influence these external causes (through lobbying, for instance), but their power is limited. Most of the firm's efforts, therefore, are directed towards the anticipation of changes in the environment.

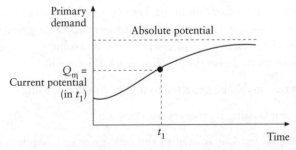

FIGURE 8.2 *Current versus absolute market potential*

8.1.4 The determinants of demand

As already underlined, market demand is not a fixed number but a function which relates the level of sales to its causes, termed demand determinants. The causes of sales are two-fold: external or uncontrollable causes and internal or controllable causes.

As indicated in Chapter 1, the *controllable factors* fall into four basic categories, popularly known as the *four P's* (McCarthy, 1960) or the marketing mix: product, place, price and promotion. This set of marketing factors constitutes the total offering of the firm to the buyers in expectation of meeting their needs at a profit. They are the main determinants of company demand.

This method of defining the marketing action variables is not really customer-oriented but rather company-oriented. Viewed from the buyer's perspective, the four P's can be redefined as follows:

- *Product*: a solution-to-a-problem and the package of benefits that the product represents.

- *Place*: a convenient access to the solution sought by the buyer.

- *Price*: all the costs, including price, supported by the buyer to acquire the solution sought.

- *Promotion*: the messages and signals communicated about the solutions available and about their distinctive qualities.

- *Selling*: the assistance given to the buyer in his search for the appropriate solution to his or her problem.

The *uncontrollable factors* constitute the constraints to be dealt with in the marketplace, which the firm does not control. These constraints can be grouped in five broad categories termed the *five C's* (Wilkie, 1990): customer, competition, company, channel, conditions.

- *Customer constraint*: the firm must understand its buyers to develop a marketing mix programme that appeals to them.

- *Competition constraint*: competitors are also striving to convince the same buyer group, and the firm must have a competitive advantage over its rivals.

- *Company constraint*: the marketing programme must be adapted to the strengths and weaknesses of the firm.

- *Channel constraint*: the channel consists of independent wholesalers, distributors and retailers who behave in their own self-interest but who are the necessary partners of the firm.

- *Conditions constraint*: this last constraint refers to a host of economic, social, political and weather conditions.

It is the task of the market analyst to identify and understand these constraints in order to adapt the marketing mix that best accounts for them.

8.2 STRUCTURE OF PRIMARY DEMAND

Demand analysis, measurement and forecast are the primary responsibilities of market research. The goal is to estimate in quantitative terms the size of the market potential and the current level of demand, and to formulate forecasts of its future development over a number of years. Aggregate estimates of total demand are rarely available and the role of the market analyst is to identify and estimate the key components of market potential. The structure of demand is different for consumer products (durable or non-durable goods), for industrial goods and for services.

8.2.1 Demand for consumer goods

Demand estimates are usually based on two factors: the number of potential users (n) and the rate of purchase (q). Thus, we have

$$Q = n \cdot q$$

where Q denotes total demand in units. Similarly, total sales revenue will be given by

$$R = n \cdot Q \cdot P$$

where R denotes the total sales revenue and P the average price per unit. The empirical measurement of these basic concepts raise different issues depending on the type of product category. We shall examine the demand structure for the main product categories.

Demand for non-durable consumer products

If the consumer good is not linked to the use of a durable good, total demand can be estimated in the following way.

- Number of potential consuming units.

- Proportion of customers using the product (market occupation rate).

- Size or frequency of purchase (market penetration rate).

The distinction between *occupation rate* and *penetration rate* is important to identify the priority objectives in a market development strategy: increase the number of users or increase the average quantity used per user.

The absolute market potential is determined by assuming a 100 per cent occupation rate and an optimum penetration per use occasion. The current level of primary demand implies data on current purchasing behaviour. These data can sometimes be obtained from trade associations, from government publications or through primary market research. A major problem in measuring current demand is the degree to which purchase rates vary among different buyer groups. Only primary sources of market research, such as consumer panels, can provide such data.

If the consumer good is linked to the use of a durable good (soap and washing machines, for instance), the equipment rate of households must also be considered, in addition to the utilization rate of the equipment. We thus have,

■ Number of potential consuming units.

■ Household rate of equipment.

■ Equipment utilization rate.

■ Consumption rate per use occasion.

Here also, the absolute market potential can be determined assuming a 100 per cent equipment rate, an average utilization rate and an average consumption rate which is technically defined in most cases. To estimate the level of current market demand, it is necessary to have primary market research data.

Demand for durable consumer goods
In this case, a distinction must be made between first equipment demand and replacement demand. The components of *first equipment demand* are:

■ The number of effective users and rate of increase of their equipment.

■ The number of new users and the rate at which they use their equipment.

The diffusion rate is an important factor in the growth of first equipment demand within the target population. The analysis of penetration curves for similar products is very useful this respect.

Replacement demand is more complex to estimate. The following components of replacement demand must be identified and estimated:

■ Size of the current population.

■ Age distribution of the current population.

■ Service life of the equipment (technical, economic or fashion obsolescence).

■ Scrappage rate.

■ Substitution effect (new technologies).

■ Mortality rate of users.

Replacement demand is directly dependent on the rate at which owners scrap a product because it wears out or is obsolescent. Market analysts can estimate *scrappage rates* either by examining the technical service life of a product or the historical long-term rate of voluntary scrappage.

If historical data on scrappage rates can be calculated from a sample of users, market analysts can use actuarial methods to estimate the replacement potential for products of different ages.

Replacement demand depends directly on the size of the current population and on the service life of the durable good. The replacement rate is not necessarily identical to the scrappage rate. Scrappage rate designates the fraction of the stock of existing durable goods which is sent to breakage or, in other words, which disappears. A durable good can be obsolete because its economic performance has become inferior or simply because it is out of fashion in the eyes of the users.

In general, one tends to consider that scrappage rates are proportional to the length of the physical life cycle of the products of a given product category. In other words, if the average duration is 12 years, the annual scrappage rate should in theory be equal to its reciprocal, i.e. 8.33 per cent.

The predictions made about the technical service life of a durable good will have a direct impact on the expected level of primary demand in the years to come. By way of an example, we can look at the car market. The average technical service life seems to be around 10 to 11 years. If the expectation is to have a service life of 12.5 years, the yearly scrappage rate will be around 8 per cent, which represents a level of replacement demand of 1.7 million cars, given the current size of the car population. If, on the contrary, the expected service life is only 9 years, the scrappage rate would be 11.1 per cent with a level of replacement demand of 2.1 million.

On the car market, one observes a continuing improvement in the technological service life. A study in Sweden has shown, for example, that the average service life has increased by 65 per cent since 1965 (OECD, 1983, p. 34).

Some of the data required to estimate the size of primary demand can be derived from times series sales data, namely the size of the population and its age distribution. The age distribution can also be estimated through a sampling of car owners when, for instance, they decide to replace their old equipment. However, the estimated replacement rates do not help us to identify the type of obsolescence responsible for the replacement decision. A technically fitted product can be replaced for economic reasons—for instance, if the operating costs of newly developed products are sharply reduced. It can also be replaced for psychological reasons when the user is sensitive to the design of the new models. Finally, at the time of the replacement decision, the buyer can also decide to switch to another product category performing the same core function.

> Significant technical progress has been made in the market of central heating systems, with low-temperature boilers which are much more economical in terms of fuel consumption. This innovation has accelerated the replacement rate of existing boilers. In parallel, other technologies have also improved their technical performance, like heat pumps which, for many applications, were substituted to traditional fuel heating systems.

In the markets of most Western economies, household equipment rates are very high and close to the maximum, and therefore the largest share of sales of durable goods corresponds to a replacement decision.

8.2.2 The demand for consumer services

The demand for services can be estimated as described above for consumer goods, and depends on the number of potential consumers and on the frequency rate of use of the service. Services have, however, a certain number of characteristics that greatly impact their marketing management. These characteristics are due to their intangible and perishable nature and to the fact that their production implies direct contact with the service person or organization. The managerial implications of these characteristics are significant (Shostack, 1977; Berry, 1980).

Intangibility of services

Services are *immaterial*. They exist only when they are produced, and are immediately consumed. They cannot be inspected before purchase and the selling activity must necessarily precede the production activity. As the consumer goods firm, the service firm is selling a promise of satisfaction. But contrary to a consumer good, the service sold has no physical support, except the organizational system of the service firm when visible to the customer. Thus, from the buyer's point of view the uncertainty is much larger and the communication role of the firm is to reduce that uncertainty by providing physical evidence, signs, symbols or indicators of quality. On this topic, see Levitt (1965) and Zeithmal *et al*. (1990).

Perishability of services

Since services are intangible, they cannot be stored. The service firm has a service production capacity that can be used only when demand is expressed. If demand peaks cannot be accommodated, potential business is lost. Similarly, if an airliner takes off with 20 empty seats, the revenue that these 20 seats could have produced is also lost for ever. Thus, a key challenge for service firms is to better synchronize supply and demand by reshaping supply or by reshaping demand through pricing incentives and promotions.

Inseparability of services

Services are produced and consumed at the same time, and the customer participates in the process of the service production. This implication is two-fold. First, the service provider necessarily has a direct contact with the customer and is part of the service. As a large human component is involved in performing services, standardization is difficult because of their personalized nature. Second, the client participates in the production process and the service provider–customer interaction can also affect the quality of the service. On this topic, see Eiglier and Langeard (1987).

An implication of these characteristics is the difficulty of maintaining services at a constant level of quality. Services' total quality control is a major issue for the service firm. The components of service quality are described in Chapter 10 (see also Lambin, 1987).

8.2.3 The demand for industrial goods

We have seen in Chapter 3 that the industrial demand is actually *derived* from the consumer marketplace. Thus, industrial marketers must not only be cognizant of conditions in their own markets, but must also be aware of developments in the markets served by their customers and by their customers' customers. Of course, many industrial products are far removed from the consumer and the linkage is difficult to see. This separation becomes more apparent as the number of intermediate customers increases between a given manufacturer and the end-user. In other cases, the linkage is quite clear, such as the impact of automobile sales on the steel industry.

> Thus, if consumers are not buying homes, autos, clothing, stereos, educational or medical services, there will be less need for lumber, steel, cotton, plastics, computer components and hospital forms. Consequently, industry will require less energy, fewer trucking services and not as many tools or machines.   (Morris, 1988, p. 390)

The planning task can become quite complex when a manufacturer's output is used in a wide variety of applications.

The demand for industrial goods is structured differently according to whether they are consumable goods, industrial components or industrial equipment. The data needed for the evaluation of demand are almost identical to the data for consumer goods, with few exceptions.

The demand for industrial consumable goods

Certain products are used by industrial firms but are not incorporated in the fabricated product. In this case, the components of demand are:

■ Number of potential industrial users (by size).

■ Proportion of effective users (by size).

■ Level of activity per effective user.

■ Usage rate per use occasion.

The usage rate is a technical norm that is easy to identify. The number of companies classified by number of employees, payroll, value of shipments, etc., can be obtained from the Census of Manufacturers.

> The Cleanchem Company has developed a water treatment chemical for paper manu-facturers. Total paper shipments in the north-east region represent a value of $700 million. Data found in trade reports and information received from local water utilities show that paper mills use 0.01 gallons of water per dollar of shipment value. Cleanchem engineers recommend a minimum of 0.25 ounces of the water treatment chemical per gallon of water and 0.30 ounces per gallon of water to be optimal. The absolute market potential is estimated to range between 1,750,000 ounces ($700 million times 0.01 times 0.25) and 2,100,000 ounces. These estimates must be adjusted for the activity level of paper mills.   (Morris, 1988, p. 183)

The current proportion of effective users in this example is the major source of uncertainty.

The demand for industrial components

Industrial components are used in the product fabricated by the customer; thus, their demand is directly related to the volume of production of the client company. The components of their demand are as follows:

- Number of potential industrial users (by size).

- Proportion of effective users (by size).

- Quantity produced per effective user.

- Rate of usage per product.

Producers of automobile parts are a good example of a sector that responds to this type of demand. A fluctuation in consumer demand for automobiles will eventually result in a variation of the demand for their components. Thus a careful observation of the evolution of demand for the end-product is imperative for the producers of industrial components who wish to predict their own demands.

The demand for industrial equipment

This relates to products such as industrial machines or computers that are necessary to the production activity. They are durable goods and thus the distinction between primary and replacement demand is important. *Primary equipment demand* is determined by the following factors:

- Number of companies equipped (by size)

- Increase of the production capacity.

- Number of new-user companies (by size)

- Production capacity.

Replacement demand is determined by the following factors:

- Size of the existing population.

- Age distribution and technology level of the population.

- Distribution of the product life span.

- Rate of replacement.

- Effect of product substitution.

- Effect of reduction of production capacity.

The acceleration effect

The demand for industrial equipment is directly related to the production capacity of the client companies, and thus even a small fluctuation in final demand can translate to a very large variation in the demand for industrial equipment. This phenomenon is known as the *acceleration effect*.

For example, suppose that the life span of a population of machines is 10 years. If the demand for the consumer goods produced by these machines increases by 10 per cent, 10 per cent of the existing population will need to be replaced and an additional 10 per cent production capacity will be needed to meet the increased demand. Thus the demand for the machines will double. If the demand for the consumer goods decreases by 10 per cent, the required production capacity will only be 90 per cent, and thus the 10 per cent that fail will not need to be replaced. Thus the demand for the machines falls to 0.

The *volatility* of the demand for industrial equipment means that for accurate demand forecasting, companies must analyse both their own demand and the final demand of the companies they supply. The data in Fig. 8.3 show evidence of an 'acceleration effect' in three different markets.

Marketing implications of industrial derived demand
In addition to the difficulty of forecasting sales, derived demand also has implications for operational marketing. The dynamic industrial firm may decide to target its selling efforts not only on the immediate customer but also towards *indirect customers* further down the production chain. For example, Recticel has advertised the benefits of its polyurethane foam to armchair and sofa distributors and to the general public as well. Its goals are two-fold: first to encourage end-users and distributors to place demands upon various furniture manufacturers to begin using the Recticel foam as a component in their production process; and, second, to provide promotional efforts for furniture manufacturers currently using Recticel's product.

By focusing efforts further down the industrial chain, the industrial firm is adopting a *pull strategy* which complements more traditional selling efforts targeted at direct customers (*push strategy*). To limit their dependence on direct customers, dynamic industrial firms have to adopt a proactive marketing behaviour and to play an active role in demand stimulations at each level of the industrial chain.

8.2.4 Growth opportunity analysis
The gap between the current and the absolute level of primary demand is indicative of the rate of development or underdevelopment of a product market. The larger the gap, the greater the growth opportunity; conversely, the smaller the gap, the closer the market is to the saturation level.

Weber (1976) has developed a framework, called gap analysis, to analyse the gaps between absolute market potential and current company sales. Four growth opportunities are identified, as shown in Fig. 8.4: the usage gap, the distribution gap, the product line gap and the competitive gap. The *competitive gap* is due to sales of directly competitive brands within the product market and also to substitute products. The other gaps present growth opportunities that will be briefly reviewed below.

Distribution gaps
The *distribution gap* is due to absence or inadequate distribution within the product market. Three types of distribution gap can be observed.

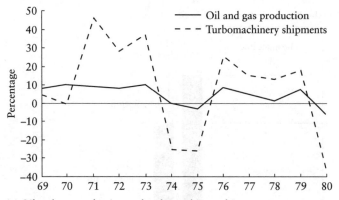

(a) Oil and gas production and turbomachinery shipments

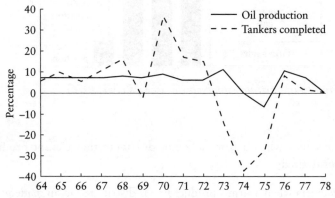

(b) Oil production and tankers completed

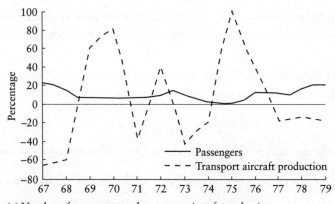

(c) Number of passengers and transport aircraft production

FIGURE 8.3 *The acceleration effect in three different markets (Source: Bishop et al., 1984)*

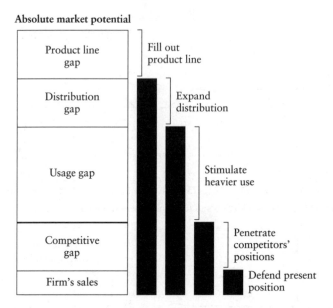

Absolute market potential

FIGURE 8.4 *Growth opportunity analysis (Source: Weber, 1976)*

■ The *coverage gap* exists when a firm does not distribute the relevant product line in all geographic regions desired.

■ The *intensity gap* exists when a firm's product line is distributed in an inadequate number of outlets within a geographic region where the firm has distribution coverage.

■ The *exposure gap* exists when a firm's product lines have poor or inadequate shelf space, location, displays, etc., within outlets where the firm does have distribution for the product.

Sales of a particular product line can be adversely affected by any or all of these distribution gaps, and before adopting new product lines, the firm should try to close these gaps.

Usage gaps

The *usage gap* is due to insufficient use of the product. Three types of usage gap can be identified:

■ The *non-user gap*, i.e. the customers who could potentially use the product but are not using it.

■ The *light user gap*, i.e. the customers who use the product but do not use it on every use occasion.

■ The *light usage gap*, i.e. the customers who use the product but by less than a full use on each use occasion.

A strategy aiming at closing these gaps will contribute to the development of primary demand and may also benefit competing firms.

Product line gaps

The product line gap is caused by the lack of a full product line. Seven types of product line gap could exist.

1. *Size-related product line gap*. Product 'size' can be defined along three dimensions: 'container size' for such consumables as soft drinks or detergents, 'capacity' for such durables as refrigerators or computers and 'power' for automobile engines or industrial machinery.

2. *Options-related product line gap*. Optional features can be offered by a firm desiring to cater to specific demands of individual customers. Automobiles serve as one good example. By offering a large number of options, car manufacturers can produce a large number of cars, each one in some way different from every other one.

3. *Style-, colour-, flavour- and fragrance-related product line gap*. Style and colour can be important for clothing, shoes, appliances, automobiles, etc.; flavours and fragrances can become important means of expanding product lines in food and drink products, tobaccos, toiletries, etc.

4. *Form-related product line gap*. One form of a product may be more attractive for customers than another. Possible dimensions of form include method or principle of operation (petrol versus electric mowers), product format (antacids: chewable, swallowable liquid, effervescent powder or tablets); product composition (corn oil, vegetable oil, margarine) and product containers (reuseable, returnable, throwaway bottles, easy-open cans).

5. *Quality-related product line gap*. Price lining is a popular practice used by marketers to provide consumers with a choice of products differentiated by overall quality and prices. Sporting goods manufacturers market tennis rackets and golf clubs in a range from beginners' models (low price) to professional models (high price).

6. *Distributor brand-related product line gap*. Many manufacturers realize a significant proportion of their sales through selling to retailers who then put their own brand names on the products, like St Michael for Marks & Spencer in the UK. For manufacturers who recognize the private brand market as a separate segment, private brands can account for product line gaps.

7. *Segment-related product line gap*. As discussed in Chapter 7, a firm can adopt different market coverage strategies. A firm has a product line gap for any segment for which it does not have a product.

Each of these identified product line gaps constitutes a growth opportunity for the firm through innovation or product differentiation.

The types of development strategies to be considered to close these gaps are briefly presented in Fig. 8.4. Those strategies will be described in more detail in Chapter 10. In addition to these development strategies operated by the firms, one must add the natural changes in the size of the industry market potential, which is linked to the product life cycle.

8.3 THE PRODUCT LIFE CYCLE

In attractiveness analysis, market potential analysis is a first, and essentially quantitative, step. The analysis must be completed by a study of the product life cycle (PLC), or the evolution of the

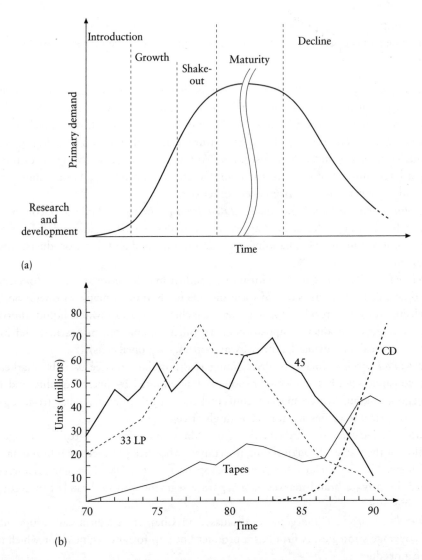

FIGURE 8.5 *The product life cycle (PLC) concept. (a) Idealized representation of the product life cycle, (b) The life cycle of audio products in France*

potential demand for a product or service over time. An essentially dynamic concept borrowed from biology, the PLC model takes the form of an S-shaped graph comprising five phases. The first phase is a take-off, or introductory phase, followed by an exponential growth phase, a shake-out phase, a maturity phase, and a decline phase. Figure 8.5(a) presents an idealized representation of the PLC, while Fig. 8.5(b) portrays the life cycle of audio products in France, and in particular long-playing records and compact discs.

8.3.1 The determinants of the product life cycle

Before moving to an explanation of the PLC, its stages and its marketing implications, it is important to explain the type of products that should be dealt with in a life-cycle analysis. Should it be a category of products (typewriters), a particular type of product within the category (electric typewriters), a specific model (portable electric typewriters) or a specific brand (Canon)? While a life-cycle analysis at any level can have value if properly conducted, the most useful level of analysis is that of a *product market*.

A product market lends itself best to a life-cycle analysis because, as we saw in the previous chapter, it best describes buying behaviours in a particular product category and most clearly defines the frame of reference: *a product seen as a specific package of benefits, targeted to a specific group of buyers*. The same product can, of course, have different life-cycle profiles in different geographic markets or different segments within the same market. Every product market has its own life cycle which reflects not only the evolution of the product, largely determined by technology, but also the evolution of primary demand and its determinants.

Once the level of analysis has been determined, the question becomes whether the PLC profile is to be treated as an independent variable determined by non-controllable factors or as a dependent variable determined by the marketing efforts of the company. In the first case, the PLC determines the strategies adopted at the different phases. In the second case, the strategies adopted must shape the life cycle (Dhalla and Yuspeh, 1976). The response to this question is different for the analysis of a product market or of a specific brand.

The product market life-cycle model

For a product market, primary demand is the principal driving force and its determining factors are both non-controllable environmental factors and industry's total controllable marketing variables. One of the most important non-controllable factors is the *evolution of technology*, which pushes towards newer, higher performance products, and makes older products obsolete. A second factor is the evolution of production and consumption norms, which makes certain products no longer suitable for the market and calls for others. Thus, the PLC model portrays the sales history of a particular product technology, which constitutes one specific solution (among many others) for a specific group of buyers to a market need.

These factors exist in all business sectors, which does not however exclude the possibility that certain better protected product markets have a much longer life cycle than others. The life cycle remains largely influenced by industry marketing efforts, particularly when the market is expanding. Dynamic companies are the driving force in a market, guiding its evolution, development and eventual relaunch sparked by modifications to the product. The PLC is thus not fixed, and research in the field has identified a great variety of life-cycle patterns (Cox, 1967; Swan and Rink, 1982).

The brand life-cycle model

For a particular brand, *selective demand* is the driving element. It is determined by the evolution of the reference market, but with an added competitive factor: the share of total marketing efforts for the particular brand compared with other competing brands. Thus it is perfectly possible to find a brand in decline in an expanding market, or vice versa.

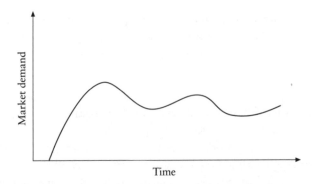

FIGURE 8.6 *The brand life cycle* (Source: *adapted from Hinkle, 1966*)

The CEO of Procter and Gamble does not believe in the product life cycle model, and cites as an example the brand Tide, launched in 1947 and still in a growth phase in 1976. In reality, the product was modified 55 times in its 26 year existence to adapt to market changes including consumption habits, characteristics of washing machines, new fabrics, etc.   (Day, 1981, p. 61)

It is clear that the life cycle of a brand is essentially determined by factors under the control of the company: the marketing strategy adopted and the amount of effort dedicated to it. Hinkle (1966) studied the historical evolution of 275 brands of food, cosmetic, and household items, and found in the majority of cases a bimodal profile. There was a first cycle, followed by a relaunch of the product, as shown in Fig. 8.6 (see also Fig. 8.7). In the following paragraphs, we shall refer to the life cycle of a product market and no longer to that of a specific brand.

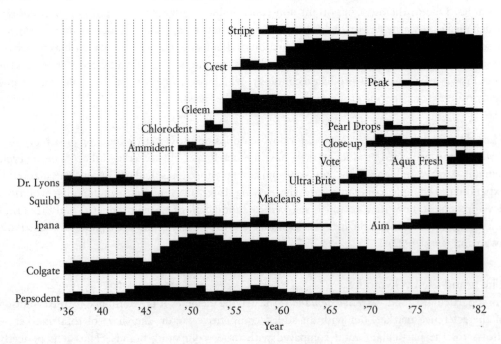

FIGURE 8.7 *Examples of brand life cycles: the toothpaste market in the USA* (Source: The Nielsen Researcher, *1984*)

8.3.2 Strategic implications of the product life cycle

As product markets grow, mature and decline over time, marketing strategy must evolve to the changing buyer's behaviour and competitive environment. To say that a product has a life cycle implies four things:

■ The economic and competitive environment is different at each phase.

■ The priority strategic objective must be redefined at each phase.

■ Cost and profit structures of products are different at each phase.

■ The marketing programme must be adapted in each stage of the PLC.

The shortening of the PLC is a major challenge for the innovative firm who has less and less time to achieve its objectives.

The introductory phase

In the introductory phase, the market is often (not always) characterized by a slow growth of sales because of various environmental factors.

■ The first of these is the *technology uncertainty*, which is often not yet entirely mastered by the innovating company. In addition, the technology may still be developing or evolving in reaction to the first applications, and thus the producer cannot yet hope to produce at maximum efficiency.

■ *Distributors* are a second environmental force, and can be very reluctant at this stage to distribute a product that has not yet proved itself on the larger market. In addition, an industrial distributor will need to familiarize itself with the product, its technical characteristics and its principal functions, which will additionally slow the process.

■ The *potential buyers* make up a third environmental factor. They can often be slow to change their consumption or production habits because of switching costs and caution towards the innovation. Only the most innovative of consumers will be the first to adopt the new product. This group constitutes a rather small initial segment for a product in the introduction phase, and is thus another contributing factor to slow sales.

■ A final environmental force is the *competition*. Typically, the innovating company is without direct competition for a period of time, depending on the strength of the patent protection, if any. Substitute product competition can still be very strong, however, except in the case of breakthrough innovation. This phase is often characterized by a high degree of uncertainty because current and potential competitors are not well known, the market is poorly defined and information is scattered.

This phase is characterized by a high degree of uncertainty because, as technology is still developing, competitors are not yet identified, the reference market is blurred and there is little market information available. The more revolutionary the innovation, the larger will be the uncertainty.

Internal company factors which also characterize the introduction phase include highly negative cash flows, large marketing expenses, high production costs, and often large research and development costs to be amortized. All of these factors put the new product in a very risky financial position. For this reason, the shorter the introduction phase of the product, the better for the company's profitability.

The length of the introductory phase of the PLC is a function of the rapidity of adoption of the less innovative potential buyers, which is influenced by various factors:

- Importance to the buyer of the new product's benefits.

- Presence or absence of adoption costs to be supported by the buyer.

- Compatibility of the product with current modes of consumption or production.

- Observable nature of the new product's benefits.

- Possibility of trying the new product.

- Competitive pressures inducing buyers to adopt the innovation.

Given these factors, the company's highest priority strategic objective is to create primary demand as rapidly as possible and thus to keep the introduction phase as short as possible. These objectives include:

- Creating awareness of the product's existence.

- Informing the market of the new product benefits.

- Inducing potential customers to try the product.

- Securing channels for current and future distribution.

Thus the marketing strategy in the early phase of the PLC typically stresses market education objectives. To respond to these priorities, the marketing programme in the introduction phase will tend to have the following characteristics:

- A basic, core version of the product.

- An exclusive or selective distribution system.

- A high price elasticity situation.

- An informative communication programme.

Several alternatives exist as to the types of launching strategies, particularly in terms of pricing: the dilemma of 'skimming versus penetration' pricing will be discussed in more detail in Chapter 14.

The growth phase

If the product successfully passes the test of its introduction to the market, it enters into the *growth phase*. This phase is characterized by growth of sales at an accelerating rate. The causes of this growth are as follows:

- The first satisfied users become repeat customers and influence other potential users by word of mouth; thus the rate of occupation of the market increases.

- The availability of the product due to wider distribution gives the product more visibility, which then further increases the product's diffusion in the market.

- The entrance of new competitors increases the total marketing pressure on demand at a moment when it is expansible and strongly elastic.

An important characteristic of this phase is the regular decrease of production costs owing to the increase in the volume produced. An effect of experience also begins to be felt. Prices have a tendency to decrease, which allows the progressive coverage of the entire potential market. Marketing expenses are thus spread over a strongly expanding sales base, and cash flows become positive.

The characteristics of the *economic and competitive environment* change markedly.

- Sales are growing at an accelerating rate.

- The target group is now the segment of early adopters.

- New competitors enter the market.

- The technology is well diffused in the market.

To meet these new market conditions, the strategic marketing objectives are changed as well. They now include:

- Expanding the size of the total market.

- Maximizing the occupation rate in the market.

- Building a strong brand image.

- Creating brand loyalty.

To achieve these new objectives, the marketing programme will also be modified, as follows:

- Product improvements and additional features strategy.

- Intensive distribution and multiple channels strategy.

- Price reductions to penetrate the market.

- Image-building communication strategy.

This primary demand development strategy requires important financial resources, and although the cash flows may be positive and profits are rising, the equilibrium breakeven point may not necessarily be reached yet.

At this time, there is no intensive competitive rivalry in the product market, since the marketing efforts of any firm contribute to the expansion of the total market and are therefore beneficial for other firms (cross-elasticity is positive).

The shake-out phase

This is a transitory phase where the rate of sales growth is decelerating, even though it remains above that of the general economy. The target group is now the majority of the market. The weakest competitors start dropping out, as the result of successive decreases in the market price, and the market is becoming more concentrated. The competitive and economic environments once again have changed:

- Demand is increasing at a slower rate.

- The target is the majority group in the market.

- The weakest competitors are leaving the market owing to the reduced prices.

- The industrial sector is more concentrated.

The key message of the shake-out phase is that things will be more difficult in the market because of the slowing down of total demand. Competing firms are led to redefine their priority objectives in two new directions.

- First, the strategic emphasis must shift from developing primary demand to building up or maximizing market share.

- Second, market segmentation must guide the product policy to differentiate the firm from the proliferation of 'me too' products and to move away from the core market. The majority rule has become the majority fallacy.

The new priority objectives are:

- To segment the market and to identify priority target segments.

- To maximize market share in the target segments.

- To position the brand clearly in consumers' minds.

- To create and maintain brand loyalty.

To achieve these objectives, the marketing programme will stress the following strategic orientations:

- Product differentiation guided by market segmentation.

- Expansion of distribution to get maximum market exposure.

- Pricing based on the distinctive characteristics of the brands.

■ Advertising to communicate the claimed positioning to the market.

The shake-out period can be very short. The competitive climate becomes more aggressive and the key indicator of performance is *market share*.

The maturity phase

Eventually, the increase of primary demand slows down and stabilizes at the growth rate of the real GNP or the rhythm of demographic expansion. The product is in the *phase of maturity*. The majority of products can be found in this phase, which usually has the longest duration. The causes of this stabilization of the global demand are as follows:

■ The rates of occupation and penetration of the product in the market are very high and very unlikely to increase further.

■ The coverage of the market by distribution is intensive and cannot be increased further.

■ The technology is stabilized and only minor modifications to the product can be expected.

At this stage, the market is very segmented as companies try to cover all the diversity of needs by offering a wide range of product variations. Over the course of this phase the probability of a technological innovation to relaunch the PLC is high, as everyone in the industry tries to extend the life of the product.

The trends observed in the shake-out period have materialized and the characteristics of the economic and competitive environment are as follows:

■ Non-expansible primary demand is growing at the rate of the economy.

■ Durable goods demand is determined by replacement demand.

■ Markets are highly segmented.

■ The market is dominated by a few powerful competitors and the market structure is oligopolistic.

■ The technology is standardized.

The firm's priority objective is to defend, and if possible to expand, market share and to gain a sustainable competitive advantage over direct competitors. The tools to be used for achieving this objective are basically of three types:

■ To differentiate the products through quality, features or style improvements.

■ To enter new market segments or niches.

■ To gain a competitive advantage through the non-product variables of the marketing mix.

The slowing of the market growth certainly has an impact on the competitive climate. Production capacity surpluses appear and contribute to the intensification of the competitive situation. Price competition is more frequent, but has little or no impact on total demand, which

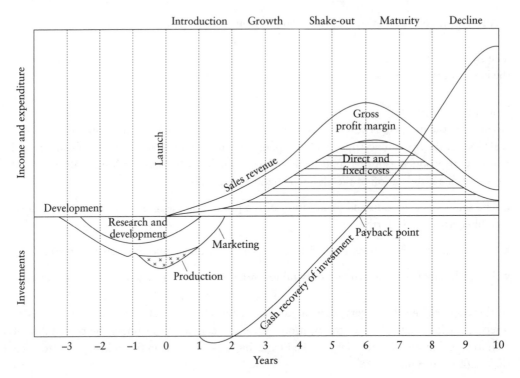

FIGURE 8.8 *Financial flows and the PLC*

has become inelastic to price. It will only affect the market share of the existing competitors. In as much as the industry succeeds in avoiding price wars, this is the phase where profitability is highest, as shown in Fig. 8.8. In theory, this profitability will be as strong as the market share retained is high.

The decline phase

The *decline phase* is characterized by a structural decrease in demand for one of the following reasons:

- New, more technologically advanced products make their appearance and replace existing products with the same function.

- Preferences, tastes, or consumption habits change with time and render products outdated.

- Changes in the social, economic and political environment, such as modifications in environmental protection laws, make products obsolete or simply prohibited.

As sales and potential profits decrease, certain companies disinvest and leave the market, while others try to specialize in the residual market. This represents a valid option if the decline is progressive. Except in a turnaround of the market, which is sometimes observed, abandonment of the technologically outdated product is inevitable. (In Table 8.1 the reader will find a PLC evaluation grid.)

TABLE 8.1 *Product life cycle evaluation grid*

Market characteristics	Phases of the product life cycle				
	Introduction	Growth	Shake-out	Maturity	Decline
Primary demand					
Slow growth	....	....	....	....	....
Fast growth	....	....	....	....	....
Slowing down	....	....	....	....	....
Decreasing	....	....	....	....	....
New competitors					
Some	....	....	....	....	....
Many	....	....	....	....	....
Few	....	....	....	....	....
Even fewer	....	....	....	....	....
Real prices					
Stable	....	....	....	....	....
Decreasing	....	....	....	....	....
Erratic	....	....	....	....	....
Range of products					
Increasing	....	....	....	....	....
Few changes	....	....	....	....	....
Decreasing	....	....	....	....	....
Distribution					
Low growth	....	....	....	....	....
Fast growth	....	....	....	....	....
Few changes	....	....	....	....	....
Decreasing	....	....	....	....	....
Product modifications					
Few	....	....	....	....	....
Many	....	....	....	....	....
Very few	....	....	....	....	....
Communication content					
Core service	....	....	....	....	....
Main attributes	....	....	....	....	....
New uses	....	....	....	....	....
Secondary attributes	....	....	....	....	....

Source: Taylor (1986, p. 28).

8.3.3 Limits of the PLC model

The PLC model is not unanimously accepted and certain market analysts recommend the complete abandonment of the concept (Dhalla and Yuspeh, 1976). Several legitimate criticisms should lead to a nuanced use of the model, though its utility remains nonetheless important.

Circular reasoning

The first criticism is methodological. It holds that the PLC model uses a circular reasoning: its phases are defined by the rate of growth of sales, then the phases are used to predict sales (Hunt, 1983). This purely endogenous definition is indeed very unsatisfactory. It is from the comprehension of the driving forces of the PLC model that one can formulate predictions. The potential explanatory variables are known, yet the measure of their influence is difficult to establish. By accumulating empirical observations, one can progressively improve this comprehension. For empirical studies of the PLC model, see notably Cox (1967), Polli and Cook (1969), Rink and Swan (1979), Swan and Rink (1982) and Tellis and Crawford (1981).

Deterministic model

A second criticism questions the deterministic nature of the model, which assumes the existence of a predefined sequence of phases in time. The company which considers the life cycle as inevitable risks acting in such a manner that the life cycle becomes a self-fulfilling prophesy (Dhalla and Yuspeh, 1976). The company's strategy should rather be to try to affect the life cycle to its greatest advantage. This criticism is based on an assumption that the life cycle is in fact a dependent variable, entirely determined by the actions of the company. This problem has already been discussed above. It stems from the fact that the life cycle model has been applied both to brands and to product markets. It is certain that, on the brand level, uncontrollable factors have relatively less impact; however, on the level of a product category or of a product market, the dependence of primary demand on environmental factors is important and cannot be overlooked in a strategic analysis.

Diversity of actual PLC profiles

A third source of difficulty comes from the fact that available experimental observations show that the PLC profile does not always follow an S-curve, as suggested by the model. Rink and Swan (1979) identified as many as 12 different profiles. Sometimes products escape the introduction phase and enter directly into growth; others skip the maturity phase and pass directly from growth to decline; still others skip decline and find a new vigour after a brief slowdown, etc. (see Fig. 8.9). Thus there is not just one type of evolution that will invariably intervene, and it is often difficult to determine the phase in which a product is currently situated. This difficulty reduces the utility of the concept as a planning tool, and even more so as the duration of the phases varies from one product to another, not to mention from one country to another for the same product. For example, in 1960, most of the European producers of TV sets had planned their production capacity for colour TV (at that time in the introductory phase) by reference to the PLC of colour TV in the USA, which had a very long introductory phase. In Europe, however, the market penetration was very rapid, the European market and environment being very different.

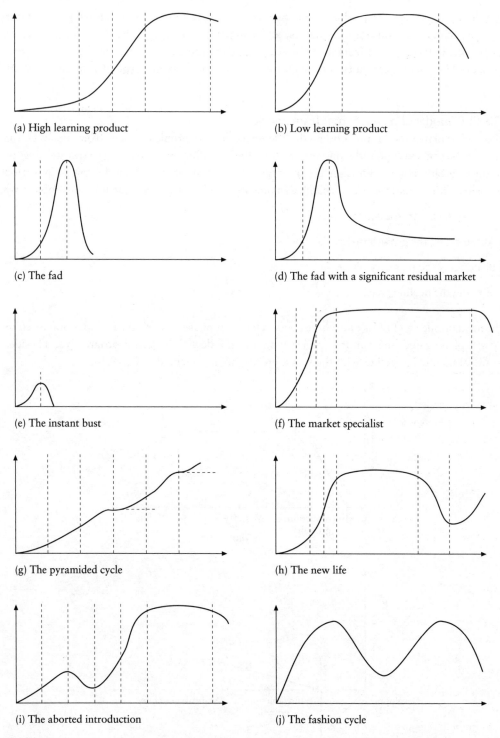

FIGURE 8.9 *Common variants of the product lifecycle* (Source: *Wasson, 1974*)

The different profiles observed can be explained by the evolution of the following explanatory factors: technology, consumption habits, and company dynamism. The PLC model does not exempt the market analyst from a systematic analysis of the driving forces at the origin of these changes. The obvious difficulty is to determine, before the facts, the type of evolution that will prevail.

The PLC model as a conceptual framework

Another explanation of the observed differences in the profiles comes from the fact that companies can act upon the pattern of the PLC profile by innovating, repositioning the product, promoting its diffusion to other groups of consumers, or modifying it in various manners. Throughout the life cycle, the dynamic firm will try to pursue the following objectives:

- Shortening the introduction phase.

- Accelerating the growth process.

- Prolonging the maturity phase.

- Slowing the decline phase.

The ideal profile of a PLC is one where the development phase is short, the introduction brief, the growth phase rapid, the maturity phase long and the decline long and progressive. The ideal profile of the PLC, together with the worst profile, are represented in Fig. 8.10.

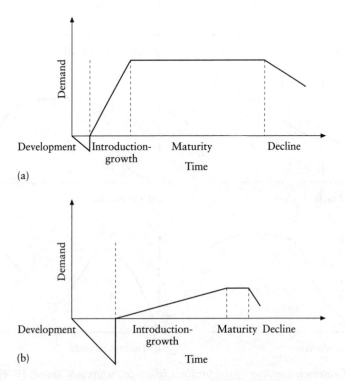

FIGURE 8.10 *Ideal profile of the PLC: The best and the worst (Source: Goldman and Muller, 1982). (a) The best PLC profile, (b) The worst PLC profile*

The initiatives taken by an innovating firm can thus modify the life-cycle profile of a product market. A classic example of a life cycle with successive product relaunches is the nylon industry, where the growth phase was prolonged several times due to successive technological modifications (Yale, 1964). It is clear that if all the competitors in a product market consider maturity or decline inevitable, the phases risk being realized sooner than expected.

More than a planning tool, the PLC model is a conceptual framework for analysing the forces which determine the attractiveness of a product market and provoke its evolution. Markets evolve because certain forces change, provoking pressures or inciting changes. Porter calls these forces *the evolutionary process*.

> Instead of attempting to describe industry evolution, it will prove more fruitful to look underneath the process to see what really drives it. . . . The evolutionary processes work to push the industry toward its potential structure, which is rarely known completely as an industry evolves. Imbedded in the underlying technology, product characteristics, and nature of present and potential buyers, however, there is a range of structures the industry might possibly achieve, depending on the directions and success of research and development, marketing innovations and the like.   (Porter, 1980, p. 163)

These changing forces are important to identify, and for that purpose the PLC model is useful (Levitt, 1965).

8.4 METHODS OF FORECASTING THE PRODUCT LIFE CYCLE

The application of the PLC model implies the ability to formulate forecasts of the evolution of primary demand in a given product market, be they qualitative or quantitative. This problem has become particularly complex in Western economies because of the turbulence of the environment and the radical nature of the changes observed over the course of the last decade. In light of these difficulties and the importance of forecasting errors, certain analysts spoke of the futility of forecasting. In reality, forecasting is an inevitable task that all companies must perform, whether explicitly or implicitly. The objective of this section is to describe the problems of forecasting demand and the conditions that must be fulfilled for the application of the principal forecasting methods.

8.4.1 Typology of forecasting methods

The different forecasting methods can be classified with reference to two dimensions: the degree of interpersonal objectivity of the forecasting process and the extent of its analytical nature. At the two extremes of these dimensions are subjective or objective methods and heuristic and analytical methods.

1. *Subjective methods*. The process used to formulate a forecast is not explicit and is inseparable from the person making the forecast.

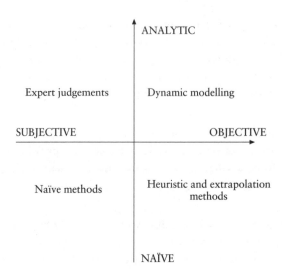

FIGURE 8.11 *Typology of demand forecasting methods*

2. *Objective methods.* The predictive process is clearly defined and can be reproduced by others who would necessarily suggest with the same forecast. The methods used here are quantitative.

This first dimension opposes quantitative to qualitative methods, where the roles of intuition, creativity and imagination are dominant.

1. *Analytic methods.* The explanatory factors of demand are identified and their probable future values predicted; one then deduces the probable value of demand, conditional upon the realization of the established scenario.
2. *Heuristic methods.* The forecast is based essentially on rules of thumb or extrapolation of historical facts, and not on an identified causal structure.

This second dimension deals with the analytical character of the forecasting approach, which opposes extrapolation methods to explanatory methods, be they qualitative or quantitative.

As shown in Fig. 8.11, the intersection of these two dimensions allows one to classify the different demand forecasting methods in four categories. Below we shall briefly review the main methods used, neglecting the case of naïve methods.

8.4.2 Forecasting methods based on expert judgements

When the forecast formulated does not rest on objective data but rather on the judgements of managers or consumers, the forecasting methods used are said to be expert judgement-based. The 'expert' is assumed to base his or her judgement on a group of explanatory factors, to estimate their chances of occurrence and their likely impact on the level of demand.

Thus, underlying this approach there is a *causal structure*, a set of judgements upon the explanatory factors of demand and their probability of occurrence, in the framework of one or several scenarios. This causal structure is unique to the expert, and another expert confronted with the same problem could reach different conclusions using the same information. The expert approach presents the advantage of allowing exchange and confrontation of ideas, because of the existence of an explicit causal structure. The three judgement-based methods most often used are: management judgements, sales force estimates and buyers' intentions.

Management judgements

The forecast is determined by the *vision, intuition* or *imagination* of the individual who formulates it. Managers are asked to give their best guesses or estimates, with their degree of uncertainty taking, for example, the form of probabilities.

This approach is, to a certain degree, always present in a company. It is frequently observed in organizations dominated by managers who orient their actions only on the basis of their own views. The value of this approach will obviously depend on the values of the experience and the intuition of the managers. The major disadvantage of this approach is its difficulty of communication and the absence of any possibility of verification or falsification. One way to reduce the subjectivity of individual judgement is to have a *panel of managers* who discuss possible forecasts and try to reach a consensus. A somewhat better way to arrive at subjective estimates is to use the *Delphi method*.

> Under this procedure, the judgments of individuals in a group of experts are solicited anonymously (usually by questionnaire). Then the median judgment is computed and communicated to the individuals in the group, who are again asked to make a new judgment. In practice, it has been found that such a procedure quickly leads to a consensus, typically within two rounds. (Phillips, 1987)

The Delphi method has been applied with some success in marketing. Its major drawback lies in the biasing influence of the feedback. An alternative is to obtain independent estimates from several individuals and to average them to yield an aggregate forecast.

Decision support systems have been developed in recent years to assist management in making judgement-based decisions and forecasts.

Salesforce estimates

Salespeople are in general very knowledgeable about future potential sales to existing customers and can provide useful estimates of the untapped market potential in their own territory as well. The simplest way to proceed is to ask salespeople for overall sales estimates in their territories for each product under a set of assumptions regarding the level of marketing support. Management then adds up the estimates to arrive at a total for the firm.

The main shortcoming of this approach is the *vested interest problem* since salespeople may systematically underestimate sales in order to keep their quota low and to appear subsequently as high sales achievers. Several remedial actions can be taken to improve the reliability of the sales estimates.

- Asking salespeople to assess their own degree of uncertainty (or confidence) in their estimates. This information can then be used to qualify the forecast.

- Combining each salesperson's estimate with an estimate provided by the regional sales manager.

- Applying a correction factor to each person's estimate based on his or her history of over- or under-reporting.

Involving the salesforce in the sales forecasting process is important for motivating the salesforce and for gaining acceptance of the sales quotas. It is also interesting to have sales forecasts available at very disaggregate levels, such as region, territory, customer, etc.

Buyers' intentions surveys

A last judgemental method is to estimate demand directly on the basis of stated intentions to purchase provided by buyers. Buyers' intentions can be analysed at two different levels: (a) the general level of buyers' expectations and confidence about their present and future personal finance and/or about the economy or (b) the level of a specific product class or brand. In the European Union two general surveys of buyers' intentions are periodically carried out.

The first is the EU quarterly survey on consumers' sentiments or confidence about the economy and about their personal economic situation. Consumers are also asked to express their intentions to purchase major durable goods within the next three months. These data are then used to construct an *index of consumer confidence* which can be used as an early indicator of shifts in retail sales (*Eurobaromètre*, 1994).

In the field of industrial goods, central banks within the EU are conducting monthly surveys among industrial firms regarding their expectations and/or intentions about investment, employment, production capacity utilization and current state of orders and shipments for both domestic and international markets. These data, available for each major industrial sector, are used to construct an *index of industry confidence*, which has proved to be a reliable early indicator of economic recession or recovery. Firms are using this information to anticipate shifts in the level of demand.

Various firms conduct their own surveys of consumer intentions, especially when testing a new product concept. A typical question on buyers' intentions looks like the one presented in Table 8.2.

TABLE 8.2 *Typical question on buyers' intentions*

Do you intend to buy a new car within the next six months?					
No chance	Slight possibility	Fair possibility	Good possibility	High probability	Certain
(0)	(0.20)	(0.40)	(0.60)	(0.80)	(1.00)

The frequencies observed for the two upper classes of this purchase probability scale can be used to generate potential market estimates and/or brand shares.

When one considers intentions about the purchase of a specific good or brand, specific intentions surveys have been found to be of more limited value than general surveys. Intentions are not always related strongly to behaviour, except when advanced planning is required, as is the case for major product or service purchases, such as automobiles, housing, holiday trips, etc.

Subjective methods have obvious limitations, but they nevertheless provide a useful starting point in demand estimation. However, they should be used conjointly with more objective methods.

8.4.3 Heuristic and extrapolation forecasting

When the analytic structure of the forecasting process is weak, but when the forecast rests on objective market data, the methods used are said to be heuristic. They are either rules of thumb, loosely based on empirical data, or extrapolations of current sales.

The chain ratio method

This method is an extension of the absolute market potential given earlier in this chapter, which calls for identifying all potential buyers (n) in the product market or segment and for assuming optimum use of (q) the product by each potential user. Two examples of application have been provided, one for a consumer good (see Box 8.1) and one for a consumable industrial good (see 'The demand for industrial goods' on p. 278). The determination of the current level of primary demand in these two examples would require estimates of the current occupation rates.

The chain ratio method involves the use of successive adjusting percentages to break down the absolute potential to come to the demand for a particular product or brand. To illustrate, let us consider the case of a company selling a compound to be used in conjunction with the usual water-softening chemicals used for treating water in boiler systems. The market is dominated by a monopolist, but many factories are still non-users of the compound. To determine the expected sales volume of this new compound in a particular geographic area, an estimate can be made by the following calculations.

■ Water consumption by factories equipped with boiler systems = 7 500 000 hl.

■ Softener use ratio per litre of water = 1 per cent.

■ Percentage of factories using water-softening products = 72 per cent.

■ Compound use ratio per litre of softener = 9 per cent.

■ The current market potential is

  7 500 000 hl × 0.01 × 0.72 × 0.09 = 486 000 litres.

■ Percentage of factories using the chemical compound = 54 per cent.

■ The current level of primary demand is

  750 000 000 hl × 0.01 × 0.72 × 0.09 × 0.54 = 262 440 litres.

If the target market share for Company A is 40 per cent, the expected sales volume in this particular area will be 104 976 litres.

The difficulty of this method is the choice of the different multipliers if no primary research data are available. Moreover, error in any one multiplier will carry throughout the analysis, given the dependency of each level on preceding levels. The way out is to adopt different multipliers to generate, not a single estimate, but a range of estimates. In any case, this method should be used along with other procedures or complementary analyses.

Buying power index

In the field of consumer goods a popular technique is the buying power index (BPI) method. The objective is to measure the attractiveness of a market by a weighted average of the three key components of any market potential, i.e.

■ The number of potential consuming units.

■ The purchasing power of these consuming units.

■ The willingness to spend of these consuming units.

Indicators of these components are identified by region, province, district, community or city and a weighted average index is computed for each area.

Two approaches are possible: use a standard BPI developed by market research companies or develop an index tailored to the specific products and market of a particular firm.

Standard BPIs are in general based on the following three indicators: total population, per capita income and retail sales. The relative buying power of any area i is given by

$$BPI_i = 0.5(C_i) + 0.3(Y_i) + 0.2(W_i)$$

where C is the percentage of total population in area i, Y is the percentage of income originating from area i and W is the percentage of retail sales in area i.

The weights adopted in the BPI equation are those used by the *Sales & Marketing Management* magazine which, in the USA, publishes BPIs in July of each year. They are derived empirically through regression analyses and apply mainly to mass products moderately priced. Other weights can be adopted if necessary, as well as additional indicators. Similar BPIs are published by Chase Econometrics for the main regions of the EU, and by Business International for 117 countries throughout the world.

Tailor-made BPIs would typically keep the same three basic components of buying power, but would include indicators more directly related to the business plus possibly other indicators to reflect competitive conditions or local characteristics. An example of a tailor-made BPI is presented in Table 8.3.

TABLE 8.3 *Sales performance evaluation per territory*

Territory	Brand A sales	Percentage of total sales	Buying power index (%)	Performance index
1	2533	3.53	4.31	0.82
2	8458	11.80	7.84	1.51
3	3954	5.52	5.89	0.94
4	19 619	27.37	20.28	1.35
5	3780	5.27	4.75	1.11
6	3757	5.24	13.24	0.40
7	5432	7.58	8.74	0.87
8	3701	5.16	3.97	1.30
9	3028	4.22	3.19	1.32
10	3820	5.33	9.16	0.58
11	2433	3.39	3.70	0.92
12	5736	8.00	8.32	0.96
13	2569	3.58	2.96	1.21
14	2861	3.99	3.65	1.09
Total	71 681	100.00	100.00	–

The market studied in Table 8.3 is the soft drinks market. The indicators used to compute the buying power index are number of households with children, private disposable income, and number of hotels, restaurants and cafés within each area. These data, expressed in percentages of the total, are available for 14 sales territories. The buying power index is a simple average of the three percentages of each territory. Its predictive value has been verified by correlating the BPI with product category sales in each area.

In the table, the BPI is used to assess the market penetration of brand A within each area. To estimate potential sales of each territory, the BPI is multiplied by the expected national sales for the brand. Other strategic goals or local conditions must, of course, be considered. Some firms also use the BPI as a guide to allocate their total advertising budget among the different sales territories.

Trend decomposition and extrapolation

The purpose of trend analysis is to decompose the original sales series into its principal components, to measure the past evolution of each component and to project this evolution into a near future. It is evident that this projection has no meaning beyond the short term—that is, the period of time for which one can consider that the characteristics of the phenomenon being studied do not change measurably. However, these conditions exist rather often in practice, because inertia also exists in the environment. Five different components can be identified in a typical sales time series:

■ A *structural* component, i.e. the long-term trend, generally linked to the life cycle of the product market.

- A *cyclical* component, represented by fluctuations around the long-term trend, provoked by medium-term changes in economic activity.

- A *seasonal* component, or recurrent short-term fluctuations due to diverse causes (weather, holidays, calendrical structure, etc.).

- A *marketing* component reflecting short-term promotional actions, temporary price cuts or out-of-stock situations.

- An *erratic* component, which reflects the impact of complex phenomena, poorly understood, unpredictable and non-quantifiable.

For each component, a parameter is estimated on the basis of the regularities observed in the past: long-term average growth rate, short-term fluctuations, seasonal coefficients and special events. These parameters are then used to generate a sales forecast, assuming that their past values will remain unchanged during the next period.

Exponential smoothing

This approach forecasts sales as a weighted average of sales observed in a number of past periods, with the largest weights being placed on sales observed in the most recent periods. The sales forecast for the next period is given by

$$\bar{Q}_t = \alpha\, Q_t + (1 - \alpha)\, \bar{Q}_{t-1}$$

where $\bar{Q}_t$ is the smoothed sales for the current period, α is the smoothing constant $(0 < \alpha < 1)$, Q_t is the current sales in period t, and $\bar{Q}_{t-1}$ is the smoothed sales as computed in period $t - 1$.

The smoothing constant is a number between 0 and 1 and must be selected by the market analyst. Low values of α are appropriate when sales change slowly, and high values are relevant for rapid changes in sales. Computer programs are available to select the best value of α by trial and error on historical data.

To illustrate, let us examine the data presented in Table 8.4, in which quarterly sales in volume have been seasonally adjusted. The objective is to find the optimal value for α, the smoothing constant. The data of 1992 are used to test the predictive value of the model.

TABLE 8.4 *Seasonally adjusted quarterly sales*

Quarter	1987	1988	1989	1990	1991	1992	Seasonal index
1	105	106	112	121	124	130	0.908
2	101	111	115	117	125	127	0.996
3	100	110	110	117	129	132	1.153
4	108	110	117	118	122	124	0.943

To forecast sales for the first quarter of 1992, we need the smoothed sales as estimated for the preceding periods. For example, the smoothed sales for the first quarter of 1988 are then,

$$\bar{Q}_{88} = [0.10(106)] + [0.90(105)] = 105.1$$

where seasonally adjusted sales for 1987 have been used for the smoothed sales because the smoothed sales are not available when one begins exponential smoothing. Similarly, for the other quarters we have successively,

$$\bar{Q}_{89} = [0.10(112)] + [0.90(105.1)] = 105.9$$

$$\bar{Q}_{90} = [0.10(121)] + [0.90(105.9)] = 107.3$$

$$\bar{Q}_{91} = [0.10(124)] + [0.90(107.3)] = 109.0$$

Thus, the forecast for the first quarter of 1992 is based on past sales and is equal to

$$E(Q_{92}) = Q_{91} = 109.0$$

Note that the sales forecast is always included between current sales and smoothed sales for the current period.

The error of forecasting can be computed as

$$\text{Forecasting error} = \frac{109.0 - 130}{130} = 16.2 \text{ per cent}$$

This a very large prediction error, which can be caused by the small value of the smoothing constant α since, in this example, sales are rapidly increasing. A value of 0.80 for α gives smoothed sales for 1991 equal to 128.60, reducing the forecasting error to 1.1 per cent, a much better performance.

A large number of different techniques exist, incorporating more than one smoothing constant. For an overview of these methods, see Makridakis and Wheelwright (1973). The main shortcoming of exponential smoothing methods is their inability to really 'forecast' the evolution of demand, in the sense that they cannot anticipate a turning point. At most, they can rapidly integrate a modification in sales. This is why these methods are termed 'adaptive forecasting model'. For numerous management problems, this 'after the fact' forecast is nonetheless useful since the causes of sales tend to operate in a regular manner. Thus, the use of previous sales levels as predictors of future levels often works satisfactorily.

8.4.4 Dynamic modelling

'Objective' and 'analytical' forecasting methods are the most advanced methods, scientifically speaking. They are based upon the construction of *explicative mathematical models*, which allow the simulation of market situations in alternative scenarios. In its basic philosophy, mathematical modelling is very similar to the expert approach described above: identifying a causal structure, constructing one or several scenarios and deducting the probable level of demand in each of them. The difference comes from the fact that *the causal structure was established and validated experimentally in objectively observable and measurable conditions.*

Identification of the causal structure

The identification of the causal structure of the phenomenon under study is the starting point for any model-building exercise. Let us take as an example the case of a distributor who wishes to increase the loyalty rate of his or her customers and is trying to identify the best means of reaching this result. The questions to be asked are as follows:

■ What are the determining factors behind the *image* of a distributor?

■ How does this image influence the *visit frequency* of stores?

■ What other factors explain customer *satisfaction*?

■ To what extent does the level of satisfaction generate long-term customer store *loyalty*?

Rather typically, we are faced here with successive causal relationships where the first dependent variable (*image*) becomes the explanatory variable of a second dependent variable (*visit frequency* and *satisfaction*), which then explains *loyalty*. This is obviously a set of hypotheses based on the understanding of buyer behaviour and on *a priori* questions suggested by behavioural theory. These hypotheses should be verified (or disproved) on the basis of empirical data gathered by the market analyst. If confirmed, the model could then be used to guide the distributor's decisions.

Multi-equations models

When the phenomenon under study is too complex, as in the preceding example, the analyst must use estimation methods which explicitly recognize the interdependence of variables.

By way of illustration, let us look at the problem of measuring the impact of brand advertising on market share for a FMCG sold by large retailer chains. Previous works on the effect of advertising have shown that there is a direct effect of advertising on the brand presence in supermarkets and also on the behaviour of the sales representatives responsible for the presence and the exposure of the brand at the point of sales. The causal structure of the phenomenon is described in Fig. 8.12. We then have three basic relationships:

1. The retailer's behaviour (y_1) is determined by the level of the distribution margin (x_1) and by the intensity of the advertising efforts made in support of the brand (x_2).
2. The behaviour of sales personnel (y_2) is determined by the behaviour of the retailers (y_1), brand advertising intensity (x_2) and by competition actions (x_3).
3. The level of market share (y_3) is determined by the behaviour of distributors (y_1), the behaviour of sales personnel (y_2) and by the relative price of the brand (x_4).

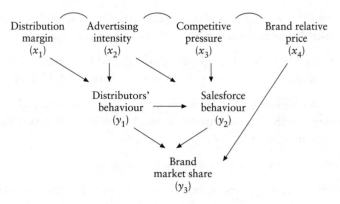

FIGURE 8.12 *Example of causal structure: the impact of brand advertising on market share*

Thus, we have,

$$y_1 = f(x_1, x_2)$$

$$y_2 = f(x_2, x_3, y_1)$$

$$y_3 = f(y_1, y_2, x_4)$$

The structural equations to estimate are,

	Exogenous variables				Endogonous variables			Error
	x_1	x_2	x_3	x_4	y_1	y_2	y_3	
y_1	b_1x_1	$+ b_2x_2$						$+ e_1$
y_2		b_3x_2	$+ b_4x_3$		$+ b_4y_1$			$+ e_2$
y_3				b_5x4	$+ b_6y_1$	$+ b_7y_2$		$+ e_3$

Powerful computing methods are now available to estimate this equation system.

Dynamic modelling
Peeters (1992) has developed a dynamic model for estimating the demand for lorries on different European markets. The demand function adopted is:

$$\text{Demand} = F(\text{Production, Interest rates, Prices, Error term})$$

where

Demand	=	monthly registrations of lorries weighing 15 tonnes and more
Production	=	monthly index of industrial production
Interest rates	=	monthly interest rate of state guaranteed bonds
Price	=	index of fuel prices.

Data are de-seasonalized and expressed as logarithms. The mathematical model used is a dynamic model which describes the structure of the market response as follows:

- The *production* variable is introduced under a distributed lag model taking the shape of a decreasing geometric progression from t to $t - k$ with a rate of 0.4557 (Koyck model).

- The *interest rate variable* comes into the model with an eight-month lag, which means that the time lag of a change in the interest rate on demand is eight months; this lag was identified through an iteration procedure.

- The *price* variable is also introduced with an eight-month lag.

- The *error term* also has a dynamic structure as it is composed of a weighted sum of the preceding error terms (U) and of a random term (e).

The demand equation, estimated through a numerical method of maximum likelihood, is as follows:

$$Q_t = -5.503 + (1.7479 \cdot Prod_t) + (0.7960 \cdot Prod_{t-1}) + (0.3630 \cdot Prod_{t-2}) + (...)$$
$$- (0.1899 \cdot Interest_{t-8}) - (0.4767 \cdot Price_{t-8})$$
$$+ (0.2463 \cdot U_{t-1}) + (0.1389 \cdot U_{t-2}) + (0.2602 \cdot U_{t-3}) + e_t$$
$$N = 86 \qquad DW = 1.989 \qquad R^2 = 0.865$$

The quality of the statistical fit is measured by the usual statistical indicators. The determination coefficient here is 0.865. The '*t-tests*' measuring the precision of the individual coefficients are also statistically significant at the 5 per cent level of higher.

The interpretation of the coefficients is straightforward since they are elasticities. Thus, as an example,

- The cumulative total effect (sum of effects for all lags) of the industrial production variable is 3.2114, which means that a 1 per cent increase of the industrial production index generates an increase of 3.2 per cent of truck registrations.

- A decrease in interest rate of 10 per cent causes an increase of 1.9 per cent in the demand for trucks eight months later.

- A 120 per cent increase in the price of fuel causes a decrease of 4.8 per cent in the demand for trucks eight months later.

A comparison of the observed and calculated sales via the model for the last ten months is shown in Fig. 8.13.

Limitations of mathematical model building

The strength of this approach is that the model becomes an instrument of discovery and exploration of numerous and varied situations that the human mind could not exhaustively explore.

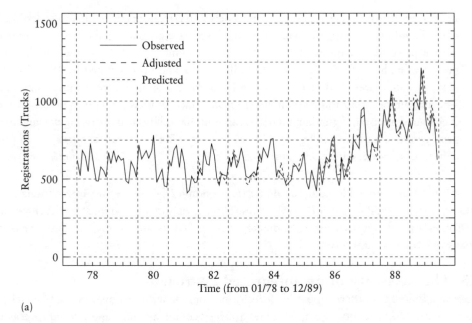

(a)

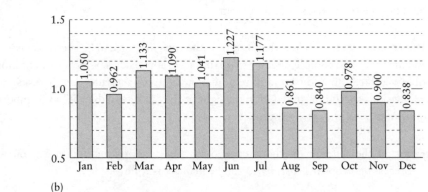

(b)

FIGURE 8.13 *Comparison of observed and calculated demand for heavy trucks (Source: Peeters, 1992). (a) Observed, adjusted and predicted dependent variable, (b) Seasonal profile of dependent variable*

It is important to note that this approach is only valid as long as the causal structure identified remains stable. Forecasting with an explicative model thus also implies an extrapolation, but of second degree. In a rapidly and profoundly changing environment, a mathematical model is incapable of anticipating the effect of a change in the model when the cause has not been taken into account. A mathematical model thus lacks the ability to improvise, and cannot adapt to a profoundly modified environment, whereas an expert can.

The majority of forecasting errors are due to the fact that, at the moment of formulation of the forecast, it has been implicitly considered that the current tendencies will more or less be maintained in the future. This is rarely the case in the reality of social and economic life.

In 1983 and 1984, 67 new types of business personal computers were introduced to the US market, and most companies were expecting explosive growth. One industry forecasting service projected an installed base of 27 million units by 1988; another predicted 28 million units by 1987. In fact, only 15 million units had been shipped by 1986. By then, many manufacturers had abandoned the PC market or gone out of business altogether. The inaccurate suppositions did not stem from a lack of forecasting techniques. Instead, they shared a mistaken fundamental assumption: that relationships driving demand in the past would continue unaltered. The companies didn't foresee changes in end-user behaviour or understand their saturation point.   (Barnett, 1988, p. 28)

History can be an unreliable guide as domestic economies become more international, new technologies emerge and industries evolve. These abilities of anticipation must be developed and this assumes a good comprehension of the key driving factors and of the vulnerability of the company to environmental threats.

8.4.5 The necessity of an integrated approach

The examination of the different possible forecasting approaches has shown the advantages and limitations of each. In reality, the approaches are very complementary and a good forecasting system should be able to make use of all of them.

In a turbulent environment, it is clear that intuition and imagination can be precious instruments of perception of reality and complementary to quantitative approaches, which, by definition, rely solely on observed facts. In addition, a purely qualitative approach runs certain risks, and the intuitions and visions should be analysed in the light of the facts available. What is important is thus the confrontation of these two approaches.

The integration of the different methods evoked by the scenarios method is a good way to approach a forecasting problem. A *scenario* can be defined as follows:

> a presentation of the key explanatory factors to be taken into consideration, and a description of the manner(s) in which these factors could affect demand.

A scenario is thus different from a forecast. A forecast is more a judgement which tends to predict a specific situation and which is to be taken or left on its own value. A scenario, on the other hand, is an instrument which is conceived for analysis and reflection—namely,

- To give a better understanding of a market's situation and its past evolution.

- To sensitize the company to its interactions with the environment.

- To evaluate its vulnerability to threats.

- To identify possible lines of action.

Thanks to this sensitization, the method allows the company to improve its anticipation capability and to develop its flexibility and adaptability (de Boisanger, 1988, p. 63). A scenario

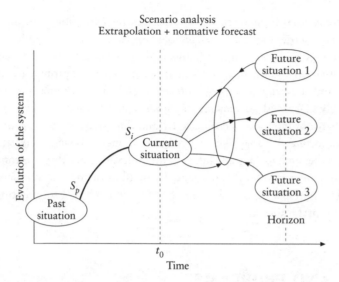

FIGURE 8.14 *The scenario approach* (Source: *de Boisanger, 1988*)

should be regarded together with other scenarios: one basic scenario and other alternative scenarios based on key factors, as illustrated in Fig. 8.14.

This approach, which is based upon the conviction that the future can never be completely measured and controlled, presents several advantages for management:

■ It sensitizes the company to the uncertainties which characterize any market situation; in a turbulent environment, sound management implies the *ability to anticipate* the evolution of the environment.

■ The scenario method facilitates *integration of the different forecasting approaches*, qualitative or quantitative.

■ The practice of this approach introduces more flexibility in management and induces the company to develop alternative plans and a system of *contingency planning* (see Chapter 11).

The spectacular development of microcomputer technology has largely facilitated the application of this method, notably in allowing its decentralization within the company.

SUMMARY

The key demand concepts are 'primary' versus 'company' demand, 'absolute' versus 'present' market potential, 'end' versus 'derived' demand, 'first equipment' versus 'replacement' demand for durable goods. The objective of demand analysis is to give an empirical content to these concepts through market research in order to objectively assess the attractiveness of each potential target segment and to identify the determinants of demand. These concepts are useful for detecting growth opportunities in the reference market through gap analysis. The product life cycle model is a conceptual framework which describes the evolution of primary demand in a dynamic perspective. A large variety of profiles exist for the PLC which can be explained by the evolution of technology and consumption habits and by the size of industry marketing efforts. The competitive situation and the financial structure (turnover and profits) are different at each stage of the PLC and the priority strategic objective and the marketing programme must be adapted accordingly. Demand forecasting methods can be classified by reference to two dimensions: the degree of interpersonal objectivity and the extent of the analytical approach. A distinction is made between 'subjective' and 'objective' methods and 'heuristic' or 'analytic' methods. Each of these methods has advantages and limitations but they are complementary. A good forecasting system should be able to make use of all of them. In a turbulent environment, the emphasis is placed on flexibility and speed of adaptation. Thus, a foresighting rather than a forecasting system is preferable.

QUESTIONS AND PROBLEMS

1. What is the relationship between current market potential and absolute market potential? Describe the factors that determine the level and the evolution of these market potential concepts.
2. You must estimate the size of the absolute market potential as well as the current level of equipment of households for microwaves in a given country. Describe the information as well as the methods needed to gather this information.
3. How does the price elasticity of primary demand develop during the various phases of its product life cycle? What are the factors explaining this evolution and what are the managerial implications for the firm?
4. How would you proceed to develop a buying power index that would allow you to evaluate the market potential for life insurance on a regional base within a given country?
5. You are asked to measure young people's attitudes towards advertising in general. Describe the causal structure that should guide the search for information.

REFERENCES

Barnett, F.W. (1988), 'Four Steps to Forecast Total Market Demand', *Harvard Business Review*, July–August, pp. 28–37.
Berry, F.W. (1980), 'Services Marketing is Different', *Business Magazine*, May–June.
de Boisanger, P. (1988), 'Réduire l'imprévu à l'imprévisible', *Futuribles*, March, pp. 59–68.
Cox, W.E. (1967), 'Product Life Cycle as marketing models', *Journal of Business*, vol. 40, October, pp. 375–84.
Day, G.S. (1981), 'The Product Life Cycle: Analysis and Application Issues', *Journal of Marketing*, vol. 45, Autumn, pp. 60–7.
Dhalla, N.K. and S. Yuspeh (1976), 'Forget the Product Life Cycle Concept', *Harvard Business Review*, January–February, pp. 102–12.
Eiglier, P. and E. Langeard (1987), *Servuction*. Paris: McGraw-Hill.
Eurobarometre (1994), 'Public Opinion in the European Community: Trends 1976–1994'.

Goldman, A. and E. Muller (1982), Measuring Shape Patterns for Product Life Cycles: Implications for a Marketing Strategy. Unpublished Paper, quoted in Kotler, P. (1984), *Marketing Management*, 5th edn., Englewood Cliffs, NJ: Prentice-Hall Inc.

Hinkle, J. (1966), *Life Cycles*. New York: Nielsen Co.

Hunt, S.D. (1983), General Theories and the Fundamental Explananda of Marketing, *Journal of Marketing*, vol. 47, Autumn, pp. 9–17.

Lambin, J.J. (1987), 'Le contrôle de la qualité dans le domaine des services', *Gestion 2000*, vol. 1, pp. 63–75.

Levitt, T. (1965), 'Exploit the Product Life Cycle', *Harvard Business Review*, vol. 43, November–December, pp. 81–96.

Makridakis, S. and S.C. Wheelwright (1973), *Forecasting Methods for Management*. New York: John Wiley & Sons.

McCarthy, J. (1960), *Basic Marketing: A Managerial Approach*, 1st edn. Homewood, Ill.: R.D. Irwin.

Morris, M.H. (1988), *Industrial and Organizational Marketing*. Columbus: Merrill Publishing Co.

OECD (1983), *Perspectives à long terme de l'industrie automobile mondiale*. Paris.

Peeters, R. (1992), *Total Truck Demand in Europe: A Case Study*. IAG, Université Catholique de Louvain, Louvain-la-Neuve, Belgium.

Phillips, L.D. (1987), 'On Adequacy of Judgemental Forecasts', in Wright, G. and Aytol, P. (eds), *Judgemental Forecasting*. New York: John Wiley & Sons.

Polli, R. and V. Cook (1969), 'Validity of the Product Life Cycle Concept', *Journal of Business*, vol. 42, October, pp. 385–400.

Porter, M.E. (1980), *Competitive Strategy*. New York: The Free Press.

Rink, D.R. and J.E. Swan (1979), 'Product Life Cycle Research: A Literature Review', *Journal of Business Research*, September, pp. 219–42.

Shostack, G.L. (1977), 'Breaking Free from Product Marketing', *Journal of Marketing*, vol. 41, April, pp. 73–80.

Swan, J.E. and D.R. Rink (1982), 'Fitting Market Strategy to Varying Product Life Cycles', *Business Horizons*, January–February, pp. 72–6.

Taylor, J.W. (1986), *Competitive Marketing Strategies*. Radnor, Penn.: Chilton Book Co.

Tellis, G.J. and C.M. Crawford (1981), 'An Evolutionary Approach to Product Growth Theory', *Journal of Marketing*, vol. 45, Autumn, pp. 125–34.

Wasson, C.R. (1974), *Dynamic Competitive Strategy and the Product Life Cycle*. St Charles: Challenge Books.

Weber, J.A. (1976), *Growth Opportunity Analysis*. Reston, Virginia: Reston Publishing Co.

Wilkie, W.L. (1990), *Consumer Behavior*, 2nd edn. New York: John Wiley & Sons.

Yale, J.P. (1964), 'The Strategy of Nylon's Growth: Create New Market', *Modern Textiles Magazine*, February.

Zeithmal, V.A., A. Parasuraman and L.L. Berry (1990), *Delivering Quality Service*. New York: The Free Press.

FURTHER READING

Bishop, W.S., J.L. Graham and M.H. Jones (1984), 'Volatility of Derived Demand in Industrial Markets and its Management Implications', *Journal of Marketing*, vol. 48, Autumn, pp. 95–103.

Business International (1991), 'Indicators of Market Size for 117 Countries, Weekly Report', 8 July.

Kotler, P. (1991), *Marketing Management*, 7th edn. Englewood Cliffs, New Jersey: Prentice Hall Inc.

Lambin, J.J. and R. Peeters (1977), *La gestion marketing de l'entreprise*. Paris: Presses Universitaires de France.

Levitt, T. (1981), 'Marketing Intangible Products and Product Intangibles', *Harvard Business Review*, vol. 59, May–June, pp. 94–102.

Sizer, J. (1972), 'Accountants, Product Managers and Selling Price Decisions' in 'Multi-Consumer Product Firms', *Journal of Business Finance*, vol. 4, Spring, p. 76.

Stoffaès, C. (1985), 'Filières et stratégies industrielles', *Annales des Mines*, January, pp. 9–20.

CHAPTER 9

COMPETITIVE-NESS ANALYSIS

LEARNING OBJECTIVES

After reading this chapter, you should be able to:

■ define a competitive advantage which is sustainable in a target market

■ describe the nature and strengths of the competitive forces at play in an industry

■ assess the impact of the competitive situation on the strategic and operational marketing objectives

■ predict the type of competitive behaviour to expect, given the competitive environment

■ explain the importance of differentiation as a source of competitive advantage

■ use the experience curve to measure the extent of a cost advantage or disadvantage over direct competitors.

*H*aving evaluated the intrinsic appeal of the product markets and segments in the reference market, the next stage of strategic marketing is to analyse the climate or the *competitive structure* of each of the product markets, and then evaluate the nature and intensity of the *competitive advantage* held by the various competitors in each market. A product market may be very attractive in itself, but not so for a particular firm, given its strengths and weaknesses and compared to its most dangerous competitors. Therefore, the aim of measuring business competitiveness is to identify the kind of competitive advantage that a firm or a brand can enjoy and to evaluate the extent to which this advantage is sustainable, given the competitive structure, the balance of existing forces and the positions held by the competitors.

9.1 THE NOTION OF COMPETITIVE ADVANTAGE

Competitive advantage refers to those characteristics or attributes of a product or a brand that give to the firm some superiority over its direct competitors. These characteristics or attributes may be of different types and may relate to the product itself (the core service), to the necessary or added services accompanying the core service, or to the modes of production, distribution or selling specific to the product or to the firm.

When it exists, this superiority is relative and is defined with respect to the best-placed competitor in the product market or segment. We then speak of the most dangerous competitor, or the *priority competitor*.

A competitor's relative superiority may result from various factors. Generally speaking, these can be classified into two main categories, according to the competitive advantage they provide. This can be internal or external.

> A competitive advantage is 'external' when it is based on some distinctive qualities of the product which give superior value to the buyer, either by reducing its costs or by improving its performance.

An external competitive advantage gives the firm increased market power. It can force the market to accept a price above that of its priority competitor which may not have the same distinctive quality. A strategy based on an external competitive advantage is a *differentiation strategy*, which calls into question the firm's marketing know-how, and its ability to better detect and meet those expectations of buyers which are not yet satisfied by existing products.

> A competitive advantage is 'internal' when it is based on the firm's superiority in matters of cost control, administration and product management, which bring 'value to the producer' by enabling it to have a lower unit cost than its priority competitor.

Internal competitive advantage results from better productivity, thus making the firm more profitable and more resistant to price cuts imposed by the market or by the competition. A strategy based on internal competitive advantage is a *cost-domination strategy*, which mainly calls into question the firm's organizational and technological know-how.

To succeed with an external advantage strategy, the price premium the customer is willing to pay must exceed the cost of providing that extra value. Similarly, a cost strategy must offer acceptable value to customers, so that prices are close to the average of competitors. If too much quality is sacrificed for achieving a low-cost position, the price discount demanded by customers will more than offset the cost advantage.

These two types of competitive advantage have distinct origins and natures, which are often incompatible because they imply different abilities and traditions. Figure 9.1 shows the two aspects of competitive advantage, which can be expressed as questions.

1. *Market power.* To what extent are buyers willing to pay a price higher than the price charged by our direct competitor?
2. *Productivity.* Is our unit cost higher or lower than the unit cost of our direct competitor?

The horizontal axis in Fig. 9.1 refers to the maximum acceptable price and the vertical axis to unit cost. Both are expressed in terms of percentages compared to the priority competitor.

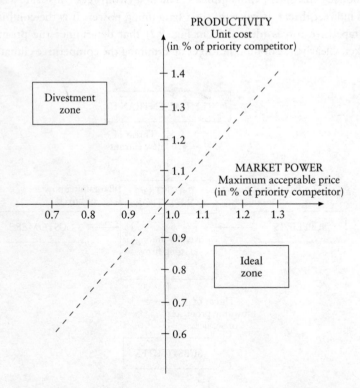

FIGURE 9.1 *Competitive advantage analysis*

- Positioning in the upper left quadrant and lower right quadrant are extreme cases, disastrous or ideal, respectively.

- Positioning in the lower left quadrant implies cost domination.

- Positioning in the upper right quadrant implies successful differentiation.

- The bisecting line separates the favourable and unfavourable zones.

The purpose of measuring business competitiveness is to allow the firm to find its own position on these axes and deduce its strategic priority objectives for each of the products of its portfolio. To find the position along the 'market power axis', the firm will use information provided by brand image studies which, as seen in Chapter 5, help to measure the brand's perceived value and estimate price elasticities. As for the 'productivity axis', the experience law can be used when applicable (see section 9.3) or the firm can use information provided by the marketing intelligence unit which has, among other things, the task of monitoring competition.

9.2 FORCES DRIVING INDUSTRY COMPETITION

The notion of extended rivalry, due to Porter (1985), is based on the idea that a firm's ability to exploit a competitive advantage in its reference market depends not only on the direct competition it faces, but also on the role played by rival forces, such as potential entrants, substitute products, customers and suppliers. The first two forces constitute a direct threat; the other two an indirect threat, because of their bargaining power. It is the combined interplay of these five competitive forces (described in Fig. 9.2) that determines the profit potential of a product market. Clearly, the dominant forces determining the competitive climate vary from one

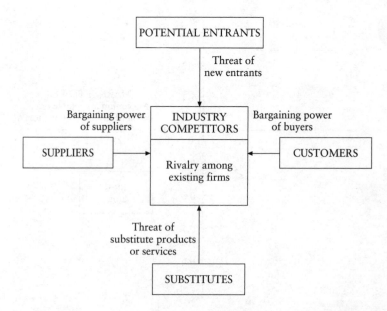

FIGURE 9.2 *The forces driving industry competition* (Source: *Porter, 1980*)

market to another. Using Porter's analysis, we shall examine the role of these external competitive forces successively. The analysis of rivalry between direct competitors will be discussed later in the chapter.

9.2.1 Threat of new entrants

Potential competitors constitute a threat that the firm must limit, and protect itself against, by creating barriers to entry. Potential entrants can be identified as follows:

- Firms outside the product market which could easily surmount the barriers to entry.

- Firms for which entry would represent a clear synergy.

- Firms for which entry is the logical conclusion of their strategy.

- Clients or suppliers who can proceed to backward or forward integration (Porter, 1980, p. 55).

The importance of the threat depends on the *barriers to entry* and on the strength of reaction that the potential entrant can expect. Possible barriers to entry are as follows:

- *Economies of scale*, which force the entrant to operate on a large scale or risk having to bear cost disadvantage.

- *Legal protection* obtained through patents, as we have seen in the case of the conflict between Kodak and Polaroïd.

- *Product differentiation* and brand image, leading to a high degree of loyalty among existing customers who show little sensitivity to newcomers.

- *Capital requirements*, which can be considerable, not only for production facilities but also for inventories, customer credit, advertising expenses, start-up losses, etc.

- *Switching costs*, that is, one-time real or psychological costs that the buyer must bear to switch from an established supplier's product to that of a new entrant.

- *Access to distribution channels*, as distributors might be reluctant to give shelf space to a new product; sometimes the new entrant is forced to create an entirely new distribution channel.

- *Experience effects* and the cost advantage held by the incumbent, which can be very substantial, especially in high labour-intensive industries.

Other factors which may influence the entrant's degree of determination are the expectation of sharp reactions from existing firms and of the dissuasive nature of the retaliations they may organize. The following factors will in particular influence the degree of deterrence in the response:

- A history and reputation of aggressiveness *vis-à-vis* new entrants.

- Degree of commitment of established firms in the product market.

- Availability of substantial resources to fight back.

- Possibility of retaliation in the entrant's home market.

Put together, sustainable entry barriers and the ability to respond are the elements that determine the entry deterring price.

9.2.2 Threat of substitute products

Substitute products are products that can perform the same function for the same customer groups, but are based on different technologies. Referring back to the distinctions made in Chapter 6, substitute products go hand in hand with the definition of a market which is the 'set of all technologies for a given function and a given customer group'. Such products are a permanent threat because a substitution is always possible. The threat can be intensified, for instance, as a result of a technological change which modifies the substitute's quality/price as compared to the reference product market. For example, the price decline in the microcomputer market has helped to stimulate the development of electronic communication at the expense of traditional typographic equipment. Desktop publishing is taking over and many documents are no longer printed on paper.

Prices of substitute products impose a ceiling on the price firms in the product market can charge. The more attractive the price-performance alternative offered by substitutes, the stronger the limit on the industry's ability to raise prices (Porter, 1982, p. 25). This phenomenon is observable, for instance, in the market of primary energy sources. The successive increases of oil prices has stimulated the development of alternative energy resources like solar and nuclear energy.

Clearly, substitute products that deserve particular attention are those that are subject to trends improving their price-performance trade-off with the industry's product. Moreover, in such a comparison, special attention needs to be given to switching costs (real or psychological) which can be very high and, as far as the buyer is concerned, offset the impact of the price differential.

Identifying substitute products is not always straightforward. The aim is to search systematically for products that meet the same generic need or perform the same function. This can sometimes lead to industries far removed from the main industry. It would be insufficient simply to look at the uses made in the major customer groups, because that information may appear too late. Therefore, it is necessary to have a permanent monitoring system of major technological developments in order to be able to adopt a proactive rather than a reactive behaviour.

9.2.3 Bargaining power of buyers

Buyers have a bargaining power *vis-à-vis* their suppliers. They can influence an activity's potential profitability by forcing the firm to cut prices, demanding more extensive services, better credit facilities or even by playing one competitor against another. The degree of influence depends on a number of conditions (Porter, 1980, pp. 24–7):

- The buyer group is concentrated and purchases *large volumes* relative to seller sales; this is so for large distributors and large shopping centres.

- The products that buyers purchase from the industry represent a significant fraction of their *own costs*, which drives them to bargain hard.

- The products purchased are standard or *undifferentiated*. Buyers are sure that they can always find alternative suppliers.

- The buyers' *switching costs*, or costs of changing suppliers, are few.

- Buyers pose a credible threat of *backward integration*, and are therefore dangerous potential entrants.

- The buyers have *full information* about demand, actual market prices and even supplier costs.

These conditions apply equally to consumer goods as well as industrial goods; they also apply to retailers as against wholesalers, and to wholesalers as against manufacturers. Such a situation, where buyers' bargaining power is very high, is seen in Belgium and France in the food sector, where large-scale distribution is highly concentrated and can even dictate its terms to manufacturers (Messinger and Chakranarthi, 1982).

These considerations underline the fact that the choice of buyer groups to whom to sell is a crucial strategic decision. A firm can improve its competitive position by a *customer selection policy*, whereby it has a well-balanced portfolio of customers and thus avoids any kind of dependence on the buyer group.

9.2.4 Bargaining power of suppliers

Suppliers can exert bargaining power because they can raise the prices of their deliveries, reduce product quality or limit quantities sold to a particular buyer. Powerful suppliers can thereby squeeze profitability out of an industry unable to recover cost increases in its own prices. For instance, the increase in the price of basic steel products, imposed in Europe between 1980 and 1982 by the Davignon plan, contributed to profit erosion in the downstream steel transformation sector. Intense competition prevented firms in this sector from raising their prices.

The conditions that make suppliers powerful are similar to those that make buyers powerful (Porter, 1980, pp. 27–9).

- The supplier group is dominated by a few companies and is more concentrated than the industry it sells to.

- It is not facing other substitute products for sale to the industry.

- The firm is not an important customer of the supplier.

- The supplier's product is an important input to the buyer's business.

- The supplier group has differentiated its products or has built up switching costs to lock the buyers.

- The supplier group poses a credible threat of forward integration.

Note that the labour force used in a firm must also be recognized as a supplier. As such, and according to its degree of organization and unionization, labour exercises a significant bargaining power that can greatly affect potential profits in an industry.

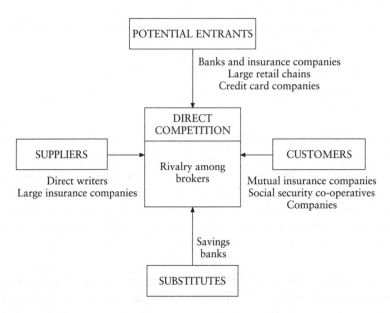

FIGURE 9.3 *An example of competition analysis: the market for private insurance brokers*
(Source: *MDA Consulting Group, Brussels*)

These four factors of external competition, together with rivalry among existing firms within the same product market, determine a firm's potential profitability and market power.

By way of illustration, the results of a competitive structure analysis in the private insurance brokerage market is presented in Fig. 9.3.

9.3 ACHIEVING COMPETITIVE ADVANTAGE THROUGH MARKET POWER

The intensity and form of the competitive struggle between direct rivals in a product market varies according to the nature of the actual competitive structure. This defines the degree of interdependence between rivals and the extent of market power held by each competitor. To analyse a particular market situation, it is convenient to refer to the various competitive structures proposed by economists, for which numerous theoretical and empirical studies exist. Four competitive structures are generally distinguished: pure (or perfect) competition, oligopoly, monopolistic (or imperfect) competition and monopoly. We shall examine each of these alternatives successively and underline the expected competitive behaviour in each case.

9.3.1 Pure or perfect competition

Perfect competition is characterized by the existence in the market of a large number of sellers facing a large number of buyers. Neither of the two groups is powerful enough to influence prices. Products have clearly defined technical characteristics, are perfect substitutes and sell at the market price, which is strictly determined by the interplay between supply and demand. In this kind of market, sellers have no market power whatsoever, and their behaviour is not affected by their respective actions. Key features are therefore the following:

■ Large number of sellers and buyers.

■ Undifferentiated and perfectly substitutable products.

■ Complete absence of market power for each player.

This kind of situation can be seen in industrial markets for unbranded products, and in the 'commodities' market, such as soft commodities and the minerals and metals market. These are normally organized markets (terminal markets) such as the London Metal Exchange (LME) or the various commodity futures exchange.

In a perfectly competitive market, the interplay between supply and demand is the determinant factor. As far as the firm is concerned, price is given and the quantity supplied is the variable of interest. The demand function is therefore an inverse function of the form

$$P = f(Q)$$

where the market price, P, is the dependent variable and the quantity, Q, is the independent variable.

To improve performance, the firm's only possible courses of action are either to modify its deliveries to the market, or to change its production capacity upward or downward, depending on the market price. In the short term, it is essential for the firm to keep an eye on competitors' production levels and on new entrants in order to anticipate price movements.

In the long term, it is clearly in the firm's interest to release itself from the anonymity of perfect competition by differentiating its products to reduce substitutability, or by creating switching costs to the buyers in order to create some form of loyalty. One way of achieving this, for example, is to exercise strict quality control accompanied by a branding policy. A number of countries exporting food products follow this kind of strategy to maintain their product's price and demand levels: Columbian coffee, Spanish oranges, Cape fruits and Swedish steel are attempts at this type of differentiation.

Another way is to develop, downstream in the industrial chain, higher added value activities incorporating the commodity, with the objectives of stabilizing the level of demand and gaining protection from wild price fluctuations.

9.3.2 Oligopoly

Oligopoly is a situation where the number of competitors is low or a few firms are dominant. As a result, rival firms are highly interdependent. In markets concentrated in this way, each firm knows well the forces at work and the actions of one firm are felt by the others, who are inclined to react. Therefore, the outcome of a strategic action depends largely on whether or not competing firms react. Box 9.1 describes the notion of reaction elasticity, which measures the force of the reaction.

BOX 9.1

Reaction elasticity defined

Reaction elasticities measure the intensity of competitive reaction to a decision taken by a rival firm. If we denote by 'i' the firm initiating the change, and by 'r' the reacting firm, we obtain the following function:

$$M_{r,t} = f(M_{i,t})$$

where M is a marketing variable and t is the period. This function assumes an instantaneous reaction, which is more likely to occur in the case of price modifications than for non-price variables, where an adjustment period is necessary, for instance, for quality change, creation of a new advertising campaign, etc.

In the general case, we have

$$M_{r,t} = f(M_{i,t-k})$$

The reaction elasticity is defined as

$$\varepsilon_{r,i} = \frac{\% \text{ of variation of } M_r}{\% \text{ of variation of } M_i}$$

The interpretation of the order of magnitude of a reaction elasticity is straightforward.

- An elasticity close to 0 implies a lack of reaction from rivals, and we have independent competitive behaviour.
- An elasticity between 0.20 and 0.80 implies a partial adaptation.
- An elasticity between 0.80 and 1.00 implies a quasi-full adjustment.
- An elasticity larger than 1 reveals an escalation strategy or over-reaction among rivals.

Retaliation strategies can be complex and based on different marketing factors (direct versus indirect reaction) or based on a single or several marketing variables (simple versus multiple reactions).

Source: Lambin and Peeters (1977).

The more undifferentiated the products of existing firms, the greater will be the dependence between them; in this case we talk about *undifferentiated oligopoly*, as opposed to *differentiated oligopoly*, where goods have significant distinctive qualities of value to the buyers. Oligopolistic situations tend to prevail in product markets having reached the maturity phase of their life cycle, where total demand is stagnant and non-expansible.

The mechanisms of a price war

In undifferentiated oligopoly, products are perceived as 'commodities' and buyers' choices are mainly based on price and the service rendered. These conditions are therefore ripe for intense price competition, unless a dominant firm can impose a discipline and force a leading price. This

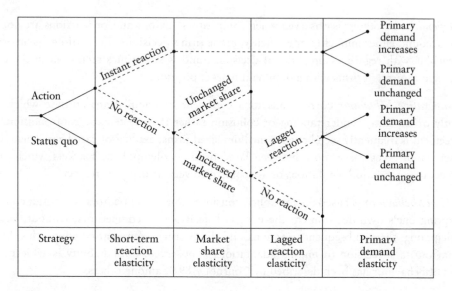

FIGURE 9.4 *Structuring a reaction strategy (Source: Lambin and Peeters, 1977, p. 282)*

situation is one of *price leadership*, in which the dominant firm's price is the reference price used by all competitors. On the other hand, if price competition does develop, it generally leads to reduced profitability for everyone, especially if total demand is non-expansible. A *price war* then develops, as follows:

1. A price cut initiated by one firm creates an important market share movement due to buyers attracted by the reduced price.
2. The firm's market share increases. Other firms feel this immediately, given that their own shares drop. They begin to adopt the same price cut to overturn the movement.
3. Price equality between rivals is restored, but at a lower level, which is less profitable for all.
4. Since total demand is non-expansible, the price cut has not contributed to increasing the market size.

Lack of co-operation or discipline causes everyone's situation to deteriorate. The decision tree in Fig. 9.4 describes the sequence of actions and reactions, as well as the main demand concepts involved at each mode.

In a non-expansible market, competition becomes a *zero sum game*. Firms seeking to increase sales can only achieve that at the expense of direct competitors. As a result, competition is more aggressive than when there is growth, where each firm has the possibility of increasing its sales by simply growing at the same pace as total demand—that is, with constant market share.

Alternative competitive behaviours

In a stagnant oligopolistic market, explicit consideration of competitors' behaviour is an essential aspect of strategy development. *Competitive behaviour* refers to the attitude adopted by a firm in its decision-making process with regard to its competitors' actions and reactions. The attitudes observed in practice can be classified into five typical categories.

- *Independent behaviour* is observed when competitors' actions and/or reactions are not taken into account, either implicitly or explicitly, in the firm's decisions. This attitude is observed in particular with regard to operational decisions, and is sometimes seen even in the case of strategic choices, in firms with a dominant market position.

- *Co-operative behaviour* corresponds to a confident or complaisant attitude which seeks, tacitly or explicitly, understanding or collusion rather than systematic confrontation. Tacit agreement is frequently seen between medium-sized firms; explicit or cartel agreement, on the other hand, takes place more between large firms in oligopolistic markets which are not subject to competition regulations or are controlled very little in this respect.

- *Follower behaviour* is based on an explicit consideration of competitors' actions; it consists of adapting one's own decisions to the observed decisions of competitors, without, however, anticipating their subsequent reactions. If all existing competitors adopt this kind of behaviour, a succession of mutual adaptations is observed, until stability is achieved. This kind of behaviour has been described by Cournot (1897), among others.

- *Leader behaviour* is more sophisticated. It consists of anticipating competitors' reactions to the firm's own decisions, assuming they have the previous type of behaviour; here, the firm is assumed to know its rivals' reaction function and to incorporate it when elaborating its strategy. As strategic marketing develops, it is seen ever more frequently in oligopolistic markets, where competition laws are strictly enforced.

- *Aggressive or warfare behaviour* also consists of anticipating competitors' reactions to the firm's decisions. But in this case, rivals' behaviour is assumed to be such that they always adopt the strategy most harmful to the adversaries. This type of behaviour is mainly observed in oligopolistic markets where total demand is stagnant and any one firm's gains must be at the expense of the others. This kind of situation is analysed in game theory as a 'zero sum' game, with the optimal strategy being the one with the lowest risk of loss.

The most frequent behaviours in undifferentiated oligopoly are of the follower or leader kind. It is, however, not rare to observe aggressive behaviours of the kind described in game theory, especially as regards price decisions, with the risk of leading to price wars which are generally harmful to all.

Marketing warfare

In industrialized economies, oligopolistic situations are frequent. In many industrial sectors, firms face each other with weakly differentiated products, in stagnant and saturated markets, where one firm's gains are necessarily another's losses. A key factor of success is thwarting competitors' actions. This kind of competitive climate obviously breeds the adoption of *marketing warfare*, which puts the destruction of the adversary at the centre of preoccupations. Kotler and Singh (1981), Ries and Trout (1986), and Durö and Sandström (1988) have taken the analogy with military strategy even further and proposed various typologies of competitive strategies directly inspired from von Clausewitz (1908). As put by Ries and Trout (1986, p. 7): 'The true nature of marketing is not serving the customer, it is outwitting, outflanking and outfighting your competitors.'

TABLE 9.1 *Competitive reaction matrix*

Brand A actions	Competing Brand B's reactions		
	Price (*p*)	Advertising (*a*)	Quality (*x*)
Price	$\varepsilon_{p,p}$*	$\varepsilon_{p,a}$	$\varepsilon_{p,x}$
Advertising	$\varepsilon_{a,p}$	$\varepsilon_{a,a}$	$\varepsilon_{a,x}$
Quality	$\varepsilon_{x,p}$	$\varepsilon_{x,a}$	$\varepsilon_{x,x}$

*The first subscript is for the brand initiating the move; the second for the rival's response.
Source: Lambin (1976, p. 24).

This point of view is in conflict with the market-driven orientation, which suggests that a balance should be maintained between customer and competitor orientations. What is the advantage of beating competitors in products that the customer does not want?

Competitive reaction matrix

Firms compete with one another by emphasizing different elements of the marketing mix and by insisting differently on each component of the mix. The competitive reaction matrix presented in Table 9.1 is a useful instrument for analysing alternative action–reaction patterns among two competing companies (Lambin, 1976, pp. 22–7). The matrix might include two brands—the studied brand and its priority competitor—and three or four components of the marketing mix, such as price, media advertising, promotion or product quality.

In Table 9.1, the horizontal rows designate the actions initiated by our brand A. The alternative actions might be to cut price, increase advertising or improve quality. The responses of brand B, the direct competitor, are represented by the vertical columns. The coefficients in the matrix are the reaction elasticities or the probabilities of brand B reacting to brand A's move. A definition of reaction elasticity can be found in Box 9.1.

On the one hand, we have the *direct reaction elasticities*, or the likelihood of brand B responding to a move by brand A with the same marketing instrument, i.e. meeting a price cut with a price cut. On the other, we have the *indirect reaction elasticities*, or the probabilities of brand B responding to brand A with another marketing instrument, for example, meeting a price cut with increased advertising. These reaction elasticities can be estimated by reference to past behaviour or by seeking management's judgement concerning the strengths and weaknesses of competition. Once the matrix is developed, management can review each potential marketing action in the light of probable competitor reactions.

The entries of the matrix can also be probabilities. In this case, their horizontal sum must be equal to 1. For example, if management considers that there is a 70 per cent chance that competition will meet a price cut, but only a 20 per cent chance that it will meet a quality increase, it might consider that a quality increase programme will help more to develop a unique marketing approach than the price cut, since it is less likely to be imitated.

The competitive matrix is useful in helping to develop a distinctive marketing approach of the market and to anticipate competitors' reactions. More columns can be added representing other marketing instruments. Delayed responses can also be analysed. For an example of an application in the electric razor market, see Lambin *et al.* (1975).

Competitor analysis system

The attitude to be adopted towards competitors is central to any strategy. This attitude must be based on a refined analysis of competitors. Porter (1980, p. 47) describes the purpose of analysing competitors as follows:

> The objective of a competitor analysis is to develop a profile of the nature and success of the likely strategy changes each competitor might make, each competitor's probable response to the range of feasible strategic moves other firms could initiate, and each competitor's probable reaction to the array of industry changes and broader environmental shifts that might occur.

There are four areas of interest which constitute the structure to guide the collection and analysis of information about competitors. The relevant questions are:

- What are the competitors' major objectives?

- What is the current strategy being employed to achieve the objectives?

- What are the capabilities of rivals to implement their strategies?

- What are their likely future strategies?

The first three parts of the analysis form the background data needed to predict the future strategies. Together, these four areas of information collection and analysis compose an almost complete report of the competitors' activities.

Some companies have discovered the importance of competitor analysis; for example:

- IBM has a commercial analysis department with thousands of branch office representatives responsible for reporting information about the competition.

- Texas Instruments has a section that analyses government contracts won by competitors to discern their technological strengths.

- Citicorp has an executive with the title 'manager of competitive intelligence'.

- McDonalds distributes a Burger King and Wendy's Competitive Action Package to its store managers.

Strong competitive interdependence in a product market is not very attractive, because it limits the firm's freedom of action. To escape it, the firm can either try to differentiate itself from rivals, or seek new product markets through creative market segmentation.

9.3.3 Imperfect or monopolistic competition

Monopolistic competition is halfway between competition and monopoly (Chamberlin, 1950). There are many competitors whose market powers are evenly distributed, but their products are differentiated in the sense that, from the buyer's point of view, they possess significantly distinct characteristics and are perceived as such by the whole product market. Differentiation may take different forms: for example, the taste of a drink, a particular technical characteristic, an innovative combination of features which provides the possibility of a variety of different uses, quality and extent of customer services, the distribution channel, power of brand image, etc. Monopolistic competition is therefore founded on a *differentiation* strategy based on external competitive advantage.

Conditions for successful differentiation

For a differentiation strategy to be successful, a number of conditions need to be present:

- The differentiation should provide something that is *unique*, beyond simply offering a low price.

- The element of uniqueness must represent some *value* to buyers.

- This value can either represent a better *performance* (higher satisfaction) or reduced *cost*.

- The value to buyers must be high enough for them to be prepared to pay a *price premium* to benefit from it.

- The element of differentiation must be *sustainable*; in other words, other rivals should not be able to imitate it immediately.

- The price premium paid by buyers must exceed the *cost supplement* borne by the firm to produce and maintain the element of differentiation.

- Finally, insofar as the element of differentiation is not very apparent and is unknown by the market, the firm must produce *signals* to make it known.

The effect of differentiation is to give the firm some degree of market power, because it generates preferences, customer loyalty and weaker price sensitivity. The buyer's bargaining power is thus partially neutralized. Differentiation also protects the firm from rival attacks, given that, as a result of the element of differentiation, substitution between products is reduced. The monopolistic firm is relatively independent in its actions *vis-à-vis* its rivals. Finally, it also helps the firm to defend itself better against suppliers and substitute products. This is the typical competitive situation that strategic marketing seeks to create.

In monopolistic competition, the firm offers a differentiated product and thus holds an external competitive advantage. This 'market power' places it in a protected position, and allows the firm to earn profits above the market average. Its strategic aim is therefore to exploit this preferential demand, while keeping an eye on the value and duration of the element of differentiation.

Measuring market power

The degree of market power is measured by the firm's ability to dictate a price above that of its priority competitors. One measure of this sensitivity is the price elasticity of the firm's or differentiated product's selective demand. The lower this demand elasticity, the less volatile or sensitive will market share be to a price increase.

> If brand A has price elasticity equal to -1.5 and brand B an elasticity of -3.0; the same price increase of 5 per cent will lower demand for A by 7.5 per cent and demand for B by 15 per cent.

Therefore, a firm or brand with market power has a less elastic demand than a poorly differentiated product. As a result, it is in a position to make the group of buyers or consumers who are sensitive to the element of differentiation accept a higher price. In fact, economic theory shows that the less elastic (in absolute value) the demand for a product, the higher is the optimal price, that is the price that maximizes profits. If we know the elasticity, the optimal price can be calculated as follows:

$$P_{opt} = C[\varepsilon/(1 + \varepsilon)]$$

or

$$\text{Optimal price} = \text{Unit direct cost} \times \text{Cost mark-up}$$

where

$$\text{Cost mark-up} = \text{Price elasticity} / (1 + \text{Price elasticity})$$

Thus, the optimal price is obtained by multiplying the unit variable cost (marginal cost) by a percentage which depends on the price elasticity and is independent of costs. The derivation of this optimization rule is presented in Appendix 9.1.

Table 9.2 shows that the optimal cost mark-up is higher when price elasticity is lower in absolute value, i.e. closer to unity, and gives some comparisons of mark-up coefficients corresponding to given price elasticities. When price elasticity is high, which is the case in highly competitive markets of undifferentiated products, mark-up is close to unity; the firm's market power is weak and the price accepted by the market is close to unit costs. Conversely, the closer elasticity is to unity, the higher is the price acceptable by the market.

To illustrate, Table 9.3 presents estimated price elasticities for six brands of a feminine hygiene product, as well as the mark-up on unit costs that each brand could adopt when calculating the optimal price. A measure of market power is obtained by calculating the ratio of the brand's mark-up to the average mark-up observed in the market.

TABLE 9.2 *Optimal cost mark-up as a function of price elasticity*

Price elasticity $\lvert \varepsilon_{qp} \rvert$	Optimal cost mark-up $\varepsilon_{qp}/(1 + \varepsilon_{qp})$	Price elasticity ε_{qp}	Optimal cost mark-up $\varepsilon_{qp}/(1 + \varepsilon_{qp})$
1.0	–	2.4	1.71
1.2	6.00	2.6	1.00
1.4	3.50	–	–
1.6	2.67	3.0	1.50
1.8	2.22	4.0	1.33
2.0	2.00	5.0	1.25
2.2	1.83	–	–
–	–	15.0	1.07

TABLE 9.3 *Measuring brand market power: The market of feminine hygiene products*

Brands	Estimated price elasticity	Implied optimal cost mark-up	Indicator of market power
Brand A	−1.351	3.849	1.334
Brand B	−1.849	2.178	0.755
Brand C	−1.715	2.399	0.832
Brand D	−1.624	2.603	0.902
Brand E	−1.326	4.067	1.410
Brand F	−1.825	2.212	0.767
Average	−1.615	2.885	–

Source: Lambin (1983).

Price elasticity coefficients can be estimated either by experimentation (field or laboratory), by survey research or on the basis of time series data by an econometric method.

The value chain in differentiation analysis

In the search of a source uniqueness on which to base a differentiation strategy, two pitfalls should be avoided: (a) identifying elements of uniqueness that customers value but the firm is incapable of supplying; (b) identifying elements of uniqueness that the firm is able to supply but are not valued by customers. For this purpose the value chain model (Porter, 1985) provides a particularly useful framework.

Every firm is a collection of activities that are performed to design, produce, market, deliver and support its products. As shown in Fig. 9.5, these activities can be divided into two broad types: *primary activities* and *support activities*. A value chain is constructed for a particular firm on the basis of the importance and of the separateness of different activities and also on the basis of their capacity for creating differentiation.

FIGURE 9.5 *The generic value chain model (Source: Porter, 1985, p. 37)*

By way of illustration, representative sources of differentiation for primary activities could be:

- *Purchasing*: quality and reliability of components and materials.
- *Operations*: fast manufacturing, defect-free manufacturing, ability to produce to customer specifications, etc.
- *Warehousing and distribution*: fast delivery, efficient order processing, sufficient inventories to meet unexpected orders, etc.
- *Sales and marketing*: high advertising level and quality, high salesforce coverage and quality, extensive credit to buyers, etc.
- *Customer service*: in-use assistance, training for customers, fast and reliable repairs, etc.

Similarly, for support activities, potential sources of differentiation are:

- *Human resources*: superior training of personnel, commitment to customer service, stable workforce policies, etc.
- *Research and development*: unique product features, fast new product development, design for reliability, etc.
- *Infrastructure*: corporate reputation, responsiveness to customers' needs, etc.

The objective is to identify the drivers of uniqueness in each activity, i.e. the variables and the actions through which the firm can achieve uniqueness in relation to competitors' offerings and provide value to the buyer. The merit of the value chain model is to suggest that the search for a sustainable competitive advantage is the role of every function within the organization and not only of the marketing function.

9.3.4 Monopoly

This type of competitive structure is a limiting case, as for perfect competition. The market is dominated by a single producer facing a large number of buyers. Its product therefore, for a limited period of time, has no direct competitor in its category. This kind of situation is observed in the introductory stage of a product's life cycle, namely in emerging industries characterized by high technology innovations.

If monopoly exists, the firm has a market power which in principle is substantial. In reality, this power is rapidly threatened by new entrants who are attracted by the possibility of growth and profits. The foreseeable duration of monopoly then becomes an essential factor. It will depend on the innovation's power and the existence of sustainable barriers to entry. A monopoly situation is always temporary, due to the rapid diffusion of technological innovations. We saw in the previous chapter the strategic options and the risks that characterize innovation monopoly. A monopolist is also subject to competition from substitute products.

The logic of state or government monopolies is different from that of private firms. It is no longer the logic of profit, but that of public good and public service. Fulfilling these objectives in public services is difficult because there is no incentive for adopting a market orientation. On the contrary, the public or state organization favours the adoption of a self-centred or internal orientation. This is one of the reasons in favour of the policy of deregulations adopted in many European countries.

This problem is dealt with in the field of social marketing, or marketing of non-profit organizations, which has developed quite substantially over the last few years (Kotler, 1982; Bon and Louppe, 1980).

The dynamics of competition

Concluding the analysis of competitive forces, it is clear that market power and profit potential can vary widely from one market situation to another. We can thus put two limiting cases aside: in one case the profit potential is almost zero; in the other it is very high. In the first case, the following situation will be observed:

■ Entry into the product market is free.

■ Existing firms have no bargaining power against their clients and suppliers.

■ Competition is unrestrained because of the large number of rival firms.

■ Products are all similar and there are many substitutes.

This is the model of *perfect competition* which is so dear to economists. The other limiting case is where profit potential is extremely high:

■ There are powerful barriers that block entry to new competitors.

■ The firm has either no competitors or a few weak competitors.

■ Buyers cannot turn to substitute products.

■ Buyers do not have enough bargaining power to force prices down.

■ Suppliers do not have enough bargaining power to make increased costs acceptable.

This is the ideal situation for the firm that has very strong market power. Market reality is obviously somewhere between these two limits. It is the interplay of competitive forces that favours one or the other of these situations.

9.4 ACHIEVING COMPETITIVE ADVANTAGE THROUGH COST DOMINATION

Gaining market power through successful product differentiation is one way to obtain a competitive advantage. Another way is to achieve cost domination *vis-à-vis* competition through better productivity and cost controls. Cost reductions can be achieved in many ways. In many industries, where the value added to the product accounts for a large percentage of the total cost, it has been observed that there is an opportunity to lower costs as a firm gains experience in producing a product.

The observation that there exist *experience effects* was made by Wright (1936) and the Boston Consulting Group (1968) who, towards the end of the 1960s, verified the existence of such an effect for more than 2000 different products, and deduced a law known as the *experience law*. This law, which has had great influence on the strategies adopted by some firms, translates and formalizes at the firm level what economists study at the aggregate level: improvements in productivity. We shall first present the theoretical foundations of the experience law, then discuss its strategic implications.

9.4.1 The experience law defined

The strategic importance of the experience law stems from the fact that it makes it possible not only to forecast one's own costs, but also to forecast competitors' costs. The law of experience stipulates that:

> The unit cost of value added to a standard product, measured in constant currency, declines by a constant percentage each time the accumulated production doubles.

A certain number of points in this definition deserve further comment:

- The word 'experience' has a very precise meaning: it designates the *cumulative number of units produced* and not the number of years since the firm began making the product.

- Thus the growth of production per period must not be confused with the growth of experience. Experience grows even if production stagnates or declines.

- The experience law is a *statistical law* and not a natural law; it is an observation that is statistically verified in some situations, but not always. Costs do not spontaneously go down; they go down if someone reduces them through productivity improvements.

- Costs must be measured in *constant monetary units*, that is, they must be adjusted for inflation, which can hide the experience effect.

■ The experience effect is always stronger during the *launching and growth stages* of a new product's development cycle. Later improvements are proportionally weaker as the product market reaches maturity.

■ The experience law applies only to *value added costs*, that is, costs over which the firm has some control, such as costs of transformation, assembly, distribution and service. Recall that value added is equal to selling price minus input costs: the cost of value added is given by unit cost minus input costs.

In practice, total unit cost is often used as the basis of observation of experience effects, especially because it is more easily accessible than value added costs. The error introduced in this way is not too high when the cost of value added represents a large proportion of the total unit cost.

Causes of experience effects

Several factors contribute to drive unit costs down the experience curve (Fig. 9.6). They are the improvements adopted by management in the production process as a result of learning from accumulated output. Abell and Hammond (1979, pp. 112–13) have identified six sources of experience effects:

1. *Labour efficiency*. As workers repeat a particular task, they become more dextrous and learn improvements and short-cuts which increase their efficiency.
2. *Work specialization and method improvements*. Specialization increases worker proficiency at a given task.
3. *New production processes*. Process innovations and improvements can be an important source of cost reductions, such as the introduction of robotics or of computer-assisted systems.
4. *Better performance from production equipment*. When first designed, a piece of production equipment may have a conservatively rated output. Experience may reveal innovative ways of increasing its output.
5. *Changes in the resource mix*. As experience accumulates, a producer can often incorporate different or less expensive resources in the operation. For instance, less skilled workers can replace skilled workers, or automation can replace labour.
6. *Product redesign*. Once the firm has a clear understanding of the performance requirements, a product can be redesigned to incorporate less costly materials and resources.

These factors are all under the control of the firm. They are part of the general policy of the firm for productivity improvements aiming at making an equivalent product for less cost or at making a better product for the same cost, or a combination of the two. Thus experience *per se* does not generate cost reductions, but rather provides *opportunities for cost reductions*. It is the task of management to exploit these opportunities.

To what extent are experience effects different from *scale effects*? Scale effects are different from experience effects, even if in practice it is difficult to separate them. Two major differences exist:

- Scale effects arise from the size of the operation, while experience effects accrue over time. The time dimension is what makes them different. Confusion between the two effects arises because size increases as experience accumulates.

- Cost advantages due to size always exist: fixed costs are divided by a larger number of units, thereby diminishing the unit cost. Cost advantages due to experience do not occur naturally: they are the result of concerted efforts to diminish costs.

Thus, scale effects can exist as a consequence of experience effects. For instance, the cost of capital (relative to that of its competitors) should decline as the firm gets bigger and gains access to more and cheaper sources of capital. But scale effects can also exist independently of experience effects and vice versa.

The mathematics of experience curves

The mathematical expression for the experience curve is as follows:

$$C_p = C_b(Q_p/Q_b)^{-\varepsilon}$$

where C_p is the projected unit cost, C_b is the base unit cost, Q is experience (the cumulated volume of production) and ε is a constant (unit cost elasticity). Thus we have

$$\text{Projected cost} = \text{Base cost} \times \left(\frac{\text{Projected experience}}{\text{Base experience}}\right)^{-\varepsilon}$$

The cost elasticity (ε) can be estimated as follows:

$$\frac{C_p}{C_b} = \left(\frac{Q_p}{Q_b}\right)^{-\varepsilon}$$

and hence

$$\varepsilon = \frac{\log C_p - \log C_b}{\log Q_p - \log Q_b}$$

In practice, it is convenient to refer to a doubling of experience. When the ratio of projected experience to base experience is equal to 2, i.e. $Q_p/Q_b = 2$, we obtain

$$\frac{C_p}{C_b} = 2^{-\varepsilon}$$

where $2^{-\varepsilon}$ is defined as lambda (λ), the *slope of the experience curve*. If, in the above equation, ε is 0.515, then λ is equal to 0.70 and C_p will be equal to 0.70(C_b); that is, the projected cost of the future unit of output C_p, when cumulative experience doubles, will be equal to 70 per cent of the base cost, C_b.

TABLE 9.4 *Relationship between ε and λ*

Slope of experience (λ)	1.00	0.95	0.90	0.85	0.80	0.75	0.70
Unit cost elasticity (ε)	0	0.074	0.152	0.234	0.322	0.450	0.515

Thus, the experience curve slope, λ, measures the percentage reduction in costs compared to the base value. Table 9.4 shows the relationship between ε, the unit cost elasticity, and λ, the experience curve slope, for values of λ ranging from 70 to 100 per cent.

In Fig. 9.6, we can see that, in any currency, the cost of the first unit is 100 and that of the second is 70. When the cumulative quantity has doubled from 1 to 2, unit cost has decreased by 30 per cent; the cost of the fourth unit will therefore be 49, the cost of the eighth unit 34.3, of the sixteenth 24.0, etc. In this example, the rate of cost decline is 30 per cent for each doubling, and the experience slope is 70 per cent. This corresponds to a cost elasticity of -0.515.

Often, the co-ordinates of an experience curve are expressed on a logarithmic scale, in order to represent it as a straight line. The larger the slope of the curve, the steeper the straight line. Experience slopes observed in practice lie between 0.70 (high degree of experience effect) and 1.00 (zero experience effect). The Boston Consulting Group observes that most experience curves have slopes between 70 and 80 per cent.

> A review of 190 experience curve analyses has shown that experience curve slopes vary from one industry to the other; in the automobile industry, the cost reduction rate was 12%, 15% for colour television, 20% for steel and related industries, 40 to 50% for semi-conductors and integrated circuits. (Thompson, 1981, p. 64)

For a given firm, the impact of experience effects depends not only on its experience slope, but also on the speed at which experience accumulates. The possibility of reducing costs will be higher in sectors which have rapidly growing markets; similarly, for a given firm, the potential

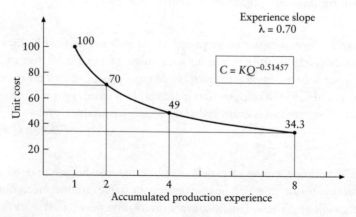

FIGURE 9.6 *Example of an experience curve*

TABLE 9.5 *Annual percentage of cost reduction due to experience effects*

Experience curve slope	Annual market growth rate				
	2%	5%	10%	20%	30%
90%	0.3	0.7	1.4	2.7	3.9
80%	0.6	1.6	3.0	5.7	8.1
70%	1.0	2.5	4.8	9.0	12.6
60%	1.4	3.5	6.8	12.6	17.6

for cost reduction is high if its market share increases sharply, irrespective of whether or not the reference market is expanding. The figures in Table 9.5 give expected percentage reductions in annual costs for different experience slopes and different rates of sales growth.

Statistical estimation of experience curves

The statistical estimation of experience curves is made with historical data on unit costs (sometimes on the basis of unit prices) and on cumulative quantities, which should ideally cover several doublings of cumulated volume. The analysis of different cost components should in principle be carried out separately in order to pinpoint those that are behaving differently. For each group, unit costs are considered against cumulative volume, and after logarithmic transformations a line is fitted by the method of least squares. The estimated function is then used to forecast future costs for each of the components.

Two measurement problems occur regularly in estimating experience curves: the non-availability of competitors' cost data and the choice of the experience measurement units. To overcome the first problem, average prices for the industry as a whole are used. An alternative is to accept the assumption that all players in a particular product market are driving the same experience curve, an acceptable assumption if the same technology is prevalent. As to the experience measurement unit, the total number of units produced may not always be the most appropriate basis for measuring cumulative experience.

> For instance, the experience curve phenomenon may not be readily discernible if a firm manufacturing refrigerators in various sizes ranging from 2 cubic feet to 26 cubic feet of storage space were to employ the number of units produced as a measure of cumulative experience. Cubic feet of refrigeration space may be a more appropriate measure when the experience phenomenon is examined at the aggregate product level.
>
> (Kerin *et al.*, 1990, p. 117)

The estimated experience curves are only valid if the conditions that gave rise to past observations remain stable: the firm manufactures the same product according to the same process and technology. These conditions are in reality never fully satisfied. Like many management tools, the experience law is more a tool of analysis than an accurate forecasting instrument. Nevertheless, it is of great value in analysing disparities in competitive capacity and evaluating the significance of competitive cost advantage.

9.4.2 Strategic implications of the experience law

The experience law helps to illustrate how a competitive advantage can exist based on a disparity in unit costs between rival firms operating in the same market, and using the same means of production. The strategic implications of the experience law can be summarized as follows:

■ The firm with the largest cumulated production will have the *lowest* costs if the experience effect is properly exploited.

■ The aggressive firm will try to drive down as *rapidly* as possible its experience curve, in order to build a cost advantage over its direct competitors.

■ The goal is to grow faster than priority competitors, which implies *increased* relative market share.

■ This growth objective is best achieved *at the start*, when gains in experience are most significant.

■ The most effective way of gaining market share is to adopt a *price penetration* strategy, whereby the firm fixes the price at a level that anticipates future cost reductions.

■ This strategy will give the firm *above normal* profit performance.

Thus, in an experience-based strategy, building market share and penetration pricing are the key success factors for achieving a competitive advantage based on cost domination.

Figure 9.7 illustrates the mechanism of a price penetration policy. The firm anticipates the movement of its unit cost in terms of cumulative production. It sets itself a target to reach which implies a faster sales growth than in the reference market and hence an increase in its relative market share. The selling price, when launching the product, is determined with respect to this anticipated volume. Once the level of experience has been reached, future cost decreases will be reflected in the price to maintain the advantage over priority competitors.

Assessing competitive costs disparities

If cumulative production does lead to the expected cost reduction, and if the dominant firm manages to protect the benefit of the experience it acquires, the experience effect creates an entry barrier to new entrants and a cost advantage for the leader. Firms with low market shares will inevitably have higher costs, and if they fix their prices at the same level as the dominant competitor they have to suffer heavy losses. Furthermore, the firm with the highest market share also enjoys larger cash flows. It can reinvest in new equipment or new processes and thus reinforce its leadership.

To illustrate, let us examine the data in Table 9.6. A comparison is made of movements in unit costs as a function of experience, for experience slopes equal to 70, 80 and 90 per cent respectively.

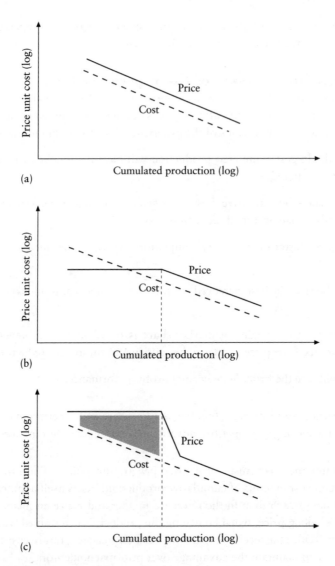

FIGURE 9.7 *Price penetration strategy*

Let us consider the case of two firms, A and B, using the same technology and having the same initial conditions; they both have an experience slope of 70 per cent. Firm A is at its first doubling of cumulative production, while firm B is at its fourth. Their costs are 70 and 24, respectively. One can imagine that it might be quite difficult for firm A to close this gap, given that it needs to increase its market share quite considerably to achieve cost parity.

Now let us assume that the two firms A and B have the same experience; they are both at their fourth doubling. However, firm A has better exploited cost reduction opportunities and is on an experience curve of 70 per cent, whereas firm B's experience curve has a slope of only 90 per cent; their unit costs are 24 against 66. Here too, it would be difficult to close the gap. Experience

TABLE 9.6 *Evolution of unit cost as a function of experience effects*

Cumulative production (× 1000)	Number of doublings	Slope of the experience curve		
		70%	80%	90%
1	–	100	100	100
2	1	70	80	90
4	2	49	64	81
8	3	34	51	73
16	4	24	41	66
32	5	17	33	59
64	6	12	26	48

effects can therefore create large disparities in costs of firms which are of equal size, but have failed to incorporate this potential equally in productivity improvements.

Experience curves as an early warning system

As mentioned above, the main usefulness of the experience curve is to assess the dynamics of cost competition between two or more firms operating in the same reference market and to alert management to the necessity of making timely strategic changes. The example of Fig. 9.8, proposed by Sallenave (1985, p. 67), illustrates this last point.

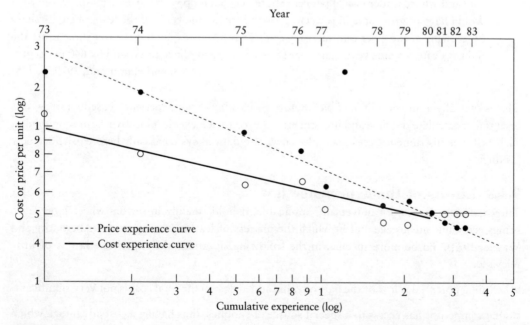

FIGURE 9.8 *The experience curve as an early warning system (Source: Sallenave, 1985)*

The chart shows the cost and experience curves of a polyester fibre manufacturer. Prices and costs are expressed in constant \$/kg. Prices declined on a 75 per cent experience curve while the slope of the cost curve was only 86 per cent. In this example, management of the plant could have predicted, years before it was too late, that the cost and price curves were converging rapidly. In 1980, the plant made no profit. Its management immediately embarked on a cost reduction programme, but at the same time demand slowed down. The plant was unable to operate at capacity level, which would have made the cost reduction programme effective. Unit costs remained unchanged. The plant closed down in 1983.

Had management read the early warning given by the experience curve analysis, it would have reacted early enough to decide between several possible remedial actions.

■ Increase the capacity of the plant to accumulate faster and drive the unit cost down.

■ Retool and/or improve the production process to operate on a 75 per cent cost slope, i.e. a slope compatible with the price slope.

■ Specialize in special-purpose fibres and sell them at a higher price than the normal price for regular polyester fibre.

■ Sell the plant while it was profitable or convert it to another production line.

Thus, the experience curves can be used to anticipate future developments and to *simulate contemplated strategies*. The simulation exercise can be very instructive, as the following example shows.

> Consider a firm with 6 per cent of a market that is growing at an 8 per cent real growth rate and whose leader has 24 per cent share. To catch up with the leader's share, our firm would have to grow at a 26 per cent growth rate in nine years, if the leader held its share by growing at the 8 per cent industry rate. That means expanding at over three times the industry rate for nine years, and that sales and capacity have to expand by 640 per cent.
>
> (Abell and Hammond, 1979, p. 118)

This is typically a 'mission impossible'. Before embarking on an experience-based strategy, it is essential to calculate the time and investment required to achieve the objective. Some companies, such as Texas Instruments, use experience curve simulations systematically before pricing a new product.

9.4.3 Limits of the experience law

The experience law is not universally applicable; it holds mainly in sectors where large scale brings economic advantage and in which the process of learning is important (Abernathy and Wayne, 1974). To be more specific, in the following situations the experience law is of little relevance:

■ Learning potential is low or the part of value added cost in the total cost is not very significant.

■ One competitor has access to a special source of supplies, thus having a cost advantage which bears no relation to its relative market share.

- Technology changes rapidly and neutralizes the experience-based cost advantage.

- The market is not price-sensitive.

- There is large potential for product differentiation.

Thus, if a firm is dominated by a competitor having a major cost advantage, two basic strategies can be adopted to circumvent the experience advantage:

- A *differentiation strategy* offering distinctive features valued by the buyer, who is ready to pay a premium price that would offset the cost handicap.

- A *technological innovation strategy* that would place the firm on a new and steeper experience curve, thereby neutralizing the cost advantage of the current market leader.

The experience law is not of general application. To avoid misuse of the experience curve theory, it is important to verify the validity of the assumptions on which the theory is based.

9.4.4 The competitive advantage matrix

A competitive advantage can be obtained in different ways, depending on the competitive structure and on the market characteristics. The Boston Consulting Group (Lochridge, 1981), which greatly contributed towards spreading the law of experience, has proposed a classification of market situations which helps in identifying the type of competitive advantage to pursue. Two classification criteria are used:

- The size of the competitive advantage.

- The number of ways of achieving competitive advantage.

One then obtains a matrix such as that presented in Table 9.7. Horizontally, we have the size of the advantage, which can be small or large. Vertically, we have the number of ways to achieve advantage, which can be few or many. To each of the quadrants corresponds a particular market situation requiring a specific strategic approach. The four types of industry are: volume, specialization, fragmented and stalemate.

Volume industries are those where sources of competitive advantage are few and where cost advantage is the major opportunity. It is typically in this market situation that experience and/or

TABLE 9.7 *The competitive advantage matrix*

Number of ways to achieve competitive advantage	Size of the competitive advantage	
	Small	Large
Many	Fragmented	Specialization
Few	Stalemate	Volume

Source: Lochridge (1981).

scale effects manifest themselves, and where a large relative market share is a precious asset. Profitability is closely related to the size of market share, as postulated by the experience curve theory.

Specialization industries are those with many ways of obtaining a sizeable competitive advantage. In these markets, the potential for differentiation is high, as is the case in situations of monopolistic competition, described earlier. Products have significant distinctive qualities from buyers' points of view, and they in turn are prepared to pay prices above those of direct competitors. In this kind of situation, the scale/experience effect brings no particular advantage. It is the value of differentiation or specialization that counts and determines profitability. Total market share has little value; it is market share in a specific segment or niche which is critical, even if the size of the niche is small.

In *fragmented industries*, sources of differentiation are many, but no firm can create a sustainable and decisive advantage over its rivals. Scale brings no significant economies and a dominant market share does not lead to lower costs. On the contrary, increased costs, linked to the complexity of the situation, limit the optimal size of the firm. Many service firms are good examples of a fragmented sector.

Large and small firms can co-exist with very different profitability. Market share has no effect, irrespective of the way it has been calculated. In this category, one can classify women's clothing, restaurants and car repair and maintenance services. In many cases, the best strategy is to transform a fragmented activity into a volume or specialized activity.

In *stalemate industries*, the ways of obtaining a competitive advantage are few, as in the case of volume industries. But unlike these, accumulated experience does not constitute a competitive advantage. On the contrary, it is sometimes the newcomers who have the most efficient tools of production, because they have the most recent investment. In situations where technology is easily available, as in the steel industry or basic chemicals, competitiveness is more dependent on the age of the investment rather than the size of the firm: the last firm to invest benefits from lowest operating costs.

We can therefore see that an experience-based strategy can in fact only be applied in commodity-based, volume-sensitive industries, in which low cost is one of the few potential sources of achieving competitive advantage.

9.5 INTERNATIONAL COMPETITIVE ADVANTAGE

International trade theory has traditionally placed the emphasis on country comparative advantages. The focus was on a country's natural endowments, its labour force, its currency values as main sources of competitiveness. Recently, economists have turned their attention to the question of how countries, governments and even private industry can alter the conditions within a country to create or reinforce the competitiveness of its firms. The leader in this area of research is Michaël Porter (1990).

> A nation's competitiveness depends on the capacity of its industry to innovate and upgrade. Companies gain advantage against the world's best competitors because of pressure and challenge. They benefit from having strong domestic rivals, aggressive home-based suppliers and demanding customers.   (Porter, 1990, p. 70)

Four broad attributes contribute to shape the environment in which local firms compete. These attributes promote or impede the creation of competitive advantage.

■ *Factor conditions*: the nation's position in factors of production such as skilled labour or infrastructure, necessary to compete in a given industry. Porter notes that although factor conditions are very important, the ability of a nation to continually create, upgrade and deploy its factors is more important, and not only the initial endowment.

■ *Demand conditions*: the nature of home demand for the industry's product or service. The quality of home demand is more important than the quantity of home demand in determining competitive advantage. By quality, Porter means a highly competitive and demanding local market.

■ *Related and supporting industries*: the presence or absence in the nation of supplier and related industries that are internationally competitive. A firm that is operating within a mass of related firms and industries gains and maintains advantages through close working relationships, proximity to suppliers, and timeliness of product and information flows.

■ *Firm strategy, structure and rivalry*: the conditions in the nation governing how companies are created, organized and managed and the nature of domestic rivalry. Porter notes that there is no operational strategy that is universally appropriate; it depends on the fit and flexibility of what works for that industry in that country at that time.

In the analysis of home demand composition, Porter identifies three home demand characteristics that are particularly significant to achieving a national competitive advantage.

1. *Large share of home demand*. A nation's firms are likely to gain competitive advantage in global segments that represent a large share of home demand but account for a less significant share in other nations. These relatively large segments receive the greatest and the earliest attention by the nation's firms, but tend to be perceived as less attractive by foreign competitors. The nation's firms may gain advantages in reaping economies of scale.

   A good example is Airbus Industries' entry into commercial airliners. Airbus identified a segment of the European market that had been ignored by Boeing: a relatively large capacity plane for short hauls. Such a need was quite significant in Europe with its numerous capital cities within short flying distances and served by few airlines, in sharp contrast with the US situation.

2. *Sophisticated and demanding buyers*. A nation's firms gain competitive advantage if domestic buyers are, or are among, the world's most sophisticated and demanding buyers for the product or service. Such buyers provide a window into the most advanced buyer needs. Demanding buyers pressure local firms to meet high standard in terms of product quality and services.

The Japanese pay great attention to writing instruments, because nearly all documents have until recently been handwritten in Japan due to the impracticality of typewriters in reproducing Japanese characters. Penmanship is an important indication of education and culture. Japanese firms have been the innovators and have become world leaders in pens.

(Porter, 1990, p. 91)

3. *Anticipatory buyer needs.* A nation's firms gain advantages if the needs of home buyers anticipate those of other nations. This means that home demand provides an early warning indicator of buyer needs that will become widespread.

Scandinavian concern for social welfare and the environment tends today to be ahead of that in the United States. Swedish and Danish firms have achieved success in a variety of industries where the heightened environmental concern anticipates foreign needs, such as in water pollution control equipment.   (Porter, 1990, p. 92)

The composition of home demand is at the root of national advantage. The effect of demand conditions on competitive advantage also depends on other parts of the 'diamond', as illustrated in Fig. 9.9. Without strong domestic rivalry, for example, rapid home market growth or a large home market may induce complacency rather than stimulate investment. Without the presence of appropriate supporting industries, firms may lack the ability to respond to demanding home

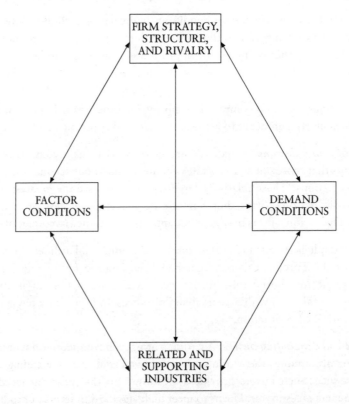

FIGURE 9.9 *The determinants of national competitive analysis (Source: Porter, 1990, p. 127)*

buyers. The 'diamond' is a system in which the role of any determinant cannot be viewed in isolation (Porter, 1990, p. 99).

SUMMARY

Competitive advantage refers to a product superiority held by the firm over its direct competitor. Competitive advantages can be classified in two main categories: external advantages based on market power due to superior value to the buyer, and internal advantages based on productivity generating a cost advantage. A firm's ability to exploit a competitive advantage depends on the strength not only of direct competition but also of other rival forces, such as potential entrants, substitute products, customers and suppliers. The intensity of direct competition varies according to the extent of market power held by each competitor. In an oligopoly, the degree of interdependence among rivals is high and explicit consideration of competitors' behaviour is an essential aspect of strategy development. In a monopolistic situation, products are differentiated in a way which represents a value to the buyer, either by reducing its cost or by improving its performance. The effect of product differentiation is to give the firm some degree of market power, customer loyalty and weaker price sensitivity. This is the typical competitive situation that strategic marketing seeks to create for the firm. Another way to get a competitive advantage is cost domination through better productivity and cost controls. In many industries, there is an opportunity to lower costs as experience increases in producing a product. The strategic importance of the experience law stems from the fact that it is possible not only to forecast one's own costs, but also to forecast competitors' costs. Porter has identified four determinants of international competitive advantage which can be used by governments or management to create a favourable context in which a nation's firms can compete.

QUESTIONS AND PROBLEMS

1. Which differences do you see between a differentiated oligopoly and a situation of monopolistic competition? More specifically, what will be the expected competitive behaviour in each case?
2. What are the reaction strategies to be contemplated by a firm leader in a market in which it is confronted with a price-cutting strategy initiated by a competitor having a very low market share?
3. Give an example of a sustainable external competitive advantage for each of the following sectors: mineral waters, fire insurance, highly specialized machine tools.
4. What type of development strategy can be adopted by a small firm dominated in its reference market by an aggressive and powerful competitor having a strong cost advantage?
5. The Springer Manufacturing Corporation is considering producing and delivering 40 units of an industrial plating machine to a new customer. The customer has indicated that the maximum feasible price for each plating machine is $5000. The average cost of building the first unit is estimated by research and development to be $8000. In the past, the company has usually operated along an experience curve of 85 per cent. Several executives believe the potential price of $5000 is to low. Prepare an analysis that answers their concern. In your

analysis show the average and the total costs and the total revenue received for the following units: 1, 2, 3, 4, 8, 16, 32, 40.

6. Try to identify the competitive threats of the competitive environment for one of the following industrial sectors: private insurance brokerage, typographic industry, television.

REFERENCES

Abell, D.E. and J.S. Hammond (1979), *Strategic Market Planning*. Englewood Cliffs, New Jersey: Prentice Hall Inc.

Abernathy, W. and K. Wayne (1974), 'The Limits of the Experience Curve', *Harvard Business Review*, vol. 52, September–October, pp. 109–19.

Bon, J. and A. Louppe (1980), *Marketing des services publics: l'étude des besoins de la population*. Paris: Les Éditions d'Organisation.

Boston Consulting Group (1968), *Perspectives on Experience*. Boston.

Chamberlin, E.H. (1950), *The Theory of Monopolistic Competition*. Cambridge, Mass.: Harvard University Press.

Cournot, A.A. (1897), *Researches into the Mathematical Principles of the Theory of Wealth*. New York: The Macmillan Co.

Durö, R. and B. Sandström (1988), *Le marketing de combat*. Paris: Les Éditions d'Organisation.

Kerin, R.A., V. Mahajan and P.R. Varadjan (1990), *Contemporary Perspectives on Strategic Market Planning*. Boston, Mass.: Allyn & Bacon.

Kotler, P. (1982), *Marketing for Non-Profit Organizations*, 2nd edn. Englewood Cliffs, NJ: Prentice-Hall International.

Kotler, P. and R. Singh (1981), 'Marketing Warfare in the 1980s', *Journal of Business Strategy*, Winter, pp. 30–41.

Lambin, J.J., P.A. Naert and A. Bultez (1975), 'Optimal Marketing Behavior in Oligopoly', *European Economic Review*, vol. 6, pp. 105–28.

Lambin, J.J. (1976), *Advertising, Competition and Market Conduct in Oligopoly over Time*. Amsterdam: North-Holland and Elsevier.

Lambin, J.J. (1983) Unpublished CESAM Working Paper. Louvain-la-Neuve: IAG.

Lambin, J.J. and R. Peeters (1977), *La gestion marketing des entreprises*. Paris: Presses Universitaires de France.

Lochridge, R.K. (1981), *Strategies in the Eighties*. The Boston Consulting Group Annual Perspective.

Messinger, P.R. and N. Chakravarthi (1995), 'Has Power Shifted in the Grocery Channel?', *Marketing Science*, vol. 14, no. 2, pp. 189–223.

Porter, M.E. (1980), *Competitive Strategy*. New York: The Free Press.

Porter, M.E. (1985), *Competitive Advantage*. New York: The Free Press.

Porter, M. (1990), *The Competitive Advantage of Nations*. London: The Macmillan Press.

Ries, A. and J. Trout (1986), *Marketing Warfare*. New York: McGraw-Hill.

Sallenave, J.P. (1985), 'The Use and Abuse of Experience Curves', *Long Range Planning*, vol. 18, January–February, pp. 64–72.

Thompson, D.H. (1981), 'The Experience Curve Effect on Costs and Prices: Implications for Public Policy', in Balderston, F.E., J.M. Carman and F.M. Nicosia (eds), *Regulation of Marketing and Public Interest*. New York: Pergamon Press.

von Clausewitz, C. (1908), *On Wars*. London: Routledge & Kegan Paul.

Wright, T.P. (1936), 'Factors Affecting the Cost of Airplanes', *Journal of Aeronautical Sciences*, vol. 3, pp. 16–24.

FURTHER READING

Carman, J.M. and E. Langeard (1980), 'Growth Strategies for Service Firms', *Strategic Management Journal*, vol. 1, pp. 7–22.

di Sciullo, J. (1993), *Le marketisme*. Paris: Les Éditions Juris Service.

Hamermesh, R.G., M.J. Anderson and J.E. Harris (1978), 'Quand les plus petits sont les plus rentables', *Harvard-L'Expansion*, Autumn.

Hax, A.C. and N.S. Majiluf (1984), *Strategic Management: An Integrative Perspective*. Englewood Cliffs, New Jersey: Prentice Hall Inc.

Kotler, P., L. Fahey and S. Jatuskripitak (1985), *The New Competition*. Englewood Cliffs, New Jersey: Prentice Hall Inc.

APPENDIX 9.1

Derivation of the Price Optimization Rule

We have the following demand function:

$$Q = Q\,(P/M, E)$$

where Q denotes quantity, P the selling price, M other marketing variables and E environmental factors. Assuming that M and E are constant, the problem is to derive the optimum price.

The profit function is as follows:

$$\pi = (P - C)Q - F$$

where π is the gross profit, C the direct unit cost and F the fixed costs specific to the activity considered.

To identify the optimum price, let us calculate the first derivative of π with respect to price and set the derivative equal to zero:

$$\frac{\delta\pi}{\delta P} = (P - C) \cdot \frac{\delta Q}{\delta P} + Q = 0$$

Multiplying each term by the ratio P/Q and rearranging terms we have

$$P(1 + \varepsilon_{qp}) = C \cdot \varepsilon_{qp}$$

which is the *marginal revenue–marginal cost equality rule* expressed by reference to price elasticity. Solving for P^*, the optimum price, we have

$$P^* = C\left(\frac{\varepsilon_{qp}}{1 + \varepsilon_{qp}}\right)$$

The *second-order condition* stipulates that the price elasticity in absolute value should be larger than 1. By way of illustration, if $\varepsilon = -2.1$ and $C = 105$, the optimum price is

$$P^* = 105 \times \left(\frac{-2.1}{1 + (-2.1)}\right) = 105 \times 1.9 = \text{FF205}$$

The optimal cost mark-up is therefore 1.9.

CHAPTER 10

FORMULATING A MARKETING STRATEGY

LEARNING OBJECTIVES

After reading this chapter, you should be able to:

■ conduct a product portfolio analysis, using either the BCG growth–share matrix or the multi-factor portfolio matrix

■ discuss the merits and limitations of these two product portfolio analysis methods

■ describe the objectives and risks associated with the choice of a specific generic strategy

■ define the different strategic options a firm can contemplate in designing a development or growth strategy

■ describe the different competitive strategies a firm can consider *vis-à-vis* its rivals and their conditions of application

■ discuss the objectives and the various forms of international development.

*T*he objective of this chapter is to examine how a market-driven firm can select the appropriate competitive strategy to achieve an above-average profit performance in the different business units included in its product portfolio. Two sets of factors determine the performance of a particular business unit: first, the overall attractiveness of the reference market in which it operates and, second, the strength of its competitive position relative to direct competition. The reference market's attractiveness is largely determined by forces outside the firm's control (see Chapter 8), while the business unit's competitiveness can be shaped by the firm's strategic choices (see Chapter 9). Product portfolio analysis relates attractiveness and competitiveness indicators to help guide strategic thinking by suggesting specific marketing strategies to achieve a balanced mix of products that will ensure growth and profit performance in the long run. In this chapter, we shall first define the conceptual bases of portfolio analysis and then describe the types of mission or objectives the firm should assign to each of its business units, given their differentiated positions along the attractiveness–competitiveness dimensions. Finally, we shall discuss the strategic alternatives open to the firm in the field of international development.

10.1 PRODUCT PORTFOLIO ANALYSES

The purpose of a product portfolio analysis is to help a multi-business firm decide how to allocate scarce resources among the product markets in which they compete. In the general case, the procedure consists in cross-classifying each activity with respect to two independent dimensions: the attractiveness of the reference market in which the firm operates, and the firm's capacity to take advantage of opportunities within that market. Various portfolio models have been developed, using matrix representations where different indicators are used to measure attractiveness and competitiveness. Here we shall concentrate on the two most representative methods: the Boston Consulting Group's method (BCG), called the 'growth–share' matrix (Boston Consulting Group, 1972; Henderson, 1970) and the 'multi-factor portfolio' matrix attributed to General Electric and McKinsey (Hussey, 1978; Abell and Hammond, 1979). Although the two methods have the same objectives, their implicit assumptions are different and the two approaches will probably yield different insights (Wind *et al.*, 1983).

10.1.1 The BCG growth–share matrix

The BCG matrix is built around two criteria: the reference market's growth rate (corrected for inflation), acting as an indicator of attractiveness, and the market share relative to the firm's largest competitor, measuring competitiveness. As shown in Fig. 10.1, we have a double entry table where a cut-off level on each axis creates a grid with four quadrants.

■ Along the 'market growth rate' axis, the cut-off point distinguishing high-growth from low-growth markets corresponds to the growth rate of the GNP in real terms, or to the (weighted) average of the predicted growth rates of the different markets in which the products compete.

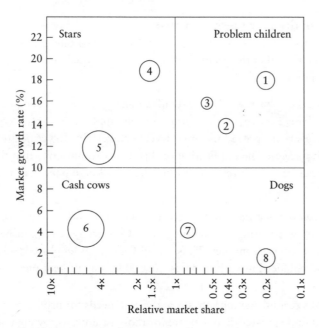

FIGURE 10.1 *The BCG growth–share matrix. (Source: Boston Consulting Group, 1972)*

In practice, high-growth markets are often defined as those growing by more than 10 per cent per year. Markets growing by less than 10 per cent are deemed to be of low growth.

■ Similarly, on the 'relative market share' axis the dividing line is usually put on 1 or 1.5. Beyond this level, relative market share is high; below, it is low.

Thus the matrix relies on the concept of relative market share to leading competitor (see Chapter 6), which calculates the ratio of unit sales for one firm with unit sales for the largest share firm. For example, if company A has a 10 per cent share of the market and the largest share belongs to company B, with 20 per cent, then company A has a relative market share of 0.5 (10/20 per cent). It has a low market share since the ratio is less than 1. Similarly, company B has a relative market share of 2 (20/10 per cent). It has a high share of the market.

The use of relative market share is based on the assumption that market share is positively correlated with experience and therefore with profitability (see Chapter 9). Therefore the competitive implications of holding a 20 per cent market share are quite different if another competitor is holding 40 per cent or only 5 per cent.

We thus obtain four different quadrants, each of which defines four fundamentally different competitive situations in terms of cash flow requirements and which need to be dealt with by specific objectives and marketing strategies.

Basic assumptions of the growth–share matrix

There are two basic assumptions underlying the BCG analysis; one concerns the existence of experience effects, and the other the product life cycle (PLC) model. These two assumptions can be summarized as follows:

■ Higher relative market share implies cost advantage over direct competitors because of experience effects; where the *experience curve concept* applies, the largest competitor will be the most profitable at the prevailing price level. Conversely, lower relative market share implies cost disadvantages. The implication of this first assumption is that the expected cash flow from products with a high relative market share will be higher than those with smaller market shares.

■ Being in a *fast-growing market* implies greater need for cash to finance growth, added production capacity, advertising expenditures, etc. Conversely, cash can be generated by a product operating in a mature market. Thus, the PLC model is employed because it highlights the desirability of a balanced mix of products situated in the different phases of the PLC.

The implication of this second assumption is that the cash needs for products in rapidly growing markets are expected to be greater than they are for those in slower growing ones.

As discussed in Chapters 8 and 9, these assumptions are not always true. On this topic, see Abell and Hammond (1979, pp. 192–3).

Defining the type of business

Keeping in mind these two key assumptions, we can identify four groups of product markets having different characteristics in terms of their cash flow needs and/or contributions:

1. *Low growth/high share or 'cash cow' products.* These products usually generate more cash than is required to sustain their market position. As such, they are a source of funds for the firm to support diversification efforts and growth in other markets. The priority strategy is to 'harvest'.
2. *Low growth/low share or 'dogs' or 'lame ducks' products.* Dogs have a low market share in a low-growth market, the least desirable market position. They generally have a cost disadvantage and few opportunities to grow, since the war is over in the market. Maintaining these products generally results in a financial drain with no hope of improvement. The priority strategy here is to 'divest' or, at least, to adopt a low profile and live modestly.
3. *High growth/low share or 'problem children' products.* In this category we find products with low relative market shares in a fast-growing market. Despite their handicap *vis-à-vis* the leader, these products still have a chance of gaining market share, since the market has not yet settled down. However, supporting these products implies a large financial commitment to finance share-building strategies and offset low profit margins. If the support is not given, these products will become dogs as market growth slows down. Thus, the alternatives here are to build market share or divest.
4. *High growth/high share or 'stars' products.* Here we have the market leaders in a rapidly growing market. The growth of these activities also requires to be heavily financed, but because of their leading position they generate significant amounts of profits to reinvest in

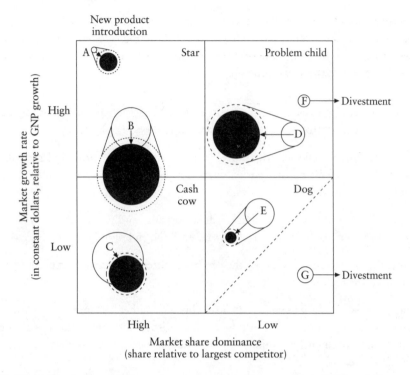

FIGURE 10.2 *Product portfolio trajectory analysis (Source: Day, 1977, p. 34)*

order to maintain their market position. As the market matures, they will progressively take over as cash cows.

Every activity can be placed in a matrix similar to that shown in Fig. 10.1. The significance of an activity can be represented by a circle of size proportional to sales volume, sales revenue or profit contribution. This analysis should be made in a dynamic way, i.e. by tracking the progression or movements of each business unit over a period of time, as illustrated in Fig. 10.2.

Diagnosing the product portfolio

In this approach, it is important to define accurately the reference market in which the activity is competing. Relative market share compares the strength of a firm relative to its competitors. If the market is defined too narrowly the firm appears as the segment leader; if it is too wide, the firm appears too weak. The following points arise from the analysis.

■ The position in the matrix indicates the *credible strategy* for each product: maintain leadership for stars; abandon or adopt a low profile for dogs; selective investment and growth for problem children; maximum profitability for cash cows.

■ The position in the matrix helps evaluate *cash* requirements and profitability potential. Profits are usually a function of competitiveness; cash requirements generally depend on the phase of the product's life cycle—that is, on the reference market's degree of development.

■ Allocation of the firm's total sales revenue or profit contribution according to each quadrant allows balancing of the product portfolio. The ideal situation is to have products that generate cash and products in their introductory or growing stage that will ensure the firm's long-term viability. The needs of the second category will be financed by the first.

Based on this type of diagnosis, the firm can envisage various strategies to maintain or restore the balance of its product portfolio. To be more specific, it allows the firm:

■ To develop *portfolio scenarios* for future years on the basis of projected growth rates and tentative decisions regarding the market share strategies for the various activities, assuming different competitive reaction strategies.

■ To analyse the potential of the existing product portfolio and predict the *total cash-flow* that can be expected from each activity, every year, until the end of its planning horizon.

■ To analyse the *strategic gap*—that is, the observed difference between expected performance and desired performance.

■ To identify the *means to be employed* to fill this gap, either by improving existing product performances, or by abandoning products that absorb too much cash with no realistic potential for improvement, or, finally, by introducing new products that will rebalance the portfolio structure.

Too many ageing products indicate a danger of decline, even if current results appear very positive. Too many new products can lead to financial problems, even if activities are quite healthy, and this type of situation inevitably risks loss of independence.

Figure 10.3 describes two successful and two unsuccessful trajectories that can be observed for new or existing business units.

■ The *innovator* trajectory, which uses the cash generated by the cash cows to invest in R&D and enter the market with a new product that will take over from existing stars.

■ The *follower* trajectory, which uses the cash generated by the cash cows to enter as a problem child in a new market, dominated by a leader, with an aggressive market share build-up strategy.

■ The *disaster* trajectory, whereby a star product evolves to the problem children quadrant as a consequence of insufficient investment in market share maintenance.

■ The *permanent mediocrity* trajectory involves a problem child product evolving to the dogs quadrant as a consequence of the failure to build market share for the product.

Let us remember that this type of diagnosis is only valid if the underlying assumptions mentioned earlier hold true. However, as already mentioned, the links between market share and profitability on the one hand and growth rate and financial requirements on the other are not always observed (see Abell and Hammond, 1979, pp. 192–3).

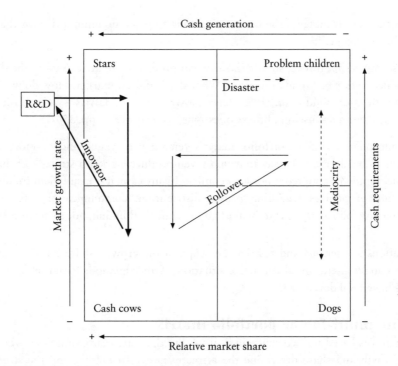

FIGURE 10.3 *Portfolio scenarios alternative*

Limitations of the growth–share matrix

The most important merit of the BCG method is undoubtedly that it provides an appealing and elegant theoretical development which establishes a clear link between strategic positioning and financial performance. It is true that the initial assumptions are restrictive, but if they are true, they allow accurate analysis and valuable recommendations. General managers can thus concentrate on the major strategic problems and analyse the implications of alternative business strategies. Furthermore, the method is based on *objective indicators* of attractiveness and competitiveness, thus reducing the risk of subjectivity. Finally, it should also be added that the matrix provides a visual, vivid and easy to comprehend synthesis of the firm's activities, thus facilitating communication.

There are, however, a number of limitations and difficulties which need to be emphasized because they reduce the generality of the approach.

■ The implicit hypothesis about the relation between relative market share and cash flows means that this technique can only be used when there is an experience effect, that is in *volume industries*, as we saw in the previous chapter (see Table 9.7). Thus the experience effect might be observed in only some product markets and not all the product markets in the firm's portfolio.

■ The method is based on the notion of 'internal' competitive advantage only and takes no account of any 'external' competitive advantage enjoyed by the firm or the brand as a result of a successful differentiation strategy. Thus, a so-called 'dog' could very well generate cash despite its cost disadvantage if the market is willing to pay a premium price for the product, given its distinctive qualities.

- Despite its simple appearance, some *measurement* problems can arise. Should the definitions of the product market be broad or narrow? What share of what market? How do we determine market growth rate? Wind *et al.* (1983) have shown that the analysis is very sensitive to the measures used. For a discussion of these questions, see Day (1977, pp. 35–7).

- The recommendations of a portfolio analysis remain very vague and at most constitute *orientations* to be clarified. To say that in a given product market a strategy of 'harvest' or 'low profile' should be adopted is not very explicit. In any case, it is insufficient for an effective determination of policies regarding prices, distribution, communication, etc. The main purpose of a portfolio analysis is to help to guide strategic thinking, not to act as a substitute.

These limitations are serious and restrict the scope of the growth–share matrix significantly, which is not equally useful in all corporate situations. Other methods based on less restrictive assumptions have been developed.

10.1.2 The multi-factor portfolio matrix

The BCG matrix is based on two single indicators, but there are many situations where factors other than growth and share determine the attractiveness of a market and the strength of a competitive position.

Clearly, a market's attractiveness can depend also on such factors as market accessibility, size, existing distribution network, structure of competition, favourable legislation, etc. For example, the market for portable computers is in principle highly attractive if we judge it by its high growth rate. There are, however, many other factors, such as rapid change in demand, expected price changes, fast rate of obsolescence, intensity of competition, etc., which make this a risky and therefore relatively less attractive market.

A firm's competitive advantage may also be the result of strong brand image or commercial organization, technological leadership, distinctive product qualities, etc., even if its market share is low relative to the major competitor. For example, when IBM introduced its personal computer in 1982, its competitiveness was very low according to the BCG matrix, since its market share was zero. Yet many analysts perceived IBM's competitive potential as very high because of its reputation in the computer market, its important technological know-how, its available resources and its will to succeed.

It is clear that several factors need to be taken into account to measure correctly the market's attractiveness and the firm's competitive potential. Instead of using a single indicator per dimension, multiple indicators can be used to assess attractiveness and competitiveness and to construct a composite index for each dimension. For an extensive list of possible factors, see Abell and Hammond (1979, p. 214). Thus, the BCG matrix described in the preceding section may be viewed as a special case of a more general theory relating market attractiveness and business competitiveness.

Development of a multi-factor portfolio grid

To illustrate, Table 10.1 presents a battery of indicators selected to measure the attractiveness of five product markets from the textile industry, as well as a series of indicators evaluating the competitiveness of the company Tissex, which operates in these five product markets.

Since each situation is different, the relevant list of factors has to be identified and a multi-factor portfolio grid is necessarily company-specific. The selection of the relevant factors is a delicate task and should involve several persons from the strategic marketing group and from other departments as well. Precise definition of each indicator must be given and the nature of the relationship should be clearly determined. Once the grid is developed, each product market is evaluated against each indicator.

- A scale of 5 points is used, with 'low', 'average' and 'high' as reference points for scores equal to 1, 3 and 5, respectively.

TABLE 10.1 *Multi-factor portfolio grid*

Indicators	Weight (100)	Weak 1	2	Moderate 3	4	Strong 5
		Evaluation scale				
Attractiveness						
Market accessibility	–	Outside Europe and USA		Europe and USA		Europe
Market growth rate	–	≤5%		5–10%		≥10%
Length of the life cycle	–	≤2 years		2–5 years		≥5 years
Gross profit potential	–	≤15%		15–25%		≥25%
Strength of competition	–	Structured oligopoly		Unstructured competition		Weak competition
Potential for differentiation	–	Very weak		Moderate		Strong
Concentration of customers	–	Very dispersed		Moderately dispersed		Concentrated
Competitiveness						
Relative market share	–	≤1/3 leader		≥1/3 leader		Leader
Unit cost	–	>Direct competitors		=Direct competitors		<Direct competitors
Distinctive qualities	–	'Me too' product		Moderately differentiated		'Unique selling proposition'
Technological know-how	–	Weak control		Moderate control		Strong control
Sales organization	–	Independent distributors		Selective distribution		Direct sales
Image	–	Very weak		Fuzzy		Strong

- As far as indicators of competitiveness are concerned, ratings are not attributed 'in abstract', but relative to the most dangerous competitor in each product market or segment.

- If some indicators appear to be more important than others, weighting can be introduced, but the weights must remain the same for every activity considered.

- The ratings should reflect, as much as possible, future or expected values of the indicators and not so much their present values.

- A summary score can then be calculated for each product market's global attractiveness and the firm's potential competitiveness.

Contrary to the BCG approach, subjective evaluations enter into these measures of attractiveness and competitiveness. But the process may nevertheless gain in interpersonal objectivity, to the extent that many judges operate independently. Their evaluations are then compared in order to reconcile or to explain observed differences and disagreements. This process of reconciliation is always useful in itself.

Interpretation of the multi-factor grid

We then obtain a two-dimensional classification grid similar to the BCG matrix. It is current practice to subdivide each dimension into three levels (low, average, high), thus forming nine squares, each corresponding to a specific strategic position.

Each zone corresponds to a specific positioning. The firm's different activities can be represented by circles with an area proportional to their share in the total sales revenue or profit contribution. The four most clearly defined positionings are those corresponding to the four corners of the matrix in Fig. 10.4.

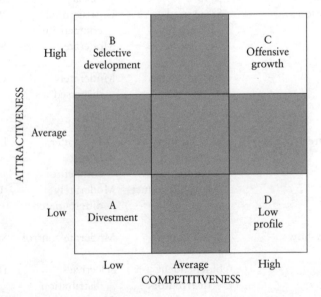

FIGURE 10.4 *Multi-factor portfolio grid*

■ In quadrant C, both the product market's attractiveness and the firm's competitive potential are high; the strategic orientation to follow is *offensive growth*. The characteristics are similar to those of 'stars' in the BCG matrix.

■ In quadrant A, both attractiveness and competitiveness are low; strategic orientation is *maintenance without investment* or *divestment*. We have the case of 'dogs' of Fig. 10.1.

■ Quadrant B depicts an intermediate situation: competitive advantage is low, but the reference market's attraction is high. This is typically the case of 'problem children'. The strategy to follow is *selective growth*.

■ In quadrant D, we have the opposite situation. Competitive advantage is high but market attractiveness is low. A skimming and maintenance strategy without major new investment is required. This is the equivalent of the 'cash cows' positioning in the BCG matrix.

The other intermediate zones correspond to strategic positions that are less clearly defined and are often difficult to interpret. The fuzzy value of the summary scores can reflect either very high marks on some indicators and very low marks on others, or simply an average evaluation on all the criteria. The latter case is often observed in practice and reflects imprecise information or simply a lack of information.

Choice of future strategy

We thus have a visual representation of the firm's growth potential. By extrapolating each activity's expected growth under the assumption of 'no change' strategy, the firm can then assess its future position. Alternative strategic options can also be explored:

■ *Investing to hold* aims at maintaining the current position and keeping up with expected changes in the market.

■ *Investing to penetrate* aims at improving the business position by moving the business unit to the right of the grid.

■ *Investing to rebuild* aims at restoring a position that has been lost. This revitalization strategy will be more difficult to implement if the market attractiveness is already medium or low.

■ *Low investment* aims at harvesting the business, i.e. the business position is exchanged for cash, for example, by selling the activity at the highest possible price.

■ *Divestment* aims at leaving markets or segments of low attractiveness where the firm does not have the capacity to acquire or sustain a competitive advantage.

Figure 10.5 shows an example of multi-factor portfolio analysis. It represents the portfolio of a firm from the food industry. Note that the product market's attractiveness is very average and the firm's competitiveness is evaluated as low for most of the products considered. The future of this firm is clearly very bleak.

Evaluation of the multi-factor portfolio grid

The multi-factor portfolio model leads to the same kind of analyses as the BCG matrix, with one major difference: the link between competitiveness and financial performance (i.e. cash flow) is

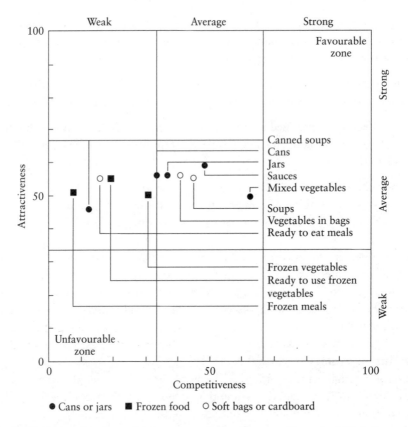

FIGURE 10.5 *Example of a multi-factor portfolio. (Source: Brussels, MDA Consulting Group)*

lost. However, since this model is not based on any particular assumption, it does overcome many of the shortcomings of the BCG method and it is more widely applicable. Furthermore, it is much more flexible because the indicators used are company-specific.

The use of these types of matrix suffers nevertheless from certain limitations.

■ Measurement problems are more delicate and the *risk of subjectivity* is much higher. This shows up not only in the choice of indicators and their possible weighting, but especially in the marking of the criteria. The risk of subjectivity is greater for indicators of competitiveness, where there is necessarily self-evaluation.

■ When the number of indicators and the number of activities to evaluate are high, the procedure becomes heavy and demanding, especially when information is scarce or imprecise.

■ The results are sensitive to the ratings and to the weighting systems adopted. Manipulation of weights can produce a desired position in the matrix. It is therefore important to tes• the sensitivity of results to the use of alternative weighting systems.

■ As for the BCG matrix, recommendations remain very general and need to be clarified. Furthermore, the link with financial performance is less clearly established.

The two approaches will probably yield different insights, but as the main purpose of a product portfolio analysis is to help to guide, and not be a substitute for, strategic thinking, the process of reconcilation will be useful. Thus it is desirable to employ both approaches and compare results (Day, 1977, p. 38).

10.1.3 Benefits of product portfolio analyses

Portfolio analysis is the outcome of the whole *strategic marketing process* described in the last four chapters of this book. A portfolio analysis rests on the following principles, irrespective of the method used:

- An accurate division of the firm's activities into product markets or segments.

- Measures of competitiveness and attractiveness allowing evaluation and comparison of the strategic values of the different activities.

- Links between strategic position and economic and financial performance, mainly in the BCG method.

Matrix representations help to synthesize the results of this strategic thinking exercise and to visualize them in a clear and expressive manner. Contrary to appearances, they are not simple to elaborate. They require complete and reliable information about the way markets function, and about the strengths and weaknesses of the firm and its rivals. More specifically, this analysis implies:

- Considerable effort to *segment the reference market*. This is particularly important, because the validity of the recommendations is conditioned by the initial choice of segmentation.

- Systematic and careful collection of *detailed information*, which does not normally exist as such and needs to be reconstituted by cross-checking and probing; quality of results also depends on the reliability of this information.

This kind of analysis cannot be improved and it relies particularly on top management's complete support. Such a tool is obviously not a panacea, but it has the merit of emphasizing some important aspects of management:

- It moderates *excessively short-term* vision by insisting on a balance being maintained between immediately profitable activities and those that prepare the future.

- It encourages the firm to keep both market *attractiveness* and *competitive potential* in mind.

- It establishes *priorities* in allocation of human as well as financial resources.

- It suggests *differentiated development strategies* per type of activity on a more data-oriented basis.

- It creates a *common language* throughout the organization and fixes clear objectives to reinforce motivation and facilitate control.

The main weakness of methods of portfolio analysis is that they can give an image of the present, or indeed of the recent past, and devote insufficient time to the assessment of future changes and

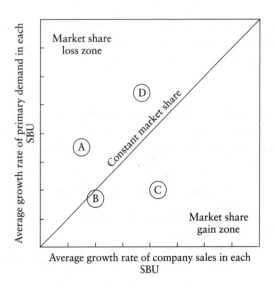

FIGURE 10.6 *The growth matrix (Source: Hussey, 1987)*

strategic options for dealing with these changes. There is also a risk of too mechanistic an application of these methods. As already emphasized, different methods could lead to very different classifications. The tools described here must be viewed more as guides to informed reasoning than as prescriptive tools.

These matrices can also be used in a dynamic perspective, for instance in comparing the present market positions held within each product market with the targeted positions for the next period. The matrix presented in Fig. 10.6 is useful in this respect because it permits analysis of the changing competitive positions of each strategic business unit (SBU) over time (Hussey, 1978).

Portfolio models in practice

In a survey of the Fortune 1000 industrial firms, Haspeslagh (1982) studied the usefulness of portfolio analysis. Some of his findings are given below:

■ As of 1979, 36 per cent of the Fortune 1000 firms and 45 per cent of the Fortune 500 firms had introduced the portfolio model approach to some extent. About 14 per cent of the Fortune 1000 were engaged in the process of portfolio planning in which the portfolio became a central part of the management process.

■ The decision as to which portfolio model to use was not regarded as critical. Considered fundamental to portfolio planning were: (a) defining the business units; (b) classifying those business units according to their attractiveness and competitiveness; and (c) using this framework to assign financial objectives.

■ One-third of the respondents felt that the most important benefit of a portfolio analysis was the achievement of a better understanding of their businesses, which in turn led to better strategic decision making. Another one-third felt that the key benefits were improved resource allocation, strategic reorientation and exit and entry decisions.

The survey also showed that firms using product portfolio models clearly had a longer time horizon than those who conducted no portfolio planning. A more recent survey by Hamermesch (1986) reached the same conclusions.

A portfolio analysis leads to different strategic recommendations according to the positioning of activities in the portfolio. As we saw, such recommendations are mainly general guidelines, such as invest, maintain, harvest, abandon, etc., which require clarification and need to be put in a more explicit operational perspective.

10.2 THE CHOICE OF A GENERIC STRATEGY

The first step in elaborating a development strategy is to clarify the nature of the *sustainable competitive advantage* that will serve as the basis for later strategic actions and tactics.

We saw in the previous chapter that competitive advantage can be described by reference to two aspects (see Fig. 9.1): *productivity* (cost advantage) and *market power* (advantage in terms of maximum acceptable price). The question is to know which of these two aspects should be given priority, considering the firm's characteristics—strengths and weaknesses—and those of its rivals. In other words, which advantage is 'sustainable' in a given product market?

Identifying this sustainable competitive advantage requires an analysis of the competitive structure and, more specifically, answers to the following questions.

■ What are the *key success factors* in a given product market or segment?

■ What are the firm's *strengths and weaknesses* with regard to these factors?

■ What are the strengths and weaknesses of the firm's *direct rival(s)* with regards to the same key success factors?

On the basis of this information, the firm can: (a) assess the nature of the advantage for which it is best placed; (b) decide to create competitive advantage for itself in a particular domain; or (c) attempt to neutralize rivals' competitive advantage.

Generic strategies will therefore be different according to the type of competitive advantage sought—that is, whether they are based on productivity (and therefore cost advantage), or rest on an element of differentiation and are therefore based on a price premium.

Porter (1980, p. 35) suggests that there exist three generic competitive strategies to outperform other firms in an industry: overall cost leadership, differentiation or focus (Fig. 10.7).

10.2.1 Overall cost leadership

This first generic strategy is based on *productivity* and is generally related to the existence of an experience effect. This strategy implies close scrutiny of (a) overhead costs, (b) productivity investments intended to enhance the value of experience effects, (c) product design costs and

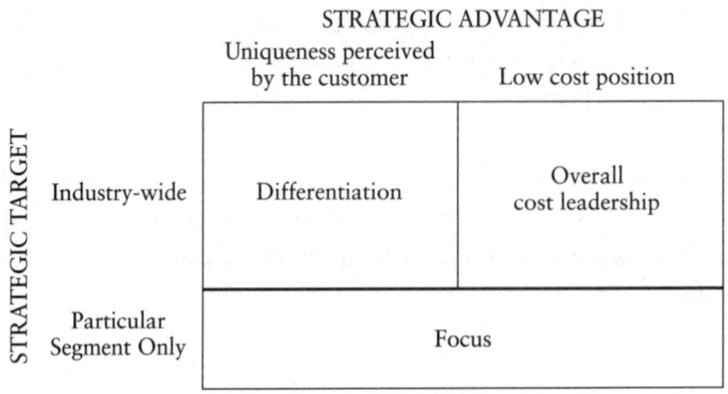

STRATEGIC ADVANTAGE

	Uniqueness perceived by the customer	Low cost position
Industry-wide	Differentiation	Overall cost leadership
Particular Segment Only	Focus	

STRATEGIC TARGET

FIGURE 10.7 *Three generic strategies (Source: Porter, 1980)*

(d) cost minimization in service, selling, advertising and so on. Low cost relative to competitors is the major preoccupation of the entire strategy.

Having a cost advantage constitutes an effective protection against the five competitive forces (see Fig. 9.2).

■ Relative to its *direct competitors*, the firm is in a better position to resist a possible price war and still make a profit at its rivals' minimum price level.

■ Powerful *buyers* can only drive down prices to the level of the most efficient competitor.

■ Low cost provides a defence against powerful *suppliers* by providing more flexibility to cope with input cost increases.

■ A low-cost position provides substantial *entry barriers* in terms of scale economies or cost advantage.

■ A low-cost position usually places the firm in a favourable situation *vis-à-vis substitutes* relative to competitors in the industry (Porter, 1980, p. 36).

Thus, cost leadership protects the firm against all five competitive forces, because the least efficient firms are the first to feel the effects of the competitive struggle.

10.2.2 Differentiation

In differentiation the objective is to give the product distinctive qualities that are significant to the buyer and create something that is perceived as being unique. The firm tends to create a situation of monopolistic competition in which it holds some market power because of the distinctive element (Chamberlin, 1950).

We saw before that differentiation can take many forms: design or brand image, technology, features, customer service, dealer network, and so on (see Levitt, 1980). Differentiation, like cost domination, protects the firm from the five competitive forces, but in a very different way.

- Relative to its *direct rivals*, differentiation provides the firm with insulation against competitive rivalry because of brand loyalty and resulting lower price sensitivity. It also increases margins, which avoids the need for a low-cost position.

- The resulting customer loyalty, and the need for a competitor to overcome uniqueness, provide *entry barriers*.

- Higher profitability increases the firm's ability to resist cost increases imposed by powerful *suppliers*.

- Finally, the firm that has differentiated itself to achieve customer loyalty should be better positioned *vis-à-vis substitutes* than its competitors (Porter, 1980, p. 37).

Successful differentiation enables the firm to realize higher profits than its rivals because of the higher price the market is willing to accept and despite the fact that costs are generally higher. This type of strategy is not always compatible with high market share, since most buyers are not necessarily prepared to pay a higher price, even though they recognize product superiority.

Differentiation strategies generally imply large investments in operational marketing, particularly in advertising expenditures to inform the market about the product's distinctive qualities.

10.2.3 Focus

A third generic strategy is focusing on the needs of a particular segment, group of buyers or geographic market, without claiming to address the whole market. The objective is to take a restricted target and serve its narrow strategic target more effectively than competitors who are serving the whole market. It implies either differentiation or cost domination, or both, but only *vis-à-vis* the particular target. For example, a paint manufacturer can decide to address professional painters only, excluding the public at large, car manufacturers and the naval industry. In the car industry, Mercedes only addresses the high end of the market, but it covers that segment more effectively than other car manufacturers who have a full line of models.

The focus strategy always implies some limitations on the overall market share achievable. A focus strategy can give the firm a large share of the market in the targeted segment, but it may be low relative to the whole market.

10.2.4 Risks associated with generic strategies

The choice of one strategy against another is not a neutral decision, in the sense they involve differing types of risks and also different priority preoccupations in the organization. Box 10.1 summarizes the risks inherent in each generic strategy.

The implementation of these strategies implies different resources and different know-how:

BOX 10.1

Risks associated with generic strategies

Risks of overall cost leadership

- Technological changes that nullify past investments or learning.

- Low-cost learning by industry newcomers or followers, through imitation or through their ability to invest in state-of-the-art facilities.

- Inability to see required product or marketing change because of the attention placed on costs.

- Inflation in costs that narrows the firm's ability to maintain enough of a price differential to offset competitors' brand images or other approaches to differentiation.

Risks of differentiation

- The cost differential between low-cost competitors and the differentiated firm becomes too great for differentiation to hold brand loyalty. Buyers sacrifice some of the features, services or image possessed by the differentiated firm for large costs savings.

- Buyers' needs for the differentiating factor fall. This can occur as buyers become more sophisticated.

- Imitations narrow the perceived differentiation, a common occurrence as industries mature.

Risks of focus

- The cost differential between broad range competitors and the focused firm widens to eliminate the cost advantages of serving a narrow target or to offset the differentiation achieved by focus.

- The differences in desired products or services between the strategic target and the market as a whole narrows.

- Competitors find submarkets within the strategic target and out-focus the focuser.

Source: Porter (1980, pp. 45–6).

- A cost domination strategy assumes sustained investment, a high degree of technological competence, close control of manufacturing and distribution costs and standardized products to facilitate production.

- A differentiation strategy assumes significant marketing know-how as well as technological advance. The ability to analyse and anticipate trends in market needs plays a fundamental role. Interfunctional co-ordination between R&D, production and marketing is vital.

lly, a *concentration* strategy also assumes the previous characteristics *vis-à-vis* the targeted
ent.

ASSESSING GROWTH OPPORTUNITIES

e are growth objectives in most strategies considered by firms, whether the strategies are of
growth, market share, profits or size. Growth is a factor that influences firm vitality,
ulates initiatives and increases motivation of personnel and management. Independent of
element of dynamism, growth is necessary in order to survive assaults from competitors,
ks to the economies of scale and experience effects it generates.

m can envisage growth objectives at three different levels:

growth objective within the reference market it operates—that is, *intensive growth*.

growth objective within the industrial chain, lateral expansion of its generic activity,
ckwards or forwards—that is, *integrative growth*.

growth objective based on opportunities outside the normal field of activity—that is, *growth
diversification*.

ach of these growth objectives correspond a number of possible strategies. It is interesting to
ine them briefly.

.1 Intensive growth

rategy of intensive growth is called for when a firm has not yet fully exploited the
rtunities offered by its products within its 'natural' reference market. Various strategies
be envisaged: market penetration, market development and product development.

ket penetration strategies

rket penetration strategy consists of trying to increase or maintain sales of current products
sting markets. Several options are open:

ary demand development This method increases the size of the total market by expanding
ary demand, for example:

adening the customer base by converting non-users into users.

reasing the frequency of purchase among present users.

reasing the average quantity purchased per use occasion.

ntifying and promoting new uses.

that this strategy can benefit all competitors since it influences primary demand more than
tive demand.

Market share increase strategy   This method increases sales by attracting buyers from brands, through significant spending on marketing mix variables. For example:

■ Improved product or service offering.

■ Repositioning the brands.

■ Aggressive pricing.

■ Significant reinforcement of the distribution and service network.

■ Major promotional efforts.

This more aggressive strategy will be mainly observed in market situations where pri demand is non-expansible, having reached the maturity phase of the product life cycle.

Market acquisition   This can increase market share substantially by acquisition or venture. For example:

■ Acquisition of competitor to obtain its market share.

■ Joint venture to achieve control of a significant market share.

Market position defence   This method is used to defend current market position (i.e. custo relationships, network, share, image, etc.) by adjusting the marketing mix. For example:

■ Product or service minor modifications or repositioning.

■ Defensive pricing.

■ Sales and distribution network reinforcement.

■ Stepped-up or redirected promotional activities.

Market rationalization   This is used to modify significantly the markets served, to reduce and/or increase marketing effectiveness. For example:

■ Concentration on most profitable segments.

■ Use of the most effective distributors.

■ Limiting individual customers served via minimum volume requirements.

■ Selective abandonment of market segments.

Market organization   Using legally accepted practices, market organization can influenc level of competition within one's industry to enhance economic viability. For example:

■ Establishment of industry-wide competitive rules or guidelines, usually under govern supervision.

■ Creation of joint marketing research organizations to improve information systems.

■ Agreement on capacity stabilization or reduction.

These last three strategies are more defensive, aiming at maintaining the level of market penetration.

Market development strategies

A market development strategy refers to a firm's attempt to increase the sales of its present products by tapping new markets. This objective can be achieved using three alternative approaches.

New market segments This is an attempt to reach new groups of buyers within the same geographic market. For example:

- Introducing an industrial product to the consumer market or vice versa.

- Selling the product to another consumer age group (sweets to adults).

- Selling the product to another industrial sector.

New distribution channels These are introduced to distribute the product through different channels to those in current use. For example:

- Adopting a direct marketing system for specific groups of buyers.

- Distributing the products through vending machines.

- Developing a franchise system parallel to the existing network.

Geographic expansion This extends the sales area of the product to include other parts of the country, or other countries. For example:

- Shipping existing products to foreign markets relying on local agents or on an independent worldwide trading company.

- Creating an exclusive network of distributors to handle foreign business.

- Acquiring a foreign company in the same sector.

Market development strategies rely mainly on the distribution and marketing know-how of the firm.

Product development strategies

A product development strategy consists of increasing sales by developing improved or new products aimed at current markets. Several different possibilities exist.

Features addition strategy This is used to add functions or features to existing products in order to expand the market. For example:

- Increasing the versatility of a product by adding functions.

- Adding an emotional or social value to a utilitarian product.

- Improving the safety or convenience of the product.

Product line extensions strategy   This strategy will increase the breadth of the product line by introducing new varieties to improve or maintain market share. For example:

■ Launching different packages of different sizes.

■ Increasing the number of flavours, scents, colours or composition.

■ Offering the same product in different forms or shapes.

The strategy of line extension can lead to product proliferation and the question of cannibalization and synergistic effects should be addressed explicitly.

Product line rejuvenation strategy   This is used to restore the overall competitiveness of obsolete or inadequate products by replacing them with technologically or functionally superior products. For example:

■ Developing a new generation of more powerful products.

■ Launching environmentally friendly new models of existing products.

■ Improving the aesthetic aspects of the product.

Product quality improvement strategy   This strategy aims to improve the way a product performs its functions as a package of benefits. For example:

■ Determining the package of benefits sought by each customer group.

■ Establishing quality standards on each dimension of the package of benefits.

■ Establishing a programme of total quality control.

Product line acquisition   This is used to complete, improve or broaden the range of products through external means. For example:

■ Acquisition of a company with a complementary product line.

■ Contracting for the supply of a complementary product line to be sold under the company's name.

■ Joint venture for the development and production of a new product.

Product line rationalization   This is a method of modifying the product line in order to reduce production or distribution costs. For example:

■ Product line and packaging standardization.

■ Selective abandonment of unprofitable or marginal products.

■ Minor product redesign.

The lever used in product development strategies is essentially R&D. These strategies are generally more costly and risky than market development strategies.

10.3.2 Integrative growth

An integrative growth strategy is justified when a firm can improve profitability by controlling different activities of strategic importance within the industrial chain. It describes a variety of make-or-buy arrangements that firms use to obtain a ready supply of strategic raw materials and a ready market for their outputs. Examples include ensuring stability of supplies, controlling a distribution network, or having access to information in a downstream activity to secure captive markets. There is a distinction between backward integration, forward integration and horizontal integration.

Backward integration

A *backward integration* strategy is driven by the concern to maintain or to protect a strategically important source of supplies, be it raw or semi-processed materials, components or services. In some cases, backward integration is necessary because suppliers do not have the resources or technological know-how to make components or materials that are indispensable to the firm.

Another objective may be to have access to a key technology that might be essential to the success of the activity. For example, many computer manufacturers have integrated backwards in the design and production of semiconductors in order to control this fundamental activity.

Forward integration

The basic motivation for a *forward integration* strategy is to control outlets without which the firm will choke. For a firm producing consumer goods, this involves controlling distribution through franchises or exclusive contracts, or even by creating its own chain stores, such as Yves Rocher or Bata. In industrial markets, the aim is mainly to ensure the development of downstream industries of transformation and incorporation that constitute natural outlets. This is how some basic industries actively participate in creating intermediary transformation activity.

In the steel industry, for example, Cockerill in Belgium has created Phoenix Works, specializing in coating and galvanizing sheet steel, Polypal developing and manufacturing industrial storage systems and Polytuile, manufacturing roof coverings with steel sheet.

In some cases, forward integration is conducted simply to provide a better understanding of the needs of buyers of manufactured products. To understand the problems of users, and in order to meet their needs more effectively, the firm creates a subsidiary playing the role of a pilot unit.

Horizontal integration

A *horizontal integration* strategy has a totally different perspective. The objective is to reinforce the competitive position by absorbing or controlling some competitors. There can be various arguments for this: neutralizing a dangerous rival, reaching the critical volume so as to benefit from scale effects, benefiting from complementarity of product lines and having access to distribution networks or to restricted market segments.

10.3.3 Growth by diversification

A strategy of growth by diversification is justified if the firm's industrial chain presents little or no prospect of growth or profitability. This may happen either because competitors occupy a powerful position, or because the reference market is in decline. Diversification implies entry into new product markets. This kind of growth strategy carries a high degree of risk as it involves a leap into the unknown. It is usual to establish a distinction between concentric diversification and pure diversification.

Concentric diversification

In a concentric diversification strategy, the firm goes outside its industrial and commercial network and tries to add new activities that are technologically and/or commercially related to its current activities. The objective is therefore to benefit from synergy effects due to the complementarity of activities, and thus to expand the firm's reference market.

For example, the Sports Division of Fabrique Nationale (FN) in Belgium, the leading European manufacturer of hunting weapons, has gradually diversified and added to its product line other sporting goods, such as golf clubs, fishing rods, tennis racquets and windsurfing boards. The aim was, on the one hand, to compensate for the decline in the hunting market and, on the other, to take full advantage of a specialized distribution network of sporting goods controlled by FN, the Browning network in the USA in particular.

A concentric diversification strategy usually has the objectives of attracting new groups of buyers and expanding the reference market of the firm.

Pure diversification

In a pure diversification strategy, the firm enters into new activities which are unrelated to its traditional activities, either technologically or commercially. The aim is to turn towards entirely new fields in order to rejuvenate the product portfolio. For this very reason, Volkswagen, at the end of 1978, bought Triumph-Adler, which specializes in computer science and office equipment.

Diversification is undoubtedly the most risky and complex of all strategies, because it leads the firm into unknown territory. To be successful, diversification requires important human as well as financial resources. Drucker (1981, p. 16) considers that a successful diversification requires a common core or unity represented by common markets, technology or production processes. He states that without such a unity core, diversification never works; financial ties alone are insufficient. Other organizational management specialists believe in the importance of a 'corporate culture' or a 'management style' which characterizes every organization but may only be effective in some fields and not others.

The rationale of diversification

Calori and Harvatopoulos (1988) studied the rationale of diversification in the French industry. They identified two dimensions. The first dimension relates to the *nature* of the strategic objective: diversification may be defensive (replacing a loss-making activity) or offensive

TABLE 10.2 *The rationales of diversification*

Type of objective	Expected outcome	
	Coherence	Economic value
Offensive	Expansion (Salomon)	Deployment (Taittinger)
Defensive	Relay (Framatome)	Redeployment (Lafarge)

Source: Calori and Harvatopoulos (1988).

(conquering new positions). The second dimension involves the *expected outcomes* of diversification: management may expect great economic value (growth, profitability) or first and foremost great coherence and complementarity with their current activities (exploitation of know-how).

Cross-classifying these two dimensions gives rise to four logics of diversification, as shown in Table 10.2.

■ *Expansion*, whereby the firm tries to reinforce its activity (offensive aim) while taking full advantage of its know-how (coherence). This kind of diversification strategy has been followed by Salomon, for example, world leader in ski bindings, which has gone into the market for ski boots, then the market for cross-country skiing and more recently into manufacturing golf clubs and ski poles.

■ *Relay*, which seeks to replace a declining activity (defensive objective), while using high quality staff (coherence). Framatome followed this strategy at the end of the 1970s when the market for nuclear plant started to shrink.

■ *Deployment* is an offensive strategy seeking high economic value. This was the case for Taittinger diversifying into the deluxe hotel business.

■ *Redeployment*, which is defensive in nature but seeks a new channel for growth. This strategy was followed by Lafarge which merged with Coppée and entered into biotechnology when faced with decline in the building industry.

In addition to the above, there is diversification driven by image improvement (the logic of image), and diversification driven by the will to watch the growth of a new promising technology (the logic of window).

It is important that management should define the logic of diversification from the outset and as clearly as possible. Upon this logic will depend the criteria for assessing and selecting potential activities. The alternative growth strategies are summarized in Box 10.2.

BOX 10.2

Alternative growth strategies

1. *Intensive growth: to grow within the reference market*

   1.1. Penetration strategy: increase sales of existing products in existing markets

- Primary demand development
- Market share increase
- Market acquisition
- Market position defence
- Market rationalization
- Market organization

   1.2. Market development strategy: increase sales of existing products in new markets

- Target new market segments
- Adopt new distribution channels
- Penetrate new geographic markets

   1.3. Product development strategy: increase sales in existing markets with new or modified products

- Features addition strategy
- Product line extensions strategy
- Product line rejuvenation strategy
- Product quality improvement strategy
- Product line acquisition
- Product line rationalization
- New product development strategy

2. *Integrative growth: to grow within the industrial chain*

   2.1. Backward integration
   2.2. Forward integration
   2.3. Horizontal integration

3. *Growth by diversification: to grow outside the industrial chain*

   3.1. Concentric diversification
   3.2. Pure diversification

10.4 COMPETITIVE STRATEGIES

An important element of a growth strategy is taking explicit account of competitors' positions and behaviours. Measuring business competitiveness (Chapter 9) helps to evaluate the importance of the firm's competitive advantage compared with its most dangerous rivals, and to identify their competitive behaviour. The next task is to set out a strategy based on a realistic assessment of the forces at work, and to determine the means of achieving defined objectives.

Kotler establishes a distinction between four types of competitive strategy; his typology is based on the level of market share held and comprises four different strategies: market leader, market challenger, market follower and market nicher (Kotler, 1991, p. 319).

10.4.1 Market leader strategies

In a product market, the market leader is the firm that holds a dominant position and is acknowledged as such by its rivals. The leader is often an orientation point for competitors, a reference that rival firms try to attack, to imitate or to avoid. The best-known market leaders are IBM, Procter & Gamble, Kodak, Benetton, Nestlé, L'Oréal, etc. A market leader can envisage different strategies.

Primary demand development

The market leader is usually the firm that contributes most to the growth of the reference market. The most natural strategy that flows from the leader's responsibility is to *expand total demand* by looking for new users, new uses and more usage of its products. Acting in this way, the market leader contributes to expanding the total market size which, in the end, is beneficial to all competitors. This type of strategy is normally observed in the first stages of the product's life cycle, when total demand is expansible and tension between rivals is low due to high potential for growth of total demand.

Defensive strategies

A second strategy open to a firm with large market share is a *defensive strategy*: protecting market share by countering the actions of the most dangerous rivals. This kind of strategy is often adopted by the innovating firm which finds itself attacked by imitating firms once the market has been opened. This was the case for IBM in the mainframe computer market, for Danone in the fresh products market, for Coca-Cola in the soft drinks market, etc. Many defensive strategies can be adopted:

- Innovation and technological advance which discourages competitors.

- Market consolidation through intensive distribution and a full line policy to cover all market segments.

- Direct confrontation—that is, direct conflict through price wars or advertising campaigns.

We have seen this type of strategy between firms such as Hertz and Avis, Coca-Cola and Pepsi Cola, and Kodak and Polaroïd.

Aggressive strategies

A third possibility available to a dominant firm is an *offensive strategy*. The objective here is to reap the benefits of experience effects to the maximum and thus improve profitability. This strategy is based on the assumption that market share and profitability are related. In the previous chapter, we saw that this relationship was mainly observed in volume industries, where competitive advantage is cost-based. Its existence has also been empirically established by works of PIMS (Buzzell *et al.*, 1975) and confirmed by Galbraith and Schendel (1983). Although increasing market share is beneficial to a firm, there exists a limit beyond which the cost of any further increase becomes prohibitive. Furthermore, an excessively dominant position also has the inconvenience that it attracts the attention of public authorities who are in charge of maintaining balanced competitive market conditions. This, for instance, is the task of the Competition Commission within the European Union, and of anti-trust laws in the USA. Dominant firms are also more vulnerable to attacks by consumer organizations, who tend to choose the most visible targets, such as Nestlé in Switzerland and Fiat and Montedison in Italy.

Demarketing strategy

There is also a fourth strategy open to a dominant firm: *reduce* its market share to avoid accusations of monopoly or quasi-monopoly. Various possibilities exist. First, it can use *demarketing* to reduce the demand level in some segments by price increases, or reduce services as well as advertising and promotion campaigns.

10.4.2 Market challenger strategies

A firm that does not dominate a product market can choose either to attack the market leader and be its challenger, or to become a follower by falling into line with the leader's decisions. Market challenger strategies are therefore aggressive, with the declared objective of taking the leader's position.

The challenger faces two key decisions: (a) the choice of battleground from which to attack the market leader and (b) evaluation of the latter's reactive and defensive abilities.

In the choice of battleground, the challenger has two possibilities: frontal attack or lateral attack. A *frontal attack* consists of opposing the competitor directly by using its own weapons, and without trying to use its weak points. To be successful, a frontal attack demands a balance of power heavily in favour of the attacker. In military strategy, this balance is normally put at 3 to 1. For example, when in 1981 IBM attacked the microcomputer market with its PC, its marketing tools, advertising in particular, were very clearly superior to those of Apple, Commodore and Tandy, which dominated the market (*Business Week*, 25 March 1985). Two years later IBM had become the leader.

Lateral attacks aim to confront the leader over one or another strategic dimension for which it is weak or ill prepared. A lateral attack may, for example, address a region or a distribution network where the leader is not well represented, or a market segment where the leader's product is not well adapted. A classic market challenger strategy is to launch an attack on the leader by offering the same product at a much lower price. Many Japanese firms adopt this strategy in electronics or cars (Kotler *et al.*, 1985, p. 91).

This strategy becomes even more effective when the leader holds a large market share. If the latter were to take up the lower price, it would have to bear important costs, whereas the challenger, especially if it is small, only loses over a low volume. For example, the major European steel producers severely suffered from price cuts offered by the Italian Bresciani mini-steelworks. The same phenomenon is observed in the oil market with 'cut-price firms' such as Seca in Belgium, Uno-X in Denmark and Conoco in Great Britain; dominant firms (BP, Exxon, Shell, etc.) had more to lose in a price war.

Lateral or indirect attacks can take various forms. There is direct analogy with military strategy and one can define strategies of outflanking, encircling, guerrilla tactics, mobile defence, etc. See, on this topic, Kotler and Singh (1981) and Ries and Trout (1986).

Before starting an offensive move, it is essential to assess correctly a dominant firm's *ability to react and defend*. Porter (1980, p. 68) suggests using the three following criteria:

- *Vulnerability*: to what strategic moves and governmental, macro-economic or industry events would the competitor be most vulnerable?

- *Provocation*: what moves or events will provoke a retaliation from competitors, even though retaliation may be costly and lead to marginal financial performance?

- *Effectiveness of retaliation*: to what moves or events is the competitor impeded from reacting to quickly and/or effectively, given its goals, strategy, existing capabilities and assumptions?

The ideal is to adopt a strategy against which the competitor cannot react because of its current situation or priority objectives.

As was emphasized earlier, in saturated or stagnant markets the aggressiveness of the competitive struggle tends to intensify as the main objective becomes finding a method to counter rivals' actions. The risk of a strategy based only on 'warfare marketing' is that too much energy is devoted to repelling rivals and there is a risk of losing sight of the objective of satisfying buyers' needs. A firm that is focusing entirely on its rivals tends to adopt a reactive behaviour which is more dependent on rivals' actions than the developments in market needs. A proper balance between the two orientations is therefore essential (Oxenfeld and Moore, 1978).

10.4.3 Market follower strategies

As we saw before, a follower is a competitor with modest market share who adopts an adaptive behaviour by falling into line with competitors' decisions. Instead of attacking the leader, these firms pursue a policy of 'peaceful co-existence' by adopting the same attitude as the market leader. This type of behaviour is mainly observed in oligopolistic markets where differentiation possibilities are minimal and cross price elasticities are very high, so that it is in no one's interest to start a competitive war that risks being harmful to all.

Adoption of a follower's behaviour does not prevent the firm from having a competitive strategy, quite the contrary. The fact that the firm holds a modest market share reinforces the importance of having clearly defined strategic objectives that are adapted to its size and its strategic ambition. Hamermesch *et al.* (1978) analysed strategies of small firms and showed that these firms can overcome the size handicap and achieve performances that are sometimes superior to dominant rivals. In other words, not all firms with low market share in low-growth markets are necessarily 'dogs' or 'lame ducks'.

Hamermesch *et al.* (1978, pp. 98–100) have uncovered four main features in the strategies implemented by companies with high performance and low market share:

1. *Creative market segmentation.* To be successful, a low market share company must compete in a limited number of segments where its own strengths will be most highly valued and where large competitors will be most unlikely to compete.
2. *Efficient use of R&D.* Small firms cannot compete with large companies in fundamental research; R&D should be concentrated mainly on process improvements aimed at lowering costs.
3. *Think small.* Successful low market share companies are content to remain small. Most of them emphasize profits rather than sales growth or market share, and specialization rather than diversification.
4. *Ubiquitous chief executive.* The final characteristic of these companies is the pervasive influence of the chief executive.

A market follower strategy, therefore, does not imply passivity on the part of the chief executive of the firm; rather the concern to have a growth strategy which will not entail reprisals from the market leader.

10.4.4 Market nicher strategies

A nicher is interested in one or few market segments, but not in the whole market. The objective is to be a large fish in a small pond rather than a small fish in a large pond. This competitive strategy is one of the generic strategies we discussed earlier, namely focus. The key to a focus strategy is specialization in a niche. For a niche to be profitable and sustainable, five characteristics are necessary (Kotler, 1991, p. 395):

- Sufficient profit potential.

- Growth potential.

- Unattractive to rivals.

- The market corresponds to the firm's distinctive competence.

- A sustainable entry barrier.

A firm seeking a niche must face the problem of finding the feature or criterion upon which to build its specialization. This criterion may relate to a technical aspect of the product, to a particular distinctive quality or to any element of the marketing mix.

10.5 INTERNATIONAL DEVELOPMENT STRATEGIES

We emphasized in the first chapter that internationalization of the economy means that a growing number of firms operate in markets where competition is global. As a result, international development strategies concern all firms, irrespective of whether they actively participate in foreign markets or not. In this section we shall examine the stages of international development as well as the strategic reasoning of a firm that pursues an international marketing development strategy.

10.5.1 Objectives of international development

International development is no longer limited to large enterprises. Many small firms are forced to become international in order to grow, or simply to survive. Objectives in an international development strategy may be varied.

■ To enlarge the *potential market*, thus being able to produce more and achieve better results owing to economies of scale. For many activities, the critical volume is at such a level that it demands a large potential market.

■ To extend the product's *life cycle* by entering markets that are not at the same development stage and still have expansible total demand, whereas in the domestic market of the exporting firm demand has reached the maturity phase.

■ To diversify *commercial risk* by addressing buyers in different economic environments and enjoying more favourable competitive conditions.

■ To control *competition* through diversification of positions on the one hand and surveillance of competitors' activities in other markets on the other.

■ To reduce *costs of supplies and production* by exploiting different countries' comparative advantages.

■ To exploit *excess production capacity* by exporting goods at low (marginal cost) prices.

■ To achieve *geographic diversification* by entering new markets with existing products.

■ To *follow key customers* abroad to supply or to service them in their foreign locations.

The phenomenon of globalization of markets, already mentioned in Chapter 2, must also be added to these basic objectives: take advantage of the progressive liberalization of world trade.

10.5.2 Forms of international development

A firm's internationalization does not happen overnight, but results from a process that can be subdivided into six levels of growing internationalization (Leroy *et al.*, 1978).

1. *Exporting* is the most frequent form. Often, the first attempts to export result from a necessity to clear surplus production. Later, exports can become a regular activity, but one which is reconstituted every year without there being any kind of medium- or long-term commitment to foreign countries. Relations are purely commercial.

2. The second stage is the *contractual stage*. Here the firm seeks more long-term agreements in order to stabilize its outlets, especially if its production capacity has been adjusted in terms of the potential to export. It will then sign long-term contracts, either with an importer or with a franchised distributor, or with a licensed manufacturer if it is an industrial firm.

3. In order to control the foreign partner or to finance its expansion, the firm may directly invest its own capital; this is the *participatory stage* which leads to commercial companies or co-ownership production.

4. After a few years, involvement can become absolute, with the firm owning 100 per cent of the capital of the foreign subsidiary; this stage is *direct investment* in a subsidiary with controlled management.

5. Gradually, the foreign subsidiary looks for ways of autonomous development, using local finance, national managers and its own programme of R&D which is distinct from the parent company. This is the *autonomous subsidiary stage*. If the parent company has many subsidiaries of this kind, this subsidiary becomes a multinational company. It would probably be more appropriate to use the term 'multi-domestic', because it emphasizes the point that each of these companies is more concerned about its own internal market, and the group's various companies co-exist independently of each other.

6. The final stage of development is the one that is taking shape at the moment. It is the stage of the *global enterprise* that addresses the international market as if it were a single market. This kind of firm bases itself on interdependence of markets, and the latter are therefore no longer administered autonomously.

Stages of international organization

To the various stages of international development there often correspond specific forms of organization at the international level which reflect different views of international marketing. Keegan (1989) suggests the following typology:

1. *Domestic organization*. The firm is focused on its domestic market, and exporting is viewed as an opportunistic activity. This type of organization is frequent in the 'passive marketing' stage described in Chapter 1.

2. *International organization*. Internationalization takes place more actively, but at this stage the firm's orientation is still focused on the home market, which is considered as the primary area of opportunity. The *ethnocentric* company, unconsciously, if not explicitly and consciously, operates on the assumption that home country methods, approaches, people, practices and values are superior to those found elsewhere in the world. Attention is mostly centred on similarities with the home country market. The product strategy at this stage is 'extension', i.e. products that have been designed for the home country market are 'extended' into markets around the world.

3. *Multi-domestic organization*. After a certain period of time, the company discovers that the difference in markets demands adaptation of its marketing in order to succeed. The focus of the firm is now multinational (as opposed to home country) and its orientation is *polycentric*. The polycentric orientation is based on the assumption that markets around the world are so different and unique that the only way to succeed is to adapt to the unique and different aspect of each national market. The product strategy is adaptation, i.e. to change or adapt products

to meet local differences and practices. Each country is managed as if it were an independent entity.

4. *Global organization.* A global market is one that can be reached with the same basic appeal and message and with the same basic product. Both the product and the advertising and promotion may require adaptation to local customs and practices, as illustrated in Table 7.7. The *geocentric* orientation of the global corporation is based on the assumption that markets around the world are both similar and different, and that it is possible to develop a global strategy that recognizes similarities which transcend national differences while adapting to local differences as well. The basic notion of a world strategy can therefore be summarized as follows: 'Think globally and act locally.'

This last stage is at the moment taking shape in the world and in particular in the European economy. It implies important changes in the logic of strategic marketing. On this topic, see Hamel and Prahalad (1985).

SUMMARY

Product portfolio analyses are designed to help guide a multi-product firm's strategic thinking by evaluating each activity with reference to indicators of attractiveness and competitiveness. The growth–share matrix has the merit of simplicity and objectivity, but its underlying assumptions are restrictive and limit its scope of application. The multi-factor matrix is more widely applicable and more flexible because the indicators used are company-specific, but the risk of subjectivity is higher and the procedure is more demanding in terms of available information. In elaborating a development strategy, the firm should clarify the nature of the sustainable competitive advantage which will serve as the basis for later strategic actions and tactics. Three generic options exist: overall cost leadership, differentiation or focus. The choice of one generic strategy is not neutral, but implies different resources, know-how and risks. In assessing growth opportunities, growth objectives can be considered at different levels: within the reference market (intensive growth), within the supply chain (integrative growth) or outside the current field of activity (diversification). For each of these three development strategies, several options are open which should be systematically explored in a strategic thinking exercise. A development strategy should explicitly take into account competitors' positions and behaviours on the basis of a realistic assessment of the forces at work. One can distinguish four types of competitive strategy: market leader, market challenger, market follower and market nicher. As a consequence of the globalization of the world economy, international development is no longer limited to large enterprises and is motivated by a variety of strategic objectives. A firm's internationalization does not happen overnight but results from a process that can be subdivided into different stages of international involvement in various organizational forms.

QUESTIONS AND PROBLEMS

1. A manufacturer of electronic components for industrial applications has five business units shown in the table.

Strategic business units (SBU)	Sales in units (million)	Number of competitors	Sales of top 3 competitors	Market growth rate (%)
A	1.0	7	1.4 / 1.4 / 1.0	15
B	3.2	18	3.2 / 3.2 / 2.0	20
C	3.8	12	3.8 / 3.0 / 2.5	7
D	6.5	5	6.5 / 1.6 / 1.4	4
E	0.7	9	3.0 / 2.5 / 2.0	4

Using the BCG growth–share matrix, evaluate the strength of the company's current and future position. What development strategies should it consider to improve the position of each business unit? Define clearly the conditions of application of this portfolio analysis method.

2. Design a multi-factor portfolio grid for one of the following companies: Godiva International (chocolate pralines), Haagen-Dazs (ice-cream), Perrier (mineral water).

3. Which development strategy would you recommend for a small business firm having a very specialized and recognized know-how in a worldwide market, but which has very limited financial means?

4. In France and Belgium, the level of ice-cream consumption is much lower than in other European markets as well as in North America. You are responsible for a worldwide known brand of ice-cream. Which development strategy (or strategies) would you consider in these two markets?

5. You are responsible for preparing a diversification programme for a company that has a very strong know-how in the field of fruit purchase and transformation and owns a well-known brand of jam and fruit preserves. Propose different avenues for diversification and assess their risks and opportunities.

REFERENCES

Abell, D.E. and J.S. Hammond (1979), *Strategic Market Planning*. Englewood Cliffs, New Jersey: Prentice Hall Inc.

Boston Consulting Group (1972), *Perspectives on Experience*. Boston, Mass.: The Boston Consulting Group.

Buzzell, R.D., B.T. Gale and G.M. Sultan (1975), 'Market Share, a Key to Profitability', *Harvard Business Review*, vol. 53, January–February, pp. 97–106.

Calori, R. and Y. Harvatopoulos (1988), 'Diversification: les règles de conduite', *Harvard-L'Expansion*, vol. 48, Spring, pp. 48–59.

Chamberlin, E.H. (1950), *The Theory of Monopolistic Competition*. Cambridge, Mass.: Harvard University Press.

Day, G.S. (1977), 'Diagnosing the Product Portfolio', *Journal of Marketing*, vol. 41, April.

Day, G.S. (1984), *Strategic Market Planning*. St Paul West Publishing Co.

Drucker, P.F. (1981), 'The Five Rules of Successful Acquisition', *The Wall Street Journal*, 15 October, p. 16.

Galbraith, C. and D. Schendel (1983), 'An Empirical Analysis of Strategy Types', *Strategic Management Journal*, vol. 4, pp. 153–73.

Hamel, G. and C.K. Prahalad (1985), 'Do you Really Have a Global Strategy?', *Harvard Business Review*, vol. 63, July–August, pp. 139–48.

Hamermesch, R.G. (1986), 'Making Planning Strategic', *Harvard Business Review*, vol. 64, July–August, pp. 115–20.

Hamermesch, R.G., M.J. Anderson and J.E. Harris (1978), 'Strategies for Low Market Share Businesses', *Harvard Business Review*, vol. 56, May–June, pp. 95–102.

Haspeslagh, P. (1982), 'Portfolio Planning: Uses and Limits', *Harvard-L'Expansion*, Summer, pp. 58–72.

Henderson, B.B. (1970), *The Product Portfolio*, Boston, Mass.: The Boston Consulting Group.

Hussey, D.E. (1978), 'Portfolio Analysis: Practical Experience with the Directional Policy Matrix', *Long Range Planning*, vol. 11, August, pp. 2–8.

Keegan, W.J. (1989), *Global Marketing Management*, 4th edn. Englewood Cliffs, New Jersey: Prentice Hall Inc.

Kotler, P. and R. Singh (1981), 'Marketing Warfare in the 1980s', *Journal of Business Strategy*, vol. 2, Winter, pp. 30–41.

Kotler, P. (1991), *Marketing Management*, 7th edn. Englewood Cliffs, New Jersey: Prentice Hall Inc.

Kotler P., L. Fahey and S. Jatuskripiak (1985), *The New Competition*. Englewood Cliffs, New Jersey: Prentice Hall Inc.

Levitt, T. (1980), 'Marketing Success through Differentiation of Everything', *Harvard Business Review*, vol. 58, pp. 83–91.

Leroy, G., G. Richard and J.P. Sallenave (1978), *La conquête des marchés extérieurs*, Paris: Les Editions d'Organisation.

Oxenfeld, A.R. and W.L. Moore (1978), 'Customer or Competitor: Which Guide Lines for Marketing?', *Management Review*, August, pp. 43–8.

Porter, M.E. (1980), *Competitive Strategy*, New York: The Free Press.

Ries, A. and J. Trout (1986), *Warfare Marketing guerrier*. New York: McGraw-Hill.

Wind, Y., V. Mahajan and D.S. Swire (1983), 'An Empirical Comparison of Standardized Portfolio Models', *Journal of Marketing*, vol. 47, pp. 89–99.

FURTHER READING

Hax, A.C. and N.S. Majluf (1984), 'Strategic Management: An Integrative Perspective', Englewood Cliffs, New Jersey, Prentice-Hall.

McNamee, P. (1984), 'Competitive Analysis Using Matrix Displays', *Long Range Planning*, vol. 17, June, pp. 98–114.

THE STRATEGIC MARKETING PLAN

LEARNING OBJECTIVES

After reading this chapter, you should be able to:

- understand the usefulness of formal strategic planning

- define the structure and content of a strategic plan

- conduct an external and internal audit (SWOT analysis)

- define operational objectives and action programmes

- prepare a projected profit and loss statement

- test the robustness of a strategic plan.

*S*ound strategic thinking about the future must be spelled out in a written document which describes the ends and means required to implement the chosen development strategy. In the short term, the firm's success is directly dependent on the financial performance of its on-going activities. In the longer run, however, its survival and growth imply the ability to anticipate market changes and to adapt the structure of its product portfolio accordingly. To be effective, this strategic and proactive thinking must be organized in a systematic and formal way. The role of strategic marketing planning is the design of a desired future and of effective ways of making things happen. Its role is also to communicate these choices to those responsible for their implementation. This planning task is, of course, particularly difficult when great uncertainties prevail in the firm's environment. Anticipating the unexpected is also part of the strategic planning process. In this chapter, we shall build on the concepts and procedures described in previous chapters and examine the steps needed to make strategic marketing happen in the firm.

11.1 OVERVIEW OF STRATEGIC PLANNING

The *raison d'être* of a strategic plan is to formulate, in a clear and concise way, the main strategic options taken by the firm in order to ensure its long-term development. These strategic options must be translated into decisions and action programmes. We shall briefly examine the overall structure of a plan and the benefits expected from strategic planning.

11.1.1 Overall structure of the strategic marketing plan

As shown in this book, the strategic marketing process can be summarized around six key questions. The answers provided to these questions constitute the backbone of the plan and also the objectives for the firm.

1. What business are we in and what is the *firm's mission* in the chosen reference market?
2. Within the defined reference market, what are the targeted product markets or segments and what *positioning strategy* is likely to be adopted within each segment?
3. What are the key business *attractiveness* factors in each segment and what are the opportunities and threats presented by the environment?
4. Within each segment, what are the firm's distinctive qualities, strengths and weaknesses and *competitive advantages*?
5. Which *development strategy* and strategic ambition should be adopted for each activity in the firm's product portfolio?
6. How do these strategic options translate into *operational marketing programmes* defined in terms of product, distribution, pricing and communications decisions?

Once the answers to these questions are obtained as the result of a strategic marketing audit, it is still necessary to summarize the options taken, to define the means required to achieve the stated objectives, to design the specific action programmes and, last but not least, to prepare projected profit and loss statements for each activity and the company as a whole.

In fact, a strategic marketing plan is nothing more than a financial plan, but with much more information on the origins and destinations of the financial flows. As discussed in Chapter 1 (see Fig. 1.2), the strategic marketing plan has direct implications on all the other functions of the firm, and vice versa.

- *Research and development*: market needs must be met through new, improved or adapted products and services.

- *Finance*: the marketing programme is subject to financial constraints and availability of resources.

- *Operations*: sales objectives are subject to production capacity and physical delivery constraints.

- *Human resources*: the implementation of the plan implies the availability of qualified and well-trained personnel.

Thus strategic planning will result in a better integration of all the company's functions and contribute to maximization of efforts in reaching corporate goals. In a market-driven organization, the mission of strategic marketing is to identify prospects for growth and profit, given the company resources and *savoir faire*. As already emphasized in this book, this role is much broader than the traditional domain of marketing management, and implies interfunctional co-ordination.

11.1.2 Importance of strategic planning

Every company, even those reluctant to the idea of formal planning, has to formulate forecasts in a minimum of three areas:

- The calibration of the *investment programme* required to meet the level of market demand or to penetrate a new product market.

- The *production programme* organization needed, given the seasonality of sales and the periodicity of orders.

- The *financial liquidity*, based on income and expenses forecasts, which is required to meet the financial liabilities.

These managerial problems are common to all companies and they imply that reliable sales forecasts must be handled properly.

In addition to this argument of necessity, other arguments in favour of formal strategic planning exist.

- The plan expresses the value system, philosophies and views of top management. This information gives people a *sense of direction* and a sense of how to behave.

- The plan presents the facts on 'where the business has come from and where it stands'. The situation analysis helps to understand the *reasons* for the strategic options taken by top management.

- The plan *facilitates co-ordination* among the different functions, maintains consistency in the objectives, and facilitates trade-offs among conflicting goals.

- The plan is a *monitoring instrument* which provides the opportunity to review the progress made in implementing the plan and to redirect parts of the action programme that are off target.

- The plan minimizes the degree to which the company is taken by surprise to the extent that 'best case–worst case' scenarios have been explored.

- The plan encourages a more *rigorous management* of scarce resources by using standards, budgets, schedules, etc., thereby reducing the risk of improvisation.

Most strategic plans are complemented by some form of *contingency plan* to be activated if certain events occur. Contingency plans are developed for factors that are essential to the survival of the company.

11.1.3 Objections to formal planning

Although strategic planning is a widely adopted practice, a certain number of firms avoid the use of formal written strategic plans. Three types of objections to formal planning are usually given: the lack of relevant information; the futility of forecasting in a fast-changing environment; and the rigidity of planning.

Lack of needed information

Ideally the planner would have at hand all the pertinent information required on industry and market trends, competitive intentions, market share, technological innovations and so forth. The most common complaint concerns the lack of adequate information for the purpose of planning. On deeper investigation, however, it is usually found that there is too much information rather than too little. The real problem is more often the lack of in-depth analysis.

The existence of a market information system, similar to the one described in Chapter 5 (see Fig. 5.1), is today a vital necessity to maintain the firm's competitiveness. Market information and business intelligence systems must exist in any case, and these are costly operations with or without formal planning.

Futility of forecasting

In a turbulent environment, how beneficial are strategic plans that will be contradicted by future events? This attitude results from a misunderstanding of the nature of forecasting, which is erroneously compared to a crystal ball. As emphasized in Chapter 8, a forecast is a quantitative or qualitative estimate of what one expects, given a set of assumptions on the environment. A forecast is not an end in itself, but a *forward thinking exercise*, a tool used to increase the company's responsiveness and adaptability to the unexpected. This objective can be achieved even if the predicted outcome is not attained.

Bureaucratic rigidity

Formal planning would commit the firm to a given direction, whereas adaptability and flexible response are required in a fast-changing environment. This objection questions more the authoritarian planning style than planning itself. A plan should be designed to enhance creativity and quick reaction to changes. The mere fact of having analysed possible changes in the market in advance will help to revise programmes and objectives more quickly, when it is desirable to do so.

In practice, strategic planning is widely used, as evidenced by various surveys conducted in Europe and in the USA (Haspeslagh, 1982; Hamermesch, 1986; Greenley, 1987; Caeldries and Van Dierdonck, 1988). For an analysis of the main barriers to the development of marketing plans, see McDonald (1991).

11.2 CONTENT OF A STRATEGIC MARKETING PLAN

A strategic marketing plan typically sets out to answer the six key questions presented at the beginning of this chapter. In this section, we shall describe the basic elements of a strategic marketing plan and the type of information required on which to base recommendations.

11.2.1 The mission statement

Sometimes called a *creed statement* or a *statement of business principles*, a mission statement reveals the company's long-term vision in terms of what it wants to be and who it wants to serve. It defines the organization's value system and its economic and non-economic objectives. The mission statement is important from both an internal and an external point of view.

- Inside the company, it serves as a focal point for individuals to identify with the organization's direction and to ensure unanimity of purpose within the firm, thereby facilitating the emergence of a *corporate culture*.

- From an external point of view, the mission statement contributes to the creation of *corporate identity*, i.e. how the company wants to be perceived in the marketplace by its customers, competitors, employees, owners and shareholders, and the general public.

A mission statement should include at least (a) a history of the company, (b) a business definition, (c) the corporate goals and restraints, and (d) the basic strategic choices.

History of the company

Knowledge of the past history of the company, its origin and successive transformations is always useful to understand its present situation and the weight given to some economic or non-economic goals and objectives.

> Materne-Confilux celebrated its 100th anniversary in 1987. This company has accumulated a broad experience in the field of purchase and transformation of fruits and has succeeded in maintaining a family managerial structure. This strong foothold in the fruit sector is a key factor to consider when exploring alternative diversification strategies.

In searching for a new purpose, a company must remain consistent with its past achievements and fields of competence.

Business definition

This is a key component in the mission statement. As emphasized in Chapter 4, what customers buy and consider valuable is never the product, but rather its utility, i.e. *what a product or a service does for them* (Drucker 1973, p. 61). Thus, the market definition should be written in terms of the benefit provided to the buyer. As discussed in Chapter 7, the three relevant questions to examine here are:

■ What business(es) are we in?

■ What business(es) should we be in?

■ What business(es) should we not be in?

These are not easy questions to answer, particularly when the environment is changing very quickly. Examples of business definitions were presented on p. 227.

Every organization has a unique purpose and reason for being. This uniqueness should be reflected in the market definition. In a market-driven organization, the market definition will reflect the degree of customer orientation of the firm. By adopting a business definition formulated in terms of generic need or in terms of 'solution-to-a-problem', the firm emphasizes its market orientation and limits the risk of market myopia.

Corporate goals and restraints

Goals set the direction for both long- and short-term development and therefore determine the limitations and priorities with which the company should comply. These general goals, usually defined at the corporate level, are constraints within which the strategic plan must be developed. They should be clearly defined in advance to avoid proposals that contradict objectives of general management or corporate shareholders. These goals may be either economic or non-economic—for example, a minimum rate of return on investment, a growth objective, the conservation of the family ownership of the company, the refusal to enter particular fields of activity, or a minimum level of employment, etc.

The description of *available company resources* (capacity, equipment, human resources, capital, etc.) also forms part of the restraints and should be made explicit in order to avoid the adoption of a 'mission impossible' given the resources needed. *Codes of conduct and corporate ethics* for dealing with others (customers, distributors, competitors, suppliers, etc.) should also be formulated.

Basic strategic choices

Independent of the general goals imposed at the corporate level by general management, basic strategic options can be defined for each strategic business unit. For example, the extent of the strategic ambition and the role played by the firm in the target segment—i.e. leader, follower, challenger or nicher—may be defined. The strategic ambition must of course be compatible with the available resources of the firm.

Reference could be made here also to the three basic positioning strategies suggested by Porter (1980) and discussed in Chapter 10 (see section 10.2): cost advantage, differentiation or focus. The type of competitive advantage sought should also be defined. At this stage of the strategic plan, only broad orientations are given. They will be redefined in quantitative terms in the action programmes developed for each business unit.

In general

Ideally, the mission statement should be stated in terms narrow enough to provide practical guidance, yet broad enough to stimulate imaginative thinking, such as openings for product line extensions, or for diversification into adjacent product areas. At the Grumman Corporation, the guidelines for the mission statement advise:

> We should be careful not to confine the market boundaries by our existing or traditional product participation. The market definition analysis is purposely meant to create an outward awareness of the total surrounding market, and of its needs and trends that may offer opportunity for, or on the other hand challenges to, our current or contemplated position.   (Hopkins, 1981, p. 119)

In a survey conducted in the USA, out of a total of 181 responses received, 75 organizations provided a formal description of their mission statements. The main components included are summarized in Box 11.1.

BOX 11.1

What components are included in company mission statements?

Customers:	Who are the company's customers?
Products or services:	What are the firm's major products or services?
Location:	Where does the firm compete?
Technology:	What is the firm's basic technology?
Concern for survival:	What is the firm's commitment to economic objectives?
Philosophy:	What are the basic beliefs, values, aspirations and philosophical priorities of the firm?
Self-concept:	What are the firm's major strengths and competitive advantages?
Public image:	What are the firm's public responsibilities and what image is desired?
Concern for employees:	What is the firm's attitude towards its employees?

Source: David (1989).

11.2.2 External audit: market attractiveness analysis

This external audit—also called *opportunities and threats* analysis—is the first part of the situation analysis. As explained in Chapter 8, an attractiveness analysis examines the major external factors, i.e. the factors that are beyond the control of the firm but may have an impact on the marketing plan. The following areas should be reviewed:

■ Market trends.

■ Buyer behaviour.

■ Distribution structure.

■ Competitive environment.

■ Macro-environmental trends.

■ International environment.

These external factors may constitute opportunities or threats that the firm must try to anticipate and monitor through its marketing information system and business intelligence. Below we shall simply list the critical questions to raise in each of these areas. The precise type of information required will, of course, differ by product category: i.e. consumer durable or non-durable goods, services or industrial goods.

Market trends analysis

The objective is to describe, segment by segment, the total demand's general trends within a three- to five-year horizon. The task is to position each product market in its life cycle and to quantify the market size. Both unit volume and monetary values should be identified. The key demand concepts to examine have been reviewed in Chapter 8.

Questionnaire 1: total market trends

■ What is the size of the total market, in volume and in value?

■ What are the trends: growth, stagnation, decline?

■ What is the average per capita consumption?

■ How far are we from the saturation level?

■ What is the rate of equipment per household or per company?

■ What is the average lifetime of the product?

■ What is the share of replacement demand in total demand?

■ What is the seasonal pattern of total sales?

■ What are the main substitute products performing the same service?

■ What are the major innovations in the sector?

■ What are the costs per distribution channel?

- What is the structure of the distributive system?

- How will supply–demand relationships affect price levels?

- What is the level of total advertising intensity?

- What are the most popular advertising media?

- ...

This list is certainly incomplete. It simply illustrates the type of information required. If the product studied is an industrial good, several information items should pertain not only to the direct customers' demand, but also to the demand expressed further down the line in the industrial chain by the customers of the direct customers.

Buyer behaviour analysis

The task here is to examine buyer behaviour in terms of purchasing, use and possession. In addition to a description of the buyers' purchasing habits, it is also useful to know the buying process and to identify the influencing factors.

Questionnaire 2: Buyer behaviour analysis

- Per segment, what is the buyers' socio-demographic profile?

- What is the composition of the buying centre?

- Who is the buyer, the user, the decider, the influencer?

- What decision process is adopted by the buyer?

- What is the buyer's level of involvement?

- What are the main motivations of the buying decision?

- What package of benefits is sought by the buyer?

- What are the different uses of the product?

- What changing customer demands and needs do we anticipate?

- What are the purchasing frequency and periodicity?

- To which marketing factors are customers most responsive?

- What is the rate of customer satisfaction or dissatisfaction?

- ...

These descriptive data must be complemented with measures of the cognitive and affective response (recall, attitudes, preferences, intentions, etc.), as well as with brand or company image analyses.

Distribution structure analysis

This part of the external audit is probably more relevant in the field of consumer goods than in the sector of industrial goods, where direct distribution is common practice. The objective is to assess the future development of distribution channels and to understand the motivations and expectations of the company's trading partners.

Questionnaire 3: Structure and motivation of distribution

- What are industry sales by type of outlet?

- What are product type sales by type of outlet?

- What are product type sales by method of distribution?

- What is the concentration ratio of distribution?

- Is distribution intensive, selective or exclusive?

- What is the share of advertising assumed by distributors?

- What change does one observe in the assortments?

- What market share is held by private brands?

- Which market segments are covered by the different channels?

- What are the total distribution costs?

- What is the distribution margin for each channel of distribution?

- What kind of distributor support is currently provided?

- What is the potential of direct distribution?

- ...

The distributor, as a business partner, has strong negotiation powers *vis-à-vis* the firm. One of the roles of a distribution analysis is to assess the degree of autonomy or dependence of the firm in the distributive system.

Competitive environment

The competitive structure of a market sets the framework within which the firm will operate. As Porter (1980) has said: 'The essence of strategy formulation is coping with competition.' The basic attractiveness of a market segment is largely determined by the strength of competitors' capabilities. An assessment of what is driving the competition is of vital importance to the firm.

Questionnaire 4: Competition analysis

- What is the market's competitive structure?

- What market share is held by the top three to five rivals?

- What type of competitive behaviour is dominant?

- What is the image strength of competing brands?

- What is the nature of the competitive advantage of direct competitors?

- To what extent are these competitive advantages well protected?

- What are the competitors' major objectives?

- What current strategy is being used to achieve the objectives?

- What are the strengths and weaknesses of competitors?

- What are their likely future strategies?

- Are there entry barriers in this market?

- Which are the main substitute products?

- What is the bargaining power of customers and suppliers?

- ...

The collection of this type of information implies the development of a *competitor intelligence system*. For a more detailed framework of competitor analysis, see Porter (1980, ch. 3).

Macro-environmental trends

This section describes the macro-environmental trends—demographic, economic political/legal and sociocultural—that bear on the studied market's future development. These external factors can provide productive opportunities or severe limitations for the company's products.

Questionnaire 5a: Economic macro-environment

- What is the expected GNP rate of growth?

- What major economic changes could affect our business?

- What is the expected level of employment?

- What is the expected rate of inflation?

- Do these trends affect our business, and how?

- ...

Questionnaire 5b: Technological environment

- What major changes are occurring in product technology?

- How can we adjust our activities to cope with these changes?

- What major generic substitutes might replace our product?

- Do we have the required R&D capabilities?

■ Do we need to update our equipment, and at what cost?

■ ...

Questionnaire 5c: Socio-demographic and cultural macro-environment

■ What are the major demographic trends that affect our business?

■ What is the cultural climate within which our business operates?

■ Are present and future lifestyles favourable to our business?

■ Is society's attitude towards our business changing?

■ Are there changes in society's values that could affect our business?

■ ...

Questionnaire 5d: Political and legal macro-environment

■ Are there any specific changes in the law that affect our company?

■ Are there legal or political areas that affect our customers?

■ Which regulations could affect our advertising or selling strategy?

■ Is our industry subject to criticisms from consumer organizations?

■ Are there political or legal trends that could be used to our advantage?

■ ...

Questionnaire 5e: International environment

■ To what extent are we dependent on imports for key components?

■ What is the economic and political stability of the supplier country?

■ What alternatives do we have should our imports be interrupted?

■ What is the economic and political stability of the customer countries?

■ What opportunities does the European Single Market represent?

■ Are there emerging global segments in our business?

■ Is our business affected by changing world trade patterns?

■ ...

Questionnaire 5f: Ecological environment

■ Are our products environmentally friendly?

■ Do we use processes or raw materials which threaten the environment?

■ Is green marketing a potential strategy for our company?

- Is our industry a potential target for environmentalists?

- How can we improve the ecological quality of our products?

- ...

Questionnaire 5g: Industry and corporate ethics

- Does our company or industry have a stated code of ethics?

- What is the ethical level of our industry?

- Are industry values in alignment with those expected by society?

- How could our industry improve its ethical practice?

- ...

This information, dealing with the macro-environment of the firm, is indispensable for exploring alternative scenarios of market development. Generally, at least two scenarios will be explored: a base scenario, but also one or several alternative scenarios based on vulnerability factors.

In general

The sources of information are numerous and varied, but often very scattered. Professional organizations and local chambers of commerce have economic data available for their members to use in planning. In addition to national statistics and foreign trade institutes, international financial institutions like the Bank for International Settlements (BIS), the International Monetary Funds (IMF), the World Bank (WB), the Office for Economic and Co-operation Development (OECD), the United Nations (UN), etc., are the major public sources, with periodic publications readily available. University research centres and large international consulting firms, like Business International, McKinsey, the Economist Intelligence Unit, etc., also publish newsletters, articles and monographs that are very useful for planning purposes.

11.2.3 Internal audit: company competitiveness analysis

The objective of the internal audit, also called the *company strengths and weaknesses analysis*, is to assess company resources and to identify the type of sustainable competitive advantage on which to base the development strategy. Strengths and weaknesses are internal factors, in contrast with opportunities and threats, which are external factors. Company strengths (or distinctive qualities) point to certain strategies the company might be successful in adopting, while company weaknesses point to certain things the company needs to correct. A competitiveness analysis should not be abstract. Reference to competition in general is too vague. Therefore, competition should be referred to in terms of the most dangerous competitors, called priority competitors.

To illustrate, *distinctive qualities* for a brand of laptop computer, as compared to those of the priority competitor, might be:

- An excellent brand awareness and an image of high quality.

- Dealers who are knowledgeable and well trained in selling.

- An excellent service network and customers who know they will get quick repair service.

The *weaknesses* of the same brand could be:

- The screen quality of the brand is not demonstrably better than the quality of competing machines, yet screen quality can make a big difference in brand choice.

- The brand is budgeting only 5 per cent of its sales revenue for advertising and promotion while major competitors are spending twice that level.

- The brand is priced higher relative to other brands without being supported by a real perceived difference in quality.

The strengths of the company or of the brand constitute potential *competitive advantages* on which to base the positioning and the communication strategy. The weaknesses determine the *vulnerability* of the brand and require remedial action. Some weaknesses may be structural, i.e. linked to the size of the firm and therefore difficult to correct. Examples of structural weaknesses are:

- National market share leadership, if not accompanied by international distribution, creates a home country vulnerability to the extent that the local company has little freedom for retaliation in the country of foreign competitors.

- If total sales volume is generated by a single powerful distributor, the company has weak bargaining power.

- A small or medium-sized company does not have the financial capability to use the most powerful media, like television advertising.

So a distinction must be made between (a) the weaknesses the company can correct and which therefore become priority issues that must be addressed in the plan, and (b) the high risk structural weaknesses that are beyond the control of the firm and require a high degree of surveillance.

Competitiveness analysis is organized much like attractiveness analysis. The major difference comes from the fact that the company, and not the market, is the central subject of the analysis.

The following questionnaires should be used as guidelines for periodically reviewing the company's situation within the framework of a marketing audit.

Company current marketing situation
Data on the served markets for each of the products of the company's portfolio, in volume and market shares for several years and by geographical areas, are presented, as well as data on the current marketing mix.

Questionnaire 6: Product portfolio analysis

■ What is the rate of current sales per product, segment, distributive channel, region, country, etc., in volume and value?

■ What is the current market share per product category, segment, distributive channel, region, country, etc.?

■ How does the quality of our products compare with that of competition?

■ How strong is the company's product brand image?

■ Does the firm have a complete product line?

■ What is the structure of our portfolio of customers?

■ How concentrated is our total turnover?

■ What is the age profile of our product portfolio?

■ What is the contribution margin per product, segment, channel, etc.?

■ What is the current level of nominal and relative prices?

■ ...

This analysis is to be repeated for each product of the company's portfolio. Profit and loss statements of the last three years should be presented along with the current budget. A typical profit and loss statement is shown later (see Table 11.2, p. 408).

Priority competitor analysis
Priority competitor(s) should be identified for each product market. For each of these competitors, the same data collected for the company products will be gathered and compared, as shown in Table 11.1. Other information is required to assess the strength of priority competition.

Questionnaire 7: Priority competition analysis

■ What is the relative market share?

■ Does competition have a cost advantage?

■ What is the relative price?

■ What is the competitive behaviour of rivals?

■ How strong is the image of competing products?

■ On what basis are competing products differentiated?

■ How large are their financial resources?

■ What is their retaliation capacity in case of frontal attack?

■ Which are their major sources of vulnerability?

TABLE 11.1 *Priority competitors analysis form*

(Each factor must be evaluated on a 10-point scale)

Marketing variables	Our product	Competitor 1	Competitor 2	Competitor 3
Product				
Quality	....	....	....	....
Company price	....	....	....	....
Product line	....	....	....	....
Packaging	....	....	....	....
Evaluation on:				
attribute 1	....	....	....	....
attribute 2	....	....	....	....
attribute 3	....	....	....	....
Distribution				
Distribution number	....	....	....	....
Distribution value:				
channel 1	....	....	....	....
channel 2	....	....	....	....
channel 3	....	....	....	....
Facing	....	....	....	....
Margin	....	....	....	....
Discounts	....	....	....	....
Promotion	....	....	....	....
Salesforce				
Size of salesforce	....	....	....	....
Quality	....	....	....	....
Call frequency	....	....	....	....
Training	....	....	....	....
Advertising				
Size of budget	....	....	....	....
Media mix:				
medium 1	....	....	....	....
medium 2	....	....	....	....
medium 3	....	....	....	....
Advertising copy	....	....	....	....
Advertisement quality	....	....	....	....
Promotion				
Size of budget	....	....	....	....
Type of promotion:				
Consumer price	....	....	....	....
Distribution margin	....	....	....	....
Other promotions	....	....	....	....
Services				
Range of services	....	....	....	....
Delivery terms	....	....	....	....
After-sales service	....	....	....	....
Research and development				
Size of budget	....	....	....	....
Staff	....	....	....	....
Performance in R&D	....	....	....	....
Marketing research				
Quality of MIS	....	....	....	....
Data banks	....	....	....	....
Performance	....	....	....	....

- What type of aggressive actions could they take?

- What kind of retaliatory or protective actions could we adopt?

- What changes could modify the present balance of power?

- Is competition able to destroy our competitive advantage?

- ...

With the information provided by Questionnaires 6 and 7, a product portfolio analysis can be conducted using one of the procedures described in Chapter 10.

Distribution penetration analysis

Distributors—a company's partners in the marketing process—control the access to the end-users' market and play an important role in ensuring the success of the contemplated marketing programme. In addition, if they are powerful buyers they have a strong bargaining power *vis-à-vis* their suppliers. In fact, distributors must be viewed as intermediate customers just like end-user customers. The role of *trade marketing* is to analyse the needs and requirements of these intermediate customers in order to develop a mutually satisfactory exchange relationship.

Questionnaire 8: Distribution analysis

- How many distributors do we have in each channel?

- What is our penetration rate in number and value in each channel?

- What is the sales volume by type of distributor?

- What are the growth potentials of the different channels?

- What are the efficiency levels of the different distributors?

- Are the present trade terms motivating for distributors?

- What changes could modify relationships with our dealer network?

- Should the firm consider changing its distribution channels?

- What is the potential of direct marketing in our business?

- Are new forms of distribution emerging in the market?

- ...

The objectives pursued by the firm and by its distributors are not exactly the same and conflicts can arise in the channels. Distributors are no longer passive intermediaries in most markets. The role of 'trade marketing' is to ensure that distributors are viewed by the firm as partners and as intermediate customers.

Communication programme analysis

Mass media advertising, interactive advertising, personal selling, publicity, etc., are powerful competitive weapons if properly used, i.e. when the target markets are well chosen and the content of the communication programme is consistent with the product positioning, pricing and distribution strategies.

Questionnaire 9: Communication programme analysis

- What is the advertising intensity compared to direct competition?

- What is the advertising cost per thousand target buyers per medium?

- What is the communication effectiveness of media advertising?

- What are the consumers' opinions on the advertisement content?

- What is the number of reply coupons stimulated by direct advertising?

- How well are the advertising objectives defined?

- What is the sales or market share effectiveness of advertising?

- What is the impact of advertising on awareness, attitude, intentions?

- What is the average number of sales call per sales representative per week?

- What is the number of new customers per period?

- What is the salesforce cost as a percentage of total sales?

- ...

11.3 OBJECTIVES AND ACTION PROGRAMMES

At this point, management knows the major issues and has to make some basic decisions about the objectives. Using the information provided by the strategic marketing audit and by the positioning statement, the firm's identified priority objectives must then be translated into operational action programmes.

11.3.1 Definition of objectives

Every firm has several objectives which can be regrouped into two broad categories: marketing and non-marketing.

- *Non-marketing objectives* have been described in the firm's mission statement. They describe the overall value system of the company and, as such, they apply to all market targets.

- *Marketing objectives* are of three types: sales, profit and customers. They should be defined for each product market or segment.

Sales objectives

A sales objective is a quantitative measure of the impact the firm 'wants' to achieve in the future within a particular product market. It is not simply a forecast of what one 'expects' may occur in the future. It is an active, not a passive, statement about the future.

Sales objectives can be stated in currency, in volume or in market share. Here are a few sales-oriented objectives:

■ Achieve a total sales revenue of $2 150 000 by the end of 1992.

■ Attain a 20 per cent market share of the management distance learning market.

■ Reach a sales volume of 150 000 units per year.

■ *Sales revenue* objectives are the most convenient way to express a sales objective because they are easily integrated in the accounting and financial system. Sales revenue may be misleading, however, if not adjusted for inflation and also for modifications in the sales mix if, for example, the share of high-priced products has changed from one period to another.

■ *Market share*, as discussed in Chapter 6, is the best indicator of competitive performance. Also, in volume industries where experience effects occur, high market share implies a cost competitive advantage over direct competition.

■ *Unit sales* represent the best indicator provided there is no change in the volume definition. In the soft drinks sector, for example, it is current practice to think in terms of sales of cases. What about cases of 12 or 18 bottles? Conversion to 'litres equivalent cases' must be made. In many markets a meaningful unit definition simply does not exist. For example, in life insurance the number of contracts sold is not a good indicator of sales performance.

Sales data are the main elements in the projected income statement, but they must be translated into financial terms.

Profit objectives

Marketing, as for all other functions within the firm, must be accountable for profits. The inclusion of formal profit objectives forces marketing people to estimate the cost implications of the stated sales objectives. Here are some examples of profit objectives:

■ Produce net profits of $150 000 before tax by December 1996.

■ Earn an average 15 per cent return on investment during the next 5 years.

■ Produce a dollar contribution of $350 000 at the end of the fiscal year.

The definition of profit objectives implies a close interfunctional co-ordination within the firm. A statement of profitability cannot be made without a close look at the cost–volume relationship and capacity constraints. For new products, the investment in fixed costs and working capital, in addition to manufacturing and marketing costs, should be analysed before launching. Similarly, the marketing expenses involved in implementing the proposed marketing strategy must be carefully evaluated and their expected contribution to sales and/or market share development assessed. Go back to Fig 1.2 for a description of the interrelationships among the key managerial functions.

Customer objectives

Customer objectives are deduced from the positioning statement. They describe the type of behaviour or attitude the firm would want customers to have towards its brands or services. A few customer objectives are:

■ Create at least a 60 per cent awareness for brand A within the 15–25 age group by the end of 1992.

■ To increase by 20 per cent the repeat purchase rate of brand A within the 15–25 age group by the end of 1996.

■ To position the brand at the high end of the market in the minds of consumers belonging to the upper income bracket.

These customers objectives are important because they provide directions to advertising people for the development of communication strategies and for supporting the positioning theme adopted.

Integration of objectives

Kotler (1991, p. 77) suggests starting with the profit objectives and deducing the required sales and customer objectives.

> For example, if the company wants to earn $1 800 000 profit, and its target profit margin is 10 per cent on sales, then it must set a goal of $18 million in sales revenue. If the company sets an average price of $260, it must sell 69 230 units. If it expects total industry sales to reach 2.3 million units, that is a 3 per cent market share. To maintain this market share, the company will have to set certain goals for consumer awareness, distribution coverage, and so on.

Thus, the line of reasoning is as follows:

■ Define the expected net profit.

■ Identify the turnover required to achieve this result.

■ Given the current average company price, determine the required sales volume (in units).

■ Given the expected level of primary demand in the reference segment, calculate the correponding required market share.

■ Given this target market share, determine the target objectives in terms of distribution and communication.

The corresponding *marketing objectives* should therefore be:

■ To achieve a given turnover, which represents an increase over previous year of x per cent.

■ This would imply a sales volume of x units, corresponding to a y per cent market share.

- To determine the level of brand awareness required to achieve this market share objective and also the required proportion of purchase intentions within the target segment.

- To determine the increase of distribution rate.

- To maintain the average company price.

This logical and apparently simple procedure is difficult to implement in the real world because it implies complete knowledge of the functional relationships between market share and price, market share and distribution, market share and awareness, etc. The merit of this approach is to identify clearly the required information for sound marketing planning.

Characteristics of good objectives

Sound marketing objectives should have the following characteristics. They must (a) be clear and concise, avoiding long statements and phrases; they should (b) be presented in a written form to facilitate communication and to avoid altering objectives over time; they should (c) be stated within a specific time period and (d) in measurable terms; they must (e) be consistent with overall company objectives and purpose; they must (f) be attainable but of sufficient challenge to stimulate effort; and they should (g) name specific results in key areas, such as sales, profits and consumer behaviour or attitudes (Stevens, 1982, pp. 80–2).

In addition, individual responsibilities should be clearly defined as well as the calendar and the deadlines to be met.

11.3.2 Selection of the strategic path

To define an objective is one thing; to know how to reach that objective is quite another since the very same objective can be achieved in different ways. For example, a 10 per cent revenue increase can be obtained by increasing the average selling price, or by expanding total demand through a price decrease, or by increasing market share without price change but through intensive advertising or promotional actions.

Clearly these alternative actions are not substitutes and their efficiency will vary according to market and competitive situations. Thus, beyond the general directions given by the basic strategic options discussed in Chapter 10, it is necessary to specify the action programmes segment by segment.

If the strategic option is to defend current market position with existing products in an existing segment, the alternative actions to consider in a *market position defence strategy* could be:

- Product or service modifications, e.g. new features or packaging, or product repositioning through concept advertising.

- Sales, distribution and service network reinforcement.

- Increased or redirected promotional activities.

- Defensive pricing through bundling or premium pricing.

If the objective is to complete, improve or broaden the range of products, the alternative of a *product line extension strategy* could be:

- Filling gaps in the existing product line.

- Introduction of new products to serve untapped segments in related business areas.

- Systematic proliferation of brands to blanket the market.

- Acquisition of a company with a complementary product line.

- Contracting for the supply of a complementary product line to be sold under the company's name.

- Joint venture for the development and production of a new product line.

If the objective is *international development* by shipping existing products to foreign markets, the alternatives could be:

- Use of an independent, worldwide trading company.

- Use of a network of export agents to handle all foreign business.

- Establishing a network of distributors or import agents in target markets.

- Acquisition of a foreign company in the same industrial sector.

- A joint venture to enter a restricted foreign market.

These alternative strategy paths may have very different implications in terms of resources, both financial and human, and their feasibility must be carefully assessed.

The strategy statement

The strategy statement requires basic choices to be made among the various strategy alternatives. It is a summary overview designed to state 'how' the objectives for the business unit will be met. The strategy statement will govern not only marketing planning, but the manufacturing, financial and R&D functions. It is the mainstream guidance from which all subsequent planning functions flow. The strategy statement should address the following:

- Market segments selected and targeted.

- Positioning relative to direct competition.

- Product line requirements, mix, extensions, etc.

- Channels of distribution, direct, indirect, etc.

- Pricing and price structure.

- Personal selling.

- Advertising and promotion.

- After-sale, warranty, services, etc.

- Market research.

The strategy statement should not exceed two or three pages of text. At this point, general management should review and approve the objectives.

Criteria for selecting a strategic option
A certain number of simple rules, inspired by military strategy, should be followed in selecting a strategy.

- *Feasibility:* assess skills and resources constraints.

- *Strength:* always try to have a strength advantage.

- *Concentration:* avoid scattering of efforts.

- *Synergy:* ensure co-ordination and consistency in efforts.

- *Adaptability:* be ready to respond to the unexpected.

- *Parsimony:* avoid waste of scarce resources.

In the environment of the 1990s, forward thinking is a dynamic exercise which requires adaptability and flexibility (Gilbreath, 1987).

11.3.3 The marketing budget
Once the course of action is identified, a detailed description of the means required will be made for each component of the marketing mix. The strategy statement allows the product manager to prepare a supporting budget, which is basically a projected profit and loss statement. A standard structure of a projected profit and loss statement is presented in Table 11.2.

TABLE 11.2 *Projected profit and loss statements form*

Variables	$t-3$	$t-2$	$t-1$	Current	$t+1$	$t+2$	$t+3$
1. Total demand in unit							
2. Company market share							
3. Average selling price							
4. Unit direct cost							
5. Unit gross profit margin $(3-4)$							
6. Company sales in units (1×2)							
7. Company sales revenue (3×6)							
8. Total gross profit margin (5×6)							
9. Overhead							
10. Net profit margin $(5-6)$							
11. Advertising and promotion							
12. Salesforce							
13. Market research							
14. Operating profit $10-(11+12+13)$							

The strategy statement gives a general direction which must then be translated into specific actions for each component of the marketing mix with a description of the resources available to implement those actions. These resources include human and financial resources; they are described in the action programme and in the budget.

The *action programme* includes a detailed description of the actions to be undertaken. In addition to financial considerations, the budget should also specify the timing of the action programme and the responsibilities, i.e. who is in charge of what. An example of budget structure is presented in Table 11.2.

Negotiation of the marketing budget

Different budgeting modes can be adopted to design a strategic marketing plan. The ideal procedure should be as simple as possible and involve the whole organization and, in particular, the functions responsible for implementing the plan. The most popular budgeting process observed in a survey of 141 companies (Piercy 1987, p. 49), is the *bottom-up/top-down* process:

> Managers of the subunits in marketing submit budget requests, which are co-ordinated by the chief marketing executive and presented to top management, who adjust the total budget size to conform with overall goals and strategies.

A good strategic marketing plan should be a written document, taking the form of a contract. To be effective the plan should have the following characteristics:

■ To be sufficiently standardized as to permit fast discussion and approval.

■ To consider alternative solutions to be adopted if environmental conditions change or if corrective actions have to be taken.

■ To be regularly re-examined or up-dated.

■ To be viewed as a managerial aid, which implies (a) to be strict on the applications of corporate goal and on long-term strategic options, and (b) to be flexible on short-term forecasts.

The planning horizon is, in general, a three-year moving horizon and, usually, there is a monthly comparison between current and expected results in order to monitor closely the implementation of the plan and to facilitate the adoption of fast remedial action.

Gap analysis

In summarizing the objectives of each business unit, it is instructive to project the current performance trends to verify whether the projected performance is satisfactory. If gaps appear between the current and the desired performances, then strategic changes will need to be considered. The graph presented in Fig. 11.1 illustrates the contribution of growth opportunities under two growth scenarios:

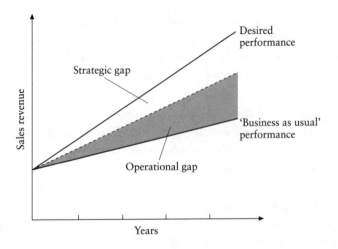

FIGURE 11.1 *Gap analysis*

- An *all things being equal performance*, where growth is achieved through a penetration strategy based on existing products and existing markets, assuming no change in the current strategy.

- A *desired performance*, where growth is the outcome of the proposed marketing programme and of different growth opportunities.

As shown in Fig. 11.1, the gap between these two performance levels can be subdivided into two parts:

- An *operational gap*, which reveals the improvement potential of existing businesses that could be achieved through a market and product rationalization strategy, i.e. reducing costs and/or improving marketing effectiveness, while keeping the structure of the product portfolio unchanged.

- A *strategic gap*, which requires new growth opportunities, i.e. new products, new markets, international development, diversification or integration.

These growth opportunities should be listed in order of priority and their potential financial contribution to the desired performance evaluated.

11.4 VULNERABILITY ANALYSIS AND CONTINGENCY PLANNING

The value of strategic planning is a continuing topic for debate. Not long ago, planning departments enjoyed a high status within the corporate organization. Today, most corporate planners downplay their formal planning roles. Experience with such largely unforeseen upheavals as the two oil crises of the 1970s, the stock market crash of 1987, the Gulf War, the East European revolutions, etc., has revealed the shortcomings and the limitations of rigid planning procedures. Under fairly static conditions planning works well, but when faced with uncertainties, turbulences, unanticipated market and competitive changes, general management becomes suspicious of the forecasts of revenue and profit performance that come from the business units.

11.4.1 Testing the robustness of a strategic plan

A strategy must be developed and implemented under turbulent and uncertain conditions, but that is no reason to abandon the discipline of structured planning. Planning is necessary for the functioning of the firm. To improve strategic planning performance, it is therefore important to test the robustness of the proposed strategy. Gilbreath (1987) suggests applying a 'shake test' to the proposed strategy.

> When structural or mechanical engineers wish to determine the reaction of a proposed design to mechanical vibrations, they either model it mathematically and calculate its response to input vibrations or, if feasible, build a prototype, put it on a special 'shaking table' and actually witness the outcome. This is called a 'shake test'. . . . It is proposed that a similar exercise be applied to strategic plans – giving them the shake test before the unforgiving test our markets and competitors will surely apply.   (Gilbreath, 1987, p. 47)

Day (1986) proposed testing the robustness of a proposed strategy through the following seven 'tough questions' to be examined by corporate management and operating managers.

1. *Suitability*. Is there a sustainable advantage given the potential threats to and opportunities for the business and in light of the capabilities of the firm?
2. *Validity*. Are the assumptions realistic? What is the quality of the information on which these assumptions rely?
3. *Feasibility*. Do we have the skills, resources and commitment?
4. *Consistency*. Does the strategy hang together? Are all elements of the strategy pointing in the same direction?
5. *Vulnerability*. What are the risks and contingencies?
6. *Adaptability*. Can we retain our flexibility? How could the strategy be reversed in the future?
7. *Financial desirability*. How much economic value is created? What is the attractiveness of the forecast performance relative to the probable risk?

(Adapted from Day, 1986, pp. 63–8)

Examples of vulnerability factors are presented in Table 11.3.

Given the rapidity of environmental change, the test should be applied periodically to facilitate adaptability and revision. A good way to proceed is to apply this shake test with the assistance of outside persons to avoid the risk of myopia and wishful thinking.

11.4.2 Vulnerability and risk analysis

The vulnerability of a strategic plan is determined by two factors: the strategic importance of risk and the degree of control the firm has over the risk factor. The risk factor is a combination of (a)

TABLE 11.3 *Identifying vulnerability factors*

Vulnerability factors	Stability factors
Reliance on fads	Projection of lasting symbols
Single use	Multiple use of products
Technology dependence	Technology transcendence
Single distribution network	Multiple distribution network
Heavy capital investment	Leasing, renting and joint ownership
Prescriptive identities	Non-restrictive identities
Building with products outside our control	Building with unchanging needs

Source: Adapted from Gilbreath (1987).

the impact of extreme but plausible values on overall performance, and (b) the likelihood that these extreme values could occur during the planning period.

The vulnerability grid presented in Fig. 11.2 can be used to position the different risk factors and to isolate those few that could cause the most damage. To each quadrant there corresponds a specific risk situation which requires appropriate action.

■ In the *strategy quadrant*, i.e. where both risk and degree of control are high, the risk factors are subject to company control, need to be understood very well, are the focus of major strategic actions and should be tightly monitored.

■ In the *vulnerability quadrant*, the risks are high but the degree of control is weak. The factors positioned here are critical and must be continuously monitored. Contingency plans should be developed.

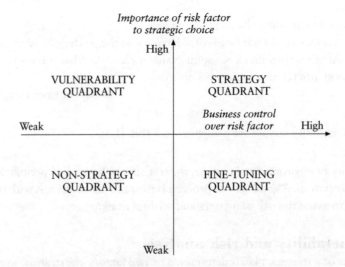

FIGURE 11.2 *Vulnerability grid (Source: Day, 1986)*

■ In the *fine-tuning quadrant*, the risks are low but the degree of control is high. These factors are controlled and managed by operational management.

■ In the *non-strategy quadrant*, both risk and degree of control are low and the factors positioned here will be included in the base scenario.

The vulnerability quadrant deserves particular attention, since major and unanticipated crises could come from these risk factors. Alternative strategies should be developed for these risk factors.

11.4.3 Strategic surprise management

In spite of the best planning efforts, some issues or unexpected changes will slip by the environmental monitoring system and become 'crises' or *strategic surprises* in Ansoff's terminology (1984). A crisis is characterized by four elements (Ansoff, 1984, p. 24):

■ The issue arrives suddenly, unanticipated.

■ It poses novel problems in which the firm has little prior experience.

■ Failure to respond implies either a major financial reversal or loss of a major opportunity.

■ The response is urgent and cannot be handled promptly enough by the normal systems and procedures.

The combination of these four elements creates major problems for the firm. A crisis or disaster can be any emergency that (a) happens suddenly, (b) disrupts the routine of the organization and (c) demands immediate attention. Examples of crises are numerous: the 'Nestlé kills babies' affair; the Tylenol incident; the Union Carbide disaster in Bhopal; the Société Générale of Belgium's takeover bid; the Pan Am Boeing 747 crash at Lockerbie; the Chernobyl and Three Mile Island nuclear accidents; the change in the Coke formula, etc.

The suddenness and the prospect of a major loss create a danger of widespread panic, and 'business as usual' managerial systems are inefficient to deal with a crisis. The firm needs to invest in a *crisis recovery plan*, because disaster recovery planning is more conducive to a rational perspective and is more cost-effective if the process is begun before a crisis, rather than pulled together in the heat of battle (Phelps, 1986, p. 6).

To develop a contingency planning system the following steps must be taken:

1. Identify the *sensitive* factors and the zones of danger through a vulnerability analysis.
2. Establish a monitoring system with *warning signals* based on early warning indicators.
3. Prepare a *crisis recovery plan* based on some previously identified alternative strategy .
4. Adopt this procedure for the *major risks*.

According to Ansoff (1984) and Lagadec (1991), a crisis recovery plan should have the following characteristics:

- An emergency communication network which crosses normal organizational boundaries, filters the information and rapidly communicates with the entire organization.

- A distribution of top management responsibilities between three groups: one in charge of the organization's morale control and maintenance; one in charge of 'business as usual'; and one in charge of the response to the surprise.

- A strategic task force, whose members cross normal organizational lines, to deal with the surprise.

- The task force and communication networks should be pre-designed and trained under non-crisis conditions before they are put to the actual test.

This procedure will not eliminate the occurrence of completely unexpected events but will contribute towards reducing the consequences of major risks that can be identified. According to Augustine (1995, p. 151), '... when preparing for crises, it is instructive to recall that Noah started building the ark before it began to rain.' To go further on the topic of crisis management, see the excellent book by Lagadec (1991).

11.4.4 The new roles of global strategic planning

In 1991, Business International conducted a survey with 18 of the world's leading global companies on three continents for gaining insights into their approaches to global planning. The 10 most frequently mentioned functions of corporate planners are:

- Compiling of information for top management.

- Competitor research.

- Forecasting.

- Consulting services.

- Creating a common language.

- Communicating corporate culture.

- Establishing and communicating corporate objectives.

- Group facilitation and team leadership.

- Guardianship of the planning system.

- Developing planning methods.

Most corporate planners downplay their formal planning roles and instead emphasize their functions as 'facilitators', 'communicators' or 'consultants'. They see their role less as representatives of corporate authority than as consultants charged with assisting the divisions in developing their own plan and strategies.

SUMMARY

This chapter has provided a scheme for developing a formal strategic marketing plan. The role of strategic planning is to design a desired future for the company and to define effective ways of making things happen. The plan summarizes, in a formal way, the marketing strategy development phase. One of the key elements of the strategic plan is the mission statement, which should reveal the company's long-term vision of what it wants to be and who it wants to serve. The strategic plan is based on an external audit. The environment is ever-changing and complex and the firm must constantly scan and monitor the environment to identify the main threats and opportunities. The assessment of strengths and weaknesses is also an essential task in the strategic process. The objective is to evaluate company resources in order to identify a sustainable competitive advantage on which to base the development strategy. Using the information collected in the external and internal audits, the next task is to define priority objectives to be translated into operational action programmes within a marketing budget. Testing the robustness of a strategic plan is useful to improve the strategic planning performance. Also, in the current turbulent environment, vulnerability and risk analysis is required to help the firm to anticipate the unexpected through contingency planning and crises management.

QUESTIONS AND PROBLEMS

1. What difference do you see between a marketing plan and a marketing strategy?
2. Select a company you know well and prepare a mission statement for its activities and its corporate goal.
3. How can you associate, as closely as possible, the different echelons within the firm to the preparation and adoption of a strategic plan? Compare the merits and the weaknesses of the 'top-down' and 'bottom-up' budgeting processes .
4. Referring to Table 11.3, give examples of three vulnerability factors and three stability factors to be used to test the robustness of a strategic plan.
5. What are the chances that strategic planning will succeed in a company whose chief executive shows no interest and delegates the task to staff members?
6. List five variables on which success in the home construction industry depends.
7. Since it is natural for managers to want to justify their actions and decisions, is it possible for a company to make a truly objective appraisal of its strengths and weaknesses?
8. A financial executive questions the need for formal planning. Prepare a defence for strategic marketing planning.

REFERENCES

Ansoff, H.I. (1984), *Implanting Strategic Management*. Englewood Cliffs, New Jersey: Prentice Hall Inc.

Augustine, N.R. (1995), 'Managing the Crisis you Tried to Prevent', *Harvard Business Review*, November–December, vol. 73, no. 6, pp. 147–58.

Caeldries, F. and R. Van Dierdonck (1988), 'How Belgian Businesses Make Strategic Planning Work', *Long Range Planning*, vol. 21, no. 2.

David, F.R. (1989), 'How Companies Define Their Mission', *Long Range Planning*, vol. 22, no. 1, pp. 90–7.

Day, G.S. (1986), 'Tough Questions for Developing Strategies', *The Journal of Business Strategy*, vol. 6, no. 3.

Drucker, P.F. (1973) *Management Tasks, Responsibilities, Practices*. New York: Harper & Row.

Gilbreath, R.D. (1987), 'Planning for the Unexpected', *The Journal of Business Strategy*, vol. 8, no. 2.

Greenley, G. (1987), 'An Exposition into Empirical Research into Marketing Planning', *Journal of Marketing Management*, vol. 3, no. 1, July.

Hamermesch, R.G. (1986), 'Making Planning Strategies', *Harvard Business Review*, vol. 64, July–August, pp. 115–20.

Haspeslagh, P. (1982), 'Portfolio Planning Uses and Limits', *Harvard Business Review*, vol. 60, January–February, pp. 58–72.

Hopkins, D.S. (1981), *The Marketing Plan*, New York: The Conference Board, Inc., Report no. 801.

Kotler, P. (1991), *Marketing Management*, 7th edn. Englewood Cliffs, New Jersey: Prentice Hall Inc.

Lagadec, P. (1991), *La gestion des crises*. Paris: Ediscience International.

McDonald, M.H.B. (1991), 'Ten Barriers to Marketing Planning', *The Journal of Consumer Marketing*, vol. 8, Spring, pp. 45–58.

Piercy, N.F. (1987), 'The Marketing Budgeting Process: Marketing Management Implications', *Journal of Marketing*, vol. 51, no. 4, October, pp. 45–59.

Phelps, N.L. (1986), 'Setting Up a Crisis Recovery Plan', *The Journal of Business Strategy*, vol. 6, no. 4.

Porter, M.E. (1980), *Competitive Strategy*. New York: The Free Press.

Stevens, R.E. (1982), *Strategic Marketing Plan Master Guide*. Englewood Cliffs, New Jersey: Prentice Hall Inc.

FURTHER READING

Taylor, J.W. (1986), *Competitive Marketing Strategies*. Radnor, Penn.: Chilton Book Co.

Weber, J.A. (1976), *Growth Opportunity Analysis*. Reston, Virginia: Reston Publishing Co. Inc.

Weitz, B.A. and R. Wensley (eds) (1986), *Strategic Marketing: Planning, Implementation and Control*. Boston: Kent Publishing Co.

APPENDIX 11.1

The search for a sustainable competitive advantage in the value chain

Managerial functions	Evaluation*				
	1	2	3	4	5
Marketing:					
High relative market share	......	......	......	......	......
Brand reputation	......	......	......	......	......
High distribution coverage	......	......	......	......	......
Size of the salesforce	......	......	......	......	......
Effective salesforce	......	......	......	......	......
Level of sales training	......	......	......	......	......
Quality sales support	......	......	......	......	......
Low relative price	......	......	......	......	......
Balanced customer portfolio	......	......	......	......	......
Size of the advertising budget	......	......	......	......	......
Advertising quality (creativity)	......	......	......	......	......
Marketing data bank	......	......	......	......	......
Fast delivery	......	......	......	......	......
Training for dealers	......	......	......	......	......
Fine-tuned segmentation	......	......	......	......	......
Customers level of satisfaction	......	......	......	......	......
Extent of product line	......	......	......	......	......
Customer service					
...					
Operations:					
Large production capacity	......	......	......	......	......
Convenient location of production units	......	......	......	......	......
Extension potential	......	......	......	......	......
Advanced technology	......	......	......	......	......
Age of equipments	......	......	......	......	......
Total quality control	......	......	......	......	......
Equipment versatility	......	......	......	......	......
Availability of quality labour force	......	......	......	......	......
Fast manufacturing	......	......	......	......	......
Quality, reliability of components	......	......	......	......	......
Flexible manufacturing	......	......	......	......	......
Production to customer specifications	......	......	......	......	......
Defect-free manufacturing	......	......	......	......	......
Fast, reliable service	......	......	......	......	......
...					

*1 = not at all important; 5 = very important

Managerial functions	Evaluation*				
	1	2	3	4	5
Finance:					
High cash flow	......	......	......	......	......
Good profitability	......	......	......	......	......
Availability of credit	......	......	......	......	......
Availability of capital	......	......	......	......	......
Low debt ratio	......	......	......	......	......
High stock turnout	......	......	......	......	......
No long term debt	......	......	......	......	......
Good return on equity	......	......	......	......	......
Efficient invoicing	......	......	......	......	......
Good customer credit	......	......	......	......	......
...					
Administration:					
Qualification of personnel	......	......	......	......	......
Sufficient inventory	......	......	......	......	......
Strategic, attractive location of office	......	......	......	......	......
Low operating costs	......	......	......	......	......
Good customer after-sales service	......	......	......	......	......
Good training programmes	......	......	......	......	......
Up-to-date office equipment	......	......	......	......	......
Office automation	......	......	......	......	......
Efficient order processing	......	......	......	......	......
...					
Technology:					
Fast new product development	......	......	......	......	......
Up-of-date technology	......	......	......	......	......
Engineering know-how	......	......	......	......	......
Product patents	......	......	......	......	......
Process patents	......	......	......	......	......
High creativity in R&D	......	......	......	......	
Good management of R&D	......	......	......	......	......
High R&D budget	......	......	......	......	......
Performance of R&D	......	......	......	......	......
...					

*1 = not at all important; 5 = very important

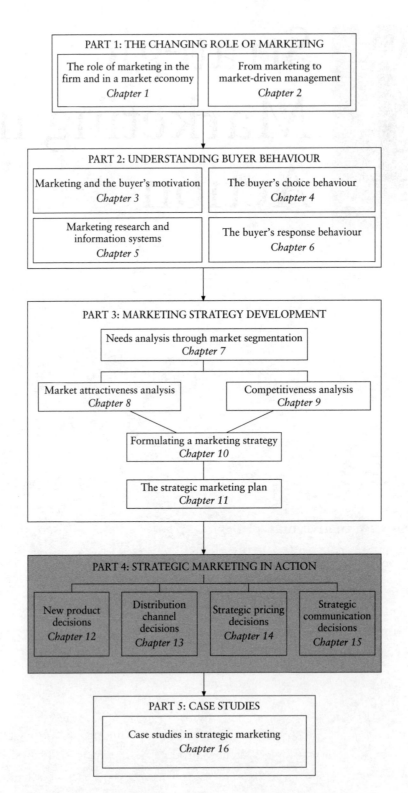

FIGURE PT4.1 *The structure of this book*

CHAPTER 12

NEW PRODUCT DECISIONS

LEARNING OBJECTIVES

After reading this chapter, you should be able to:

■ describe the nature, risks and success factors of innovations

■ define the organizational procedure which reduces the risk of failure throughout the new product development process

■ list and discuss the steps in new product development

■ develop alternative marketing programmes for a new product and evaluate their expected profitability

■ describe the concept of portfolio of projects

■ explain the concept and the dimensions of quality viewed from the buyer's perspective.

*T*he objective of this chapter is to analyse the concepts and procedures which allow a firm to implement new product development strategies. Redeployment, diversification and innovation are at the heart of all development strategies. In a constantly changing environment, a company must continuously re-evaluate the structure of its portfolio of activities—making decisions to abandon products, to modify existing products or to launch new products. These decisions are of the utmost importance to the survival of the company and involve not only the marketing department, but also all the other functional areas. In this chapter, we shall examine methods of establishing a dialogue between the various functional areas that play a role in the development of a new product. This must be conducted in such a way as to minimize the strategic risks during the innovation process.

12.1 ASSESSING THE RISK OF INNOVATIONS

The expression 'new product' is used loosely to describe a whole spectrum of innovations ranging from very minor, such as a change in an existing product, to very major, such as perfecting a new medicine resulting from years of research and development. Clearly, the risk varies greatly in these two examples and the nature of the risk in each is completely different. Therefore, it is important to evaluate accurately the diversity of innovations and their specific risks. After having defined the elements that constitute innovation, we shall examine the different classifications of innovation as well as the principal factors that explain the success or failure of new products.

12.1.1 Components of an innovation

In Chapter 2 we saw that there was a distinction between an invention and an innovation. The latter is defined as the original implementation of a concept, discovery, or invention. According to Barreyre (1980, p. 10), an innovation (see Box 12.1) may be subdivided into three elements:

BOX 12.1

Components of an innovation: two examples

The disengageable T-bar and downhill skiing
- The *need*: to avoid the long and tiresome process of climbing back up snow-covered slopes.
- The *concept*: traction by a disengageable cable with a seat.
- The *technology*: mechanics

The problem of aeronautic vibrations
- The *need*: to eliminate the vibrations that affect electronic equipment in an aeroplane.
- The *concept*: a sort of mesh covering.
- The *technology*: a resilient steel weave.

Source: Barreyre (1980).

- A *need* to be satisfied, or a function(s) to be fulfilled.

- The *concept* of an object or entity to satisfy the need, in other words, the 'new idea'.

- The *inputs*, comprising of a body of existing knowledge as well as materials and available technology, which allow the concept to become operational.

The degree of risk associated with an innovation will thus depend on two factors:

- The degree of originality and complexity of the concept, which will determine the reception by the market and transfer costs for the user (market risk).

- The degree of technological innovation pertaining to the concept, which will determine the technical feasibility of the innovation (technology risk).

Added to these two intrinsic risks is the degree of familiarity that the firm has with the market and technology (strategy risk).

Three possible criteria for classifying innovations emerge: (1) the degree of newness for the firm; (2) the intrinsic nature of the concept based on the innovation; and (3) the intensity of the innovation.

12.1.2 Degree of newness for the company

Assessing the degree of newness for the company is important because it is this newness which determines, at least in part, the company's competitiveness or competitive capacity. As Table 12.1 suggests, the more a company explores new territory, the greater the strategy risk becomes. Four distinguishable levels of risk for a new product are as follows:

1. *Known market and technology.* The risk is doubly limited because the firm relies on its distinctive abilities.
2. *New market, known technology.* The risk is essentially a commercial one and success relies heavily on the marketing know-how of the firm.
3. *Known market, new technology.* The risk is technical in nature and success relies on the firm's technical know-how.
4. *New market, new technology.* The risks increase and we find the characteristics for a strategy of diversification.

TABLE 12.1 *Assessing the newness of an innovation*

	Product or technology	
Market	Known	Unknown (new)
Known	Concentration	Technological risk
Unknown (new)	Commercial risk	Diversification

When considering product *newness*, it is important to distinguish between products 'new-to-the-world' and 'new-to-the-company'. Booz *et al*. (1982) established the following typology, based on a study of 700 companies and 13 000 new industrial and consumer products.

- New-to-the-world products   10 per cent

- New product lines   20 per cent

- Additions to existing product lines   26 per cent

- Improvements in/revisions to existing products   26 per cent

- Repositionings   7 per cent

- Cost reductions   11 per cent

Note that a small percentage of innovations is new-to-the-world (10 per cent), while the majority of innovations (70 per cent) essentially involve line extensions or modifications of existing products.

Choffray and Dorey (1983, p. 9) propose a classification based on the nature of the changes in the physical or perceptual characteristics. The proposed distinctions are as follows:

- *Original products:* products whose physical as well as perceptual characteristics are defined in new terms.

- *Reformulated products:* products whose physical characteristics have been redefined while leaving the basic perceptual characteristics unchanged.

- *Repositioned products:* the way in which the potential buyer perceives the product is modified, thus only changing the perceptual dimensions.

The first two classifications are complementary; the third one describes more precisely the notions of reformulated versus repositioned products, recalling that a product is viewed by the potential buyer as a 'bundle of attributes', including both physical and perceptual dimensions. However, this typology does not state the extent of risk involved as clearly as that by Booz *et al*.

12.1.3 Nature and origin of innovations

A second classification of innovations deals with the intrinsic nature of the new idea. Based on this, we distinguish between commercial and technological innovations.

Technological versus Commercial Innovations

Technological innovation deals with the physical characteristics of the product, whether at the level of the manufacturing process (float glass), the use of a new ingredient (steel cord in radial tyres), the use of a new primary material (polyurethane foam), completely new products (composite materials), new finished products (compact disc), new physical conditioning of the product (instant coffee) or complex new systems (the high-speed train).

The technological innovation results in the application of exact sciences for industrial practices. These innovations usually come from the laboratories or the R&D department. Some of these innovations require a lot of technology and capital (nuclear industry, space industry), while others require a lot of technology and very little capital (consumer electronic industry).

Commercial innovation deals mostly with the modes of organization, distribution and communication inherent in the commercialization process of a product or service. For example, the new presentation of a product (paperback books), a new means of distribution (cash and carry), a new advertising medium (posters at bus stops), a new combination of aesthetics and function (Swatch watches), a new application of an existing product, a new system of payment (credit card) or a new way of selling (telemarketing).

Thus commercial innovation deals with all that is linked to getting the product from the manufacturer to the end-user. It also results in the application of the human sciences. In this sense, it is organizational in nature and does not concern itself specifically with scientific and technical progress. Commercial innovation examines matters of imagination, creativity and know-how more so than those of financial resources. Often these innovations require very little capital outlay and technology. However, some commercial innovations may require considerable financial resources, such as the installation of a computerized banking network.

Admittedly, the boundary between these two types of innovation is blurred in the sense that technological innovations sometimes lead to commercial innovations. For example, the progress achieved in information technology has led to the development of credit cards which have revolutionized systems of payment and sales.

The inverse is also true: certain organizational changes encourage technological innovations. For example, the generalization of self-service in distribution contributed to the development of scanning and computerized banking systems.

Technological innovations are generally considered 'heavier', i.e. they require greater financial means and are therefore more risky. Commercial innovations are generally 'lighter' and less risky, but also more easily copied.

Market-pull versus technology-push innovations
Concerning technological innovations, the degree of risk will vary according to the origin of the idea of the new product. A distinction can be made between a *market-pull* product, i.e. one that directly answers observed needs, or a *technology-push* product, i.e. one that results from research and technological opportunities.

A synthesis of American and European contributions in the area of innovations, notably in the industrial sectors, reveals that (Urban *et al.*, 1987, p. 23):

■ About 60 to 80 per cent of successful products in many industries have been developed in response to market demand and needs against 40 to 20 per cent for technology-push innovations.

■ Consumer-based innovations often results in better sales growth.

These observations suggest that consumer needs and demand are a prime source of successful products.

> R&D isn't worth anything alone, it has to be coupled with the market. The innovative firms are not necessarily the ones that produce the best technological output, but the ones that know what is marketable. (E. Mansfield, published in *Business Week*, June 8, 1976)

Thus, while a proactive strategy must include research and development, it must also have a strong marketing component that is critical to the successful development of new products.

Fundamental versus applied research

On the other hand, an innovation strategy based on fundamental research, however risky it may be in the short term, may unleash the opportunity for a technological breakthrough. This could place the firm at a considerable advantage, with an advanced technology that the competition would have a difficult time catching up with. This brings up the argument that was touched on in Chapter 1, which dealt with the limitations of the marketing concept. A new product strategy which is based solely on the needs felt and expressed by the market inevitably leads to innovations which are less revolutionary, but also less risky, and which are therefore viewed as more attractive (Bennett and Cooper, 1979).

Therefore it is important to keep a balance between these two innovation strategies. An emphasis on applied research versus fundamental research can lead to a technological disadvantage from which it is difficult to recover. For example, the R&D strategy adopted by Japan (Mihaies, 1983) bears fruit, as is evidenced by the rapid improvement in Japan's high-technology industry.

12.1.4 Degree of newness to the marketplace

A third classification of innovations places emphasis on the degree of newness to the marketplace. A distinction is made between 'radical' or breakthrough innovations and 'relative' innovations. The originality of the concept results from the newness of the concept, as well as the technology used to produce the innovation (see Table 12.2). The concept or the technology can be classified as traditional, improved or brand new. Obviously, the closer one moves to the bottom right-hand corner of the table, the riskier the innovation.

TABLE 12.2 *Assessing the innovation intensity*

	Concept		
Technology	Traditional	Improved	New
Traditional		*Increasing risks*	
Improved			
New			→

Technology plays a key role in the competitive game. The acceleration of technological change has made it increasingly important to evaluate the strategic role that these technologies play. A study conducted by Arthur D. Little has suggested that there is a distinction between key technologies, basic technologies and emerging technologies (Ader, 1983).

■ *Key technologies* are those put to use by a company and which have a major impact on the firm's competitive performance, expressed in terms of the quality of the product or productivity.

■ *Basic technologies* are those which are readily available and no longer constitute the foundation for competition.

■ *Emerging technologies* are those which are still in the experimental stage, but which could play a part in changing the basis of competition.

Note that these distinctions are not intrinsically linked to the relevant technologies, but rather to the way in which they are used in an industry. For example, computer-aided design (CAD) is now a key technology in the automobile industry, an emerging technology in the textile industry and a basic technology in aeronautics.

Taking the technological dimension into consideration in planning a strategy allows one to assign priorities with respect to technological choices. Ideally, competitive firms should always (a) aim to control all their key technologies, (b) be involved in at least one of the emerging technologies of the industry and (c) be ready to reduce and even to divest its basic technologies.

12.1.5 High-technology marketing

As emphasized in Chapter 2, the pace of technological change has considerably accelerated in recent years, and technology-push innovations have become the major source of competitive advantage in many fast-growing markets. A question often raised is whether the marketing of high-technology innovations—or high-technology marketing—is different from traditional marketing.

High-technology industries have specific characteristics which differentiate them from more classic industrial sectors. They are science-intensive activities in continuous change, leading to unexpected applications often ahead of expressed market needs, striding across the boundaries of economic activity and upsetting the established balance of existing industrial sectors.

1. *Shorter product life cycles.* Most industrial products have 10- to 15-year life cycles, while high-technology products rarely last more than three to five years. Moreover, copying and 'reverse engineering' from competition is common practice. Thus, speed in market development is a strategic issue.

2. *Creative supply.* It is rarely clear where fundamental research will lead, and innovations are often impossible to predict. At the early stage of an emerging technology, it is not even apparent where the new technology will find applications. Once the technology is developed, the goal is to move quickly to the market and to apply the 'meta-technology' or 'technology platform' to as many products as possible. Thus the technology creates the market.

3. *Blurred competitive environment.* The market boundaries are not well defined and competitive threats can come from very different technological horizons. Technological uncertainties remain high and entry and exit of competitors is constant. The boundaries of existing sectors or market segments are modified and one observes either regrouping of segments into a new reference market—e.g. the office automation market—or upsetting a traditional market into specialized segments.

These characteristics of high-technology industries have implications for the new product development process—namely, speed and flexibility in product development (Stalk, 1988), close co-operation with customers and systematic monitoring of the technological environment.

Thus, in high-technology markets, strategic marketing has a crucial role to play, particularly in the R&D–Production–Marketing interface.

12.1.6 Strategic role of innovations

New product decisions are complex and risky, but they are of vital importance for the development and survival of the firm. The acceleration of technological change has reinforced this importance. In 1995, the share of sales derived from new or improved products commercialized within the previous five years was 45 per cent on average (Page, 1993). This percentage is even higher for high-technology products and tends to increase with time: 1976–81, 33 per cent; 1981–86, 40 per cent; 1986–90, 42 per cent; 1990–95, 45 per cent.

New products also have a decisive impact on corporate profits. A study made by the Product Development and Management Association (PDMA) indicated that,

> ... on average 33.2% of 1990 profits came from internally developed new products introduced during the previous five years. Furthermore, this percentage is expected to increase to 45.6% for new products introduced during the 1990–1994 period.
>
> (Page, 1993, p. 285)

These data, observed in the United States, cannot be transposed as such on the European markets, but they remain nevertheless very instructive.

12.2 THE DIMENSIONS OF NEW PRODUCT SUCCESS OR FAILURE

The available information on the success rate of new products is limited and sometimes contradictory.

- In 1971, the Nielsen Research Company observed a 47 per cent success ratio of new brands in a study based on a sample of 204 new products from the health and beauty aids (106), household (24) and grocery (74) markets. In a similar study done in 1962, but based on a smaller sample of 103 new brands, the observed success ratio was 54.4 per cent (*The Nielsen Researcher*, 1971, p. 6).

- In the study performed by Booz *et al.* (1982), the success rate observed over the 1977–81 period was 65 per cent, against 67 per cent in the same study done over the 1963–68 period (Booz *et al.*, 1982, p. 7).

- In a UK study conducted in 1990 on a sample of 86 British firms and of 116 Japanese firms operating in the United Kingdom, the success rate was 59.8 per cent for the Japanese firms and 54.3 per cent for the British firms (Edgett *et al.*, 1992, p. 7).

- The most recent observations come from the PDMA study (Page, 1993, p. 284) where the success rate observed on a sample of 189 firms was 58 per cent.

Obviously, the estimations fluctuate widely. In the best cases, the probability of success is a little better than one in two. This implies that investing a large proportion of available funds in R&D and spending a great deal on commercialization are unproductive. In other words, there is no correlation between large investments in R&D commercial spending and the success rate of a product.

12.2.1 Effective management of an innovation

Booz *et al.* also analysed the success rate of innovations at different stages of the new product development process. As seen in Fig. 12.1, this process is composed of five stages. The observed success and failure rates from both the 1968 and 1981 studies are represented.

On examining the data, one can observe that the success rate increases continuously from 36 per cent in the first phase to 71 per cent in the fifth phase. This implies that the evaluation process was effective. It is also instructive to compare these data with the same observations found in the 1968 study. It reveals that the selection process has become more discriminating, as the probability for success in the last phase rose from 50 per cent in 1968 to 70 per cent in 1981. This improvement in new product selection is probably due to the change in spending distribution from 1968 to 1981. In other words, a different proportion of money was spent during each phase.

Indeed, one can observe that a large proportion of resources was spent during the early phases (21 per cent in phases 1 and 2 during 1981, as compared to 10 per cent in 1968). In contrast, 37 per cent of resources was spent in phase 3 in 1981, compared with 28 per cent in 1968. On the other hand, 25 per cent of resources was allocated to the commercial phase in 1981, as compared to 48 per cent in 1968.

These data suggest that the companies have increased upfront strategic marketing analysis while reducing the share of the total expended on commercialization efforts.

> Companies that have excellent records of successful new product introductions conduct more analyses early in the process and focus their idea and concept generation. And they conduct more rigorous screening and evaluation of the ideas generated.
>
> (Booz *et al.*, 1982, p. 12)

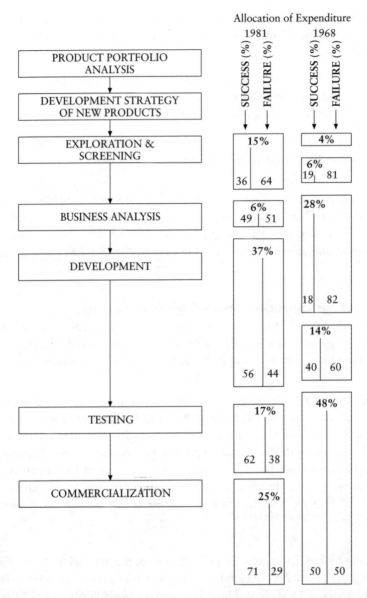

FIGURE 12.1 *The new product development process (Source: Booz et al., 1982)*

To reinforce the strategic marketing analysis at the beginning of the new product development process seems to be profitable. Using the data published by Booz *et al.* (1982) and computing the weighted average of the success rates observed at each phase, the estimated success rate in 1981 is 57 per cent against 37 per cent in 1968, a 54 per cent improvement. This gain in new product management effectiveness is dramatically illustrated in Fig. 12.2, which compares the mortality rate of new product ideas in 1968 and 1981. The data were taken from a 1982 study performed by Booz *et al.*

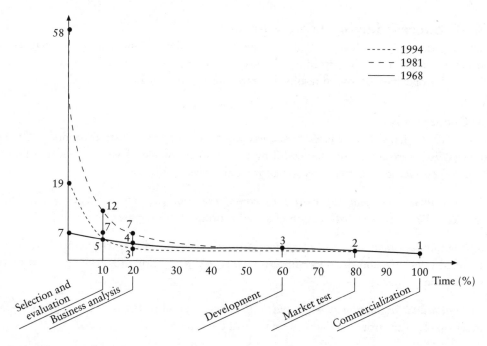

FIGURE 12.2 *Mortality curve of new product ideas* (Source: *Booz et al., 1982; Theys 1994*)

- In 1968, on average, out of 58 new product ideas, 12 passed the initial filtering test. Of these, seven remained after an extensive study of their profitability potential. Only three of these progressed to the product development stage, two to market testing and only one was a commercial success. It can therefore be concluded that 58 new product ideas were considered for every successful new product.

- In 1981, as a result of increased attention to the market and of increased sophistication in segmenting the market, only seven ideas were required to generate one successful new product.

The more up-to-date PDMA study (Page, 1993, p. 284) is less optimistic and report a 9 per cent rate.

> Out of 100 new product ideas that enter their development process, 26.6 of them are typically tested in some formal manner, 12.4 of them are introduced into the market, and 9.4 are typically commercially successful.

In a similar study conducted in the metallurgical sector in Belgium, Theys (1994) observed about the same mortality curve: Out of 19 ideas, one product was introduced into the market.

Increased strategic marketing is therefore profitable for the company since it improves the productivity of its investments in the conception and development phases. This allows the company to reduce its spending in operational marketing in the launch and commercialization.

12.2.2 Success factors of new products

Analysing the factors which explain the success or failure of innovations is particularly instructive and confirms the preceding conclusions. Several available studies, done in both the USA and Europe, have produced results that are remarkably similar.

The Cooper study

Cooper (1979) analysed the causes of success and failure of 195 industrial products. Of these products, 102 were considered successful by the company, while 93 were considered failures. Three success factors or dimensions appear to be the keys to success:

■ *Product uniqueness and superiority to competing products*, i.e. existence of distinctive qualities allowing for the conception of superior products for the user.

■ *Strong market orientation and marketing proficiency:* detailed market potential study, well targeted salesforce and distribution, test market and trial prior to launching and a market orientation.

■ *Technical and production synergy and proficiency:* a good fit between the engineering and design skills of the firm and the requirements of the project.

Cooper's study shows that two out of three key factors directly relate to the quality of strategic marketing, which plays here a crucial role in the success of an innovation.

> The observed success rates for new products that perform well in one of the above three dimensions are 82%, 79.5% and 64%, respectively. Moreover, if a new product is strong in all three dimensions, it has a success rate of 90 per cent; if it is weak in all three areas, the success rate is 7 per cent.   (Cooper, 1981, p. 75)

It is also important to emphasize that these three key success factors are all under the firm's control. Thus, success is directly determined by the quality of management and not just by chance, or by the situation, or by the environment the firm is facing. The message is clear: 'It matters not what situation you face; it matters more what you do about it.'

The *NewProd* methodology developed by Cooper in 1979 has since been applied to a large number of companies and the results available in 1993 in the NewProd III project are based on retrospective analysis of 203 actual new product projects in 125 industrial product firms (Cooper, 1993, p. 57). As in the initial study, some of these projects were successes and others failures. The results broadly confirm the observations made in 1979 and also bring some additional information.

As in the initial study, the key success factor is clearly *the existence of a superior product that delivers unique benefits to the user*. When the high-advantage products (the top 20 per cent) were contrasted with those with the least degree of differentiation (the bottom 20 per cent), it was found (Cooper, 1993, p. 58) that:

- they had an exceptional success rate of 98.0 per cent, versus only 18.4 per cent for undifferentiated ones.

- they had a market share of 53.5 per cent, versus only 12.6 per cent for 'me too' new products.

- they had a rate of profitability of 8.4 out of 10 (versus only 2.6 out of 10 for undifferentiated products).

- they met company sales and profit objectives to a greater degree than did undifferentiated products.

Fifteen key lessons for success of new product development were identified by Cooper. They are summarized in Box 12.2.

BOX 12.2

Fifteen key lessons for new product success

1. The number one success factor is a unique superior product: a differentiated product that delivers unique benefits and superior value to the customer.
2. A strong market orientation – a market-driven and customer-focused new product process – is critical to success.
3. Look to the world product: an international orientation in product design, development and target marketing provides the edge in product innovation.
4. More pre-development work – the homework – must be done before product development gets under way.
5. Sharp and early product definition is one of the key differences between winning and losing at new products.
6. A well-conceived, properly executed launch is central to new product success; and a solid marketing plan is at the heart of the launch.
7. The right organizational structure, design and climate are key factors in success.
8. Top management support doesn't guarantee success, but it certainly helps. But many senior managers get it wrong.
9. Synergy is vital to success – 'step-out' projects tend to fail.
10. Products aimed at attractive markets do better; market attractiveness is a key project-selection criterion.
11. New product success is predictable; and the profile of a winner can be used to make sharper project-selection decisions to yield better focus.
12. New product success is controllable: more emphasis is needed on completeness, consistency, and quality of execution.
13. The resources must be in place.
14. Speed is everything! But not at the expense of quality of execution.
15. Companies that follow a multi-stage, disciplined new product game plan fare much better.

Source: Cooper (1993, p. 76).

TABLE 12.3 *The causes of new product failure*

Causes for failure		Frequency of occurrence
1. *Superficial market analysis*		50%
■ Underestimation of delays in distributing the product on the market	60%	
■ Overestimation of the size or resources of the potential market	40%	
2. *Production problems*		38%
■ Difficulties in moving from the prototype to the test market	50%	
■ Difficulties in final product development	50%	
3. *Insufficient financial resources*		7%
4. *Commercialization problems*		5%
	Total	100%

Source: Daudé (1980).

The French CNME study

A French study conducted by the CNME (Caisse Nationale des Marchés de l'Etat) analysed the principal reasons for the failure of new products and came to the same conclusions (Daudé, 1980, p. 44). The principal causes for failure that were identified, along with the frequency of occurrence, are presented in Table 12.3.

Note here again that market knowledge is a much more basic factor than massive advertising, promotion and selling efforts behind the new product. The 'upfront' activities, i.e. those activities that precede the usual selling and launching efforts, have a vital role to play in a market-oriented new product process.

The Davidson study in the UK

Davidson's statistical study (1976) of a series of new products or new brands launched in the UK market largely confirms the results observed by Cooper. Analysing 100 new consumer products belonging to 38 categories that were launched between 1960 and 1970 in Great Britain, 50 were successes and 50 were failures. Davidson (1976) identifies three factors of success:

1. *Significant price or performance advantage*. Of the successes, 74 per cent offered the consumer better performance at the same or higher price, while only 20 per cent of the failures fitted this category.
2. *Significant difference from existing brands*. The study revealed a close correlation between a brand's success and its distinctiveness. Out of the 50 successes, 68 per cent were dramatically or very different from existing products.
3. *New, untried idea*. In 18 UK grocery categories largely developed since 1945, the pioneer company was still market leader in 12 cases.

The rules for developing a successful new brand are therefore simple and uncontroversial: (1) offer consumers better value for money than existing brands do, (2) ensure that your new brand has an important point of difference and, if possible, (3) be there first with a new idea (Davidson, 1976, p.120). For another view on new brand performance see Saunders (1990).

The Booz, Allen and Hamilton study in the USA

The previously mentioned Booz et al. study (1982) identified the following factors as contributing to the success of new products:

Product fit with market needs	85 per cent
Product fit with internal functional strengths	62 per cent
Technological superiority of product	52 per cent
Top management support	45 per cent
Use of new product process	33 per cent
Favourable competitive environment	31 per cent
Structure of new product organization	15 per cent

The two most important factors in successful new product introductions are the fit of the product with market needs and with internal functional strengths. Having a technologically superior product, receiving support from top management and using a multiple-step new product process are additional factors contributing to new product success. The relative importance of these factors, however, varies significantly by industry and by type of product being introduced.

The British study of Edgett, Shipley and Forbes

When respondents were asked in this study to identify factors that have contributed to a successful new product, the most frequently cited variable overall was that successful new products were well matched to customer needs. This reflects the need for a consumer-oriented approach to development programmes rather than a production-oriented approach. Only one in four respondents considered skilful marketing to be a factor in new product success. A comparison of the success factors is presented in Table 12.4.

Compared with British companies, the Japanese rated the need to develop a superior product significantly higher in terms of product quality, reliability and offerability at highly competitive prices This suggests that Japanese firms believe that to be successful in an increasingly cluttered marketplace, the product must also have a competitive advantage (Edgett et al., 1992, p. 8).

12.3 ORGANIZATION OF THE NEW PRODUCT DEVELOPMENT PROCESS

The data presented in the previous section illustrate the high risk involved in launching a new activity. This risk may be reduced, however, by implementing a systematic evaluation and development procedure for new products. The principal success factors are those which are controllable by the company. The purpose of this section is to examine the procedures and

TABLE 12.4 *Factors contributing to new product success*

Success factor of product	Percent of companies	
	Japanese (n = 116)	British (n = 86)
■ Well matched to customer needs	69.8	75.6
■ Superior to competition:		
− in quality	79.3	59.3[a]
− in reliability	69.8	45.3[b]
− in value for money	58.6	61.6
− in design	55.2	48.8
■ Highly price competitive	41.4	27.9[c]
■ Well matched to company objective and image	39.7	34.9
■ Unique	36.2	29.1
■ Skilfully marketing	27.6	25.6
■ Based on good market research	27.6	18.6
■ Launched into large markets	20.7	16.3
■ Created synergy in production or marketing	16.4	18.6
■ Avoiding competitive markets with satisfied customers	7.8	10.5
■ Avoiding dynamic markets where product launches are common	2.6	4.7

a: $P = 0.01$ b: $P = 0.001$ c: $P = 0.05$
Source: Edgett *et al*. (1992).

organizational methods which reduce the risk of failure throughout the innovation process. The objective is to organize a *systematic and continuous dialogue* between the relevant functions within an organization, i.e. R&D, marketing, operations and finance. In a market-driven company, developing a new product is a *cross-functional* effort which involves the entire organization.

12.3.1 A workable organizational structure

If it is true that top management bears the final say in decisions concerning new product launches, it remains that an organizational structure with specific responsibilities is essential in managing and co-ordinating the entire innovation process. Different organizational structures are possible. Large companies have created 'new product management' functions or 'new product departments', as Nestlé, Colgate Palmolive, Johnson & Johnson and General Foods have done.

Light organizational structures

A more flexible solution, which is available to all companies regardless of their size, is the 'new products committee' or 'venture team' in charge of a specific project.

■ A *'new products committee'* is a permanent group of persons who meet periodically, say, once a month. It is composed of individuals from different functions (i.e. R&D, operations,

TABLE 12.5 *Organizational structures used for new product development*

Organizational structures	Percent
Multi-disciplinary team	76.2
New product department	30.2
Product manager	30.2
New product manager	25.9
New product committee	16.9
Venture team	6.9

Source: Page (1993, p. 277).

marketing, finance and human resources). Ideally, it is presided over by the managing director, whose responsibility is to organize and to manage the development process of a new product from its conception to its launch.

■ A '*self-organizing project team*' or 'venture team' is a group formed for the development of a specific project (task force). The group is composed of people from various departments, from which they are temporarily separated, either completely or partially. This allows better concentration on the creation of a new activity.

The PDMA study is instructive on the evolution observed on the organizational structures used for new product development. The respondents were asked to indicate which of six forms of new product organization structure best described the ones used by their firm. The multi-disciplinary team was by far the most widely used organization with a score of 76 per cent of the sample businesses while the new product department had a score of only 30 per cent (Table 12.5).

No matter which organizational structure is adopted, the most important thing is to have a *structure open to the ideas of new activities*. The objective is to institutionalize a new products' system within the company and to do so in a way that is flexible and favours an entrepreneurial approach to problems.

Two processes are currently adopted by innovative companies: the sequential or the parallel development process.

Sequential development process The *sequential development process*, evidenced by the Booz *et al.* study (1982), is where the project moves step by step from one phase to the next: concept development and testing, feasibility analysis, prototype development, market test and production. The whole process is described in Fig. 12.3.

The merits of the sequential approach have already been discussed, but although it contributes towards a reduction in the new product failure rate, it also has some shortcomings.

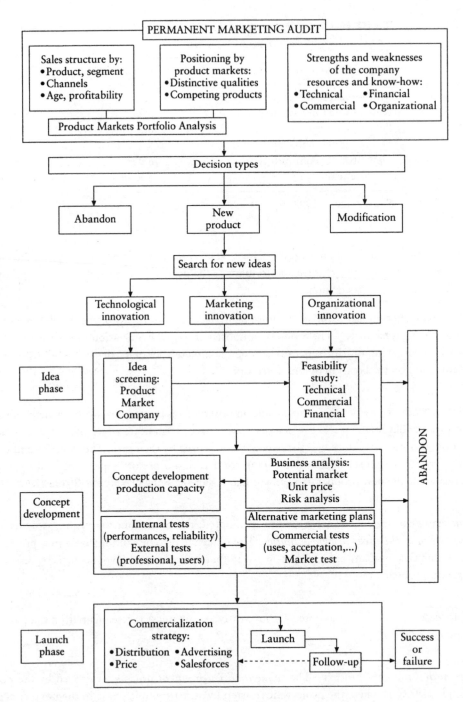

FIGURE 12.3 *The sequential development process of new products*

- First, the sequential process in itself leaves little room for integration since each functional specialist passes the project on to the next.

- The move to the next phase is done only after all the requirements of the preceding phase are satisfied. A bottleneck in one phase can slow or even block the entire process.

- Moreover, this product planning process is slow and requires long lead times. It avoids errors, but is very time consuming.

Changes in the market, entry of new competitors and risk of copying often result in a product arriving too late in the market. Thus long lead times can very well increase rather than reduce the risk of failure. This will be particularly important for high-technology products, where speed is a key success factor.

Parallel development process The *parallel development process* advocated by Takeuchi and Nonaka (1986) speeds the process by relying on self-organizing project teams whose members work together from start to finish. Under this organizational scheme, the process development process emerges from the constant interaction of a multi-disciplinary team. Rather than moving in defined, highly structured stages, the process is born out of the team members' interplay. One of the potential benefits of the parallel development process is the *overlapping of the tasks* assumed by the different departments. While design engineers are still designing the product, production people can intervene to make sure that the design is compatible with production scale economies and marketing people can work on the positioning platform to communicate to the market.

The parallel development process is described in Fig. 12.4. The merits of this organizational structure are important.

- The system facilitates a better cross-functional co-ordination since each function is associated in the entire development process.

- Several activities can be organized simultaneously which accelerates the process because the amount of recycle and rework—going back and doing it again—is greatly reduced.

- Each activity is better controlled since it directly determines the subsequent activities.

- Substantial time savings are made due to the more intensive work and to the improved spontaneous co-ordination.

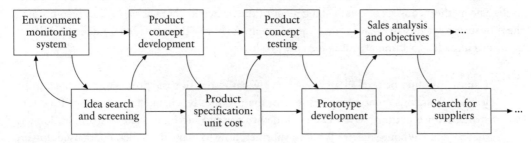

FIGURE 12.4 *Parallel development of new products*

This type of organizational structure, because it stresses multi-functional activities, promotes improved teamwork. To go further on this topic, see Larson and Gobeli (1988).

12.3.2 Idea generation

Naturally, the development process for innovation begins with researching new product ideas which are in line with the chosen development strategy. Some companies adopt an empirical approach to this problem, relying on a spontaneous stream of ideas originating from external and internal sources. However, the mortality rate of these ideas is very high; therefore, it is essential to feed on new ideas regularly. Generally, ideas, especially good ones, do not happen by themselves; organization and stimulation are needed to generate them. A company may use different methods for collecting ideas. These methods try to anticipate the change in needs and not simply respond to the demands expressed by the market. This is a 'proactive' versus a 'reactive' approach.

A creative idea is nothing but an unexpected combination of two or more concepts. Creativity can therefore be defined as 'the intellectual exercise of linking information in an unpredictable way so as to produce a new arrangement'.

Idea generation methods can be regrouped into two broad categories: (a) functional analysis methods which analyse products in order to identify possible improvements, (b) and methods which interview directly or indirectly buyers or consumers to detect unsatisfied needs or ill-resolved problems with the existing products.

Methods of functional analysis

The rationale behind functional analysis methods is that a product's users can provide useful information on how the product could be modified and improved.

Problem/opportunity analysis starts with the consumer. It is linked to the study of user behaviour in order to identify the kinds of problems a user may encounter during use of the product. Every problem or difficulty brought up could give rise to a new idea for improvement or modification. This modification is frequently used in industrial market studies with a panel of user clients.

The 'attribute listing' method has the same objectives as problem analysis, but instead of examining how the consumer uses the product, it examines the characteristics of the product itself. The method consists of establishing a list of the principal characteristics and recombining them in such a way as to create some improvement. Osborn (1963, pp. 286–7) defined a list of questions intended to stimulate ideas for new products.

> Can the product be used in any new way? What else is like the product and what can be learned from this comparison? How can the product be changed in meaning, function, structure, use pattern? What can be added to the product? To make it stronger, longer, thicker, etc.? What to delete? What to subtract, how to make it smaller, condensed, lower, shorter, lighter, etc.?

Morphological analysis consists of identifying the most important structural dimensions of a product and examining the relationship between these dimensions in order to discover new and interesting combinations.

Suppose we are studying a cleaning product. The six key structural dimensions are as follows: product support (brush, rag, sponge, etc.), ingredients (alcohol, ammonia, disinfectant, etc.), things to be cleaned (glass, carpet, sinks, walls, cars, etc.), substance to be got rid of (grease, dust, blood, paint, etc.), product texture (cream, powder, salt, liquid, etc.), and packaging (box, bottle, aerosol, bag, etc.). Paired combinations of these dimensions are evaluated and considered in terms of their potential value as new products.

A last method for idea generation—one that is old but very effective—must be added: the *suggestion box*. This can prove to be very helpful if certain rules are followed. Two rules are particularly important: follow up promptly on the proposed ideas and provide a complete recognition system to motivate employees.

There are other and varied methods for idea generation. Systematic analysis of competitive products through 'reverse engineering' is also widely used. For a more exhaustive description of these methods, see Wind (1982, ch. 9). The most important objective for a firm is to keep a permanent portfolio of new product ideas which is sizeable enough to allow the firm to face the competition in an environment where innovation is omnipresent.

Creativity groups and brainstorming

Methods that are likely to stimulate creativity can be grouped in two categories: unstructured and structured. Unstructured methods are essentially based on imagination and intuition, they are usually implemented in the form of *creativity groups*, relying on the hypothesis that a group of individuals is usually more creative than a person working alone. This assumption is based on the synergy effect or the interaction between group members.

Brainstorming is probably the most popular method, mainly because it is easy to organize. The only goal of a brainstorming session is to produce as many ideas as possible. Six to ten participants with diverse backgrounds and experience, from both within and outside the company, are gathered together and are given the objective of generating the greatest possible number of ideas on a particular theme in a spontaneous manner. The major rules governing a brainstorming session, according to Osborn (1963, p. 156), are the following:

■ No evaluation of any kind is permitted, since criticism and judgement may cause people to defend their ideas rather than generate new and creative ones.

■ Participants should be encouraged to think of the wildest ideas possible.

■ Encourage a large number of ideas.

■ Encourage participants to build upon or modify the ideas of others, as combinations or modifications of previously suggested ideas often lead to new ideas that are superior to those that sparked them.

TABLE 12.6 *Typology of idea generation methods*

Nature of customer need	Accessibility of new product opportunity to manufacturer-managed action	
	Low	High
Overt	Customer active only	Customer and/or manufacturer active
Latent	Neither	Manufacturer active only

Source: von Hippel (1978).

This type of exercise is usually very effective; it is not out of the ordinary for a group to generate more than 100 ideas during a brainstorming session. Another somewhat more structured method is synectics (Gordon, 1965).

New product generation from customer ideas

The idea generation methods presented so far are usually 'manufacturer-active'; i.e. the manufacturer plays the active role. In industrial markets, von Hippel (1978) has shown that a customer's request for a new product can often generate a new product idea, at least in situations where the industrial customer is overtly aware of his new product need (Table 12.6).

In the consumer goods sector, the role of the consumer is essentially that of a respondent, 'speaking only when spoken to'. It is the role of the manufacturer to obtain information on needs for new products and to develop a responsive product idea. In the industrial good sector, it is often the role of the *would-be customer* to develop the idea for a new product and to select a supplier capable of making the product. We have here a *customer-active paradigm*.

Any statement of need made by a professional customer contains information about what a responsive solution should be. Consider the following statement of need of manufacturing firm X:

(a) ... we need higher profits in our semi-conductor plant; (b) ... which we can get by raising output ... (c) ... which we can best do by getting rid of the bottleneck in process step D ... (d) ... which can best be done by designing and installing new equipment, ... (e) ... which has the following functional specifications, ... (f) ... and should be built according to these blueprints.   (von Hippel, 1978, p. 41)

This need statement already contains the key elements of the solution-to-a-problem sought by the would-be customer. The firm needs only to instruct its R&D and manufacturing people to manufacture the product according to the customer's specifications spontaneously provided. This example underlines the importance of a systematic dialogue with customers to generate new product ideas.

In the field of industrial goods, there are also several markets in which everyone knows what the customer wants, but progress in technology is required before the desired product can be realized. For example, in the computer, plastics and semi-conductor industries, everyone knows that the customer wants more calculation per second and per dollar in the computer business; everyone knows that the customer wants plastics which degrade less quickly in sunlight; and everyone knows that the semiconductor customer wants more memory capacity on a single chip of silicon. In these sectors, a customer request is not required to trigger a new product, only an advance in technology.

Idea generation methods are numerous and varied. Cooper (1993, p. 133) proposes a list of 25 different methods. It is important that the firm should have permanently a *portfolio of new product ideas* sufficiently diversified to enable the firm to meet the challenge of competition in an environment where innovation is not only permanent but is also a key success factor for survival and development.

12.3.3 Idea screening

The objective of the second stage in the development process is to screen the ideas generated in order to eliminate those that are incompatible with the company's resources or objectives or are simply unattractive to the firm. The purpose is to spot and drop unfeasible ideas as soon as possible. This is therefore an *evaluation phase* which presupposes the existence of criteria for choice. The goal of this screening is not to do an in-depth analysis, but rather to make a quick, inexpensive, internal evaluation about which projects merit further study and which should be abandoned. Therefore this is not yet a feasibility study, but simply a preliminary evaluation.

Typically, the new product committee is in the best position to do the screening. A single and effective method is the *evaluation grid* which has the following basic principles:

■ An exhaustive inventory of all the key success factors (KSF) in each functional area: marketing, finance, operations and R&D.

■ Each factor or group of factors is weighted to reflect its *relative importance*.

■ Each new product idea is scored against each KSF by the *judges* of the new product committee.

■ A desirability or *performance index* is calculated.

This procedure ensures that all the important factors have been systematically and equally considered and that the objectives and constraints of the company have been attended to.

When computing the performance index, it is preferable to adopt a 'conjunctive method' and not a simple weighted average procedure (compensatory approach). As seen in Chapter 6, the conjunctive method does not result in a global score, but aids in identifying ideas which are or are not compatible with the company's objectives or resources. The conjunctive approach presupposes that a maximum and minimum level of performance for each project has been specified. Only those ideas which satisfy each specified threshold are retained.

New product idea:_____   Score:____

INDICATORS OF ATTRACTIVENESS	SCORES				Not relevant
	Very good	Good	Weak	Very weak	
1. Market trend	Emerging	Growing	Stable	Declining	
2. Product life	10 years plus	5–10 years	3–5 years	2–3 years	
3. Spread of diffusion	Very fast	Fast	Slow	Very slow	
4. Market size (volume)	> 10000 T	5000–10000 T	1000–5000 T	1000 T	
5. Market size (value)	1 billion	0.5–1 billion	100–500 M	> 100 million	
6. Buyer's needs	Not met	Poorly met	Well met	Very well met	
7. Receptivity of distribution	Enthusiastic	Positive	Reserved	Reluctant	
8. Advertising support required	Weak support	Moderate support	Important support	Strong support	
9. Market accessibility	Very easy	Easy	Difficult	Very difficult	

INDICATORS OF COMPETITIVENESS	SCORES				Not relevant
	Very good	Good	Weak	Very weak	
1. Product's appeal	Very high	High	Moderate	Weak	
2. Distinctive qualities	Exclusivity	Major distinctive quality	Weak distinctive quality	'me too' product	
3. Strength of competition	Very weak	Weak	High	Very high	
4. Duration of exclusivity	> 3 years	1–3 years	–1 years	–6 months	
5. Compatibility with current products	Very good	Good	Weak	Very weak	
6. Level of price	Lower price	Slightly lower	Equal price	Higher price	
7. Compatibility with existing distribution network	Fully compatible	Easily compatible	Compatible but difficult	New network	
8. Capacity of the salesforce	Very good	Good	Weak	Very weak	
9. Level of product quality	Clearly superior	Superior	Same	Inferior	

FIGURE 12.5 *Example of a new product screening grid* (Source: Brussels, MDA Consulting Group)

Several standard evaluation grids exist in the marketing literature, the most well known being those of O'Meara (1961) and of Steele (1988). Such checklists provide a useful guideline for ideas evaluation. Ideally, an evaluation grid should be tailor-made and be adapted to the company's own needs. It is up to the new product committee to establish an appropriate structure which reflects the corporate objectives and the unique situational factors of the firm. Figure 12.5 shows an evaluation grid used in a consumer goods company to evaluate the marketing feasibility of new product ideas. Similar grids have been developed for the other functions: R&D, operations and finance.

Cooper (1993, App. C, p. 335) has also developed a diagnostic and screening grid. The questionnaire comprises 30 questions to be answered by several judges who evaluate the project on each criterion on a 10-point scale and who express their degree of confidence on their own evaluation, also on a 10-point scale. The profile of the project is then evaluated and compared to the observed profiles of hundreds of projects which belong to the NewProd data bank. The simulation model provides a probability of success and also analyses the strong and the weak points of the project.

12.3.4 Concept development

At this phase of the development process, we move from 'product ideas' to 'product concepts'. The ideas having survived to the screening phase are now defined in more elaborated terms. A product concept can thus be defined as:

> A written description of the physical and perceptual characteristics of the product and of the 'package of benefits' (the promise) it represents for the identified target group(s) of potential buyers.

This is more than a simple technological description of the product, since the product's benefits to the potential user are emphasized. The product concept definition highlights the notion of a product as a package of benefits. In defining the concept, a company is forced to be explicit about its strategic options and market objective.

A clear and precise definition of the product concept is important in many respects:

■ The concept definition describes the *positioning sought* for the product and therefore defines the means required to achieve the expected positioning.

■ The product concept is a kind of *specification manual* for R&D, whose job it is to examine the technical feasibility of the concept.

■ The description of the product's promise serves as a *briefing* for the advertising agency who is in charge of communicating the new product's claims to the marketplace.

Thus, the product concept defines the reference product market in which the future product should be positioned. Four questions come to mind:

■ To which attributes or product characteristics do potential buyers react favourably?

■ How are competitive products perceived with regard to these attributes?

■ What niche could the new product occupy, considering the target segment and the positions held by competition?

■ What are the most effective marketing means that will achieve the desired positioning?

The answers to these questions presuppose the existence of a fine-tuned market segmentation analysis which is able to quantify the size of the potential market.

12.3.5 Designing a green product concept

Sensitivity towards the environment is today essential for business success, and on this issue the accountable firm should assess the environmental implication of a new product at the concept development phase and at each phase of the product life cycle from 'cradle to grave', as discussed in Chapter 2. Numerous opportunities exist for refining existing products or developing new ones that meet environmental imperatives and satisfy consumers' expectations. These opportunities must be considered proactively very early in the development process. Ideas for action are presented hereafter (Ottman, 1993, ch. 5).

- Source reduce and packaging:
  - eliminate or lightweight packaging
  - concentrate products
  - use bulk packaging or large sizes
  - develop multi-purpose products.

- Use recycled content.

- Conserve natural resources, habitats and endangered species.

- Make products more energy efficient.

- Maximize consumer and environmental safety.

- Make products more durable.

- Make products and packaging reusable or refillable.

- Design products for remanufacturing, recycling and repair.

- Take products back for recycling.

- Make products and packaging safe to landfill or incinerate.

- Make products compostable.

While adopting the green product concept, the firm has to be careful and must prove its environmental credentials in scientific terms by reference to the entire life cycle of the product. This is not always easy, because green is relative and also because large uncertainties remain on the ecological impact of products and raw materials.

According to a study conducted in France (Peixoto, 1993), 33 per cent of consumers—the True-Blue Greens and the Greenback Greens—are active environmentalists. These consumers avoid buying products from a company with a questionable environmental reputation and are much more likely to buy greener types of products. According to an American study, active environmentalist consumers, on average, would pay a 4.6 per cent price premium for certain environmentally sound products (Ottman, 1993, p. 43). The size of this segment of green activists is growing regularly.

12.3.6 Concept testing

Concept testing represents the first investment (other than managerial time) a firm has to make in the development process. It consists of submitting a description of the new product concept to an appropriate group of target users to measure the degree of acceptance.

The product concept description may be done in one of two ways: neutrally, i.e. with no 'sale', or by a mock advertisement which presents the concept as if it were an existing product. The former is easier to do and avoids the pitfall of the inevitable and uncontrollable creative element inherent in an advertisement. The advantage of the advertisement, however, is that it more accurately reproduces the buying atmosphere of a future product and is therefore more realistic.

The following descriptions illustrate 'neutral' and 'advertising' forms of concept testing, respectively, for a new dessert topping.

> Here is a new dessert topping made of fruit and packaged in a spray can. It comes in four flavours: strawberry, cherry, apricot and redcurrant. It can be used in cakes, puddings and frozen desserts.

> Here is a new delicious fruit topping for desserts conveniently packaged in a spray can. These new toppings will enhance the desserts you serve your family. Your choice among four flavours—strawberry, cherry, apricot and redcurrant—will certainly embellish all your desserts including cakes, puddings, frozen desserts and more.

Twenty to fifty people with varying socio-demographic profiles are gathered to assess the degree of concept acceptance. They are shown slides or videos on the new concept and asked to react to it with questions similar to those below (Kotler, 1991, p. 325).

1. Are the benefits clear to you and believable?
2. Do you see this product as solving a problem or filling a need for you?
3. Do other products currently meet this need and satisfy you?
4. Is the price reasonable in relation to the value?
5. Would you (definitely/probably/probably not/definitely not) buy the product?
6. Who would use this product, and how often would it be used?

Obviously, the key question in the above list is the one dealing with intentions to buy (Question 5). A score of positive intentions (i.e. 'would definitely buy' and 'would probably buy' responses grouped together) that adds up to less than 60 per cent is generally considered insufficient, at least in the field of consumer goods.

Predictive value of intentions
Results from concept testing should be interpreted with care, especially when the concept is very new. Consumers are asked to express their interest in a product they have never seen or used. They are therefore often unable to judge whether or not they would like the new product. Numerous products that received mediocre scores during the concept testing phase actually proved to be brilliant successes. Inversely, expensive failures were avoided using concept testing.

Measuring intentions to buy is not always the best indication of the respondents' degree of conviction regarding a new product's ability to solve problems or to satisfy unmet needs. Yet, this is clearly a key success factor. In a test situation, respondents may express a willingness to purchase a new product out of simple curiosity or concern for keeping up with the latest innovation, or a need for variety. In light of this, scores for intention tend to overestimate the true rate of acceptance.

In order to deal with this problem, Tauber (1973) suggests using concept testing results based on measurements of perceived needs as well as of purchase interest. In an experiment on eight new product concepts, Tauber observed that virtually all the respondents who claimed that a product solved a problem or filled an unmet need had a positive intention to purchase the new product, while a considerable number of respondents who expressed purchase interest did not believe the product solved a problem or filled an unmet need. This observation suggests that overstatement of purchase intent may be simply those with curiosity to try but with little expectation of adopting. Thus, basing new product decisions on purchase intent data could be misleading in predicting the true rate of product adoption for regular use.

A more reliable way to estimate the adoption rate of a new product for regular use would be to base the decision on the percentage of people giving an affirmative answer to both questions, i.e. they *do intend* to buy and they are convinced that the new product solves a problem or fills an unmet need.

The adjusted purchase intent rates of Table 12.7 illustrate the argument. The ranking of the eight product concepts is significantly different from the ranking observed for the positive purchase intention.

12.3.7 Conjoint analysis

More elaborate approaches to concept testing may be used, including *conjoint analysis* which has been successfully used over the last few years (Green and Srinivasan, 1978). The distinctive value of conjoint analysis is to allow the impact of the product concept's key characteristics on product preferences, information which is not revealed by an overall reaction to the concept. The basic principles of this method were described in Chapter 4 and an example was presented in Chapter 6).

TABLE 12.7 *Interpretation of intention-to-buy scores*

New product concepts	A	B	C	D	E	F	G	H
Gross intentions Percentage of respondents with positive buying intention	71	62	60	60	51	46	44	22
Adjusted intentions Percentage of respondents with positive intentions and convinced of the novelty of the product	45	37	18	19	27	37	10	19
Rate of conviction Percentage of respondents convinced within the group with positive intentions	63	59	30	31	53	79	26	86

Source: Tauber (1973).

In concept testing, conjoint analysis helps to answer the following questions:

■ What is the partial utility or *value* that a target group attaches to different characteristics of the product concept?

■ What is the *relative importance* of each product characteristic?

■ What kind of *trade-offs* are potential buyers ready to make between two or several product characteristics?

■ What will be the *share of preferences* with regard to different product concepts each representing a different bundle of characteristics?

The collected data are simple rankings of preference for the various concept combinations. Each concept constitutes a different assortment of characteristics. These preference data are submitted to one of the conjoint analysis algorithms and the output is partial utilities for each component of the product concept and for each individual respondent.

Conjoint analysis results provide the market analyst with four useful results:

■ The identification of the *best concept*, i.e. the combination of concept components with the highest utilities, among all possible combinations.

■ Information on the *utility or disutility of any change* in the concept characteristics. This enables a selection of the most attractive trade-offs among concept components.

■ Information on the *relative importance* of each component.

■ Possibility of constructing *segments* based on the similarity of the respondents' reactions to the tested concepts.

On the basis of these results, alternative scenarios can be developed and the expected share of preferences estimated in each case.

The problems raised by concept testing are usually less subtle in industrial markets, since the needs of industrial clients' are generally more clearly specified. Moreover, the respondent is a professional, and trade-off analysis is a more natural way of thinking. Conjoint analysis has many applications within industrial markets; for an interesting application see the Clarke Equipment Case (Clarke, 1987).

Example of a concept test

To illustrate the contribution of conjoint analysis, let us examine the following example. The product studied is a hairspray, targeted to the Belgian market and defined in terms of the following five characteristics:

■ *Design*: two designs are considered—the existing one and a new one.

■ *Product's claim*: 'styling spray', 'extra strong hair spray' or 'fixing spray'.

■ *Price*: three price levels are considered—109, 129 and 149 Belgian francs.

- *Product range*: the product may be offered singly or included in a range comprising a gel, a mousse and a styling cream.

- *Brand*: the brand may be A, B or C.

These variables give a total of 108 possible combinations for new product concepts ($2 \times 3 \times 3 \times 2 \times 3$). Using a fractional factorial design we can reduce the number of concepts to be tested to 18. All pertinent information on each of the characteristics is retained, but information on interactions of orders greater than 2 is lost. In order to estimate partial utilities, regression analysis is conducted, using binary variables (0, 1) for describing the presence or absence of the product characteristics at each level. Figure 12.6 shows the average utility curves obtained from the sample examined.

The results show that consumers are very sensitive to the brand name and that they noticeably prefer Brand B to the other brands. They also show the price elasticity to be -0.81. The new design is also clearly preferred over the old one. With regard to the product's claim, there appears to be very little sensitivity on the part of the respondents, who probably do not really understand the claim (Rochet, 1987).

These results are useful to develop alternative launching scenarios and to obtain estimates of the likely rate of adoption of the new product concept.

12.4 BUSINESS ANALYSIS AND MARKETING PROGRAMMING

Once the product concept has been developed and accepted by top management, it is the task of the marketing department to quantify the market opportunity and to develop alternative marketing programmes. This implies sales forecasting and market penetration objectives under different marketing budgets. The economic viability of the new product within the chosen time horizon must be assessed and the risk of the new venture must be evaluated.

12.4.1 Estimating sales volume

Estimating the sales projection for the first three years is the first problem to examine, as this will condition the remainder of the analysis. Given estimates of total potential sales in the target segment, what will be the expected sales volume or market share of the new product under different assumptions regarding the size of the marketing efforts? Different methods can be used to approach this question: subjective methods, feasibility studies and methods based on a test market.

- *Subjective methods* rely not only on the marketing information system of the firm, but also on experience, judgement and information accumulated more or less informally within the firm. This accumulated knowledge is based on sales history of similar products, on information from distributors, on the salesforce, on comparison with competing products, etc.

- *Feasibility studies* aim to gather the missing information in the field by interviewing directly potential users, distributors, retailers, etc. Purchasing intention scores are collected and used to estimate the sales volume.

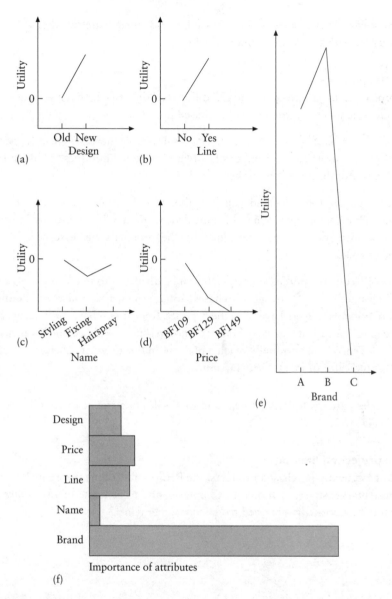

FIGURE 12.6 *Example of conjoint analysis: hairspray products* (Source: *Rochet, 1987*)

■ *Market tests* permit the observation of buyer behaviour in the real world. Trial and repeat purchase rates can be estimated and used for early projection of sales. Alternatives to market tests are in-home use tests, mini-test panels, laboratory experiments and regional introduction (see Wind, 1982, ch. 14).

These three methods are not exclusive and may be used jointly where uncertainty and the degree of newness for the company are high. Regardless of the approach adopted, the marketing department needs to set a sales revenue objective and to estimate whether sales will be high enough to generate an acceptable profit to the firm.

Typical sales patterns

The new product sales pattern over time will differ according to whether it is a one-time purchase product, a durable good or a frequently purchased product.

■ For one-time purchased products, the expected sales curve increases steadily, peaks and then decreases progressively as the number of potential buyers diminishes. Thus, in this case, the occupation rate of the market is the key variable.

■ For *durable goods*, total demand can be subdivided into two parts: first equipment and replacement. First equipment demand is time dependent and determined by income variables, while replacement demand is determined by the product's obsolescence, be it technical, economic or style.

■ Purchases of frequently purchased products can be divided into two categories: first-time and repeat. The number of first-time purchases initially increases and then diminishes as the majority of potential buyers have tried the product. Repeat purchases will occur if the product meets the requirements of a group of buyers who eventually will become loyal customers, and the total sales curve will eventually reach a plateau. In this product category, repeat purchases are the best indicator of market satisfaction.

The typical sales patterns for trial, repeat and total sales of a frequently purchased product are presented in Fig. 12.7.

Panel data projection methods

In the case of frequently purchased products, the Parfitt and Collins theorem (1968) can be used to decompose market share, as shown in Chapter 6, and to generate *market share projections*. These measures are normally obtained from a consumer panel.

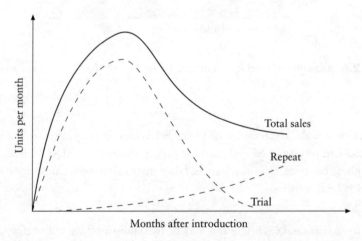

FIGURE 12.7 *Typical sales pattern for trial and repeat sales*

As previously discussed, market share can be divided into three distinct components:

■ The *penetration rate* for a brand is defined as the cumulative trial, i.e. the percentage of buyers having made a trial purchase at time t; this rate first increases after the launch and then tends to stabilize fairly rapidly as the stock of potential first-time buyers diminishes.

■ The *repeat purchasing rate* is expressed as the proportion of total puchases in the product field by those buyers having tried the product. After a certain number of purchases, the repeat purchase rate will level off to some equilibrium state.

■ The *intensity rate*, or buying level index, compares the rate of quantities purchased of the studied brand to the average quantities purchased within the product category. A distinction can be made here between heavy, light or average buyers (by volume) in the product field.

The *expected market share* is estimated by multiplying these three values.

Suppose that the estimated rate for trial purchase is 34 per cent and that the repeat purchase rate is around 25 per cent. If the average quantities purchased are the same for the brand and the product category, the expected market share will be:

$$34 \text{ per cent} \times 25 \text{ per cent} \times 1.00 = 8.5 \text{ per cent}$$

In cases of segmented markets, the expected market shares are calculated for each group. For example, the buying index-level may vary according to the type of buyer. It may reach 1.20 for heavy buyers and 0.80 for light buyers. The expected market share in each of these cases will be around 10.2 and 6.8 per cent, respectively.

This kind of market share projection can be quickly formulated after the first few months of launching a new product. This method also allows for measurement of the impact that advertising and promotional activities have on market share. For more on this topic, see the seminal article by Parfitt and Collins (1968).

No method can estimate future sales with certainty. Therefore, it is useful to give a range of estimations, with minimum and maximum sales, in order to assess the extent of risk implied by the new product launch.

12.4.2 Determination of the base marketing mix

The expected level of sales for a new product will depend on the intensity and continuity of operational marketing support. The marketing programme should be described in precise terms and summarized in a projected profit and loss statement.

To illustrate this point, let us examine the case of a new, highly nutritional food product which has a variety of uses. This product can be used as a snack, a camping food or as a diet food. This illustration is based on the Newfood Case developed by Eskin and Montgomery (1975, pp. 49–50). Early product and concept tests have been very encouraging, but the company has great difficulty in defining the market. The product manager of the Newfood Corporation must now analyse the economic data of the problem and propose a marketing programme.

STRATEGIC MARKETING MANAGEMENT

The product tests have led the product manager to believe that the product could easily sell 2 million cases (24 packages in a case) under the proposed marketing programme, involving a 24 cent package price and an advertising budget involving $3 million in expenditure per year. The distribution margin is 30 per cent and the direct cost for the product is $1 per case. Fixed manufacturing costs are $1 million. It is company policy not to introduce new products with profit expectations of less than $0.5 million per year. A three-year planning horizon is usually considered.

Sales volume beyond the first year is mainly determined by the repeat purchase rate, which is difficult to estimate in this particular case. Historically, products in this category have had sales that decayed over time after the first year at a decay rate that varies with the size of marketing efforts. The average decay rate observed for similar products is 20 per cent. Third-year sales would then be 80 per cent of second-year sales or, equivalently, 64 per cent of first-year sales. Thus total sales over all three years would be 2.44 times first-year sales. This number (2.44) is called the sales multiplier or 'blow-up factor'.

A projected profit and loss statement over three years based on these assumptions and on the base marketing programme is presented in Table 12.8. On the whole, the project seems attractive and generates a $1.7 million net cumulative contribution. Note that the break-even point for the first year is around 1.5 million cases.

Value of perfect information
The projected profit and loss statement of Table 12.8 is based on assumptions about the sales growth rate and the size of the marketing budget. Management knows that this information is imperfect and risk analysis consists of testing the sensitivity of these assumptions on expected sales and profit.

TABLE 12.8 *The Newfood case—base scenario: projected profit and loss statement*

	Year 0	Year 1	Year 2	Year 3
1. Expected sales (cases)	–	1 925 000	1 540 000	1 232 000
2. Blow-up factor	–	1.00	0.80	0.64
3. Price	–	4.03	4.03	4.03
4. Unit cost	–	1.00	1.00	1.00
5. Gross margin	–	3.03	3.03	3.03
6. Sales revenue	–	7 757 750	6 206 200	4 964 960
7. Total gross margin	–	5 832 750	4 666 200	3 732 960
8. Marketing expenditure	–	3 000 000	3 000 000	3 000 000
9. Fixed cost	–	1 000 000	1 000 000	1 000 000
10. Gross contribution	–	1 832 750	666 200	– 267 040
11. R&D expenditure	– 500 000	–	–	–
12. Net cumulated contribution	– 500 000	1 332 750	1 998 950	1 731 910
13. Break-even point (1st year)	–	1 485 148	–	–

Given the absence of reliable information on the trial and repeat purchase rates of the product, the first year's and subsequent years' sales cannot be determined with precision, and it is therefore useful to have a range of likely sales, and not only a point estimate, to assess the risk implications of the project.

> The product manager is satisfied with the sales estimate of 2 million cases for the first year, although admitting that it contains some uncertainty. When pressed, however, the product manager will admit that sales could be as low as 1 million cases in the first year, but points out that sales might also exceed the estimate by as much as 1 million cases. The operational definition of these extremes is that each has no more than a 1 in 10 chance of occurring.

Using these estimates, one can derive a probability distribution for first-year sales and calculate the expected value of sales. The objective is to assess the risk of having a sales volume inferior to the break-even volume during the first year. The probability distribution is presented in Table 12.9.

The expected value of sales is 1.925 million cases, which is very close to the deterministic estimation. There is, however, a 3 in 10 ten chance that the sales volume in the first year will fall below the break-even volume. This is a significant risk.

Risk can also be measured in financial terms by computing the value of perfect information or the cost of uncertainty. The expected value of the choice given perfect information (VPI) is obtained by computing the expected value of the best conditional pay-offs of Table 12.9.

$$E(VPI) = 0.10(0) + 0.20(0) + 0.25(0.938) + 0.25(4.635) + 0.10(8.331) + 0.10(12.028)$$

That is,

$$E(VPI) = \$3.430 \text{ million}$$

TABLE 12.9 *The newfood case: expected value of sales and profit*

Sales*			Expected	Conditional	Expected
Classes	Mid-point	Probability	sales	payoffs*	profit
0.5–1.0	0.75	0.10	0.075	−6.455	−0.646
1.0–1.5	1.25	0.20	0.250	−2.759	−0.552
1.5–2.0	1.75	0.25	0.438	+0.938	+0.235
2.0–2.5	2.25	0.25	0.562	+4.635	+1.159
2.5–3.0	2.75	0.10	0.275	+8.331	+0.833
3.0–3.5	3.25	0.10	0.325	+12.028	+1.203
Total	–	1.00	E(q) = 1.925	–	E(π) = 2.232

*In million cases or dollars.

Without perfect information, the optimal action is to go ahead, with an expected pay-off of $2.232 million. Thus the expected gain from perfect information (or the uncertainty cost) is:

$$\$3.430 \text{ million} - \$2.232 \text{ million} = \$1.198 \text{ million}$$

One observes that the uncertainty cost is high compared to the expected gain. Another way to assess the risk is simply to observe, referring to column 5 in Table 12.9, that there are 30 chances out of 100 to have a loss of at least $2.759 million on this project.

The cost of uncertainty measures in a way the opportunity cost of a decision taken under imperfect information. This amount also measures the value of additional information.

In the Newfood case, there is the possibility of conducting a market test before proceeding with the launch. The cost will not exceed $75 000 and the test allows for a more precise estimation of the first-year sales volume. The level of risk measured by the uncertainty cost suggests that postponing the decision to collect additional information should be considered by the product manager.

Comparing alternative marketing plans

There are also other marketing plans under consideration. Instead of trying the improve the precision of the first-year sales forecast (often an illusive pursuit), it would probably be better to try to develop a more aggressive and effective marketing programme. Several alternatives can be explored.

- Adopt a *higher price*, for example, 34 cents instead of 24 cents. This would support a bigger advertising budget, $6 million instead of $3 million for the first year. This strategy could induce a higher trial rate and therefore increase sales during the first year. There is a risk, however, that repeat sales will decline faster during the second year owing to the higher price.

- Keep the same initial price of 24 cents, but *increase* the advertising budget during *the second and third years* in order to slow down the decline in sales after the first year.

- Try to *combine* the preceding two strategies by adopting a price of 29 cents and increasing the advertising budget by 50 per cent over the three years.

Each strategy has its implications for the shape of the response curve.

The product manager feels that doubling the advertising will lead to 500 000 more cases sold in the first year and will increase repeat sales in the following two years. This will reduce the decay rate from 20 to 15 per cent. The manager estimates, however, that a higher price of 34 cents would increase the decay rate of sales during the first year from 20 to 30 per cent.

The profit and risk implications of these alternatives plans can be easily estimated by changing the price and advertising variables in the profit and loss statement. This simulation exercise is greatly facilitated through the use of spreadsheet software packages, such as Lotus 1–2–3, Microsoft or Excel.

12.4.3 Dynamic performance analysis

The launch of a new product is a strategic decision process which concerns every function within the firm, and not only the marketing function. The success of this process largely depends on a sound co-ordination of each function involved. Moreover, the time factor is important and may modify the profitability of the new product. To ensure a good co-ordination, the firm must have at its disposal analytical tools to monitor the development process step by step and to assess its conformance with the profitability and timing objectives.

Assessing the financial risk

For each strategy, it is important to determine as precisely as possible when the elimination of risk is supposed to occur. There are three levels of risk, identified in Fig. 12.8.

■ The *simple break-even point*, i.e. the moment where the new activity leaves the zone of losses and enters the zone of profits.

■ The *equilibrium break-even point*, when the present value of total receipts covers the present value of total expenses. The company has recouped its capital layout.

■ The *capital acquisition point*, i.e. the point where the new activity generates a financial surplus allowing for reinvestments to prolong the economic life of the activity or for supporting the development of other businesses within the firm.

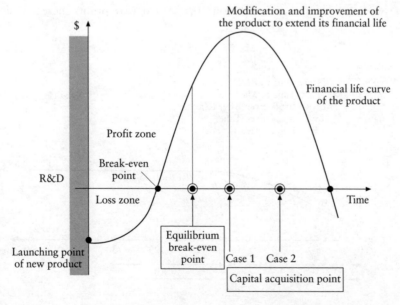

FIGURE 12.8 *Assessing the financial risk of a new product* (Source: *Daudé, 1980*)

Ideally, the capital acquisition point should be reached before the maturity phase of the product's life cycle in order to allow the company timely redeployment, i.e. before competitive pressure begins to erode profit margins. These three criteria will eventually determine the economic viability of the project. To be operational these criteria must be viewed in a dynamic perspective.

Dynamics of the development process

House and Price (1991) have developed a tracking system, called the 'return map', which is used at Hewlett-Packard. This allows people working in cross-functional teams to assess the impact of their decisions and of their colleagues' decisions on the entire development process, both in terms of time and money.

The return map is simply a dynamic break-even chart. It is a two-dimensional graph displaying time and money on the x and y axes respectively, The x axis is usually drawn on a linear scale, while the y axis is drawn most effectively on a logarithmic scale, because, for successful products, the difference between sales and investments costs will be greater than $100 : 1$. The x axis is divided into three segments showing partitioned tasks and responsibilities: investigation, development and manufacturing. An example of application is presented in Fig. 12.9.

Investigation took 4 months and costs about $0.4 million; development required 12 months and $4.5 million. Hence the total product development effort from beginning to manufacturing and sales release took 16 months and cost $4.9 million. See the 'investment' line in Fig. 12.9. The manufacturing–sales phase has started in period 16.

Sales for the first year was $56 million and for the second year $145 million. Cumulative sales gives a sense of how quickly the product was introduced and sold; In the first year, net profits of $2.2 million were less than expected. During the second year profits increased significantly,

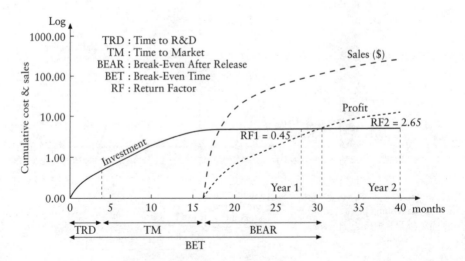

FIGURE 12.9 *Dynamic analysis of the development process (Source: House and Price, 1991)*

reached $13 million and passed through the investment line about 16 months after manufacturing. Thus—in dollars and in months—the chart tracks R&D, manufacturing, sales and profit.

Several indicators of performance can be derived from the chart in Fig. 12.9:

■ Time to R&D (or TRD) gives the time and cost of the investigation phase until the start of the development phase.

■ Time to Market (or TM) is the total development time from the start of the development phase to manufacturing release.

■ Break-Even After Release (or BEAR) is the time from manufacturing release until the project investment costs are recovered in product profits.

■ Break-Even Time (or BET) is defined as the time from the start of the investigation until product profits equal the investment in development.

■ Return Factor (or RF) is a calculation of profit dollars divided by investment dollars at a specific point of time after the product has moved into manufacturing and sales.

In the example presented, the performance indicators are as follows:

TRD:	4 months and a cost of $0.4 million.
TM:	12 months and a cost of $4.5 million.
BEAR:	16 months.
BET:	32 months.
RF (year 1):	2.2/4.9 = 0.45.
RF (year 2):	15.2/4.9 = 2.65.

The effectiveness of the return map hinges on the involvement of all three major functional areas in the development and introduction of new products. The map captures the link between the development team and the rest of the company and the customer. It is a typical situation where a high level of market orientation of the entire firm is required.

12.4.4 Project evaluation procedure

How should a firm proceed to select priority projects when financial resources are limited, opportunities too many and the risks very different from one project to the other?

There is a vast literature in the field of capital budgeting on this topic, but the methods proposed are strictly financial, quantitatively oriented and do not consider qualitative criteria which are often very important when assessing the attractiveness of a particular project. Moreover, they required precise financial data which often are not available at the evaluation phase of a project.

A crude but useful financial indicator is the *payback period index* (in years) which answers the question 'When shall I get all my money back?' This index is calculated as follows:

$$\text{Payback} = \frac{\text{Development and commercial costs}}{\text{Annual sales ($/year)} \times \text{profit margin as a \% of sales}}$$

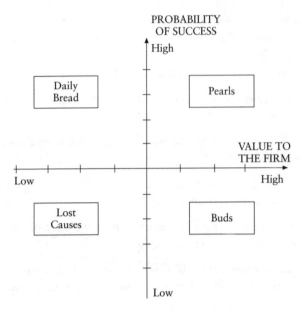

FIGURE 12.10 *Portfolio analysis of new product concepts*

This criterion is simple, easily understood and is based on data usually available at the evaluation phase. The reciprocal of this index gives a very crude estimate of the return as a percentage. Alternative and more rigorous methods are Net Present Value (NPV) or Discounted Cash Flow (DCF) as well as Internal Rate of Return (IRR).

It is often useful to add explicitly a risk factor and qualitative indicators similar to those used in the screening grid (see Fig. 12.5). We would then have a new projects evaluation matrix similar to the one presented in Fig. 12.10.

In this matrix the projects are evaluated along two dimensions:

■ The horizontal dimension measures the value to the firm of each project, using a multi-attribute composite index based on quantitative and qualitative indicators reflecting the value of the project to the firm.

■ A vertical dimension measures the probability of technological and/or commercial success of each project as evaluated by management after the investigation or development phase.

We thus have a two-dimensional grid composed of four quadrants, where each project is represented by a bubble denoting the size of the resources to be devoted to each project.

■ In the upper right quadrant are the *Pearls*, i.e. projects having a high value to the firm and a high probability of success.

■ In the lower right quadrant are the *Buds*, very desirable projects for the firm but having still a low probability of success.

- In the upper left quadrant are the *Bread and Butter* projects, with a good probability of success (and a low risk) but of ordinary or low value to the firm.

- In the lower right quadrant are the *Lost Causes*, the bad projects, with a low commercial pay-off and a low probability of success.

This project portfolio grid is used during the annual budgeting exercise to identify the priority projects. Decision rules might be:

- Allocate resources by priority to the development and the launching of Pearls projects.

- Invest in some Buds projects to reinforce their competitiveness by gathering additional market information or by redesigning the product concept.

- Cut back on Bread and Butter projects which often absorb too much time and resources.

- Delete from the portfolio the Lost Causes projects.

This type of portfolio analysis is also useful to help the firm to allocate research and development efforts towards new projects.

12.5 TOTAL QUALITY STRATEGY

Quality control has traditionally been considered as a purely defensive measure whose objective was to prevent flaws in manufacturing and to eliminate defective products. This function was normally included in the production department. Today, however, following the Japanese industry example, quality management is seen as a competitive weapon of great strategic importance, actively employed to gain market share. As such, quality strategy calls directly on marketing to define the *expected excellence level* for each of its manufactured products.

12.5.1 Quality from the buyer's point of view

For the buyer, a quality product does not necessarily mean a luxury good, but could simply mean a product that pleases, i.e. that fits the needs and expectations of a specific target group. Product quality can thus be defined as follows (Groocock, 1986, p. 27):

> The quality of a product is the degree of conformance of all of the relevant features and characteristics of the product to all of the aspects of a customer's need, limited by the price and delivery he or she will accept.

Comparisons in quality only make sense between products designed to meet the same needs and sold at the same price level. Buyer satisfaction is a function of the degree of conformance between the buyer's expectations of the product and the perception of the product's overall performance.

Buyers dictate to the company the level of excellence to be attained, as a function of their own needs. Quality management implies, above all, a knowledge of the expectations and motivations to buy of the target group. For example, the person who buys a Renault 5 does not expect the same kind of performance from the car as does the person who purchases a Mercedes 190E. Both products, however, may be quality products in the sense that they both meet the excellence level expected by the buyers, given the price paid.

Considering the diversity of needs, the level of excellence for each product must be defined for each target segment. This implies a different package of benefits or 'set of values' corresponding to the expected quality level and to the accepted price range. Thus, designing a quality strategy presupposes a market segmentation analysis.

12.5.2 The key dimensions of quality

We have seen that buyers perceive a product as a bundle of attributes likely to supply the core service sought as well as other added services or benefits. Quality management implies breaking down total quality into components so as to establish norms or performance standards for each component.

The components of product quality

Garvin (1987) proposes eight dimensions or components of product quality:

- *Product or service performance*: the ability of a product to perform its basic function.

- *Proprietary features*: the range of other advantages a product offers in addition to its basic function.

- *Conformance*: adherence to norms or standards corresponding to a determined level of excellence (with a reduced tolerance margin).

- *Reliability*: the absence of failure or defective operation within a given time frame.

- *Durability*: the useful life span of a product or the frequency of product use before the product deteriorates.

- *Serviceability*: the extent, speed and efficiency of services offered before, during and after purchase.

- *Appearance or aesthetics*: the design, look, colour, taste, etc., of a product (i.e. a much more subjective component).

- *Perceived quality*: the reputation or perceived image of a product or brand.

A quality control programme will consist of establishing norms for each of these components and monitoring conformance to these norms. Each of these components represents an opportunity to differentiate the product with respect to competition.

The components of service quality

The same kind of process can be used in managing the *quality of services*—a much more complicated task because of its intangible nature (Lambin, 1987; Horovitz, 1987). This complexity is described in Fig. 12.11.

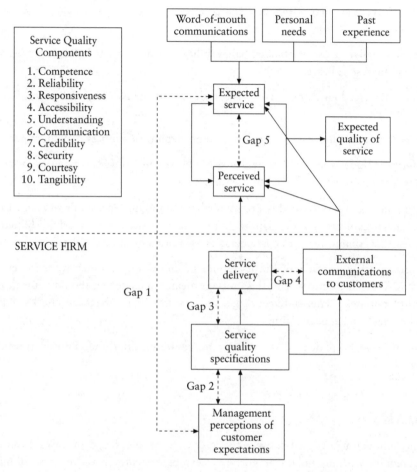

FIGURE 12.11 *The components of service quality (Source: Zeithaml et al., 1990, p. 46)*

The empirical studies conducted in France (Eiglier and Langeard, 1977) and in the United States (Parasuraman *et al.*, 1985) identified 10 factors which determine the perception of the quality of a service.

- *Competence* means the possession of the required skills and knowledge to perform the service.

- *Reliability* involves consistency of performance and dependability, and performing the service right the first time. It also means that the firm honours its promises.

- *Responsiveness* concerns the willingness or readiness of employees to provide service. It involves timeliness of service.

- *Accessibility* refers to both physical and psychological accessibility. Access involves approach-ability and ease of contact.

- *Understanding* or knowing the customer involves making the effort to understand the customer's needs.

- *Communication* means keeping customers informed in a language they can understand and listening to them. It may mean that the company has to adjust its language for different customers.

- *Credibility* involves trustworthiness, believability and honesty. It involves having the customer's best interest at heart.

- *Security* is the freedom from danger, risk or doubt. It involves physical safety, financial and moral security.

- *Courtesy* involves politeness, respect, consideration and friendliness of contact personnel.

- *Tangibility* includes the physical evidence of the service: physical facilities, appearance of personnel, physical representation of the service, etc.

These components of service quality are somewhat redundant (Parasuraman *et al.*, 1985, Table 1, p. 47). Each organization must adapt them to its specific situation and establish quality norms which constitute commitments to customers. These norms must be measurable.

> Lufthansa has just included in its service promise: 'Businessmen want to get there, not wait.' Translated into norms, this message means: 'a passenger should not wait more than thirty minutes'. This statement also induces norms for baggage checks, flight times, schedules and baggage claim.   (Horovitz, 1987, p. 99)

Once norms have been defined, they must be communicated and diffused throughout the company.

SUMMARY

The term 'innovation' is used loosely to describe a whole range of cases from minor to breakthrough innovations and it is important to evaluate accurately the diversity of innovations and their specific risks. The distinction between market-pull and technology-push innovations is particularly useful. Data available on new product success or failure show that the risk of failure is very high and that success is directly determined by the quality of management of the new product development process and not just by chance or by the environment the firm is facing. The new product development process consists of three phases: (a) idea phase (idea generation and screening); (b) concept phase (concept development, concept testing, business analysis); and (c) launching phase. In market-driven companies this process tends to be more a parallel than a sequential development process in order to ensure better interfunctional co-ordination. The concept development phase is crucial for incorporating the market orientation upfront and also for adopting a thorough approach to product greening. In the business analysis, the economic viability of the new product must be assessed in a dynamic perspective under alternative marketing programmes and the risk of the new venture evaluated. The market-oriented firm tries to have a permanently balanced portfolio of projects, a useful tool for identifying priority projects. Total quality from the buyer's point of view refers to the degree of conformance between the product's perceived performance and the buyer's expectations. Quality is a multidimensional concept and a quality control programme will consist of establishing norms for each component of quality.

QUESTIONS AND PROBLEMS

1. Proceed to the morphological analysis of one of the following three products: office chair, an electric fryer, a document binding system.
2. You are responsible for the launching of a new electronic device for automatic video recording of TV programmes through a system of code numbers (type Show-View). Prepare a written description of the product concept (a) to be communicated as a brief to the advertising agency and (b) to be used in a product concept test within a sample of housewives owing a video and belonging to the 40 years and over age group.
3. The Agrifood company specializes in the manufacture and sale of snacks and every year introduces into the market several products under its brand name. The PLC of this type of product is typically one of a fad with a stable residual market after three years. Typically, first-year sales are on average 10 000 cases (35 packages per case); sales decline at a 30 per cent annual decay rate for two years to stabilize at the level reached. According to product types, first-year sales can be 20 per cent higher or lower in 20 cases out of 100. The first-year advertising support is FF10 million and FF3 million during the two subsequent years. Retail price is FF90 per package and the unit direct cost FF33. Each new product generates a fixed cost of about FF3 million per year. Compute the break-even and the general equilibrium points over a period of three years given a target profit rate of 10 per cent on an investment of FF50 million. How would you proceed to assess the risk of this new product launch?
4. Give three examples of products new-to-the-world; show the key components of these innovations; and the type of risk that will confront the innovating firm.
5. In your opinion, what are the merits and demerits of the parallel and sequential approaches in the organization of a new product development process?
6. A travel agency has developed different tourist concepts using three characteristics— activity, site and price—each at three levels. These service concepts have been tested within three segments of potential customers: juniors, families and seniors. Through conjoint analysis, the utilities in Table Q6 were identified. Analyse the sensitivity of each segment to

Table Q6

Characteristics	Segment		
	Juniors	Families	Seniors
Activity:			
Culture	+0.10	−0.20	+0.20
Sport	+0.30	−0.10	−0.20
Leisure	−0.40	+0.30.	0
Prices (by following week):			
20 000	+0.50	+0.40	+0.30
40 000	−0.10	−0.10	−0.10
50 000	−0.40	−0.30	−0.20
Sites:			
Sea	+0.10	+0.50	−0.30
Mountain	+0.10	+0.10	−0.10
Cities	−0.20	−0.60	+0.40

the different service characteristics. Which tourist service should be given priority in each segment? Would it be possible to develop a service concept that would suit the three segments?

REFERENCES

Ader, E. (1983), 'L'analyse stratégique et ses outils', *Futuribles*, vol. 72, Décember, pp.3–21.

Barreyre, P.Y. (1980), 'Typologie des innovations', *Revue Française de Gestion*, January–February, pp. 9–15.

Bennett, R.C. and R.G. Cooper (1979), 'Beyond the Marketing Concept', *Business Horizons*, vol. 22, June, pp. 76–83.

Booz, Allen and Hamilton (1982), *New Product Management for the 1980's*. New York.

Choffray J.M. and F. Dorey (1983), *Développement et gestion des produits nouveaux*. Paris: McGraw-Hill.

Clarke, D.G. (1987), *Marketing Analysis and Decision Making*. Redwood City, Cal.: The Scientific Press.

Cooper, R.C. (1979), 'The Dimensions of Industrial New Products Success and Failure', *Journal of Marketing*, vol. 43, Summer, pp. 93–103.

Cooper, D.G. (1981), 'The Myth of the Better Mousetrap: What Makes a New Product a Success', *Business Quarterly*, Spring, pp. 69–81.

Cooper, R.G. (1993), *Winning at New Products*, 2nd edn. Reading, Mass.: Addison Wesley Publishing Co.

Daudé, B. (1980), 'Analyse de la maîtrise des risques', *Revue Française de Gestion*, January–February, pp. 38–48.

Davidson, J.H. (1976), 'Why do most New Consumer Fail?, *Harvard Business Review*, vol. 57, March–April, pp.117–22.

Edgett, S., D. Shipley and G. Forbes (1992), 'Japanese and British Companies Compared: Contributing Factors to Success and Failure', in 'New Product Development', *Journal of Product Innovation Management*, vol. 9, pp. 3–10.

Eiglier, P. and Langeard E. (1977), *Servuction: le marketing des services*. Paris: McGraw-Hill.

Eskin, G.J. and D.B. Montgomery (1975), *Cases in Computer and Model Assisted Marketing*. Palo Alto: The Scientific Press.

Garvin, D.A. (1987), 'Competing on the Eight Dimensions of Quality', *Harvard Business Review*, vol. 65, November–December, pp. 101–9.

Gordon, J.J. (1965), *Stimulation des facultés créatrices dans les groupes de recherche synectique*. Paris: Hommes et Techniques.

Green, P.E. and V. Srinivasan (1978), 'Conjoint Analysis in Consumer Research: Issues and Outlook', *Journal of Consumer Research*, September, pp. 103–23.

Groocock, J.M. (1986), *The Chain of Quality*. New York: John Wiley & Sons.

House, C.H. and R.L. Price (1991), 'The Return Map: Tracking Product Teams', *Harvard Business Review*, vol. 69, January-February, pp. 92–100.

Horovitz, J. (1987), *La qualité des services*. Paris: InterEditions.

Kotler, P. (1991), *Marketing Management*, 7th Edn. Prentice Hall International.

Lambin, J.J. (1987), 'Le contrôle de la qualité dans le domaine des services', *Gestion 2000*, No. 1.

Larson, E.W. and D.H. Gobeli (1988), 'Organizing for Product Development Projects', *Journal of Product Innovation Management*, vol. 5, pp. 180–90.

Mansfield, E. (1976), *Business Week*, June 8.

Mihaies, G. (1983), 'La stratégie japonaise de RD', *Futuribles*, July–August, pp. 59–69.

Nielsen Researcher, The (1971), New Product Success Ratio', vol. 5, pp. 4–9. Chicago: The Nielsen Company.

O'Meara, J.T. (1961), 'Selecting profitable products', *Harvard Busines Review*, vol. 39, January–February, pp. 110–18.

Osborn, A.F. (1963), *Applied Imagination*. New York: Charles Scribner's Sons.

Ottman, J.A., (1993), *Green Marketing*, Lincolnwood, Ill.: NTC Business Books.

Parasuraman A., V.A. Zeithaml and L.L. Berry (1985), 'A Conceptual Model of Service Quality and Its Implications for Future Research', *Journal of Marketing*, vol. 49, Autumn, pp. 41–50.

Parfitt, J.M. and J.K. Collins (1968), 'Use of Consumer Panels for Brand Share Prediction', *Journal of Marketing Research*, vol. 5, May, pp. 131–45.

Page, A.L. (1993), 'Assessing New Product Development Practices and Performance: Establishing Crucial Norms', *Journal of Product Innovation Management*, vol. 10, No. 4, September, pp. 273–90.

Peixoto, O. (1993), 'Conscience verte des Français et Eco-marketing', *Revue Française du Marketing*, no. 142–143, pp. 198–202.

Rochet, L. (1987), *Diagnostic stratégique du potentiel d'extension d'une marque de laque*. IAG, Louvain-la-Neuve, Belgium.

Saunders, J. (1990), 'Brands and Valuations', *International Journal of Advertising*, vol. 66, pp. 95–110.

Stalk, G. (1988), 'Time: The Next Source of Competitive Advantage', *Harvard Business Review*, July–August, pp. 41–51.

Steele, L.W. (1988), 'Selecting R&D Programs and Objectives', *Research & Technology Management*, March–April, pp. 17–36.

Takeuchi, H. and I. Nonaka (1986), 'The New Product Development Game', *Harvard Business Review*, January–February, pp. 137–46.

Tauber, E.M. (1973), 'Reduce New Product Failures: Measure Needs as well as Purchase Interest', *Journal of Marketing*, vol. 37, July, pp. 61–70.

Theys, F. (1994), *Succès et échecs de l'innovation dans l'IFME*. IAG, Louvain-la-Neuve, Belgium.

Urban, G.L., J.R. Hauser and N. Dholakia (1987), *Essentials of New Product Management*. Englewood Cliffs, New Jersey: Prentice Hall Inc.

von Hippel, E. (1978), 'Successful Industrial Products from Customer Ideas', *Journal of Marketing*, vol. 42, January, pp. 39–49.

Wind, Y.S. (1982), *Product Policy: Concepts, Methods and Strategy*. Reading, Mass.: Addison-Wesley Publishing Co.

Zeithaml, V., A. Parasuraman and L.L. Berry (1990), *Delivering Quality Service*. New York: The Free Press.

13

DISTRIBUTION CHANNEL DECISIONS

LEARNING OBJECTIVES

After reading this chapter, you should be able to:

■ explain the role and the functions performed by distribution channels in a market economy

■ describe why companies use distribution channels and the tasks performed by these channels

■ identify the main configurations of a distribution channel and analyse the distribution cost structure of each possible channel

■ explain the different market coverage and communication strategies open to the manufacturer

■ explain the strategic marketing issues facing the retailer

■ understand the potential of interactive marketing

■ describe the alternative entry strategies in foreign markets open to the international firm.

*I*n most markets, the physical and psychological distance between producers and end-users is such that intermediaries are necessary to ensure an efficient matching between the segments of demand and supply. Distributors and facilitating agencies are required because manufacturers are unable to assume by themselves, at a reasonable cost, all the tasks and activities implied by a free and competitive exchange process. The use of intermediaries means a loss of manufacturer control of certain distributive functions, since the firm subcontracts activities that could, in principle, be assumed by marketing management. Thus, from the firm's point of view, channel decisions are critical decisions which involve developing a channel structure that fits the firm's strategy and the needs of the target segment. The design of a channel structure is a major strategic decision, neither frequently made nor easily changed. In this chapter, we shall first examine the channel design decisions from the manufacturer's point of view, and then analyse the type of positioning strategies available to retailers in consumer markets.

13.1 THE ECONOMIC ROLE OF DISTRIBUTION CHANNELS

A distribution channel is a structure formed by the interdependent partners participating in the process of making goods or services available for consumption or use by consumers or industrial users. These partners are the producers, intermediaries and end-users. Distribution channels are organized structures performing the tasks necessary to facilitate exchange transactions. Their role in a market economy is to bridge the gap between manufacturers and end-users by making goods available where and when they are needed and under the appropriate terms of trade. The functions of a distribution channel are to create time, space and state utilities which constitute the added value of distribution (Fig. 13.1).

13.1.1 The tasks of distribution

Many functions are provided by channels of distribution. These occur for the benefit of the producer or consumer, or both. For producers, distribution channels perform seven different functions.

■ *Transporting*: to make the goods available in places near to consumers or industrial users.

■ *Breaking of bulk*: to make the goods available in quantity or volume adapted to consumers' purchasing habits.

■ *Storing*: to make the goods available at the time of consumption, thereby reducing the manufacturer's need to store its own products in company-owned warehouses.

■ *Assorting*: to constitute a selection of goods for use in association with each other and adapted to the buyer's use.

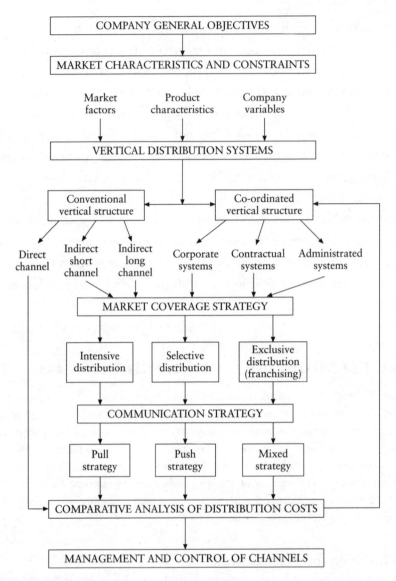

FIGURE 13.1 *Overview of distribution channel decisions*

- *Contacting*: to establish personalized relationships with customers who are numerous and remote.

- *Informing*: to collect and disseminate information about market needs and about products and terms of trade.

- *Promoting*: to promote the products through advertising and promotions organized at the point of sales.

In addition to these basic functions, intermediaries also provide services such as financial credit, guarantees, delivery, repairs, maintenance, atmosphere, etc. The main economic role of distribution channels is to overcome the existing *disparities* between demand and supply.

13.1.2 The distribution flows

These functions give rise to distribution flows between partners in the exchange process. Some of these flows are forward flows (ownership, physical and promotional), others are backward flows (ordering and payment), and still others move in both directions (information). The five main flows are:

- *Ownership flow*: the actual transfer of legal ownership from one organization to another.
- *Physical flow*: the successive movements of the physical product from the producer to the end-user.
- *Ordering flow*: the orders placed by intermediaries in the channel and forwarded to the manufacturer.
- *Payment flow*: successive buyers paying their bills through financial institutions to sellers.
- *Information flow*: the dissemination of information to the market and/or to the producer at the initiative of the producer and/or the intermediaries.

The key question in designing a channel of distribution is not whether these functions and flows need to be performed, but rather who is to perform them. These functions and the management of the distribution flows can be shifted among the channel's partners. The problem is to decide who could perform these economic functions most efficiently: the producer, the intermediary or the consumer.

13.1.3 The rationale for marketing channels

The distribution functions cannot be eliminated, but rather simply assumed by other more efficient channel members. Innovations in distribution channels largely reflect the discovery of more efficient ways to manage these economic functions or flows. Various sources of efficiency enable intermediaries to perform distribution functions at a lower cost than either the customer or the manufacturer could individually. This is particularly true for consumer goods, which are distributed to a large number of geographically dispersed customers.

Contactual efficiency

The complexity of the exchange process increases as the number of partners increases. As shown in Fig. 13.2, the number of contacts required to maintain mutual interactions between all partners in the exchange process is much higher in a decentralized exchange system than in a centralized system. Figure 13.2 shows that, given three manufacturers who buy goods from five retailers, the number of contacts required amounts to 15. If the manufacturers sell to these retailers through one wholesaler, the number of necessary contacts is reduced to 8. Thus, a centralized system employing intermediaries is more efficient than a decentralized system of exchange, by reducing the number of transactions required for matching segments of demand and supply.

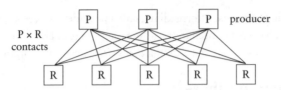

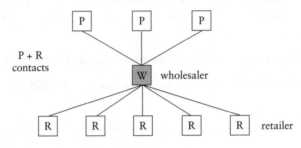

(a) Direct marketing system

(b) Indirect marketing system

FIGURE 13.2 *Contactual efficiency of distributors* (Source: *Lambin and Peeters, 1977*)
(a) *Direct marketing system* (b) *Indirect marketing system*

Economies of scale

By regrouping the products of several manufacturers, intermediaries can perform one or several distribution tasks more efficiently than manufacturers. For example, a wholesaler's sales representative can spread costs over several manufacturers and perform the selling function at a lower cost per manufacturer than if each firm paid its own company sales representative.

Reduction of functional discrepancies

By purchasing large volumes of goods from manufacturers, storing them and breaking them down into the volume customers prefer to purchase, wholesalers and retailers enable manufacturers and their customers to operate at their more efficient scale. Rather than having to make small production runs to fill the orders of individual customers, manufacturers can achieve economies of scale. Similarly, their customers can buy small quantities without having their capital tied up in large inventories.

If a particular organization is responsible for two separate functions (for instance manufacturing and distribution) that have different optimum levels of operations, there is a risk that one of the two functions, or even both of them, may operate at a suboptimum level. Costs go up and prices have to be higher. When some functions are subcontracted to third parties the producer's costs and prices are lower.

Better assortments

At the manufacturer's level, the assortment of goods produced is largely dictated by technological considerations, whereas the assortment of goods consumers usually desire is dictated by the use situation. Typically, consumers desire *a limited quantity of a wide variety of goods*. The role of intermediaries is to create wide assortments and to make it possible for consumers to acquire a large variety of products from a single source with one transaction. This reduces the time and effort that consumers must expend in finding the goods they need. The same economy of efforts also exists on the manufacturer's side. For example, a manufacturer of a limited line of hardware items could open its own retail outlets only if it were willing to accumulate a large variety of items generally sold at this type of outlet. In general, hardware wholesalers can perform this assortment function more efficiently than individual manufacturers.

Better services
The intermediary is close to the end-users and therefore can have a better understanding of their needs and desires and adapt the assortment to local situations.

The superior efficiency of intermediaries in a market system is not absolute however. A particular intermediary will survive in the channel structure as long as the other channel partners in the exchange process consider that there is no other more efficient way to perform the function. Thus, the issue of who should perform various distribution tasks is one of relative efficiency.

13.2 CHANNEL DESIGN ALTERNATIVES

The design of a channel structure implies decisions regarding the responsibilities to be assumed by the different participants in the exchange process. From the manufacturer's point of view, the first decision is whether or not to subcontract certain distribution tasks and, if so, to what extent and under which trade conditions.

13.2.1 Types of intermediary
There are four broad categories of intermediary that a firm might include in the distributive network of its product: wholesalers, retailers, agents and facilitating agencies.

Wholesalers
These intermediaries sell primarily to other outlets such as retailers or institutional or industrial customers, rather than to individual consumers. They take title of the goods they store and can provide quick delivery when the goods are ordered because they are usually located closer to customers than the manufacturers. The case of wholesalers in the pharmaceutical industry described in Box 13.1 is illustrative in this respect.

They purchase in large lots from manufacturers and resell in smaller lots to retailers. Wholesalers generally bring together an assortment of goods, usually of related items, by dealing with several sources of supply. In the food industry, full-service wholesalers have been confronted with competition from mass retail distributors who have taken over the wholesaling function. Wholesalers have reacted by creating *voluntary chains* which consist of a wholesaler-sponsored group of independent retailers engaged in bulk buying and in common merchandising.

BOX 13.1

Wholesalers in the pharmaceutical industry

How can 350 pharmaceutical laboratories and 250 suppliers of para-pharmaceutical products respond as rapidly as possible to the needs of 2000 French pharmacies, knowing that 12 million health products are required every day?

To do the job, speciality wholesalers have networked the French territory with warehouses to meet this demand. As a result, 81 per cent of health products are now distributed by these wholesalers. The remaining 19 per cent are delivered directly to hospitals (12 per cent) or to pharmacies (7 per cent).

Twice a day, pharmacists place their orders through teletransmission, to be served early afternoon before the end of the schools' closing time, or the following morning before the store's opening time. The distributor's staff has less than two hours to handle the orders.

Source: 'Le Monde', 16 March 1993.

Retailers

Retailers sell goods and services directly to consumers for their personal, non-business use. Retailers take the ownership of the goods they carry, and their compensation is the margin between what they pay for the goods and the price they charge their customers. There are several schemes for classifying retailers. A traditional classification makes a distinction between three types of independent retailers: food retailers, specialty retailers and artisan retailers (bakers and butchers).

They can also be classified according to the level of service they provide (self-service versus full service retailing) or according to their method of operation (low margin/high-turnover or high margin/low turnover). Low-margin/high-turnover retailers compete primarily on a price basis, while high-margin/low-turnover retailers focus on unique assortments, specialty goods, services and prestigious store image. The number of independent retailers has drastically decreased in most European countries due to the competition of mass merchandisers.

Integrated distribution

Since the beginning of the century, profound changes have taken place in the distribution sector and it is useful to give a brief summary of this evolution.

■ The first revolution goes back to 1852 with the establishment in Paris of the first *department store*. The innovating principles were broad assortment, low mark-ups and rapid turnover, marking and displaying the prices, free entry without pressure or obligation to purchase. The best-known department stores are, today, Harrods in London, Galeries Lafayettes in Paris, Macy's in New York, La Renascente in Milan, etc.

■ The next generation of stores was the *specialty-stores chain* located in suburban shopping centres closer to consumers. This was a store concept based on a limited assortment and economies of scale due to the purchase of large quantities.

- The next generation was the *popular store* which sold goods at low prices by accepting lower margins, working on higher volumes and providing minimum service (typically Prisunic in France and Belgium).

- The fourth revolution was the *supermarket*, a store concept based on self-service operations and designed to serve the consumer's total needs for food, laundry and household maintenance products. This was the one-stop shopping concept. Supermarkets have moved towards larger stores, the superstore or hypermarché, as Carrefour in France.

The supermarket concept has been extremely successful in Europe, particularly in the fast-moving consumer goods sector. Six managerial rules characterized this selling formula.

- A broad assortment and wide variety of popular merchandise to facilitate multiple-item purchases and rapid stock rotation.

- A low purchase price resulting from to the high volume of goods purchased, and a strong bargaining power *vis-à-vis* suppliers.

- Low margins and low sales prices.

- Dynamic promotional activities in order to stimulate store traffic.

- Economies of scale on physical distribution (in transportation, handling and packaging)

- Long credit terms (typically 90 days) for products usually sold within 15 days in order to generate substantial financial by-products.

This selling formula has given a substantial competitive advantage to integrated distributors over independent retailers. The situation is changing today as new expectations emerge among consumers and as independent distributors propose new store concepts (de Maricourt, 1988).

Agents

Agents are functional intermediaries who do not take title of the goods with which they deal but negotiate sales or purchases for clients or principals. They are compensated in the form of a commission on sales or purchases. They are independent business people or freelance salespeople who represent client organizations. Common types of agent include import or export agents, traders, brokers and manufacturers' representatives. Manufacturers representatives usually work for several firms and carry non-competitive, complementary goods in an exclusive territory or foreign country.

Facilitating agencies

Facilitating agencies are business firms that assist in the performance of distribution tasks other than buying, selling and transferring title. From the firm's standpoint, they are subcontractors carrying out certain distribution tasks because of their specialization or special expertise. Common types of facilitating agencies are: transportation agencies, storage agencies, advertising agencies, market research firms, financial agencies, insurance companies, etc. These agencies are involved in a marketing channel on an as-needed basis and they are compensated by commissions or fees paid for their services.

Many different types of institutions participate in a distribution channel. The channel structure will be determined by the manner in which the different distribution tasks have been allocated among the channel participants.

13.2.2 Configurations of a distribution channel

Distribution channels can be characterized by the number of intermediary levels that separate the manufacturer from the end-user. Figure 13.3 shows the different channel designs commonly used to distribute industrial or consumer goods. A distinction can be made between direct and indirect distribution systems.

- In a *direct* distribution system, the manufacturer sells directly to the end-user and there is no intermediary in the channel. This structure is also known as a direct marketing system.

- In an *indirect* distribution system, one or several intermediaries participate and bring the product closer to the final buyer. An indirect system is said to be 'short' or 'long' depending on the number of intermediary levels.

In the field of consumer goods, distribution channels tend to be long and involve several intermediaries, typically wholesalers and retailers. In industrial markets, channels are generally shorter, particularly when buyers are large and well identified. From the producer's point of view, the longer the channel, the more difficult it is to control.

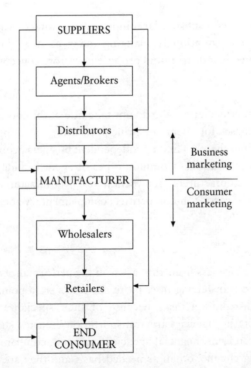

FIGURE 13.3 *Structure of a conventional vertical marketing system*

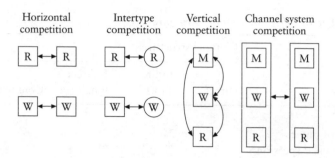

FIGURE 13.4 *Types of competition among distributors (Source: Palamountain, 1955)*

In most market situations, companies use *multiple channels* to reach their target segments, either to create emulation among distributors or to reach separate target segments with different purchasing habits. For example, many industrial companies use distributors to sell and service small accounts and their own salesforce to handle large accounts.

Types of competition among distributors

In a distributive network several types of competition may exist, as shown in Fig. 13.4.

■ *Horizontal competition*: the same type of intermediaries at the same channel level competing with each other.

■ *Intertype competition*: different types of intermediaries at the same channel level competing with each other (self-service versus full service).

■ *Vertical competition*: channel members at different levels in the channel competing with each other, such as retailers integrating the wholesaling function or vice versa.

■ *Channel system competition*: complete channel systems competing with each other as units; for instance, the competition between indirect distribution through wholesalers and retailers and direct marketing through direct mail.

Distribution has experienced important changes over the last 30 years which have contributed to reinforce the competitive struggle among intermediaries. The growth of vertical marketing systems illustrates this evolution.

13.2.3 Factors affecting the channel structure

The selection of a particular channel design is largely determined by a set of constraints related to market and buyer behaviour factors and to product and company characteristics. These factors and their implications for the channel configuration are described in Table 13.1.

Market factors

The number of potential buyers determines the size of the market. A very general heuristic rule about market size relative to channel structure is: if the market is large, the use of intermediaries is more likely to be needed; conversely, if the market is small, a firm is more likely to avoid the use of intermediaries and assume most of the distribution tasks. Also, the more *geographically*

TABLE 13.1 *Factors affecting channel structure*

Influencing factors	Channel structure			Comments
	Direct	Indirect short	Indirect long	
Market factors				
■ Large number of buyers		**	***	
■ High geographical dispersion		**	***	
■ Purchase in large quantity	***			
■ Buying highly seasonal		**	***	
Product characteristics				
■ Perishable products	***			
■ Complex products	***			
■ Newness of product	***	**		
■ Heavy and bulky products	***			
■ Standardized products		**	***	
■ Low unit value		**	***	
Company variables				
■ Large financial capacity	***	**		
■ Complete assortment	***	**		
■ High control sought	***	**		

Source: Adapted from Rosenbloom (1978, pp. 119–27)
Note:
** important
*** very important

dispersed the market, the more difficult and expensive will be the distribution. In a geographically dispersed market, intermediaries will almost certainly be used because of the high costs involved in providing adequate services to many dispersed customers.

Patterns of buying behaviour also influence the channel structure. If customers typically buy in very small quantities and if demand is highly *seasonal* a long distribution channel involving several intermediaries will be more appropriate.

Product variables
Characteristics of the product also determine the channel structure. Channels should be as short as possible for *highly perishable* products. Heavy and bulky products have very high handling and shipping costs and the firm should try to minimize these costs by shipping the goods only in truck-load quantities to a limited number of places; the channel structure should also be short.

Short structures are also desirable for *complex* and *technical* products requiring extensive after-sales service and assistance in use. Similarly, for *innovative* products requiring aggressive promotion in the introductory stage of the PLC, a shorter channel will facilitate the development and control of promotion activities aiming at creating product acceptance by the market. Long channel structures will be more adequate, on the other hand, when products are highly standardized and when they have *low unit value*. In this latter case, the costs of distribution can be shared by many other products handled by the intermediaries. For example, it would be difficult to imagine the sales of packages of crisps by the Smiths Company to the consumer. Only by spreading the costs of distribution over the wide variety of products handled by wholesale and retail intermediaries is it possible to buy a packet of crisps at a low price.

A manufacturer's channel choice is also influenced by the extent of its product line. The manufacturer with only one item may have to use wholesaling intermediaries, whereas it could go directly to retailers if it made several products that could be combined on a large scale. A retailer ordinarily cannot buy a truck-load of washing machines alone, but it might buy a truck-load of mixed appliances.

Company variables

The key variables here are the size and financial capability of the producer. Large firms in general have large financial resources and therefore the capacity to assume several distribution tasks directly, thereby reducing their dependence on intermediaries. Several distribution activities, such as transportation and storage, imply fixed costs. Large companies are better able to bear these costs. On the other hand, the use of intermediaries implies a cost which is proportional to the volume of activity, since their compensation takes the form of commissions on actual sales revenue. Therefore, small firms will be inclined to have extensive recourse to intermediaries. In some cases, the entire output is sold under the retailer's brand. The disadvantage of this arrangement is that the producer is completely at the mercy of its one large retailer.

Other considerations are also important. For example, the lack of marketing expertise necessary to perform the distribution tasks may force the firm to use the services of intermediaries. This happens frequently when the firm is penetrating new markets. Also, high-technology companies built upon the engineering abilities of management often rely heavily on distributors to do their marketing. A manufacturer may establish as short a channel as possible, simply because it wants to *control* the distribution of its product, even though the cost of a more direct channel is higher.

13.2.4 Vertical marketing systems

If the adopted channel structure is indirect, some degree of co-operation and co-ordination must be achieved among the participants in the channel. Two forms of vertical organization can exist: conventional vertical structures and co-ordinated vertical structures, known as vertical marketing systems.

■ In a *conventional* vertical structure each level of the channel behaves independently as a separate business entity seeking to maximize its own profit, even if this is at the expense of the overall performance of the distribution channel. This is the traditional operation of a distribution network, where no channel member has control over the other members.

■ In a *co-ordinated* vertical structure, the participants in the exchange process behave like partners and co-ordinate their activities in order to increase their bargaining power and achieve operating economies and maximum market impact. In this type of vertical organization, a channel member takes the initiative of co-ordination, be it the manufacturer, the wholesaler or the retailer.

Several forms of vertical marketing system have emerged, and a distinction is usually made between corporate, contractual and administered systems.

Corporate vertical marketing systems

In corporate vertically integrated marketing systems a particular firm achieves co-ordination and control through corporate ownership. The firm owning and operating the other units of the channel may be a manufacturer, wholesaler or retailer. Firms such as Bata in shoes and Rodier in clothing own their own retail outlets. However, it is not always the manufacturer that controls the channel system through forward integration. Backward integration occurs when a retailer or a wholesaler assumes ownership of institutions that normally precede them in the channel. Sears in the USA, for example, and Marks & Spencer in the UK have ownership interest in several manufacturing firms that are important suppliers of their private brands.

Contractual vertical marketing systems

In a contractual vertical marketing system, independent firms operating at different levels of the channel co-ordinate their activities through legal contracts that spell out the rights and duties of each partner. The three basic types of contractual system are: retail co-operatives, wholesale-sponsored voluntary chains and franchise systems. Franchise systems have expanded the most in recent years, and their organization is discussed in more detail in the next section.

Administered vertical marketing systems

In this third system, firms participating in the channel co-ordinate their activities through the informal guidance or influence of one of the channel members (and not through ownership or contractual agreements). The leading firm, usually the manufacturer, bases its influence on the brand or company reputation or managerial expertise. Companies such as L'Oréal in cosmetics and Procter & Gamble in detergents are examples of firms having successfully achieved this form of co-operation.

Vertical marketing systems have become the dominant mode of distribution in the field of consumer marketing over the last 20 years. They can be viewed as a new form of competition *channel system competition*, setting complete channels against other complete channels, as opposed to traditional vertical competition in which channel members oppose each other at different levels of the same channel—i.e. retailers versus wholesalers, manufacturer versus wholesaler, etc. Vertical marketing systems help to eliminate the sources of conflict that exist in conventional vertical structures, and increase of the market impact of their activities.

13.3 MARKET COVERAGE STRATEGIES

If the producer decides to use intermediaries to organize the distribution of its products, the firm must then decide on the number of intermediaries to use at each channel level to achieve the market penetration objective. Three basic market coverage strategies are possible:

■ Hollywood distributes its chewing gums wherever possible: in food stores, tobacconists, drug stores, through vending machines, etc.

■ Pierre Cardin distributes his dresses and women's suits in carefully selected clothing stores and tries to be present in the most elegant shops.

■ VAG distributes its cars through exclusive dealership; each dealer has an exclusive territory and no other dealer is authorized to carry the VAG products.

Hollywood is adopting an *intensive* distribution strategy, Cardin a *selective* strategy and VAG an *exclusive* strategy. The best strategy for a given product depends on the nature of the product itself, on the objective being pursued and on the competitive situation.

13.3.1 Consumer goods classifications

In the field of consumer goods, the choice of a particular market coverage strategy is largely determined by the shopping habits associated with the consumers of the distributed product. Consumer goods fall into four subgroups: convenience goods, shopping goods, specialty goods and unsought goods. The purchasing behaviour associated with these products varies primarily in the amount and type of effort consumers exert in buying these products.

Convenience goods

Convenience products are purchased with as little effort as possible, frequently and in small quantities. In these products there is a routine buying behaviour. Convenience goods can be further subdivided into staple goods, impulse goods and emergency goods.

■ *Staple goods* are purchased on a regular basis and include most food items. Brand loyalty facilitates routine purchase and the goods must be pre-sold, namely through repetitive advertising.

■ *Impulse goods* are purchased without any planning (crisps, magazines, sweets, etc.). These goods must be available in many places; the packaging and the in-store displays in super-markets are important in the sale of these products.

■ *Emergency goods* are those needed to fill an unexpected and urgent need. These goods are purchased immediately as the need emerges and therefore they must be available in many outlets.

For these product categories, the firm has practically no alternative. These products require an intensive market coverage. If the brand is not found at the point of sale, consumers will buy another brand and the sales occasion will be lost.

Shopping goods

Shopping goods are high perceived-risk products. For these products, consumers are willing to spend time and effort to shop around and to compare product alternatives on criteria such as quality, price, style, features, etc. Examples include major appliances, furniture and clothing, i.e. expensive and infrequently bought products. Prospective buyers visit several stores before making a decision and sales personnel have an important role to play by providing information and advice. For shopping goods maximal market coverage is not required and a selective distribution system will be more appropriate, more especially as the co-operation of the retailer is necessary.

Specialty goods

Specialty goods are products with unique characteristics which are sufficiently important to consumers that they make a special effort to purchase them. Examples would include specific brands, fancy goods, exotic foods, deluxe clothings, sophisticated photographic equipment, etc. For those products, prospective buyers do not proceed to comparisons; they search for the outlet carrying the wanted product. Brand loyalty or the distinctive features of the product are the determining factors. For specialty goods, retailers are especially important; thus the producers of such goods will tend to limit their distribution to obtain strong support from the retailers. A selective or exclusive distribution system is the best option for the producer.

Unsought goods

Unsought goods are products that consumers do not know about or know about but do not consider buying. Examples are heat pumps, smoke detectors, encyclopaedias and life insurance. Substantial selling efforts are required for those products. The co-operation of the intermediaries is indispensable, or the firm must adopt a direct marketing system.

Other factors must be taken into consideration in the choice of a market coverage strategy. As a general rule, selective and exclusive distribution systems imply a higher level of co-operation among distributors, a reduction of distribution costs for the supplier and a better control over sales operations. On the other hand, in both cases, there is a voluntary limitation of the product retail availability. Thus potential buyers will have to actively search for the product. The firm must therefore maintain a good balance between the benefits and the demerits of each distribution system.

13.3.2 Intensive distribution

In an intensive distribution system, the firm seeks the maximum possible number of retailers to distribute its product, the largest number of storage points to ensure a maximum market coverage and the highest brand exposure. This strategy is appropriate for convenience goods, common raw materials and low-involvement services. The advantages of intensive distribution are to maximize product availability and to generate a large market share due to the brand's broad exposure to potential buyers. There are, however, significant disadvantages or risks associated with this strategy.

■ The sales revenue generated by the different retailers varies greatly, while the contact cost is the same for each intermediary. If the firm receives many small orders from an intensive network of small retailers, distribution costs (order processing and shipping) can become extremely high and undermine the overall profitability.

■ When the product has an intensive distribution in multiple and very diversified sales points, it becomes difficult for the firm to control its marketing strategy: discount pricing, poor customer service and lack of co-operation from retailers are practices difficult to prevent.

■ Intensive distribution is hard to reconcile with a brand image-building strategy and with a specific product positioning strategy due to the lack of control of the distributive network.

For these reasons, market-driven companies are induced to adopt a more selective distributive system once the brand awareness objectives have been achieved.

13.3.3 Selective Distribution

In a selective distribution system, the producer uses fewer distributors than the total number of available distributors in a specific geographic area. It is an appropriate strategy for shopping goods that customers buy infrequently and compare for differences in price and product features.

A selective distribution may also be the result of the refusal from distributors to carry the product in their assortment. To have a selective distribution, the firm must decide the criteria upon which to select its intermediaries. Several criteria are commonly used.

■ The *size of the distributor*, measured by its sales revenue, is the most popular criterion. In the majority of markets, a small number of distributors achieve a significant share of total sales revenue. In the food sector, for instance, the concentration ratio is very high in Switzerland, the UK and Belgium, where the first five distributors in the food sectors account for 82, 53 and 52 per cent, respectively, of the total turnover (Nielsen, 1995). In these conditions, it is obviously unprofitable to contact all distributors.

■ The *quality of the service* provided is also an important criterion. Intermediaries are paid to perform a certain number of well-defined functions and some dealers or retailers are more efficient than others.

■ The *technical competence* of the dealer and the availability of up-to-date facilities, mainly for complex products where after-sales service is important, is a third significant criterion.

In adopting a selective distribution system, the firm voluntarily agrees to limit the availability of its product in order to reduce its distribution costs and to gain better co-operation from the intermediaries. This co-operation can take various forms.

■ Participating in the advertising and promotion budget.

■ Accepting new products or unsought products requiring more sales effort.

■ Maintaining a minimum level of inventory.

■ Transferring information to the producer.

■ Providing better services to customers.

The main risk of a selective distribution system is to have insufficient market coverage. The producer must verify whether the market knows the distributors handling the brand or the product. If not, the reduced availability of the product could generate significant losses of sales opportunities. The firm may, on occasion, have no alternative and be forced to maintain a certain degree of selectivity in its distributive network. For example:

- A new product which is not yet a proven success will be accepted by a retailer only if it receives an exclusive right to carry the product in its territory.

- If the assortment is large because the consumer must be able to choose among several product forms (design, colour, size), selectivity will be necessary, otherwise the expected sales revenue will be too low to motivate the retailer.

- If the after-sales service implies long and costly training of the dealers, selectivity will be necessary to reduce the costs.

If the firm decides to adopt a selective distribution system, it is important to realize that this decision implies the adoption of a 'short' indirect distribution channel. It is very unlikely, indeed, that wholesalers will agree to voluntarily limit their field of operation simply to meet the strategic objectives of the producer.

13.3.4 Exclusive distribution and franchise systems

In an exclusive distribution system, the manufacturer relies on only one retailer or dealer to distribute its product in a given geographic territory. In turn, the exclusive dealer agrees not to sell any competing brand within the same product category. Exclusive distribution is useful when a company wants to differentiate its product on the basis of high quality, prestige or excellent customer service. The close co-operation with exclusive dealers facilitates the implementation of the producer's customer service programmes. The advantages and disadvantages of exclusive distribution are the same as in selective distribution, but amplified. A particular form of exclusive distribution is franchising.

Franchising is a contractual, vertically integrated marketing system which refers to a comprehensive method of distributing goods and services. It involves a continuous and contractual relationship in which a *franchisor* provides a licensed privilege to do business and assistance in organizing, training, merchandising, management and other areas in return for a specific consideration from the *franchisee*. Thus, the franchisee agrees to pay an initial fee, plus royalties calculated on the sales revenue, for the right to use a well-known trade-marked product or service and to receive continual assistance and services from the franchisor. In fact, the franchisee is buying a proven success from the franchisor.

Types of franchise systems

The franchisor may occupy any position within the channel; therefore there are four basic types of franchise system:

- The *manufacturer–retailer* franchise is exemplified by franchised automobile dealers and franchised service stations. Singer in the USA, and Pingouin and Yves Rocher in France are good examples.

- The *manufacturer–wholesaler* franchise is exemplified by the soft drinks companies like Coca-Cola and 7-Up who sell the soft drink syrups they manufacture to franchised wholesalers who, in turn, carbonate, bottle, sell and distribute to retailers.

- The *wholesaler–retailer* franchise is exemplified by Rexall Drug Stores, by Christianssens in toys and Unic and Disco in food.

- The *service sponsor–retailer* franchise is exemplified by Avis, Hertz, McDonald's, Midas and Holiday Inn.

The faster growing franchises include business and professional services, fast food, restaurants, car and truck rentals, and home and cleaning maintenance (Shangavi, 1991).

Characteristics of a good franchise

A good franchise must be above all a *transferable proven success*, which can be replicated in another territory or environment. According to Sallenave (1979, p. 11), a good franchise must:

- Be related to the distribution of a *high quality* product or service.

- Meet a *universal need* or want which is not country or region-specific.

- Be a *proven success* in franchisor owned and operated pilot units which serve as models for the other franchisees.

- Ensure the full transfer of *know-how* and to provide the training of the franchisee in the methods of doing business and modes of operation.

- Offer to the franchisees *initial and continuing service* to gain immediate market acceptance and to improve modes of operation.

- Have a regular *reporting and information system* which permits effective monitoring of the performance and collection of market information.

- Specify initial franchise *fees* and the royalty fees based on the gross value of a franchisee's sales volume (generally 5 per cent).

- Involve the franchisee in the *management* and development of the franchise system.

- Specify *legal provisions* for termination, cancellation and renewal of the franchise agreement, as well as for the repurchase of the franchise.

Franchise systems constitute a viable alternative to completely integrated corporate vertical marketing systems. In a franchise system, *funds are provided by the franchisees*, who invest in the stores and in the facilities. From the franchisor's point of view, the establishment of franchised dealers is an ideal means to achieve rapid national or international distribution for its products or services without committing large funds but keeping control of the system through contractual agreements.

> John Y. Brown, President of Kentucky Fried Chicken Corporation, has stated that it would have required $450 million for his firm to have established its first 2700 stores if

they had been company-owned. This sum was simply not available to his firm during the initial stages of its proposed expansion. The use of capital made available from franchisees, however, made the proposed expansion possible.   (McGuire, 1971, p. 7).

Thus a franchise system is an integrated marketing system controlled by the franchisor but financed by the franchisees. A successful franchise is a partnership in which the mutual interests of both franchisor and franchisees are closely interdependent.

Benefits to the franchisor
The motivations of the franchisor for creating and developing a franchise system are as follows:

■ To acquire funds without diluting control of the marketing system.

■ To keep high flexibility in the use of the capital collected for developing the system.

■ To avoid the fixed overhead expenses associated with distribution through company-owned branch units or stores.

■ To co-operate with independent business people, the franchisees, who are more likely to work hard at developing their markets than salaried employees.

■ To co-operate with local business people well accepted and integrated in the local community or in the foreign country.

■ To develop new sources of income based on existing know-how and marketing expertise.

■ To achieve faster sales development owing to the snowball effect generated by the franchising of a successful idea.

■ To benefit from economies of scale with the development of the franchise system.

Franchisors provide both initial and continuous services to their franchisees (McGuire, 1971). *Initial services* include: market survey and site selection; facility design and layout; lease negotiation advice; financing advice; operating manuals; management training programmes and franchisee employee training. *Continuous services* include: field supervision; merchandising and promotional materials; management and employee retraining; quality inspection; national advertising; centralized purchasing; market data and guidance; auditing and record keeping; management reports; and group insurance plans.

The franchise system is present in almost all business fields, and total franchise system sales have grown dramatically over the last decade. The number of franchise companies and franchisees active in each of the major market of the EU in 1991 is summarized in Table 13.2.

Benefits to franchisees
From the perspective of the potential franchisee, the most important appeal is to benefit from the franchisor's reputation of quality and corporate image. Franchising has several other strong appeals which explain the success of this distribution arrangement.

TABLE 13.2 *Number of franchise companies in the EU*

Country	Number of franchisors	Number of franchised units
Belgium	82	4100
Denmark	10	30
France	700	30 300
Italy	210	13 500
Holland	255	8800
Spain	100	9000
UK	295	16 600
West Germany	190	9100

Source: Shangavi (1991).

- Franchising enables an individual to enter a business which would be prohibitively expensive if the individual tried to do it alone.

- The amount of uncertainty is reduced, since the business idea has been successfully tested.

- The extensive services provided by the franchisor, both initial and continuous, reduce the risks of the operation.

- Franchising offers better purchasing power, the access to better sites and the support of national advertising.

- The introduction of new products and the constant rejuvenation of the product portfolio are made possible.

- Managerial assistance in marketing and finance is provided.

- The opportunity is provided for individuals to operate as independent business people within a large organization.

Franchising is a very flexible organization and many variants exist. Three basic rules must be met to have a successful arrangement:

- The will to work as partners.
- The right to mutual control.
- The value of the business idea.

This last condition is crucial. Franchising will work only if the business idea is a proven success. It is not a solution for a firm to declare itself a franchisor if there is no proven success.

13.4 COMMUNICATION STRATEGIES IN THE CHANNEL

Gaining support and co-operation from independent intermediaries is a key success factor for the implementation of the firm's marketing objectives. To get this co-operation, two very distinct

TABLE 13.3 *Incentives for motivating channel members*

Functional performance	Examples of channel incentives
Increased purchases or carry large inventories	Large margins, exclusive territories, buy-in promotions, quantity discounts, buy-back allowances, free goods, shelf-stocking programmes
Increased personal selling effort	Sales training, instructional materials, incentive programmes for channel members' salespeople
Increased local promotional effort	
■ Local advertising	Co-operative advertising, advertising allowance; print, radio, TV ads for use by local retailers
■ Increased display space	Promotion allowances tied to shelf space
■ In-store promotions	Display racks and signs, in-store demonstrations, in-store sampling
Improved customer service	Service training programmes, instructional materials, high margins on replacement parts, liberal labour cost allowance for warranty service.

Source: Boyd and Walker (1990).

communication strategies can be adopted by the firm: a push strategy or a pull strategy. A third alternative is a combination of the two.

13.4.1 Push strategies

In a push communication strategy, the bulk of the marketing effort is devoted to incentives directed to wholesalers and retailers to induce them to co-operate with the firm, to carry the brands in their assortments, to keep a minimum level of inventory, to display the products and to give them enough visibility on their shelf spaces. The objective is to win *voluntary co-operation* by offering attractive terms of trade, i.e. larger margins, quantity discounts, local or in-store advertising, promotional allowances, in-store sampling, etc. Personal selling and personal communication are the key marketing instruments in this strategy. The role of the sales representatives and of the merchandisers will be particularly important. Table 13.3 lists a variety of incentives the firm can use to increase the number of channel members.

A programme of incentives is indispensable to get the support of intermediaries. The greater their negotiating power, the more difficult it will be for the firm to obtain the support of distributors. In markets where distribution is highly concentrated, it is the intermediary who specifies the conditions for carrying the brand. The risk of an exclusive push strategy is the absence of countervailing power and the dependence of the firm on the intermediary who controls the access to the market.

The only alternative for the firm is the adoption of a direct marketing system which completely by-passes intermediaries. This is a costly operation, however, since all distribution tasks must then be assumed by the firm. Recent developments in communication technologies present new opportunities, however. The potential of direct or interactive marketing will be discussed in section 13.8.

13.4.2 Pull strategies

When adopting a pull strategy, the manufacturer focuses its communication efforts on the end-user, by-passing intermediaries and trying to build company demand directly among potential customers in the target segment. The communication objective is to create strong customer demand and brand loyalty among consumers in order to pull the brand through the distribution channel, forcing the intermediaries to carry the brand to meet consumers' demand.

To achieve these objectives, the manufacturer will spend the largest proportion of its communication budget on media advertising, consumer promotions and direct marketing efforts aimed at winning end-customer preferences. If this branding policy is successful, the manufacturer has the power to influence channel participants and to induce them to carry the brand, since a substantial sales volume will be achieved. The strategic objective is to neutralize the bargaining power of the intermediary who could block the access to the market. For example, Procter & Gamble generally adopts a pull strategy in its new product launching strategies. However, the consumer advertising campaign starts only when the new brand has achieved almost 100 per cent distribution at retail. It goes without saying that such a result can be achieved only because P&G's sales representatives are in position to demonstrate to retailers the advertising that will be organized to support the new product market introduction. Thus, retailers are willing to co-operate with the company.

Pull strategies imply in general large financial resources to cover the costs of brand image advertising campaigns. These costs are fixed overhead expenses, while the costs of a push strategy are proportional to volume and therefore easier to bear, particularly for a small firm.

In fact, a pull strategy must be viewed as a long-term investment. The goal of the firm is to create a capital of goodwill, a *brand equity*, around the company name or around the brand. A strong brand image is an asset for the firm and is the best argument for obtaining support and co-operation from intermediaries.

In practice, these two communication strategies are used in combination, and it is difficult to imagine a market situation where no incentives would be used to motivate intermediaries. With the development of marketing expertise and the increased cost of personal selling, the trend among market-driven companies is to reinforce branding policies and pull communication strategies. As the average cost of a call to customer made by a salesperson is constantly increasing, the selectivity of mass media tends to improve and therefore to lower the unit cost of a contact through advertising.

13.5 DISTRIBUTION COSTS ANALYSIS

The distribution cost is measured by the difference between the unit sales price paid by the end-user and the unit cost paid to the producer by the first buyer. Thus, the distribution margin

BOX 13.2

Definitions of trade margins

Trade margins:

      Trade margin = Selling price − Purchase cost

$$D = P - C$$

Trade margin as percentage:

    'of selling price' (discount)   'of purchase cost' (mark-up)

$$D^* = (P - C)/P \qquad\qquad D^0 = (P - C)/C$$

Conversion rules:

$$D^* = D^0/(1 + D^0) \qquad\qquad D^0 = D^*/(1 - D^*)$$

measures the *added value* brought by the distribution channel. If several intermediaries participate in the distribution process, the distribution margin is equal to the sum of the different distributors' margins. The margin of a particular distributor is equal to the difference between its selling price and its purchase cost. The two definitions coincide when there is only one intermediary in the channel.

13.5.1 Trade margins

A trade margin is often expressed as a percentage. This is sometimes confusing, since the margin percentage can be computed on the basis of purchase cost (C) or on the basis of selling price (P). The trade margin (D) is then referred to as a 'mark-up' or as a 'discount'. The conversion rules are presented in Box 13.2.

    Suppose a retailer purchases an item for £10 and sells it at a price of £20, that is, at a £10 margin. What is the retailer's margin percentage ? As a percentage of the selling price, it is

$$£10/£20 \times 100 = 50 \text{ per cent}$$

As a percentage of cost, it is

$$£10/£10 \times 100 = 100 \text{ per cent}$$

    Trade margins are usually determined on the basis of selling price, but practices do vary between firms and industries.

Trade margins are based on a distributor's place in the channel and represent payment for performing certain distribution tasks. In some cases, several margins are quoted to distributors, as illustrated in Box 13.3. The manufacturer's problem of suggesting a list price, i.e. the final suggested price of the product, is more complex, as the number of intermediaries between the producer and the final consumer increases.

BOX 13.3

Developing a price structure

1. Trade margins are based on a distributor's place in the channel and represent payment for performing certain distribution tasks.
2. Prices are usually quoted to distributors as a series of numbers depending on the number of functions performed.
3. In the case of large retail chains, we would have the following quotation:

30, 10, 5, and 2/10, net 30

The first three numbers represent successive discounts from the list price:

- 30 per cent: as functional discount for the position the retailer occupies in the channel;
- 10 per cent: as compensation for performing the storage function, usually performed by the wholesaler;
- 5 per cent: as an allowance for the retailer's efforts to promote the product through local advertising;
- 2/10: as cash discount, 2 per cent, as reward for payment of an invoice within 10 days;
- Net 30: the length of the credit period; if the payment is not made within 10 days, the entire invoice must be paid in full within 30 days.

Source: Adapted from Monroe (1979, p. 169).

13.5.2 Comparison of distribution costs

The distribution margin compensates the distribution functions and tasks assumed by the intermediaries in the channel. If some of these distribution tasks are assumed directly by the producer, it will have to support the organization and the costs implied. By way of illustration, Table 13.4 shows a cost comparison of two indirect distribution channels: a 'long' indirect channel involving two intermediaries, wholesalers (W) and retailers (R), and a 'short' indirect channel involving only retailers, the wholesaling function being assumed by the manufacturer (M).

In the *indirect long channel*, most of the physical distribution tasks (storage and transportation) are assumed by wholesalers and the distribution costs are largely proportional to the rate of activity and covered by the margin of the wholesalers' distributor. The manufacturer has to maintain a minimum sales administration unit and the overhead costs are minimized. In this type of conventional vertical marketing organization, however, the producer is dependent on the goodwill of the distributors and has only limited control on the sales organization. To offset this handicap, the producer can create its own salesforce (merchandisers) to stimulate sales at the retailers' level and also to use mass media advertising to create brand awareness and brand preference among end-users through a 'pull communication' strategy.

TABLE 13.4 *Distribution cost analysis of two distribution channels*

Distribution tasks	Indirect long channel		Indirect short channel	
	Cost	Comments	Cost	Comments
Transport	Covered by the wholesaler margin: 16% of the manufacturer's sales revenue	M → W: in charge of M—more expensive W → R: in charge of R—cheaper	—	M → warehouses: in charge of M—cheaper Warehouses → R: in charge of R—more expensive
Assortment		In charge of W and R: complete assortment	—	In charge of R: risk of incomplete assortment
Storage		Warehouses: in charge of W Stocks: in charge of W Customer: in charge of W	$750 000 2.5% of sales revenue 1.25% of sales revenue	7 warehouses (fewer) 4 rotations/year (rate 10%) Payment at 45 days (rate 10%)
Contact		In charge of W—risk of inertia	$500 000	25 sales people at $20 000 more dynamic (push strategy)
Information	2.5% of sales revenue	Push strategy on W and R	1.5% of sales revenue	Pull strategy
Sales administration	$30 000	Principally in charge of W; small team	$200 000	Principally in charge of M; large team
Total cost	$30 000 + 0.185 (sales revenue)	Cost proportional to the activity rate	$1 450 000 + 0.0525 (sales revenue)	Largest part of cost is fixed

Source: Adapted from Brown *et al.* (1968).

Note: M = manufacturer; W = wholesaler; R = retailer.

Examining now the cost structure of the *indirect short channel*, one observes that overheads or fixed costs represent the largest share of total distribution costs. It means that the manufacturer has to support the costs of the physical distribution functions and organize a network of warehouses plus a much more extensive sales administration unit. The financial costs involved by the inventory management and by the customers' accounts receivable are also completely assumed by the producer, as well as the selling function. By adopting a selective distribution strategy, the firm has to contact 2500 retailers at least once a month. One sales representative can perform on average 4.8 calls per day during 250 working days per year. The firm therefore requires 25 sales representatives to achieve the market coverage objective.

Thus, the adoption of an indirect short distribution channel implies a major financial risk for the producer. The benefits of this strategy, however, are better control of the commercial organization and a closer contact with the end-users.

The two cost equations are compared in Fig. 13.5. One sees that the costs of distribution are the same at a certain level—the break-even level—of the total sales revenue. If the expected sales revenues are the same in both cases, the 'longer' channel will be preferred for any turnover inferior to the break-even level and conversely for any higher turnover. This observation is in line with the common observation that small companies tend to favour long distribution channels, their financial capacities being in general too weak to support the costs of a short distribution channel.

In general, the sales revenue expectations are not the same for each distribution channel. The profitability rate of each channel will be determined as follows:

$$R = \frac{\text{Sales revenue} - \text{Distribution costs}}{\text{Distribution costs}}$$

where R is an estimate of the expected rate of return when all the costs are taken into account for each channel. This quantitative indicator must, of course, be interpreted with care and with due consideration of the more 'qualitative' factors discussed above.

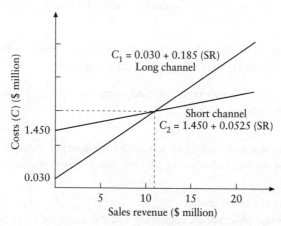

$C_1 = 0.030 + 0.185 \text{ (SR)}$
Long channel

Short channel
$C_2 = 1.450 + 0.0525 \text{ (SR)}$

Costs (C) ($ million)

1.450

0.030

5   10   15   20

Sales revenue ($ million)

FIGURE 13.5 *Comparing the cost structures of two distribution channels*

13.6 THE RETAILER'S STRATEGIC MARKETING

Significant changes have occurred during the 1990s in the way retailers, and in particular large retailers, perceive their roles in the exchange process. Traditionally, retailers have limited their role to intermediaries, acting rather passively between the producer and the consumer by simply performing the physical tasks of distribution and by making the goods available to consumers in the required condition, place and time. From this rather passive role, intermediaries are increasingly adopting an innovative and active role, thereby modifying the balance of power between manufacturers and retailers.

This evolution has coincided with significant sociocultural changes in affluent economies which have induced retailers to redefine their roles as economic agents and to adopt a more market-driven perspective. From a traditional 'shop' or 'in-house' orientation, retailers are now discovering strategic marketing and are moving away from a business philosophy where the marketing function is confined to the physical distribution tasks and to the purchasing function.

13.6.1 Major changes in the distribution sector

The major changes of the macro-environment have been described in Chapter 2. In addition to these structural changes, significant evolutions in government regulations, purchasing habits and in retailing have also influenced the development of the distribution sector.

Legislation regulating business

Because the distribution sector has an important social and economic role in the economy, government authorities have regulated distributive activities in different fields in most Western European countries. The forms of regulation include:

- Controls of prices and distribution margins in order to reduce inflation either through authoritarian price freezes and controls or through sectoral agreements.

- Consumer protection against unfair business practices through consumerist legislation on labelling, product safety, deceptive advertising, unit pricing, promotions, etc.

- Legislation aiming at the protection of small businesses by limiting further expansion of large retail chains.

- Laws to define and prevent unfair competition based on the Treaty of Rome and enforced by the European Commission's general directorate for competition.

- Legislations on waste collection, recycling and reduction which constitute a challenge for manufacturers and distributors.

Within the European Union, substantial efforts are being made to standardize these regulations to meet the objective of the Single European Market which came into force in 1993.

Changing Sociocultural environment

These changes are demographic, social, economic and cultural, and have occurred at a different rate within each West European country.

- Although the world population is showing explosive growth, in Western Europe one observes a slow-down in the birth rate, smaller families and ageing populations.

- The number of single-adult households is growing as well as the number of working wives; the rate of equipment in household appliances is very high and the number of better educated people continues to rise.

- In terms of values, radical changes are emerging; more attention is given to the quality of life, to high-touch products and services, to more personalized services, and to the value of time, change and stimulations.

- Regarding the economic situation in the OECD countries in 1996, the recession is still present, with a modest 2.5 per cent growth of real GNP, persistent unemployment and a slow-down in consumption expenditures.

The new consumers are better educated and informed and more professional in their buying behaviour. They seek gratifying experiences and are strongly differentiated in their preferences and expectations. In this context, mass-marketing techniques become ineffective and retailers are confronted with highly *fragmented markets* and *smarter shoppers* searching for the best value for money. Clearly, these changes constitute important challenges for the distribution sector, and in particular for the retailer.

Changes in the retailing industry

In many West European countries, retailing has become a mature industry, and several indicators confirm this observation.

- Keeping pace with the growth of the economy, the retailing industry has experienced zero or minimal growth for several years, particularly in the food sector. The share of large retail chains has reached a plateau and is even declining in some markets.

- The proliferation of retailers has created over-capacity, and today a retailer must compete against a crowd of tough competitors, not only in the food sector but also in such sectors as clothing, household appliances and even in the newest product categories like home computers.

- Competition is intensive and based almost exclusively on price for all the branded products. In most product categories, consumers can buy exactly the same product or brand at a discount store at bargain prices as they can at a department store at its full price.

- In several European countries, a high level of concentration is observed among large distributors. Table 13.5. displays the concentration ratios of the top five and top ten distributors in the food sector. These distributors have substantial purchasing power (and bargaining power), reinforced recently by the creation of joint purchasing units at the European level (Dupuis, 1991; Ducrocq, 1991).

All these characteristics—maturity, over-capacity, concentration and price competition— are typical of commodity markets and suggest that the retailing industry has become

TABLE 13.5 *Concentration of European distribution in the food sector (measured by value of sales)*

Countries	Market share of the 2% best self-service stores	Market share of the 10% best self-service stores
UK	52	83
France	49	80
Spain	48	66
Portugal	47	65
Greece	46	71
Italy	43	66
Belgium	39	80
Austria	28	49
Germany	28	55
Switzerland	26	58
Denmark	21	50
Sweden	19	48
Norway	19	46
Finland	17	45
Holland	17	44

Source: Nielsen (1995, p. 16).

'commoditized'. This conclusion must be qualified, however, by country and by product category. As suggested by Wortzel (1987, p. 46), several factors explain this evolution.

■ During the 1960s, *manufacturers' brand names* became prominent in a broadening range of product categories, and more and more retailers began featuring these brands. Thus, the presence of the brand in the retailer's assortment became the determining choice criterion in choosing a particular store. In the process, retailers abdicated much of their stores' marketing and positioning responsibilities to the manufacturers.

■ This situation has stimulated the development of *hard discounters,* who sell well-known brands exclusively at bargain prices with minimum services.

■ The proliferation of slightly differentiated brands and the adoption of *intensive distribution strategies* by manufacturers have also contributed to reducing store differentiation, with most stores carrying the same assortment of brands.

■ Retailers once had the major responsibility for *after-sales service,* and choosing a retailer was important when one bought such products as appliances and consumer electronics. Now consumers can obtain after-sales service for most products independently of the retailer, and this type of store differentiation is also waning.

■ The lack of customer services at retail to improve productivity has generated an important *self-production of services* by consumers which contribute towards increasing the 'total price' of mass distribution (de Maricourt, 1988).

■ Finally, the tremendous growth in *bank credit cards* also contributes to undermining store loyalty. Consumers no longer choose a store because they have established credit there: bank cards entitle customers to buy items almost anywhere they please.

These factors have all contributed to reducing store differentiation and loyalty, to killing the concept of 'shopping for enjoyment' and to modifying consumer's buying behaviour, particularly for working housewives attracted by other more rewarding and stimulating activities.

Changes in consumer's retail buying behaviour

Retail consumers today behave differently, not only because of the social and demographic changes described above, but also because they are more educated and professional in their purchase decisions. As suggested by Wortzel (1987, p. 47), one of the biggest changes is the rise of the 'smart shopper'. Being a smart shopper implies several capabilities:

■ Being informed about the products one wants to buy and being able to compare and choose independently of brand, advertising, store and salesperson's recommendations. It means finding the best value for money.

■ Being able to separate the product features and the benefits and services provided by a store to augment the product value. Smart shoppers distinguish between what is inherent in the product and can therefore be obtained anywhere they buy it, and what a specific store adds to the purchase. They routinely compare stores as well as brands on this basis.

■ Being able to recognize that brands have become increasingly similar. They will not necessarily choose a well-known brand over a less-well-known brand simply because it is familiar or because of its image. The product must also be viewed as offering superior value.

In addition, for many consumers, and for a broadening range of goods, shopping is no longer viewed as fun or recreational, but rather as a tedious task to be performed as economically and efficiently as possible. In their search for value, an expanding group of consumers seek not only good merchandise but also savings of time and effort.

13.6.2 Positioning strategies of the retailer

Confronted with these changes, the retailer has to review its traditional strategic positioning by redefining its 'store concept' and by adopting a positioning which provides unique value to consumers. The adoption of a store differentiation strategy becomes a necessity in a marketplace where retailing has become commoditized. Thus the concepts of strategic marketing developed for product marketing can be directly applied to retail marketing.

The multi-attribute concept of a store

From the consumer standpoint, the store concept can be viewed as a package of benefits, and the *multi-attribute product concept* described in Chapter 4 is useful here to help design the store concept. In any store, six different characteristics or attributes can be identified which constitute as many action variables for the retailer:

1. *Location.* This defines the territorial coverage or trading area within which to develop business relations. The alternatives are downtown location, community, suburban or regional shopping centres.
2. *Assortment.* The number of product lines that will be sold, which implies decisions on the product assortment breadth (narrow or wide) and product assortment depth (shallow or deep) for each product line.
3. *Pricing.* The general level of prices (high or low gross margins) and the use of loss-leaders, discount pricing and price promotions.
4. *Services.* The extent of the service mix. A distinction can be made between pre-purchase services (telephone orders, shopping hours, fitting rooms, etc.), post-purchase services (delivery, alterations, wrapping, etc.) and ancillary services (credit, restaurants, baby sitting, travel agencies, etc); see de Maricourt (1988).
5. *Time.* The time required for a shopping trip. Proximity is the key factor, but this also involves opening and closing hours, accessibility, ease of selection, fast completion of transaction and queuing time at checkout counters.
6. *Atmosphere.* The layout of the store, but also the light, the space the musical ambience, the look and the interior decoration, etc.

These store attributes are used by consumers when they compare retail stores. It is the retailer's task to define a store concept—based on some innovative combination of these attributes—which constitutes a package of benefits differentiated from the competition.

Store positioning strategies
The positioning strategies to be adopted by the retailer vary with sectors. Retail outlets can be classified according to two dimensions: the level of the gross margin (high or low) and the type of benefit sought by the consumer: symbolic or functional. We thus have a two-dimensional map as shown in Fig. 13.6, which describes four distinct positioning strategies.

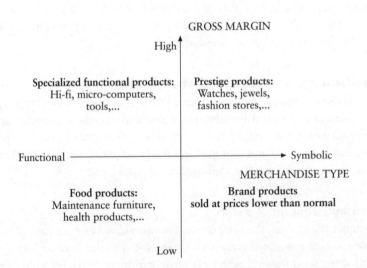

FIGURE 13.6 *Retail positioning strategies (Source: Wortzel, 1987)*

- Among the functional products sold with a high gross margin (upper left quadrant) are the *specialty stores*, having selected or specialized assortments in food or in audiovisuals, computers, tools, etc.

- Among the functional products with low margins are the 'every day' food products sold in supermarkets and superstores, low-price furniture (Ikea), Do-It-Yourself centres, cheap audio-visual goods, etc.

- The symbolic products with high margins are sold through *prestige specialty stores*, like fashion stores (Benetton, Rodier), jewellery, watches, etc.

- Symbolic products sold at low prices are distributed through *discount stores* selling national brands at prices lower than those prevailing in conventional stores.

Three basic store positioning strategies can be adopted by the retailer: product differentiation, service and personality augmentation, and price leadership.

- A *product differentiation* strategy is based on offering products that are intrinsically different, e.g. different brands or different styles from those in the same product category offered by other stores.

- In a *service and personality augmentation* strategy, a retailer offers products that are intrinsically similar to those offered by competitors, but adds specific services and personality to differentiate the store.

- A *price leadership* strategy means offering the same products as the competition at lower prices.

Several alternative positioning strategies can be contemplated by the retailer who has under his control several action variables. Thus, a strategic marketing plan can be elaborated and implemented through an action programme consistent with the chosen objectives to gain a sustainable competitive advantage over competition.

Private labels development

Differentiation strategies based on private brand development have been successfully implemented by large retailers during the last decade. In Belgium, for instance, the market shares of private labels increased from 11.4 per cent in 1983 to 19.8 per cent in 1992 (Nielsen, 1995). Private label market shares in the other European countries are presented in Table 13.6. See also the McKinsey study (Glémet and Mira, 1993a, 1993b).

This development coincides with the growth of the market power held by large retailers, owing to three groups of factors:

- The creation of powerful *purchasing centres* at the European level, which has substantially increased the bargaining power of large retailers.

- The development of *centralized warehousing and delivery systems* which has created a physical barrier between the supplier and the local supermarket.

TABLE 13.6 *Market shares of private labels*

Countries	Market shares (%)	Countries	Market shares (%)
Switzerland	41.2	Italy	6.8
United Kingdom	37.1	Germany	6.8
Belgium	19.8	Austria	6.3
France	16.4	Finland	5.4
Holland	16.3	Norway	5.0
Sweden	10.7	Ireland	3.6
Spain	7.7	Portugal	2.3

Source: Nielsen (1993).

■ The generalization of *electronic point of sales* (EPOS), a computerized system for recording sales at retail checkouts which give the retailer instant information on each product sold at the retail outlet.

As a result of these technological changes, one observes a shift in the balance of power between suppliers and retailers (Messinger and Chakravarthi, 1995)

This increased market power has induced retailers to develop their own branding policies in order to improve their profitability. This private label strategy has been used for more than 20 years in Western Europe, but has recently gained a new dimension. Several types of private labels exist in the European market.

1. *Store brand names*. These are intended to provide the same performance as national brands, but at more moderate prices. Typical examples are Delhaize, St Michael from Marks & Spencer, Casino, etc. The brand name is that of the chain and is used as a method of furthering the store's image.
2. *Generic brands*. These products are unsophisticated, presented in simple package at lowest prices and without a brand name. Typical examples are the white products from GB in Belgium.
3. *Invented brand names*. They are presented as regular brands by the retailer but are distributed exclusively in the stores of the chain. Many retail chains sell invented brands such as Beaumont at Monoprix, O'Lacy at Asko and Saint Goustain and Chabrior at Intermarché.
4. *'Premiers prix'*. Their role is to stave off the invasion of the hard discounters, namely Aldi. The name of the store is not mentioned.

It is worth noting that the development of private labels has been stimulated by the growth of the *premiers prix* brands and by the dynamism of the new breed of hard discounters such as Aldi and Idl (Germany and Denmark) and Kwik-Save (UK) which operate through warehouse retail stores.

This offensive of private labels has been fruitful and, as a consequence, national brand loyalty is decreasing, forcing suppliers to reduce their price differentials.

- In the USA, the Roper Organization regularly measures brand loyalty. In 1988, 56 per cent of respondents claimed to know which brands to buy in entering the store; this figure dropped to 53 per cent in 1990 and to 46 per cent in 1991 (Liesse, 1991).

- Marlboro's market share in the US dropped from 30 to 22 per cent, largely in favour of generic brands whose market share reached more than 30 per cent. To stop this erosion, Philip Morris reduced its price by 22 per cent (*The Economist*, April 10, 1993, pp. 61–62).

Retailers' marketing strategies tend to become more sophisticated. They do not simply imitate existing products but develop new product concepts targeted to well-defined market segments, which are then produced by international manufacturers specializing in private labels. Most large retailers list three product classes:

- *National brands*, and preferably the brand leaders in the product category (the A brands), supported by heavy advertising and promotional activities.

- *Own labels*, *store* or *umbrella brands* (the B brands) created by the retailer to improve profitability and to build the store image.

- *'Premiers prix'* (the C brands) which are used as price-fighters to stop the hard discounters by offering an alternative to customers.

In this competitive struggle, the weakest manufacturer's brands are the first to be eliminated from the supermarkets. For retailers, three objectives can be pursued with private labels.

- To reduce the power of manufacturers by reducing their volume and their brand franchise and to eliminate small competitors.

- To enhance category margins since private labels can deliver 5–10 margin points more than national brands.

- To provide a differentiated product to build retailer's image.

This last objective is now gaining in importance among the most sophisticated and dynamic retailers.

Trade marketing

Confronted with the growing power of large supermarket retailers, what are the defence strategies for the consumer brand manufacturer? Four strategic options exist.

1. *Pull strategy*. To promote an innovative (unique) product or well-differentiated brand through creative segmentation and media advertising targeted to the end-consumer, in order to induce the distributor to list the brand in his assortment.
2. *Direct marketing*. To by-pass the retailers by adopting a non-store marketing strategy where purchases are made from the home and delivered to the home.
3. *Subcontracting marketing*. To concentrate on R&D and manufacturing and to leave the marketing function to a well-diversified group of retailers.
4. *Trade marketing*. To view distributors as intermediate customers and to design a retailer-driven marketing programme.

Thus, trade marketing is simply the application of the marketing concept to distributors who are no longer viewed as intermediaries in the channel but as partners or customers in their own right. In order to manage this relationship with retailers, suppliers will have to develop an in-depth understanding of their logistic problems, their desired store image and the perceived importance of a particular product category for the chain store's positioning. A good understanding of the objectives and constraints of the intermediate customer is a prerequisite for the development of a successful relationship marketing strategy.

The term *channel partnership* has been used to designate a variety of relationships between buyers and suppliers. Buzzell and Ortmeyer (1995, p. 86) define channel partnership in the following way: '... an ongoing relationship between a retailer and an independent supplier in which the parties agree on objectives, policies and procedures for ordering and physical distribution of the supplier's products.'

The most fundamental change is the shift from an adversarial practice to one of partnership that will enable the industry to optimize the whole supply chain, minimizing inventory levels and optimizing product availability through EDI (Electronic Data Interchange). To go further on this topic, see Buzzell and Ortmeyer (1995).

13.7 INTERACTIVE OR DIRECT MARKETING

Direct marketing (i.e. a zero intermediary level channel) is current practice in industrial markets when potential buyers are few and products are sophisticated or custom made and of high unit value. The surprising fact in recent years is the growth of this selling system in the field of consumer goods, largely as a result of the development of new communication media, such as telemarketing, direct response radio and television, electronic shopping (Mintel), etc.

Direct marketing is defined by the Direct Marketing Association as: 'An interactive system which uses one or more advertising media to effect a measurable *response and/or transaction at any location.*'

Thus, according to this definition, direct marketing does not necessarily imply non-store marketing, i.e. a marketing system without using intermediaries. To clarify the field, a distinction must be made between 'direct-order' marketing and 'direct-relationship' marketing.

- In *direct-order* marketing purchases are made from the home and delivered to the home, and the firm distributes directly without using intermediaries. This is non-store marketing, and the techniques used are mail order catalogues, direct mail, telemarketing, electronic shopping, etc.

- In *direct-relationship* marketing, the objective is to stimulate sales by establishing direct contacts with prospects and customers to create or maintain a continuing relationship.

Thus, direct-relationship marketing can very well co-exist with a conventional vertical indirect marketing system. For this reason, the expression *interactive marketing* seems more appropriate than 'direct marketing', which refers essentially to non-store marketing practices.

The development of interactive marketing is indicative of a significant change in the exchange and communication process between producers and consumers in affluent economies. It suggests that the marketing monologue which prevails in most market situations tends to be replaced by a marketing dialogue, customized marketing being substituted for mass or segment marketing.

13.7.1 Rationale of direct-order marketing

Several factors explain the development of more direct marketing and communication systems.

■ First, the considerable cost increase of personal communication. According to a study by Forsyth (1988), the average cost of a business sales call rose to $251.63 in 1987, i.e. 160 per cent increase over the 1977 cost of $96.79.

■ Simultaneously, the effectiveness of mass media advertising has been weakened by the proliferation of advertising messages and changing viewing habits in TV (zapping, VCR) combined with the rising cost of brand image advertising campaigns.

■ Shopping is no longer associated with fun and excitement, and is perceived as a time-consuming bore by educated consumers who tend to give their time higher value. For consumers, catalogue shopping is a convenient shopping alternative.

■ For the manufacturers, direct marketing presents several potential advantages. It allows greater selectivity in communicating with the market, personalization of messages and the maintenance of a continuous relationship. From a strategic point of view, interactive marketing gives the producer a way to by-pass intermediaries and reduce the firm's dependence on the goodwill of too-powerful retailers.

■ Finally, the formidable development of low-cost computers, with their immense storage and processing capabilities, has greatly facilitated the use of databases to record and keep track of commercial contacts with customers. This information is then used to reach them individually with highly personalized messages.

The economic incentive of increasing the productivity of marketing expenditure is very appealing.

13.7.2 Organization of direct-order marketing systems

Direct-order marketing supposes the development of a marketing database system. The essence of the system is to communicate directly with customers and ask them to respond in a tangible way. A database system can be defined as follows: from a marketing perspective, database marketing uses information about consumers in order to improve the efficiency of what might be called the Three Ts: *targeting*, *tailoring* and *tying* (Cespedes and Smith, 1993, p. 7).

The development of a direct marketing campaign implies the creation of personalized messages containing an *offer* and an *invitation to respond*. The database is then used to record the response of customers and to adapt the next message. The components of a direct marketing system as follows:

The message content.   The end objective is, of course, to achieve a sale, but the immediate objective is to create a dialogue and to maintain a relationship. The intermediate objective may be to obtain prospect leads, to reactivate former customers, to acknowledge receipt of an order, to welcome new customers, to inform customers and prepare them for later purchase, to generate requests for catalogues or leaflets, to propose a visit to a showroom, etc.

Personalized messages.   This is the main superiority of direct marketing over mass media advertising. Instead of using standardized advertising messages and a 'shotgun' approach, a marketing database makes possible a 'rifle' approach and, at the limit, a truly personalized message by including details relevant to the target customer and not to others.

The offer.   To obtain a positive behavioural response from the prospect, the message must include an offer or a proposition sufficiently attractive to induce prospects to respond. In the simplest case, it is an offer to purchase the product. It could also be the proposal to inspect the product, a free sample or a free credit, participation in a contest or in a club, etc. The attractiveness of the offer is a key success factor.

Measurable response.   In an interactive marketing system, the key objective is to engage in a dialogue with individual customers, and it is therefore essential to obtain some kind of response. The ideal response is placing an order, but other forms of response are sought, such as agreeing to a sales appointment, returning a reply coupon, confirming receipt of information, agreeing to attend an exhibition, providing more information about needs and wants, etc. In an interactive marketing system, potential customers are self-selected since only potentially interested customers will respond.

Database marketing.   Any interactive marketing system implies the existence of a computerized database. A marketing database is

> an organized collection of data about individual customers, prospects or suspects that is accessible and actionable for such marketing purposes as lead generation, lead qualification, sale of a product or of a service, or maintenance of customer relationships.
>
> (Kotler, 1991, p. 627)

In addition to the personal identification elements, the database must include information on past purchase behaviours, preferred brands, size of orders, etc. Thus, the firm must have the capacity to handle prospects' reactions and personal orders. This implies a considerable reinforcement of the sales administration and logistics departments.

Communication mix.   The communication media used are mainly the personalized media like direct mail, catalogue marketing and telemarketing. Then come radio, magazine and television direct-response marketing and electronic shopping. Direct mail remains the most important medium. The total expenditure for direct marketing in most of the EU countries (1993) can be seen in Table 13.7.

TABLE 13.7 *Total expenditure in direct marketing*

Countries	Direct mail (million ECU)	Direct advertising (million ECU)	Tele market-ing/others (million ECU)	Total (million ECU)	ECU/ Per capita	Per cent of total
Germany	5 730	3540	1720	10 990	136	37
France	4 010	750	780	5 540	96	18
UK	1 390	1940	770	4 100	70	14
Italy	1 380	460	1100	2 940	193	10
Holland	1 220	1240	190	2 650	47	9
Spain	510	1250	80	1 840	47	6
Denmark	670	100	90	850	164	3
Belgium/Lux.	570	200	50	820	81	3
Portugal	20	100	10	130	13	–
Greece	20	80	10	110	11	–
Ireland	70	30	10	100	31	–
TOTAL	15 580	9690	4810	30 080	87	100
% Total	52%	32%	16%	100%	–	–

Source: European Direct Marketing (1993).

One of the greatest advantages of direct marketing is that responses to campaigns are measured, enabling marketing management to identify the effectiveness of different approaches. It is testable and permits privacy in that the marketing offer is not visible to the competition (Roscitt and Parket, 1988).

Limits of direct-order marketing

Convenience is the major benefit for the consumer, but many consumers can be less interested in convenience than in product quality, reliable delivery and being able to touch, feel and smell the merchandise. In addition, as direct marketing becomes more and more popular, many consumers view the techniques of direct marketing—the unsolicited telephone calls, the junk mail and the trading and renting of mailing lists—as an *invasion of privacy*.

Quelch and Takeuchi (1981, p. 84) questioned the future of non-store marketing by raising the following questions:

■ What if postal rates double?

■ What if privacy laws prevent direct marketers from selling or buying mailing lists?

■ What if a freeze is placed on credit card usage?

These questions are more relevant than ever with the spectacular development of direct marketing, and the European Commission is currently examining proposals to regulate this ever-increasing field and to request the prior assent of the subject. A firm could not use the data

BOX 13.4

Rules for database marketing fairness

Rule 1

Data users must have the clear assent of the data subject to use personal data for Database Marketing (DBM) purposes.

- Companies should avoid deception and secrecy in data collection.
- Targeted consumers should know the marketer's source for information about them.
- Individuals should have the opportunity to opt out of subsequent uses of data.
- A consumer's assent to data use by one company does not automatically transfer to companies sharing that information.

Rule 2

Companies are responsible for the accuracy of the data they use, and the data subjects should have the right to access, verify and change information about themselves.

Rule 3

Categorizations should be based on actual behaviour as well as the more traditional criteria of attitudes, lifestyles and demographics.

Source: Cespedes and Smith (1993, p. 16)

for subsequent purposes unless overt permission is granted for each use. Cespedes and Smith (1993, p. 16) have proposed rules for the fair use of database marketing. Those rules are summarized in Box 13.4.

Direct marketing is probably less controversial in the field of business-to-business marketing than in the field of consumer marketing.

Relationship marketing

Interactive marketing does not necessarily imply direct-order marketing. *Relationship marketing* is oriented towards a strong, lasting relationship with individual customers, in contrast with *transaction marketing,* where the firm has a more short-term orientation and is mostly interested in achieving immediate sales (see Dwyer *et al.*, 1987).

In a relationship marketing system, *the profit centre is the customer* and not the product, and attracting new customers is viewed as an intermediate objective. Maintaining and cultivating the existing customer base is the key objective, in order to create a long-term mutually profitable relationship. Relationship marketing is particularly useful in industrial marketing, where buyers' and sellers' relationships are frequently close, long-lasting and important for both parties.

Jackson (1985) establishes a distinction between two types of customer behaviour: the 'lost-for-good' model and the 'always-a-share' model.

■ The *lost-for-good* model assumes that if a customer does decide to leave a supplier, the account is lost forever, or, alternatively, that it is at least as difficult and costly for the vendor to win back such an account as it was to win the customer in the first place. Because of high switching costs, the customer changes suppliers very reluctantly.

■ The *always-a-share* model assumes that buyers can maintain less intense commitments than they do in the 'lost-for-good' model and that they can have commitments to more than one vendor at the same time. The account can easily switch part or all of its purchases from one vendor to another, and therefore it can share its patronage, perhaps over time, among multiple vendors.

These two models provide the end-points of a spectrum of behaviour of industrial customers. Relationship marketing is sensible for customers behaving as in the 'lost-for-good' model; transaction marketing is appropriate for customers behaving as suggested by the 'always-a-share' model (Jackson, 1985, p. 16).

Relationship marketing is especially promising in the field of business marketing where the supplier–customer relationships are long-lasting and important for each party. Relationship marketing is also the business philosophy presiding over trade marketing. On relationship marketing, see Dwyer *et al.* (1987), Jackson (1985) and Payne (1995).

13.8 ENTRY STRATEGIES IN FOREIGN MARKETS

The key role of international development was discussed in Chapter 10, in view namely of the globalization of the European and world economy. One of the critical questions to examine in establishing an international development strategy is to select the entry mode in the target foreign country and the distribution channel. Several alternative entry strategies can be considered, as shown in Fig. 13.7, from a base of either domestic production or foreign production.

13.8.1 Indirect export

The market-entry technique that offers the lowest level of risk and the least market control is indirect export when products are carried abroad by others. The firm is not engaging in international marketing and no special activity is carried on within the firm. The sale is handled like a domestic sale. There are different methods of indirect exporting.

1. The simplest method is to treat foreign sales through the *domestic sales organization*. For example, if a firm receives an unsolicited order from a customer in Spain and responds to the request on a one-time basis, it is engaging in casual exporting. Or if a foreign buyer comes to the firm, the products are sold in the domestic market but used or resold abroad. It is the case of buyers of foreign department stores having buying offices in the firm's home country. If the exporting firm does not follow up the contact with a sustained marketing effort, it is unlikely to gain future sales.

2. A second form of indirect exporting is the use of *international trading companies* with local offices all over the world. Perhaps the best-known trading companies are the *sogo sosha* of

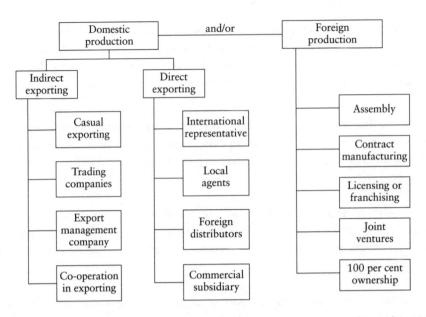

FIGURE 13.7 *Entry strategies in foreign markets* (Source: *Terpstra and Sarathy, 1991, p. 362)*

Japan such as Mitsui or Mitsubishi. The size and market coverage of these trading companies make them attractive distributors, especially with their credit reliability and their information network. The trading companies of European origin are important primarily in trade with former European colonies, particularly Africa and Southeast Asia. The drawback to the use of trading companies is that they are likely to carry competing products and the firm's products might not receive the attention and support the firm desires.

3. A third form of indirect exporting is the *export management company* which is located in the same country as the producing firm and plays the role of an export department—that is, the firm gains the facilities of an export department without having to establish one. The economic advantage arises because the export company performs the export function for several firms at the same time. The producer can establish closer relationships and gains instant foreign market contacts and knowledge. The firm is spared the burden of developing in-house expertise in exporting. The method of payment is by commission and the costs are variable. Export management companies handle different but complementary product lines which can often get better foreign representation than the products of just one manufacturer.

Exporting in this indirect way can open up new markets without special expertise or investment. Both the international know-how and the sales achieved by these indirect approaches are generally limited. In this approach, the commitment to international markets is very weak.

13.8.2 Direct exporting

In direct exporting the firm becomes directly involved in marketing its products in foreign markets. The firm performs the export task rather than delegating it to others. Thus, this implies the creation of an export department responsible for market contact, market research, physical distribution, export documentation pricing, and so on. This approach requires more corporate resources and also entails greater risks. The expected benefits are increased sales, greater control, better market information and development of expertise in international marketing.

To implement an direct exporting strategy, the firm must have representation in the foreign markets. Different solutions can be considered.

■ To send *international sales representatives* to the foreign market to establish contact and directly negotiate sales contracts.

■ To select *local representatives or agents* to prospect the market, to contact potential customers and to negotiate on behalf of the exporting firm.

■ To use *independent local distributors* who will buy the products and resell them in the local market with or without exclusivity.

■ To create a fully owned *commercial subsidiary* in order to have greater control over the foreign operations.

In most cases, the commercial subsidiary will be a joint venture created with a local firm to gain access to local relationships.

13.8.3 Foreign manufacturing

Under certain conditions, the firm may find it either impossible or undesirable to supply foreign markets from domestic production sources. For example, transportation costs may be too high for heavy or bulky products, custom rates or quotas on imports can render products uncompetitive, or government preferences for local products can prevent entry into the foreign market. Any of these conditions could force the firm to manufacture in a foreign market in order to sell there. Other positive factors can also induce the firm to produce abroad, among them, the size and attractiveness of the market, lower production costs, economic incentives given by public authorities, etc.

Varied approaches can be adopted to foreign manufacturing, as was shown in Fig. 13.7 opposite. Each implies a different level of commitment from the firm.

Assembling

Assembling is a compromise between exporting and foreign manufacturing. The firm produces domestically all or most of the components or ingredients of its product and ships them to foreign markets to be assembled as a finished product. By shipping CKD (Completely Knocked Down), the firm is saving on transportation costs and also on custom tariffs which are generally lower on unassembled equipment than on finished products. Another benefit is the use of local employment which facilitates the integration of the firm in the foreign market.

Notable examples of foreign assembly are the automobile and farm equipment industries. In similar fashion, Coca-Cola ships its syrup to foreign markets where local bottling plants add the water and the container.

Contract manufacturing

The firm's product is produced in the foreign market by a local producer under contract with the firm. Because the contract covers only manufacturing, marketing is handled by a sales subsidiary of the firm, which keeps control of the market. Contract manufacturing obviates the need for plant investment, transportation costs and custom tariffs and the firm gets the advantage of advertising its product as locally made. Contract manufacturing also enables the firm to avoid labour and other problems that may arise from its lack of familiarity with the local economy and culture.

A drawback to contract manufacturing is the loss of profit margin on production activities, particularly if labour costs are inferior in the foreign market. There is also the risk of transferring the technological know-how to a potential foreign competitor. This risk is lessened, however, where brand names and the marketing know-how are the key success factors. A frequent problem is also quality control.

Licensing

Licensing is another way to enter a foreign market with a limited degree of risk. It differs from contract manufacturing in that it is usually for a longer term and involves greater responsibilities for the local producer. Licensing is similar to franchising except that, as described above, the franchising organization tends to be more directly involved in the development and control of the marketing programme. The international licensing firm give the licensee patent rights, trademark rights, copyrights, or know-how on products and processes. In return, the licensee will (a) produce the licensor's products, (b) market these products in the assigned territory and (c) pay the licensor royalties related to the sales volume of the products.

The benefits of licensing for the two partners are those described above for franchising. This type of agreement is generally welcomed by foreign public authorities because it brings technology into the country.

The major drawback of licensing is the problem of controlling the licensee owing to the absence of direct commitment of the international firm granting the licence. After a few years, once the know-how is transferred, there is a risk that the foreign firm may decide to operate on its own and thus the international firm may lose that market.

Joint ventures

Foreign joint ventures have much in common with licensing. The major difference is that, in a joint venture, the international firm has an equity position and a management voice in the foreign firm. A partnership between host- and home-country firms is formed, usually resulting in the creation of a third firm. This type of agreement gives the international firm better control over operations and access to local market knowledge. The international firm has also access to the network of relationships of the franchisee and, owing to the partnership with the local firm, is less exposed to the risk of expropriation.

This type of agreement is very popular in international management. Its popularity stems from the fact that it avoids the problems of control inherent in the other types of foreign market entry strategies. In addition, the presence of the local firm facilitates the integration of the international firm into the foreign environment.

Direct investments

The international firm can make a direct investment in a production unit in a foreign market. This is the greatest commitment since there is a 100 per cent ownership. The international firm can obtain wholly foreign production facilities in two primary ways: (a) it can make a direct acquisition or merger in the host market or (b) it can build and develop its own facilities. In some countries, governments prohibit 100 per cent ownership by an international firm and only permit licensing or joint ventures.

Foreign market entry strategies are numerous and imply a varying degree of risk and commitment from the international firm. In general, an international development strategy is a process that is implemented in several steps. Indirect exporting is the starting point. If the results are satisfactory, further committing agreements can be made with local firms.

SUMMARY

Distribution channels are organized structures performing the tasks necessary to facilitate exchange transactions. The functions of distribution channels are to create time, space and state utilities which constitute the added value of distribution. Distributors (wholesalers, retailers, agents, brokers, etc) are required because manufacturers are unable to assume by themselves, at a reasonable cost, all the tasks implied by a free and competitive exchange process. Distribution channels can be characterized by the number of intermediary levels that separate the supplier from the end-user. The selection of a particular channel design is determined by factors related to market, buyer behaviour and company characteristics. When the channel structure is indirect, some degree of co-operation and co-ordination must be achieved among the partici-pants in the vertical marketing system. Regarding the number of intermediaries necessary, three market coverage strategies are possible: intensive, selective or exclusive distribution. Exclusive distribution through franchising is a popular system present in almost all business fields. The distribution margins, or trade margins, compensate the distribution functions and tasks assumed by the intermediaries in the channel. Significant changes have occurred in the 1990s in the way retailers, and in particular large retailers, perceive their roles in the channel. Today, they are discovering strategic marketing, developing innovative store concepts and sophisticated own brand policies. The development of interactive marketing (i.e. direct-order and relationship marketing) suggests that the traditional marketing monologue tends to be replaced by a marketing dialogue, customized marketing being substituted for mass or segment marketing. In designing its international development strategy, the firm can contemplate different foreign market entry strategies, from indirect export to direct local investment.

QUESTIONS AND PROBLEMS

1. You are responsible for the organization of the distribution of a new chemical compound to be used for the maintenance of water in swimming pools. Suggest alternative distribution channels to be considered to reach the different potential customer groups and describe the functions to be performed by the producer and distributor(s) of each alternative.

2. *'Middlemen are parasites.'* This charge has been made by many, and particularly by Marxists. Referring to a market economy system, how would you react to this charge?

3. Godiva chocolates are sold exclusively through company-owned or franchised boutiques. The company wishes to maintain the positioning of Godiva chocolates as a luxury item. What changes in distribution strategy could be contemplated by management in order to increase Godiva's market share?

4. In view of the dynamism and the growing power of mass merchandisers in the FMCG sector, what type of defence or redeployment strategies can be adopted by brand manufacturers? Analyse the merits and difficulties of each possibility.

5. A supplier gives a 5 per cent promotional discount to a distributor who already receives a 7 per cent quantity discount. The list price is $4. Calculate the distributor's purchase price with the 7 per cent quantity discount and then with the 5 per cent promotional discount.

6. A distributor's purchase price before taxes is $120. For this product category, VAT is 20.5 per cent and the distribution margin before taxes is 30 per cent. What will the retail price of this product be?

REFERENCES

Boyd, H.W. and O.C. Walker Jr (1990), *Marketing Management: A Strategic Approach*, Homewood, Ill.: Irwin.

Buzzell, R.D. and G. Ortmeyer (1995), 'Channel Partnerships Streamline Distribution', *Sloan Management Review*, Spring, pp. 85–9.

Cespedes, F.V. and H.F. Smith (1993), 'Database Marketing: New Rules for Policy and Practice', *Sloan Management Review*, Summer, pp. 7–22.

de Maricourt, R. (1988), 'Vers une nouvelle révolution de la distribution: de l'hypermarché à l'hyperservice', *Revue Française du Marketing*, no. 118.

Ducrocq, C. (1991), 'Concurrence et stratégies dans la distribution. Paris: Librairie Vuibert.

Dupuis, M. (1991), *Marketing international de la distribution*. Paris: Les Editions d'Organisation.

Dwyer, F.R., P.H. Schurr and Oh Sejo (1987), 'Developing Buyer–Seller Relationships', *Journal of Marketing*, vol. 51, April, pp. 11–27.

The Economist (1993), 'When Smoke Got in Their Eyes', April 10, pp. 61–62.

Federation of European Direct Marketing (1994), *Direct Marketing In Europe: An Examination of the Statistics 1993*, December, NTC Research Ltd.

Forsyth, D.P. (1988), 'Sales Calls Cost More According to McGraw-Hill', *Direct Marketing*, August, p. 67.

Kotler, P. (1991), *Marketing Management*. New Jersey: Prentice Hall Inc.

Glémet, F. and R. Mira (1993a), 'The Brand Leader's Dilemma', *The McKinsey Quarterly*, no. 2, pp. 3–15.

Glémet, F. and R. Mira (1993b), 'Solving The Brand Dilemma', *The McKinsey Quarterly*, no. 3.

Jackson, B.B. (1985), *Winning and Keeping Industrial Customers*. Lexington, Mass.: Lexington Books.

Liesse, J. (1991), 'Brands in Trouble: As Brand Loyalty Crumbles, Marketers Look for New Answers', *Advertising Age*, 2 December.

McGuire, E.P. (1971), *Franchised Distribution*. New York: The Conference Board, Report no. 523.

Messinger, P.R. and N. Chakravarthi (1995), 'Has Power Shifted in the Grocery Channel?', *Marketing Science*, vol. 14, no. 2, pp. 189–223.

Nielsen (1995), *L'univers alimentaire en Belgique*. AC. Nielsen, Belgium.

Palamountain, J.C. (1995), *The Politics of Distribution*. Cambridge, Mass.: Harvard University Press.

Payne, A. (ed.) (1995), *Advances in Relationship Marketing*. London: Kogan Page.

Quelch, J.A. and H. Takeuchi (1981), 'Non-store Marketing: Fast Track or Slow', *Harvard Business Review*, vol. 59, July–August, pp. 75–84.

Rosenbloom, B. (1978), *Marketing Channels: A Management View*. Hinsdale, Illinois: The Dryden Press.

Roscitt, R. and I.R. Parket (1988), 'Direct Marketing to Consumers', *Journal of Consumer Marketing*, vol. 5, no. 1, Winter, pp. 5–13.

Sallenave, J.P. (1979), *Expansion de votre commerce par le franchisage*. Gouvernement du Québec, Ministère du Commerce et du Tourisme: Canada.

Shangavi, N. (1991, 'Retail Franchising as a Growth Strategy for the 1990s', *International Journal of Retail & Distribution*, vol. 19, no. 2, pp. 4–9.

Terpstra, V. and R. Sarathy (1991), *International Marketing*, 5th edn. Chicago: The Dryden Press.

Wortzel, L.H. (1987), 'Retailing Strategies for Today's Mature Market-place', *Journal of Business Strategy*, vol. 7, no. 4.

FURTHER READING

Chinardet, C. (1994), *Le Trade Marketing*. Paris: Les Editions d'Organisation.

Ducrocq, C. (1988), 'Combien d'hypermarchés dans 10 ans?', *Revue Française du Marketing*, no. 119.

Ducrocq, C. (1993), 'Marques de distribution: de l'économique au marketing', *Revue Française du Marketing*, no. 141, pp. 61–5.

Ensor, J. (1994), 'Europe is the Target for UK', *The Grocer*, 10 December.

Jallais, J., J. Orsoni and A. Fady (1987), *Marketing de la distribution*. Paris: Vuibert Gestion.

Marshall, J.J. and H. Vredenburg (1988), 'Successfully Using Telemarketing in Industrial Sales', *Industrial Marketing Management*, vol. 17, pp. 15–22.

Molle, P. (1987), *La négocommunication*. Paris: Les Editions d'Organisation.

Slywotzky, A. and B.P. Shapiro (1993), 'Leveraging to Beat the Odds: The New Marketing Mind-Set', *Harvard Business Review*, vol. 71, September–October, pp. 97–107.

Stone, M. and R. Shaw (1987), 'Database Marketing for Competitive Advantage', *Long Range Planning*, vol. 20, no. 2.

U.F.P.D./Junior ESSEC (1985), '18 exemples de marketing direct dans l'entreprise', *Revue Française du Marketing*, Cahier 105, pp. 87–115.

STRATEGIC PRICING DECISIONS

LEARNING OBJECTIVES

After reading this chapter, you should be able to:

- understand the buyer's perception of price and its significance for the firm

- analyse the cost and profit implications of different pricing alternatives

- list and explain the factors affecting the buyer's price sensitivity

- describe and compare different methods of pricing in a buyer-oriented perspective

- discuss the impact of the competitive structure on the firm's pricing strategy

- describe the way to approach the problem of setting the price for a set of related products

- explain the pricing issues facing a firm operating in foreign markets.

*E*ach product has a price, but each firm is not necessarily in a position to determine the price at which it sells its product. When products are undifferentiated and competitors numerous, the firm has no market power and must take the price level imposed by the market. But when the firm has developed strategic marketing and thus has gained some degree of market power, setting the price is a key decision which conditions the success of its strategy, to a large extent. Until recently, pricing decisions were still considered from a purely financial viewpoint, and largely determined by costs and profitability constraints. This approach changed because of the upheavals in the economic and competitive situation during the crisis years: double figure inflation, increased costs of raw materials, high interest rates, price controls, increased competition, lower purchasing power, consumerism, etc. All these factors play an important part in making pricing decisions of strategic importance. After describing the strategic role of price in marketing, we shall analyse successively pricing decisions that emphasize costs, competition and demand. Figure 14.1 describes the general problem of price setting in a competitive environment.

14.1 PRICING AND THE MARKETING MIX

From the firm's point of view, the question of price has two aspects: the price is an instrument to stimulate demand, much like advertising for example, and the price is also a determining factor in the firm's long-term profitability. Therefore the choice of a pricing strategy must respect two types of coherence: an *internal coherence*, i.e. setting a product price respecting constraints of costs and profitability, and an *external coherence*, i.e. setting the price level, keeping in mind the market's purchasing power and the price of competing goods. Furthermore, pricing decisions must remain coherent with decisions regarding product positioning and distribution strategy.

14.1.1 The buyer's perception of price

Price is the *monetary expression of value* and as such occupies a central role in competitive exchange. Purchasing behaviour can be seen as a system of exchange in which searching for satisfaction and monetary sacrifices compensate each other. This behaviour results from forces that balance a need, characterized by the buyer's attitude towards the product and the product's price. From the buyer's point of view, the price he or she is willing to pay measures the intensity of the need and the quantity and nature of satisfaction that is expected; from the seller's point of view, the price at which he or she is willing to sell measures the value of inputs incorporated in the product, to which the seller adds the profit that is hoped to be achieved.

Formally, monetary price can be defined as a ratio indicating the amount of money necessary for acquiring a given quantity of a good or service:

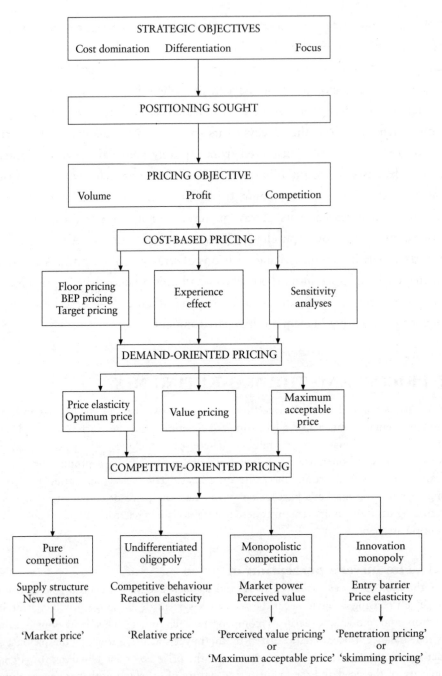

FIGURE 14.1 *Overview of pricing decisions*

$$\text{Price} = \frac{\text{Amount of money provided by the buyer}}{\text{Quantity of good provided by the seller}}$$

In fact, the notion of price is wider and goes beyond the simple coincidence of purely objective and quantitative factors. The amount of money paid is an incomplete measure of the sacrifice made, and, similarly, the quantity of good obtained is an imperfect measure of actual satisfaction.

The total value of a product

We saw in Chapter 4 that, as far as the buyer is concerned, a product is a package of benefits, and the services that are derived from the product are many. The latter not only result from the product's core service, but also from all the objective and perceptual secondary utilities that characterize the product. Therefore the price must reflect the value of all such satisfaction to the buyer.

Let us, for example, compare two watches having the same objective technical quality. Brand A is a prestigious watch with an elegant design and is sold exclusively by watchmakers. It carries a five-year guarantee and is advertised using sport and theatre personalities. Brand B, which is little known, is soberly designed and sold in department stores with a six-month guarantee. It is advertised as being 'reliable'. Although these two watches provide the same core or functional service (time measurement), we can see that they are two distinct products and their *value as perceived by potential buyers* will be very different. Therefore, seen from the demand point of view, price must be conceived as the compensation for all services rendered and set according to the total value or total utility perceived by the buyer. Hence the importance of a well-defined positioning before setting the selling price.

The total cost of acquiring a product

Just as the obtained quantity of good measures actual satisfaction imperfectly, the amount of money paid measures the importance of actual sacrifice imperfectly. In fact, the actual cost borne by the buyer not only covers the price paid, but also the *terms of exchange*. These refer to all the concrete practical procedures that lead to transfer of ownership, such as conditions of payment, delivery terms and times, after-sale service, etc. In some cases, the buyer may have to bear important costs to compare prices, transact and negotiate. This can happen if, for example, the buyer is located in isolated regions. Similarly, the buyer may face high transfer costs if he or she changes suppliers after having set the product specifications in relation to a given supplier. The main sources of transfer costs are as follows:

- Costs of modifying products to fit a new supplier's product.

- Changes in habits of consuming or using the product.

- Expenditures on training and reorientation of users.

- Investments to acquire new equipment necessary for the use of new products.

- Psychological costs related to change.

All these costs may be higher for some clients than for others. When transfer costs exist, the real cost to the buyer is much higher than the product's monetary price. Therefore, from the buyer's point of view, the notion of price goes well beyond that of monetary price. It involves all the benefits provided by the product and all the costs borne by the buyer. Hence measures of price sensitivity must take into account all these benefits and costs as well as the product's nominal price.

To illustrate the complexity of pricing, here are seven different ways of changing the above price ratio. You can change the:

1. Quantity of money or goods and services given up by the buyer.
2. Quantity of goods and services provided by the seller.
3. Quality of goods and services provided.
4. Premiums or discounts to be applied for quantity variations.
5. Time and place of transfer of ownership.
6. Place and time of payment.
7. Acceptable forms of payment.

Source: Monroe (1979).

14.1.2 Importance of pricing decisions

The following points highlight the importance of pricing strategies in the current macro-marketing environment.

■ The chosen price directly influences demand level and determines the level of activity. A price set too high or too low can endanger the product's development. Therefore, measuring price elasticity is of crucial importance, and it is difficult to achieve.

■ The selling price directly determines the *profitability* of the operation, not only by the profit margin allowed, but also through quantities sold by fixing the conditions under which fixed costs can be recovered over the appropriate time horizon. Thus, a small price difference may have a major impact on profitability.

■ The price set by the firm influences the product or the brand's general perception and contributes to the brand's positioning within potential buyers' evoked set. Buyers perceive the price as a signal, especially in consumer goods markets. The price quoted invariably creates a notion of quality, and therefore is a component of the brand image.

■ More than any other marketing variable, the price is an easy means of comparison between competing products or brands. The slightest change in price is quickly perceived by the market, and because it is so visible it can suddenly overturn the balance of forces. The price is a forced point of contact between competitors.

■ Pricing strategy must be compatible with the other components of strategic marketing. The price must allow for financing of promotional and advertising strategy. Product packaging must reinforce high quality and high price positioning; pricing strategy must respect distribution strategy and allow the granting of necessary distribution margins to ensure that the objectives of covering the market can be achieved.

Recent developments in the economic and competitive environment, which were discussed in Chapter 2, have played their part in increasing the importance and complexity of pricing strategies significantly.

- Acceleration of technological progress and shortening of product life cycles means that a new activity must recover all costs over a much shorter time span than previously. Given that correction is so much more difficult, a mistake in setting the initial price is that much more serious.

- Proliferation of brands or products which are weakly differentiated, the regular appearance of new products and the range of products all reinforce the importance of correct price positioning; yet small differences can sometimes modify the market's perception of a brand quite significantly.

- Increased prices of some raw materials, inflationary pressures, wage rigidities and price controls call for more rigorous economic management.

- Legal constraints, as well as regulatory and social constraints, such as price controls, setting maximum margins, authorization for increases, etc., limit the firm's autonomy in determining prices.

- Reduced purchasing power in most Western economies makes buyers more aware of price differences, and this increased price sensitivity reinforces the role of price as an instrument for stimulating sales and market share.

Given the importance and complexity of these decisions, pricing strategies are often elaborated by the firm's general management.

14.1.3 Alternative pricing objectives

All firms aim to make their activities profitable and to generate a possible economic surplus. This broad objective can in practice take different forms and it is in the firm's interest to clarify from the outset its strategic priorities in setting prices. Generally speaking, possible objectives can be classified in three categories, according to whether they are centred on profits, volumes or competition.

Profit-oriented objectives

Profit-oriented objectives are either profit maximization or achievement of a sufficient return on invested capital. Profit maximization is the model put forward by economists. In practice, it is difficult to apply this model. Not only does it assume precise knowledge of cost and demand functions for each product, it also assumes a stability that is seldom enjoyed by environmental and competitive factors. In Chapter 9 (see Appendix 9.1), we described the problem of calculating optimal price. The objective of target return rate on investment (ROI) is widespread. In practice it takes the form of calculating a target price, or a sufficient price; that is, a price which, for a given level of activity, ensures a fair return on invested capital.

This approach, often adopted by large enterprises, has the merit of simplicity, but is incorrect. It ignores the fact that it is the price level that ultimately determines demand level.

Volume-oriented objectives

Volume-oriented objectives aim to maximize current revenue or market share, or simply to ensure sufficient sales growth. Maximizing market share implies adopting a *penetration* price, i.e. a relatively low price, which is lower than competitors' prices, in order to increase volume and consequently market share as quickly as possible. Once a dominant position is reached, the objective changes to one of sufficient or 'satisfactory' rate of return. As we saw in Chapter 8, this is a strategy often used by firms who have accumulated a high production volume and expect reduced costs due to learning effects. A totally different strategy is that of *skimming pricing*, with the aim of achieving high sales revenue, given that some buyers or market segments are prepared to pay a high price because of the product's distinctive (real or perceived) qualities. The objective is to achieve the highest possible turnover with a high price rather than high volume.

Competition-oriented objectives

Competition-oriented objectives aim either for price stability or to be in line with competitors. In a number of industries dominated by a leading firm, the objective is to establish a stable relationship between prices of various competing products and avoid wide fluctuations in prices that would undermine buyers' confidence. The objective of keeping in line with other firms reveals that the firm is aware of its inability to exercise any influence on the market, especially when there is one dominant firm and products are standardized, as in undifferentiated oligopolies. In this case, the firm prefers to concentrate its competition on features other than price. Forms of non-price competition will prevail in the market.

To elaborate a pricing strategy, three groups of factors must be taken into consideration: costs, demand and competition. We shall now examine successively each of these factors and their implications for price determination.

14.2 COST-BASED PRICING PROCEDURES

Starting with costs analysis is certainly the most natural way to approach the pricing problem, and it is also the one most familiar to firms. Given that the manufacturer has undergone costs in order to produce and commercialize a product, it is natural that its main preoccupation would be to determine various price levels compatible with constraints such as covering direct costs and fixed costs and generating a fair profit. Figure 14.2 shows a typical cost structure in which the definitions of the main cost concepts are given.

14.2.1 Cost-based price concepts

Prices which are based on costs and make no explicit reference to market factors are called 'cost-based prices'. Cost analysis identifies four types of cost-based prices, each responding to specific cost and profit requirements.

The 'floor price'

The floor price, or the minimum price, corresponds to direct variable costs (C), also known as 'out-of-pocket costs'. It is the price that only covers the product's replacement value, and therefore implies zero gross profit margin.

Floor price = Direct variable costs

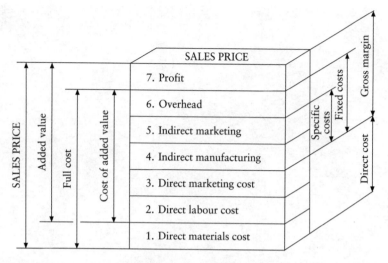

FIGURE 14.2 *The elements of price (Source: adapted from Monroe, 1979, p. 61)*

This price concept is useful for negotiating exceptional orders or for second market discounting, when the firm has unused capacity and has the possibility to sell in a new market such that there will be a negligible loss of sales in its main market. Floor price, also called *marginal price*, is the absolute minimum selling price the firm should accept. Any price above the floor price can allow a firm to use its production capacity to a maximum and still generate extra funds to cover overheads or improve profits. Exceptional orders, generics for large retail chain and foreign markets, provide opportunities for this form of discriminatory pricing strategy.

The 'break-even price'

The break-even price (BEP) corresponds to the price where fixed costs and direct costs are recovered, given the sales volume assumed. It ensures that both the product's replacement value as well as fixed costs (F) are recovered.

$$\text{Break-even price} = C + F/E(Q)$$

where $E(Q)$ denotes expected sales volume. The BEP corresponds to the full cost concept, where the level of activity is used as a criterion for allocating the fixed costs.

Break-even prices are usually calculated for different volume levels, as shown in Box 14.1, which defines a range of minimum prices. Note that the break-even price depends on the volume of activity and only coincides with the full cost at that level.

The 'target price'

The target price, or sufficient price, includes, apart from direct costs and fixed costs, a profit constraint, which is normally determined by reference to a 'normal' rate of return (r) on invested capital (K). This cost-based price is also calculated with reference to an assumed level of activity.

$$\text{Target price} = C + \frac{F}{E(Q)} + \frac{r \cdot K}{E(Q)}$$

BOX 14.1

An application of cost-based pricing

Basic data

Production capacity:	180 000 units
Capital invested (K):	BF240 000 000
Expected rate of return (r):	10 per cent
Unit direct cost (C):	BF1050 per unit
Fixed costs (F):	BF90 000 000 per year
Expected sales volume E(Q):	120 000 units
Pessimistic estimate:	90 000 units
Optimistic estimate:	150 000 units

Cost-based prices

Floor price: $P = C = BF1050$ per unit

BEP price:
$$P = C + \frac{F}{E(Q)} = 1050 + \frac{90\,000\,000}{E(Q)}$$

$$P_1 = BF2050 \qquad P_2 = BF1800 \qquad P_3 = BF1650$$

Target price:
$$P = C + \frac{F}{E(Q)} + \frac{r \cdot K}{E(Q)}$$

$$P = 1050 + \frac{90\,000\,000}{E(Q)} + \frac{(0.10) \cdot (240\,000\,000)}{E(Q)}$$

$$P_1 = BF2317 \qquad P_2 = BF2000 \qquad P_3 = BF1810$$

Break-even (BE) thresholds

Sales price: $P = BF1950$ per unit

BEV (in volume):
$$Q = \frac{F}{P - C} = \frac{90\,000\,000}{1950 - 1050} = 100\,000 \text{ units}$$

BES (in sales revenue):
$$R = \frac{F}{(P - C)/P} = \frac{90\,000\,000}{0.46} = BF195\,652\,174 \text{ units}$$

where K denotes invested capital and r, the rate of return, is considered as sufficient or normal. Like the break-even price, target price depends on the activity volume being considered.

The 'mark-up price'

The mark-up price is set by adding a standard mark-up to the break-even price. Assuming that the firm wants to earn a 20 per cent mark-up on sales, the mark-up price is given by

$$\text{Mark-up price} = \frac{\text{BEP}}{1 - \text{Desired mark-up}}$$

This pricing method, popular for its simplicity, ignores demand and competition. It will work only if the expected sales level is achieved.

The risk of circular logic

Target and mark-up prices are used widely, because of their simplicity and the apparent security arising from the illusory certainty of a margin, since mark-up and target pricing procedures promise to ensure a given return on cost. Their most important shortcoming is the lack of any relationship between price and volume. In fact, they implicitly contain a built-in circular logic: volume determines costs, which determine price, which in turn determines the level of demand.

Indeed, there is no guarantee that the adopted target price or mark-up will generate the activity volume on the basis of which it was calculated. Box 14.1 shows what happens to the target price if the firm's sales volume is below the assumed level.

In Box 14.1, the expected activity level is 120 000 units and the corresponding target price is BF2000. If demand is only 90 000 units, to maintain the desired profitability level the price would have to be increased and the product sold at BF2317.

Is raising price the appropriate response in the face of declining demand? Similarly, if the firm's sales exceed expectations, fixed costs are spread over a larger volume and the target price declines. Should management respond to excess demand by cutting prices?

This pricing behaviour runs counter to economic logic and leads to inappropriate recommendations. The firm that sets price from the sole perspective of its own internal needs generally forgoes the profit it seeks.

> During the recession of 1974–1975, the automobile industry faced such a dilemma. During 1974–1975, car prices rose on average $1000 while sales fell by 25 per cent. Yet, the automobile industry could not reduce price because of its inflexible, formularized method of pricing.
> *(Business Week, 1975)*

If all firms within a given industry adopt the same mark-up or target rate of return, the prices tend to be similar and price competition is minimized. In practice, cost-based prices are used only as a convenient starting point, because, in general, firms have more reliable information about costs than about demand factors.

14.2.2 Usefulness of cost-based pricing

Cost-orientated prices constitute a starting point for setting a price. They cannot be the only basis for determining prices because these pricing procedures ignore demand, product perceived value and competition. However, they do have a real *usefulness*, because they provide answers to the following types of question:

- What is the sales volume or sales revenue required to cover all costs?

- How does the target price or the mark-up price compare with prices of direct competition?

- To what level of market share does the level of sales at the break-even point correspond?

- What is the expected sales increase required to cover a fixed cost increase, such as an advertising campaign, assuming constant price?

- If prices go down, what is the minimum volume increase required to offset the price decrease?

- If prices go up, what is the permissible volume decrease to offset the price increase?

- What is the implied price elasticity necessary to enhance or maintain profitability?

- What is the rate of return on invested capital for different price levels?

Cost analysis is a first necessary step which helps to identify the problem by focusing attention on the financial implications of various pricing strategies. Armed with this information, the firm is better placed to approach the more qualitative aspects of the problem, namely market sensitivity to prices and competitive reactions.

14.3 DEMAND-ORIENTED PRICING PROCEDURES

Pricing based exclusively on the firm's own financial needs is inappropriate. In a market economy, it is the buyer who ultimately decides which products will sell. Consequently, in a market-driven organization an effective pricing procedure *begins with the price the market is most likely to accept,* which in turn determines the target cost. An important concept in demand analysis is the notion of *elasticity*, defined in Chapter 6 (see Appendix 6.1). We shall first examine the main factors affecting price sensitivity, and then describe various approaches that can be adopted to measure it.

14.3.1 Factors affecting price sensitivity

Every buyer is sensitive to prices, but this sensitivity can vary tremendously from one situation to another, according to the importance of the satisfaction provided by the product, or conversely depending on the sacrifices, other than price, imposed by obtaining the product. Nagle (1987) has identified nine factors affecting buyers' price sensitivity:

- *Unique-value effect*: buyers are less price sensitive when the product is more unique.

- *Substitute awareness effect*: buyers are less price sensitive when they are less aware of substitutes.

- *Difficult comparison effect*: buyers are less price sensitive when they cannot easily compare the quality of substitutes.

- *Total expenditure effect*: buyers are less price sensitive the lower the expenditure is to a ratio of their income.

BOX 14.2

Factors affecting price sensitivity

1. *The unique value effect*
   - Does the product have any (tangible or intangible) attributes that differentiate it from competing products?
   - How much do buyers value those unique, differentiating attributes?

2. *The substitute awareness effect*
   - What alternatives do buyers have (considering both competing brands and competing products)?
   - Are buyers aware of alternative suppliers or substitute products?

3. *The difficult comparison effect*
   - How difficult is it for buyers to compare the offers of different suppliers? Can the attributes of a product be determined by observation, or must the product be purchased and consumed to learn what it offers?
   - Is the product highly complex, requiring costly specialists to evaluate its differentiating attributes?
   - Are the prices of different suppliers easily comparable, or are they stated for different sizes and combinations that make comparisons difficult?

4. *The total expenditure effect*
   - How significant are buyers' expenditures of the product in cash terms and (for a consumer product) as a portion of their incomes?

5. *The end benefit effect*
   - What benefit do buyers seek from the product?
   - How price-sensitive are buyers to the cost of the end benefit?
   - What portion of the benefit does the product's price account for?

6. *The shared cost effect*
   - Do the buyers pay the full cost of the product?
   - If not, what portion of the cost do they pay?

7. *The sunk investment effect*
   - Must buyers of the product make complementary expenditures in anticipation of its continued use?
   - For how long are buyers locked in by those expenditures?

8. *The price–quality effect*
   - Is a prestige image an important attribute for the product?
   - Is the product enhanced in value when its price excludes some consumers?
   - Is the product of unknown quality, and are there few reliable cues for ascertaining quality before purchase? If so, would buyers accept a lower quality relative to the price of the product?

9. *The inventory effect*
   - Do buyers hold inventories of the product?
   - Do they expect the current price to be temporary?

Source: Nagle (1987).

■ *End benefit effect*: buyers are less price sensitive the lower the expenditure is compared with the total cost of the end-product.

■ *Shared cost effect*: buyers are less price sensitive when part of the cost is borne by another party.

■ *Sunk investment effect*: buyers are less price sensitive when the product is used in conjunction with assets previously bought.

■ *Price-quality effect*: buyers are less price sensitive when the product is assumed to have more quality, prestige or exclusiveness.

■ *Inventory effect*: buyers are less price sensitive when they cannot store the product.

The questions to examine for assessing buyers' price sensitivity are presented in Box 14.2.

Note that these determinants of price sensitivity apply equally to the decision of buying a particular product category (market demand price sensitivity) and that of buying a particular brand within a product category (interbrand price sensitivity). In the first case, the question would, for example, be to choose between a laptop computer or a hi-fi; in the second case, the alternatives would be, for example, to buy a Toshiba or an IBM laptop computer. Both kinds of decision are affected by the price level of the alternatives.

14.3.2 Price sensitivity of the organizational buyer

We saw in Chapter 3 that in industrial markets, buyers' needs are generally well defined and the functions performed by products clearly specified. In these conditions, it is sometimes easier to determine the importance of price to the organizational customer. Porter (1980, pp. 115–18) observed that buyers who are not price sensitive tend to have the following behavioural characteristics or motivations:

■ The cost of the product is a small part of the cost of the buyer's product cost and/or purchasing budget.

■ The penalty for product failure is high relative to its cost.

■ Effectiveness of the product (or service) can yield major savings or improvement in performance.

■ The buyer competes with a high-quality strategy to which the purchased product is perceived to contribute.

■ The buyer seeks a custom-designed or differentiated variety.

■ The buyer is very profitable and/or can readily pass on the cost of inputs.

■ The buyer is poorly informed about the product and/or does not purchase from well-defined specifications.

■ The motivation of the actual decision-maker is not narrowly defined as minimizing the cost of inputs.

Industrial market research studies can help in identifying these behavioural characteristics or requirements. These are useful to know in order to direct pricing policy.

To summarize, price sensitivity of demand is determined by a variety of factors closely related to the benefits or values that the product represents to the buyer. This price sensitivity is measured quantitatively by price elasticity.

14.3.3 Measuring price elasticity

Elasticity directly measures buyers' price sensitivity, and ideally allows the calculation of quantities demanded at various price levels. Recall the definition of price elasticity: it is the percentage change in a product's unit sales resulting from a 1 per cent change in its price:

$$\varepsilon = \frac{\text{Percentage change in unit sales}}{\text{Percentage change in price}}$$

Price elasticity is negative, since a price increase generally produces a decline in sales while a price cut generally produces an increase in sales. As an illustration, Table 14.1 compares the impact of price elasticity on quantities and on sales revenue for an elastic demand and an inelastic demand.

The economic and marketing literature contains many econometric studies on measuring price elasticities, as shown in Table 14.2. For a summary of elasticity studies, see Hanssens *et al.* (1990). Tellis (1988) found a mean price elasticity of -2.5. Broadbent (1980) reported an average price elasticity of -1.6 for major British brands. Lambin, covering a sample of 137 brands, reported an average price elasticity of -1.74 (Lambin, 1976, 1988).

Furthermore, if the firm is pursuing a profit maximization policy, it is also possible to determine the optimal selling price using a price elasticity estimate (see Table 8.1). In the case of a monopolistic situation, the price optimization rule is

$$P^* = C\,[\varepsilon/(1 + \varepsilon)]$$

where C is the direct cost and ε the brand price elasticity. As explained in Chapter 9, the optimal cost mark-up, $(\varepsilon/(1 + \varepsilon))$ is large if the brand price elasticity is close to 1 in absolute value, thereby denoting the existence of a strong market preference for the brand.

TABLE 14.1 *Impact of price elasticity on quantity and on sales revenue*

Elastic demand curve: $\varepsilon = -3.7$			Inelastic demand curve: $\varepsilon = -0.19$		
Price (FF)	Quantity (in 000)	Sales revenue (in 000 FF)	Price (FF)	Quantity (in 000)	Sales revenue (in 000 FF)
12 000	80	960 000	8.00	300	2400
9000	400	3 600 000	6.00	320	1920
7000	1200	8 400 000	4.00	340	1360

TABLE 14.2 *Comparing average elasticity of marketing variables*

Published sources	Number of observations	Average value of estimated elasticities			
		Advertising	Price	Quality	Distribution
Lambin (1976, 1988)	127	0.081	−1.735	0.521	1.395
Leone and Schultz (1980)	25	0.003–0.230	–	–	–
Assmus *et al.* (1984)	22	0.221 (0.264)	–	–	–
Hagerty *et al.* (1988)	203	0.003 (0.105)	−0.985 (1.969)	0.344 (0.528)	0.304 (0.255)
Neslin and Shoemaker (1983)	25	–	−1.800	–	–
Tellis (1988)	220	–	−1.760	–	–

Price optimization rules originally developed for the case of a monopoly (Dorfman and Steiner, 1954) have been extended to oligopolies (Lambin *et al.*, 1975) and to the dynamic case where market response is spread over time (Nerlove and Arrow, 1962; Jacquemin, 1973).

Usefulness of elasticity measures

Knowledge of the order of magnitude of an elasticity is on the whole useful in many ways:

- Elasticities provide information about the direction in which prices should change in order to stimulate demand and increase turnover.

- Comparing elasticities of competing brands identifies those that can more easily withstand a price increase, thus revealing their market power.

- Comparing elasticities of products in the same category helps to adjust prices within the category.

- Cross-elasticities help to predict demand shifts from one brand to another.

To illustrate, Table 14.3 shows estimated price elasticities in the car market and in the market for air transport in the USA. Although the estimates have insufficient precision for the exact

TABLE 14.3 *Price elasticity estimates: two examples from the US market*

Demand for automobiles		Demand for air transport	
Sub-compact	−0.83	First class	−0.75
Compact	−1.20	Economy	−1.40
Intermediate	−1.30	Discount	−2.10
Full-size	−1.54		
Luxury	−2.07		

Source: Automobile data from Carlson (1978); air transport data from Oum and Gillen (1981).

calculation of prices, the results are nevertheless very enlightening as far as pricing policy orientation for each product category is concerned.

Limitations of price elasticity measures

Despite the relevance of these works, there have been very few practical applications of this highly quantitative approach to the problem of pricing, except perhaps in some large enterprises. The reason is that the notion of elasticity presents a number of conceptual and operational difficulties which reduce its practical usefulness.

■ Elasticity measures a relationship based on buying behaviour and is therefore only observable *after the fact*; its predictive value depends on the stability of the conditions that gave rise to the observation; it cannot, for example, be used to determine the price of new products.

■ In many situations, the solution is not so much the ability to adapt prices to present market sensitivities, but more the ability to change and *act upon this sensitivity* in the direction sought by the firm. From this viewpoint, it is more interesting to know the product's perceived value by the targeted group of buyers.

■ Elasticity measures the impact of price on quantity bought, but does not measure the effect of price on the propensity to try the product, on repeat purchases, exclusivity rate, etc. But these are all important notions for understanding consumers' response mechanisms with respect to prices; therefore, other measures, which are less aggregate, need to be developed for marketing management.

Furthermore, in practice it is often very difficult to get sufficiently stable and reliable estimates of price elasticities which could be used to calculate an optimal selling price.

In an econometric study, an estimate having a Student t-value of 4.0 (rarely obtained) is very satisfactory, as this implies a statistical significance level of 1 per cent for degrees of freedom above 30 (rarely observed). However, at this level of precision, the coefficient of variation, which is the ratio of the standard deviation to the mean, is 25 per cent; this implies that it is highly likely that the true value of the estimated price elasticity falls in an interval of plus or minus 25 per cent, which is operationally a totally unacceptable level of imprecision.

These limitations are inherent in the economic model, which is developed more to help understand economic behaviour than as a decision-making tool (Nagle, 1987). This does not imply, however, that the economic theory of price determination has no relevance in the study of the problem of price determination. Even if imprecise, the order of magnitude of an estimated price elasticity helps to determine the direction of price changes and its impact on sales revenue.

14.3.4 Value pricing

Value pricing is a customer-based pricing procedure that has evolved from the multi-attribute product concept. From the customer's viewpoint, a product is the total package of benefits that is received when using the product. Therefore, the customer-oriented company should set its price according to customer's perceptions of product benefits and costs. To determine the price, the marketer needs to understand the customers' perceptions of benefits as well as their perceptions of the costs other than price. Customers balance the benefits of a purchase against its costs; when the product under consideration has the best relationship of benefit to cost, the customer is inclined to buy the product (Shapiro and Jackson, 1978). This customer-based pricing procedure can be implemented in different ways.

The maximum acceptable price

This approach is particularly useful for setting the price of industrial products, whose core benefit to the buyer is a cost reduction. To evaluate what the customer is prepared to pay, the procedure followed is to identify and evaluate the different satisfactions or services provided by the product as well as all the costs (other than price) it implies. Thus the procedure is as follows:

- Understand the total use of the product from the buyer's point of view.

- Analyse the benefits generated by the product.

- Analyse the costs implied by the acquisition and the use of the product.

- Make cost–benefit trade-offs and determine the maximum acceptable price.

The highest price that the customer will be willing to pay for the product is given by

$$\text{Benefits} - \text{Costs other than price} = \text{Maximum acceptable price (MAP)}$$

The benefits to consider can be functional (the core service), operational, financial or personal. Similarly, the costs other than price are just as diverse: acquisition costs, installation, risk of failure, custom modification, etc.

If the target market is segmented, this analysis should be done for different groups of buyers with non-identical behaviours. Comparing the maximum acceptable price with competitors' prices helps to evaluate the firm's margin for manoeuvre. Box 14.3 presents an application of this method. See also Ross (1984).

The product's perceived value

The basic idea behind this method is the same: it is the product or the brand's perceived value that should determine the price level. By analysing and measuring the buyers' perception and its determinants, a score of total perceived value can be derived and used to set the price. The notion of perceived value is a direct extension of the multi-attribute attitude model described in Chapter 6.

To illustrate, let us reconsider the information of Table 6.3 (already discussed in Chapter 6) where evaluations have been given by a group of potential buyers on six competing brands of laptop computers over five attributes. Respondents were asked to allocate 100 points to the five attributes in order to determine their relative importance and to rate the degree of perceived presence of each attribute on each brand on a 10-point scale.

BOX 14.3

Calculating the maximum acceptable price

Product description

■ A chemical compound to be used in conjunction with the regular water-softening chemicals.

Uses of the product

■ To disperse the water-softening compounds, thus lengthening their economic life.

■ To reduce rust formation in the boiler system.

Benefits of the product

■ Core benefit: reduces the amount of softening chemicals by 35 per cent.

■ Prevents rust formation.

■ Reduction in time and effort required to regenerate the softeners.

Costs other than price

■ Installation of a dispenser and of a storage tank in the plant.

■ Service of the installation and technical assistance.

■ Risk of breakdown.

■ Lack of reference of the supplier.

■ Custom modification.

Costs–benefit trade-off analysis

■ Average use: 40 000 gallons of softenings per year.

■ Cost per gallon: 50 cents.

■ Average cost saving: 14 000 gallons (35 per cent), or $7000.

■ Volume of Aqua-Pur: ratio: 1:7, or 3715 gallons (26 000/7).

■ Cost of installation: $450, or $90 per year over 5 years.

■ Cost of maintenance: $320 per year.

■ Total maximum acceptable cost: $7000 − ($90 + $320) = $6590.

■ Maximum acceptable unit price: $6590/3715 gallons = $1.77 per gallon.

■ Price of direct competitor: $1.36.

Source: Adapted from Leighton (1972, pp. 408–9).

The overall perceived value of each brand is then measured by multiplying the points given to each attribute by their determinance. Finally, the measures are expressed as an index based on the average of the adjusted zones (7.2033). In the example of Table 6.3 (p. 191), we obtain, respectively,

$$A = 1.07 \quad B = 1.05 \quad C = 1.09 \quad D = 1.10 \quad E = 0.98 \quad F = 0.70$$

(where $A = 7.68/7.2033 = 1.07$).

We notice that brands C and D have perceived values well above the average. In so far as these results can be assumed to be representative, and assuming that marketing pressure on the other factors is equal, these two brands could set their prices above the average offered by existing competitors. Suppose that the average price is BF33 000. Prices proportional to perceived values would therefore be

$$A = 35\,146 \quad B = 34\,700 \quad C = 35\,991 \quad D = 36\,418 \quad E = 32\,406 \quad F = 23\,216$$

If brand D adopts a price that is below the price corresponding to its perceived value, it can hope to achieve a higher market share because it would thus be increasing its relative marketing pressure.

This method, based on the *compositional approach*, is particularly appropriate when price sensitivity is determined by the presence of qualitative factors, such as perceived image effects.

Contributions of conjoint analysis

The same kind of result can be obtained with a *decompositional approach*, described in Chapter 6. Let us look again at the results obtained for the price variable in the cigarette study reported in Box 6.4. For respondent 17, the following utilities were obtained:

$$(\text{BF62: } U = -2.5), \quad (\text{BF67: } U = -3.5) \text{ and } (\text{BF72: } U = -5.0)$$

We thus have three observations and, using ordinary least squares (OLS), the average price elasticity was calculated as: $\varepsilon = -3.59$ $(R^2 = 0.958)$. For respondent 86, we obtained the following pairs of values:

$$(\text{BF62: } U = -0.25), \quad (\text{BF67: } U = -1.25) \text{ and } (\text{BF72: } U = 1.50)$$

The calculated elasticity here is: $\varepsilon = -1.11$ $(R^2 = 0.914)$. Note that the difference in price sensitivity between the two respondents is quite high. Now, suppose that we have similar information for a representative sample of 200 buyers. An average price elasticity could be estimated for the whole sample as well as for subgroups of buyers of high or low price sensitivity.

This kind of elasticity coefficient measures price sensitivity in terms of utility rather than quantity. Although more vague, it is nevertheless useful for a comparison of different buyers' relative price sensitivities.

14.3.5 Flexible pricing strategies

Firms do not have a single price, but a variety of prices adapted to different market situations. Flexible pricing strategies occur in market situations where the same product is sold to different customers at different prices. Flexible pricing strategies arise primarily because of customers' heterogeneity, showing different price sensitivities. Price flexibility can be achieved in different ways: by region, period, product form or from one segment to another. We shall examine four different ways of achieving price flexibility. In the economic literature, the term *price discrimination* has been used to designate the pricing strategies discussed here. In what follows, we shall adopt the classification of pricing strategies suggested by Tellis (1986) and *Business Week* (1977).

Second market discounting

This situation occurs when a firm with excess production capacity has the opportunity to sell in a new market such that there will be a negligible increase in fixed or variable costs and no loss of sales in its first market. The minimum acceptable selling price the firm should accept is the floor price, i.e. the unit direct cost. Opportunities for this pricing strategy exist in foreign trade, private label brands or special demographic groups, such as students, children or senior citizens. The essential requirement for this strategy is that customers of the lower price market cannot resell the product in the higher price market because of the high transaction costs implied.

Periodic discounting

In this situation the problem lies in trying to price a product confronted with different price sensitivities among potential buyers at the beginning and end of the seasonal period? Some buyers want to buy only at the beginning of the period and are not very price sensitive, while others want to buy the product at any time, but are price sensitive. To exploit the consumers' heterogeneity of demand, the firm will sell at the high price at the beginning of the period and systematically discount the product towards the end of the period. This is the principle often involved in the temporal mark-down and periodic discounting of off-season fashion goods, off-season travel fares, matinee tickets and happy hour drinks.

An essential principle underlying this strategy of periodic discounting is the manner of discounting, which is predictable over time and generally known to consumers who will, therefore, behave accordingly (Tellis, 1986, p. 150).

Random discounting

Which pricing strategy should be adopted in a market where the same product is sold at a low price by some firms and at a high price by others, knowing that some buyers are ready to spend time searching for the low price while others are not ready to do so? In this case, we have heterogeneity of demand with respect to perceived search costs among consumers. The objective of the firm is two-fold: (a) to sell at a high price to the maximum number of 'uninformed' consumers and, at the same time, (b) to prevent 'informed' consumers from buying at the low price of the competition.

In this situation, the recommended strategy is *random discounting*, which involves maintaining a high price and discounting the product periodically 'at random'. The manner of discounting is crucial: it should be indiscernible or random so that uninformed buyers will buy randomly, usually at the high price, and the 'informed' will search or wait until they can buy at the low price (Tellis, 1986, p. 150).

Price administration

Price administration deals with price adjustments for sales made under different conditions, in different quantities, to different types of intermediary in different geographic locations, with different conditions of payment, etc. These price adjustments or discounts are designed to reward customers whose buying behaviour contributes to cost reductions for the firm. This is the case for quantity discounts, cash payment discounts, seasonal discounts, functional discounts, etc. For more on this topic, see Monroe (1979, ch. 11).

14.4 COMPETITION-ORIENTED PRICING PROCEDURES

As far as competition is concerned, two kinds of factor greatly influence the firm's autonomy in its pricing strategy: the sector's competitive structure, characterized by the number of competing firms, and the importance of the product's perceived value.

- *Competitive structures* were described in Chapter 9. Clearly, when the firm is a monopoly, autonomy is great in setting its price; it tends to diminish as the number of competitors increases; we have monopoly and perfect competition at the extremes, and differentiated oligopoly and monopolistic situations at the intermediate positions.

- The product's perceived value results from the firm's efforts to differentiate in order to achieve an external competitive advantage; where an element of differentiation exists and is perceived by the buyer as a value, the buyer is usually prepared to pay a price above that of competing products. In this case, the firm has some degree of autonomy over prices.

Table 14.4 presents these two factors, each at two levels of intensity (low and high). We can thus identify four distinct situations, in each of which the question of price determination takes on a different form.

Reality is, of course, more complex and there is a continuum of situations. Nevertheless, it is helpful to place a product in one of these quadrants to understand the problem of price determination.

TABLE 14.4 *Competitive environments of pricing decisions*

Perceived value of the product	Number of competitors	
	Low	High
High	Monopoly or differentiated oligopoly	Monopolistic competition
Weak	Undifferentiated oligopoly	Pure or perfect competition

■ When the number of competitors is low and the product's perceived value is high, we are in structures close to *monopoly* or *differentiated oligopoly*. Price is a tool for the firm that has a margin for manoeuvre, varying with the buyer's perceived value of the differentiating attribute.

■ At the other extreme, where there are many competitors and products are perceived as a commodity, we are close to the *perfect competition* structure where prices are largely determined by the interplay of supply and demand. The firm has almost no autonomy in its pricing strategy.

■ The lower left quadrant, with low number of competitors and low perceived value, corresponds to an *undifferentiated oligopolistic* structure in which interdependence between competitors is often high, thus limiting their autonomy. In this instance, prices will tend to be aligned with those of the market leader.

■ Finally, in the upper right quadrant we have highly differentiated products offered by a large number of competitors; this corresponds to imperfect or *monopolistic competition* where there is some degree of autonomy, this being limited by the intensity of the competition.

These market structures are very different and they can be observed at various stages of a product market's life cycle (Box 14.4).

14.4.1 Anticipating competitors' behaviour

In many market situations, competitors' interdependence is high and there is a 'market price' which serves as reference to all. This is usually the case when there is undifferentiated oligopoly, where total demand is no longer expanding and the offerings of existing competitors are hardly differentiated. This type of competitive structure tends to prevail during the maturity stage of a product's life cycle.

In these markets, the firm can align itself with competitors' prices or those of the industry leader. It can fix its price at a higher level, thus taking the risk of losing some market share. Alternatively, it can fix its price below the market level, thus seeking a competitive advantage that it cannot find from other sources, but also taking the risk of launching a price war. The problem, therefore, is to determine a *relative price*. The outcome of these strategies largely depends on the reactions of competitors.

The objective of analysing competition in pricing strategies is to evaluate competitors' capabilities to act and react. In particular, one needs to estimate the reaction elasticity of the most dangerous competitor(s) if prices were to go up or down. We discussed the notion of reaction elasticity in Chapter 9 (see Fig. 9.4).

The direction and intensity of competitors' reactions varies when prices move upwards or downwards. As shown in Fig. 14.3, the firm faces a *kinked* demand curve. Elasticity is different on either side of the market price because of different competitive reactions. Some conditions are more favourable to price decreases and some to price increases. These are the conditions that need to be identified.

BOX 14.4

Price elasticity in an oligopolistic market situation

In an undifferentiated oligopoly, when total demand is non-expansible, the firm's demand function, Q, can be written as

$$Q = F(P_i, P_{r(i)}/M, \ldots)$$

where P is the sales price, M denotes other marketing factors, i is the firm and r denotes the direct competitors of i.

Firm i's price sensitivity is given by

$$\frac{dq_i}{dp_i} = \frac{\delta q_i}{\delta p_i} + \frac{dq_i}{dp_r} \times \frac{dp_r}{dp_i}$$

Multiplying by the ratio q/p, one gets the price elasticity:

$$\varepsilon(q_i, p_i) = \varepsilon(q_i, p_i) + \varepsilon(q_i, p_r) \times r(p_r, p_i)$$

The net price elasticity is the combined result of two effects:

- A direct price effect of i's price on i's sales volume.

- An indirect price effect of r's price on i's sales volume, the importance of which depends on the strength of firm r's reaction.

In an undifferentiated oligopoly, the strength of competitors' reactions will, in general, be larger in the case of a price cut than in the case of a price increase. Thus, the price elasticity will be higher at the upper end of the demand curve, and less price elastic at the lower end. The demand curve is said to be 'kinked'.

14.4.2 Initiating price cuts

Initiating a price cut with a view to stimulating demand is relevant only when total demand for the product can develop. Otherwise, if the firm reduces its price and if all the competitors react immediately and follow suit, the profits of each will drop and their respective market shares will remain exactly as before in a market of the same size, although average price has decreased.

There are, however, some situations that might be favourable to a price cut in a non-expansible market, without entailing rapid reactions from competitors:

- When competitors' costs are higher and they cannot lower their prices without endangering profitability; not following the price cut implies a loss of market share unless factors of differentiation neutralize the price difference.

- Smaller firms can use a price cut more easily. This represents a lighter investment for them as opposed to larger enterprises which hold a higher market share, because the cost of promoting a product via price is proportional to sales volume. Larger competitors may indeed prefer to

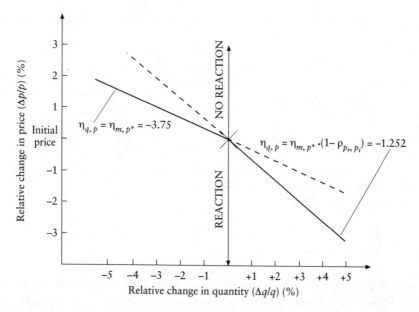

FIGURE 14.3 *The kinked demand curve: the electric shavers market in Germany (Source: Lambin et al., 1975)*

maintain their prices and react on a different front, for example by increasing advertising, which represents a fixed cost.

A firm may therefore choose not to follow a price cut, particularly when its product's perceived value is above that of its immediate competitors. It will then be protected from the effects of a price cut by differentiation factors, such as brand image, range of services or customer relations. Changing suppliers implies transfer costs which are not always compensated by the price difference. In industrial markets, for example, it is frequently observed that customers accept price differentials of up to 10 per cent without much difficulty if relationships with the usual supplier are well established.

Determining the cost of a price cut

It is important to realize that the cost of a price cut is often very high, especially for a firm with a high proportion of variable costs. The data in Table 14.5 define the necessary increases in sales revenue and in volume required to retain the same gross margin (25 per cent in this case) at different levels of price cut.

In this particular case, where the gross margin of 25 per cent before the price cut is to be held, the number of units sold must more than double to compensate for a price cut of 15 per cent. One can imagine that the necessary increase in sales can rapidly be above the impact that can reasonably be expected from a price cut.

TABLE 14.5 *Minimum volume and sales revenue increase required to offset a price decrease*

Price decrease(%)	Percentage minimum sales revenue increase required	Percentage minimum volume increase required
5	18	25
10	50	66
15	112	150
20	300	400

(Assuming a gross profit margin of 25 per cent.)
Source: Monroe (1979, pp. 70–3).

Furthermore, it can be shown that a price cut is less favourable to a firm with high variable costs, because the higher the necessary increase in sales to keep the same margin, the higher will be the proportion of variable costs (Monroe, 1979, p. 73). In general, for a price decrease, the necessary volume increase to maintain the same level of profitability is given by

$$\text{Necessary volume increase (\%)} = \left(\frac{x}{M^* - x}\right) \times 100$$

where x is the percentage price decrease expressed as a decimal and M^* is the gross profit margin as a percentage of selling price before the price cut.

To illustrate: if a price cut of 9 per cent is envisaged and the gross profit margin is 30 per cent, the required sales volume increase is

$$\text{Necessary volume increase (\%)} = \left(\frac{0.09}{0.30 - 0.09}\right) \times 100 = 42.86 \text{ per cent}$$

If the gross profit margin were to decrease to 25 or 20 per cent, the same price cut of 9 per cent would require sales increases of 56.25 and 81.82 per cent, respectively. For the derivation of the break-even formula, see Nagle (1987, pp. 44–6).

Therefore, the firm having the lowest variable costs will be induced to initiate a significant price cut, in the knowledge that other firms could not follow suit.

Computing implied price elasticity

It is also possible to derive an *implied* price elasticity from these figures. This is the price elasticity that should prevail within the targeted group of buyers before profits could be increased.

In the previous example, the price cut of 9 per cent ought to give rise to a 42.86 per cent increase in sales volume in order to retain the gross profit margin at 30 per cent. Therefore, the implied

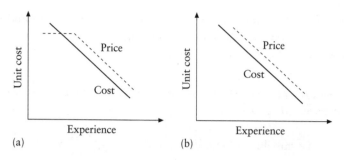

FIGURE 14.4 *Experience of curve-pricing strategies (logarithmic axes)*

price elasticity is

$$\varepsilon = \frac{+42.86\%}{-9\%} = -4.76$$

A price elasticity of -4.8 per cent is very high and assumes a very price-sensitive demand. If it is considered that the product market's demand is less elastic, and if profit is the only choice criterion, then the price cut is not economically justified.

The risk of a price war is always present in an oligopolistic market, which explains why firms are reluctant to initiate price cuts. There are, however, situations where a price cut can improve the competitive position of the firm. As discussed in Chapter 8, reducing the profit margin with price cuts may be compensated for by market share gains, which in the long run mean higher profitability because of cost reductions due to experience effects. Another reason for a price war might be to eliminate a potentially dangerous competitor.

Experience curve pricing

As discussed in Chapter 9, in sectors where the cost of value added represents a large proportion of total unit cost, substantial cost reductions can be obtained as accumulated production increases. If consumers in this market are price sensitive, a good strategy for the firm having the largest experience is to price aggressively, even below current cost, as illustrated in Fig. 14.4(a). This strategy presents several advantages. First, competing firms will have to leave the market and the leading company will be confronted with fewer rivals. Second, the firm can benefit from the sales of the other firms and gain experience more rapidly. Also, because of the lower prevailing market price, new buyers will be encouraged to enter the market.

However, pricing below cost cannot be maintained for extended periods of time. A less aggressive pricing strategy is the one depicted in Fig. 14.4(b) where a parallel is maintained between cost and price reductions.

14.4.3 Initiating price increases

Initiating a price increase is also a difficult decision. The firm initiating the increase must be certain that competitors are willing to follow suit. Generally speaking, this willingness depends on the prevailing market conditions at the time, and in particular when production capacity is fully used and demand is growing. As in the case of a price cut, before starting any initiative it is in the firm's interest to evaluate its margin for manoeuvre.

If price is increased, the permissible volume decrease—i.e. leaving the previous level of profit unchanged—is determined as follows:

$$\text{Permissible volume decrease } (\%) = \frac{x}{M^* + x} \times 100$$

where x is the percentage price increase expressed as a decimal. If a 9 per cent price increase is contemplated, and if the gross profit margin is 30 per cent, the percentage sales volume decrease is

$$\text{Volume decrease } (\%) = \left(\frac{0.09}{0.30 + 0.09}\right) \times 100 = 23.08 \text{ per cent}$$

and the implied price elasticity is -2.56. For the price increase to enhance profits, market demand must have a price elasticity below the implied price elasticity of -2.6.

Pricing in an inflationary economy

During inflation, all costs tend to go up, and to maintain profits at an acceptable level, price increases are very often a necessity. The general objective is that price should be increased to such a level that the profits before and after inflation are approximately equal. Decline in sales revenue caused by the price increase should be explicitly taken into account and the market reaction evaluated.

It should be noted that it is not always necessary for a company to increase prices to offset inflationary effects. Non-price measures can also be taken to reduce the impact of inflationary pressures, namely by improving productivity to offset the rise in costs. Also, price increases well above inflationary pressures can be justified to the market if the brand has a competitive advantage over competing brands.

14.4.4 Price leadership

Price leadership strategy prevails in oligopolistic markets. One member of the industry, because of its size or command over the market, emerges as the leader of the industry. The leading company then makes pricing moves which are duly acknowledged by other members of the reference market.

Initiating a price increase is typically the role of the industry leader. The presence of a leader helps to regulate the market and avoid too many price changes. Oligopolistic markets, in which the number of competitors is relatively low, favour the presence of a market leader who adopts an anticipative behaviour and periodically determines prices. Other firms then recognize the leader's role and become followers by accepting prices. The leadership strategy is designed to stave off price wars and 'predatory' competition, which tends to force down prices and hurt all competing firms. There are different types of leadership.

■ *Leadership of the dominant firm*—that is, the firm with the highest market share. The dominant firm establishes a price and the other producers sell their products at this price. The leader must be powerful and undisputed and must accept maintaining a high price.

■ *Barometric leadership*, which consists of initiating desirable price cuts or price increases, taking into account changes in production costs or demand growth. In this case the leader must have access to an effective information system providing him or her with reliable information on supply and demand, competition and technological change.

■ *Leadership by common accord*, where one firm is tacitly recognized as leader, without there being a formal understanding or accord. The latter would in fact be illegal. Such a leader could be the most visible firm in the sector, for example the firm that leads in technology. It should also have a sensitivity to the price and profit needs of the rest of the industry.

According to Corey (1976, p. 177), the effective exercise of leadership depends on several factors:

■ The leader must have a superior market information system for understanding what is going on in the market and reacting in a timely way.

■ It should have a clear sense of strategy.

■ It should have a broad concern for the health of the industry.

■ The price leader should use long-term measures to assess managerial performance.

■ It should want to lead and to act responsibly.

■ It will tend to behave in a way that preserves short-run market share stability.

On the whole, the presence of a leader acts as a *market stabilizer* and reduces the risk of a price war.

14.5 PRICING NEW PRODUCTS

The more a new product is unique and brings an innovative solution to the satisfaction of a need, the more delicate it is to price. This price is a fundamental choice upon which depends the commercial and financial success of the operation. Once the firm has analysed costs, demand and competition, it must then choose between two very contradictory strategies: (a) a high initial price strategy to skim the high end of the market, and (b) a strategy of low price from the beginning in order to achieve fast and powerful market penetration.

14.5.1 Skimming pricing strategy

This strategy consists of selling the new product at a high price and thus limiting oneself to the upper end of the demand curve. This would ensure significant financial returns soon after the launch. Many considerations support this strategy; furthermore, a number of conditions need to be met for this strategy to prove successful (Dean, 1950).

- When there are reasons to believe that the new product life cycle will be short, or when competition is expected to copy and to market a similar product in the near future, a skimming pricing strategy may be recommended because a low price strategy would make the innovation unprofitable.

- When a product is so innovative that the market is expected to mature slowly and the buyer has no elements on which to compare it with other products, *demand is inelastic*. It is tempting to exploit this situation by setting a high price and then readjusting it progressively as the market matures.

- Launching a new product at a high price is one way of *segmenting* the market. The segments have different price elasticities. The launching price skims the customers who are insensitive to price. Later price cuts then allow the firm to reach successively more elastic segments. This is a form of time discriminatory pricing.

- When demand is hard to evaluate, it is risky to anticipate the kind of demand growth or cost reduction that can result from a low price. This is particularly true when the manufacturing process is not yet stabilized and costs are likely to be underestimated.

- To be effective, the introduction of a new product requires heavy expenditure on advertising and promotion. When the firm does not have the financial means necessary for a successful introduction, charging high prices is one way of generating the resources.

A skimming pricing strategy is definitely a cautious strategy that is more financial than commercial. Its main advantage is that it leaves the door open for a progressive price adjustment, depending on how the market and competition develop. From a commercial point of view, it is always easier to cut a price than to increase it. The importance of the strategy lies mainly in its financial aspect, as it releases some capital that can be used for alternative activity.

14.5.2 Penetration pricing strategy

A penetration pricing strategy, on the other hand, consists of setting low prices in order to capture a larger share of the market right from the start. It assumes the adoption of an intensive distribution system, the use of mass advertising to develop market receptivity, and especially an adequate production capacity from the beginning. In this case the outlook is more commercial than financial. The following general conditions must prevail to justify its use.

- Demand must be *price elastic* over the entire demand curve; there are no upper segments to be given priority and the only strategy is to address the whole market at a price low enough to satisfy the greatest number.

- It is possible to achieve lower unit costs by increasing volumes significantly, either because of economies of scale or because of potential experience effects.

- Soon after its introduction, the new product is threatened by strong competition. This threat of new entrants is a powerful reason for adopting low prices. The penetration strategy is used here to discourage competitors from entering the market. Low prices act as very efficient barriers to entry, as discussed in Chapter 8.

- If the top range of the market is *already satisfied*, a penetration policy is the only valid policy to develop the market.

- Potential buyers can easily integrate the new product in their consumption or production; the *transfer costs* of adopting the product other than its price are relatively low and, therefore, a mass market can be developed rapidly.

A penetration pricing strategy is therefore more risky than a skimming pricing strategy. If the firm plans to make the new product profitable over a long period, it may face the situation that new entrants might later use new production techniques which will give them a cost advantage over the innovating firm.

14.6 PRODUCT LINE PRICING

Strategic marketing has led firms to adopt segmentation and diversification strategies that have resulted in the multiplication of the number of products sold by the same firm or under the same brand. Generally a firm has several product lines, and within each product line there are usually some products that are functional substitutes for each other and some that are functionally complementary. This strategy of product development brings about an interdependency between products, which is reflected either by a *substitution effect* (or cannibalism) or by a *complementarity effect*. Since the objective of the firm is to optimize the overall outcome of its activities, it is clearly necessary to take this interdependence into account when determining prices (Oxenfeld, 1966).

14.6.1 The risk of a cannibalism effect

Figure 14.5 illustrates the possible scenarios of *cannibalization* between two brands of the same firm, the old and the new. The circles represent buyers, with the intersections representing switchers. The total market is defined by the outer boundaries of all circles combined. Brand X denotes the competing brands (Traylor, 1986).

- The first case is the worst; the new brand brings no advantage whatsoever and simply shares sales with the firm's current brand. This situation might still be tolerated if the new brand's gross margin is well above that of the old brand.

- The second case is better, because the new brand has increased the size of the market and also its market share, but without going over the competitor's position. The operation will be globally profitable if the margin obtained on sales to new buyers is greater than that lost on sales of the old brand.

- In the third scenario, the new brand overlaps with the old brand's market as well as with that of the competing brand, while extending the size of the market by attracting new customers. As in the previous case, one needs to compare the margins lost and gained to evaluate whether there is a net positive gain.

- The fourth case is the ideal situation, with no cannibalization. The new brand cuts into competitors' sales and reaches new buyers. Total market share increases and the new brand is bringing in a net cash flow increment (Traylor, 1986, p. 72).

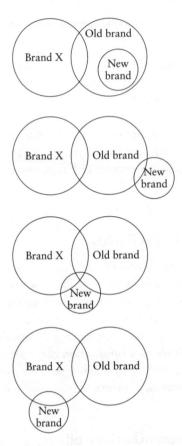

FIGURE 14.5 *Cannibalism in multi-brand firms (Source: Traylor, 1986)*

How can a multi-brand firm eliminate cannibalism? As firms look for finer and more subtle definitions of new market segments, the risk of cannibalism goes up. The main objective to pursue is to position the firm's brands against each other as well as against competitors' brands. In addition, some form of cannibalism should be tolerated if the net effect of the multi-brand strategy is in the best strategic interest of the firm as a whole.

> Coca-Cola is a good example of a company that has flipped from a very conservative protectionism to an almost reckless use of the Coke name. The intended (Diet Coke, Cherry Coke) and unintended (Coke Classic) brand extensions represent radical departures from the company's traditional reluctance to extend the Coke name.
> (Traylor, 1986, p. 73)

A firm concerned about market power may accept short-term profit losses resulting from cannibalism if it stands to increase its market power overall.

The concept of cross-elasticity
A cross-elasticity measures the degree of interdependence between products sold by the same

firm or under the same brand, and identifies the nature of this dependence when it exists: complementarity or substitution.

In the case of two products A and B, their cross-elasticity is defined as follows:

$$\text{Cross-elasticity} = \frac{\text{Percentage change of product A's sales}}{\text{Percentage change of product B's price}}$$

If cross-elasticity is positive, the products are substitutes; if elasticity is negative, then they are complementary. If elasticity is zero or very close to it, then the products are independent.

14.6.2 Contribution analysis in product line pricing

The complexity of product mix pricing is due to the fact that, apart from demand interaction, there is often also a cost interaction. For example, this is true when a change in the manufacturing process of one product affects the cost of other products. In this case, to study the implications of changing the price of one product in a range of products, it is important to take into account the effect of such a change on the overall result.

To illustrate, let us examine the data of an example presented in Table 14.6. A firm is selling three interdependent products and has a marketing programme which it is planning to modify as follows.

> By increasing advertising by F350 000, it is expected that sales of product B will increase by 6000 units at a price increased by F20, and increased packaging cost by F5. Sales of product A are expected to decrease by 1000 units because of product interdependence, and sales of product C are expected to decrease by 3000 units because of production capacity constraint. Should this change in the marketing programme for product B be adopted?
> (Blondé, 1964)

What would be the impact of such a change on the overall result? A convenient way to proceed is to reason in terms of variations (Δ). The variation in the gross margin (M) of product B is

$$\Delta M = \Delta P - \Delta C$$

TABLE 14.6 *Product line pricing: an example*

	Product A	Product B	Product C
Selling price (FF)	200	220	100
Direct cost (FF)	150	180	80
Unit profit margin (FF)	50	40	20
Volume (units)	20 000	15 000	10 000
Total profit margin (FF)	1 000 000	600 000	200 000
Fixed costs (FF)	700 000	500 000	100 000
Net profit (FF)	300 000	100 000	100 000
Total net profit (FF)		500 000	

which, in this case, gives

$$\Delta M = (+20) - (+5) = +15$$

To determine the effect on the overall result, let us use the following expression:

$$\Delta R = \sum_n (\Delta Q \cdot M + Q \cdot \Delta M + \Delta Q \cdot \Delta M - \Delta F)$$

The summation is over the n products made. In the case of this example, for the three products A, B and C we have

$$\Delta R = (-1000) \cdot (50) + (20.000) \cdot (0) + (-1000) \cdot (0) - 0$$
$$+ (+6000) \cdot (40) + (15.000) \cdot (15) + (+6000) \cdot (15) - 350\,000$$
$$+ (-3000) \cdot (20) + (10\,000) \cdot (0) + (-3000) \cdot (0) - 0$$
$$= -50\,000 + 205\,000 - 60\,000$$
$$= +F95\,000; \text{ that is, an increased profit of 19 per cent.}$$

The new marketing programme is therefore profitable. Total gross margin obtained from the new sales volume for product B with its new unit gross margin is higher than the loss of gross margins on products A and C, due to their lower sales volume and increased fixed costs.

14.6.3 Product line pricing strategies

When a firm is selling a set of related products, the price of each product must be set in such a way as to maximize the profit of the *entire product line* rather than the profit of a single product. The pricing strategy adopted will be different according to whether the related products are complementary to, or competitive with, each other.

Price bundling

When the products are related but are non-substitutes, i.e. complementary or independent, one strategic option for the firm is optional price bundling, where the products can be bought separately, but also as a package offered at a much lower price than the sum of the parts. Because the products are not substitutes, it is possible to get consumers to buy the package instead of only one product of the line. This pricing strategy is common practice, for instance, in the automobile and audiovisual markets, where packages of options are offered with the purchase of a car or of stereo equipment. A simple example will illustrate the profit implication of this pricing strategy (Tellis, 1986, p. 155).

Assume a market situation where two related products are offered to two customers, who could buy one product or both. The maximum prices they are ready to pay are presented in Table 14.7.

What is the best pricing strategy to adopt if tying contracts are excluded?

■ Charging each customer the maximum price would yield a total revenue of $76. But this strategy, if not illegal, is difficult to implement if the buyers are sufficiently informed.

TABLE 14.7 *Bundling pricing: an example*

Products	Customer 1	Customer 2	Total
Product A	$12	$15	$27
Product B	$25	$24	$49
Budgets	$37	$39	$76

■ Adopting the lowest price for each product would mean selling product A at $12 and product B at $24. This could induce buyers to buy the two products, since the total cost ($36) for them would be compatible with their budget constraints, but the total sales revenue would be only $72.

■ Adopting the highest price for each product, i.e. selling product A at $15 and product B at $25, will generate an even lower total revenue of $49 maximum (if they both buy product B), since the customers will not be able to buy the two products (at a total cost of $40) given their budget constraints.

The best solution is to price product A at $15 and product B at $25 and offer both at $37 for a total revenue of $74. Both customers will accept the package for $37 since this total cost is compatible with their budget constraints. (Adapted from Tellis, 1986.)

This strategy of 'optional bundling', in contrast with *indivisible bundling*, leaves the option to the customer to buy only one product or the total package.

> Several computer companies have adopted the indivisible bundling strategy. Under this pricing system, not only are costs of hardware and profits covered, but also included are the anticipated expenses for extra technical assistance, design and engineering of the system concept, software and applications to be used on the system, training of personnel and maintenance. (Jain, 1984, p. 740)

For the customer, this strategy is very attractive because the manufacturing firm is selling a *solution* and not simply a product. To be able to sell a solution, however, the manufacturer has to cover the anticipated expenses for providing services and assistance in use and for keeping the system in working condition. Such a bundling strategy also permits an on-going relationship with the customer and first-hand knowledge of the customer's needs.

In recent years, however, with the inflationary pressures on costs of services, many companies have begun unbundling their services and charging separately for them.

Premium pricing
This pricing strategy applies to different versions of the same product, a superior version and a basic or standard model. Potential buyers for the standard model are very price sensitive, while buyers of the superior model are not. If economies of scale exist, it is unprofitable for the firm to

limit its activity to one of the two market segments. The best solution is to exploit, jointly, economies of scale and heterogeneity of demand by covering the two segments—the lower end of the market with a low price and the high end with a premium price, as illustrated by the following example:

> Consider a firm having the following target prices: $50 at 20 units and $35 at 40 units. The cost of producing a superior version of the same product is $10. Forty consumers per period are on the market for the product. Half of them are price-insensitive and are ready to pay $50 for the superior version. The other half are price-sensitive and will not pay more than $30. In what version and at what price should the firm sell the product?
>
> (Tellis, 1986, p. 156)

Costs and profit constraints seem to exceed prices if the firm decides to sell to only one segment at only one price. If the firm targets the low-price segment, the market potential is 20 customers and the maximum acceptable price is $30, while the target price at this level of production is $50. Similarly, if the firm targets the high-price segment, the market potential is 20 customers willing to pay $50, but the target price is now $60 ($50 + $10). This strategy is also unfeasible.

A premium price strategy can solve the problem. The firm should produce 40 units and sell 20 units of the standard product for $30 and 20 units of the superior version for $50, for an average target price of $40. The target prices are respectively $35 and $45, but the market prices will be $30 and $50. Thus, the firm takes a premium on its higher priced version and a loss on its lower priced version, but can profitably produce and sell the product to both segments (Tellis, 1986, p. 156).

This pricing strategy is common practice in many markets, typically durable goods for which several versions differing in price and features cater to different consumer segments.

The same pricing strategy can be applied in the service sector by modifying the service package. For example, airlines have used this pricing strategy very successfully. Their market consists of both a price-insensitive business traveller and a very price-sensitive holiday traveller. Business people place a high value on flexible scheduling. In contrast, holiday-makers generally plan their trips far in advance.

Capitalizing on these differences, airlines set regular ticket prices high and offer discounts only to buyers who purchase their tickets well before departure. By offering lower fares only with inflexible schedules, airlines have been able to price low enough to attract price-sensitive buyers without making unnecessary concessions to those who are less price sensitive (Nagle, 1987, p. 169).

Image pricing
A variant of premium pricing is *image pricing*. The objective is the same: to signal quality to uninformed buyers and use the profit made on the higher priced version to subsidize the price on the lower priced version. The difference is that there is no real difference between products or brands, it is only in image or perceptual positioning. This is common practice in markets like

cosmetics, dresses, snacks, etc., where the emotional and/or social value of a product or a brand is important for the consumer.

Complementary pricing

The problem here is to determine the prices of complementary products, such as durable goods and accessories or supplies necessary for the use of the basic product. Examples of complementary products are razors and blades, cars and spare parts, computers and software, etc. To the extent that buyers are source loyal and want to buy supplies or accessories from the original manufacturer, low prices can be charged for the main product and high prices for the supplies. For example, Kodak prices its cameras low because it makes its money on selling film. Those camera makers who do not sell film have to price their cameras higher in order to make the same overall profit (Kotler, 1991, p. 495).

In evaluating the effect of a price change of complementary products, management must examine the changes in sales revenue and costs not only for the product being priced, but also for the other products affected by the price change. By way of illustration, let us examine the pricing problem of a company selling personal computers and software.

> In this company, the typical buyer of a personal computer also purchases on average three software packages. The gross profit margin on a computer is $1000 or 40 per cent on selling price, while the profit margin on software is $250. If management treated sales of computers and software as independent, the break-even sales quantity for a 10 per cent price cut would be 33.3 per cent $(-10\%/(40\% - 10\%) = -0.333)$. Thus sales should increase by 33.3 per cent to justify the 10 per cent price cut.

How likely is this sales increase? In fact, the profit contribution for a computer sale is much higher than 40 per cent, since each buyer of a computer also purchases on average three software packages. Thus, the relevant gross profit margin here is $1750 ($1000 + (3 × $250)), or 70 per cent of the selling price. The adjusted break-even sales change is 16.7 per cent $(-10\%/(70\% - 10\%) = -0.167)$. Thus, the company could cut its price even if it expects a percentage increase in sales much less than 33.3 per cent.

In retailing, the corresponding strategy is called *loss leadership*. It involves dropping the price on a well-known brand to generate store traffic (Tellis, 1986, p. 157).

14.7 PRICING IN INTERNATIONAL MARKETING

The pricing problem in a foreign market should be approached in the same way as in the domestic market. Costs, demand and competition factors should be taken successively into consideration. Specific issues arise, however, for an international firm exporting to foreign markets from a domestic production unit. We shall discuss the main pricing problems to be examined by an exporting firm. This section relies heavily on Terpstra and Sarathy (1991).

14.7.1 Transfer pricing

Transfer pricing refers to prices placed on goods sold within the corporate family, i.e. from division to division or to a foreign subsidiary. Transfer pricing is a problem for the large international corporation on at least two levels: pricing from (1) the production division to the international division and from (2) the international division to the foreign subsidiary.

Intracorporate transfer pricing

In setting an intracorporate transfer pricing policy, the objective should be to optimize corporate rather than divisional profit. More precisely, the two following objectives should be pursued.

- The transfer price should be high enough to motivate the production division. Thus, sales to the international division should be as attractive as sales to other parties and particularly to the domestic market through the traditional distribution network.

- The transfer price should be low enough to enable the international division to be competitive in the foreign market.

Obviously, there is room for divisional conflict here and it is the overall corporate profit that should be the determining factor. Let us take the following example given by Terpstra and Sarathy (1991, p. 429).

> Assume that the producing unit makes a product at a full cost of $50. It sells this to outside buyers for $60, but the transfer price to the international division is $58. The producing division may be unhappy because the markup is 20 per cent lower to the international division ($8 versus $10). The international division adds its various export marketing expenses of $10 for an export cost of $68. For competitive reasons, the international division cannot sell the product for more than $72, or a $4 return. Since this is less than 6 per cent sales, the international division is also unhappy. However the return to the corporation is $12 on $72 instead of $10 on $60, or almost 17 per cent ($8 from the producing division plus $4 from the international division). The corporation may find this very attractive, even though both divisions are unhappy with it.

Different approaches can be taken to solve this internal transfer pricing problem. The two extreme solutions would be the 'floor price' on the one hand and the 'market price', less the distribution margin, on the other. The market price would then be the same as that paid by any other buyer outside the firm. In general, the actual transfer price will be between these two extremes by adopting a *cost plus* transfer price. The 'plus' may be a percentage negotiated between the divisions in an attempt to conciliate the two objectives mentioned above.

Transfer pricing to foreign subsidiaries

This type of pricing decision is more complex because several new factors must be taken into consideration—namely, the foreign tax system, custom rates, exchange rates and the level of involvement of the international firm in the foreign country.

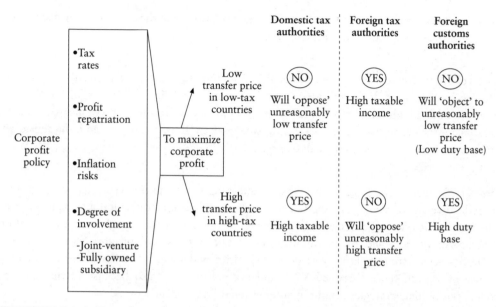

FIGURE 14.6 *Transfer pricing to foreign subsidiaries* (Source: *adapted from Terpstra and Sarathy, 1991*)

The main factors interfering with the transfer pricing decision are presented in Fig. 14.6. Given that each country has a different taxation system, it is not a matter of indifference to know where the international firm will accumulate profits. The three key questions to examine are:

- How do profit tax rates compare from one country to the other?

- What are the rules governing profit repatriation policy?

- What is the risk of inflation?

To these basic questions, one must add considerations on the attitude of tax and custom authorities, both in the domestic and the foreign countries.

As a general rule, the firm would like to use the transfer price to get more profits in low-tax countries—that is, it will use a low transfer price to subsidiaries in low-tax countries and a high transfer price in high-tax countries. This corporate profit policy will not always be accepted by domestic tax authorities who do not want to lose taxable income to other countries. On the other hand, this policy will be welcome by foreign tax authorities, since it increases taxable income. Thus, domestic tax authorities will watch for 'unreasonably low' transfer prices. A low transfer price is also used as a method of financing new subsidiaries abroad. Reasons for adopting a high transfer price, in addition to the high tax rate on corporate profits, may also be restrictions on profit repatriation or fear of devaluation.

A different attitude may be observed among foreign customs authorities who watch for transfer prices that are considered to be too low since they reduce the duty base. Customs officials in many countries refuse to accept transfer prices that are lower than the prices paid by distributors purchasing the same product at market prices.

The level of involvement of the international firm and the foreign subsidiary is also a factor to take into consideration. If the subsidiary is a joint venture or a licensee, the exporting firm will prefer to sell at a high transfer price. A low price to joint ventures or licensees means, in effect, that some of the profit is being given away outside the firm. If, on the other hand, the subsidiary is fully owned a low transfer price will be preferred.

Those are the main factors to examine when establishing an international transfer pricing policy. Given the diversity of regulations and tax systems, one realizes how difficult it may be to have the same international pricing policy for all countries. At the European Union level, the elimination of non-tariff barriers and the harmonization of tax systems will progressively facilitate a standard pricing strategy. However, deep disparities will remain for many years, not only because of the differences between VAT and tax policies, but also because of the different product positioning strategies sought by international firms for their brands.

14.7.2 Export price quotations

Export costs constitute an important part of the price that will be charged in the foreign market. Export price quotations are also important because they spell out the legal responsibilities of each party.

A number of terms covering the conditions of the delivery are commonly used in international trade (see Fig. 14.7). Many of these terms have, through long use, acquired precise meanings. Every commercial transaction is based upon a contract of sale and the trade terms used in that contract have the important function of naming the exact point at which the ownership of merchandise is transferred from the seller to the buyer. Export cost may increase substantially the price of the exported product and undermine its competitiveness abroad. The major trade terms used are defined hereafter.

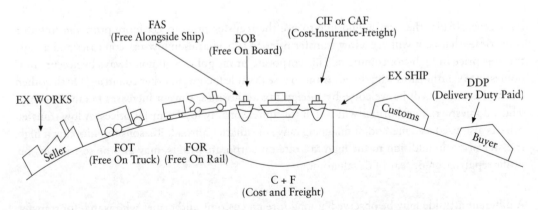

FIGURE 14.7 *Description of export costs (Source: Leroy et al., 1980)*

1. *Ex Works (ex-factory).* The buyer takes delivery at the premises of the seller and bears all risks and expenses from that point on. The seller favours this quote since it gives him or her least liability and responsibility.
2. *Free Alongside Ship (FAS).* The seller must place goods alongside the vessel or other mode of transportation and pay all charges up to that point. The seller's legal responsibility ends once he or she has obtained a clean wharfage receipt.
3. *Free on Board (FOB).* The responsibility and liability of the seller ends when the goods have actually been placed on board a ship (ship, aircraft or truck).
4. *Cost, Insurance, Freight (CIF).* The seller, in addition to the FOB obligations, has to pay the expenses of transportation for the goods up to the port of destination, including the expenses of insurance.
5. *Delivery Duty Paid (DDP).* The seller undertakes to deliver the goods to the buyer at the place he or she names in the country of import with all costs, including duties, paid. The seller is responsible under this contract for obtaining the import licence if one is required.

The seller favours a quote that offers the least liability and responsibility, such as FOB. In this case, the exporter's responsibility ends when the goods are put on a carrier at his or her plant. The importer–buyer, on the other hand, favours a CIF quote which means that his or her responsibilities begin only when the goods are in the country of destination.

14.7.3 Market-oriented export pricing

A good starting point for export price analysis is to calculate the foreign market acceptable price. At what price, or within what price range, could the firm's product sell well in the foreign market? By working back from this market price, the firm can see if it can sell at that price given the international transfer price, the export costs, the taxes and the custom duties.

Assume the firm is selling a consumer product to a foreign country and market research shows that the market acceptable price should be about $7 equivalent.

1.	Market price in the foreign market:		$7.00
2.	*Less* 40 per cent retail margin on selling price:	2.80	
	Purchase cost to the retailer:		4.20
3.	*Less* 11 per cent wholesaler mark-up on his or her cost:	0.42	
	Wholesaler cost:		3.78
4.	*Less* 5 per cent importer mark-up on his or her cost:	0.18	
	Importer cost:		3.60
5.	*Less* 10 per cent VAT on landed value plus duty:	0.33	
	DDP value of the product:		3.27
6.	*Less* 9 per cent duty on landed value CIF:	0.27	
	Landed or CIF value:		3.00

7. *Less* insurance and shipping costs to market: *0.40*

    FOB value of the product: **$2.60**

Thus, $2.60 is the FOB plant price that will allow the firm to meet the foreign market acceptable price of $7.00. Is this price close to the contemplated transfer price? If the domestic FOB plant price does not compare favourably, i.e. if it is greater than $2.60, export will be difficult and the international firm will have to consider one of the following alternatives (Terpstra and Sarathy, 1991).

■ To forget about exporting for lack of sufficient competitiveness.

■ To reduce the transfer price and consider marginal cost pricing for exports if there is excess production capacity.

■ To adopt a shorter distribution channel, for example by selling directly to wholesalers or to large retailers.

■ To design a stripped down and cheaper model for export.

■ To consider foreign manufacturing, assembling or licensing to avoid export and duty costs.

In any case, the market price in the foreign market cannot be inferior to the domestic market price to avoid the charge of dumping by foreign competitors.

SUMMARY

The choice of a pricing strategy must respect two types of coherence: an internal coherence, i.e. setting a price respecting constraints of costs and profitability, and an external coherence, i.e. setting a price compatible with the buyer's price sensitivity and with the price of competing goods. Cost-based pricing (break-even, target and mark-up pricing) is a first and necessary step which helps to identify the financial implications of various pricing strategies. Pricing based exclusively on the firm's own financial needs is inappropriate, however, since in a market economy it is the buyer who ultimately decides which product will sell. In demand-oriented pricing, the notion of price elasticity is central although difficult to estimate empirically with sufficient precision. The factors affecting buyers' price sensitivity are useful to help estimate price elasticity in qualitative terms. Value pricing is a customer-based pricing procedure that has evolved from the multi-attribute product concept. Flexible pricing strategies (second market, periodic, or random discounting) arise primarily because buyers' heterogeneity show different price sensitivities. Two kinds of factors influence competition-oriented pricing: the competitive structure of the market and the product's perceived value. One objective of analysing competition in pricing is to evaluate competitors' capacity to act and react. Special issues in pricing are: pricing new products (skimming versus penetration pricing), product line pricing (price bundling, premium pricing, image and complementary pricing) and international pricing (transfer pricing and export costs).

QUESTIONS AND PROBLEMS

1. A distributor sells an average of 300 units per week of a particular product whose purchase cost is $2.50 and sales price is $3. If the distributor gives a 10 per cent price reduction during one week, how many units should the firm sell in order to keep its gross profit margin unchanged?

2. Company Alpha distributes a product in a market which is price-inelastic. Sales are 30 000 units per year. The operating data of the product are as follows:

Direct unit cost:	$9.90
Fixed unit cost:	$3.30
Total:	$13.20
Sales price:	$19.80
Net profit per unit:	$6.60

The firm wants to increase its sales volume by 3000 units and, for that purpose, has adopted a $39 600 advertising budget per year. What minimum price increase should the firm adopt in order to leave its profit unchanged?

3. The Elix Company produces and distributes a product which is differentiated from competing products by a better design. The average market price is $50 and the total market amounts to 1 million units; Elix' market share is 10 per cent. The price elasticity for this product category is in the range −1.7 to −2.0. The operating data for Elix are as follows:

Direct unit cost:	$20
Fixed costs:	$2 000 000
Expected rate of return:	10 per cent
Invested capital:	$10 000 000

The market research department has conducted a brand image study for Elix and for its priority competitor the brand Lumina. The attributes' importance scores for the product category are, respectively: 0.50/0.25/0.25. The performance scores are: 10/6/9 for Elix; 8/7/9 for Lumina. Calculate the target price, the value price and the optimum price. What pricing strategy do you recommend?

4. X and Y are two divisions of the New Style Company. Division X manufactures the product Alpha. The operating data are:

Direct costs raw materials:	$6
Labour:	$4
Fixed costs:	$2
Total:	$12

The Alpha market is a perfect competition market and the market price is $16. Alpha is also sold to division Y. Market sales imply a selling cost of $2 per unit. Given that demand for

Alpha is sufficiently large in order to permit division X to work at full capacity, at what transfer price should division X sell the Alpha product to division Y?

REFERENCES

Assmus, G., J.V. Farley and D.R. Lehmann (1984), 'How Advertising Affects Sales: Meta-Analysis of Econometric Results', *Journal of Marketing Research*, vol. 21, February, pp. 65–74.

Blondé, D. (1964), *La gestion programmée*. Paris: Dunod.

Broadbent, S. (1980), 'Price and Advertising: Volume and Profits', *Admap*, vol. 16, pp. 532–40.

Business Week (1975), 'Detroit Dilemma on Prices', 20 January, pp. 82–3.

Business Week (1977), 'Flexible Pricing', 12 December, pp. 78–88.

Carlson, R.L. (1978), 'Seemingly Unrelated Regression and the Demand for Automobiles of Different Sizes: A Disaggregate Approach', *The Journal of Business*, vol. 51, April, pp. 243–62.

Corey, E.R. (1976), *Industrial Marketing: Cases and Concepts*. Englewood Cliffs, New Jersey: Prentice Hall Inc.

Dean, J. (1950), 'Pricing Policies for New Products', *Harvard Business Review*, vol. 28, November–December, pp. 28–36.

Dorfman, R. and P.O. Steiner (1954), 'Optimal Advertising and Optimal Quality', *American Economic Review*, December, pp. 826–33.

Hagerty, M.R., J.M. Carman and G.J. Russel (1988), 'Estimating Elasticities with PIMS Data: Methodological Issues and Substantive Implications', *Journal of Marketing Research*, vol. 25, February, pp. 1–19.

Hanssens, D.M., L.L. Parsons and R.L. Schultz (1990), *Market Response Models: Econometric and Time Series Analysis*. Boston: Kluwer Academic Publishers.

Jacquemin, A. (1973), 'Optimal Control and Advertising Policy', *Metroeconomica*, vol. 25, May.

Jain, S. (1984), *Marketing Planning and Strategy*, 2nd edn. South-Western Publishing Company, p. 740.

Kotler, P. (1991), *Marketing Management*, 7th edn. Englewood Cliffs, NJ: Prentice-Hall Inc.

Lambin, J.J., P.A. Naert and A. Bultez (1975), 'Optimal Marketing Behaviour in Oligopoly', *European Economic Review*, vol. 6, pp. 105–28.

Lambin, J.J. (1976) *Advertising, Competition and Market Conduct in Oligopoly over Time*. Amsterdam: North Holland.

Lambin, J.J. (1988), Synthèse des études récentes sur l'efficacité économique de la publicité. CESAM Unpublished Working Paper, Louvain-la-Neuve, Belgium.

Leone, R.P. and R. Schultz (1980), 'A Study of Marketing Generalizations', *Journal of Marketing*, vol. 44, pp. 10–18.

Leighton, D.S.R. *et al.* (1972), *Canadian Problems in Marketing*, 3rd edn. Toronto: McGraw-Hill Ryerson Ltd.

Leroy, G., G. Richard and J.P. Sallenave (1980),

Monroe, K.B. (1979), *Pricing: Making Profitable Decisions*. New York: McGraw-Hill Book Co.

Nagle, T.T. (1987), *The Strategy and Tactics of Pricing*. Englewood Cliffs, New Jersey: Prentice Hall Inc.

Nerlove, M. and K.J. Arrow (1962), 'Optimal Advertising Policy under Dynamic Conditions', *Economica*, vol. 29, pp. 129–42.

Neslin, S.A. and R.W. Shoemaker (1983), 'Using a Natural Experiment to Estimate Price Elasticity', *Journal of Marketing*, vol. 47, pp. 44–57.

Oum, T.H. and D.W. Gillen (1981), Demand for Fareclasses and Pricing in Airline Markets. Queen's University, School of Business Working Paper No. 80–12.

Oxenfeld, A.R. (1966), 'Product Line Pricing', *Harvard Business Review*, vol. 44, July–August, pp. 137–44.

Porter, M.E. (1980), *Competitive Strategy*. New York: The Free Press.

Ross, E.B. (1984), 'Making Money with Proactive Pricing', *Harvard Business Review*, vol. 62, November–December, pp. 145–55.

Shapiro, B.P. and B.B. Jackson (1978), 'Industrial Pricing to Meet Customers' Needs', *Harvard Business Review*, vol. 56, November–December, pp. 119–27.

Shapiro, B.P. and B.B. Jackson (1979), 'Politique de prix: le client d'abord', *Harvard-L'Expansion*, Spring, pp. 81–90.

Tellis, G.J. (1986), 'Beyond the Many Faces of Price: An Integration of Pricing Strategies', *Journal of Marketing*, vol. 50, October, pp. 146–60.

Tellis, G.J. (1988), 'The Price Elasticity of Selective Demand: A Meta-Analysis of Econometric Models of Sales', *Journal of Marketing Research*, vol. 25, November, pp. 331–41.

Terpstra, V. and R. Sarathy (1991), *International Marketing*, 5th edn. Chicago: The Dryden Press.

Traylor, M.B. (1986), 'Cannibalism in Multibrand Firms', *The Journal of Consumer Marketing*, vol. 3, no. 2, Spring, pp. 69–75.

CHAPTER 15

STRATEGIC COMMUNI- CATION DECISIONS

LEARNING OBJECTIVES

After reading this chapter, you should be able to:

■ discuss the nature and the role of marketing communication

■ describe the steps in designing an effective communication programme

■ explain the tasks and objectives of personal communication

■ define the different objectives of advertising communication

■ describe the different levels of advertising effectiveness

■ explain how advertising budget decisions can be made.

W e saw in Chapter 1 that marketing is an action-oriented process as well as a business philosophy. To be effectively implemented, the firm's strategic choices must be supported by dynamic action programmes, without which there is very little hope for commercial success. To sell, it is not enough to have a competitively priced product made available to target potential buyers through a well-structured distribution network. It is also necessary to advertise the product's distinctive features to the target segment, and to stimulate the demand through selling and promotional activities. An effective marketing strategy requires the development of a communication programme having the two interrelated objectives of *informing* potential buyers about products and services and *persuading* them to buy. Such a programme is based on various means of communication, the most important of which are personal selling, advertising, promotion and public relations. The objective of this chapter is to examine the major strategic decisions facing a firm when developing its communication programme (see Fig. 15.1).

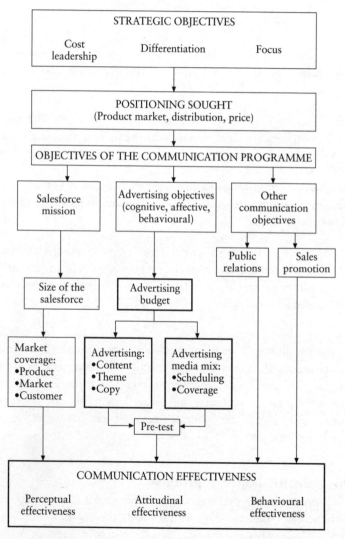

FIGURE 15.1 *Overview of communication decisions*

15.1 THE ROLE AND NATURE OF MARKETING COMMUNICATION

It was stated in Chapter 1 that to ensure an efficient matching of segments of demand and supply, communication flows must be organized between the trading partners to facilitate the exchange process. It is therefore up to the producer to initiate and control these communication flows to create a brand or a corporate image consistent with the firm's strategic objectives.

15.1.1 The marketing communication mix

Marketing communication refers to all the signals or messages made by the firm to its various publics, i.e. customers, distributors, suppliers, shareholders and public authorities, and also its own personnel. The four major communication tools, called the *communication mix*, are advertising, personal selling, promotion and public relations. Each of these communication tools has its own characteristics.

- *Advertising* is a unilateral and paid form of non-personal mass communication, designed to create a favourable attitude towards the advertised product and coming from a clearly identified sponsor.

- *Personal selling* has the objective to organizing a verbal dialogue with potential and current customers and to deliver a personal message with the short-term objective of making a sale. Its role is also to gather information for the firm.

- *Promotion* includes all short-term incentives, generally organized on a temporary and/or local basis, and designed to stimulate immediate purchase and to move sales forward more rapidly than would otherwise occur.

- *Public relations* involve a variety of actions aimed at establishing a positive corporate image and a climate of understanding and mutual trust between a firm and its various publics. Here, the communication objective is less to sell and more to gain moral support from public opinion for the firm's economic activities.

In addition to these traditional communication tools, one must also add direct mail, catalogue selling, fairs and exhibitions, telemarketing, etc. Although these methods of communication are very different, they are also highly complementary. The problem is therefore not whether advertising and promotion are necessary, but rather how to allocate the total communication budget to these various communication tools, given the product's characteristics and the chosen communication objectives.

15.1.2 The communication process

Any communication involves an exchange of signals between a sender and a receiver, and the use of a system of encoding and decoding which allows the creation and interpretation of the message. Figure 15.2 describes the communication process in terms of nine elements (Kotler, 1991, p. 568):

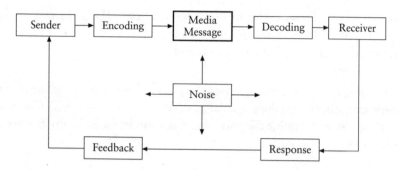

FIGURE 15.2 *The communication process* (Source: *Kotler, 1991, p. 589*)

- *Sender*: the party sending the message to another party.

- *Encoding*: the process of transforming the intended message into images, language, signs, symbols, etc.

- *Media*: the communication channel through which the message moves from the sender to the receiver.

- *Message*: the information or the claim to be communicated to the receiver by the sender.

- *Decoding*: the process through which the receiver assigns meaning to the symbols transmitted.

- *Receiver*: the target audience.

- *Response*: the receiver's reactions after exposure to the message.

- *Feedback*: the part of the target audience's response that the receiver communicates to the sender.

- *Noise*: the distortions that occur during the communication process.

Figure 15.2 describes the relationship between these nine factors and helps to determine the conditions for effective communication. Four conditions can be identified:

1. *Communication objectives.* Senders must know what audiences they want to reach and what type of response they want. This implies the choice of a target audience and the determination of specific communication objectives. These tasks are typically the responsibilities of strategic marketing people.
2. *Message execution.* Communicators must be skilful in encoding messages and able to understand how the target audience tends to process messages. This involves designing advertisements and ensuring, through testing, that they are processed by the target group in the intended manner to produce the desired communication effect.
3. *Media planning.* This involves (1) media selection, i.e. 'where' to reach the target audience most efficiently, and (2) media scheduling, i.e. 'how often' the target audience needs to be reached to produce the intended communication objective. This task and the previous task are, in general, assumed by advertising agencies and/or by agencies specializing in media planning.

4. *Communication effectiveness.* The advertiser must identify the audience's response to the message and verify the extent to which the communication objectives have been achieved. This, again, is the task of marketing management.

Applying the concept of marketing to advertising implies developing messages that relate to buyers' experiences, namely by adopting a language they can decode. These four conditions for efficient communication determine the various decisions to be taken in any marketing communication programme.

15.1.3 Personal versus impersonal communication

The two most important tools of marketing communication are personal communication, assumed by the salesforce, and impersonal communication, achieved through media advertising. The problem is to know when direct intervention by a sales representative is more effective than advertising. A comparison of the main features of each of these two means of communication is shown in Table 15.1.

This comparison suggests the following:

■ Personal selling is by far the most efficient and powerful communication tool. But it costs almost a hundred times more to contact a prospect with a salesperson's visit than with an advertising message.

■ Media advertising, however, has the advantage over personal selling in that it can reach a large number of people in a short period of time, while a sales representative can only visit a limited number of customers within a day.

TABLE 15.1 *Comparing personal and impersonal communication*

Elements of the communication process	Personal communication	Impersonal communication
Target	■ Very well identified target	■ Average profile of the target
Message	■ Tailor-made message ■ Many arguments ■ Weak control of form and content	■ Standard message ■ Few arguments ■ Strong control of form and content
Media	■ Personalized and human contact ■ Few contacts	■ Impersonalized contact ■ Several contacts
Receiver	■ Continued attention ■ Weak consequence of encoding error	■ Volatile attention ■ Strong effect of encoding error
Response	■ Immediate behavioural response possible	■ Immediate behavioural response difficult

Source: Adapted from Darmon *et al.* (1982, p. 398).

■ When a product is complex and difficult to use and is targeted to a limited number of people, a sales representative is clearly much more effective than an advertising message, which is necessarily too general and too simplistic.

■ A salesperson acts directly and can obtain an immediate order from the customer, whereas advertising works through brand awareness and attitude formation. These are often long-term effects.

Consequently, whenever the personal factor is not essential to communication, advertising is more economical in terms of costs and of time. Recent developments in the field of advertising tend to reconcile the advantages of these two communication systems, which is indeed the objective of interactive or response advertising.

It is therefore not surprising to observe that firms selling industrial goods devote a larger proportion of their communication budget to personal selling than firms operating in the field of consumer goods.

15.1.4 Costs of communication activities

It is difficult to evaluate the costs of communication activities because available information is sketchy. Furthermore, orders of magnitude vary tremendously with the field of activity. It is nevertheless generally accepted that personal communication expenses devoted to the salesforce are much greater than advertising expenditure; they are also more significant in industrial markets as compared to consumer goods markets. The following figures are quite revealing.

> In France, in 1986, total media advertising amounted to F30.6 billion and, in 1982, to more than F100 billion for personal selling. In the USA, in 1986, total advertising outlays amounted to $66 billion and, in 1982, to $100 billion in personal selling.
>
> (Xardel, 1982; Waterson, 1992)

Using the data in Table 15.2 we can evaluate the relative importance of advertising expenditure in the gross domestic product (GDP) of various economies and also compare advertising intensities in the main industrialized countries.

The cost of a salesperson is constantly increasing, especially in industrial markets, while the cost of an advertising contact tends to decrease because of better selectivity by the media. According to a study by Forsyth (1987), the average cost of a well-targeted contact through a printed industrial advertising medium is 17 cents. This cost must be compared with the average cost of an industrial sales call, which was $252 in 1987, against $97 in 1977.

This trend in communication costs calls for a reassessment of the respective roles of advertising and personal selling. It is even more urgent because of the development of new means of communication.

TABLE 15.2 *International comparison of advertising expenditures per media (1994)*

	Dailies (%)	Weeklies (%)	TV (%)	Radio (%)	Cinema (%)	Outdoor (%)	Total (in M ECU)
Austria	44.3	18.3	22.3	9.9	0.4	4.8	1 243
Belgium	26.4	25.8	30.7	7.7	0.9	8.5	1 142
Denmark	62.2	16.0	17.2	2.2	0.6	1.8	995
Finland	61.1	13.4	19.2	3.6	0.1	2.7	704
France	24.9	23.1	32.0	7.6	0.6	11.8	7 369
Germany	50.3	20.2	21.0	4.2	1.0	3.3	15 476
Greece	14.0	14.0	65.6	4.4	0	2.0	815
Ireland	57.4	4.9	24.9	7.7	0.8	4.4	390
Italy	21.5	17.0	57.4	1.4	0	2.8	4 207
Netherlands	47.1	25.4	19.7	4.1	0.4	3.3	2 514
Norway	61.8	13.1	17.6	4.5	0.8	2.2	717
Portugal	17.0	16.9	54.8	4.9	0	6.4	593
Spain	31.9	16.2	37.2	9.4	0.8	4.5	3 570
Sweden	63.9	10.8	18.6	1.4	0.7	4.7	1 332
Switzerland	58.3	16.4	8.9	2.8	1.0	12.7	1 831
UK	42.6	17.6	32.5	2.9	0.6	3.7	9 692

Source: European Association of Advertising Agencies (EAAA, Brussels) (1995).

15.1.5 Electronic communication

As a result of the impetus from developments in telematics, cable television, pay-TV, satellite communication, interactive videotext terminals, personal computers, etc., electronic communication is at present in full development. These new possibilities influence our way of life as well as the communication strategies of firms. As put by Daniel Bell (1979): '... telecommunications constitute for humanity as big a revolution as did the advent of printing, writing and language.'

The development of electronic communication not only modifies the respective roles of personal selling and of advertising, but also changes the objectives and content of advertising communication. Many significant changes are already observable in our society.

■ To begin with, the new means of communication tend to be more *interactive*, i.e. two-way rather than one-way as in the past. Today, the general public has the possibility of asking for, choosing and sending back information rather than simply being passively subjected to a bombardment of irrelevant messages. We are moving in fact towards demanded advertising.

■ Furthermore, it is now possible, in the most varied fields, to have access to huge data banks on available products, their comparative performance, their prices, etc. The firm will therefore face a more and better informed public. Such facts will further reinforce the informative and factual character of communication, which will increasingly be set up as an aid to the buyer rather than as a sales instrument.

■ Another consequence of the development of electronic communication is its *greater selectivity*. The combination of possibilities offered by the telephone, the computer and the television means that very well-defined targets can be reached with personalized messages. We are therefore moving towards personalized electronic mail systems which improve communication effectiveness and favour the development of interactive marketing.

Some sectors, such as the car industry, already use personalized mail. Access to the central file of the Road Traffic Bureau helps identify and reach, by direct mail for example, owners of a particular brand of car who purchased their vehicle more than five years ago and might thus be likely to replace it in the near future.

■ Regionalization of radio and television programmes also favours *selectivity of communication*. The introduction of local channels will allow local firms and local advertisers to have access to radio and television. Media plans could allocate different degrees of pressure from region to region and thus better adapt the brand situation from one region to another.

■ Finally, a last consequence is that the considerable increase in geographic zones covered by a transmitting station, through the use of satellites and cable, will *reinforce the internationalization* of brands and advertising campaigns.

As a result of these developments in the methods of communication, a whole series of tasks once exercised by salespersons could henceforth be achieved by impersonal means of communication at a lower cost. Well-addressed direct mail, the telephone, a catalogue that can be consulted on a TV screen or a computer can all bring more extensive and more precise information much more quickly than a salesperson's sales speech. This is why we now observe a spectacular development of direct marketing systems, as shown in Table 13.4 (p. 505).

> What we observe is a basic transformation of the selling function, which becomes more a sedentary activity. The contact with the prospect is not any more the exclusive privilege of the sales person but the role of the entire organization. The number of persons engaged in sales forces may decrease, but the number of contacts with the customer will nevertheless increase. Hence, the importance of having a market-driven orientation within the organization.   (Xardel, 1982, pp. 59–75)

Note that the growth of these new communication systems does not imply the elimination of the salesperson. A personal contact will always be necessary. Electronic communication completes the action, prepares it and makes it more productive.

15.2 PERSONAL COMMUNICATION

Personal selling is the most effective means of communication at certain stages of the buying process, especially when preferences need to be developed and the decision to buy spurred on. Owing to developments in communication technology, the role of the salesforce is now undergoing a major transformation. Its role in strategic marketing is on the increase and the more routine tasks are increasingly being assumed by cheaper, more impersonal means of communication.

15.2.1 Salesforce tasks and objectives

The first step in developing a personal communication strategy is to define the role of the salesforce in the overall marketing strategy. This can only be done by clearly defining the kind of relationship the firm wants to establish with its customers in each product market.

One can define three types of activity that any salesforce exercises:

■ *Selling*, which implies prospecting and approaching potential buyers, negotiating sales conditions and closing sales.

■ *Servicing*, which implies delivery, technical assistance, after-sale service, merchandising, etc.

■ *Information gathering*, which involves market research, business intelligence, monitoring of competitors' activities, needs analysis, etc.

Thus, the salesperson is not only the firm's commercial arm, but also an important element in its marketing information system.

In practice, the terms *salesperson* and *sales representative* can cover very different missions, depending on the emphasis placed on one or other of the three functions above. The following categories of salesperson can be identified.

■ The function of the *delivery person* is to ensure the physical delivery of the product.

■ The role of the *sales clerk* is to assist customers in their choice and to take orders. Sales clerks operate at the point of sale or stand behind the counter.

■ The *travelling salesperson* visits the retailers or the distributors, takes their orders and performs non-selling activities such as checking inventory, handling retailers' complaints, etc.

■ The role of the *merchandiser* is not to sell but rather to organize promotional activities at the sales point and to arrange point-of-purchase displays.

■ The *missionary delegate* is not permitted to take an order, but has a role to inform and educate potential users. This is typically the role played by the medical representatives in the pharmaceutical industry.

■ The *sales engineer* has a technical competence and operates as a consultant *vis-à-vis* the customer, providing assistance and advice. It is the role played by IBM sales engineers.

■ The *sales representative* is an independent salesperson selling durable goods such as cars and vacuum cleaners, or services such as insurance, where creative selling is very important.

■ The *negotiator* is in charge of the financial engineering of vast industrial projects and responsible for negotiations with government authorities and industrial partners.

Once the type of mission assigned to the salesperson is defined, the problem is to know how to organize commercial relations and which tasks to assign to the salesforce, to the distribution network and to advertising.

15.2.2 Personal selling in the marketing mix

Generally speaking, the true role of a salesperson remains first and foremost to satisfy the need for two-way communication felt by well-informed customers who have demands about how the product can be adapted to their own needs. From the firm's viewpoint, the salesforce's new effectiveness is mainly linked to their ability in collecting and transmitting information in order to increase the speed of adjustment to market changes. This is how a Japanese firm conceives the role of the salesforce:

> Salesmen are irreplaceable canvassers of information; they must be trained: (a) to listen to the customer, much more than to know seductive sales speech of the kind: 'the ten secrets of selling'; (b) to be humble when criticized, much more than display militant pride of the kind: 'the products of firm X are the best'; (c) to be in solidarity with other salesmen and with his firm to facilitate cross-checking and return of information, much more than pursue the superficial solitude of the sales person who only tries to reach his quota in order to improve his own performance. (Xardel, 1982, pp. 59–75)

This evolution in the notion of the role of the salesforce therefore tends to increase its direct participation in strategic marketing. In addition to operational marketing functions, various strategic functions are now exercised by the salesforce. The typical functions of the salesforce are:

- Winning acceptance for new products.

- Developing new customers.

- Maintaining customer loyalty.

- Providing technical service to facilitate sales.

- Communicating product information.

- Gathering information.

Several of these selling objectives—such as winning acceptance for new products, developing new customers and gathering information—are typically related to strategic marketing. The salesperson can therefore play an important role in strategic marketing, insofar as he or she participates in elaborating product policy through the information supplied regarding buyers' needs.

15.2.3 The salesforce organization

A firm can organize its salesforce in different ways. The organization can be by territory, by product, by customer or even a combination of these.

Territory-based organization   This is the most common structure and also the simplest organization. The salesperson is the firm's exclusive representative for its full product line for all current and potential customers. This structure has several advantages: first, it defines clearly the sales representative's responsibilities; second, it motivates the salesperson, who has the full exclusivity on the territory; and, finally, it minimizes costs and travel expenses.

This structure is only appropriate, however, when products are few in number or similar and when customers have the same kind of needs. A firm producing paints and varnishes, whose customers are wholesalers, retailers and industrial users (building painters, car bodies, etc.) clearly cannot use the same salesperson to cultivate these different customer groups.

Product-based organization   This structure is preferable when products are very different, technically complex and require appropriate technical competence. In this case, the salesperson is more specialized and better equipped to meet clients' needs and to counter rivals.

The problem with a product-based organization is that costs may increase manifold, since several salespersons from the same firm may visit the same customer. For example, Rank Xerox uses different salespersons for photocopying machines and for word-processing units.

Customer-based organization   Organization by customer categories is adopted when clients' needs are very different and require specific abilities. Customers may be classified by industrial sector, by size or by their method of buying. We find here the same criteria as those of segmentation presented in Chapter 7.

The advantage of a customer-based structure is that each salesforce is specialized and becomes very knowledgeable about specific customer needs. But if customers are dispersed geographically, this organization can be very costly. Most computer firms organize their salesforce by customer groups: banks and insurance, industrial customers, retailers, etc.

Others   Other more complex forms of organization combining pairs of criteria also exist. Salespersons can be specialized by product–territory, customer–territory or even by territory–customer–product. This normally happens in very large enterprises with many products and varied clients.

15.3 ADVERTISING COMMUNICATION

Advertising is a means of communication by which a firm can deliver a message to potential buyers with whom it is not in direct contact. When a firm resorts to advertising, it is effectively following a *pull* communication strategy. Its main objective is to create a brand image and brand equity, and to ensure co-operation from distributors. Just as the salesforce is the best tool for a push strategy, advertising is the best means for a pull strategy.

15.3.1 Setting the role of media advertising

In Chapter 4, we described what advertising represents for the advertiser and its utility to the buyer. Recall briefly that:

■ For the *firm*, the function of advertising is to produce knowledge for consumers and to generate interest among them in order to create demand for its product.

■ For *consumers*, advertising allows them to learn about the distinctive characteristics claimed by the manufacturer. Advertising also helps them to save personal time, since the information reaches them directly without their having to collect it.

Since the advent of the early form of advertising, advertising communication objectives have diversified considerably and different forms of advertising can be identified while using the same media.

Concept advertising

This is a media advertising message with a mainly 'attitudinal' communication objective: to influence the buyer's attitude towards the brand. Its role can be defined as follows:

> The creative efforts of many national advertisers are designed, not to induce immediate action, but to build favourable attitudes that will lead to eventual purchase.
>
> (Dhalla, 1978)

This definition implies that the effectiveness of this type of advertising can only be viewed from a long-term perspective. The notion of attitude holds a central position here. The objective is mainly to create an image based on communicating a concept.

Promotional advertising

This is a media advertising message with a mainly 'behavioural' communication objective: to influence the buyers' purchasing behaviour rather than their attitudes. The objective is to trigger the act of purchase. Its effectiveness is evaluated directly in terms of actual sales. This is the most aggressive type of communication, although it is not incompatible with image creation. However, its immediate purpose is to achieve short-term results.

Response advertising

This is a personalized message of an offer, having the objective of generating a 'relationship' with the prospect by encouraging a response on which a commercial relation can be built.

This type of advertising tries to reconcile the characteristics of the two previous ones: building an image, but also encouraging a measurable response allowing an immediate appraisal of the effectiveness of the communication. This type of media advertising is expanding rapidly now, and is directly linked to interactive marketing, discussed in Chapter 13 (see sect. 13.7).

Institutional advertising

In the first three styles of communication, the product or brand is at the heart of the advertising message. Institutional advertising does not talk about the product, but aims to create or reinforce a positive attitude towards the firm.

The objective is therefore to create an image, but that of the firm to describe the firm's profile and stress its personality in order to create a climate of confidence and understanding. The purpose is *to communicate differently* in a saturated advertising world and to fight against the fatigue of product advertising with a softer approach, by drawing attention to the firm itself, its merits, its values and talents. Clearly, the effectiveness of this kind of advertising can only be evaluated in the long-term and can essentially work on attitudes.

Sponsoring and patronage

These are two specific methods of institutional advertising, which runs the risk of tiring the public, who can become irritated and view these campaigns as attempts at self-satisfaction. Hence, these new forms of communication have developed, based on the idea that '... there is more splendour in being virtuous than taking credit for it' (Van Hecke, 1988). A typical example of one of these media stunts is the financing by American Express of the restoration of Van Eyck's masterpiece *L'agneau mystique*, which considerably increased its prestige in a way that no other campaign could have done.

The objective is to increase awareness of the firm's brand and to improve its image by association with positive values. The event being supported—which often unfolds in an unpredictable manner, thus reinforcing the credibility of the message—must have a testimony value, in the sense that a link should exist between the sponsored event and the sponsoring organization, even if the link is indirect.

> Whether the firm is sponsoring an expedition in the Himalayas or a transatlantic race, it is emphasizing its adherence to moral values such as team spirit and courage. On the one hand it proves its open-mindedness and its harmonious integration in society, and, on the other hand, with regards to internal communication, it increases support from its personnel and develops a favourable climate within the firm.   (Van Hecke, 1988)

It should be noted that sponsorship is a commercial operation, implying a two-way relation of rights and obligations: on the one hand, material or financial support for the sponsored event and, on the other, direct and methodical exploitation of the event by the firm. Thus sponsorship is distinct from patronage, in which generosity and lack of interest in profit are dominant (Chaval, 1986, p. 68).

It is clear that forms of advertising, pursued objectives and the means used to achieve them are very different. Before launching an advertising campaign, it is therefore important to have a clear view of the role that advertising is to play in the marketing programme.

15.3.2 Prerequisites of concept advertising

There are still too many firms that tend to assimilate advertising with marketing and to approach marketing by advertising. In fact, advertising is only a complement, which is sometimes but not always indispensable, to a more fundamental process of strategic marketing. For advertising to be effective, a number of prerequisites should ideally prevail:

■ Advertising is only one element of the marketing mix and its role cannot be separated from the roles of the other marketing instruments. As a general rule, advertising will be effective only when the other marketing factors have been chosen: a differentiated and clearly positioned product sold at a competitive price through a well-adapted distribution network.

■ Advertising is useful to the consumer mainly for complex products that have *internal qualities* that cannot be discovered by inspection. For experience goods, such as motor oil and hair conditioner, consumers have lots to gain from truthful advertising (Nelson, 1974).

■ To be effective, advertising should promote a *distinctive characteristic* to position the brand clearly in the minds of consumers as being different from competing brands. The distinctive characteristic can be the promise of the brand, but also its personality, its look or its symbolic value.

■ Advertising is particularly effective in markets or segments where *primary demand is expansible*. Its role is then to stimulate the need for the product category as a whole. In non-expansible markets, the main role of advertising is to stimulate selective demand and to create communication effects at the brand level.

■ The size of the reference market must be large enough to absorb the cost of an advertising campaign, and the firm must have enough financial resources to reach the *threshold levels* of the advertising response function.

Thus, the advertising communication platform is the complement of a strategic marketing programme. The advertising positioning sought must be in line with the marketing positioning adopted and based on sound strategic thinking, without which advertising cannot be effective.

15.3.3 Alternative advertising objectives

To determine the objectives of advertising communication, it is useful to refer back to the three levels of market response analysed in Chapter 6:

■ *Cognitive response,* which relates to awareness and to knowledge of the product characteristics. At this level, the advertiser can set objectives of information, recall, recognition or familiarity.

■ *Affective response,* which relates to the overall evaluation of the brand in terms of feelings, favourable or unfavourable judgements and preferences. The objectives will be to influence attitude and to create purchase intention.

■ *Behavioural response,* which refers not only to buying behaviour and post-purchase behaviour, but also to all other forms of behavioural response observed as the result of a communication, such as visiting a showroom, requesting a catalogue, sending a reply coupon.

It is common practice to consider these three levels as a sequence, as potential buyers pass successively through the three stages: cognitive, affective and behavioural (Lavidge and Steiner, 1961). This sequence of reactions is known as the *learning model*. As noted in Chapter 6, this model needs to be adjusted in terms of the buyer's degree of involvement (see Fig. 4.1, p. 177). Although not generally applicable, the learning response model nevertheless remains a useful tool for defining the priority objectives of communication (Vaughn, 1986).

Keeping this hierarchy of objectives in mind, Rossiter and Percy (1987, p. 132) have identified *five different communication effects* that can be caused, in whole or in part, by advertising. These effects reconstitute the process followed by the buyer when confronted with a purchasing decision; there can, therefore, be as many possible objectives for communication.

Development of primary demand

Existence of need is a prerequisite that determines the effectiveness of any act of communication. Every product satisfies a product category need. Perception of this need by potential buyers can be stimulated by advertising. Advertising thus helps develop total demand in the market. Three distinct situations can exist:

- The category need is *present and well perceived* by potential buyers. In this case, generic advertising is not justified. This is the case for many low-involvement, frequently purchased products, where purchasing is done on a routine basis.

- The category need is *perceived but neglected or forgotten* and the role of generic advertising is to remind the prospective buyer of a previously established need. This is the case for infrequently purchased or infrequently used products such as pain remedies.

- The perception of the category need is *weak or not established* in the target group of potential users. In this case, generic advertising can sell the benefits of the product category. A typical example is the campaign in favour of the use of condoms to combat the spread of AIDS. Selling category need is a communication objective for all new products, and in particular for new-to-the-world products.

In generic advertising campaigns, the advertising content places the emphasis on the core service of the product and/or on the product benefits. This type of communication message will benefit the advertiser, but may also benefit the competing firms.

Creating brand awareness

This is the first level of cognitive response. In Chapter 6, we defined brand awareness as the buyer's ability to identify a brand in sufficient detail to propose, choose or use a brand. Three kinds of advertising objective, based on awareness, can be identified:

- To create or maintain *brand recognition* so that buyers identify the brand at the point of sale and are induced to check the existence of a category need.

- To create or maintain *brand recall* to induce buyers to select the brand once the category need has been experienced.

- To emphasize both *brand recognition* and *brand recall*.

These communication objectives imply different advertising contents. For brand recognition, the advertising content will emphasize the visual elements (logo, colours, packaging), while for brand recall the advertising will seek to repeat the brand name in audio and visual media and in headlines and to associate the brand name with the core service.

Creating a favourable brand attitude

The objective is to create, improve, maintain and modify buyers' attitudes towards the brand. It is therefore an affective response which intervenes here. Chapter 6 describes the components of attitude (see sect. 6.3). The following communication strategies are open to the advertiser:

- To convince the target audience to give *more importance* to a particular product attribute on which the brand is well placed in comparison to rival brands.

- To convince the target audience of the firm's *technological superiority* in the product category.

- To *reinforce beliefs* and the conviction of the target audience on the presence of a determining attribute in the brand.

- To *reposition the brand* by associating its use with another set of needs or purchase motivations.

- To eliminate a *negative attitude* by associating the brand with a set of positive values.

- To call attention to *neglected attributes* by consumers in their decision-making process.

- To *alter the beliefs* of the target audience about competing brands.

The last strategy can only be adopted in countries where comparative advertising is authorized, as in the UK. A directive for comparative advertising in the EU has been recently proposed by the European Commission.

It is important to identify clearly the implicit assumptions of a communication strategy based on brand attitude. They can be summarized as follows:

- The advertiser must emphasize the features or characteristics in which it has the strongest competitive advantage.

- It is useless to try to modify buyers' perceptions when the brand does not really have the claimed characteristic.

- The major criticism directed against advertising is the adoption of arguments or themes that are totally unrelated to product attributes important to the buyer.

In other words, a market-driven communication strategy is based on the idea that advertising is mainly designed to encourage the buyer to buy and not simply to praise the advertiser. This vision of a communication strategy falls well in line with the marketing concept.

Stimulate brand purchase intention

Purchase intention is halfway between the affective and the behavioural response. Two kinds of situation may arise:

■ The buyer is not involved, or only weakly involved, in a purchasing decision and there is no conscious, prior intention to buy until the last minute at the point of purchase. This is the case for low perceived-risk products and also for routinely purchased products. In this type of situation, stimulating brand purchase intention is not an advertising objective.

■ The buyer has a conscious purchase intention during advertising exposure.

In the latter case, promotional advertising can play a role by using incentives (price reductions, special offers, etc.) that precipitate the buying decision or encourage repurchase.

Recall that the intention to buy is only expressed when there is also a *state of shortage*, that is, when the category need is felt. Thus, the two states, need and intention, are closely associated. Yet intention to buy is not a frequently recurring event in any particular consumer.

> Markets that are huge in their annual volume are made up of buying decisions made by very small numbers of people in a given period of time. For example, in a typical week in 1982, American retailers sold over $365 million worth of shoes. But during that week (as shown in our study that year) only six persons in 100 bought shoes for themselves or their children. Similarly, only 28 adults in 1,000 bought any kinds of women's slacks, jeans, or shorts in the course of a week, and only 21 bought a dress. Fourteen in 1,000 bought a small appliance; 18 in 1,000 bought furniture; 3 in 1,000 bought an article of luggage.
>
> (Bogart, 1986, p. 267)

Hence, many markets with very high turnovers, like those mentioned in the above examples, depend each week on the buying decisions of a small number of people. It is not surprising to find that advertising messages give rise to relatively few immediate purchase intentions, since in most cases the prerequisite is not there: namely, the existence of a state of need.

Purchase facilitation
This last objective of advertising communication deals with the *other marketing factors* (the four P's), without which there can be no purchase: a product that keeps its promise, retail availability of the product, acceptable price, and competence and availability of the salesforce. When these conditions are not all met, advertising can sometimes help to reduce or minimize problems by, for example, defending the market price, or by working as a substitute to distribution through direct marketing.

15.3.4 Creativity in concept advertising
Advertisers can adopt various creative approaches in their choice of communication platform. The most conventional approach, called *copy strategy* in advertising jargon, is based on four components:

1. *Target*: What target is the group to reach?
2. *Promise*: What is the distinctive proposal made to the target?
3. *Argument*: What is the support of the promise?
4. *Tone*: What style or format should be adopted for executing the message?

The *copy strategy statement* is a blueprint for creative people: it defines what must be communicated by advertising. Its strength lies in the fact that it forces marketing managers to choose an axis of communication which will be maintained over many years. As a result, the brand becomes endowed with a specific image and a positioning.

Kapferer (1985) emphasizes, in particular, the effectiveness of this strategy in the case of predominantly functional products for which there exist elements of differentiation based on technical features.

> For example, during the 1960s, when Ariel was being launched, housewives in large families (target) were promised unparalleled washing (promise) thanks to the biological agents in the powder (argument); the communication had a resolutely serious style (tone) so as to give the message credibility.   (Kapferer, 1985, p. 102)

Yet in many fields brands have proliferated, and it is difficult to find specific promises which are not already 'occupied' by competing brands. To differentiate at any price, the manufacturer might run the risk of putting out details that might be significant, but derisory to the buyer.

Star strategy

This trend has led advertisers, in France in particular, to adopt another creative approach called *star-strategy*, developed by Séguéla (1982), which emphasizes the 'tone' of the communication and its personality, the brand's character.

> No properly respected copy strategy would have allowed TBWA to launch the pen Pentel in France with its campaign based on the three following slogans referring to the green colour of the Pentel pens: *Mettez-vous au vert* (reference to ecology), *Allez les verts* (reference to a football team wearing green shirts), *Envers et contre tout* (reference to the word *vert*). Here, there is no promise. But what does Pentel exactly promise? Nothing, or nothing distinctive. On the other hand, the advertising has managed to create an attractive brand personality which drives people to try Pentel. Its actual properties will only be discovered once the pen is in the hand.   (Kapferer, 1985, p. 103)

'Star strategy' determines the axis of communication on the basis of three elements: the brand's physical characteristics (its function), its character or personality, and the style of expression. This kind of creative approach is particularly effective when the product has no significant factor of differentiation.

Other creative notions have also been proposed. Variot (1985) extends Séguéla's approach and suggests that a brand's identity can be decomposed into six facets: its physique and its personality, but also the uses to which it is associated, its cultural facet, its buyer's image (others' viewpoint) and its self-image. For example, the identity of the brand Porsche in France can be described as follows (example quoted in Kapferer, 1985, p. 104):

1. *Physical*: Performance.
2. *Personality*: Perfectionist.

3. *Use*: Personal rather than family oriented.
4. *Cultural*: German technology.
5. *Buyer's image*: Winner's car.
6. *Self-image*: Surpassing oneself.

This advertising approach is very demanding because it requires great coherence of expression. The reason is that form, style and tone are more important than substance in constructing the image.

The Maloney grid

In the USA, Maloney (1961) has developed a model that continues to be relevant today and helps to generate ideas for advertising themes. Table 15.3 classifies, on the one hand, the kinds of reward buyers seek in a product and, on the other, the source of those rewards in the use of the product. This classification identifies 12 possible axes of advertising communication and creative people can put forward a theme for each.

As emphasized above, the choice of advertising message (theme, appeal, copy) is part of the product positioning decision, since it expresses the major benefits that the brand offers to the buyer. Yet within this concept there are several possible messages, and creative people have latitude to change the message without changing the product positioning concept. Consistency in advertising communication is important for building brand image and brand equity.

The dilemma: quality versus quantity

Which is more important in an advertising campaign: the creativity factor or the amount of money spent? At least one thing is clear: only after gaining attention can an advertising message help to generate sales. Gross (1972) has shown the economic value of creative advertising and several empirical studies have confirmed his observations.

An interesting argument has been put forward in the USA by Nelson (1974) and recently confirmed in the UK by Davis *et al.* (1991). For experience goods, i.e. goods for which consumers cannot discover either quality or usefulness without buying them repeatedly over a long time period (e.g. motor oil or shampoo), the mere fact of advertising heavily is more important than the advertising content. For this type of goods, the advertiser should not simply tell consumers

TABLE 15.3 *Searching for advertising appeal*

Type of potentially rewarding experience	Potential type of reward			
	Rational	Sensory	Social	Ego satisfaction
Results of use experience	(1)	(2)	(3)	(4)
Product-in-use experience	(5)	(6)	(7)	(8)
Incidental-to-use experience	(9)	(10)	(11)	(12)

Source: Maloney (1961, pp. 595–618).

that its product is better than its rivals; everyone says that. Rather, it should signal that it believes the product will be around for a long time by spending more than its rivals on advertising. Consumers will decode the message in this sense and therefore the cost or volume of advertising can be just as important as any direct or creative message the advertising contains. For good discussions of this question, see Nelson (1974) and Davis *et al.* (1991).

15.3.5 Measuring advertising effectiveness

Once the objectives of advertising communication have been clearly defined and translated into messages, it is then much simpler to measure the advertising effectiveness. Figure 15.3 describes the process of advertising communication. Three key stages can be distinguished, defining three distinct levels of advertising effectiveness: perceptual, attitudinal and behavioural, corresponding to the three levels of market response mentioned earlier (cognitive, affective and behavioural).

Perceptual effectiveness

Effectiveness at this stage means the ability to overcome potential buyers' indifference or perceptual defences and to be seen, read, heard and memorized by the target group. Clearly, the first quality of an advertisement is to be noticed. Without it, nothing can happen to attitudes or behaviours. One can thus better understand advertisers' preoccupation—sometimes irritating to the outside observer—with 'getting across' and their willingness to achieve it using such means as humour, dreams, the unseemly, stars, etc. Also, the *proliferation of advertising messages* aggravates their worry, because it leads inevitably to reduced levels of attention from a public that rejects boring or undesirable elements.

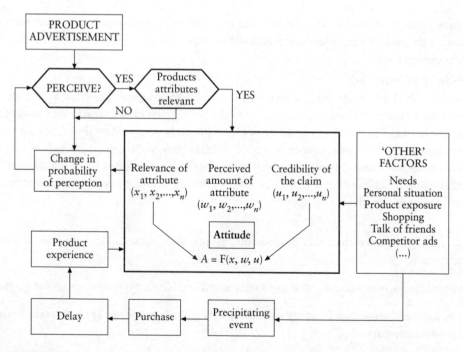

FIGURE 15.3 *The advertising communication process (Source: Dalrymple and Parsons, 1976, p. 462)*

> In the USA, the number of advertising messages had doubled between 1967 and 1982. Most experts believe that the number of messages will double again before 1997.
>
> (Bogart, 1986, p. 220)

The consequence for communication effectiveness can easily be imagined.

> In 1965, 18 per cent of TV viewers were able to remember one of the last advertising spots to which they had been exposed the previous day. In 1987, this percentage had fallen to 7 per cent.
>
> (Bogart, 1986, p. 240)

This first level of 'advertising quality'—the perceptual effectiveness—determines the *productivity* of advertising communication. Important differences between advertising campaigns of the same intensity are observed in practice. Indicators of effectiveness used are tests of brand recognition, of unaided awareness, brand recall (Beta factor), etc., described in Chapter 6.

Overemphasizing the perceptual stage, however, runs the risk of leading to unbridled advertising creations which lose sight of the fact that advertising is only to complement and support a market position. Some advertising critics even go as far as to suggest that advertising is too important to be left in the hands of creative or agency people, who are often tempted to emphasize the communicational impact of advertising at the expense of the market positioning objective.

The copy strategy approach has precisely the merit of refraining from creative outbursts, as opposed to the star strategy where the risk is less well contained.

Attitudinal effectiveness

The second level of effectiveness concerns the psycho-sociological aspect, which calls into question the affective response and the impact of the perceived message on attitudes towards the product or brand. The fact that a message has been properly perceived by the targeted group of buyers doesn't imply effectiveness in terms of attitude change. A message which is perfectly received, understood and digested, may be totally inoperative because of being maladapted, not credible or simply irrelevant. It is why knowledge of the target group's components of attitude is required to define the advertising appeal.

Twedt (1969) suggests that the proposition or promise made must have the following characteristics:

- *Desirability*: the message must first say something desirable or interesting about the product.

- *Exclusiveness*: the message must say something exclusive that does not apply to every brand in the product category.

- *Believability*: the message must be believable or provable; the credibility of the message sender is at stake in this situation.

There is no recipe in the field of creative advertising, even if there are many advertisers who claim to have one (see, in particular, Reeves, 1970 and Ogilvy, 1964). In addition to the criteria already suggested, the following questions can also be addressed regarding the quality of effective advertising.

- Is the advertising positioning in line with the *market positioning* sought for the brand?

- Is the *benefit* brought to the buyer clearly evidenced, simple to understand and, if possible, provable?

- To what extent is the promise *unique* as compared to the promises made by competing brands?

- To what extent is there *consistency* and *continuity* in the adopted advertising theme across media and over time?

- Is the message based on a *creative* idea, easy to memorize for the target audience?

- Does the advertisement succeed in gaining the *attention* of the reader or the viewer?

- Is there a clear and simple *link* between the product, the benefit, the advertising appeal and the advertisement's execution?

Generally speaking, one should beware of advertising ideas that are too original. They run the risk of obscuring the message to be put across, and of the public remembering the advertisement but not the brand name. Some agencies tend to make the advertisement the centrepiece, forgetting that the centrepiece is the product.

If these conditions are met, advertising has achieved its objectives regarding attitudes and the target group is in a state of positive receptiveness towards the product or brand. This state of receptiveness will either be reinforced by repeated exposure to the message, or, on the other hand, modified by competing messages.

Box 15.1 measures the effectiveness of the attitudinal stage of a concept advertising campaign.

The same kind of results can be obtained for institutional advertising, as shown in Table 15.4. This table compares scores of public attitude towards two types of company: those who use institutional advertising and those who do not (de Jaham, 1979).

TABLE 15.4 *Attitudinal impact of institutional advertising*

	Categories of advertiser	
Indicators of attitude	Do not use institutional advertising (%)	Use institutional advertising regularly (%)
Knowledge of the firm's existence	82	93
Familiar with the firm's activities	63	77
Positive impression of the firm	38	51

Source: de Jaham (1979).

BOX 15.1

Example of attitudinal measure of advertising effectiveness: Texas Gulf phosphoric acids and fertilizer manufacturers

Advertising objective
To increase by 10 per cent within 1 year the knowledge and conviction about the product's distinctive characteristics among fertilizer manufacturers.

Advertising theme
To gain conviction about the product's superiority. It contains fewer impurities and has a distinctive green colour: 'clean and green'.

Results of the advertising effectiveness study

	Before advertising	*After advertising*
Identification of the message	3.6%	16.3%
Knowledge to the claimed distinctive characteristics	15.3%	35.1%
Conviction of product superiority over competing products	9.4%	24.3%

Source: Bryk and Davis (1973).

Behavioural effectiveness

The third level of the process is the effectiveness of the behavioural stage—that is, purchasing behaviour directly caused by advertising, which is the ultimate objective being pursued. Indicators used are then trial purchases, sales or market share, decomposed into penetration intensity, exclusivity or loyalty rates as shown in Chapter 6 (see 'Quality of market share analysis', Table 6.6, p. 203).

The growth in the use of response advertising and direct marketing means a greater use of intermediate measures of the behavioural response, such as reply coupons, requests for catalogues and brochures, visits to showrooms, etc., which all reflect active interest caused by advertising and thus can be used to measure its effectiveness. In fact, these indicators also reveal communicational effectiveness, since it would be difficult to identify from the replies those who are motivated by the attractiveness of the offer and those who are showing real interest in the product. The only way to tell is to convert expressions of interest into actual purchases.

As mentioned previously, advertising can only give rise to purchasing behaviour if the other (non-advertising) determinants of the purchasing behaviour are also manifest, such as, for example, the need for the product, seeing the product at a point of sale, a reduction in the price, users' favourable opinions, etc. A favourable attitude created by advertising is only a predisposition which increases the *probability* of purchase of the brand. Once bought, it is mostly the buyer's degree of satisfaction or dissatisfaction and the price–quality relation which become significant and will act upon the attitude and propensity to remain loyal.

It is therefore not possible to measure directly how much advertising contributes to increasing sales. To measure its effect on sales, one would have to take into account all the relevant factors and estimate their respective weights in a dynamic context. For example, an econometric model can be used to find quantitative measures of demand elasticity with respect to each of the relevant factors, as shown in Table 6.7 (p. 206). Other methods are also available, as shown convincingly by Simon (1983). An interesting survey of empirical work in this domain is given by Assmus *et al.* (1984).

As for any kind of investment, it is essential to measure the effectiveness of advertising (Colley, 1961; Aaker and Carman, 1982). Yet one hears frequently in advertising circles that it is impossible to really measure advertising effectiveness. Negative attitudes in this respect are often due to the fact that the world of advertising is usually dominated by creative people, who, more or less consciously, refuse to be judged by anyone other than their peers. Furthermore, there is often great confusion about the level of effectiveness to which one is referring. While it is undoubtedly difficult (but not impossible) to measure sales or market share advertising effectiveness, intermediate measures of effectiveness are easier to use and they often help improve the productivity of advertising investments.

Advertising–sales effectiveness research

Two methods can be used to estimate the sales or market share effect of advertising: the econometric approach based on historical data and the experimental design approach. One study undertaken by Lambin (1969) illustrates the profit maximization approach applied to advertising.

The product concerns a well-established, frequently purchased consumer good sold on the Belgian market. The objective of the study was to examine the profitability of the advertising investment. The demand function parameters were estimated by regression analysis. The resulting equation is presented in Fig. 15.4. Since advertising spending is the object of the study, other decision variables (price, visit frequency and packaging) have already been decided upon and uncontrollable variables have been predicted or fixed. Substituting the values of these variables, the demand equation reduces to

$$q_t = 2.024 \cdot q_{t-1}^{0.565} \cdot s_t^{0.190}$$

For a one-period forecast q_{t-1} is known and we thus have the advertising sales response curve presented in Fig. 15.4. This response function can be used to assess the profitability of the advertising investment (see Lambin, 1969) and to determine the advertising budget.

If the issue is to find out if current advertising expenditure is too high, too low or about right, the model will produce a specific figure which should be used as a guideline rather than as something absolute.

$$q_t = 0.155 \cdot q_{t-1}^{0.565} \cdot y_t^{0.494} \cdot w_t^{-0.260} \cdot x_t^{0.134} \cdot p_t^{-0.588} \cdot v_t^{0.088} \cdot s_t^{0.190}$$

where q_t = per capita sales
        y = per capita disposable income
        w = weather conditions (rainfall)
        x = number of bottle sizes
        p = retail price per litre
        v = call frequency to retailer
        s = per capita brand advertising expenditures
        t = time (year)

(a)

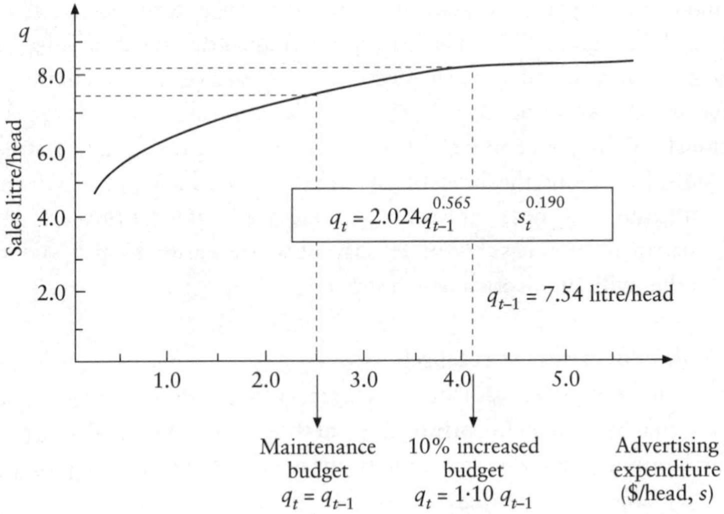

$$q_t = 2.024 q_{t-1}^{0.565} \, s_t^{0.190}$$

q_{t-1} = 7.54 litre/head

| Maintenance budget $q_t = q_{t-1}$ | 10% increased budget $q_t = 1{\cdot}10\, q_{t-1}$ | Advertising expenditure ($/head, s) |

(b)

FIGURE 15.4 (a) *The estimated demand function for brand X.* (b)*The advertising–sales relationship* (Source: Lambin, 1969)

15.3.6 Media planning

Having defined the target, the message content and the expected response, the advertiser must choose the best combination of media support that will allow it to achieve the desired number of exposures to the target within the limits imposed by the advertising budget. Different strategies of how to use the media can be envisaged. Box 15.2 shows the definition of the important terms used in the field of media planning. Different strategies of how to use the media can be envisaged.

The *first* alternative opposes the two objectives of 'reach' and 'frequency': i.e. adopting an *extensive campaign* with a view to reaching the greatest number of people through maximum reach, or adopting an *intensive campaign* to reach, as emphatically as possible, a restricted target through maximum frequency or repetition.

BOX 15.2

Definition of the parameters used in media planning

- *Target*: the specific group of prospects to be reached.
- *Circulation*: the number of physical units through which advertising is distributed.
- *Audience*: the number of people who are exposed to a particular vehicle.
- *Effective audience*: the number of people with the target's characteristics who are exposed to the vehicle.
- *Exposure*: the 'opportunity to see' (OTS) or 'opportunity to hear' (OTH) the message, which does not imply that the person actually sees or hears the advertisement.
- *Reach*: the number of different persons or households exposed to a particular medium vehicle at least once during a specified period of time.
- *Frequency*: the number of times within a specified period of time that a prospect is exposed to the message.
- *Gross rating point (GRP)*: equal to 'reach' multiplied by 'frequency' and measures the total number of exposures (weight).
- *Impact*: the qualitative value of an exposure through a given medium.

Generally, a high degree of reach is necessary when launching a new product or starting an ambitious programme of promotion. On the other hand, a high degree of frequency is required when the message is complex, the product frequently bought and brand loyalty low. However, too much repetition is useless, as it may cause boredom or irritation. Krugman (1975, p. 98), for example, considers that three 'perceived' exposures are often sufficient.

The *second* strategic option involves 'continuity' as opposed to 'intermittence' in advertising: i.e. seeking *continuity* of advertising efforts over time to overcome the forgetting rate, stimulate repeated purchases, oppose rivals' efforts, etc., or seeking *intermittence* (pulsing) in order to optimize consumer learning or reinforcement, or to 'stretch budgets' to coincide with consumption patterns.

The problem is to decide how to schedule advertising. But there is no clear answer to the dilemma. It is important to take into account the nature of the product, its purchase frequency, seasonality in sales, rivals' strategies and the distribution of memory over time. The fact that the life of a message is a function of its communication quality renders the problem even more complicated.

Finally, the *third* strategic choice is between media 'concentration' or media 'diversification': i.e. seeking *diversification* in various types of media in order to enjoy complementarity between them, obtain a better net reach, a better geographical allocation, etc., or *concentration* on a single media in order to dominate the medium best suited to the target, to personalize the campaign and the product and to benefit from economies of scale and discounts.

The solution depends on the segmentation strategy adopted. Diversification is desirable if the firm follows undifferentiated marketing, but if it follows a market niche strategy, then it is probably more effective to concentrate on a single medium.

15.3.7 Criteria for media selection

Media selection is guided by the quantitative and qualitative criteria listed below. Amongst the *quantitative* criteria, the following are important:

- *Target-audience* media habits, i.e. the proportion of the target group that can be reached through the medium.

- The *stability* of the reach over time, for instance from one week to another or from one season to another.

- The possibility of having *frequent exposures* to the message.

- The medium *selectivity* in terms of socio-demographic or lifestyle profiles.

- The *cost per thousand* persons reached, which is a function of the vehicle audience and of the medium cost.

These data are provided by the media themselves, by the media sales houses or by organizations responsible for the control of the media circulation or diffusion.

Qualitative criteria of medium selection must complement the quantitative ones. The following can be noted in particular:

- *Audience attention* probability, which is, for instance, very high for cinemas and very low for outdoor advertising.

- The duration of the *message's life*, i.e. the period during which the message can be perceived.

- The perceptual *environment* of the message.

- The *editorial quality* of the vehicle, i.e. its prestige and credibility.

- The *technical quality* of the medium, for instance, the use of colour, the quality of sound or of images, etc.

- The degree of *advertising saturation* of the vehicle and the presence of competitive advertising.

The final choice is concretized in a *media plan* describing budget allocation between the different media. Once one has chosen the medium, the next decision is to select the *specific vehicles* to advertise in within the medium. Although the choices are complex and numerous, a number of paid research services in media and vehicles selection provide data to help the decision maker. The latter choice is now increasingly made using computer models of vehicle selection.

15.4 ADVERTISING BUDGET DECISIONS

Conceptually, advertising budget decisions can be analysed using marginal rules of economic theory. Expenditure on each method of communication is increased until any further increase reduces profits. Similarly, the allocation of total budget between different methods is such that each instrument is used to the level where all marginal revenues are equal. Economists have developed optimization rules based on elasticities (Dorfman and Steiner, 1954), also extended to situations of oligopoly (Lambin *et al.*, 1975), as well as dynamic models to allow for lagged response to advertising (Palda, 1963; Jacquemin, 1973). The derivation of the optimization rule for the advertising budget is illustrated in Box 15.3.

As for the selling price, this approach is rarely operational in practice because of all the problems of estimating response functions already mentioned in the previous chapter (see sect. 14.3). It is therefore necessary to use other, more general, methods and to use marginal rules only as guidelines. When available, the analysis of elasticities can be useful *a posteriori* to evaluate the effectiveness of both advertising and the salesforce. In this section we shall examine different methods of determining the advertising budget.

15.4.1 Characteristics of advertising response functions

Advertising response curves have important characteristics which must be taken into account in advertising budget decisions.

■ Advertising response functions are typically *non-linear* and subject to the law of diminishing returns, as illustrated in Fig. 15.5(a). Thresholds exist reflecting inertia, perceptual resistance or fatigue effects.

■ The slope of the response curve is determined by the communication quality of the message. For an identical level of advertising expenditure, a very different response curve can be observed as a function of the medium used, the relevance of the message, the creativity of the advertisement, etc.

■ The advertising response is *dynamic* and its effects are distributed over time. The structure of the lagged effects also varies with media, products and advertising themes. In a way, advertising can be viewed as an investment which creates for the brand a lasting demand over time.

■ Last, but not least, the advertising effect does not exist independently of the other marketing factors, such as distribution and price. The interaction effect between these factors is multiplicative, which means that the sum of their isolated effects is different from their joint effects.

The presence of such characteristics simply reflects the complexity of buyers' behaviours. But it also seriously complicates the problem of quantitative estimation both for advertising and the salesforce. For a fuller discussion of the characteristics of sales and market share response functions, see Hanssens *et al.* (1990, chs 6 and 7).

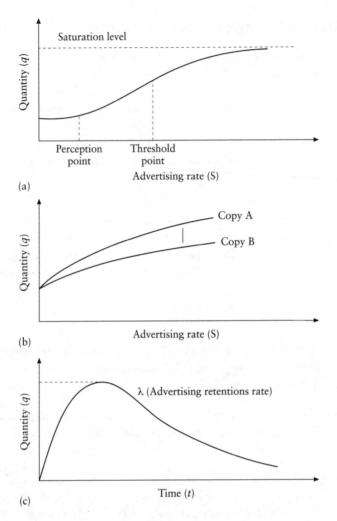

FIGURE 15.5 *Characteristics of advertising response functions*

15.4.2 Cost-oriented advertising budgets

Cost-oriented budgets are calculated on the basis of cost considerations, without explicitly taking demand reactions into account. There are three types of cost-oriented budget: affordable, break-even and percentage of sales.

Affordable budget

The budget is directly linked to the short-term financial possibilities of the company. Advertising will be appropriated after all other unavoidable investments and expenses have been allocated. As soon as things go badly, this budget can be eliminated, and if cash is abundant then it can be spent. The fiscal system also encourages this type of practice, since increased advertising expenditure reduces taxable profit. This is not a method as such, but rather a state of mind reflecting an absence of definite advertising objectives.

Break-even budget

The break-even budget method is based on the analysis of advertising's profitability threshold. The absolute increase in unit sales and in turnover necessary to recoup the incremental increase in advertising expenditure is simply obtained by dividing advertising expenditure (S) by the absolute gross profit margin or by the percentage of gross profit margin:

$$\text{Break-even volume} = S/(P - C)$$

and

$$\text{Break-even turnover} = S/[(P - C)/P]$$

For instance, if the gross profit margin is £60, or 30 per cent of the unit price, the absolute increase in unit sales to recoup a £1.5 million advertising budget will be

$$1\,500\,000/60 = 25\,000 \text{ units}$$

and the break-even turnover

$$1\,500\,000/0.30 = £5\,000\,000$$

To determine the percentage increase of sales volume or turnover necessary to maintain the previous level of profit, one can use the following expression:

$$\text{Percentage sales increase} = \delta Q/Q = 100 \times \delta S/(F + S + \text{Profit})$$

where δS is the proposed change in the budget. The advertiser can determine by how much sales must increase to retain the same level of profit, and also calculate the implicit demand elasticity to advertising, by comparing expected sales levels 'with advertising' to expected volume 'without advertising'.

Using these data, the advertiser can verify whether the proposed budget implies an unrealistic increase in market share given the state of the market, competitors' power, etc. The weakness of the method is that it is strictly an accounting exercise. But clearly some advertising objectives are not necessarily reflected in higher sales in the short-run, even if they have been reached completely. Nevertheless, this type of analysis is useful because the advertiser is encouraged to view advertising as an investment rather than an overhead cost.

The percentage of sales budget

The percentage of sales budget method is used frequently and treats advertising as a cost. In its simplest form the method is based on a fixed percentage of the previous year's sales. One advantage of this procedure is that expenditures are directly related to funds available. Another advantage is its relative simplicity.

Although this method is quite popular, it can easily be criticized from a logical point of view, because it inverts the direction of causality between advertising and sales. Relating advertising appropriation to *anticipated sales* makes more sense, because it recognizes that advertising precedes rather than follows sales. Nevertheless, this approach can lead to absurd situations, reducing the advertising budget when a downturn in sales is predicted and increasing it when turnover is growing, with the risk of overshooting the saturation threshold.

In practice, however, it seems that managements mainly use this method to control total advertising expenditure at the consolidated level of turnover, in order to keep an eye on total marketing expenditure or to make comparisons with competitors. More refined methods are used when deciding on advertising at the brand level.

Cost-oriented advertising budgets are only the first stage of the process of determining the advertising budget. They enable the firm to define the problem in terms of financial resources, production capacity and profitability. As for the determination of prices, these methods must be completed with an analysis of market attitudinal and behavioural responses.

15.4.3 Communication-oriented advertising budgets

This approach, also called the 'task and objective' method, is the one most widely used. It emphasizes communication objectives and the means necessary to reach them. Two methods can be adopted: one based on 'contact', defined in terms of reach and frequency, and one based on 'perception'.

Task and objective budgeting

The method starts either with an objective of reach and frequency for which a budget is calculated, or with a budget constraint for which the best combination of reach and frequency is sought to maximize total exposure. By trying to maximize exposure, this approach places the emphasis on the first level of advertising effectiveness, i.e. communication effectiveness, while clearly linking the communication objectives to costs.

As defined in Box 15.2, the term *exposure* has a very precise meaning, because it only refers to opportunity to see (OTS) or to hear (OTH), which does not imply perception. Newspapers only sell OTS to advertisers: a certain number of readers (maybe) will have the paper in their hands, but this does not imply that they will see the advertisement, or that they will familiarize themselves with it or assimilate it. The method ensures the productivity of the budget by searching for the best way to spend the money in the media given the target audience and given an expected creative level of the campaign. This is why the task and objective method is widely used by advertising agencies. By way of illustration, let us consider the following example.

> A company wants to reach women in the 25–49 age group. The socio-professional profile is determined by the following criteria: business, middle management, or owners of small–medium sized companies. The size of the target population is 3 332 000 women, or 16.7 per cent of women of 15 years old and more. The vehicles are magazines selected for their affinity with the target. The budget is 650 000 francs.

TABLE 15.5 *Task and objective budgeting: an example*

Media plan	Plan 1	Plan 2	Plan 3
Magazine 1	3(1 + 2)	4(1 + 3)	–
Magazine 2	2(2)	–	3(1 + 2)
Magazine 3	3(1 + 2)	4(1 + 3)	4(1 + 3)
Magazine 4	3(1 + 2)	4(1 + 3)	4(1 + 3)
Magazine 5	3(1 + 2)	4(1 + 3)	–
Magazine 6	3(1 + 2)	4(1 + 3)	4(1 + 3)
Budget (in FF)	660 500	652 120	650 130
Reach	67.07%	66.3%	65.4%
Frequency	3.7	4.1	3.7
Gross Rating Point	248.2	271.8	242.0

3(1 + 2) = 1 double page, four colours + 2 single pages, four colours.
Source: Troadec *et al.* (1984, p. 47).

The advertising agency has proposed the three media plans presented in Table 15.5. Each plan in the table shows the number of ads per magazine, the reach, the frequency, the GRP and the budget. Logically plan 2 will be preferred because it has the highest GRP.

The value of this budgeting method is its attempt to search for the best possible allocation of the budget given the profile of the target group and the structure of the audience of each medium or vehicle. Another advantage is its simplicity. The major drawback is its systematic overestimation of the number of people reached by the advertisement. The gap between the number of people 'exposed' and the number of people having 'perceived' the message may be very high.

Perceptual impact budgeting

Perceptual impact budgeting is based on psycho-sociological communication objectives. To achieve these objectives, conditions are defined in terms of the means used (medium, reach, repetitions, perceptions, etc.). Next, the cost of the various activities is calculated and the total determines the necessary budget. What is sought in this form of budget is an impact on one of the three components of attitude (cognitive, affective or behavioural).

This is a much more fundamental approach, based on the learning process (Lavidge and Steiner, 1961) and the resulting hypothesis about the hierarchy of advertising effects (Colley, 1961). The difficulty is that the advertiser must, first, be able to link the communication impact to the perceptual impact, and then the perceptual impact to the attitudinal impact and, finally, to the behavioural response. Typically, the budgeting problem can be stated in the following terms:

How many OTS or exposures to the message in a given medium are necessary to achieve, among 60 per cent of the potential buyers within the target group, the cognitive objective of 'knowing product characteristics', the attitudinal objective 'being convinced of product superiority' and the behavioural objective 'intention-to-buy'?

In the task and objective budget example given above, all the women of the target group were simply supposed to be exposed to the vehicle. This number should be corrected by two factors: first, the probability of reading, which is in general specific to each magazine; and, second, an estimate of the perception probability of the advertisement. This perception probability will be determined by the creativity of the message, its relevance for the target group, its capacity to get attention, etc.

This method is much more demanding, but has the advantage of requiring management and advertising agencies to spell out their assumptions about the relationships between money spent, exposure, perceptions, trial and repeat purchase.

Communication-oriented advertising budgets constitute the second stage of the process of determining the advertising budget. They are in fact an initial way of explicitly taking into account market response. Because it is mainly based on intermediary objectives of communication, the advantage of the method is the emphasis it places on results directly attributable to advertising, and the fact that it allows the advertiser to control the advertising agency's effectiveness.

The limitations of these methods are that there is not necessarily any link between achieving the intermediate communicational objective and the final goal of improving sales. One cannot therefore view measures of communicational effectiveness as substitutes for direct measures linking advertising to sales or market share.

15.4.4 Sales-oriented advertising budgets

Determining a sales- or market-share-oriented advertising budget requires knowledge of the parameters of the response function. In some market situations—in particular where advertising is the most active marketing variable—it is possible to establish this relationship and use it to analyse the effects of various levels of expenditure on market share and profits.

Various models of determination of advertising budget exist in the literature. The most operational among them are the model by Vidale and Wolfe (1957) and the ADBUDG model by Little (1970). Both models have some strong and some weak points which we shall consider briefly. The contribution of economic analysis will also be reviewed.

Budgeting to maximize profit

The advertising optimization rules are presented in Box 15.3. These rules can be used to verify whether the current level of advertising spending is about right or whether the firm is over-advertising. To illustrate, let us use the example presented in Fig. 15.4.

The advertising-sales elasticity is 0.190. The product currently sells for BF6 and the gross profit margin is BF3.30 (55 per cent). Average advertising per 1000 inhabitants is BF3440 with corresponding sales of 4060 units. The current advertising sales ratio is therefore:

$$\alpha = \frac{S}{PQ} = \frac{3440}{6 \times 4060} = 14.1 \, \text{per cent}$$

BOX 15.3

Derivation of the advertising optimization rule

In a monopolistic market, where primary demand is non-expansible, the brand demand function can be written as

$$Q(S) = K_s \cdot S^\varepsilon$$

and the profit function

$$\pi = (P - C) \cdot Q(S) - S - F$$

where S denotes advertising expenditures, ε advertising-sales elasticity, C variable cost and F fixed costs. The optimum is reached when

$$\frac{\delta\pi}{\delta S} = (P - C)\frac{\delta Q}{\delta S} - 1 = 0$$

Multiplying by S/PQ, we obtain the advertising optimization rule expressed by reference to advertising-sales elasticity,

$$\frac{P - C}{P} \cdot \frac{\delta Q}{\delta S} \cdot \frac{S}{Q} - \frac{S}{PQ} = 0$$

Rearranging terms, we obtain the following decision rules:

$$\text{Optimal advertising sales ratio} = \frac{S}{PQ} = (\varepsilon_{q,s}) \cdot \left(\frac{P - C}{P}\right)$$

and the optimal advertising budget is given by

$$\text{Optimum budget} = S^* = \{\varepsilon_{q,s} \cdot (P - C) \cdot K\}^{1/(1 - \varepsilon)}$$

The second-order condition stipulates that $0 \leqslant \varepsilon \leqslant 1$.

At optimality, we should have (see Box 15.3)

$$\alpha_{\text{opt}} = \varepsilon_{q,s}\left(\frac{P - C}{P}\right) = (0.190)(0.55) = 10.4 \text{ per cent}$$

Thus, when only short-term advertising effects are considered, it would appear that the firm is overspending on advertising. The optimal advertising budget would be

$$S_{\text{opt}} = (0.190) \cdot (3.30) \cdot \left[\frac{4060}{3440^{0.190}}\right]^{1/(1 - 0.190)} = \text{BF2372}$$

Thus, current advertising expenditure exceeds the optimal level by 45 per cent. At this level of expenditure, sales would be 3 783 units (-6.8 per cent) and the profit BF10 112 per 1000 inhabitants instead of BF9958 with the current budget—a 1.55 per cent increase. Thus, in this situation the firm should make a trade-off between profit gain and market share loss.

The advertising-sales elasticity estimate, however, is not guaranteed. Adopting a plus or minus 20 per cent margin of error for ε, the optimal advertising budget is included in the interval BF1 854–2 949 per 1000 inhabitants. Note that the upper limit of the budget interval is significantly inferior to the current budget.

Only short-term advertising effects have been considered so far, whereas the presence of advertising lagged effects is suggested in the demand function presented in Fig. 15.4. If the retention rate of advertising (λ) is estimated by the coefficient of lagged sales $Q_{t-1}^{0.565}$ and assuming a discount rate, r, of 10 per cent, then the present value of cumulative advertising elasticity is:

$$\varepsilon_{q,s}\left(\frac{1}{(1-\lambda)/(1+r)}\right) = 0.190\left(\frac{1}{(1-0.565)/(1+0.10)}\right) = 0.391$$

If the firm takes a long view, the optimal budget is then BF4877, which is 42 per cent above the current advertising budget. Here, again, the firm must decide which perspective is the most relevant, given its strategic objectives. For the derivation of the dynamic optimization rule, see Lambin and Peeters (1977, ch. 15).

The optimization rules used in this example are adapted to a situation of monopolistic competition where competitive advertising and reactions can be safely neglected in the analysis. For an extension of these optimization rules to oligopolies, see Lambin et al. (1975).

The normative value of this type of economic analysis is reduced, not only because of the ever-present uncertainty about the true value of the response coefficients, but also because the advertiser faces multiple objectives other than profit maximization. Also, the advertising quality (copy and media) is taken here at its average value, while large differences may exist from one campaign to another. For these reasons, the output of economic analysis should be used as a guideline for advertising budget decisions and be complemented by other approaches.

The Vidale and Wolfe advertising model

The model developed by Vidale and Wolfe expresses the following relationship between sales (in units or value) and advertising expenditure (see Box 15.4 for an explanation of the symbols):

$$\frac{ds}{dt} = \left[\beta(A)\frac{S-s}{S}\right] - (1-\lambda)s$$

The equation states that, within a given period, the increase in sales (ds/dt) due to advertising is equal to:

■ The product of the sales response constant per dollar (a) of advertising when sales are zero and (b) of the rate of advertising during the period (response effect) ...

■ ... adjusted by the proportion of the untapped market potential (saturation effect) ...

■ ... reduced by the fraction of current sales that will decrease in the absence of advertising because of product obsolescence, competing advertising, etc. (depreciation effect).

This is an interesting model because it takes into account the main features of advertising response functions while explicitly setting out the key parameters to be estimated. As an illustration, let us consider the following example.

Sales of brand X are $40 000 and the saturation level is $100 000; the response constant is $4 and the brand is losing 10 per cent of its sales per period when advertising is stopped. By adopting a $10 000 advertising budget, the brand could expect a $20 000 sales increase.

$$\frac{ds}{dt} = \left[4(10\ 000)\frac{100\ 000 - 40\ 000}{100\ 000} \right] - 0.10(40\ 000) = 20\ 000$$

One can also state the problem in terms of the advertising budget required to achieve a given sales objective. Referring to Box 15.4, the equation has to be solved for A, the advertising budget.

BOX 15.4

Comparing two advertising budget models

The Vidale and Wolfe model:

$$\frac{ds}{dt} = \left[\beta(A).\left(\frac{S-s}{S}\right) \right] - (1-\lambda)s$$

where ds/dt = sales increase per period
      β = sales response constant when $s = 0$
      A = advertising expenditures
      s = company or brand sales
      S = saturation level of sales
      λ = sales retention rate

Little's ADBUDG model

$$MS(t) = MS(min) + [MS(max) - MS(min)].\frac{Adv^{\gamma}}{\delta + Adv^{\gamma}}$$

where $MS(t)$ = initial market share
     $MS(min)$ = minimum market share with zero advertising
     $MS(max)$ = maximum market share with saturation advertising
     Adv = effective advertising (adjusted for media and copy effectiveness)
     γ = advertising sensitivity coefficient
     δ = constant

Source: Vidale and Wolfe (1957) and Little (1970).

The Vidale and Wolfe model does, however, have some weak points:

- The model does not allow explicit consideration of marketing variables other than advertising, such as price, distribution, etc.

- The model does not integrate competitive advertising and is therefore implementable only in monopolistic situations.

- The model assumes that advertising merely obtains new customers and increased customer usage is neglected.

- The model does not explicitly consider possible variations in advertising quality, unless one could assume different sales constants per medium or per advertising theme.

- In some markets, it is difficult to estimate the absolute market potential.

Vidale and Wolfe's model has an interesting conceptual structure, but its range of application is limited.

The ADBUDG model

The ADBUDG model, developed by Little (1970), can be applied to a market where primary demand is non-expansible and where advertising is a determining factor in sales and market share development. The model establishes a relationship between market share and advertising and assumes that managers are able to provide answers to the following five questions:

1. What is the current level of advertising expenditure for the brand?
2. What would the market share be if advertising were cut to zero?
3. What would the maximum market share be if advertising were increased a great deal, say to saturation (saturation advertising)?
4. What would the market share be if the current level of advertising were halved?
5. What would the market share be if the current level of advertising were increased by 50 per cent?

The market share level estimates in response to these five questions can be represented as five points on a market share response to an advertising curve, as illustrated in Fig. 15.6. The ADBUDG model can be expressed as:

$$MS_t = MS_{min} + (MS_{max} - MS_{min}) \cdot \frac{Adv^\varepsilon}{\delta + Adv^\varepsilon}$$

where MS_t is the initial market share, MS_{min} is the minimum market share with zero advertising, MS_{max} is the maximum market share with saturation advertising, Adv is effective advertising (adjusted for media and copy effectiveness), ε is the advertising sensitivity coefficient and δ is a constant. The expected market share in any given period is then equal to:

- The *minimum* market share expected at the end of the period if advertising is cut to zero (depreciation effect) ...

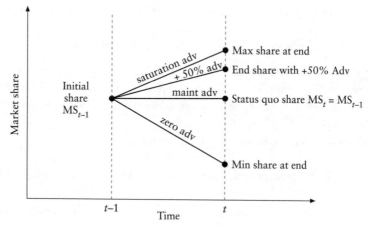

(a) Static advertising–sales response curve: input data

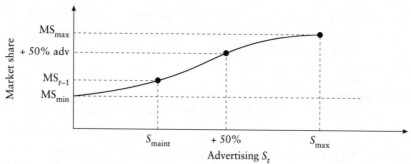

(b) Static advertising–sales response curve: graphic representation

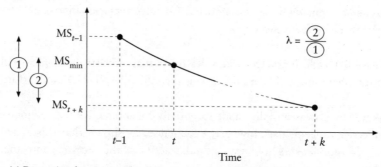

(c) Dynamic advertising–sales response curve: graphic deduction of retention rate

FIGURE 15.6 *The ADBUDG model* (Source: *Little, 1970*)

■ ... plus a *fraction* of the maximum market share change due to advertising; this maximum change is equal to the difference between the maximum share expected with saturation advertising and the minimum share expected with zero advertising.

■ The intensity of the response is determined by an 'advertising sensitivity coefficient' characterized by two parameters: ε, which influences the shape of the response function and δ, which is a moderator factor. Both parameters are determined by input data.

Effective advertising is given by the following expression:

$$\text{Adv}(t) = \{\text{Medium efficiency}(t)\} . \{\text{Copy effectiveness}(t)\} . \{\text{Adv dollars}\}$$

Both indices will be assumed to have a reference value of 1.0. These indices can be determined on the basis of copy testing and media exposure data.

This is an interesting model in many respects, and has most of the features of advertising response functions. Furthermore, it can be easily estimated on microcomputers in interactive mode. Thus, users can test the model themselves without any help from outside experts. The model's strong points are as follows:

■ The model parameters can be estimated either on the basis of management judgements using the five-questions procedure outlined above, or through econometric analysis of historical or experimental data.

■ The dependent variable can be sales, market share or measures of cognitive response, such as awareness.

■ The advertising input data can be adjusted for advertising quality using indices of media efficiency and copy effectiveness.

It is also possible to add marketing variables other than advertising, which make the models more difficult to manipulate. The model used is then the BRANDAID model (Little, 1979).

The ADBUDG model was initially made essentially for interactive use relying on the decision maker's subjective judgements. However, experience has shown that this approach is elusive because most decision makers hold only a small fraction of the necessary information.

On the other hand, it forms a useful framework for integrating objective information coming from various sources and for simulating the implications of different advertising strategies on market share and profits (for a similar approach, see Lambin, 1972).

15.4.5 Deciding the size of the salesforce

Determining the number of salespeople required is a problem logically similar to the advertising budget. In practice, however, it can be resolved more simply because market response is easier to measure. Different approaches are possible. The simplest no doubt is the one based on the salesperson's *workload*. An example of its application was shown in Chapter 13 (see Table 13.4, p. 192). The procedure is as follows.

- The underlying philosophy in the call-load approach is that large customers should be serviced differently from medium-sized customers, and medium-sized customers differently from small customers. Thus, the first step is to have a *breakdown of customer by class*.

- The next step is to develop a theoretical *call frequency* for each class. Experience shows that as a customer grows larger, the number of sales calls does not grow in direct proportion to the increase in sales. Talley (1961, p. 8) suggested that the relationship between customer size and sales calls can be clearly seen when these two factors are plotted on semi-log paper, which reflects the presence of diminishing returns. For every customer class, a specific call frequency is provided and the total workload is obtained by multiplying the call frequency times the number of accounts in any class.

- In the third step, the *number of calls* made by an average salesperson during one year must be determined. The factors to consider here are: number of working days after deducting holidays, weekends, vacations, etc.; percentage of non-selling time devoted to sales meetings, sick leave, laboratory training, etc.; number of calls made per day by salesperson and by territory; and variation in call capacity between urban and rural territories.

Given the number of visits that a salesperson can make in a given customer class, it is then possible to determine the size of the necessary salesforce from the following expression:

$$\text{Size of salesforce} = \frac{\text{Number of customers per class} \times \text{call frequency}}{\text{Average number of calls per salesperson}}$$

The calculation is repeated for each customer class. This approach is valid for current customers but should also be extended to prospective customers. For other methods of setting the size of the salesforce, see Semlow (1959) and Lambert (1968).

Other methods are based on direct or indirect measures of market response to an increase in the frequency of calls through the salesforce. The method developed by Semlow is based on several indicators of buying power within each sales territory. A successful application of this method in the insurance sector is presented by Lambin (1965).

In business-to-business markets, direct sales measures of visit frequency are more easily obtainable. An econometric study conducted by Lambert (1968) in the hospitals market has contributed towards a significant improvement in the overall allocation of selling efforts among sales territories.

15.5 INTERNATIONAL ADVERTISING

The debate on whether to customize or standardize the marketing mix (see Chapter 2) is particularly acute in the field of international advertising. Academics and practitioners alike are still divided on the advisability of using a standardized (universal) or localized (individualized) advertising approach in international campaigns. Advertisers who use the standardized approach argue that consumers anywhere in the world have the same basic needs and desires and can therefore be persuaded by universal appeals. On the other hand, advertisers who follow the localized approach assert that the success of an advertising campaign in a global environment requires *cultural empathy* (the ability to identify with different cultures) and that consumers differ from country to country and must accordingly be reached by advertising that is specific to their respective countries. In this section, we shall first briefly review the limitations and obstacles to global advertising and then examine the alternative international advertising strategies.

15.5.1 Limitations on global advertising

In the theory of communication it is well established that an individual's cultural environment significantly affects the way he or she perceives information. Consequently, if a sender of a message lives in a cultural environment different from his or her intended receiver and wishes to communicate effectively, a knowledge of the receiver's culture is necessary (Schramm, 1954). To test this argument different empirical studies have attempted to measure the extent to which advertising practitioners are standardizing their offerings.

The most recent research results reveal that the majority of the studied firms are guided by the localized approach (Kanso, 1992; Shao *et al.*, 1992). The findings of these studies suggest that if human wants and needs are in effect more or less universal, the way to address these wants and needs is not.

> ... although the story of Boy meets Girl is as old as time, the 'body language' of how Boy meets Girl varies considerably from culture to culture. If we get the language even subtly wrong, the local consumer rejects the whole concept.   (Perry, 1992)

In addition to the cultural issue, many other obstacles exist to discourage attempts at advertising standardization.

Language   Language diversity in world markets is a major issue in communication. Difficulties with language can arise through carelessness in translation, but also because of the capability of languages to convey meaning. Also, some brand names may have a strong resemblance to a word *not used in polite company* in another country. Examples in French are Pet milk products and a toothpaste called 'Cue'. Similarly in Spanish, with the Chevrolet brand called 'Nova'.

A standardized global advertising campaign is therefore vulnerable to distortion, as a result not only of language but of local slang or regional dialect. For a global brand, the ideal is to search out a nonsense word that is pronounceable everywhere but has no specific meaning anywhere; 'Kodak' is a famous example. Another good example, with a positive meaning, is 'Visa'.

Use of foreign language   In several countries the use of foreign words is prohibited. For example, France prohibits totally the use of English words that already have an equivalent in the French language, such as 'jumbo jet', 'supermarket', 'cash-and-carry', etc.

Media availability   The ability to standardize a campaign internationally presupposes the international media availability. Television is by far the most important media internationally, yet two-thirds of Western Europe may be said to be under-served in terms of programme choice, with government controlling the number of television channels, amount of broadcasting hours and availability of advertising. There are also wide differences in television viewing rates.

> Television viewing habits vary broadly in Europe, with 230.6 minutes yesterday in the UK, 202.9 in Portugal, 198.2 in Spain and 126.0 in Switzerland, 137.6 in Denmark, etc.
>
> *(Source: Euro Time Survey*, 1994)

Similar differences or restrictions also exist for the press and for radio. See the European Planning Guide, 1995–96 in *Media & Marketing Europe* (1995).

Legal considerations   In most countries, there are restrictions on the use of advertising for certain product categories. For example, alcohol advertising is banned in Austria, Denmark, Finland, France, Norway and Switzerland. It is restricted by law in Ireland, Italy, Luxembourg, Portugal and Spain. It is restricted voluntarily in Germany and Holland. It is permitted in Belgium and Greece (*Source:* Carat, 1994).

Symbols   Symbols are abstract characters that represents ideas, feelings and other aspects of culture. The way symbols are perceived varies among countries. For example, snakes symbolize 'danger' in Sweden and 'wisdom' in Korea.

Colours   The significance of colours can vary from culture to culture. In Western European countries colours may be used to identify emotions: to 'see red', to be 'green with envy' or to 'feel blue'. Also, black signifies mourning in Western countries, whereas white is often the colour of mourning in Eastern nations. Green is popular in Muslim countries, while red and black are unpopular in several African countries. The marketer needs to know these patterns in planning products, packages and advertising as some international firms have been obliged to change their logos.

Family structure   In Europe, what constitutes a household is the nuclear family of two parents and two children; while in Africa, the extended family includes grandparents, uncles, aunts, etc. It can be seen, therefore, that even the target group may differ from one country to another.

Consuming habits   In the USA, orange juice is consumed at breakfast but not in most areas of France. Thus, an orange juice's brand should be positioned as a breakfast drink in the USA and as a refreshment in France. Similarly, toothpaste is a cosmetic product in Italy and Greece, but a domestic product in Holland.

Social roles   Gender roles are sometimes very different from one country to another. For example, in Arabian countries, shopping is always done by women and never by men.

Tradition   What is viewed as 'appropriate' in one country may be very different in another.

15.5.2 Alternative international advertising strategies

As already mentioned in Chapter 2 (see 'From international to transnational marketing', p. 56), too often the standardization versus customization issue is presented in terms of an *all or nothing*

TABLE 15.6 *Alternative international branding and advertising strategies*

	International advertising	
Brand name	Standardized	Non-standardized
Same brand name	*Strategy 1:* Brand and advertise globally	*Strategy 2:* Brand globally and advertise locally
Different brand names	*Strategy 3:* Brand locally and harmonize advertising	*Strategy 4:* Brand and advertise locally

Source: Adapted from Sandler and Shani (1992).

question. In reality, intermediate solutions exist and the real question is to know how to reconcile the two approaches.

For example, in most cases brand and advertising standardization are implicitly considered as interdependent decisions. Thus two basic options are available: to standardize both or not to standardize both. Following Sandler and Shani (1991), we support the idea that branding and advertising are two independent decisions that can occur in varying combinations, as shown in Table 15.6.

Brand globally and advertise globally

Strategy 1 standardizes both brand names and advertising. This situation will tend to prevail in a global environment where the global forces are strong and the local forces are weak. Classical examples of this strategy are: Marlboro, Hermès, Coca-Cola, Gillette Sensor, Sony Walkman, Levi's, Gucci, Ariel, etc.

These genuinely global brands deliver benefits to the consumers who value them in all countries: 'Coke' for the convenience and the appeal of American young imagery; Sony for the attraction of 'music on the move'; Hermès for fashion and romance. The benefits can be hard-to-copy innovations like Pampers or Polaroïd instant cameras, or emotional benefits like Dunhill or Cartier.

> An especially strong kind of positioning to be exploited globally involves national stereotypes: German quality in cars, for example, or French style and romance in perfume, or English conservatism in men's tailoring, or American youth and fun in fast food.   (Riesenbeck and Freeling, 1991)

Procter & Gamble seems to have adopted this policy regarding brand names since 70 per cent of its turnover is made by brands such as Oil of Ulay, Ariel, Pampers, Clearasil and Vicks, that are sold all over the world. There is one exception: the P&G shampoo 'Wash & Go' is launched in

60 different countries, but under six different brand names. The concept 'two in one' is the same in each market, however. Slight variations in the advertising expressions also exist. This last example illustrates the fact that a complete standardization will probably never be possible.

Brand globally but advertise locally

Strategy 2 standardizes brand names but localizes advertising campaigns. This situation will probably prevail in transnational environments where both global and local forces are strong. Examples of this strategy are given by Bacardi and Volvo and also, to a lesser degree, by P&G with the shampoo 'Wash & Go'. These firms use the same brand name worldwide but the advertising themes and/or expressions are adjusted for each country.

In instances where brand standardization tends to be high, localized advertising enables the firm to consider local culture and sensitivity and to position the brand in the local market.

Brand locally and harmonize advertising globally

Strategy 3 harmonizes advertising but keeps local brand names. This is a strategy adopted by European firms, like Unilever and Kraft who have developed their portfolio of brands through acquisitions. Unilever management, for example, seems to believe (see Fraser, 1990) that as long as core brand values can be harmonized, the name does not really matter. Unilever tends to draw the line in its harmonizing policy at changing names. As mentioned in Fraser (1990):

> Unless the original name is meaningless, it would be very dangerous to drop it. Names that have been built up over years and years are an essential part of brand's franchise or equity.

This is the justification of the approach taken with a Unilever fabric softener called Cajoline in France, Coccolino in Italy, Kuschelweich in Germany, Mimosin in Spain and Snuggle in the USA. Although the name is different in each country, it suggests cuddly softness everywhere, and the product benefits are always presented by a talking teddy bear—a universally understood symbol of softness. Far from being a disadvantage, the different names actually bring the brand closer to the hearts of local consumers.

The 'same advertising–different name' approach has also been used for the fish fingers of Unilever. The well-known salty sea captain has appeared in commercials throughout Europe even though he is variously known as Birds Eye, Findus or Iglo. All he has to do is change his cap and speak a different language in each country, which leads to significant cost savings in the production of television commercials.

Kraft General Food also manages to combine centralized European marketing with local brand sensitivity. It does not, for example, market a multinational ground coffee brand, but it does own over a dozen such brands in various European countries where it is the uncontested number one.

> Because of the way the company grew, mainly via acquisitions, we control many local brands. There was a tentative effort by Klaus Jacobs (the former proprietor of Jacobs Suchard which was bought by General Foods) to internationalize them. But it has been

abandoned. Discouraged by the costs of such an alignment, management also recognized the gigantic waste that killing off the local brands, rich in capital and heritage, would represent.   (Subramanian, 1993)

This attitude is very different from the one adopted by Mars. Has Mars carried things too far by investing major sums in the name changes of successful brands: Raider to Twix, Marathon to Snickers, Kal-Kan to Whiskas? Too much centralization leads naturally to excessive standardization.

In Europe, the dominant concept to manage diversity seems to be: 'Brand locally, harmonize advertising globally'. For the Americans, on the contrary, the natural concept seems to be: 'Brand globally, advertise locally'.

Brand locally and advertise locally

Strategy 4 will be adopted in environments where the local forces are strong and the global forces are weak. In general, it is considered that this situation prevails in the food sector where tastes, flavours and colours are important factors.

This was typically the strategy adopted by Unilever until recently as explained above (Omo, All, Persil, Skip, Via, ...). This strategy of complete decentralization seems more and more difficult to maintain for an international firm, because *'speed and scale'* are, and will become, more and more crucial success factors in the newly integrated European market.

We were at trouble competing well with companies like P&G because we needed speed and scale—and we didn't have that when we had to go through 16 or 17 countries, explains Alfred Jung, one of Lever's first Euromanagers.   (Dalgic, 1992)

In the European context, the word *harmonization* of branding policies rather than *standardization* is probably more appropriate.

SUMMARY

Marketing communication refers to all the signals and messages made by the firm to its various publics. The four major communication tools, called the communication mix, are personal selling, advertising, sales promotion and public relations. The four tasks in designing a communication programme are communication objective, message execution, media planning and communication effectiveness. Owing to developments in communication technology, the role of the salesforce is undergoing a major transformation and is on the increase in strategic marketing, the more routine tasks being assumed by cheaper, impersonal means of communication. When a firm resorts to advertising, it is effectively following a pull communication strategy. Its main objective is to create a brand image and brand equity and to ensure co-operation from distributors. Advertising objectives can be defined by reference to the three levels of market response; cognitive, affective and behavioural. There are three types of measure of advertising effectiveness: perceptual, attitudinal and behavioural. The selection of media is based on a set of criteria, quantitative and qualitative. Different methods of setting the advertising budgets are used in practice, the most popular being the task and objective method. Two mathematical models, Vidale and Wolfe and ADBUDG, can be used when the key parameters of the advertising response function are known. One of the key issues in international advertising is the standardization versus customization question. In reality several alternative solutions exist to this problem, namely the strategy of 'harmonized advertising'.

QUESTIONS AND PROBLEMS

1. Re-examine the five objectives of advertising communication described in this chapter. Look for examples of advertising messages that illustrate these objectives in two different vehicles or media.
2. Select a brand of a consumer good you know well and use the Maloney grid to identify three communication platforms to suggest to your advertising agency.
3. Sales representatives of a FMCG company visit hypermarkets once every fortnight and supermarkets once a month. The company is rethinking the organization of its salesforce for an area with 200 supermarkets and 30 hypermarkets. Knowing that it takes a sales representative an average of 90 minutes to visit a hypermarket and 60 minutes to visit a supermarket, how many sales representatives will the company need for this area? (A representative works 8 hours a day, 5 days a week.)
4. Compare the goals of product advertising, institutional advertising, response advertising and publicity.
5. The advertising manager of a large consumer goods company proposes to the management committee a FF1 million advertising budget increase that should generate a FF5 million increase in sales revenue. The general manager asks you to prepare a note and to formulate a recommendation to the committee. How would you proceed to prepare this recommendation?
6. A manufacturer wishes to determine the level of advertising that will maintain his current sales growth rate at 4 per cent. Current sales are $50 000 and it is estimated that sales could reach a level of $150 000 at saturation. Sales response to advertising dollars is estimated at 1.1, and it has been determined that the company would lose 0.2 of its sales per period if no advertising were made. How much advertising is needed to maintain the desired growth rate? What rate of growth would be sustained if $20 000 was spent per period for advertising?
7. The ABC Company has been selling its highly rated line of System X colour TV sets for $700, $500 and $300 respectively. These prices have been relatively uncompetitive in the market. After some study the company substitutes several cheaper components (which engineering says may reduce the quality of performance slightly) and passes on the savings to the consumer in the form of a $100 price reduction on each model. Company ABC institutes a price-oriented promotional campaign that neglects to mention that the second generation System X sets are different from the first. Is the company's competitive strategy ethical?

REFERENCES

Aaker, D.A. and J.M. Carman (1982), 'Are You Overadvertising?', *Journal of Advertising Research*, vol. 22, August–September, pp. 57–70.

Assmus, G., J.U. Farley and D.R. Lehman (1984), 'How Advertising Affect Sales?: Meta-Analysis of Econometric Results', *Journal of Marketing Research*, vol. 21, February, pp. 65–74.

Bell, D. (1979), 'L'avenir: la société de communication', *Harvard-L'Expansion*, vol. 57, Winter, pp. 9–19.

Bogart, L. (1986), *Strategy in Advertising*. Lincolnwood, Ill.: NTC Business Books.

Bryk, C.S. and R. Davis (1973), 'Ads Work: Texasgulf Proves in Positioning Campaigns for Acids', *Industrial Marketing*, vol. 58, August, pp. 52–62.

Carat (1994), *European Televisions Minibook*. London: NTC Publications.

Chaval, B. (1986), *Publicité institutionnelle et sponsoring*. Unpublished memoir, IAG, Louvain-la-Neuve, Belgium.

Colley, R.H. (1961), *Defining Advertising Goals for Measured Advertising Results*. New York: Association of National Advertisers.

Dalgic, T. (1992), 'Euromarketing: Charting the Map for globalization', *International Marketing Review*, vol. 9, no. 5, pp. 31–42.

Dalrymple, D.J. and L.J. Parsons (1976), *Marketing Management: Text and Cases*. New York: J. Wiley & Sons.

Darmon, R.Y., M. Laroche and J.V. Petrov (1982), *Le marketing, Fondements et Applications*, 2nd edn. Montréal: McGraw-Hill.

Davis, E., J.O. Kay and J. Star (1991), 'Is Advertising Rational?', *Business Strategy Review*, vol. 2.

de Jaham, M.R. (1979), 'Le défi de la publicité institutionnelle', *Revue Française du Marketing*, Cahier 77, pp. 33–41.

Dhalla, N.K. (1978), 'Assessing the Long Term Value of Advertising', *Harvard Business Review*, vol. 56, January–February, pp. 87–95.

Dorfman, P. and P.O. Steiner (1954), 'Optimal Advertising and Optimal Quality', *American Economic Review*, vol. 44, December, pp. 826–33.

European Planning Guide, 1995–96, 'Media & Marketing Europe', August 1995.

Forsyth, D.P. (1987), *Cost of a Business-to-Business Sales Call*. McGraw-Hill Research, Laboratory of Advertising Performance, LAP Report 8013.9.

Fraser, I. (1990), 'Now only the Name's Not the Same', *Eurobusiness*, April, pp. 22–5.

Gross, I. (1972), 'The Creative Aspects of Advertising', *Sloan Management Review*, vol. 14, Autumn, pp. 83–109.

Hanssens, D.M., L.J. Parsons and R.L. Schultz (1990), *Market Response Models: Econometric and Time Series Analysis*. Boston: Kluwer Academic Publishers.

Jacquemin, A. (1973), 'Optimal Control and Advertising Policy', *Metroeconomica*, vol. 25, May, pp. 200–7.

Kanso, A. (1992), 'International Advertising Strategies: Global Commitment to Local Vision', *Journal of Advertising Research*, January–February, pp. 10–14.

Kapferer, J.N. (1985), 'Publicité: une révolution des méthodes de travail', *Revue Française de Gestion*, September–December, pp. 102–11.

Kotler, P. (1991), *Marketing Management*, 7th edn. Englewood Cliffs, New Jersey: Prentice Hall Inc.

Krugman, H.E. (1975), 'The Impact of Television Advertising: Learning without Involvement', *Public Opinion Quarterly*, Autumn, pp. 349–56.

Lambert, Z.V. (1968), *Setting the Size of the Sales Force*. University Park, Pennsylvania University Press.

Lambin, J.J. (1965), *La décision commerciale face à l'incertain*. Paris: Dunod.

Lambin, J.J. (1969), 'Measuring the Profitability of Advertising: An Empirical Study', *Journal of Industrial Economics*, vol. 17, April, pp. 86–103.

Lambin, J.J. (1972), 'A Computer On-Line Marketing Mix Model', *Journal of Marketing Research*, May, pp. 119–26.

Lambin, J.J., P.A. Naert and A. Bultez (1975), 'Optimal Advertising Behavior in Oligopoly', *European Economic Review*, vol. 6, pp. 105–28.

Lambin, J.J. and R. Peeters (1977), *La Gestion Marketing des Enterprises*. Paris: Presses Univérsitaires de France.

Lavidge, R.J. and G.A. Steiner (1961), 'A Model of Predictive Measurement of Advertising Effectiveness', *Journal of Marketing*, vol. 25, October, pp. 59–62.

Little, J.D.C. (1970), 'Models and Managers, the Concept of a Decision Calculus', *Management Science*, vol. 16, April, pp. 466–85.

Little, J.D.C. (1979), 'Decision Support for Marketing Managers', *Journal of Marketing*, vol. 43, Summer, pp. 9–26.

Maloney, J.C. (1961), 'Marketing Decisions and Attitude Research', in Baker, G.L. (ed.), *Effective Marketing Coordination*. Chicago: American Marketing Association.

Nelson, D. (1974), 'Advertising as Information', *Journal of Political Economy*, vol. 82, July–August, pp. 729–54.

Ogilvy, D. (1964), *Les confessions de David Ogilvy*. Paris, Hachette: Collection Entreprise.

Palda, K.S. (1963), *The Measurement of Cumulative Advertising Effects*. Englewood Cliffs, New Jersey: Prentice Hall Inc.

Perry, M. (1992), *Investing in Brands*. Barcelona, IAA 33rd World Congress, September 29.

Reeves, R. (1970), 'Reality in Advertising', in Klepner, O. and I. Settel (eds), *Exploring Advertising*. Englewood Cliffs, New Jersey: Prentice Hall Inc.

Riesenbeck, H. and A. Freeling (1991), 'How Global are Global Brands?', *The McKinsey Quarterly*, no. 4, pp. 3–18.

Rossiter, J.R. and L. Percy (1987), *Advertising and Promotion Management*. New York: McGraw-Hill Book Co.

Sandler, D.M. and D. Shani (1992), 'Brand Globally but Advertise Locally, An Empirical Investigation', *International Marketing Review*, vol. 9, no. 4, pp. 18–31.

Schramm, W. (1954), *The Process and Effects of Mass Communication*, 1st edn. Urbana, Ill.: University of Illinois Press.

Séguéla, J. (1982), *Hollywood lave plus blanc*. Paris: Flammarion.

Semlow, W.J. (1959), 'How Many Salesmen Do You Need?', *Harvard Business Review*, vol. 37, May–June, pp. 126–32.

Shao, A.T., L.P. Shao and D.H. Shao (1992), 'Are Global Markets with Standardized Advertising Campaigns Feasible?', *Journal of International Consumer Marketing*, vol. 4, no. 3, pp. 5–16.

Simon, J. (1983), 'Advertising Sales Effects Can be Measured and Evaluated Very Well', *International Journal of Advertising*, vol. 2, October–December, pp. 331–41.

Subramanian, D. (1993), 'In Search of Eurobrands', *Media & Marketing*, pp. 22–3.

Talley, W.J. (1961), 'How to Design Sales Territories?', *Journal of Marketing*, vol. 25, January, pp. 7–13.

Troadec, L. *et al.* (1984), *Exercices de marketing*. Paris: Les Editions d'Organisation.

Twedt, D.W. (1969), 'How To Plan New Products, Improve Old Ones and Create Better Advertising', *Journal of Marketing*, vol. 33, pp. 53–7.

Van Hecke, T. (1988), 'Avis aux mécènes: la brique est porteuse', *La Libre Belgique*, 11 June.

Variot, J.F. (1985), *L'identité de marque*. Paris: Institut de Recherches et d'Études Publicitaires, Journées d'Études de l'IREP, June.

Vaughn, R. (1986), 'How Advertising Works: A Planning Model', *Journal of Advertising Research*, vol. 20, October, pp. 27–33.

Vidale, M.L. and H.B. Wolfe (1957), 'An Operation Research Study of Sales Response to Advertising', *Operations Research,* June, pp. 370–81.

Waterson, M.J. (1992), 'International Advertising Expenditures', *International Journal of Advertising*, vol. 11, no. 1, pp. 14–67.

Xardel, D. (1982), 'Vendeurs: nouveaux rôles, nouveaux comportements', *Harvard-L'Expansion*, Summer, pp. 59–75.

FURTHER READING

Chandon, J.L. (1976), L'état de l'art en matière de planification publicitaire. Unpublished paper, Université de Nice.

Clothier, P. (1992), *Multi-Level Marketing: A Practical Guide to Successful Network Marketing Selling*, 2nd edn. London: Kogan Page.

Davis, E., J.O. Kay and J. Star (1991), 'Is Advertising Rational?', *Business Strategy Review*, vol. 2.

Dayan, A. *et al.* (1985), *Marketing*. Paris: Presses Universitaires de France.

Lambin, J.J. (1975), 'What is the Real Impact of Advertising?', *Harvard Business Review*, May–June, pp. 139–47.

Lambin, J.J. (1976), *Advertising, Competition and Market Conduct in Oligopoly Over Time*. Amsterdam: North Holland Publishing Co.

Lambin, J.J. (1989), 'La marque et le comportement de choix de l'acheteur', in Kapferer, J.N. and Thoenig, J.P. (eds), *La marque*. Paris: McGraw-Hill.

Lilien, G.L., P. Kotler and S. Moorthy (1992), *Marketing Models*. Prentice-Hall International.

McNiven, M.A. (1980), 'Votre budget de publicité est-il efficace?', *Harvard-L'Expansion*, Summer, pp. 96–105.

Serieyx, H. (1985), 'Mobiliser l'intelligence dans l'entreprise: le management participatif', *Futuribles*, pp. 21–34.

Waterson, M.J. (1992), 'International Advertising Expenditures', *International Journal of Advertising*, vol. 11, no. 1, pp. 14–67.

Xardel, D. (1985), 'Les cinq mutations de la vente', *Revue Française de Gestion,* September–December, pp. 112–16.

Xardel, D. (1986), *Le marketing direct, Collection Que sais-je?* Paris: Presses Universitaires de France.

PART 5

Case Studies

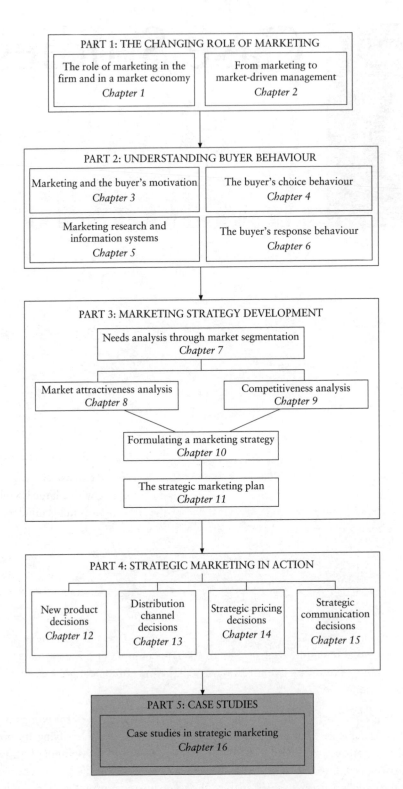

FIGURE PT5.1 *The structure of this book*

16 CASE STUDIES IN STRATEGIC MARKETING

CASE STUDY 1

The Lander Company

[This case was prepared by W.J. Stanton in *Fundamentals of Marketing*, McGraw-Hill Book Co.]

In the fall of 1970, Mr Luis Lander, president and majority stockholder of Lander Ltd, returned from a business trip to the United States. While there, he had visited extensively with a number of former business associates one of whom was a marketing executive with a large US oil company. His discussions with this particular individual had raised some doubts in his mind as to whether or not his company was sufficiently conscious of the value of marketing.

Mr Luis Lander's father, a prominent South American businessman, had founded Lander Ltd in 1927 to weave cotton cloth. The company remained a family-held enterprise until 1940 when the public was invited to subscribe to the new capital required to finance the company's expansion.

Immediately following the Second World War, the company experienced a remarkable growth. By 1970, the number of employees had risen to 4000, the number of spindles to over 100 000, and the number of looms to over 4200. Investment in plant and equipment increased ten-fold during this 15-year period.

In the late 1940s and early 1950s, Mr Luis Lander widened the scope of the company's activities through both backward and forward integration and, also, by diversifying its product line. Backward integration was accomplished by Lander's entry into the spinning business so as to supply its own yarn. Forward integration was undertaken through the introduction of printing, finishing, and dyeing processes which enabled the company to control the entire production cycle of its products.

Lander sold its products through a network of 46 independent distributors. Cloth was shipped to these distributors who held it on consignment until sold to retailers and to small manufacturers who produced limited lines of ready-to-wear apparel. Consigned goods were usually sold within 30 days of delivery to distributors. Another group of customers consisted of some 72 large garment manufacturers who were served directly from the company's plant.

Mr Lander's oil company friend had surprised him considerably with his views on the marketing concept. 'In essence,' his friend told him, 'this concept holds that marketing is literally the most important part of a business. You're in business to make a sale, and you can best do this by understanding the wants and needs of the ultimate consumer of your products. Once this much is understood, all of your actions—and certainly all of your decisions—must be geared to finding ways to satisfy these wants. Everybody in the organization must focus on the consumer and must strive constantly to find new and better ways of serving him or her.'

While Mr Lander thought that he understood what his friend was saying, he was not too sure of how this concept should be implemented within his own organization. His friend had pointed out that Lander Ltd really had no marketing organization and that its product line was made up largely by designers and colour experts who had very little contact with the housewives or the male consumers who ultimately purchased the fabrics in one form or another produced by the company. It was also pointed out that Lander Ltd had no marketing research department, did no consumer advertising, and did little or nothing to help its customers to sell the merchandise in which their products were incorporated.

In attempting to apply the concept to his company, Mr Lander considered setting up a separate company which could be likened to a sales agent. Essentially, this new company would serve solely as a marketing agency and would be responsible for 'ordering out' all production. It would be responsible for selling all company products, researching the market to determine what new patterns to produce and in what quantities, and advertising the various company products to the consumer—often in co-operation with the larger garment manufacturers and retailers. Under such an arrangement, the company's present salesforce of five men and the entire staff of designers would be transferred to the new organization. The present organization—minus those personnel shifted—would literally function solely as a production unit.

The sales agency would be a wholly owned subsidiary. It would include the company's name in its title and would establish separate offices in the heart of a nearby city. It would buy all merchandise from the plant at cost plus 10 per cent. Its responsibilities would include, however, the setting of all prices—including quantity discounts. It would be responsible for making profits—in fact, its profits would be an important part of the company's overall profits.

Mr Lander recognized that this type of organizational change would meet considerable resistance within the company, and yet the more he thought about it, the more he was convinced that it was a good idea.

Questions

1. Do you believe that the Lander Company has a problem?
2. What do you think of the new organizational structure proposed by Mr Lander?

Analyse the merits and the disadvantages of the proposed structure.

3. Suggest other possible organizational structure(s) aiming at reinforcing the level of market orientation of the firm.

4. How would you proceed to implement such an organizational change?

CASE STUDY 2

The WILO Company

[This case was prepared by Professor Dr R. Köhler, Universität zu Köln, and is used with permission.]

WILO is an internationally leading manufacturer of pumps for heating systems. The corporation's business spreads over the whole of Europe with 14 subsidiaries and several agencies abroad. WILO's activities are divided into four business units, defined mainly by customer groups and partly by product features:

- Domestic (private one- or two-family houses)

- Commercial (commercial or public builders)

- OEM (Original Equipment Manufacturer = industrial customers)

- Customer Service and Maintenance (including recycling).

Recently, the new business unit 'Systems' was created; it includes pressure-intensifying installations, transfer stations for district heating, filters for private swimming pools and collectors for the use of rainwater. However, after having shifted the entire OEM production to France, there are still four business units remaining in Germany.

Until 1990 WILO was organized in the 'classical' functional structure, as indicated in Fig. CS2.1. The functional division 'Marketing/Sales' included departments for sales in Germany, sales abroad and export. The central marketing department (Marketing Services) was in charge of market research, advertising, and sales promotion as well as the corporation's representation at trade fairs. Additional marketing specialists were working for the business units 'Domestic' and 'Commercial', just as 'OEM' and 'Customer Service' were supported by special marketing and sales units. Figure CS2.2 shows this structure valid until 1990.

The functional structure shown in Figs CS2.1 and 2.2 was suffering a significant disadvantage: too many organizational levels between work bench and customer caused co-ordination problems and time delays. For that reason a fundamental reorganization was implemented in 1991.

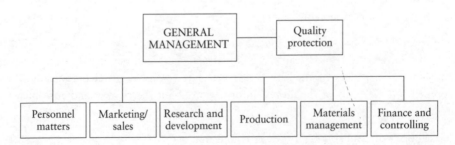

FIGURE CS2.1 *Functional organization at WILO until 1990*

FIGURE CS2.2 *The organization of marketing/sales at WILO until 1990*

The new structure was aiming for the following improvements:

■ Priority for market and customer orientation.

■ Short distances between market and production.

■ Comprehensive process orientation instead of functional departments.

■ Delegation of responsibilities to small co-operative groups within the company.

■ Higher motivation of the staff.

As the main element of the reorganization, the so-called *CIF teams* were created ('CIF' standing for 'Customer in the Focus'; German, 'Kunde im Mittelpunkt' (KIM). Each of the above-mentioned business units was assigned its own CIF team, led by an expert in Marketing/Sales or Customer Service. The rest of the team members have been recruited from Research and Development, Materials Management, Production, and Controlling, to ensure that experts from all relevant business functions contribute to the creation of customer benefit throughout the whole value chain of the corporation.

The CIF teams' work is mainly strategy-oriented: designing marketing strategies taking into consideration the competitive situation and the market development. However, they are also supposed to supervise the implementation of these strategies (e.g. by introducing new products to the market). In addition, the CIF teams are responsible for establishing long- and short-term objectives and the supervision of their realization.

The immediate closeness to customers is provided by the external organization of WILO, which consists of 16 sales and service teams, 3 regional managers and one key account management section. Since the leaders of the CIF teams are part of the external organization, strategy development on the basis of the newest information about the market and customer needs is ensured.

The so-called 'Round Table' is a further committee, which works as a link between the CIF teams and the modularly designed production. Members of the 'Round Table' are: one delegate

	Optimizing closeness to customers	Strategy development and implementation	Improved reactions to the market	Higher flexibility
Market	External organization	CIF teams	'Round Table' as a link between Sales and Production	Factories
Customer	Key account management 3 Regional managers 16 Sales and service teams	4 CIF areas with team members from • Sales • R&D • Materials management • Production • Controlling	1 delegate from the sales indoor staff 1 Member of the purchasing department 1 Production manager 1 Controller	Production planning Production (motor production, installation, mechanical processing) Quality control

FIGURE CS2.3 *Customer- and process-oriented CIF organization at WILO since 1991*

from the sales department (indoor staff), one expert from the purchasing department, one manager from the production department and one controller. They have to ensure that production reacts in a flexible way to market needs and consider the strategic priorities marked by the CIF teams. The field staff pass customers' orders immediately on to the competent production unit. Figure CS2.3 offers an overview of the new CIF organization.

The 'classical' marketing department, to be seen in Figs CS2.1 and 2.2, was given up at WILO. Merely market research and advertising are still centralized. Otherwise, the process organization, which overcomes traditional department limits, provides the framework for market orientation. The reorganization was combined with an intensive 'internal marketing' with the goal of creating a customer-oriented mentality among the staff. This new pattern of organization has proved its worth over the last four years.

The current plan is to group the 14 European subsidiaries into four larger regions: Central Europe, Northern Europe, Southern Europe and Eastern Europe. The managers of these regions will have a seat and a vote on the CIF teams if their regions are involved or if adjustment to local particularities (e.g. of product innovations) is concerned. The CIF teams shall guarantee a balance between central control and local adjustments, corresponding to a 'transnational marketing' approach (suggested by Bartlett and Ghoshal Nohria).

Question
Compare the advantages and disadvantages of a functional organization over a cross-functional organization similar to the one adopted by the WILO Company.

TV: Cold Bath for French Cinema
Alan Riding

[*Source:* International Herald Tribune, Jan 10, 1996. Reproduced with permission.]

France's troubled movie industry has long resisted change because change would mean abandoning its artistic tradition and surrendering to the commercialism of Hollywood. But change may be coming anyway, not from Hollywood but from the television companies that are fast emerging as leading financiers of French films. In truth, television companies have already saved the industry because they are required by law to invest in French movies and to broadcast a quota of French films each year. 'French cinema would have died 10 or 15 years ago without television,' said Ronan Giree, who runs the movie branch of the government-owned France 3 television channel. But, tiring of handing out money for intellectual 'auteur' movies with minimal box-office appeal, the TV companies have begun using their financial leverage to press producers and directors into making more commercial and popular films that have a chance of winning back lost audiences. 'If movie attendance in France has fallen from 200 million to 130 million per year since 1980, it's not because American films are better, but because ours are worse,' said Guillaume de Vergès, Head of the Movie Department at TF1, the country's largest television network. 'We should have some self-criticism and recognize that we don't make films people want to see.'

The television companies, which last year accounted for one-third of the $575.8 million invested in new French movies and which often act as a first step in getting other financing, have a clear interest in shaking up the movie industry. Led by the pay-TV channel Canal Plus, they need viewers to watch French movies if they are to draw advertisers. And where the companies are involved in co-productions, they want a better return on their money. But they are also couching their message to the industry in 'for-your-own-good' terms. Sooner or later, they warn, the artificial world of quotas and government subsidies will be swept away by European Union deregulation and by satellite broadcasting outside French government control. So, they say, the movie inustry must learn to compete or face extinction.

Alain Sarde, who produces films for Studio Canal Plus, the channel's movie production company, said he found it irritating to hear French directors constantly griping that Hollywood is 'stealing' their audiences. 'Let's make good films,' he said. 'Of 120 French films in a good year, 20 to 25 are interesting. In the 1970s, there'd be 50 interesting ones. It's a question of talent.' Still, under pressure mainly from Canal Plus and TF1, change is coming slowly. 'We work with name directors who now include box-office in their plans,' said Brahim Chioua, who runs Studio Canal Plus and co-produces films. De Vergès said television's influence was already significant. 'Producers are beginning to see that people want commercial films,' he said. 'The auteur world will not last because of television. Television and television fiction have produced a lot of new talent that sees cinema in a different way.' But resistance to change also runs deep. French auteurs, for example, have always viewed television with hostility, not only because its arrival undermined French moviegoing habits, but also because it is regarded as being vulgar. 'The difference between cinema and television,' Jean-Luc Godard, one of France's New Wave

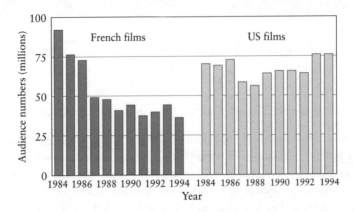

FIGURE CS3.1 *La Cinématographie: the type of films French cinema-goers watch*

directors of the 1960s, once noted, 'is that you raise your eyes for cinema and lower your eyes for television.' Claude Miller, a respected director now preparing an adaptation of Emile Zola's novel *Nana*, said that television companies preferred to back more conventional productions because they want films that can draw huge prime-time audiences. 'The negative, even perverse, effect of television is that it aims overwhelmingly for family entertainment,' he said. 'But prime-time appeal is not what characterizes the best of French cinema.' Further, for many French directors, any hint of adopting Hollywood's commercial approach is a potential threat. After all, under the current system, there is no easier place than France for a young director to make a first or second film, while known directors can find financing for a new film every year or two—notwithstanding whether their previous movie lost money. The justification is that their work is art and not entertainment.

In 1994, France won exclusion of the audio-visual industry from new international free-trade rules, and it is now fighting to preserve the European Union regulation that European productions constitute at least half of movies shown on television in the region. Yet, despite protection and subsidies, there is no disguising that the French movie industry is in crisis. From 1984 to 1994, the annual number of moviegoers in France fell from 190 million to 126 million, the number of new French films each year fell from 134 to 89 and their share of the French market fell from 49.3 per cent to 27.8 per cent. Further, while the industry routinely complains that France is being flooded with Hollywood 'trash', in the last decade annual attendance of American movies has risen only from 70 million to 75 million. In that period, tickets sold for French films have fallen from 94 million to 35 million. Put differently, the French industry has lost its edge.

But it lives on thanks to the French government—and television. Under French law, which goes further than European Union regulations, 60 per cent of films shown on television must be European, including 40 per cent French, which means that television is now the principal market for French films, with 639 French films (old and new) bought and broadcast by the five non-pay channels and Canal Plus in 1994. Because Canal Plus, which has 4 million subscribers, is largely a film and sports channel, showing no fewer than 195 French films in 1994, it has emerged as the pivotal force in the movie industry. And because it is obliged to spend 20 per cent of its annual revenue on film purchases, its pre-purchase policy means it can virtually decide what films are made. René Bonnell, who as Canal Plus's director of cinema last year spent $150 million purchasing new French films, said producers and directors turn first to the channel for support. 'We see about 500 screenplays a year and pick around 100,' he said. 'Because we represent 30, 40 or even 50 per cent of a film's budget, if you don't have Canal Plus, you can't make your film or else you take a tremendous risk.' For de Vergès of TF1, intellectual snobbery is still a problem. 'We're not there to make art, we're there to get people into movie theatres,' he said, noting that the most successful post-war French film, Jean-Marie Poiré's *Les Visiteurs*, was dismissed by intellectuals because it was a slapstick comedy. 'Do you think', he asked, 'it's nice for those who succeed to be told their work is rubbish because it isn't art?'

Questions

1. What would imply the adoption of a market-orientation by the French film industry?
2. Should the French film industry be market-oriented, or is it too different? Explain your answer.

Ecover

[This case was prepared by D. Develter (1992), *The Ecological Factory Manual*. Ecover Publications.]

Ecover, the manufacturer of green cleaners and detergents based in Belgium, grew out of the green washing products marketing and distribution business set up by entrepreneur Frans Bogaerts in 1979. In 1982 the business became Ecover, and in 1988 it began manufacturing its own liquid cleaners. Ecover has an explicit aim of striving towards 'minimum environmental impact' during each stage of product manufacture and use. When it comes to raw materials the company, whenever possible, sources natural raw materials and avoids the synthetic petrochemical products which have become the mainstay of the cleaning products industry. For example, surfactants based on sugar and soap are used which use renewable sources and quickly biodegrade unlike their more modern petrochemical counterparts. To keep pollution and waste during usage down to a minimum, the company uses minimum packaging, modular packaging of washing powder bleach (to allow it to be used in white washes but not in coloured washes) and even warns its customers against using too much of its product.

The Ecover vision went far beyond the usual concept of green products. The company saw its product range as:

> far more than a series of ecological products. It is a symbol, a statement, a point of view: we can no longer continue like this. We want to be able to swim again in our rivers, drink water from the tap without being afraid, and look forward to our children's future with confidence.

The only difficulty with developing a strategy of minimal environmental harm which went beyond the product itself was that conventional production processes and facilities could not provide the sort of green production performance that the Ecover vision entailed.

The company therefore set about creating the world's first 'ecological factory' based on a number of green principles. It aims for 'closed-loop processes' and has neither a chimney nor a polluting discharge pipe. The 1.5 million litres of water used each year is purified and recycled using a reed bed. Energy consumption is kept to a minimum through the use of solar power and heat recovery. Solid waste is sorted to maximize recycling opportunities. The building itself is a product of 'organic architecture'. It is made from entirely biodegradable materials including an insulating and aesthetically pleasing lawn roof garden supported by wooden rafters (sustainably sourced), and exterior walls made from recycled coal slag. In the choice of building materials, criteria for environmental quality pioneered by the Technical University of Eindhoven were used in addition to the conventional technical parameters. The building was also designed to cater for the health and welfare of its inhabitants through good thermal and acoustic insulation, and good natural ventilation and lighting.

Company policies include car-pooling, the provision of company bicycles and allowances for using public transport or switching to a fuel efficient car. (Although it might seem inappropriate that any workers at a factory like Ecover's should contribute to global warming by commuting to work, the company has calculated that the volume of carbon released into the atmosphere by the journeys of their staff will equate to the annual atmospheric carbon absorbed by the grass roof.) Office staff are networked on computers to reduce consumption of recycled stationery, and can take advantage of flexible hours and working from home via their portable computers.

Building the ecological factory involved a premium of 30 per cent additional cost compared to a conventional plant. However, due to its choice of materials for reuse, recycling or easy disposal, decommissioning the plant will cost only one-tenth of that for a conventional plant.

Questions

1. Is Ecover really better for the environment?
2. How can the firm communicate its superiority?
3. How do you get the consumer to pay for the product superiority?

CASE STUDY 5

Which company is truly global?

[This case was prepared by Professor W.J. Keegan in *Global Marketing Management* (1989), 4th edn. Prentice Hall International. Used with permission.]

Four senior executives of companies operating in many countries made the following comments.

Company A

'We are a truly global company. We sell our products in over 100 countries, and we manufacture in 15 countries. Some of our divisions have worldwide responsibility for their business, and others focus on the huge US market. In the latter case, we rely upon our country subsidiaries to pursue business opportunities in their territory.

'We're proud of our international reach, but we are concentrating on defending our position in the US market. This doesn't mean that we are trying to defend all of our threatened positions in the United States. I admit that we've lost market share in many of our traditional manufacturing businesses both in the United States and in overseas markets. But the United States is still where it's at, and the United States is a service economy. Even though we started out as an electrical equipment manufacturer, today we're very excited about our success in financial services. There's no point in fighting city hall and trying to hang on to the old manufacturing businesses like power generation and power distribution. It's just too hard to compete in those industries. Services are where it's at, and we want to be a leader in the fast growing financial services industry.'

Company B

'We are a global company. We are a unique media company. We do not dominate any particular area, but we have an important presence on three continents, in magazines, newspapers, and television. We have a global strategy. We are a global communications and entertainment company. We're in the business of informing people around the world on the widest possible basis. We know how to serve the needs of our customers who are readers, viewers, and advertisers. We transfer people and money across national boundaries, and we know how to acquire and integrate properties as well as how to start up a new business. We started out as Australian, and then the weight of our effort shifted to the UK and today our main effort is in the United States. We go where the opportunity is because we are market driven.

'Sure, there are lots of Australians in the top management of this company, but we started in Australia, and those Aussies know our business and the company from the ground up. And, look around and you'll see more and more Americans and Brits taking the top jobs. We stick to English because I don't believe that we could really succeed in foreign print or broadcast. We know English, and so far the English-speaking world is big enough for us. The world is shrinking faster than we all realize, and to be in communications is to be at the centre of all change. That's the excitement of what we're doing—and also the importance.'

Company C

'We're a global company. We are committed to being the number one company in our industry worldwide. We do all of our manufacturing in our home country because we have been able to achieve the lowest cost and the highest quality in the world by keeping all engineering and manufacturing in one location. The constantly rising value of our home currency is forcing us to invest in overseas manufacturing in order to maintain our cost advantage. We are doing this reluctantly, but we believe that the essence of being global is dominating markets and we plan to do whatever we must do in order to maintain our position of leadership.

'It is true that all of our senior managers at home and in most of our foreign markets are home country nationals. We feel more comfortable with our own nationals in key jobs because they speak our language and they understand the history and the culture of our company and our country. It would be difficult for an outsider to have this knowledge which is so important to smooth working relationships.'

Company D

'We are a truly global company. We have 24 nationalities represented on our headquarters staff, we manufacture in 28 countries, we market in 92 countries, and we are committed to leadership in our industry. It is true that we are backing off on our commitment to develop business in the Third World, but as you may know we have found it extremely difficult to increase sales and earnings in the Third World, and we have been criticized for our aggressive marketing in these countries. It is also true that, by law, only home country nationals may own voting shares in our company. So, even though we are global, we do have a home and a history and we respect the traditions and sensibilities of our home country.

'We want to maintain our number one position in Europe, and over time achieve the same position of leadership in our target markets in North America and Japan. We are also keeping a close eye on the developing countries of the world, and whenever we see a country make the move from LDC (less developed country) to DC (developing country) we commit our best effort to expand our position, or, if we don't have a position, to establish a position. Since our objective is to achieve an undisputed leadership position in our industry, we simply cannot afford *not* to be in every developed and advanced country market.

'We have always had a European CEO, and this will probably not change. The executives in this company from Europe tend to serve all over the world, whereas the executives from the United States and Japan serve only in their home countries. They are very able and valuable executives, but they lack the necessary perspective of the world required for the top jobs here at headquarters.'

Questions

1. Which company is truly global?
2. What are the attributes of a truly global company?
3. Why quibble about the extent to which a company is global?

Avocado

[This case was prepared by Bernard Dubois in *10 cas de marketing management*, Paris, Publi-Union. Translated and used with permission.]

In the 1960s and 1970s, avocado was almost an unknown fruit in Europe. In 1964, the Agriculture Export Company (Agrexco) decided to make an attempt to introduce it into the European market.

The first stage in this attempt was to conduct a feasibility study and make a forecast of potential sales in the various countries. The second stage was an introduction, on a limited basis, of fruit starting in France and later on spreading to other countries.

Table CS6.1 presents the sales of avocados for the 1957–72 period as well as the forecasts for the two years to come.

On the basis of these results, Germany was selected in 1972 as the major target market and a wide promotional campaign was suggested. However, in order to make the campaign effective, reliable data on present market penetration and potential consumers were required. Thus a consumer research project was conducted.

The research was designed to answer the following questions:

■ What are the stages of the consumer's decision-making process in eating and purchasing foreign fruits and vegetables in general and avocado in particular, and what are the determinants and factors influencing this process?

■ What is the level of penetration of avocado in the market and what should be the target groups for the promotion?

■ What should be the most effective channels of communication and messages to influence the target groups?

TABLE CS6.1 *Import of Israeli Avocado to Europe (tons)*

Years	England	France	Germany	Others	Total
1957/58	9	6	–	3	18
1959/60	64	12	1	5	83
1964/65	248	214	26	45	533
1969/70	614	902	197	413	2126
1970/71	1001	1753	332	584	3670
1971/72	1266	3038	533	1263	6100
1972/73	1300	3100	600	1500	6500
1973/74	1500	3200	700	1600	7000

TABLE CS6.2 *Preference of vegetables and fruits**

Vegetables	%	Fruit	%
Asparagus	41	Apples	51
Cauliflower	30	Oranges	43
Carrot	26	Strawberries	40
Beans	21	Cherries	21
Peas	20	Peaches	19
Cabbage	20	Pears	16
Fennel	18	Grapes	15
Brussels sprouts	16	Citrus	10
Kohlrabi	10	Apricots	8
Avocado	3	Grapefruit	8

*The percentages indicate the proportion of respondents who have mentioned the vegetable or fruit as their favourite.

Avocado is considered to be a luxury product, with a relatively high price. It is also an innovative and unfamiliar product. Therefore, it is more likely to be consumed by high-income, high-education groups in the population. Due to this assumption and due to the relatively limited budget for research, it was decided that the first consumer study conducted in Germany would concentrate on a high-income, high-education group and in a limited geographical area.

Consequently, a sample of 300 Munich housewives of the upper and upper-middle classes was selected. The respondents were chosen by means of the Quota sampling method in which the selection criteria were age, social grouping, size of household and whether or not the respondent went out to work.

Recognition and usage

In order to find out the level of penetration of avocado, two questions were asked:

1. Which are your favourite vegetables and fruit? (open-ended question)
2. Which of the following foreign vegetables and fruit (a list of names) do you know, have you eaten or have you purchased?

The responses to the foregoing questions are presented in Tables CS6.2 and CS6.3 respectively.

Attitude

The attitude towards avocado was examined by two different questions:

1. The intention to buy, indicated on a 1 to 7 scale (7 = maximum intention to buy).
2. The general effect, measured by an answer to the question. 'How much do you think you and your family would enjoy eating Avocado?'—also indicated on a 1 to 7 scale.

For purpose of comparison the two questions were asked not only with respect to avocado but with respect to oranges, bananas and eggplants as well. The distributions of answers are

TABLE CS6.3 *Recognition and usage of foreign fruits and vegetables*

Fruit or vegetables	Aided awareness (%)	Bought (%)	Eaten (%)
Oranges	100	100	100
Lemons	100	100	100
Grapefruit	100	99	100
Bananas	100	99	100
Olives	100	95	99
Melons	100	94	99
Green paprika	99	97	99
Red paprika	99	97	99
Dried figs	99	94	97
Chicory	99	96	97
Dried dates	99	92	95
Sweet corn	99	72	88
Artichokes	98	73	88
Fennel	98	68	79
Eggplants	95	63	77
Raw fresh figs	93	58	75
Pomegranates	85	42	62
Avocado	84	48	62
Zuchini	79	50	63
Fresh raw dates	76	37	48
Mangos	75	23	37
Kakis	68	41	50
Broccoli	56	34	43
Cactus figs	50	16	26
Papayas	24	7	11
Guavas	21	3	7
Lychees	17	8	14
Kiwi	14	3	5
Maracuya	8	2	4

presented in Table CS6.4 while Table CS6.5 compares the attitudes of those who have eaten avocado and those who have not.

The determinants of behaviour

What are the criteria by which the consumers make their decisions regarding fruit and vegetables? In order to find out, the respondents were asked to rate the importance of 12 attributes of fruit and vegetables on a 1 to 7 scale. The list of attributes is presented in Table CS6.6 and the importance ratings are presented in Table CS6.7.

Beliefs about avocado

The image of avocado was examined by means of ranking the attributes on a 1 to 7 scale of True–False statements. The answers are presented in Table CS6.8.

TABLE CS6.4 *Attitude distributions (per cent of sample, n = 300)*

Scale	Oranges	Bananas	Eggplants	Avocado
		Intention to buy		
Rating: 1	–	2	15	23
2	–	2	14	11
3	2	2	15	19
4	2	9	18	18
5	2	11	15	11
6	8	13	11	6
7	86	61	12	12
Total	100	100	100	100
Mean	6.81	6.09	3.82	3.50
Standard deviation	0.58	1.42	1.93	1.96
		Affect ('will enjoy eating')		
Rating: 1	–	1	14	16
2	–	2	10	9
3	–	3	13	14
4	1	5	18	15
5	3	14	18	18
6	5	16	14	13
7	91	59	13	15
Total	100	100	100	100
Mean	6.86	6.13	4.10	4.06
Standard deviation	0.48	1.34	1.93	2.00

TABLE CS6.5 *Those who have/have not eaten avocado*

	Oranges		Bananas		Eggplants		Avocado	
Attitude	Mean	S.D.	Mean	S.D.	Mean	S.D.	Mean	S.D.
Intention to buy								
Entire sample	6.81	0.58	6.09	1.42	3.82	1.93	3.50	1.96
Have eaten avocado	6.76	0.69	5.97	1.52	4.16	1.93	3.99	2.02
Have not eaten avocado	6.89	0.34	6.30	1.21	3.25	1.81	2.69	1.57
Would enjoy eating								
Entire sample	6.86	0.48	6.13	1.34	4.10	1.93	4.06	2.00
Have eaten avocado	6.83	0.53	5.97	1.41	4.31	1.93	4.28	2.04
Have not eaten avocado	6.90	0.38	6.38	1.18	3.76	1.89	3.69	1.88

TABLE CS6.6 *List of attributes*

Code	Statement
Fresh	(a) Always fresh in the shop
Vitamin	(b) Has a high vitamin content
Digestible	(c) Easily digestible
Inexpensive	(d) Inexpensive
Everyday	(e) Goes well with everyday meal
Obtainable	(f) Obtainable everywhere and always
Versatile	(g) Versatile (multiple ways of using it)
Special	(h) Something special and makes a change
Quickly	(i) Quickly prepared
Calories	(j) Low in calories
Guests	(k) Can be served to guests with high standards
Nutritional	(l) Nutritional and satisfying
Attractive	(m) Look attractive
Men	(n) Men like them
How	(o) One is not sure how to prepare them
Keep	(p) Keep for a long time
Children	(q) Children like them
Snobs	(r) Just for snobs

TABLE CS6.7 *Importance ratings of attributes (per cent, N = 300)*

Attribute	Rank	Mean	S.D.	Scale						
				1	2	3	4	5	6	7
Fresh	1	6.41	0.82	0	1	0	1	8	35	55
Vitamin	2	6.23	0.91	0	0	1	4	14	34	48
Digestible	3	5.26	1.49	2	7	2	13	22	36	18
Inexpensive	4	5.18	1.52	2	7	4	13	26	26	21
Everyday	5	4.96	1.37	1	7	5	17	33	27	10
Obtainable	6	4.91	1.56	3	8	9	11	27	29	13
Versatile	7	4.89	1.51	1	11	6	14	27	30	11
Special	8	4.81	1.45	1	10	6	24	21	29	9
Quickly	9	4.80	1.61	1	14	6	17	22	27	14
Calories	10	4.48	1.97	8	16	8	14	15	21	19
Guests	11	4.21	1.70	5	18	9	20	19	22	6
Nutritional	12	4.12	1.77	7	19	11	16	20	19	8

The numbers in this table should be interpreted as follows: 55% of respondents have given a score of 7 to the attribute 'fresh' (maximum score); 35% of respondents have given the mark 6; 8% the mark 5; 1% the mark 4; 1% the mark 2. The average score is therefore equal to 6.41, while the standard deviation is equal to 0.82.

TABLE CS6.8 *Beliefs about avocado (per cent, N = 300)*

| Attribute | Mean | S.D. | Scale | | | | | | |
			1	2	3	4	5	6	7
Fresh	4.22	1.45	5	8	17	33	12	18	7
Vitamin	5.52	1.36	0	1	1	34	9	19	36
Digestible	4.41	1.32	4	3	6	53	12	14	8
Inexpensive	2.90	1.31	0	22	15	23	34	5	2
Everyday	3.42	1.58	15	15	19	26	13	10	2
Obtainable	2.81	1.38	18	23	36	10	5	5	2
Versatile	5.12	1.39	1	2	3	37	12	22	22
Special	5.93	1.28	2	1	3	8	16	31	41
Quickly	5.10	1.33	1	1	3	39	14	23	20
Calories	3.51	1.56	19	5	10	50	5	6	4
Guests	6.00	1.21	0	2	1	11	12	28	46
Nutritional	5.06	1.33	3	2	5	35	18	20	19
Attractive	5.97	1.16	7	1	4	3	17	35	39
Men	4.79	1.65	6	2	7	35	12	16	21
How	4.12	2.10	18	10	10	14	11	21	14
Keep	4.06	1.34	5	7	12	46	12	14	3
Children	3.40	1.50	16	12	16	42	6	6	3
Snobs	2.62	1.66	35	23	11	21	3	5	3

Figures in this table should be interpreted in the same manner as those in Table CS6.7.

Questions

1. How would you use the data provided in the case to analyse the brand image of avocado?
2. Using the attitude data, construct the importance–performance matrix for the different fruit and vegetables?
3. Which type of promotional activity would you recommend?

CASE STUDY 7

The Petro-Equipment Company

[This case was prepared by J.J. Lambin on the basis of an example presented by M. Porter (1989) in *Competitive Advantage*, New York: The Free Press.]

Mr Bill Spencer is the marketing manager of the Petro-Equipment Company specialized in the development and manufacturing of oil-drilling equipment. The oil field equipment industry offers two types of drilling equipment to its customers: standard electro-mechanical equipment and sophisticated electronic and computer-based equipment. Electro-mechanical equipment is highly versatile and can be used for deep and shallow drilling as well, whereas the electronic systems are used for deep drilling only. The Petro-Equipment Company is specialized in advanced electronic systems and has a worldwide market organization.

Mr Spencer is currently developing a strategic plan for its line of oil-drilling equipment and has to decide the type of market coverage to adopt. For that purpose, he is trying to segment the market in a meaningful way.

In a first step, Mr Spencer tries to identify the main characteristics of potential customers and he realizes that there are several ways in which buyers can be classified. The types of end-buyers that purchase the company's products are oil companies which are geographically located both in developed and in developing countries. It is common practice in the petroleum industry to classify oil companies by size and to adopt three categories: major oil companies, large independent and small independent. A further complication comes from the fact that the ownership status also differs: some companies are private, others are state-owned. Finally, the technological sophistication of the end-buyers is also a relevant criterion to consider when segmenting the market. Some oil companies clearly have the required know-how, while others don't.

Mr Spencer is convinced that all these criteria are useful to describe the purchasing behaviour of potential customers, but he also realizes that some combinations of these segmentation criteria are infeasible combinations. For instance, all independent oil companies are by definition private-owned, and state-owned companies are generally large companies. Similarly, he is aware that it is very unrealistic to propose sophisticated technologies to oil companies operating in developing countries. The company has an excellent reputation, not only for the quality of the equipment sold, but also for the technical assistance provided to its customers—a service highly appreciated mainly by small oil companies.

Questions

1. Using the three-dimensional macro-segmentation procedure, define the market in terms of functions, technologies and buyers.
2. Build a segmentation grid describing the market of oil-drilling equipment and presenting all the 'existing' potential segments.
3. Propose a market coverage strategy adapted to the distinctive characteristics of the Petro-Equipment Company.

CASE STUDY 8

Sierra Plastics Company

[This case was prepared by W.J. Stanton in *Fundamentals of Marketing*, McGraw-Hill Book Co.]

Over a period of two years, the price of polyethylene pipe had dropped steadily and significantly. This fact, coupled with the recognition that his company was operating in an industry chronically faced with excess capacity, made Mr Walter Riley, the marketing manager of Sierra Plastics Company, realize that his company might have to alter its pricing policy. Located in San Francisco, the Sierra Plastics Company was a relatively small manufacturer of polyethylene and other plastic products. The company's main product, accounting for 60 to 70 per cent of annual sales, was polyethylene pipe which was manufactured in a variety of sizes ranging from $\frac{1}{2}$ inch to 6 inches in diameter. About 30 to 40 per cent of the company's sales came from a variety of plastic compounds intended for industrial uses such as wall panels, electrical installations, and soundproofing. Polyethylene is also widely used by other manufacturers in the production of sheeting, bottles, toys, appliance components, and automotive parts, but the Sierra Plastics Company had not entered these markets.

Compared with metal pipe, the plastic product was lighter, easier to install, non-corrosive and less expensive. Polyethylene pipe was an excellent product for farm irrigation, wells, lawn sprinklers, and other uses where the liquid pressure requirements were relatively low—up to 100 pounds per square inch. For the transmission of potable water, the only polyethylene pipe used was made from virgin materials and carried the National Sanitation Foundation (NSF) seal. Pipe not made from virgin material was considered the 'second-grade line'. About 60 to 80 per cent of the polyethylene pipe produced was of the second-grade, non-NSF, lower-priced variety intended for consumer and industrial market uses other than transmitting drinking water.

Since the end of the Second World War, the growth of the plastic pipe industry had been phenomenal, as many new uses for the product were quickly developed. Because of the attractiveness of this market, many new firms entered the industry and generated a production capacity well in excess of the level which even the expanding market could absorb. A major factor enabling this over-capacity to develop was the ease of entry into the industry. Initial investment requirements were low, and the basic technical knowledge could be acquired easily. The engineering and production information was eagerly supplied by the raw materials producers and the manufacturers of the extrusion machines used in making the pipe. The extrusion rates on a mixed basis of pipe $\frac{1}{2}$ to 6 inches in diameter were such that one machine operating 24 hours a day, seven days a week, could produce in excess of 1 million pounds of finished pipe per year. Two major producers alone had more than 50 machines, each capable of producing 1 million pounds of finished polyethylene pipe per year.

There were about 60 manufacturers of polyethylene pipe located over the entire United States, but only a small number marketed their products nationally. Most of the manufacturers were regional extruders, making only a limited line of polyethylene pipe. The Sierra Plastics Company fell in this category, operating 12 machines and marketing in California, Oregon and Arizona. The machine used by Sierra Plastics Company for extruding polyethylene pipe could also be used for the production of other plastic products. By marketing in a limited geographic area, the Sierra Plastics Company could fill orders faster and give better service generally than the large, national firms.

The company's financial position was strong. However, its profit margin, while adequate, was endangered by price-cutting in the industry. Sierra Plastics had a salesforce of 10 men. They reached the consumer market by selling to sprinkler installation firms, to lawn equipment dealers and distributors, and to landscape contractor-gardeners. In the industrial market the salesmen sold to agricultural co-operatives, agricultural equipment dealers, and plumbing and heating wholesalers. In many cases, Sierra sold directly to large farms, to businesses which wanted to install a lawn-sprinkling system, and to manufacturers with industrial watering systems.

The conditions of excess capacity in the plastic pipe industry had induced many firms to cut their prices in an attempt to broaden their market share and thus utilize some of the excess production capacity in their plants. Because it was difficult, if not impossible, to differentiate its products from those of its competitors, the Sierra Plastics Company had been forced to cut its prices to meet competition. Over the past two years Sierra's price for non-virgin polyethylene pipe had dropped from 52 cents a pound to 38 cents a pound. During the most recent year, unit sales remained relatively constant, so the potentially depressing effect on profits was evident. Currently, the cost of raw materials was 40 to 50 per cent of the selling price. High-quality pipe meeting NSF standards sold for proportionately more than the second-grade product line.

Mr Riley was studying several alternative courses of action in an attempt to stimulate sales and to stem the profit decline. His first thought was to reduce prices further and try to do a better job of promoting the Sierra brand. He hoped to bring the product into a price range that would attract a new market, not heretofore users of polyethylene pipe. He believed that these actions would increase unit sales volume enough to more than compensate for the unit price reductions. Mr Riley realized that competitors undoubtedly would retaliate if Sierra's prices were reduced. The speed and effectiveness of this price retaliation would be a function of Sierra's ability to differentiate its product, the ability of the customer to judge product quality, and the importance of price in the consumer's buying decisions. Another unknown was the extent to which prices, once cut, could ever be restored to their former levels. Mr Riley was also considering the alternative of reducing product quality and thus reducing costs enough so that unit prices could be cut without any loss of unit gross or net profit.

The production manager, Mr Pope had recommended an almost polar-opposite plan. He suggested that Sierra produce and market a new high-quality line made from superior resins. This new pipe would be sold at a price above even that of the premium pipe now produced to NSF standards. The intention would be to break away entirely from the 'price-football' image of the second-grade and the virgin product line. Mr Pope believed that the company's distributors and ultimate users could be convinced that this new product was truly of higher quality and thus warranted a higher price. To help convince the distributors and the users, Mr Pope would institute a distinctive warranty programme. Under it, Sierra Plastics would pay for all labour and materials charges incurred in replacing or repairing defective pipe.

Question

What course of action should the company follow to counter the problems of price reductions and excess capacity?

Tissex

[This case was prepared by Gilles Marion from ESC Lyon. Translated and used with the permission of Centrale de cas et de medias pédagogiques (Paris).]

Tissex is a French company whose sole activity is the production and sales of fabrics composed of artificial and synthetic fibres. In spite of a turnover of FF536 million and a gross profit margin of 17 per cent in 1983, the net result was not very high. Its know-how in production processes (gluing, weaving, dying, finishing), combined with advanced technical collaboration with manufacturers of fibres, have so far been sufficient to maintain its position in comparison with both French, European or Japanese competitors. A turnover of FF200 million from exports, mainly to the Common Market but also to the US, gives the group an international dimension.

Tissex offers a large range of products which includes fabrics for clothing (polyester silks), linings, sportswear (anoraks, clothes, etc.) and household linen (quilts, bedspreads, etc.) as well as safety fabrics (technical fabrics for the army, the police, the chemical and oil industries, etc.), printing ribbons (ready to be inked) for typewriters and computers. Over the past three years Tissex has invested in modern equipment and machinery. This policy should be sustained if Tissex wants to maintain its position in the international market.

Henry Bonnet, the new CEO, must evaluate the company's overall performance and develop a strategy for the next three years. This is what he says about the situation of his company:

> We have five factories, mainly in the Lyon area. However, by acquiring St Renard in 1980, we now have two other plants in Roubaix, in the north of France.

> This acquisition brought us a turnover of FF123 million in 1983, mainly from linings, but we are, however, more interested in St Renard's technical fabrics. Up until then our activity in this area has been secondary, let's say from FF4 million to FF5 million in 1980. We have concentrated all of this activity in Roubaix so that today we have 30 per cent of the market with a turnover of FF33 million. This is really good for a market with an average annual growth rate of 9 per cent, especially as the gross margin for this activity is over twice that of the group's average.

> Competition rose quickly! Particularly textile companies of northern France and among them Guillez with a turnover of FF20 million in 1983. They followed our example and started to export their goods. The other competitors are smaller companies with a 5 to 10 per cent market share each. Most of them are French. So far, however, we are well protected because of the highly specialized demands of our customers. Exporting is slow to get off the ground but we're not in a hurry; we are confident in our know-how. The Germans and English cannot catch up with us right away. Furthermore, each country still has its own standards. There are approximately 100 potential clients in all of Europe and what they are looking for is 'service'.

> As for linings, the situation is completely different: this is a depressed market, as is the case for the traditional garment industry. It will decline from 2 to 3 per cent next year, as it did

in previous years. Womenswear was in a somewhat better position, but as a whole the sector is doing poorly. We have over 2000 clients in this activity but every year there are several bankruptcies. Our sales representatives have standing orders not to deliver unless they have the go-ahead from Sales Information Service. The price war is fierce and when you're the leader in the European market, with only 12 per cent of the market, you have a hard time maintaining your position. Belgian companies are the toughest to compete with: they have invested a lot over the past few years. For example, Deckerman, who has only 7 per cent of the market, earned more money than we did. Up until now we have tried to hold on even if the gross margin for linings is largely inferior to that of the group average: 10 per cent, this is worrying. Luckily the Japanese can't come in on this market as the price per metre is too low.

Our objective is clear: slightly increase prices to maintain the same level of turnover (FF160 million) without affecting the volume of production and without losing our French clients who represent 45 per cent of our turnover. We will also reach some new markets because our weaker competitors will have disappeared—in France, Germany, England and maybe outside the Common Market as well. We have 12 multicard agents in France and our headquarters are in charge of foreign markets. The Roubaix plant delivers to Paris, northern France, the Benelux and Great Britain. Roanne sends goods out to southern France and to all other countries. Germany receives special treatment because an own sales subsidiary was created in 1977 for some obscure reasons. Results there are very poor and we now plan on dealing directly from France for large orders.

Roanne is a real headache. Last year we had to lay off 90 people, mostly working on polyester. Globally Roanne had a 1983 turnover of FF256 million with FF70 million for linings and the rest for clothing. Moreover, weaving of polyester fabric is divided between two workshops equipped with different weaving machinery. One-third of production comes from very modern and rapid machines and two-thirds are produced traditionally. With a gross margin of 7 per cent the polyester activity is the worst of our group and the market has not increased for the past few years.

The Japanese have hurt us in this area. They now have over 5 per cent of the European market with good quality products they can sell at a higher price than we can. We are far behind with just 1 per cent of the market. However, we do export 40 per cent of our production thanks to the quality of our sales network but at very low prices. And we can't ask our clients to pay more. However, we can observe that this market is also being concentrated: many clients have disappeared. Five years ago we had 2500 clients; today there are 800 in France and 600 in the other European countries. These numbers will decrease until we have only the most interesting companies as clients.

Luckily there is the Lyon factory: a FF157 million turnover in 1983 and 6 to 7 per cent of growth in value every year. The sportswear activity is advancing rapidly, 8 per cent per year as compared to 6 per cent for printing ribbons for computers and typewriters (but ribbons in the US are increasing by 20 per cent annually). As a matter of fact, the Lyon factory has two really distinct activities and I wonder if we shouldn't separate them completely. The factory manager has a real problem with his production planning.

We keep very little stock on hand for printing ribbons. Whatever is produced is delivered immediately and we have three eight-hour shifts. The looms are rapid, with air or water jets, and, most important, high quality is constant. Our clients know us very well; there are only 90 throughout the world including 10 in France. We export 60 per cent of our production. In 1980, the Japanese were the first to drastically reduce their prices by 30 per cent but in this activity we were able to follow their lead and we invested in very modern Swiss equipment. We have 5 per cent of the market, just a bit lower than the two world leaders who are Japanese and German. The Spaniards and English are now beginning to invest. This is going to be a running battle. We just hope that the market can be maintained long enough for us to write off our investments over the next two or three years. In five years the market will have changed and we'll have to re-adapt but a 30 per cent gross margin is acceptable today.

The sportswear fabric is less risky. Profit is still to be made, mainly for the special quality features we propose, and our clients seem to maintain their positions. The FF67 million turnover is spread evenly over 30 customers and, even if we do have a low export profile here, our clients export their goods pretty well. The Sporting company is the top competitor with 20 per cent of the French market, but two or three of us are close behind. We must pass the others and I believe we can catch up with Sporting as they have had a problem with deliveries and quality when there was a strike at their fibre supplier's. We always have several supply sources so as to avoid this kind of problem. Thanks to Sporting's difficulties we have been able to reach customers who, up until now, were out of reach. If we can develop these contacts we'll go from 15 to 20 per cent of the market next year or the following year.

The Italians of course have tried to compete with us but this market fluctuates too fast for them; you really have to be on the spot to anticipate demand and to manage your stock correctly. Most clients are located around Lyon or Paris and we know them very well. Our sales network is excellent and we work well with each of its members.

Our sales director will retire at the end of this year and I think that we will then no longer call upon the two multicard agents who now work for us. The gross margin is even higher than for technical fabrics (36 per cent) and I am planning on maintaining the same level of sales.

Questions
1. Define the strategic segments that are relevant for Tissex's activities.
2. Make a strategic analysis of Tissex's portfolio of activities according to whatever method is, to your mind, the most appropriate (BCG matrix, multi-factors portfolio matrix, etc.). According to this method, is there a problem facing Tissex? If so, what is this problem?
3. Identify the various strategies that could be developed for each of Tissex's activities. Choose the ones you think are the most appropriate.

Newfood

[This was prepared by G.S. Day *et al.* (1983), in *Cases in Computer and Model Assisted Marketing Planning*, The Scientific Press. Used with permission.]

Mr Ulcer, newly appointed New Products marketing director of Concorn, is considering the possibility of marketing a new highly nutritional food product which has widely varied uses. This product can be used as a snack, a camping food, or as a diet food. The product is to be generically labelled Newfood.

Because of this wide range of possible uses, the company has had great difficulty in defining the market. The product is viewed as having no direct competitors. Early product and concept tests have been very encouraging. These tests have led Mr Ulcer to believe that the product could easily sell 2 million cases (24 packages in a case) under the proposed marketing programme involving a 24c package price and an advertising programme involving $3 million in expenditures per year. The projected P&L for the first year national is:

Sales:	2.00 million cases
Revenue:	$8.06 million (assumes 70 per cent of the retail price is revenue to the manufacturer)
Manufacturing costs:	$3.00 million ($1 million fixed manufacturing costs plus $1 per case variable)
Advertising:	$3.00 million
Net margin:	$2.06 million

There will be no capital expenditures required to go national, since manufacturing is to be done on a contract pack basis. These costs have been included in the projected P&L. Concorn has an agreement with the contract packer requiring that once a decision to go national is made, Concorn is obligated to pay fixed production costs ($1 million per year) for three years even if the product is withdrawn from the market at a later time. Even though there are no capital requirements, it is the company's policy not to introduce new products with profit expectations of less than $0.5 million per year (a three-year planning horizon is usually considered).

Mr Ulcer is quite confident of his sales estimates (and hence his profit estimate) although he does admit that they contain some uncertainty. When pressed, he will admit that sales could be as low as 1 million cases in the first year, but points out that sales might also exceed the estimate by as much as 1 million cases. His operational definition of these extremes is that each has no more than a 1 in 10 chance of occurring. He is more concerned about sales after the first year. Historically, most new products with which he is familiar have had sales that decayed over time. After some effort, he summarized his feelings about the sales for the new product in Table CS10.1.

There are also other marketing plans under consideration. A second alternative involves a 10c price increase (34c retail) to be used to finance higher advertising expenditures ($6 million) in the first year. The advantage of this second plan is that higher advertising could bring as many people into the market as the lower price and that in subsequent years advertising expenditures

TABLE CS10.1 *First year sales estimates*

First year's sales	Probability	Decay rates per year	Probability
0.5–1.0	0.10	+10% to −10%	0.25
1.0–1.5	0.20	−10% to −30%	0.50
1.5–2.0	0.25	−30% to −50%	0.25
2.0–2.5	0.25		
2.5–3.0	0.10		
3.0–3.5	0.10		

could then be cut back to the $4 million level. There is some concern that the higher price would affect repeat sales, hence sales might decay even faster over time under this plan. A casual estimate is that the decay rate might increase by 50 per cent due to the higher price. There is also some discussion of coupling the lower price with high advertising ($6 million) or using a middle price (29c) and a middle level of advertising expenditures ($4.5). These alternatives have not as yet been fully explored.

Mr Ulcer believes that the potential of the product is so high that national introduction should be started as soon as possible. His primary concern is the choice of a strategy.

Mr Rank, the director of market research suggests that a market test be performed. Although he agrees that the project looks good, his sales estimates are somewhat lower than Ulcer's. He agrees to the sales range of 0.5 to 3.5 but, based on the history of new product failures, assigns the probabilities shown in Table CS10.2.

Mr Rank argues that not only would the market test reduce the uncertainty in the sales estimate, but it would provide an opportunity to find out more about how prices and advertising affect sales. He has not as yet worked out a test plan, but believes he could conduct a 6-month test that would cost no more than $75 000 in which it would be possible to estimate national first-year sales within 0.25 million cases (the estimated sampling error of his instrument).

Mr Ulcer is hesitant to accept the proposal, not only because of costs and time delays but also because he is concerned about the usefulness of the results. He notes that the proposed test could

TABLE CS10.2

First year's sales (million cases)	Probability
0.5–1.0	0.15
1.0–1.5	0.25
1.5–2.0	0.35
2.0–2.5	0.20
2.5–3.0	0.05
3.0–3.5	0.00

at best give him information on first-year sales while he is most concerned about future sales. He also questions Rank's ability to test within the stated error range.

Questions

1. If Mr Ulcer has to decide whether to introduce Newfood without the aid of a market test, how should he decide; if his planning horizon is 1 year or if his planning horizon is 3 years?
2. How would you use Mr Ulcer's probability estimates in the analysis?
3. Should a market test be conducted? How much would a 'perfect' market test be worth?

CASE STUDY 11

Nico Duin BV

[This case was prepared by R.J.H. Meyer and A.T. Pruyn in *Marketing in Europe*, London: Page.]

Much of the literature and research on internationalization is focused on large companies. This bias is reflected in the educational programmes offered by business schools, the concepts that are employed and the cases that are discussed. Yet the internationalization of small companies reveals much about the fundamental motives and problems accompanying the processes of internationalization. This case explores the situation of a small Dutch company taking its first steps into the international arena. It addresses the strategic steps faced by the company as it considers how it should go about entering the German market.

As Peter Duin puts down the phone on this sunny April morning in 1991, he wonders whether the approach to the German market he has just decided upon is the best one. As head of Nico Duin BV, a small Dutch machine factory started by his father, Peter Duin has just called his forwarder to ship a number of standard machines to Germany for the Hanover Messe (trade fair). This biannual trade show for industrial machinery companies, which will be held in May, will bring together many buyers and suppliers in this industry, and could therefore be a very suitable starting-point for active penetration of the German market. More particularly, Peter Duin is hoping to make contacts with a number of German distributors, who could sell and service his machines in key regions of Germany. However, Peter Duin isn't quite sure whether exporting via distributors is the best entry mode, especially given the mixed success of using distributors in the Dutch market. Maybe, he asks himself, the use of an alternative entry strategy would make more sense.

History of the company, 1955–87

After the destruction during the Second World War, a period of reconstruction took place in the Netherlands, which, together with the post-war baby boom, led to a sharp increase in the demand for housing. The consequent wave of construction, in turn, led to a substantial growth in the demand for related tools and machines. Nico Duin, a technically trained entrepreneur living in Wormerveer, just north of Amsterdam, exploited this surge in demand by founding a machinery company in 1955, specializing in equipment for the wood-processing industry. Duin's products included frame cramps, glue presses and tenoners, which could be used by carpenters, construction companies, door factories and window-frame producers—basically anyone using wood as a building material (see Box CS11.1 for a description of these machines).

While initially a purely domestic company, after a few years Nico Duin made his first foreign sales, although they were based on unsolicited orders from abroad, by customers who had seen his products in the Netherlands. However, these export sales never amounted to more than a few per cent of turnover. Nico Duin had very little reason to internationalize, since the Dutch market was far from mature, and all the machines he produced could easily be sold domestically.

BOX CS11.1

Nico Duin's product assortment

Nico Duin BV makes three categories of product:

1. *Frame cramps*. Frame cramps are used to hold wooden doors and window frames in the right position under the right pressure, so work can be carried out and glue can dry. The smallest machine is approximately 2×3 metres and can hold a frame of up to 1.5×2.5 metres. The biggest machines are approximately 4×7 metres. All cramps come in pneumatic and hydraulic versions. Prices range from about 7000 to 20 000 guilders. Nico Duin's frame cramps are sometimes more expensive than those of the competition, but have a better price/quality ratio and are well known for their flexibility in usage. This product category represents more than 50 per cent of Nico Duin's sales.
2. *Glue presses*. These products are related to the frame cramps, but are used to hold together large wood surfaces, such as table tops, while the glue between various layers or parts is hardening. These machines are also highly standardized, and sizes and prices are similar to those of the frame cramps. Glue presses account for approximately 30 per cent of turnover.
3. *Tenoners*. These are actually milling-machines solely used on window frames. This relatively new addition to Nico Duin's product assortment comes in a conventional manually guided version, but also in a computer-guided version. Peter Duin is particularly proud of this CNC 900 tenoner, which he developed himself. This machine is extremely flexible; any type of window frame can be made with the same machine, and the set-up time for each new product is a fraction of that of conventional machines. The gross profit on the sale of each of these machines is quite high, but it will take a couple of years before the R&D costs are earned back.

'The focus of our export efforts is on the first two categories of machines,' states Duin, 'because I have the most experience with them and I see the fewest problems ... they all work at the flick of a switch.' These standard products can be easily installed and serviced by a third party. As for the tenoner, however, it is still a complex specialized product, with the occasional start-up problems, so 'We'll slowly ease it into the Dutch market, while we'll be more aggressive abroad with the frame cramps and glue presses.'

Like father, like son? (1987 to the present)

In 1987 Nico Duin's only son, Peter, took over the flourishing company, but left the company's name unchanged. In contrast to his father, Peter Duin was more committed to growing and internationalizing the company, which already had an annual turnover of 1.5 million guilders. He set the following objectives for his company:

1. Increase profits.
2. Consolidate market share in the Netherlands.
3. Enlarge market share outside the Netherlands.

helped the market a little bit.' Yet Hess shouldn't be ignored. His turnover is three to four times higher than Duin's, and 'You know how German companies work. They're *gründlich*; in other words, an enormous warehouse and lab.'

Whether product adaptations are needed for the German market, time will tell, but Peter Duin isn't worried. 'We had the same problem when selling a few machines in England. The window frames needed an extra ridge and had to be stapled on the back. So you adapt, but the basic product is the same.'

Duin's distributors

When it comes to distribution, Peter Duin would like to approach the German market in the same way he does in the Netherlands. The physical distribution and installation in the Netherlands are left to a forwarder, while most of the sales and after-sales service is left to distributors. Some orders for machines are taken by the company directly, without a third party, but the large majority of sales go through a few large distributors, who have been given exclusivity within a certain geographic region. The prices of products sold directly to the customer are at the same level as the prices the distributors ask, to avoid a channel conflict. This does mean, however, that the direct sales are significantly more profitable, since Duin can pocket the distributors' margin.

Still, Peter Duin isn't enthusiastic about starting his own salesforce. He sees many advantages of working through distributors. One important point is that the distributor bears the risk of non-payment. 'The distributor knows his customers' financial situation, while most customers are new to me, so I have to check them out financially if I don't want to mess up'. A second advantage is that the distributor saves Duin considerable organizational work, such as quoting prices, so that Duin's employees can spend their time on more important business. Furthermore, distributors are better at maintaining customer relationships:

> The distributor doesn't only visit the customers to sell machines, but also to sharpen a saw. He's constantly around the customers and knows what they need and when they need it. He knows his area, does his daily rounds, hands out a brochure here and there, and can slowly soften up the customers for a sale.

Because of these benefits, Duin has given his distributors a high level of autonomy. 'In foreign markets I sell my machines to the distributors and that's that. I don't want to get involved any more. They have a sales office, they know their customers, so it's their business. I just make sure they get the machine they order from me.'

Duin does keep an eye on his distributors, however, and if they don't sell enough, he sacks them. Often this is necessary because a distributor, once armed with the exclusive rights to a region, can 'put you in a drawer and forget about you'. Since they're often also the representative of your competitor, with whom they may have a long-term relationship, they have no motivation to sell your products. This makes for a love–hate relationship between Duin and his distributors:

> I'm a technician, not a salesman, and I can't really get along with traders. They're the smart guys in blue blazers . . . I also notice that the Dutch distributor doesn't particularly like producers. Why? Because he's caught in the middle, between the customer and the producer. They know they're dependent on you. But if I keep my word there's no

problem. But they also know damn well that if they try something funny, they're out. For a distributor that's not a nice position to be in.

Deciding on a market entry strategy

As Peter Duin has his machines shipped to the Hanover Messe to test the extent of customer demand and scout for possible distributors, he is still wondering whether exporting via distributors is the best approach to the German market. And if it is, how can he find good distributors, motivate them and keep an eye on them as well?

While he is not entirely sure about the answers to these questions, at least he is sure about the German market. He is willing to try and, if he fails, to try again, since a strong position in this market is essential for the long-term success of Nico Duin BV.

Questions

1. Evaluate Peter Duin's motives for internationalization and his choice of Germany as the priority export market. Are there other, more appropriate, markets that Duin might enter?
2. What are the various alternative strategies open to Peter Duin to enter the German or another identified market? Which of these would be the most appropriate, why, and with what organizational implications?

Hudson Chemical Company

[This case was prepared by D. Leighton *et al.* in *Canadian Problems in Marketing*, 3rd edn, McGraw-Hill Ryerson Ltd. Used with permission.]

Hudson Chemical Company of Canada Limited began to manufacture a product brand-named 'Aqua-Pur' early in 1963. Aqua-Pur was a chemical agent used as part of the softening process for commercial boiler feed water. Of immediate importance to the company's executives was the problem of establishing a price policy. The company was at a severe competitive disadvantage, as their competition was an established firm which had enjoyed a virtual monopoly in the industry over the past 20 years. The General Manager knew that the establishment of a sound pricing policy would be instrumental in determining the company's success in entering the Canadian market.

Hudson Chemical Company of Canada Limited was a wholly-owned subsidiary of the Hudson Chemical Company Incorporated, a large US chemical firm with annual sales in excess of $500 million. The company, in addition to its eight plants in the United States, operated subsidiary firms in seven countries including Canada. On a consolidated basis Hudson's total assets were reported at just under $300 million. For some time the company had been noted for its excellent research and development facilities which were thought by many to account for its spectacular growth over the past 20 years. As a result of this research, Hudson had followed a policy of wide diversification within the chemical industry.

Hudson's largest foreign operation was in Canada, where Hudson Chemical Co. of Canada reported sales of almost $10 million a year. This firm operated one plant in Montreal but distributed its products nationally. The sales organization was divided into six product groups, each with a product manager and from two to five specialized salesmen. In 1963, the water treatment product group was relatively small, although the company felt it had a great potential. In addition to Aqua-Pur, the group handled a chemical fungus control for industrial water treatment and two other products, both of which represented relatively small volumes.

Most industrial concerns operated their own boiler plants and were continually facing the problems of treating boiler feed water. In hard water areas the problem was acute, as the chemicals within the water formed a sediment inside both pipes and tanks. Eventually this sediment clogged the system and often forced a programme of costly replacement. To overcome this, many firms installed water-softening devices on their boiler systems. Water softening was simply a chemical process which removed the hardening chemicals from the water before it was fed into the boiler.

In the early 1940s, Chicago Chemical Company developed a compound to be used in conjunction with the regular water-softening chemicals. This product did not in itself soften the water but rather dispersed the water-softening compounds, thus lengthening their economical life. It provided not only a saving in water-softening chemicals but also a reduction in the time and effort required to continually regenerate the softeners. Chicago Chemical patented the product in both United States and Canada under the name of Purafax.

Chicago Chemical was a relatively small firm specializing in certain water treatment chemicals. The company did not manufacture or sell water-softening chemicals as such. Trade sources reported that a large proportion of its business was in the sale of Purafax, while the remainder was made up of a variety of small-volume items such as a slime control agent and a fungi control chemical.

Since 1951, Hudson Chemical Co. had been working on a compound that would compete with Purafax. By 1957, a satisfactory compound had been developed, but to market it would have violated Chicago Chemical's patent rights. By 1961, however, these patent rights would terminate. Thus Hudson continued work on the product. During this period, two major findings were made. First, it was found that the major raw material in the compound could be extracted from brewer's spent grain. From the brewer's standpoint, this was waste material and could therefore be purchased by Hudson very cheaply. Second, Hudson developed an additive for the dispersing compound that would reduce rust formation in the boiler system. A number of the company officers felt this would be an excellent feature when the product was introduced into the market, particularly as Chicago Chemical's Purafax did not contain a rust-reducing agent. It was believed that with these refinements Aqua-Pur could readily compete with Purafax.

Tests with Aqua-Pur indicated that the proper formula for addition to softening chemicals was one gallon of Aqua-Pur for every seven gallons of water-softening chemical. Use of Aqua-Pur would reduce the amount of softening chemical required to do an equivalent job by 35 per cent. Water-softening chemical cost about 50 cents a gallon and a firm operating a boiler might use anywhere from $100 to $50 000 worth of softening chemical a year. The company realized Aqua-Pur would be of interest primarily to firms using between $10 000 and $50 000 worth of softening chemical, but that this range included most of the large production plants in the country. The savings in softening chemical by the use of Aqua-Pur for a firm initially using $20 000 worth of chemical would be:

	Before Aqua-Pur	With Aqua-Pur
Gallons of softening chemical	40 000	26 000
Aqua-Pur	0	3715

In late 1962, a decision was made to introduce Aqua-Pur to the Canadian market. The basis for this decision was a study conducted by the market research department which estimated Canadian sales of Purafax in 1961 at the equivalent of approximately 6 million gallons (of Aqua-Pur), or $4.5 million f.o.b. the Chicago Chemical Plant. A geographical breakdown of these figures is given in Table C11.1. The report noted that Chicago had concentrated its effort in the largest plants and had made few attempts to develop the smaller customers currently consuming $10 000 to $20 000 worth of softening chemical annually. It was the researchers' opinion that the potential might be at least twice current Purafax sales, particularly if a considerable cut in prices could be achieved.

In preparation for the new product the company had hired two new salesmen who were experienced in the water treatment field, and were considering hiring additional sales help. It was decided that the product would be most efficiently handled through distributors, at least until the product became established in the market. The salesmen would be responsible for training distributor personnel, providing technical assistance to the distributor and missionary work at

TABLE CS12.1 *The Canadian market 1961 (in gallons)*

British Columbia	900 000
Alberta	900 000
Saskatchewan	100 000
Manitoba	400 000
Ontario	2 000 000
Quebec	1 300 000
Maritimes	400 000
Total	6 000 000

the customer level. In addition, a man was brought in from the American company to act as product sales manager and to be directly responsible to the general manager of Hudson Chemical Co. of Canada. Mr Roberts, the new product sales manager, had several years' experience in both the development and sale of Aqua-Pur in the United States and was therefore considered a valuable asset to the Canadian company.

Immediately upon his arrival, Mr Roberts was called in by Mr Morton, the general manager, and together they started to plan a marketing programme for the new product. The first problem was to arrange for tests on the product by independent laboratories in each locality. Until such a time as a favourable report had been received from these laboratories, few customers could be interested in the new product. The company salesmen and the distributor's salesmen would have to contact both company purchasing agents and boiler or stationary engineers to make a sale. The latter had proved to be most influential from the company's experience in the United States.

Based on their experience in the US, it was decided that the distributor would have to install a dispenser and storage tank in the client's plant. The total cost of each installation ranged between $400 and $500. While some distributors considered this to be a definite problem, others realized the advantages it provided. There would be a sense of permanence in the supplier–customer relationship when such a physical installation had been made. The distributor would also have to service the installation and provide continuous technical assistance at a cost of from $200 to $500 a year or more depending in part upon the size of the account.

By May 1963, the company's plans to enter the Canadian market with Aqua-Pur were well launched. Several pilot runs had been put through the plant and a number of independent laboratory tests had been conducted. The results of these tests had been most satisfactory and would act as certification to the company's claim that the performance of their product was equal to, if not better than, that of Chicago Chemical's Purafax. As the product was introduced in each local market, however, additional tests would have to be conducted by local laboratories. The company did not anticipate any problems in this regard. Although price had not been mentioned, the company had obtained favourable reactions from a number of distributors after a series of informal meetings.

The more Mr Morton and Mr Roberts studied the situation, the more they realized the importance of establishing a sound pricing policy at the outset. Both executives felt that this would be the deciding factor in determining the success of the venture. As a basis from which to start, Mr Roberts suggested that serious study be given to each of the basic pricing alternatives open to them.

Before considering the alternatives individually, Mr Morton instructed the accountant to analyse the costs of the new product. The accountant presented the following facts:

1. The cost of direct labour, packaging, and raw materials amounted to 45c per gallon.
2. It was estimated that the new product should absorb $40 000 of general administrative overhead and $20 000 of general factory overhead per annum.
3. Grouped under fixed expenses were the following items:
   - A new 10 000 square foot addition to the existing plant had just been added at an average cost of $8 per square foot.
   - The new machinery for the process had cost $70 000 installed.
   - Early in June a new salesman had been hired which brought the salesforce complement to three men excluding the new product manager, Mr Roberts. Each salesman cost the company an estimated $15 000 per year including salary, expenses and fringe benefits.
   - Two laboratory men had been added, one of whom doubled as a plant supervisor for the new process, at an estimated $12 000 each.
   - Mr Robert's salary plus expenses was calculated at $20 000 per year.

Mr Roberts noted that the present machinery and plant had a capacity to produce 1.2 million gallons per year, and that an additional investment of approximately $50 000 could double this capacity.

Given these financial facts, the two executives started their analysis of three alternatives:

1. Mr Morton suggested that they first consider the pros and cons of simply meeting their competitor's prices. He noted that some changes would be necessary inasmuch as Aqua-Pur was in liquid form while Purafax was a powdered substance. However, a gallon equivalent to the pound price basis would be all that was required. By converting Chicago Chemical's price list from pounds to gallons, it was calculated that Hudson Chemical would receive an average price of 76 cents per gallon for its product f.o.b. the Montreal plant. Average freight costs would be about 20 cents a gallon and distributor margins about 40 cents a gallon, giving an estimated consumer price of $1.36 a gallon. This price would likely vary somewhat from customer to customer depending on size, location, competitive circumstances and distributor pricing policies but overall was roughly equivalent to delivered prices for Purafax. Mr Roberts stated that he believed this alternative would be the most suitable: first, because of its obvious simplicity it would be easy to explain to potential customers and, second, he did not feel the company knew the market sufficiently well either to judge the effect of a premium price on the consumer or to estimate what competitive retaliation might result should they cut the price. Although Mr Morton did agree that it was the alternative involving the least risk, he believed there were strong arguments for another alternative.
2. As a second alternative Mr Morton suggested that a price lower than Chicago Chemical's might be the best method of getting an initial foot-hold in the market. He noted that although they could expect some retaliation from Chicago, even a short lag would be of great assistance in getting established, and, in addition, a lower price might tend to enlarge the total market. It could quite conceivably make the product of interest to potential users who currently

considered it too expensive. Mr Roberts agreed that this was quite possible and that operating margins at the existing price level were sufficiently large to permit the reduction. However, he noted that to reduce prices would incur the wrath of the softener chemical companies, as it would mean further inroads into their sales. In other words, more firms would use Aqua-Pur to increase the life of normal softener chemicals. Mr Roberts attached considerable importance to this point, as the firms producing softening chemicals were for the most part large and could quite conceivably influence the consumer against Aqua-Pur. Mr Morton, on the other hand, questioned the importance of this threat. He believed that the consumer would not be influenced even if the chemical companies launched a campaign against Aqua-Pur.

3. The final alternative that the company considered was that of a premium price. Neither executive was particularly impressed with this possibility but they did recognize some of its merits. In the first place, the rust preventative included in Aqua-Pur gave them an advantage over Purafax. They could price just below what a combination of Purafax and a recognized rust preventative would cost the consumer. A premium price would mean even higher margins and, as a consequence, a lower volume would be sufficient to cover the overhead. This had much to recommend it because, for some time at least, the large Quebec and Ontario markets would be most difficult to enter.

Both Mr Roberts and Mr Morton knew that there were other factors that should be studied in each alternative. They also knew, however, that a decision had to be reached quickly if they were to get underway during 1963.

Questions

1. What type of competitive advantage does the Hudson Company have over the Chicago Company?
2. How would you proceed to segment this market?
3. Analyse the cost and profit implications of the three price levels contemplated by Hudson's management.
4. What is the maximum acceptable price for an average user of Aquapur?
5. Analyse the likely reactions of Purafax for each pricing alternative.
6. Which pricing strategy do you recommend and why?

Pagoda Chemical Company

[This case was prepared by W.J. Stanton in *Fundamentals of Marketing*, McGraw-Hill Book Co.]

Mr Stephen Martin, the general sales manager in the resins division of the Pagoda Chemical Company, was trying to decide how to meet competitive price-cutting tactics that were siphoning off several of his division's largest accounts. Pagoda Chemical Company was a large manufacturer and marketer of a wide variety of chemicals and plastics—both non-differentiated, standardized commodities as well as specialized, branded products. Annual sales were approximately $600 million.

Pagoda was organized into seven operating divisions and 14 staff-supporting departments. The seven operating divisions were engaged in manufacturing and sales and were divided along product lines. Each operating division was treated as an individual business; the assistant vice-president who headed a division was responsible for all phases of its operations, much like the president of a smaller company. Each division had its own production, sales, and development groups, each headed by a general manager. Each division also had its own national salesforce.

Through its resins division the Pagoda Chemical Company was the world's largest producer of a chemical, PX, which was used in the manufacture of synthetic resins. These resins were the basis for the production of paints, lacquers and varnishes. The quality of most domestically produced PX was about the same. Thus, Pagoda was marketing a non-differentiated, standardized commodity in this case. Until 1956 PX showed a sharply rising growth curve. With the advent of water-based paints, however, the use of PX levelled off and since then had shown only a minimal growth pattern.

Pagoda Chemical had traditionally spent more money than its competitors for research on (1) new uses for PX, (2) production facilities to improved quality, and (3) sales efforts to market PX. There were five domestic and several foreign competitors. Installed domestic capacity to produce PX was about 91 million pounds a year. Actual domestic production was on the order of 70 million pounds annually.

The resins division salesforce sold PX directly to other chemical companies and also to some large manufacturers of paints, lacquers and varnishes. In marketing PX, Pagoda regularly followed a policy of 'one price for all customers'. Under this policy, however, the company had lost several important accounts to competitors who were offering below-list prices to selected customers. In fact, Pagoda was the lone producer holding to the list price. Because of the raiding of its accounts, Pagoda had already been forced to make three price reductions on PX during the preceding three years.

In spite of the losses of some customers, Pagoda's sales of PX had shown a modest increase over the past few years. The increase was not satisfactory, however. Moreover, Mr Martin was worried that even this modest rate of increase would not continue in view of the fact that currently 25 per cent of the total domestic sales of PX were at less than list price.

Mr Martin identified five alternatives which he felt could be considered reasonable courses of action to meet this competitive price-cutting. One possibility was simply to continue the one-price policy and lower the list price only if important volume was being lost. One limit to this alternative was the risk that some customers, once lost, might never be regained even if the list price was later reduced. Selling at only one price, on the other hand, had earned Pagoda a bigger share of some large customers' requirements. Pagoda was finding that some previously loyal customers were becoming increasing reluctant to tell Pagoda of better offers received on PX.

A second, and completely opposite, alternative was to abandon the one-price policy and to meet competitive prices when and where they appeared. This policy would probably retain the business of accounts who were 'price buyers'. But it might result in the loss of those customers who admired Pagoda for being the lone industry adherent to a one-price policy. Furthermore, some customers threatened to cut their purchases of other Pagoda products if they ever heard that Pagoda was selling PX 'off list' to other buyers.

A third suggestion was to raise the list price and hope that no more 'raiding' would occur than already existed. The cost-price squeeze on PX and other chemicals produced by Pagoda would make a price increase particularly attractive to top management. Because of Pagoda's dominant position in the industry, some executives in the firm felt that Pagoda would always be holding a price umbrella over its competitors. Therefore, perhaps the best course would be to take some volume losses but to sell at a higher unit price. Of course, once this umbrella was raised, competitors with higher manufacturing costs would have more room to manoeuvre on price. A further deterrent to a price increase was the fact that all other chemicals used with PX to make synthetic resins had dropped sharply in price and continued under severe price pressure. Also, an increase could encourage some users to seek an already lower-priced chemical which, in some cases, might be used in place of PX.

Another possible choice was to meet competitive offers for short terms to assess whether the price-cutting would then stop. If so, Pagoda could then return to its list-price policy. If not, the list price could again be lowered. Legally and ethically Pagoda felt it had the right to use this approach, if it advised its customers that it was making this slight shift in order to assess the market tone accurately. By making it clear to its customers that Pagoda could and in all probability would meet bona fide competitive offers, the company hoped to play on loyalty so that a customer would notify Pagoda of lower prices before placing Pagoda's share with the lower-priced competition. By meeting these competitive prices head on, Pagoda hoped to signal to its competition that the umbrella was down and that Pagoda did not intend to lose any additional volume of PX. If competition did receive Pagoda's signal, it could stop a serious price war that was adversely affecting every PX producer's profits.

Finally, Mr Martin was considering keeping the one-price policy but seeking to expand the export market to make up for lost domestic volume. The quality of Pagoda's PX was generally better than that of most PX being consumed in foreign countries. Also, world-wide demand for PX was less than the total available. Pagoda's export volume had shown a good growth for the past two years, and the company had an excellent export marketing division. On the other hand, as was true of most exported chemicals, the net prices Pagoda received on PX were considerably lower than domestic prices. And credit problems in many countries were usually greater than those in the United States.

Question

What should Pagoda Chemical do to meet the competitive price-cutting on PX?

Volvo Trucks Europe

[This case was prepared by Professor Jean-Jacques Lambin and Tammy Bunn Hiller. Copyright © by Lovanium International Management Center, Belgium. Used with permission.]

In early May 1989, Ulf Selvin, vice-president of marketing, sales and service for Volvo Truck Corporation Europe Division (VTC Europe), was deep in thought. European Community (EC) directives aimed at creating a single internal EC market by the end of 1992 were reshaping the truck market in Europe. Truck buyers' sales support and service needs and demands were changing and becoming more pan-European. Competition was growing fiercer and increasingly pan-European as well.

VTC Europe had historically operated as a multi-domestic marketer, with each national importer management team responsible for the marketing, sales and service of Volvo trucks within its country. Recently, however, programmes had been initiated at both headquarters and importer level that were aimed at moving VTC Europe towards pan-European marketing. As Selvin reviewed the progress of these programmes, he deliberated over whether or not VTC Europe should attempt to become a 'Euro-marketer' and, if so, what the appropriate mix was between pan-European, regional, and national marketing of Volvo trucks in Europe. If he and his management team decided to move VTC Europe from multi-domestic to pan-European marketing, they would have to identify the critical steps that the company would need to take in order to make such a transition successful, including the implementation implications for VTC Europe's marketing strategy, marketing organization structure, marketing information systems, and human resource development policies.

Background

Volvo Truck Corporation (VTC) is a wholly owned subsidiary of AB Volvo (Volvo). Head-quartered in Göteborg, Sweden. Volvo is the largest industrial group in the Nordic region. Established in 1927 as an automobile manufacturer, the company gradually expanded its production to include trucks, buses, an extensive range of automotive components, and marine, aircraft, aerospace and industrial engines. Beginning in the late 1970s, Volvo diversified into the food industry, finance, and the oil, fruit and chemicals trade in order to increase the group's opportunities for growth and profitability and to counteract economic fluctuations. Volvo's structure and organization are characterized by decentralization and delegation of responsibility. Its myriad operations are united by the shared values of quality, service, ethical performance, and concern for people and the environment. The group's products are marketed around the world, with almost 90 per cent of sales occurring outside Sweden in 1988. Volvo's sales and net income totalled Swedish kronor (SEK) 96 639 million and SEK 4953 million, respectively, in 1988, up from 1987 levels of SEK 92 520 million and SEK 4636 million, respectively.

The first Volvo truck was manufactured in 1928. It was an immediate success and was met with high demand. Volvo's truck production expanded rapidly in the 1930s and 1940s. The profits from truck building financed the company's total operations for most of its first 20 years. It was not until the late 1940s that Volvo's automobile production became more than marginally viable.

By the late 1960s, however, this situation had reversed. Despite market leadership in Sweden and the rest of Scandinavia, Volvo's truck operations had become unprofitable because of heavy competition in new export markets, combined with problems with state-of-the-art truck models, which were placing severe stresses on Volvo's design and service departments. The truck business had become a drag on the company's automobile operations. Management contemplated divesting Volvo's truck operations but decided instead to form a separate truck division (VTC).

The creation of VTC marked the beginning of major investment in and continued expansion and profitability of Volvo's truck operations. During the 1970s and 1980s, VTC replaced its entire product line with new models and intensified its marketing efforts in international markets. Between 1979 and 1986, VTC became the first truck manufacturer to win the coveted 'Truck of the Year' award three times. In 1981, VTC acquired the truck assets of the White Motor Company in the United States and formed the Volvo White Truck Corporation. In 1987, White Volvo joined with General Motors' heavy-truck division to form a joint venture, the Volvo GM Heavy Truck Corporation, with Volvo as the majority shareholder, with responsibility for management.

VTC's truck production grew dramatically between 1970 and 1980, from 16 300 to 30 200 trucks. By 1988, production had doubled to 60 500 units. During the 1980s, VTC's share of the world market for trucks in the heavy class—gross vehicle weight (GVW) of greater than 16 tons—doubled to 11 per cent, and VTC became the world's second-largest producer of heavy trucks. In both 1987 and 1988, demand for Volvo trucks exceeded VTC's production capacity.

In 1988, VTC sold (delivered) 59 500 trucks worldwide. Table CS14.1 shows the breakout of VTC's 1987 and 1988 unit sales (deliveries) by market area. The two largest markets were

TABLE CS14.1 *Sales (deliveries) of Volvo trucks by market area and size*

Market area	Number of trucks delivered	
	1987	1989
Europe	29 300	31 600
North America	13 200	21 500
White Autocar/WHITEGMC	11 100	9 800*
Volvo	2 100	1 700
Latin America	3 300	3 300
Middle East	500	700
Australia	400	800
Other markets	1 000	1 600
Total	47 700	59 500
of which less than 16 tons GVW	6 500	6 500
of which greater than 16 tons GVW	41 200	53 000

*Includes GM's product line.

Western Europe and North America, which accounted for 52 and 36 per cent of sales, respectively. Almost 90 per cent of unit sales were in the heavy class. VTC earned SEK2645 million on sales of SEK22762 million in 1988, which represented 34 per cent of Volvo's 1988 operating income, up from 14 per cent in 1986. Figure CS14.1 contains graphs of VTC's sales, operating income, return on capital, and capital expenditure and development costs for the years 1984 through 1988.

VTC's organization chart is shown in Fig. CS14.2. Separate divisions are responsible for the manufacture and marketing of trucks in Europe, overseas, the United States and Brazil. Trucks are produced in ten Volvo-owned assembly plants. Of the 60 500 trucks manufactured by VTC in 1988, 20 000 were produced in the United States, 17 200 in Belgium, 14 400 in Sweden, 3700 in Scotland, 3200 in Brazil, 1500 in Australia and 500 in Peru. VTC's trucks are sold through a network of 850 dealers operating with 1200 service workshop in over 100 countries.

The product development division is responsible for the design and development of global truck concepts and components. It has development departments in Sweden, the United States, Belgium, the United Kingdom, Brazil and Australia. About 6 per cent of sales is invested in product development annually.

VTC Europe

VTC Europe is responsible for the production and marketing of Volvo trucks in Europe. The Western European market for heavy trucks grew 13 per cent in 1988, to 175 000 vehicles, based on new truck registration statistics. Despite full capacity utilization of its plants, VTC Europe was unable to keep pace with the market growth. Its share of the Western European heavy truck market declined from 14.3 per cent to 14 per cent. The Western European medium-truck market (10–16 tons GVW) grew by 4.5 per cent in 1988 to 42 000 vehicles. Volvo's share of this market declined from 10.6 per cent to 9.0 per cent. Table CS14.2 shows a comparison of new Volvo truck registrations and market shares by European country for 1987 and 1988.

Early 1989 registration figures indicated that Volvo was regaining lost shares in Europe in both the heavy- and medium-truck markets, as shown in Table CS14.3. VTC Europe began 1989 with a large delivery backlog. The division dramatically improved its delivery precision between January and March 1989, moving from 56 per cent to 80 per cent of trucks being delivered within one week of scheduled delivery. However, delivery precision varied widely by country. As of March 1989, it ranged from 54 per cent in Spain to 94 per cent in Austria and Finland.

Distribution system

Two layers in the distribution system separate Volvo truck factories from Volvo truck customers. Each country's distribution network is headed by an importer that is responsible for marketing, sales and service of Volvo trucks, parts distribution, and the creation and maintenance of a dealer network within its country. Of VTC Europe's 15 importer organizations, only four—Austria, Spain, Portugal and Greece—are independent importers. The other 11 are Volvo-owned. Importers purchase trucks from VTC Europe's corporate headquarters and sell them to the Volvo truck dealers within their countries, which in turn sell them to Volvo truck customers. VTC's European dealer network includes approximately 400 dealers and about 800

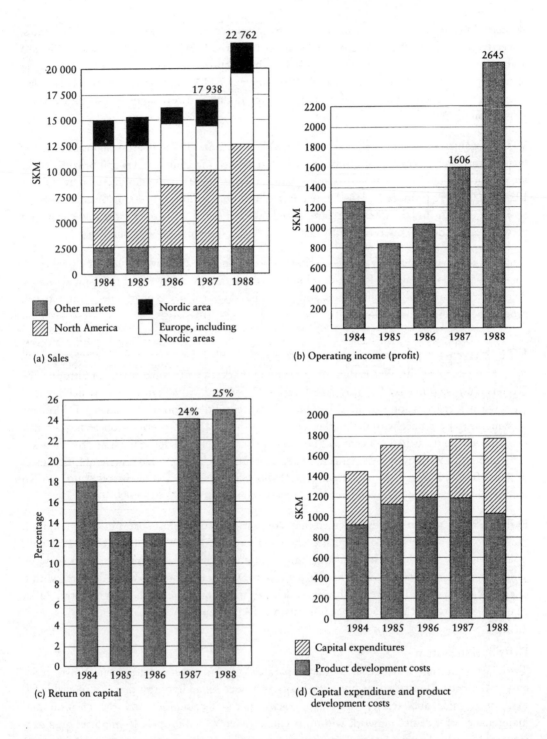

FIGURE CS14.1 *VTC financial trends, 1984–88. (a) Sales, (b) Operating income (profit), (c) Return on capital, (d) Capital expenditure and product development costs*

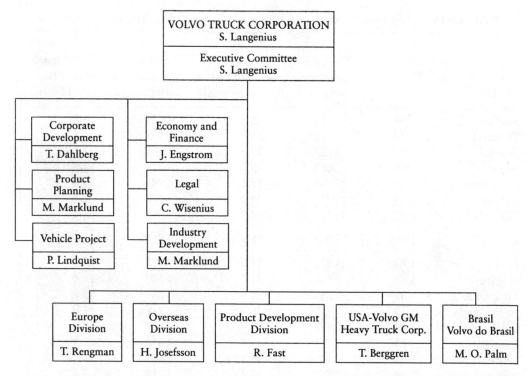

FIGURE CS14.2 *VTC organization chart*

TABLE CS14.2 *VTC Europe sales (registrations) and market share by country, 1987 and 1988*

Market	GVW class†	Numbers of new Volvo trucks registered*		Market share (percentage)	
		1987	1988	1987	1988
Great Britain	> 10 tons	5720	6610	15.5	15.4
France	> 9 tons	4340	4580	10.9	10.3
Sweden	> 10 tons	2970	3030	50.9	53.7
Netherlands	> 10 tons	2140	2070	17.7	16.4
Italy‡	> 9 tons	1490	1780	6.5	6.8
Spain	> 10 tons	1010	1700	6.5	8.4
Belgium	> 10 tons	1600	1600	21.6	20.1
Portugal	> 10 tons	1020	1280	29.9	27.1
Denmark	> 10 tons	1310	1130	29.8	33.0
Finland	> 10 tons	1060	1120	32.2	32.4
West Germany	> 10 tons	950	1030	3.0	3.2
Norway	> 10 tons	1280	800	40.6	37.5

*According to official registration statistics.

†Countries differ as to how they group their registration statistics by weight.

‡Preliminary information.

TABLE CS14.3 *Total market new truck registrations and Volvo share by country*

Market	For year ending*	Total market registration (>16 tons)	Volvo market share (%) (>16 tons)	Total market registrations (10–16 tons)	Volvo market share (%) (10–16 tons)
Sweden	3/89	5 541	51.5	938	74.1
Denmark	2/89	2 317	34.7	1 379	42.6
Finland	2/89	3 827	30.3	609	34.3
Norway	3/89	1 064	45.1	203	51.9
Great Britain	2/89	39 637	19.6	5 942	8.8
Ireland	1/89	1 782	14.2	672	1.4
Germany	2/89	28 157	4.2	5 593	2.4
Europe I	2/89†	83 962	18.1	14 851	14.8
France	3/89	35 921	11.3	8 371	7.3
Belgium	3/89	7 838	21.7	1 568	19.4
Luxembourg	12/88	385	31.9	86	19.8
Netherlands	1/89	9 419	16.0	1 489	22.0
Italy	2/89	27 198	7.5	13 328	2.0
Austria	2/89	3 751	14.5	1 072	7.8
Switzerland	12/88	3 349	15.4	476	19.7
Portugal	2/89	3 752	37.3	1 758	5.4
Spain	3/89	19 227	9.7	2 959	7.5
Greece	12/88	88	28.4	76	36.8
Israel	3/89	764	45.5	284	35.2
Europe II	2/89†	111 537	12.4	29 150	7.4
Europe Total (excl. Israel)	2/89†	195 263	14.4	44 288	9.6

*The most current registration information available was used for each market.

†Markets with late information on registrations were estimated as of 2/89 for Europe I, Europe II, and Europe Total.

service points. Almost all dealers are independent, although a few are Volvo-owned. All dealers are dedicated—that is, they sell only Volvo brand trucks.

The normal distribution network is rarely circumvented. Almost all sales are conducted through a dealer. VTC Europe headquarters sold directly to end-customers only when selling to the governments of state-controlled countries like the former Soviet Union. Similarly, importers by-pass their dealers infrequently. For example, the only customer to whom Belgium's importer makes direct sales is the Belgian army.

As a matter of course, importer organizations are headed and staffed by local nationals, although in a few cases a Swedish manager has headed an importer temporarily, during the transition from independent to Volvo-owned importership. Historically, importer managers are never transferred to work in the Swedish headquarters or in the importer organizations of other countries.

As one VTC Europe manager stated: 'importers are responsible for their country—period.' Each importer's management is evaluated and rewarded on the sales volume, market share and profit earned within its country. Importers regulate transfer prices for the trucks they purchased from VTC Europe headquarters. These transfer prices vary from country to country. Importers have the responsibility to set the prices at which they sell trucks to their dealers. Prices to dealers and, consequently, prices to truck-buying customers, vary considerably by country, depending on local competitive pressures. For example, Belgium has no national truck producer. Consequently, the Belgian importer prices Volvo's trucks significantly higher than does the French importer, which faces fierce competition from a local manufacturer.

Marketing communications

Prior to 1987, importers had complete control of the design and execution of marketing communications programmes employed within their countries. In early 1987, Roger Johansson, marketing support manager for VTC Europe, developed a corporate communication platform. His objective was two-fold. First, he hoped to encourage consistency in the visual presentation and underlying message of sales promotion and advertising materials across Europe, so as to enhance the total impact on customers of Volvo truck communications. Second, he aimed to improve the efficiency and cost effectiveness of the production of advertising and sales support materials. According to the communication platform, sales promotion and advertising activities were to be divided among all levels of the marketing organization—headquarters, importers and dealers—based on which level was best suited for a given activity.

The platform was designed to remain in effect through 1989. Every three years a new communication platform was to be introduced. The platform did not dictate the actual content of messages that importers and dealers could use in their communications. Instead, it encouraged creativity in designing messages that took account of local circumstances, as long as the thinking behind the message was consistent throughout Europe. Consistency was also encouraged by a visual identity programme that strictly specified the logotypes, emblems, symbols, colours, typefaces and layouts that were authorized for use throughout the marketing organization. Responsibility for complying with the precepts of the communications platform and visual identity programme rested with the management of each importer organization.

Personal selling occurs almost solely at the dealer level. Each importer runs its own training programmes for its dealer's salespeople. In addition, a state-of-the-art training facility in Göteborg is used to train both importer and dealer management whenever a new Volvo truck product is introduced. Importers and dealers are taught the features of the new truck, how those features translate into benefits for the potential buyers, and how to determine the bottom-line impact that the new truck will have on the potential buyer's profit-and-loss-statement.

Service

In addition to selling trucks, Volvo dealers maintain and repair them. Each dealer is responsible for designing its local service system to suit its customers' needs. Each importer is responsible for co-ordinating service on a national level and ensuring consistency in dealer service offerings throughout its country. Volvo's service philosophy is based on the principle of preventive maintenance. Volvo dealers offer their customers service agreements with fixed prices for maintenance service and repair. Trucks that operate internationally can participate in Volvo Action Service Europe, which provides 24-hour assistance throughout Europe in the event of a breakdown. Volvo offers a DKV/Volvo credit card to its customers, which can be used at most Volvo workshops in Western Europe and at thousands of gas and service stations.

Volvo's service systems are not consistent across Europe. Service agreements made with a dealer in one country are not automatically valid at service centres in another country. Even when they are honoured, prices for the same service or part often differ dramatically across countries, as does parts availability. Opening hours of service centres vary within and across countries, and the work habits and quality of mechanics differ significantly from country to country. According to importer management in Belgium, few Volvo truck owners use the DKV/Volvo credit card when travelling internationally. A customer explained why: 'We do not use the DKV card any more, except for fuel. Outside Belgium, we do not have the same discount; sometimes we find a difference of up to 22 per cent in exchange rate and sometimes the card is simply not accepted.' According to Jean de Ruyter, after-market manager of Volvo's Belgian importer, repairs made outside of a Volvo truck owner's home country typically result in a communication nightmare involving discussions among the customer, the repairing dealer, the importer, the customer's local dealer, and the importer in the customer's home country.

Market segmentation
Historically, VTC Europe segmented its market solely on the basis of GVW. It divided the European truck market into three segments: heavy trucks (more than 16 tons GVW), medium trucks (7–16 tons GVW), and light trucks (less than 7 tons GVW). Volvo does not produce trucks for the light-truck market. Medium-duty trucks are further split into a 10–16 ton market, where Volvo has a truck range across Europe, and a 7–10 ton market, where Volvo sells a model on selected markets. Therefore, marketing management ignores this segment and concentrates on the other two, emphasizing the heavy-truck segment in which Volvo has achieved the bulk of its success concentrating on tractors for international transport.

Marketing information systems
VTC Europe does not have a standardized method of forecasting sales across Europe. Each importer develops its annual sales forecast using its own forecasting technique. The importers' forecasts are sent to VTC Europe's marketing planning and logistics department, which uses them as a starting point for making a total forecast. Forecasts are used to plan production and for long-term capacity planning. In both 1987 and 1988, several importers underestimated annual sales by as much as 25 per cent, leading VTC Europe to underestimate its total sales substantially.

VTC Europe's marketing planning and logistics department conducts market research and market analysis. Market research includes both Europe-wide surveys and individual country surveys. Much of it is qualitative research intended to reveal how Volvo is performing relative to competitors. Results are shared with importer marketing managers. The department regularly tracks new truck registration statistics to try to discern market trends. It buys competitive production figures in order to learn the kinds of trucks that Volvo's competitors are building.

The department also tracks Volvo's production, delivery precision, turnover rate and market share by country.

In addition to research conducted by headquarters, importers commission marketing research in their own countries as needed. Most importer-initiated market research is conducted on a project-by-project basis, rather than on a recurrent basis. There is no standardized method of gathering data across countries.

The European truck market

Between 1970 and 1988, truck sales made by Western European manufacturers grew at a compound annual rate of almost 1 per cent. During that time, however, there were two exaggerated cycles. Sales boomed in the 1970s, peaking at 422 000 trucks (3.5 tons GVW and larger) in 1979. In the early 1980s, depression in Western Europe combined with collapse in demand from Middle East and African export markets. Sales bottomed out at 333 000 vehicles in 1984. Between 1984 and 1988, the Western European truck industry made a strong recovery. In 1988, sales reached 485 000 trucks. As Fig. CS14.3 shows, market growth was propelled by expansion in the heavy (greater than 16 tons GVW) and light (3.5–7.5 tons GVW) truck segments. Medium-truck sales (7.5–16 tons GVW) appeared to be in long-term decline. In 1988, approximately 310 000 new trucks (3.5 tons GVW and larger) were registered in Western Europe.

In 1950, there were 55 independent truck manufacturers in Western Europe. In 1989, there were 11. During the 1980s, several structural changes occurred in the European truck market. The most significant ones took place in the United Kingdom. Since the 1930s, both Ford and General Motors had based their European truck manufacturing in the United Kingdom. In 1986, Ford entered into a strategic alliance with Iveco, the truck subsidiary of Italy's Fiat, which led to the formation of Iveco-Ford. Ford ceded management control of both its UK operations and marketing to Iveco. A few months later, General Motors (Bedford-brand trucks) withdrew

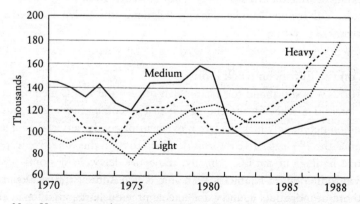

Note: Heavy = more than 16 tons GVW; medium = 7.5–16 tons GVW; light = 3.5–7.5 tons GVW.

FIGURE CS14.3 *Western European truck manufacturers' sales by truck size* (Source: *Financial Times*, 3 May 1989)

completely from truck manufacture in Europe after failed attempts to buy Enasa, MAN and Leyland Trucks. The state-owned Leyland Trucks was losing more than $1 million per week when, in 1987, the UK government wrote off Leyland's substantial debts in order to facilitate its merger with the Dutch truck maker DAF. DAF received 60 per cent of the equity of the merged company and effective control. The Rover Group received the remaining 40 per cent equity stake.

In continental Europe, structural changes were less dramatic. West Germany's Daimler-Benz, the market leader in Western Europe truck sales, reduced production capacity in the early 1980s. The other West German truck manufacturer, MAN, had been heavily reliant on Middle East markets. The 1983 cancellation of a half-completed contract with Iraq left MAN financially crippled in the early 1980s. MAN's management fought off a takeover attempt by General Motors, completely reorganized the company, concentrated on building up market presence in Western Europe, and regained profitability. In 1984, Iveco closed its unprofitable Unic truck plant in France, making RVI, the truck subsidiary of Renault, the sole truck producer in France. During the 1980s, RVI underwent a severe rationalization programme. By 1987, it was profitable for the first time since its formation in the mid-1970s. Enasa, Spain's only independent truck producer, entered into a joint venture with DAF for the development of a modern truck cab range, which was introduced in 1987. Both of Sweden's truck manufacturers, Volvo and Saab-Scania, survived the recession in very good shape without restructuring in Europe.

There is no common classification of trucks throughout Western Europe. Although the definition of the truck market varies by country, each country maintains new truck registration statistics, which industry members use to calculate market shares. In 1988, the top five truck manufacturers accounted for almost 75 per cent of total Western European truck sales (greater than 3.5 tons GVW). Daimler-Benz (23.7 per cent) was the market leader, followed by Iveco (20.6 per cent), RVT (11.4 per cent), DAF (9.4 per cent) and Volvo (9.0 per cent). In the two segments in which Volvo competed, heavy trucks and medium trucks (10–16 tons GVW only), Volvo was number two and number four in the Western European market, respectively, as shown in Table CS14.4. In 1988, the market leaders by individual country were as follows: DAF (Leyland) in the United Kingdom, Daimler-Benz in West Germany, RVT in France, Iveco in Italy, Enasa in Spain, DAF in the Netherlands, Volvo and Daimler-Benz in Belgium, and Volvo in Sweden, Denmark, Finland and Norway.

Impact of 1992 on the European truck industry

The expression '1992' was shorthand for a campaign to turn the 12 EC member countries into one barrier-free internal market by the end of 1992. The community's goal was to create a market of 322 million people in which the free movement of goods, services, people and capital was ensured. Among the 286 legislative reforms designed to fulfil this objective were ones aimed at liberalizing road haulage in the EC. Already, transport delays at customs posts had been shortened by the introduction on 1 January 1988 of a 'Single Administrative Document', which replaced the plethora of individual country documents previously required for inter-EC border crossings. Historically, inter-EC transport was strictly limited by a system of quotas that restricted the number of trips that haulers of one country could make into other EC countries in a given year. In June 1987, the EC member nations agreed to increase these quotas by 40 per cent per year in 1988 and 1989 and to abolish all road transport quotas to EC and non-EC

TABLE CS14.4 *Western European truck market shares by manufacturer based on new truck registrations*

Manufacturer	Market share (%) (>16 tons GVW)		Market share (%) (10–16 tons GVW)	
	1987	1988	1987	1988
Volvo	14.3	14.0	10.6	9.0
Daimler-Benz	20.1	18.9	23.9	23.7
Iveco	12.8	13.6	24.9	27.6
RVI	11.9	12.3	14.3	16.3
DAF	10.8	11.6	8.0	8.7
Scania	12.4	11.0	1.3	0.8
MAN	8.5	8.3	6.2	5.0
Pegaso	4.2	4.7	1.7	0.6
ERF	1.6	2.1	0	0
WRIGT	1.7	2.0	1.0	1.0
EBRO	0	0	2.0	2.7
Other	1.7	1.5	6.1	4.6

destinations by 1 January 1993. As a result of these two measures, industry analysts expected a 30 to 50 per cent increase in inter-EC trade by the year 2000.

The European Commission supported unrestricted cabotage—that is, freedom for a trucker registered in one EC country to collect and deliver loads between two points inside a second EC country. EC member states had not reached agreement on allowing unrestricted cabotage, but the Commission was pushing for agreement and implementation by the end of 1992. In 1989, restrictions on cabotage were partially responsible for 35 per cent of all trucks on EC roads travelling empty. Unrestricted cabotage would give trucks more flexibility to contract short hauls on their return trips, which would enable them to avoid returning from a long trip with an empty truck.

Trucking companies had already begun to vie for position in the EC's post-1992 transport market. Industry analysts expected concentration in the road haulage industry via mergers, acquisitions, and strategic alliances, particularly among fleets specializing in international traffic. Many observers believed that medium-sized fleets would be squeezed out in favour of small specialized haulers and large efficient international haulers. Most believed that the scramble for business would result in a major shake-up of the EC transport industry, after which there would be likely to be fewer total competitors and, perhaps, a smaller total market for heavy trucks.

The implications for European truck manufacturers were several. Inter-European transporters had already begun to demand that truck producers supply consistent systems of service and sales support across Europe. As 1992 approached, pressures to harmonize both truck and parts prices throughout Europe would probably increase, as large fleet owners attempted to negotiate Europe-wide prices. In addition, 'artificial' differences in truck product standards—that is, unique product standards that were designed solely to protect national markets—would likely disappear over time. Eventually, new trucks might be built to 'Euro-specifications', in contrast with the existing situation in which 'every European country had two unique possessions—a national anthem and a brake system standard'. As large trucking companies became increasingly international, the loyalty of their truck buyers to locally produced vehicles would likely wane. Competition between truck producers was expected to intensify as was concentration within the industry.

VTC Europe's moves towards pan-European marketing
Market segmentation and sales forecasting

In 1984, VTC Europe took over its previously independent Belgian importer. Throughout the early 1980s, VTC had experienced heavy price competition and low profitability in Belgium. In order to develop a sound marketing strategy designed to increase the profitability of VTC's Belgian operation, while at the same time satisfying its customers, André Durieux, then marketing manager of VTC Belgium, commissioned an outside consultant, Professor Robert Peeters of the Université Catholique de Louvain, to perform a brand image study in the Belgian truck market. Peeters designed and executed a quantitative survey of a representative sample of truck owners in Belgium.

The first objective of the study was to conceive a truck market segmentation scheme that would help Belgian management decide the right customer groups to target in order to increase the profitability of its sales. The study also aimed to discover the criteria that were determinant to truck owners when choosing a make of truck and, for each criterion, the position that Volvo and each of its competitors held in owners' minds. A third goal of the study was to determine the marketing mix through which VTC Belgium could send the right message to its target segments in the ways which would best reach them and influence them to buy Volvo trucks.

One of the outcomes of this research was the development of a truck industry segmentation scheme that Belgian management used in reshaping its marketing strategy. In 1987, Pol Jacobs, VTC Belgium's marketing and business development manager, commissioned a follow-up study in order to assess the impact of Volvo's post-1984 marketing efforts on brand image in Belgium and to reveal any changes that had occurred in the makeup of the market by segment. Comparing the results of the second survey with those of the first showed that the pattern of Volvo's penetration of different market segments in Belgium had changed significantly between 1984 and 1987. Between 1984 and 1989, VTC Belgium improved its profitability almost ten-fold. Jacobs was convinced that use of Peeter's segmentation scheme as a starting point from which to design Volvo's marketing strategy for Belgium had contributed to VTC Belgium's success. This segmentation scheme identified 60 unique segments based on four variables:

1. Fleet size
   a. Small (3 or fewer trucks)
   b. Medium (4–10 trucks)
   c. Large (10 or more trucks)
2. Gross vehicle weight (GVW)
   a. Less than or equal to 16 tons
   b. More than or equal to 16 tons

3. Transporter type
   a. Professional (firms whose primary business was transportation)
   b. Own account (firms that operated a truck fleet to conduct their primary business, for example, construction firms)
4. Principal truck usage
   a. Distribution (firms using trucks to transport goods)
   b. Construction (firms in the construction industry, where truck usage was primarily 'off-the-road')
   c. National (firms that used trucks exclusively within a country's borders)
   d. International (firms that shipped across country borders)
   e. Others (firms not otherwise categorized)

Table CS14.5 shows the distribution of truck registration in Belgium, which was believed to be similar in other countries in the European Community. This analysis indicated that (1) truck registrations were almost equally split between professional and own-account transporters, (2) about 35 per cent of trucks were operated within country borders, (3) 58.9 per cent of trucks were under 16 tons GVW, and (4) about 43 per cent of trucks were registered by large fleet (10 or more trucks) operators.

Peeters and Jacobs had also worked together to develop an econometric forecasting model, the intent of which was to improve the accuracy of Belgium's short-term (less than two years) sales

TABLE CS14.5 *Market segmentation grid (in percentages of total truck population)*

	Fleet size and weight						
	Small (⩽ 3)		Medium (4–10)		Large (⩾ 10)		
Activity or function	⩽16 t	⩾16 t	⩽16 t	⩾16 t	⩽ 16 t	⩾ 16 t	Total
Own-account transporters							
Distribution	7.3	4.5	1.1	1.8	0.4	2.1	17.2
Construction	0.1	1.1	0.9	1.4	1.7	1.6	6.8
National	4.7	1.6	1.4	3.8	1.7	3.6	16.8
International	1.3	0.9	0.2	1.3	–	1.4	5.1
Others	–	0.6	0.3	–	2.5	–	3.4
Professional transporters							
Distribution	1.1	0.8	0.9	1.6	–	1.6	6.0
Construction	0.2	1.6	–	0.4	–	1.2	3.4
National	1.4	1.5	1.4	3.0	2.5	8.5	18.3
International	0.2	0.7	0.5	6.1	0.4	14.7	22.6
Others	–	0.4	–	–	–	–	0.4
Total	16.3	13.7	6.7	19.4	9.2	34.7	100.0

Note: First entry, for example, means that 7.3 per cent of all truck registrations were less than or equal to 16 tons GVW, fleet owner-operators engaged in distribution.
Source: Dealer survey and truck registrations (disguised data).

forecasts. In 1989, the model was being tested in both Belgium and the United Kingdom. Ulf Norman, VTC Europe's manager of marketing planning and logistics, was supportive of expanding the model's use throughout Europe if it proved successful and reliable in the United Kingdom and Belgium.

Volvo Euro Truck Dealer and Eurofleet task forces

In late 1988, Selvin organized the 'Volvo Euro Truck Dealer' (VETD) project. Its steering committee was made up of two VTC Europe headquarters service managers and five importer after-sales and service managers (from Belgium, France, Italy, the Netherlands and the United Kingdom). Chaired by John de Ruyter, the steering committee was charged with establishing the project's objectives: co-ordinating the working process of the project among VTC, Volvo Parts Corporation (VPC), Volvo Dealer Facilities (VDF), and the importers; organizing and providing education for the importers; advising VTC and VPC in policy matters relating to the project; allocating specific tasks to work groups; and motivating all parties involved to take an active part in the project.

By the end of March 1989, the VETD steering committee had established the project's objectives and the procedures that were to be followed at the importer level in order to realize those objectives. The fundamental objective of the VETD project was to create a common Volvo truck environment at all Volvo dealers in the EC (Switzerland and Austria were included in the project although they were not EC members). The desired Volvo environment was translated into specific 'Euro Dealer Standards' that applied to the external, internal and service environments of all Volvo dealers. The importers were charged with evaluating their existing dealerships, establishing an action plan for each dealer and following up to ensure that the plans were correctly executed.

Both the objectives and the importer working procedures were presented to VTC Europe's importer truck division managers in April 1989. Each manager was directed to appoint within his organization a VETD staff that included one specialist who would be responsible for the project. The next step would be taken in June, when the importer's newly appointed VETD specialists were scheduled to be trained.

Around the time that the VETD project was initiated, Selvin created a 'Eurofleet task force' composed of the truck division managers of each of VTC Europe's six largest importers and a headquarters liaison. The purpose of the task force was for the importers to work together to satisfy the needs of VTC's international fleet customers. Through May 1989, the Eurofleet task force had operated unsystematically, attending to each issue individually as it arose.

Pan-European management training

Selvin had identified 200 VTC importer and headquarter managers throughout Europe whom he targeted to attend a three-day training seminar at the Lovanium International Management Center in Belgium. The purpose of the seminar was for the managers to think through, and discuss together, the changes that were occurring in the European truck industry due to '1992' and the impact of those changes on VTC's business. Managers were to be trained in groups of approximately 35. The groups were to be cross-sectional, made up of managers from different countries and different functional areas, in order to foster the interchange of ideas and co-operation throughout the organization. The first seminar had been conducted in March 1989. The second one was scheduled for June 1989.

The future of pan-European marketing in VTC Europe

Selvin strongly believed that, in order to be successfully implemented, any attempts to move VTC Europe towards pan-European marketing would require the full support of both head-quarters and importer management. Importer managers would not likely support a pan-European strategy that conflicted with their local interests or was perceived as being dictated from Sweden. Therefore, Selvin was convinced that it was crucial to involve managers from throughout the organization in the development and implementation of any future steps towards pan-European marketing.

Godiva Europe

[This case study has been prepared by Professeur Jean-Jacques Lambin, of Louvain University, Louvain-la-Neuve, Belgium, with the co-operation of Jean-François Buslain and Sophie Lambin. Certain names and data have been disguised and the case cannot be used as a source of information for market research. Used with permission.]

In July 1991, Charles van der Veken, president of Godiva Europe, examined with satisfaction the financial results of Godiva Belgium for the last period, which showed an operating profit of BF13 million (in 1991, US$1 = 34 Belgian francs). 'We've come a long way,' he thought to himself, remembering the financial situation he inherited just one year ago, which showed a loss of BF10 million. Over the course of the past year van der Veken had completely restructured the company. He started by firing the marketing and sales staff and then changed the retail distribution network by removing Godiva's representation from numerous stores. He then completely rethought the decoration and design of the remaining stores, and established precise rules of organization and functioning applicable to those stores. These changes made the Godiva-Belgium network of franchises comparable to those in the United States and Japan. For, while in all countries Godiva stores conveyed an image of luxury and of high scale products, in Belgium, where the Godiva concept was originally conceived, this image was scarcely maintained. Fearing what he called the 'boomerang effect', van der Veken had first focused on restructuring the Godiva retail network, an objective that was today on the road to realization. 'It is time', thought van der Veken, 'to communicate the desired image of Godiva more widely, now that we have a retail network capable of maintaining that image on the level of the Triad Countries.' (The Triad countries include the USA, Japan and countries in Western Europe.)

The Godiva Europe company

Godiva has its roots in Belgium, where the hand crafting of chocolates stems from a long tradition. Joseph Draps, founder of Godiva in the 1920s, took control of the family business upon the death of his father and created an assortment of prestigious chocolates for which he lacked a name. He finally chose the name 'Godiva' because it had an international sound and a history, that of Lady Godiva:

> Lady Godiva is the heroine of an English legend. She was the wife of Leofric, Count of Chester in the 11th century, whom she married around 1050. Roger de Wendower (13th century) tells that Godiva implored Leofric to lower the taxes that were crushing Coventry. The Count would not consent unless his wife would walk through the town completely naked, which she did, covered only by her long hair. John Brompton (16th century) added that nobody saw her. According to a ballad from the 17th century, Godiva ordered all the inhabitants to remain at home. The only one to see her was an indiscreet Peeping Tom. Since 1678, every three years in Coventry, a Godiva Procession is held.
>
> (*Grand Larousse*, Vol. 5, p. 522)

Godiva was purchased in 1974 by the multinational Campbell Soup Company. Godiva International is made up of three decision centres: Godiva Europe, Godiva USA, and Godiva

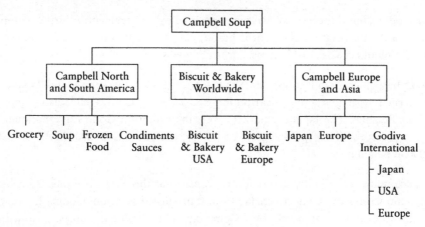

FIGURE CS15.1 *Campbell Soup organizational structure*

Japan, as shown in Fig. CS15.1. An essentially Belgian company in the beginning, Godiva has become an almost entirely triadic enterprise with a presence in the United States, Japan and Western Europe.

Godiva Europe is headquartered in Brussels, Belgium. The company's factory, which has 3000 tons of annual production capacity, is also situated in Brussels, from where products are exported to more than 20 countries throughout the world, including Japan. There is another production unit in the United States, which can provide about 90 per cent of the needs of the US market, with the remainder being imported from Belgium.

In 1990, Godiva Europe had annual sales of BF926 million. The company is well placed to serve Belgium, its largest market. After Belgium, the principal European markets are France, Great Britain, Germany, Spain and Portugal. Godiva USA and Godiva Japan distribute Godiva products to their respective markets and constitute the two other most important markets.

The largest part of European production volume (55 per cent) is sold under the Godiva brand name, about 10 per cent is sold through private label arrangements, and another 10 per cent is sold under the brand Corné Toison d'Or; 25 per cent of Godiva Europe's production is sold directly to Godiva Japan and Godiva USA at a company transfer price. Thus, only 65 per cent of the total sales are made in Europe, under the brand name Godiva. A significant share of Godiva Europe's sales are made through more than 20 airport duty-free shops throughout the world. Those sales, free of value-added tax (VAT), are made at the expense of local country sales, but they help to establish the international image of Godiva.[1]

Godiva Europe also owns the Corné Toison d'Or brand, which is distributed through 40 stores in Belgium, which are mostly located in the Brussels area. This brand has an image very similar to Godiva: a refined, hand-made, luxury product. The acquisition of Corné Toison d'Or was made in 1989 to fully exploit the production capacity of the Brussels plant modernized two years earlier. The original objective was to differentiate the positioning of the brand Corné Toison

---

[1] A value-added tax is a government tax levied upon the value that is added to products as they progress from raw material to consumer goods.

d'Or from Godiva, but this objective was never pursued by management. A further complication stemmed from the fact that another Corné brand, Corné Port Royal, also exists in the Belgian market with a retail network of 18 stores.

Godiva USA has a factory in Pennysylvania that services the US market. Godiva Japan, which is solely concerned with marketing, distribution and sales of Godiva chocolates, imports the product from Belgium. The Japanese market is very important for Godiva International because of the high price level, BF4000 per kilogram (= 2.2 lbs) compared to BF2000 in the United States, and BF1000 in Belgium.

The reference market of Godiva International consists of the Triad Nations. As a branch of Campbell Soup Company, Godiva benefits from a privileged position. Godiva International is directly attached to the Campbell Soup Company Vice President Europe-Asia without an intermediary who facilitates communication.

The world chocolate market

Unlike coffee or tea, chocolate lends itself to multiple preparations. It can be eaten or drunk, munched or savoured. The official journal of the European Community divides chocolate into four categories: bars of chocolate that are filled or not filled, chocolate candies or chocolates (called 'pralines' in Belgium) such as Godiva's chocolates and other chocolate preparations.

Chocolate consumption stabilized in the mid-1980s as a result of increasing raw material costs and an ensuing price rise of finished products. As depicted in Table CS15.1, the past three years have shown very good performances with worldwide consumption of confectionery chocolate (all categories included) of just over 3 million tons in 1989, or an increase of 30.7 per cent compared with 1980 consumption. Over-proportional consumption was observed in Japan (+54.2 per cent), Italy (+102.1 per cent), Australia (+45.1 per cent) and the United States since 1980.

A distinction is made between industrial and chocolate pralines within the chocolate candies category. Industrial chocolates are sold in pre-wrapped boxes with or without brand names. The generic boxes are mostly sold through large retail chains at Christmas or Easter; brand boxes are luxurious, offer a high-quality assortment of chocolates, and emphasize the brand name in the package and through mass-media advertising. Typical of this subcategory is the brand Mon Chéri from Ferrero. The sales of generic boxes are stable in Europe, while sales of brand boxes are increasing. This suggests that consumers pay attention to brand names and to the quality image communicated by chocolate packaging and advertising.

TABLE CS15.1 *Chocolate confectionery world consumption (in thousands of tons)*

Years	1980	1985	1986	1987	1988	1989
Tons	2359.6	2778.1	2780.2	2862.0	2990.8	3083.6
Index	100	118	118	121	127	131

Source: IOCCC, December 1990, p. 45.

Chocolate pralines, on the other hand, designate chocolate products that are hand-made or decorated by hand. The distinctive characteristics of pralines are their delicate flavour and luxurious packaging. They are also highly perishable and fragile with regard to conservation and transport. Typically, Godiva chocolates belong to this last product category.

Chocolate consumption per country

The per capita consumption of chocolate varies among countries as shown in Table CS15.2. Chocolate consumption is higher in the northern part of Europe and lower in the Mediterranean region. In 1990, Switzerland had the highest per capita consumption with 9.4 kilograms per person. The lowest per capita consumption rate is observed in Spain with 1.2 kilograms per person.

Table CS15.2 also shows that the share of chocolate candies (namely, pralines), with respect to total chocolate confectionery consumption, is strongest in Belgium with 44 per cent against 41 per cent in Great Britain, 37 per cent in France, 35 per cent in Italy and 34 per cent in Switzerland. Switzerland is the largest consumer of chocolate candies, followed close by the United Kingdom and Belgium, while the other countries are found far behind these three leaders.

In examining the level of consumption reached in countries such as Switzerland, the United Kingdom and Belgium, it is possible to get an idea of the enormous potential that the world chocolate market holds. In fact, countries like Spain, Italy and Japan are susceptible to one day reaching such a level of consumption roughly comparable to Switzerland, the United Kingdom and Belgium provided effective marketing programmes are implemented. Available industry statistics do not allow more precise estimates of the share of 'chocolate pralines' in the category of chocolate candies.

TABLE CS15.2 *Chocolate confectionery consumption per country*

	Per capita consumption in kilograms in 1989		Share of chocolates in confectionery chocolate (%)
Country	Chocolate candies	Chocolate confectionery	
Belgium	2.65	6.09	43.5
Denmark	1.17	5.61	20.9
France	1.69	4.59	36.8
Spain	0.14	1.21	11.6
Italy	0.65	1.84	35.3
Japan	0.44	1.59	27.8
German Federal Republic	1.64	6.81	24.1
Switzerland	3.17	9.41	33.9
United Kingdom	2.96	7.15	41.4
United States	1.14	4.77	23.9

Source: IOCCC, Statistical bulletin, Brussels, December 1990. Chocolate candies, candy bars, pralines and other chocolate products. Solid and filled bars and chocolate products.

TABLE CS15.3 *Evolution of chocolate confectionery consumption: average yearly growth rate, 1980–89*

Country	Consumption (kilograms per person)		Average growth	
	1980	1989	1980 = 100	Average growth rate (%)
Belgium	6.04	6.09	100.8	1.76
Denmark	4.80	5.61	116.9	1.79
France	3.96	4.59	115.9	1.65
Spain	nd	1.21	nd	–
Italy	0.92	1.84	200.0	8.00
Japan	1.09	1.59	145.9	4.28
German Federal Republic	6.56	6.81	103.8	0.42
Switzerland	8.44	9.41	111.5	1.22
United Kingdom	5.48	7.15	130.5	3.00
United States	3.69	4.77	129.3	2.89

nd = no data.
Source: IOCCC, December 1990, p. 49.

Evolution of consumption

Growth rates of chocolate confectionery are also very different among countries as shown in Table CS15.3. Countries experiencing the highest growth rates are Italy, Japan, the United Kingdom and the United States. With the exception of the United Kingdom, these are the countries where the per capita consumption is the lowest. The largest consumer countries like Belgium, Germany and Switzerland have probably reached a plateau in terms of per capita consumption.

Purchase behaviour of the chocolate consumer

Chocolate was imported to Europe by the Spanish at the time of the exploration of the New World. At that time, only the wealthy ate chocolate.

Today, chocolate is a mass-consumption product, accessible to everyone. Consumers are demanding and desire variety. In making chocolate a luxury product, chocolatiers have given chocolates a certain nobleness. The hand-worked character of production and refined decoration give chocolates their status. Chocolates are offered at holidays and other special occasions, and are eaten among friends in an atmosphere of warmth. They are not purchased like bars of chocolate; the behaviour of the consumer of chocolate pralines is much more deliberate and involved. The higher prices of chocolate pralines with respect to the other categories of chocolate do not inhibit the consumer but limit more impulsive purchases.

The consumption of chocolate of all categories is associated with pleasure. A qualitative study of the Belgian market shows that this pleasure is associated with the ideas of refinement, taste pleasure and gift: '... chocolate pralines are offered as a gift while chocolate bars are purchased for self-consumption. A praline would be mainly feminine, ... women seem to appreciate them more and pralines are described by them as refined and fine.' In addition, the strong and powerful taste, a particular form, the consistency of chocolate that melts in the mouth, and the feel of the chocolate to the touch are also factors to which the consumer is sensitive. Finally, the idea of health, of a pure product devoid of chemicals, is also in the consumer's mind.

Godiva chocolates in the world

The ancestry of chocolates can be traced to the chef of the Duke of Choiseul de Plessis-Praslin, an ambassador of Louis XIII of France, when he prepared almonds browned in caramelized sugar. However, chocolates as we know them today, a filling surrounded by chocolate, were born in Belgium. It was at the end of the nineteenth century that Jean Neuhaus, son of a confectioner from Neuchatel living in Brussels, created the first chocolates that he named 'pralines'.

The current concern of Godiva International is to convey a similar image of Godiva chocolates across the world: the image of a luxury chocolate that is typically Belgian. In what follows, the main characteristics of consumers in each country where Godiva is distributed will be briefly presented.

Belgium

Belgium is the birthplace of chocolates and where their consumption is strongest. While there are no significant differences in the consumption rate among the different Belgian regions, differences do exist among the four main socioprofessional categories, as shown in Table CS15.4.

In 60 per cent of purchases, chocolates are offered as gifts and consumers make a clear distinction between a purchase for self-consumption and for a gift. The customer prefers a package where he or she may select the assortment. However, the image of chocolate pralines has aged; chocolates have become a product more comparable to flowers than to a luxury product. The results of a brand image study conducted in the Brussels ares (see Appendix A) shows that, while Godiva is strongly associated with the items 'most expensive', 'nicest packaging' and 'most beautiful stores', it is not clearly perceived as very different from its main competitors, Neuhaus namely, on items associated with superior quality or a significant quality differential. Neuhaus and Corné, two directly competing brands, are perceived in a very similar way as shown in the perceptual map presented in Fig. CS15.2.

TABLE CS15.4 *The demand for pralines in Belgium: average expenditure per household in 1988 (BF)*

Regions	Belgium	Brussels	Wallonie	Flanders
	814	884	812	793
Households	Independent	White collar	Blue collar	Inactive
	1239	800	567	755

Source: INS, *Enquête sur les budgets des ménages* (1988). The total population includes 3 876 549 households.

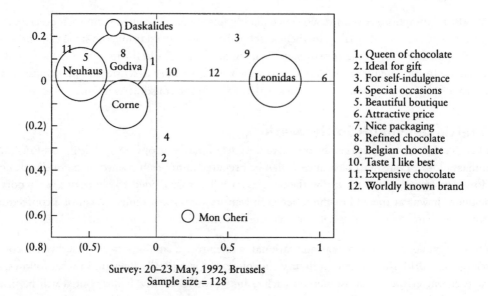

FIGURE CS15.2 *Brand image study: chocolate pralines in Belgium (encircled area = awareness)*

In Belgium, Godiva holds a 10 per cent market share and Léonidas 43 per cent. Léonidas also has a large international coverage with more than 1500 outlets throughout the world and a production capacity of 10 000 tons, or three times that of Godiva Europe. In 1991, the size of the total Belgian market for chocolate pralines is estimated to be BF3.6 billion (VAT included) or about 8800 tons. This estimate is based on the data presented in Table CS15.4.

France
French chocolate is darker, dryer and more bitter than Belgian chocolate. Belgian chocolates are, however, well known and appreciated due to Léonidas, which introduced chocolates in France and today holds the largest market share and sells through 250 boutiques. Belgian chocolates are represented as well by Jeff de Bruges, which belongs to Neuhaus. Godiva has a share in a small niche, which is also occupied by several French chocolatiers, none of whom have national market coverage. In France, chocolates are above all regarded as a gift that is offered on certain special occasions, and their purchase is very seasonal (60 per cent of all purchases are made at Christmas), which poses problems of profitability during periods of lower sales. Estimates of market size are presented in Table CS15.5.

United Kingdom
An assortment of confectionery products, in which different types of chocolate are mixed, is most appreciated in the United Kingdom. Godiva is currently being introduced to the British market and seeks to create the concept of high-quality and more refined Belgian chocolates. The change of mentality is progressing, but the British are viewed as rather conservative and the economic climate is not very favourable for a luxury product. Marks & Spencer, an upscale British retailer, is selling Belgian chocolates under the private brand name Saint Michael. The Belgian origin of the chocolates is clearly indicated in the packaging, however.

TABLE CS15.5 *Estimated consumption of chocolates in France; 1988–90 (in tons)*

Year	1988	1989	1990
Production	44 302	47 660	50 720
Imports (+)	9677	10 478	11 546
Exports (−)	3788	5739	7970
Total consumption	50 191	52 399	54 365
Per capita consumption	0.900 kg	0.935 kg	0.965 kg

Source: 'Production des IAA': *SCEES* (December 1991): 61 (bonbons de chocolat). Eurostat 'Foreign Trade'—Categories: 1806.90.11 and 1806.90.19. The category 'bonbons de chocolat' includes products other than chocolate pralines: Thus, total consumption is overestimated.

Spain and Portugal

In Spain and Portugal, chocolate pralines are a completely new concept. Godiva was the first to introduce chocolates a few years ago, and the reception was excellent. Godiva chocolates immediately acquired the image of a refined, luxury product. In Spain, Godiva is sold through the upscale department store Corte Inglese and by several franchises. Consumers' attitudes towards chocolate is very positive. Chocolates are principally offered as gifts and most often in luxurious boxes.

Germany

In Germany, a 'chocolates culture' does not really exist. Germans appear to be satisfied with a classic chocolate bar and do not yet place much importance on the distinctive qualities of fine chocolates. Godiva pralines are distributed through five franchised dealers.

Other European countries

In Holland, chocolate pralines are perceived as too expensive. In Italy and in the Nordic countries, chocolate praline consumption is still a very marginal phenomenon.

United States

Chocolates are very popular in the United States. Chocolates are given as presents on special occasions such as birthdays, Valentine's Day and Christmas. Chocolates are typically offered in pre-wrapped packages, with an interior form to house them. The output of the Godiva facility in Pennsylvania almost suffices to cover the needs of present domestic consumption. A small proportion of the Brussels plant output is exported to the United States. The Belgian factory delivers only new products or some products that cannot be produced by the Pennsylvania plant, such as the Godiva golf balls and the chocolate cartridges. In addition to 95 company-owned stores, 800 outlets carry Godiva chocolates in the United States. These outlets are generally located in upscale department stores situated in suburban shopping malls, like Lord & Taylor, Neiman Marcus, Saks Fifth Avenue, Pilenes and I Magnin.

Japan

In Japan, the Godiva chocolate is perceived foremost as European (60 per cent as Belgian and 40 per cent as Swiss or French). Chocolates are a prestigious and luxury gift. A large problem of seasonality exists in Japan as 75 per cent of purchase take place near Valentine's Day. A unique feature of this market is that Japanese women give Japanese men chocolates on Valentine's Day. The Japanese market is a very attractive market for Godiva International and is still expanding.

The duty-free market

In addition to these countries, one must also include the duty-free market, which represents a very significant market segment in terms of output. The number of duty-free stores is still increasing, and sales are closely linked to the development of passenger traffic. Godiva holds a very strong position in this market where Léonidas is not present.

Generally speaking, the annual growth potential in Europe is very different and varies from country to country. In the United States, growth varies between 5 and 10 per cent annually, while in Japan growth is very strong, varying between 20 to 25 per cent annually.

Godiva's marketing strategy

Godiva pralines are produced by four methods of fabrication: those that are formed in a mould, those that are hollowed then filled, those where a solid filling is coated with chocolate and, finally, those that are produced entirely by hand: hand-made chocolates. Seventy per cent of Godiva pralines are machine-made, and 30 per cent are hand-made. However, 60 per cent of the 70 per cent machine-made chocolates must be decorated by hand. Hand decoration is necessary to assure the quality level and the look of the praline.

Godiva strives to find an optimal compromise between automation and hand-work, hoping both to ensure the profitability and to perpetuate the name of Godiva as a producer of hand-made luxury chocolates. However, the difference in production costs between machine-made and hand-made chocolates is considerable (hand-made chocolates can cost up to seven times more than machine-made). Charles van der Veken often had second thoughts about the wisdom of maintaining this product policy. He thought:

> Isn't the investment in making hand-made chocolates disproportional to the expectations of our customers? Do they really perceive the added value of these hand-made chocolates? Aren't these chocolates just a bit too sophisticated?

Whatever the case, the objective pursued by Godiva is to convert the European market to the quality level of the Godiva praline. The Belgium consumer is the reference point: 'Shouldn't a product that has passed the test of the Belgian consumer, a fine connoisseur of chocolate and a demanding customer, be assured of success throughout the world?'

The Godiva facility in Belgium produces chocolates for the entire world, with the exception of the United States. Products exported from Belgium are identical for all countries, but sales by items are different. For example, in France, the demand for drier and more bitter chocolates is stronger while in the United Kingdom, cream and white chocolates are more popular. The production capacity of the Belgian factory is not fully utilized, and there is a significant available capacity. Today, the US factory still produces a slightly different and more limited assortment of chocolate pralines. These differences will progressively vanish, and the trend is towards similar production. The planning of production is particularly complex, however, because of the high seasonality of consumption combined with the emphasis on chocolate freshness.

Packaging policy

Only packaging will distinguish one country from another in order to better meet national and local chocolate consumption habits. In the United States, the tradition is to purchase chocolates pre-wrapped, while in Europe and Japan the custom-made assortment dominates. What's more, in Japan, chocolates are purchased in very small quantities (given the price); thus the beauty of the packaging becomes predominant, whereas in Europe and more precisely in Belgium, the value of the gift is more often related to the judicious assortment of chocolates that were chosen. As stated by a Godiva dealer, 'Customers have very precise ideas on the type of assortment they want, even for gifts, and they don't like to buy prewrapped standard assortments.'

Currently, the trend in packaging at Godiva is packaging by themes called 'collections'. With these 'collections' Godiva leaves the food industry for the luxury products sector. These hand-made creations constitute a research and development activity that ensures continuous innovation, and provides renewed promotional displays in the Godiva boutiques. In these 'collections', beautiful fabric boxes, hand-crafted according to the principles of 'haute couture', will illustrate through the calendar Valentine's Day, Spring, Easter, Mother' Day, Christmas, etc. In Belgium, the price of such a box (BF1000) is exorbitant with respect to the price of the chocolates: thus these boxes serve more often for in-store decoration than for sales.

For several years, Godiva has also tried to develop tea rooms attached to Godiva boutiques where customers can eat fine pastries or ice cream. The people who stop here see these rooms as havens of peace where they can rest between purchases while shopping and buy a few chocolates or even a box of chocolates.

Pricing policy

Making a Godiva chocolate incorporates an enormous amount of manual labour and the gross margins are modest (35 to 40 per cent on average), while top management of Campbell Soup requires a 15 per cent rate of return on capital invested for Godiva, a normal rate of return for a luxury product.

From one country to another, the price differences are great as shown in Table CS15.6. One of the main preoccupations of Godiva Europe is to standardize retail prices at the European level, in view of the unified European Community in 1993.

Previously, Godiva franchisees were held to a contract with the Godiva national and had to be supplied within that country. From 1993 on, it will no longer be possible to keep French franchisees from getting their supplies directly from the Belgian factory, which sells its chocolates at a much lower price. This is why prices must be modified. This adaptation has been started in Belgium with a 10 per cent increase in prices effective 1 August 1991. The price of one kilo of Godiva chocolates is BF1080, whereas the average market price for chocolates in Belgium is BF450 per kilo.

TABLE CS15.6 *Price of one kilo of Godiva pralines (BF)*

Country	Price to franchisees	Retail price (VAT included)	VAT (%)
Belgium	640	1080	6.0
France	763	1920	18.6
Spain	640	2145	6.0
United Kingdom	757	1782	17.5
Italy	640	2009	9.0
Holland	640	1261	6.0
Germany	640	1641	7.0
Portugal	640	2408	16.0
United States	n.a.	2040	–
Japan	n.a.	4000	–

Source: Trade publications.

This price policy, however, has not been easily accepted by the market, particularly in Belgium, where the price gap between the high and the low end of the market is already very large (see Table CS15.7). Charles van der Veken observed that, in Belgium, a 10 per cent increase has generated a loss in volume of about 7 per cent. He is also aware that this lost volume goes to Léonidas for the most part.

Distribution policy

The ultimate goal that Godiva is pursuing in its distribution policy is to obtain across the world something akin to the Benetton model: boutiques with a uniform look. This 'look' includes a logo with golden letters on a black background, a façade incorporating these same colours, interior fixtures in pink marble, glass counters, and so forth.

The current retail distribution problem lies in the great disparity between the Godiva boutiques in different countries, mainly in Europe and even more particularly in Belgium (Table CS15.8

TABLE CS15.7 *Retail price comparison among brands*

Belgium		France		United Kingdom	
Brands	Price (BF/kg)	Brands	Price (FF/kg)	Brands	Price (£/kg)
Godiva	1080	Godiva	320	Godiva	13.50
Neuhaus	980	Hédiard	640	Gérard Ronay	20.00
Corné PR	880	Fauchon	430	Valrhona	16.80
Corné TO	870	Maison ch.	390	Charbonel	14.00
Daskalidès	680	Le Notre	345	Neuhaus	12.00
Jeff de Bruges	595	Fontaine ch.	327	Léonidas	6.75
Léonidas	360	Léonidas	120	Thornton's	5.80

Source: Trade publications.

TABLE CS15.8 *The Godiva distribution network*

Country	Company-owned stores	Franchised dealers	Department stores and others	Total outlets
Belgium	3	54	–	57
France	1	19	–	20
Spain	–	6	18	24
United Kingdom	2	–	15	17
Italy	–	2	–	2
Holland	–	2	–	2
Germany	–	4	1	5
Portugal	–	3	7	10
Total Europe	6	90	41	137
United States	95	–	800	895
Japan	–	22	67	89

Source: Trade publications and yellow pages.

shows the Godiva distribution network). Through the years the boutiques in Belgium have become less and less attractive. As a consequence, the Godiva brand image has aged. Abroad, however, Godiva benefits from an extremely prestigious image, and the boutiques merit their name. Nevertheless, Charles van der Veken fears the worst:

> If we don't react quickly, we could compromise the world brand image of Godiva. What would a Spanish tourist think in comparing the boutique of a local distributor in Brussels to the refined boutiques that he finds in Spain, although Belgium is the birthplace of chocolates?

Godiva's retail distribution action plan for Belgium covers a period of 18 months. A contract has been made with the franchises in which Godiva imposes both exclusivity and design; all the boutiques must have completed renovations. Once the movement is well established in Belgium, Godiva hopes this will create a spillover effect to all of Europe, because the new boutiques will constitute a reference for the recruitment of new franchises or for spontaneous requests for renovations.

This renovation movement has already begun and every two weeks a 'new' boutique is inaugurated. The renovated boutiques have been transformed so that everything is in black and gold, and the entire interior decoration is redone according to the same single standard of luxury.

Generally, consumer reactions in Belgium seem favourable, although in certain respects consumers find the stores almost too beautiful. As for the franchisees, they feel as though they have a new business, and appear to be changing some of their former bad habits. If the effects remain favourable in the medium term, van der Veken said he will increase the margin provided to franchises, which is still different from one country to the other (see Table CS15.6).

The chairman of Godiva International, Mr Partridge, has frequently questioned the wisdom of this costly exclusive distribution system because he believes chocolate is not really a destination purchase. In Europe, the adoption of a broader distribution system is difficult, however, because of the reluctance of consumers *vis-à-vis* pre-wrapped assortments of chocolates. van der Veken is convinced, however, that the Godiva boutique is a key component of the Godiva image of a luxury good.

The competitive environment

The hand-made luxury chocolate segment is occupied by many other brands. Table CS15.9 presents a ranking of the specialty brands for Belgium, France and Germany, in descending order of market share. The strength of the Léonidas competitive position in Europe is clearly shown by this comparison. Léonidas was created in 1910. It did for chocolate pralines what Henry Ford did for the car: a mass-consumption product sold at a low price. Their recipe is simple: a price of BF360 per kilogram, 8600 square metres of industrial space and a production capacity of 10 000 tons. Léonidas is a very important competitor for Godiva. With total sales of over BF2.6 billion and a 32 per cent operating profit margin, Léonidas has 1500 stores worldwide and is now expanding rapidly in the international market. The next major competitor is Neuhaus, which recently merged with Mondose and Corné Port Royal and is also pursuing an international development strategy. The 'others' include the many small confectionery-chocolatiers who nibble at the market share of the larger companies in offering fresh, original products made from pure cocoa.

However, given its broad market coverage, Charles van der Veken believes that Godiva has a significant competitive advantage due to its integration into Campbell Soup 13 years ago, which provided Godiva with an opportunity for global expansion much more quickly than its competitors. Thus Godiva is present everywhere, and even if it often skirts a competitor in a particular market, it is rarely the same one across the world. Godiva can thus currently be considered the global leader in the luxury chocolate segment.

Only in Belgium is Godiva having difficulties making use of its competitive advantage. The volume growth has proved important everywhere, except in Belgium. According to Charles van der Veken, the market is already too saturated, and it is up to the best to make the difference.

TABLE CS15.9 *Main European competitors*

Belgium		France		United Kingdom	
Brands	Share (%)	Brands	Share (%)	Brands	Tons
Léonidas	42.8	Léonidas	62.0	Thornton's	1200
Godiva	10.3	Thornton's	18.0	Léonidas	300
Neuhaus	7.1	Jeff de Bruges	14.0	Godiva	40
Mondose	5.4	Godiva	3.0		
Corné TO	2.7	Le Notre	1.0		
Others	31.7	Others	2.0		

Source: Industry trade publications (market shares are calculated on sales revenues).

Advertising strategy

Today Godiva does not need to make itself known on the international level: its brand name is already globally recognized. Its current concern, in line with the policy that has been pursued for the past several months, is to create a common advertising message for the entire world. However, this will not be an easy task as evidenced by a comparison of the situation in Belgium, the United States and Japan. In the United States and Japan the product is relatively new, and has a strong image inasmuch as there is no direct competitor. In Belgium the consumer has followed the evolution of Godiva chocolates, and the progressive commoditization of the brand. It is therefore more difficult to impress Belgians with a product that is already well known. What's more, Belgians are in daily contact with other brands of chocolates, with which they can easily compare Godiva.

Thus, as van der Veken pointed out, Godiva finds itself faced with very different worlds. Until now, in the United States, advertising was focused on prestige, luxury, refinement, with a communication style similar to the one adopted by Cartier, Gucci or Ferrari. These advertisements were presented in magazines well adapted to the desired positioning: gourmet, fashion or business magazines that cater to higher-income echelons (see Fig. CS15.3).

In Belgium, however, this type of advertising tended only to reinforce the aged, grandmotherish image of Godiva chocolates. What's more, the gap between the 'perceived image' (a food item interchangeable with others of the same type) and the 'desired image' (an exceptional luxury product) was so large that spectacular results could not be expected.

A study performed by Godiva seems to show that nobody could remember these advertisements, or the promises that were made. In Belgium, Godiva had also made use of event marketing, being represented at events at which the target population had a large chance of being present. Thus, two years ago, Godiva was the sponsor of a golf competition in Belgium that held its name (Godiva European Master). Such actions are, however, extremely costly, and their effectiveness is difficult to measure. The total advertising budget of Godiva Europe is BF31 million per year.

The advertising decision

Aware of this problem, Godiva Europe is in the process of evaluating its advertising strategy. The following situation had to be solved: creating a common advertising message targeted at the three main markets while taking into consideration the inevitable cultural differences among countries.

Godiva USA had just sent Charles van der Veken the briefing of an international advertising campaign, which is summarized in Box CS15.1. He said that adopting this advertising style on the European market worried him to a certain degree:

> The least one can say is that differences of mentality exist between our two continents. We certainly need to wake up our old-fashioned Godiva, but we should also be careful of overly radical changes.

Reflecting with his marketing staff, van der Veken tended to define the advertising objective in the following manner.

FIGURE CS15.3 *Typical Godiva print advertisement in the USA*

The objective of Godiva USA is to increase the frequency of the purchase of chocolates for gifts as well as for self-consumption, whereas Belgium wants to make its brand image more youthful. Thus, the United States should adjust its advertising slightly 'downward', in making the product more accessible through convivial advertising and less 'plastic beauty', while Belgium should strive, jointly with other marketing efforts (redesign of boutiques, increased quality of service, creation of 'collections'), to adjust its advertising slightly 'upward', in affirming itself as a prestigious luxury product, only younger.

The upward adjustment for Belgium was a daring challenge. Charles van der Veken wondered if it would not be preferable to pass through a transitory period before beginning a global marketing campaign, which would take into consideration the historical and cultural context of Belgium.

Just then, Mrs Bogaert, van der Veken's assistant, entered his office holding a fax from Godiva International:

The campaign cannot be launched in time for Christmas: prepare as quickly as possible your advertising campaign for Belgium and contact your agencies. Meeting in five weeks in New York for the confirmation of our projects.

Charles van der Veken immediately called his director of marketing, informed her of the freshly arrived news, and asked her to submit for the Belgian market a campaign project based upon the American model, targeted in a first step to the Belgian market, but which could be extended to the other European markets, if not to the entire world. Together they agreed upon objectives in three main categories:

1. *Qualitative objectives:*
   - Rapidly reinforce the luxury image of Godiva.
   - Make visibility a priority.
2. *Quantitative objectives:*
   - Increase the frequency of purchase.
3. *Other objectives:*
   - Concentrate all efforts on Belgium for several months (months of peak sales).
   - Synergy of all other methods of promotion and advertising.

An additional BF13 million advertising budget would be allocated to the campaign. After some thought, it seemed possible to Mr van der Veken that a triad campaign would, on a long-term basis, be feasible in spite of cultural differences. He did not believe, however, that business generated in the other European countries would be high enough today to justify the same advertising budget as for Belgium. This became even more obvious when one considered that, in terms of media costs and for the same impact, 1 Belgian franc in Belgium is equivalent to BF1.6 in France and BF1.9 in the United Kingdom.

Charles van der Veken was also convinced that a European advertising campaign is useless without having first improved and reinforced the Godiva European distribution.

Questions

1. How would you characterize consumer purchasing behaviour and consumption in the chocolate praline market and the major differences observed among countries?
2. How would you characterize the strengths and weaknesses of Godiva in Europe and particularly in Belgium?
3. How might you characterize Godiva's existing marketing strategy on a 'standardization–customization' continuum?
4. Propose two advertising themes based on the briefing of Godiva International and compatible with the objectives of Charles van der Veken. Use successively the 'copy strategy' and the 'star strategy' to develop you advertising proposals.
5. What is your assessment of Charles van der Veken's views on Godiva's advertising objectives and strategy? Does a single global advertising campaign make sense?
6. Are the economics of the proposed incremental expenditure for advertising sound? Why or why not?

BOX CS15.1

The briefing from Godiva International

1. *Current positioning*
   - ■ To adults who want a quality product for special moments, Godiva is an accessible luxury branded by Godiva Chocolatier and distinguished by superior craftsmanship.

2. *Consumer benefit*
   - ■ Whether you give Godiva or consume it yourself, you will relish its uniquely sensual pleasures: taste and presentation.

3. *Promise*
   - ■ Using the finest ingredients and Belgian recipes for a remarkable taste experience.
   - ■ Godiva heritage of fine chocolate making.
   - ■ Beautifully crafted packaging.
   - ■ Handcrafted in fine European heritage/style.
   - ■ Created by an expert chocolatier.

4. *Psychographic characteristics*
   - ■ Godiva purchasers are discerning and driven by quality expectations. While they are value-oriented, they will pay a higher price if a significant quality differential exists, since they aspire to have or share the best.
   - ■ Godiva men and women are sensual individuals, enjoying the pleasures that things of exceptional look, feel taste, sound and smell can offer them.

5. *Competitive frame*
   - ■ Gift: flowers, perfume, wine, other fine chocolates, giftables of the same price range.
   - ■ Self-consumption: any item meant to provide a range of self-indulgences at Godiva's basic price-points.

6. *Target audience*
   - ■ The Godiva target covers a range of demographic characteristics:
   - ■ Broad age range (25–54 primarily).
   - ■ Women and men.
   - ■ Across a breadth of income levels, but with reasonable to high disposable incomes.

7. *Advertising objectives*
   - ■ To revitalize Godiva's worldwide premium position most specifically as it pertains to the superior quality of the chocolate product.
   - ■ To motivate our current Godiva franchise to purchase on more frequent occasions (gifting and self-consumption).
   - ■ To motivate current purchasers of competitive chocolates and nonchocolate giftables to convert to the Godiva franchise.

8. *Message*
   - ■ Godiva chocolates are expertly crafted to provide an unparalleled sensory experience.

9. *Tone and manner*
   - ■ Luxurious—Energetic—Modern—Upscale—Emotionally involving.

Appendix A: Results of the brand image study in the Brussels market area

TABLE CS15.10 *Aided brand awareness**

Brand name	Not at all	Only by name	By experience	Total
Corné	24.2	28.9	46.9	100
Corné Toison d'Or	31.3	25.8	43.0	100
Corné Port Royal	69.3	16.5	14.2	100
Daskalides	54.3	26.0	19.7	100
Godiva	2.3	19.5	78.1	100
Léonidas	2.3	10.9	86.7	100
Mon chéri	4.7	23.6	71.7	100
Neuhaus	13.3	25.0	61.7	100

*All figures are percentages of total survey.

Don't know any of the brands Corné, Corné Toison d'Or, Corné Port Royal: 22.7%. Known 'by name' or 'by experience' at least one of the following brands: Corné, Corné Toison d'Or, Corné Port Royal: 77.3%.

TABLE CS15.11 *Brand image analysis**

	Brand associated most with each attribute									
Attribute	Corné	Corné Toison D'or	Corné Port Royal	Corné total	Daska- lides	Godiva	Léoni- das	Mon Chéri	Neu- haus	Total
The queen of chocolates	7.1	5.5	0.8	(13.4)	–	37.8	27.6	1.6	19.7	100
Ideal for gift	11.0	3.1	–	(14.1)	–	29.1	26.8	10.2	19.7	100
For self-indulgence	4.8	3.2	0.8	(8.8)	0.8	26.4	48.0	1.6	14.4	100
For special occasions	6.5	8.9	0.8	(16.2)	0.8	26.8	28.5	8.1	19.5	100
The most beautiful boutique	6.0	9.4	–	(15.4)	–	40.2	12.0	0.9	31.6	100
The most attractive price	3.3	2.5	–	(5.8)	0.8	5.7	81.1	4.9	1.6	100
The nicest packaging	7.2	7.2	0.8	(15.2)	0.8	49.6	6.4	3.2	24.8	100
The most refined chocolate	8.8	7.2	1.6	(17.6)	0.8	35.2	18.4	0.8	27.2	100
Typically Belgian chocolate	6.5	2.4	–	(8.9)	–	30.1	48.1	2.4	10.6	100
Taste I like best	5.6	4.0	1.6	(11.2)	–	32.3	37.9	3.2	15.3	100
The most expensive chocolate	6.7	8.4	–	(15.1)	2.5	40.3	5.9	0.8	35.3	100
Worldly known brand	4.0	0.8	–	(4.8)	0.8	42.7	39.5	4.8	7.3	100

*All figures are percentages of total survey.

TABLE CS15.12 *Brand preferences by situation*

For self-consumption	%	For gift	%
Corné:	2.4	Corné:	3.9
Corné Toison d'Or:	4.1	Corné Toison d'Or	3.9
Corné Port Royal:	0.8	Corné Port Royal	0.8
Daskalidès:	–	Daskalides:	0.8
Godiva:	24.4	Godiva:	29.1
Léonidas:	48.0	Léonidas:	27.6
Mon Chéri:	2.4	Mon chéri:	5.5
Neuhaus:	12.2	Neuhaus:	25.2
Other:	5.7	Other:	3.2
	100		100

SUBJECT INDEX